Acquisitions, Mergers, Sales
Buyouts and Takeovers:
A Handbook with Forms,

Fourth Edition

Acquisitions, Mergers, Sales, Buyouts and Takeovers: A Handbook with Forms,

Fourth Edition

Charles A. Scharf
Edward E. Shea
George C. Beck

PRENTICE HALL
Paramus, New Jersey 07652

Library of Congress Cataloging-in-Publication Data

Scharf, Charles A.
    Acquisitions, mergers, sales, buyouts, and takeovers : a handbook
with forms / Charles A. Scharf, Edward E. Shea, George C. Beck.—
4th ed.
        p. cm.
    Includes bibliographical references and index.
    ISBN 0-13-005596-4
    1. Consolidation and merger of corporations—United States—
Handbooks, manuals, etc.   2. Sale of business enterprises—United
States—Handbooks, manuals, etc.   3. Business enterprises—United
States—Purchasing—Handbooks, manuals, etc.   I. Shea, Edward E.
II. Beck, George C.   III. Title.
    HD2741.S35   1991   91-14266
    658.1′6′0973—dc20   CIP

Printed in the United States of America

10   9   8   7   6   5   4

ISBN 0-13-005596-4

9 780130 055965   90000>

 PRENTICE HALL
Career & Personal Development
Paramus, NJ 07652
A Simon & Schuster Company

On the World Wide Web at http://www.phdirect.com

Prentice-Hall International (UK) Limited, *London*
Prentice-Hall of Australia Pty. Limited, *Sydney*
Prentice-Hall Canada Inc., *Toronto*
Prentice-Hall Hispanoamericana, S.A., *Mexico*
Prentice-Hall of India Private Limited, *New Delhi*
Prentice-Hall of Japan, Inc., *Tokyo*
Simon & Schuster Asia Pte. Ltd., *Singapore*
Editora Prentice-Hall do Brasil, Ltda., *Rio de Janeiro*

Charles A. Scharf is a practicing attorney, a member of the New York, Florida and Connecticut Bars. He has been involved for many years in all aspects of purchases, sales and mergers of businesses. He is the author of the book *Techniques for Buying, Selling and Merging Businesses* (1964) and a contributor to the *Encyclopedia of Tax Procedures*, both published by Prentice-Hall. His many articles include "Tax Aspects" in *Trademark Problems in Acquisitions and Mergers*, United States Trademark Association, Mellon Press, Inc., New York, 1968: "Brokerage. Negotiation, and the Contract" in the *Business of Acquisition and Mergers*, President's Publishing House, Inc., 1968; and "Merging and Selling a Business to Complete an Estate Plan," in *The Practical Lawyer*, October, 1966. Mr. Scharf is at present practicing law in Old Greenwich, Connecticut.

Edward E. Shea, this edition's revisor, is a partner concentrating on acquisitions and mergers with the law firm of Windels, Marx, Davies & Ives in the City of New York. He is also an Adjunct Full Professor, teaching courses in Mergers and Acquisitions and Securities Regulation in the Finance Department of the Graduate School of Business of Pace University. Mr. Shea previously served as Chairman of the Board of Reichhold Chemicals, Inc. for over nine years and as Senior Vice President, General Counsel and a director of GAF Corporation. He has written a number of articles for professional publications including *Mergers & Acquisitions*, *Standard & Poor's Review of Financial Services Regulation*, the *American Bar Association Journal*, the *National Law Journal*, *The New York Law Journal* and *The Practical Lawyer*. He is also a member of the board of directors of the New York State Small Business Development Program. He is a graduate of the University of Michigan Law School.

George C. Beck is a member of the New York Bar and a partner in the law firm of Burns and Beck. He has been involved in all aspects of business combinations and divestitures, and the securities law problems relating to the purchase or sale of business.

What This Book Will
Do for You

Acquisitions, mergers, sales, buyouts and takeovers are challenging, interesting and complex transactions. They require a concentrated effort by a team of business managers and professionals working in close cooperation to achieve a successful result. Business managers and professionals must be able to plan and perform their own responsibilities rapidly and effectively. They also need to understand the overall transaction and the objectives and roles of the other business managers and professionals working with them.

The fields of knowledge involved in buying and selling businesses reflect the great variety found in modern business itself. Many specialized books and articles about acquisitions exist in each of these fields. They are typically written in detail in the language of the field and assume the reader is experienced in the field. They seldom alert the reader to the wide range of relationships with overall business objectives and other specialized fields.

Acquisitions, Mergers, Sales, Buyouts and Takeovers is a guide to all phases of buying and selling businesses. Beginning with internal business and financial buying, the book guides you through identification and investigation of a business to be acquired; negotiations and financial valuation methods; structuring considerations; accounting treatment; antitrust securities and other legal considerations; tax-free reorganization, liquidations and other tax planning techniques; leveraged buyouts; foreign company acquisitions and joint ventures and the negotiation, preparation and closing of contracts.

The book uses a practical "how-to-do-it" method and includes numerous forms, practical examples, sample calculations, model agreements and checklists. It is designed for use by business executives and managers, attorneys, accountants, investment bankers, financial analysts, investors, tax planners, graduate business and law school students and anyone who participates or is interested in buying and selling businesses.

This is the fourth edition of a book originally published in 1964. In this new edition, you will find of special interest:

- A new Chapter 1 on corporate development including growth strategies, internal expansion, establishing a corporate development department and recommended reference sources. Seller strategies and methods for divestitures are also discussed.
- A new Chapter 2 on financing and structuring acquisitions including financial sources, intermediaries, new types of securities and traditional and recently developed structures with diagrams.
- Additional discussion of the roles of intermediaries in Chapter 3.
- Additional discussion of valuation methods using cash flow multiples and the discounted cash flow method in Chapter 4.
- A new and expanded Business "Due Diligence" Checklist in Chapter 5.
- Updated discussion of antitrust and other legal steps in Chapter 6.
- Introduction to some of the special problems of leveraged buyout accounting in Chapter 7.
- Updated discussion of Regulation D and Rule 144 and the major new Rule 144A and Regulation S in Chapter 8.
- Refocused discussion of takeovers in Chapter 9 including corporate governance, state antitakeover laws, going private transactions and proxy contests.
- Updated discussion of tax-free reorganizations in Chapter 10.
- New and restructured discussion of taxable acquisitions including corporate liquidations as affected by the tax reforms since 1986, allocation of basis under Sections 338 and 1060, original issue discount, limitations on use of net operating losses related to built-in gains and corporate equity deductions, partial denial of interest deductions on high yield debt instruments and other updated information.
- Extensive revision of Chapter 12 (formerly Chapter 15) to reflect recent developments in leveraged buyouts including ESOP transactions.
- Updated discussion of foreign company acquisitions and joint ventures in Chapter 13 (formerly Chapter 16).
- Major revision of Chapters 14, 15 and 16 (formerly Chapters 12, 13 and 14) to add modern and more sophisticated forms including a letter of intent, stock purchase agreement, assets purchase agreement, triangular merger agreement (tax-free), triangular merger agreement (cash out), exchange agency agreement and escrow agreement. A contract checklist is also added.
- Extensive revision of Chapter 17 to describe closing procedures. An example of a closing memorandum and checklists are included.
- A new Chapter 18 to describe post-closing events and methods for handling important post-closing projects, including integration of the acquired business; shutdowns, cutbacks and layoffs; maintaining seller's insurance coverage; integrating pension plans and handling claims. Checklists are included.

Who Can Benefit from Using This Book

The background of the authors includes many years of experience in business, finance, and law including the planning and coordination of numerous acquisition transactions. The book is designed to be useful to all members of acquisition teams.

Business executives and managers will benefit from the information on planning, investigation and negotiation of acquisitions and will gain better understanding of the activities and problems of the professional specialists who work with them.

Corporate development managers will benefit from the new materials discussing their role in fostering internal expansion as well as acquisitions. They will also find suggested strategies, methods and source materials.

Attorneys will benefit from the up-to-date coverage of the numerous forms, references, "real life" examples, model agreements and checklists. They will see how their activities relate to the objectives of business executives and managers and the roles of financial analysts, accountants, investment bankers, tax planners and other specialists.

Accountants will benefit from the materials describing the "purchase" and "pooling of interests" methods of accounting for acquisitions and the materials on financial analysis and tax planning. They will also gain understanding of the roles of businessmen, lawyers, investment bankers and other specialists.

Investment bankers will benefit from the materials on investigation of businesses, financial analysis and structuring of transactions and the information on arrangements and compensation of business finders, brokers and financial consultants. They will also better understand the roles of the businessmen and professionals who carry out the acquisitions originated and financed by investment bankers.

Financial analysts, venture capital firms and lending institutions will benefit from the focused description of their methods and their role in evaluating an acquisition and negotiating the purchase price. The materials alert businesspersons and other specialists to the variety of methods available to introduce greater precision to the measurement of business values and the practical limits of those methods. Financial analysts will also gain understanding of the objectives of businessmen and the roles of attorneys, accountants, investment bankers and other professionals.

Tax planners will benefit from the chapters on tax-free reorganizations, liquidations and other tax-planning techniques. They will specially benefit from the readily available materials in accounting treatment, business investigation, financial analysis and securities regulation that will enable them to coordinate decisions in their complex field with objectives in other fields.

Graduate business and law school professors and students will benefit from the readable overview presentation of the materials, the numerous "real life" examples, and the length of the book, which can comfortably be covered in one semester. The book will enable students to see how other specialized courses find application in the practical steps taken to buy and sell businesses.

Charles A. Scharf
Edward E. Shea
George C. Beck

Table of Contents

1

Corporate Development and Strategies for Buyers and Sellers

Part 1.
THE BUYER'S POINT OF VIEW

GROWTH

As population increases and technology changes, it is difficult for any business to stand still. Success brings new customers and also new competitors willing to serve both new and old customers. Motivated employees who contribute to success want increased compensation, promotions and new challenges. For these reasons, most successful businesses want and need to grow.

Growth brings some inherent advantages. To the extent that fixed cost can be spread over a higher volume of products or services, cost per unit is reduced and products or services can be sold more profitably or at lower prices to increase sales. Successful growth tends to build confidence in customers, employees, suppliers, lenders and others. It limits opportunities for competitors. It enables a business to purchase higher volumes of supplies at lower prices and attract better customers and employees.

Growth also presents risks. Some risks are similar to those of the existing business and should readily be anticipated. Others result from growth itself and can be difficult to identify and control. Most difficult are the adjustments which management must make to select, motivate and delegate to new managers and employees while continuing to guide the business effectively. Some businesses in declining or cyclical industries or whose products and manufacturing processes cannot meet the state of the art may decide that the risks are too great.

1

A decision to reject growth is not risk free. It encourages competitors and risks loss of customers and motivated employees. If contraction follows, incremental costs will increase and make it more difficult to compete.

The result is that most businesses seek to grow. However, they must plan and manage the growth to minimize risks.

METHODS AND STRATEGIES TO ACHIEVE GROWTH

Specific methods to achieve growth are very numerous. Some examples are as follows:

Add sales and advertising programs.
Improve market shares of existing products.
Find new markets for existing products.
Improve product design.
Improve product quality and performance.
Add products complementing existing products.
Add distribution facilities and equipment.
Add manufacturing facilities and equipment.
Develop improved manufacturing processes.
Add component and raw material manufacturing facilities.
Add R&D personnel and facilities.
License technology.
Protect intellectual property developed by R&D personnel.
Introduce new management policies.
Adopt employee incentive programs.
Promote and hire employees.
Reduce taxes.
Reduce the cost of debt and equity capital.
Reduce the cost of supplies and services.
Improve effectiveness of internal administrative, financial and other support programs.
Resolve regulatory compliance problems, litigation and other disputes hindering business progress.

As the examples show, growth is achieved by specific expansion projects and also through daily improvements and reductions of problems and costs.

Broader strategies include vertical integration, horizontal expansion, diversification, specialization and combination strategies:

Vertical Integration is achieved by expanding backwards into components, raw materials and services previously obtained from suppliers or forward into products and services produced by customers.

Horizontal Expansion is achieved in its simplest form by adding new sales, warehouse and eventually manufacturing facilities in new geographical areas. It can also be accomplished by introducing new product and service groups.

Diversification is achieved by expanding into unrelated products, services and businesses in order to shelter a company from cyclicality.

Specialization is achieved by concentration on a product or service of clearly higher quality or lower price than those available from competitors. Specialization is difficult to maintain except for brief periods. Once a premium product or service is successfully marketed, competitors are attracted. However, companies in industries such as computers and pharmaceuticals use intense R&D effort, patents, marketing and capital investment to operate specialty businesses successfully over long periods.

Most businesses expand by a combination of strategies. For example, some grocery companies opened new stores carrying both groceries and small appliances, thus achieving both horizontal expansion and diversification. Later, after adding a variety of new lines such as clothing, books, and pharmaceuticals, their business became general retailing. By that time, they often had acquired a truck fleet, warehouse facilities and plants making some of their largest volume products. Thus, they maintained a unified structure, but benefited from synergies created by three growth strategies.

Growth strategies can also be combined at the manufacturing level. For example, chemical manufacturers producing synthetic resins for the paint industry found that their technology and equipment could be used with modifications to produce products for the adhesive, ink and plastic industries. As they built new plants to serve these industries, they often added equipment to manufacture acids and alcohols formerly bought from suppliers. Considerable synergy resulted because research and development to improve products for one customer industry often benefited products for other customers.

"Synergy" is the incremental effectiveness, sometimes major, which can be obtained by combining work of several persons over the sum of the work which they can achieve separately. Some say it is the ability to cause $1 + 1$ to equal 3.

"Conglomerates" are companies which achieve diversification by investing in wholly unrelated businesses. The retail and chemical companies described earlier achieved some diversification, but would be adversely affected by a broad downturn in their industries. Conglomerates simultaneously engage in businesses as diverse as banking, electronics, and oil and gas. Many conglomerates were developed through opportunistic acquisitions by financially oriented managements who then claimed protection from cyclical downturns as their strategy. In general, conglomerates have not done well because they had no synergies and were difficult to manage. Financially oriented managers at the holding company level managed for the "bottom line," a policy which frustrated operating management who wanted to build for the future. The conglomerates suffered losses of operating management and eventually suffered for lack of future-oriented investment. In recent years, conglomerate acquisitions have been less common. Many conglomerates have restructured and divested businesses until those remaining had a synergistic "fit."

Finally, some businessmen believe that the key to growth and profitability is to increase market shares. Antitrust enforcement policy was based for years on this belief. It is true that a business needs product market shares sufficient to keep incremental costs in line with those of competitors. However, experience shows that market shares at dominant levels may produce stagnation. Nothing makes an industry grow faster than skilled and vigorous competition. As better products are designed, manufactured and sold for lower prices, markets grow. Few could disagree that Henry Ford was a major benefactor to the business careers of Louis Chevrolet and Walter Chrysler. Apple Computer built its business based on the work of IBM, Sperry Rand (Unisys) and other computer manufacturers.

INTERNAL EXPANSION

Internal expansion is usually the method first considered to achieve growth. Management and employees who conceive an opportunity ordinarily want to develop and commercialize it. In smaller businesses, they may be able to develop the opportunity informally and indeed may find it necessary to do so. For example, one of the authors is aware of a major chemical manufacturing process which was developed with funds budgeted for maintenance and repair of older facilities.

In larger businesses, especially public corporations, internal expansion proposals are prepared and reviewed in detail. Depending on amount, they may be reviewed by one or more levels of operating management and by committees and the board of directors. To establish a new business, a proposal will include a business plan supported by a capital expense budget, projected operating statements, and financial analysis designed to measure financial contributions and burdens by several methods.

In some businesses, operating management controls the preparation of internal expansion proposals and financial personnel assist to assure that income and costs are fully and correctly included. In other businesses, financial personnel are actively involved and may perform the preparation.

During review, senior management and committee and board members raise questions about a proposal. Especially in the early stages, it is often returned for more investigation or clarification. For example, additional support for sales projections may be required. Additional equipment and related costs may be added after review by environmental and safety personnel. Experienced management will properly question the adequacy of funds for startup costs and unexpected contingencies because it is common to underrate these items.

At the final stage, the financial projections in the proposal must meet return on investment (ROI), payback and other criteria established by the senior management and the board of directors. During the 1970s and 1980s, there was a trend to increase "hurdle rates" for ROI and shorten payback periods to assure that overoptimism by proponents of internal expansion projects would not adversely affect "bottom line" earnings performance.

A simplified outline of an internal expansion proposal is shown in Exhibit 1-A.

Exhibit 1-A

OUTLINE OF BUSINESS EXPANSION PROPOSAL

Background
Present Status
Proposal
      General
      Marketing Data
      Competition
      Technology
      Capital Equipment
      Land and Buildings
      Personnel Requirements
      Raw Materials, Utilities, etc.
      Transportation
      Other Support Items
      Environment and Safety
      Scope and Timing
Financing (Availability, Methods and Costs)
Areas of Risk and Uncertainty
Alternatives Considered
Business Justification
Economic Justification
Capital Cost Budget
Projected Operating Statements
      (GAAP and Cash Flow)
Return on Investment (CAPM), Internal Rate of Return and
      Payback Period
Sensitivity Analysis
      Price Graph
      Volume Graph
      Break-Even Point
      "Worst Case" Analysis
Effects on Existing Business
Effects on the Overall Corporate Business, Earnings and
      Financial Condition

DECIDING WHETHER AND WHAT TO EXPAND

A sound decision to grow must begin with a realistic evaluation of the existing business. The evaluation should include all components including sales and marketing, advertising, manufacturing, research and development, purchasing, transportation and distribution, finance, credit, accounting, insurance and administration. The evaluation should also include the industry as a whole including customers, suppliers, competitors and other influences such as government regulation and public relations.

A few examples of the pitfalls will illustrate the importance of in-depth planning to avoid surprises:

• A consumer product manufacturer may establish through a consultant's survey that its products would be welcomed in a new region of the United States, but then learn after months of poor sales that its sales representatives are unacceptable to customers who perceive them as too aggressive or too laid back to build good relations in the region.

• A manufacturer may confirm that all essential raw materials are available at favorable prices, but later find that local transportation and utilities such as electricity, fuel or waste disposal are unexpectedly costly and unreliable.

• Research and development managers may use accelerated testing to confirm that products designed for temperate weather conditions can perform under cold, wet conditions or hot, dry conditions. However, they may later find that the accelerated testing under laboratory conditions did not adequately measure the stresses of field performance over a period of years.

• Urban manufacturers moving to a rural area may be delighted to establish rapid cordial relationships with new employees and local officials, but later be mystified by widespread absences during planting, harvesting and hunting seasons and on holidays differing from those of city customers.

Evaluation of a business considering expansion is especially difficult when it is part of a company having several divisions, facilities, products or services. Accountants labor to prepare accurate internal financial statements and controllers labor to prepare meaningful operating and capital budgets. However, limited information, misunderstanding, and business politics frequently result in allocations of income and expenses in ways which temporarily or permanently distort the reported financial performance of internal operations.

For example, if one facility supplies components or raw materials to another, the transfer price will be related to cost or market. If related to cost, one operation is probably subsidizing the other.* When operations share common facilities or services, a variety of systems to allocate the costs are used; *i.e.,* a percentage of dollar

---

*One of the authors recalls a financial vice president who commenced negotiations to sell an unprofitable subsidiary. He received a call from the general manager of another subsidiary asking that the sale be reconsidered. Belatedly doing his homework, the financial vice-president learned that half of the volume of the unprofitable subsidiary was sold at cost to the other subsidiary. Negotiations were halted.

sales or a percentage of actual use measured by units such as hours, weight or volume. Various systems are also used to credit incidental income such as royalties. These systems almost invariably create temporary, and often permanent, differences between the performance of corporate divisions reflected in internal financial statements and the performance they would achieve as independent businesses.

Internal operating results can also be distorted by policy decisions. Like corporate management, division managers make policy decisions on matters such as maintenance and improvement of facilities and research and development. A dedicated division manager who spends for the future may suffer in comparison to the manager who cuts costs to inflate current income. On the other hand, it should be remembered that division managers can bury mistakes in long-term capital and research budgets.

In the authors' experience, distortions in internal financial statements are a real and common problem. They lead to management decisions to expand bad businesses and to neglect and even divest good businesses. While distortions in internal financial statements should be corrected whenever discovered, "real world" evaluation is especially important when management decisions to expand or divest are made.

DECIDING BETWEEN INTERNAL EXPANSION AND A BUSINESS ACQUISITION

When a growth opportunity has been identified and evaluated, management should also evaluate whether it should be undertaken as an internal expansion project or as a business acquisition. This step is often overlooked.

For example, operating personnel sometimes develop and successfully present an expansion opportunity. If financial and staff personnel then recommend an acquisition survey, the operating personnel may object to the delay and urge that they be authorized to handle the opportunity as an internal expansion project. With no attractive acquisition candidate at hand, senior management will often approve internal expansion.

As a second example, an acquisition opportunity sometimes becomes available before management has made decisions on growth or the methods by which it should be undertaken. Rushing to compete against other bidders, management may insufficiently evaluate whether the acquisition is really its best growth opportunity and may give no thought at all to an internal expansion alternative.

Some of the factors which should be weighed in a decision between internal expansion and an acquisition are as follows:

Factors Favoring Internal Expansion

- Confidentiality.
- Control of the size, scope, location, time schedule and planned cost of the expansion project and its long-term operation.

- Opportunity to install equipment and processes which match the state of the art or perhaps go on to the next generation.
- Standardization of products, processes and equipment.
- Growth of existing managers and employees who gain experience from both success and errors during the expansion project.

Factors Opposing Internal Expansions

- Necessity to divert project personnel from their regular duties on a full or part-time basis and risk that part-timers may do neither job well.
- Risk that project managers or personnel may be underqualified, but be selected and allowed to perform inadequately because of long-standing good reputations.
- Difficulty in obtaining financing for a project which does not itself have a successful operating history, although existing similar businesses may be successful.
- Risk of delays, cost overruns or operational difficulties which sacrifice profitability, quality, customer goodwill and sometimes the project itself.

Factors Favoring Acquisitions

- Opportunity to evaluate all aspects, including management, at arm's length before making a commitment.
- Freedom to set a definite price and closing date after which the acquired business should promptly begin to make contributions.
- Existence of many businesses which can be acquired at a price which is reasonable measured by book value, earnings, cash flow or other valuation standards, but is far less than replacement cost, in light of the enormous cost increases which have resulted from inflation and the strict application of environmental and safety laws to new facilities.
- Relative ease in obtaining financing if the seller's business has an established operating history and/or bankable assets.
- No need to divert existing managers and employees from their duties except as needed to integrate operations, provided that the acquired business has capable management and employees.

Factors Opposing Acquisitions

- Difficulty maintaining confidentiality even in private transactions.
- Delays during negotiations and other acquisition steps which mean that important expansion objectives may not be within control for unexpectedly lengthy time periods.
- Misjudgments during negotiations including overbidding or failure to detect and protect against risks of the acquired business.

- Loss of the opportunity to install advanced processes or equipment unless the seller's business is doing so.
- Loss of an opportunity for growth of present managers and employees.
- Need to integrate the acquired business with the existing businesses while keeping commitments to grant autonomy to managers of the acquired business.

It is widely recognized that internal expansion of U.S. industry has been insufficient during the past two decades. U.S. industry did not match the effort of industry in Japan, Germany and some other nations in long-term research and development spending programs. Operating executives blame the slow pace of R&D and growth-oriented capital investment on the financial community which demands constant short-term earnings improvement. The financial community also supports accounting rules treating R&D and capital investment by conservative methods which depress earnings. Growing emphasis on discounted cash flow valuation methods adds to the trend. In articles such as "Managing as if Tomorrow Mattered," *Harvard Business Review,* Hayes and Garvin, 1982, critics have pointed out that gains in technology and employee training have great value, but are not measured by discounted cash flow methods.

The authors agree that management should not make expansion decisions solely by the "numbers." Senior management should also remember that existing businesses provide the funds and resources which support expansion projects. Some managements have hurt basic businesses by treating them as "cash cows" whose funds could be applied without limit to expansion of unrelated businesses.

CORPORATE DEVELOPMENT DEPARTMENTS

Background

For small companies and many large companies, corporate development is a part-time responsibility of the chief executive and other senior managers. They turn to outside advisers when needs and opportunities are identified. Many feel that a banker, investment banker, corporate lawyer or retired executive on their board of directors will provide adequate support to management in corporate development. Many believe that periodic contacts with bankers, investment firms and other financial professionals fill the need.

Some companies have come to a different conclusion. After reviewing mistakes and lost opportunities, they found that management and its advisors had not assembled all necessary information and evaluated it objectively. Outside professional advisors had a bias toward acquisitions they introduced or transactions in which their skills would be used. They seldom had enough information to evaluate an expansion project or acquisition fully or compare a proposed acquisition to alternatives such as internal expansion.

Similarly, management sometimes learned by reading *The Wall Street Journal* that a competitor had acquired a business with excellent synergy. They also learned that the opportunity was well-known in the financial community, but the "fit" had not been recognized by their investment banker. Other managements learned, even more painfully, that a business acquired based on financial analysis by an investment banking firm had achieved its earnings by neglecting research, development and capital expenditures.

Beginning a New Department

During the 1980s, many companies established corporate development departments, often beginning with one professional and a secretary. The work was challenging and difficult. If the new department manager came from the financial community, he was besieged with calls about acquisition candidates. If he came from R&D, marketing or other internal background, he received calls from the "street" and also many "good ideas" from internal sources.

Corporate development managers with an instinct for survival avoided a premature role as advocates of particular transactions. Instead, they began to create resources enabling management to set sound objectives and evaluate opportunities.

Learning the Business and the Industry

How should a new corporate development manager begin his responsibilities? The authors recommend a thorough initial study of the existing business and its industry. This is not as easy as it might seem. Many early contacts will offer conclusions rather than information. The best sources of early information are non-political working professionals who will take time to teach the essentials of their job to a new manager if he is sincerely interested. Trips to plants and laboratories are invaluable once the visit goes deeper than the customary visitor's presentation. Each manager, of course, has his own bias, but each can contribute valuable information. For example, a sales manager may obviously exaggerate in describing his sales prowess, but also give a remarkable description of customer processes and specific needs for product improvement.

To learn about an industry, a corporate development manager should subscribe for his own copies of industry publications. Every industry has one or more; i.e., *Adhesives Age, Aerosol Age, Advertising Age, American Banker, American Inkmaker, Aviation Week, Biotechnology, Business Insurance, Chemical Week, Cosmetics and Toiletries, Drug and Cosmetic Industry, Elastomerics, Green Markets, Journal of Food Science, Metal Finishing, Mining Magazine, Modern Plastics, Oil and Gas Journal, Perfumer and Flavorist, Pulp and Paper, Rubber World, TAPPI Journal* and *Women's Wear Daily.*

As familiarity grows, the new manager will be able to read more technical publications. For example, a subject covered briefly in *Chemical Week* may be described more fully in *Chemical & Engineering News* or the *Chemical Marketing Reporter.* A full study may be available in the *Chemical Economics Handbook.*

Each industry also has scientific publications where research papers are published. The technical language, charts and graphs used in some scientific papers can be a barrier. However, many scientists have learned to write articles which are readable by a wider audience than their fellow scientists. As time passes, a corporate development manager will find he can read the significant parts of scientific papers with some help from friends in corporate research.

Obviously, the corporate development manager cannot become a salesman, engineer or research scientist. However, he can learn enough to communicate with them. He can also create confidence that corporate development will be a participatory process.

Modeling

With a sound grasp of the business, corporate development managers who are financial analysts will develop financial models as tools for future-oriented evaluation of expansion projects.

The personal computer with spreadsheet capability is a valuable tool because extensive data can be analyzed at high speed and presented in usable form. Data, assumptions and methods can be changed repeatedly and run again. Through modeling, forecasts can be upgraded from possibilities to probabilities. While probability is not certainty, business management must make decisions for the future. Tools which reduce the margin for error are vital to the intelligent allocation of corporate resources.

Modeling follows the general principle of computer use: "Garbage in, garbage out." That is why the authors stress that corporate development managers obtain the greatest possible knowledge of the business and the industry as well as the projects to be evaluated. Such knowledge will minimize use of inaccurate data and unrealistic assumptions.

The authors also recommend that corporate development managers resist the temptation to build a mystique about the capability of their models. Reports should clearly describe for management the assumptions used and the limitations of the model.

For readers interested in the mechanics of modeling, the authors recommend *Corporate Financial Analysis,* Harrington and Wilson, BPI/Irwin, 1989. Appendix A introduces the modeling process using a Lotus 1-2-3 spreadsheet program. Appendix B guides the reader through the steps from data entry to printout. Some complex examples are given and alternate modeling systems are identified.

Reference Materials

Corporate development managers interested in further information can refer to a multitude of sources. The authors recommend the following:

Periodicals

> *Acquisitions Monthly,* Euromoney Publications
> *Federal Reserve Bulletin*

The Harvard Business Review
Mergers & Acquisitions, MLR Publishing
Monthly Labor Review, U.S. Department of Labor

Books

Accountant's Handbook, 6th Ed. Ronald Press
Accounting Standards, Original Pronouncements, FASB, McGraw-Hill
The Acquisitions Manual, New York Institute of Finance
The Acquisition Yearbook—1991, New York Institute of Finance
Corporate Financial Analysis, Harrington and Wilson, BPI/Irwin
Corporate Finance, Brudney and Chirelstein, Foundation Press
Corporate Restructuring, Rock, McGraw-Hill
Creating Shareholder Value, Rappaport, Freedom Press
Employee Stock Ownership Plans, Prentice-Hall
Essentials of Managerial Finance, Weston and Brigham, Dryden Press
Federal Income Taxation of Corporations and Shareholders, Bittker & Eustice, Warren, Gorham & Lamont
Financial Management and Policy, Van Horne, Prentice-Hall
Handbook of Mergers, Acquisitions & Buyouts, Lee & Coleman, Prentice-Hall
International Mergers and Acquisitions, Euromoney Publications
Modern Portfolio Theory, Harrington, Prentice-Hall
Financial Valuation: Business and Business Interests, Maxwell MacMillan/Rosenfeld Launer
Principles of Corporate Finance, Brealey and Myers, McGraw-Hill
Securities Regulation, Loss and Seligman, Little, Brown & Co.
Trademark Law Handbooks, USTA, Clark Boardman Co.
Valuing a Business, Pratt, Dow Jones-Irwin, 1989
Valuation: Business and Business Interests, Maxwell McMillan/Rosenfeld Launer Publication, 1990

Newspapers

Financial Times
The National Law Journal, M&A Dealmaker
The New York Law Journal, M&A Quarterly Insets
The New York Times
The Wall Street Journal

Magazines

Barron's
The Economist
Forbes
Industry Week

Reference Sources

        Bureau of National Affairs:
           Daily Report for Executives
           Environmental Reporter
        Business Insurance
        Commerce Clearing House:
           Securities Regulation Reporter
           Blue Sky Law Reporter
           Trade Regulation Reporter
           Federal Tax Reporter
           State Tax Reporters
        Directory of Intermediaries, Business Publications
        Directory of LBO Financing Sources, Business Publications
        Dun & Bradstreet Reports; Million Dollar Directory; Key Business Ratios
        Encyclopedia of Business Information Sources, Gale Research
        LEXIS, Mead Data Central
        Lloyd's List
        M&A Database, ADP Data Services
        Mergerstat Review, W.T. Grimm & Co.
        Moody's Manuals; Moody's Investors Service
        NYSE Daily Stock Price Record
        Patent Intelligence and Data Report
        Standard Industrial Classification Manual—1987
        Standard & Poor's Corporation:
           Industry Surveys
           Register of Corporations, Directors and Executives
           Analyst's Handbook
           Corporation Records
        Securities and Exchange Commission (Disclosure, Inc.):
           Registration Statements
           Proxy Statements
           10-K, 10-Q, 8-K Reports
           Schedules 13D, 13E-1 and 14 D-1
           Forms 3 and 4
        Thomas' Register of American Manufacturers
        Value Line Investment Survey, Arnold Bernhard & Co.
        Ward's Business Directory
        WESTLAW, West Publishing
        The Wyatt Company, *Annual Review of Pension Plans*

ACQUISITION STRATEGIES

    As the title indicates, this book is primarily devoted to corporate acquisitions. Acquisitions are an important part of the U.S. economy. During the late 1980s, acquisitions of sufficient size to be reported by *Mergers & Acquisitions* and the *Mergerstat Review* of W. T. Grimm & Co. exceeded 3,000 in number and reached an annual $200 billion level in total price.

At the simplest level, an active market for the sale of businesses reduces business risk. If businesses could not be sold as owners reach retirement age or encounter competitive opportunities and problems, the risk of starting and maintaining a business would be much higher. The risk of being a worker, customer, supplier or financier for a business would also be much higher.

Critics decry the sometimes painful dislocation created by business acquisitions. However, who would wish to return to a feudal system under which businesses were operated until death by founders and then by their heirs regardless of their abilities? Who would wish to continue with a failing business until its doors were closed in bankruptcy? Who would wish to remain with a small company which has created a business, but is doomed to fail because it cannot obtain resources adequate to match its opportunity?

Many major companies contributing to the U.S. economy grew primarily because of acquisitions. For example, General Motors grew through acquisitions of Durant, Chevrolet, Oakland and Olds into a company larger than Ford Motor Company which was dedicated to internal expansion and even made its own steel and glass. Most successful companies grew through a mix of internal expansion and acquisitions. Examples are Merck & Co. Inc., The Dow Chemical Company and Merrill Lynch.

A remarkable example of a company which completely repositioned its businesses by acquisitions and divestitures is Whitman Corporation, formerly IC Industries. Over two decades, management restructured a highly regulated and declining railroad business in the north central United States. Initial acquisitions entered growing southern railroad markets and related heavy manufacturing industries. Gradually, consumer businesses were acquired and industrial businesses divested. Eventually, the ICG railroad business was divested by a spinoff to shareholders. The company then adopted the name of its well-known confectionery product "Whitman."

Earlier in this chapter, the authors have described growth strategies which apply to internal growth and to acquisitions. There are other strategies unique to acquisitions. The authors specially recommend the "five rules of successful acquisition" prescribed by Peter Drucker in *The Wall Street Journal*, October 15, 1981. As part of a series of cover story articles reviewing acquisitions in the 1980s, *Business Week* provided simple and sound strategies on page 54 of its January 15, 1990 issue. Most M&A experts agree on the importance of strategy itself, synergy, knowledge of the business and the industry, negotiation of a realistic purchase price, prudence in matching availability of cash flows to debt obligations and post-acquisition steps to realize the objectives of the acquisition.

The authors also recommend the following strategies:

• An acquisition should be based primarily on affirmative synergies which offer employees a credible chance to prosper. Acquisitions based entirely or primarily on cost-cutting will probably fail. If cost cutting is necessary after an acquisition, it should be completed promptly. It should be accompanied by adoption of realistic action plans with meaningful roles and rewards for the employees retained.

• Financial analysis and negotiation of price and terms are vital short-term elements. It can be fatal to underrate them.

• Financial analysis and negotiation of price and terms are only short-term elements. Financial analysis sometimes shows the best results for a "cash cow" business which has limited or no future potential. A bargain price and favorable financing terms cannot justify the purchase of a failing business unless the buyer is prepared to lead a turnaround or to liquidate on favorable terms.

• An acquisition has a better chance of success where the managers have modest qualifications, but are devoted to their work rather than compensation and perquisites. The resulting savings can be used to fund their efforts to develop the business including additions to their own qualifications. When success is achieved, the buyer should be sure that all who contribute share in the rewards, not just a few senior managers.

Part 2.
THE SELLER'S POINT OF VIEW

MAKING DIVESTITURE DECISIONS

Owners and managers of businesses reach a decision to sell them for many reasons:

• Founders and other individual owners sometimes sell as part of retirement and estate planning programs.

• Young founders sometimes sell because they have an unusual business opportunity that cannot be realized without access to the sales, technological, financial or other resources of a larger organization.

• Large corporations sometimes divest businesses which do not fit into their strategic business plans, even though the businesses are sound.

• Large corporations sometimes divest businesses which once were sound but have become a problem because corporate management did not know how they should be managed. They will explain the sale by saying the business does not fit their strategic plans, but this may be a rationalization.

• Venture capital firms cause the sale of businesses as part of an "exit strategy" which calls for realization upon an investment based on time and return on investment objectives.

• Executors, administrators, trustees of the estate of deceased owners sell businesses to realize funds for taxes and distributions to heirs and beneficiaries.

• Companies being reorganized in bankruptcy and trustees for companies being liquidated sell businesses to realize funds for creditors.

• Owners of all kinds sell businesses that are in trouble. They frequently do not know whether the problems can be arrested and the business turned around. Some will seek a buyer with resources to achieve a turnaround. Others will sell to anyone who takes the problems away for an acceptable price.

General Seller Objectives

All sellers have several criteria to which they will give priority in various degrees:

• Price and payment terms.
• Certainty, simplicity and prompt completion of the acquisition.
• Other considerations including continued performance of arrangements, formal or informal, between the seller and a variety of people associated with its business including management, employees, customers and suppliers.

Sellers often make important concessions in price and payment terms to a seller whose offer responds strongly to the other two general objectives. In the author's experience, sellers frequently reject bidder from whom the highest price might be obtained. For example, sellers often reject a buyer who offers an impressive price because it needs time to raise financing, lacks reputation in the industry or plans to reduce the net cost of its bid by cutting corners in its future operation of the business. Sellers who developed a business with a reputation for quality often refuse to sell to a buyer who may use its tradename to sell lower quality products. Sellers often refuse to sell an entrepreneurial business to a large-structured corporate organization because talented employees accustomed to using their own judgment might be stifled by the buyer organization.

When planning a sale, it is wise to identify specific objectives within each of the general objectives and assign targets and priorities for each of them. They should also be discussed with advisers and any broker retained as an intermediary. These discussions will help the seller to set realistic objectives and negotiating strategies. They also will help to obtain qualified bids and avoid the risk and waste of dealing with bidders and offers doomed to be unacceptable.

Sellers typically develop initial objectives that are both numerous and highly optimistic. If they are within the upper limits of realism, it is a good strategy to do so. They can be revised during negotiations. They can also be scaled down if experience shows that some of the objectives are deterring bids.

The Retiring Founder's Decision

No business decision involves more human drama than the decision by business founders to sell as part of retirement and estate plans. A substantial number of the M&A transactions during the past two decades resulted from the sale of businesses founded during the years after World War II by independent-minded entrepreneurs. Operating as benevolent autocrats, many achieved remarkable success and became leaders in existing and new industries. Their businesses tended to be relatively unstructured, providing the advantages of speed and flexibility. However, many of these businesses remained heavily reliant on the talent and energy of the founders and a limited team of managers who shared their goals.

As founders near retirement age, some are able to bring their children successfully into the business. When this happens, succession to ownership by the children becomes clear. The remaining problems become arrangements to fund estate taxes, how to achieve sound management transition and fairness among children who participate in the business and those who do not.

Other founders do not have children or have children who do not go into the business. As retirement nears, these founders often consider a sale of the business to a younger group of managers who helped them build or sustain the business. While publicity has centered on transactions involving large public companies, a large number of the management buyouts have involved sales by founders to second generation managers and employees. One reason why Congress has granted tax relief to employee stock ownership plans has been to aid in financing employee buyouts of privately owned businesses.

Some founders find answers to succession, estate taxes and other problems by going public rather than selling the business. If done successfully, a public market for a company's stock can provide liquidity to raise funds for estate taxes and enable a surviving spouse and children to meet their financial needs. The effort required to become a successful public company often leads to development of structured operations and arrangements for orderly management transition. However, going public is far from a universal solution. Many businesses are not suitable for public ownership. The stock markets fluctuate and go through periods of several years when initial public offerings are difficult to achieve. Founders of some businesses want to remain private because of the restrictions imposed by public ownership. Others go public, but are not successful in operating as a public company and do not achieve the benefits described earlier. Many articles and books have been written about "going public" and its benefits and obligations. Two of the most practical are "Going Public: Practice, Procedure and Consequences," Schneider, Manko and Kant *Villanova Law Review,* Vol. 27, page 1 (November 1981) and "Now that You are Publicly Owned," Schneider and Shargel, *The Business Lawyer,* Vol. 36, page 1631 (July 1981). These articles were updated in 1988 and 1989 and are available at the financial printing firm, Bowne & Co., Inc., 345 Hudson Street, New York, New York 10014 through Ms. Frances Felix.

Returning to founders' decisions to sell, the authors recommend that founders plan carefully before any decision to authorize a management buyout effort. A successful management buyout can be a wonderful experience, but a failure can lead to personal bitterness and lasting harm to the business. Some founders have made a mistake by attempting a management buyout at the same time as efforts were being made to sell to third parties without recognizing that the situation creates severe conflicts of interest for both the owners and managers. Almost all management buyouts begin with an educational process in the "school of hard knocks" before realistic plans can be developed. In the meantime, managers hoping to buy the business are in a poor position to build the confidence of competing outside bidders. Some bidders decide to withdraw rather than rely on operating managers who oppose them. At times, an aggressive bidder will present an attractive and well-financed offer that can be closed on a schedule much quicker than that of a management buyout. If accepted, management may harbor bitter feelings of disappointment together with a newly born urge for a greater participation in ownership and top decision-making authority. The result may be a loss of some of the managers who may leave to set up their own businesses or join competitors and take with them customers and key employees.

The experiences described should not discourage founders from management buyouts because they are often the best and most satisfying method for sale. Rather, the authors recommend that founders ensure that the managers have a realistic opportunity to do their homework with capable advisers and satisfy themselves that they either can or cannot develop a financeable offer on terms satisfactory to owners, lenders and themselves. A decision to solicit competitive offers from outsiders may be necessary and desirable, but should be carefully planned to recognize and handle conflict of interest situations.

Even when selling only to independent bidders, the objectives of founders are often unique and highly personal. For all their experience, skills and toughness, many founders react like a mother placing a baby for adoption. Within realistic limits, their feelings can and should be respected. A bidder who commits to fulfill for reasonable periods of time the moral obligations of the founders to employees and long-standing customers and suppliers may be selected over a bidder who offers a higher price but may want to clean the house. A bidder who can find a genuinely interesting and useful role for a founder or founders after the closing will be favored over a bidder who offers a ceremonial consulting contract.

Founders should recognize that it is important to begin a sale process when the business is strong and before pressures of health and age limit their freedom to be selective. An early start means that the business can be taken off the market if offers do not meet realistic expectations. It also can mean an offer of a meaningful role in the activities of a larger organization rather than consulting contracts predestined to fall into disuse.

The Young Founder's Decision

Over the years, the authors have known young entrepreneurs who developed attractive growing businesses in a wide variety of fields. They included computer systems, *haute couture* clothing styles, LASER systems, public relations, motels, audio and video cassettes and a wide variety of other products. Most of these founders had a strong sense of independence and a deep mistrust of the financial community and of the large companies whom they had known as employers and then as competitors. Their viewpoint is humorously known as Route 128, Ann Arbor or Silicon Valley Paranoia.

Young founders who begin a valuable business soon encounter a problem they recognize—need for capital. Over the years, investment bankers (such as Hambrecht & Quist and Rodman & Renshaw), small business investment companies (such as American Research & Development and Greater Washington Industrial) and venture capitalists (such as Arthur Rock) helped to fill that need at considerable risk and cost. The risk was most often the failure of young founders to recognize that they needed more than capital or that the capital raised would not be enough to fill their needs. Some eventually succeeded in grand style and their stories are well-known. Others returned to the well again and again until their credibility was lost and the business failed.

As they develop business plans, some young founders decide that they cannot realistically accomplish their objectives without support from a larger company that can provide needed resources such as sales distribution, efficient production, and continuing technical support as well as financial backing.

The young founder faces a challenging task in negotiating a sale. First, the founder must negotiate a fair price for the business, a step that is specially important if the existing corporation has shareholders who will not be employed with the buyer. Second, the founder will want commitments that the buyer will (1) provide the resources necessary to develop the business, (2) employ the founder for sufficient time and with sufficient authority to permit successful development of the business and (3) provide the founder with a fair share of the benefits if the business is successful.

To achieve these objectives, the young founder must negotiate not only a sale contract, but also a management contract or employment contract of a kind that most large corporations do not regard as customary. The buyer representatives will urge that the young founder accept standard terms and rely on the buyer organization to act in good faith. Before accepting, however, the young founder must realize that even the most sincere buyer representatives do not necessarily control the individual attitudes of many people within their organizations whose cooperation is essential. If some or all of these people perceive the new business as a threat, they may refuse to help and even oppose the new business.

One solution is for the young founder to perform a "due diligence" review of the buyer organization that is as careful as the buyer's review of the business being sold. If the young founder learns that the buyer organization is unaware or not fully ready to support development as promised by the buyer representatives, the review can become the basis for contractual commitments to provide the promised resources. If the buyer representatives will not make reasonable commitments, the young founder may find it better to continue as an independent business rather than risk being "put on the shelf."

Divestiture Decisions by Diversified Corporations

A common divestiture objective of large diversified corporations is to sell a business which is draining resources from other more promising businesses and to obtain funds that can be used to strengthen the other businesses. Even a profitable business contributing cash flow may be sold if it is outside the core businesses which are part of overall corporate development strategy. Methods used in corporate development are described earlier in this chapter.

In the authors' experience, companies have serious difficulties in making divestiture decisions even when strategy and analysis indicate that a business should be divested. Senior management is often hesitant for reasons which involve pride, loyalty or inertia. Entrepreneurial division or subsidiary management often supports a divestiture to their own buyout group or to a buyer that can provide resources and opportunities. Conservative division or subsidiary management, fearing change, may urge senior management to reject a sale. If corporate management rejects a sale, they should have a definite plan which will establish the retained business as a vital element in future corporate strategy. If they simply defer a hard decision, the result can be a downward spiral as valuable division or subsidiary employees find other opportunities and the business becomes less attractive to buyers.

In recent years, many large diversified corporations have divested businesses suffering losses and other problems. Special steps required to accomplish these divestitures are discussed later under the caption "Decisions When Selling a Troubled Business."

Venture Capital "Exit" Decisions

While venture capital investors take pride in their role as sponsors of new businesses, they are, first and foremost, investors. Their investments in stock or subordinated debt do not have the senior or secured status usually obtained by institutional lenders. They may have seats on the board of directors, but rarely are active in daily management. They often pay more cash than management for their investment, but do not share in the compensation for services paid to management or in their potential for career advancement. Thus, venture capitalists bargain not only for equity participation, but also for contractual rights to realize on their investment by means such as an IPO, a "put" option to sell their investment to the company or other investors, or a right to require a sale of the business.

Representatives of venture capital firms seeking to realize an investment may create pressure for a sale. Depending on the extent of ownership and participation in management, the pressure will be large or small. At times, a venture capital firm may press for a sale opposed by operating management and other owners and will use voting and contractual rights to support its position. It is important to resolve outstanding internal disagreements, if at all possible, before commencing the divestiture process so that seller's management and ownership can speak with one voice to the bidders. It is possible to sell a business despite the opposition of minority shareholders and some or all members of management, but it is difficult to do so and everyone is likely to lose money, tax benefits and other advantages as a result of the disunity.

Executors', Administrators' and Trustees' Decisions

Some executors, administrators and trustees acting for decedent's estate are spared a decision whether or not to sell. The deceased may have directed a sale in the will or trust and granted broad discretionary powers to carry out the sale. The heirs or beneficiaries may agree that a sale is best and even on the methods for sale. Thus, the task will be to conduct the sale in a manner which is commercially sound, but also complies with probate law and procedures.

Other executors, administrators or trustees can face extremely difficult decisions. They may receive little or no guidance from a will or trust agreement. Heirs and beneficiaries may be sharply divided whether to keep the business or to sell. Family members who work in the business may have viewpoints sharply different from those who are passive investors. The differences may be slow to surface because of respect for the deceased and family ties.

Unresolved questions can be referred to the probate judge. However, judges look to their appointed fiduciaries for evidence and sound recommendations. Thus, the executor, administrator or trustee should become familiar with the business and should obtain advice from independent advisers experienced in the industry and in the accounting, financial and legal aspects of the business sale. Family members active in the business sometimes oppose independent review, usually claiming that the expense is needless and that the advisers do not have their practical experience. However, those responsible to the court are entitled to independent advice which considers the business and the interests of the heirs and beneficiaries as a whole.

When a decision to sell a business is made, an executor, administrator or trustee can use the normal methods. The price and terms may be subject to approval by the court after notice to heirs and beneficiaries. Notice to estate creditors may also be necessary. This should not present an obstacle for most buyers because acquisitions customarily require approval by a board of directors, stockholders, government agencies, lenders and other third parties. However, the executor, administrator or trustee must be able to demonstrate to the buyer that approval can reasonably be expected without undue delay.

Bankruptcy Divestiture Decisions

Businesses are often sold during bankruptcy proceedings by management or an operating trustee appointed under Chapter 11 or by a trustee carrying out a liquidation under Chapter 7. *In re Lionel Corp.,* 722 F.2d 1063 (1983).

In Chapter 11 reorganization proceedings, management often remains in control for a lengthy time period while preparing a plan of reorganization. During this time, they may sell businesses to raise cash and to advance the plan of reorganization. Their decisions will be made by customary methods, but will be subject to approval by the bankruptcy court after notice and a hearing which is frequently contentious. Creditors committees, equity committees, secured creditors, labor unions and other groups (with and without official standing) tend to use any proposal as an opportunity to pursue their own objectives. Thus, management must expect objections on technical grounds and perhaps on broadly based social or political grounds. While these objections may eventually be overruled, they create delay and uncertainty that can lose buyers. Experienced bankruptcy lawyers build support for a proposal by agreeing to help committee representatives and others to achieve their objectives. Anticipation of opposition and tradeoffs to win support are a necessary part of the planning for any divestiture (or other action) in a bankruptcy proceeding.

Under Chapter 11, management will rarely propose any divestiture of the entire company or of businesses so significant that their own positions would be threatened. However, if management cannot operate profitably with the benefit of the automatic stay and develop a credible reorganization plan, even the most magnanimous judge will lose patience and appoint an operating trustee under Chapter 11 or a trustee to carry out a liquidation under Chapter 7.

A trustee appointed under the Bankruptcy Code has extensive authority. The trustee replaces the entire board of directors and officers of the bankrupt company. Subject to approval by the Bankruptcy Court after notice and hearing, the trustee can sell the bankrupt corporation or its assets. The trustee can even offer tax benefits not available in other business sales.

Nevertheless, the trustee must overcome serious obstacles in arranging divestitures. The first will sometimes be objections to his or her appointment and compensation. The displaced management and its counsel will object and may refuse thereafter to cooperate except when their actions are visible to the court. Committee representatives and other groups who have a variety of understandings with management and its counsel may oppose a trustee at every opportunity unless the trustee reconfirms earlier understandings, a step that is not always possible.

While a bankruptcy trustee can expect controversy, he has several advantages. His appointment means that the judge has ruled that previous management and its strategies have failed and that a new plan, probably requiring a sale, is necessary. The trustee is usually in a situation where expectations are not high and a fresh and realistic plan may be welcome. Indeed, if the trustee finds unrealistic expectations, it is best to present the facts at the earliest opportunity and to decline or resign the appointment if support for feasible plans seems unlikely.

The trustee and bidders face some practical difficulties during negotiations. Committee representatives and other interest groups insist on information about negotiations and frequently interject themselves into the negotiations or develop alternative proposals. Creditors entitled to relatively high payment priority will urge an early sale and distribution of the proceeds. Lower ranking creditors and equity holders will urge that sale be made only at a price which realizes a recovery for them. Employee groups and labor unions will urge sale on terms protecting their employment, pay and benefits. The trustee should, if possible, seek to satisfy reasonable objectives of these diverse groups, but must ultimately follow the priority system of the Bankruptcy Code when negotiation reveals that some objectives cannot be obtained.

In view of the obstacles and acrimony, it seems miraculous that businesses can be sold in bankruptcy. However, trustees and their counsel regularly sell businesses during bankruptcy proceedings and realize funds to pay administrative costs, taxes, secured and unsecured creditors, and sometimes equity holders. To do so, they emphasize strategies using the inherent advantages of a bankruptcy sale:

> • The court's power to provide a fresh start to the business by discharging debts and other obligations such as executory contracts. When necessary and with careful planning, even environmental liabilities and labor obligations can be reduced or renegotiated.

- Special tax benefits afforded by the Internal Revenue Code such as the Section 368(a)(1)(G) reorganization and exceptions to the limits on use of loss carryforwards in Section 382.
- Freedom to issue securities pursuant to Section 1145 of the Bankruptcy Code subject to only limited compliance with the Securities Act of 1933.
- Emphasis on the love of a bargain that influences everyone from weekend shoppers to corporate executives.
- Support from the appointing bankruptcy judge. Experienced bankruptcy judges tend to be practical and oriented to preserving businesses and employment. Up to a point, bankruptcy judges will often grant delays, encourage compromises, and apply strictness or leniency in administering the bankruptcy proceedings in a manner which protects a reorganization or divestiture from contentious attacks by parties seeking narrow advancement of their own interests.

Decisions When Selling a Troubled Business

A threshold question which should be asked before taking steps to sell a troubled business is whether it should be sold at all. First, does the business, although unprofitable, provide supplies, services, shared costs or benefits to other company businesses which would become unprofitable after the sale? If so, internal cost allocations should be reevaluated and a sale, if any, should perhaps involve a larger business unit. Second, would a shutdown be more realistic than a costly effort to prepare and negotiate a sale? If a sale would take many months to complete and realize only a small net price, a shutdown may be best. Funds that would have been spent in the sale attempt can be devoted to an orderly shutdown program including severance pay and placement assistance for workers who would otherwise suffer months of uncertainty. Third, would a sale create potential future problems? For example, sale of a part of a business sometimes creates a competitor more troublesome than expected. For another example, sale of a business manufacturing or using hazardous products to a buyer lacking experience and financial resources to manage the risks could lead to product or environmental liability for the seller.

Once the decision to sell is made, the seller can often improve the price and terms by initiating some of the steps that a buyer must inevitably take. Alert seller representatives often inquire during negotiations how potential buyers plan to operate the business. While the bidders will not disclose their full business plans, they often provide information and clues that are valuable. While a seller would rarely undertake a costly upgrading program, elimination of expenses with no value to buyers and commencement of conservative rebuilding efforts can cut losses and improve sale prospects. These improvement efforts can also preserve morale and help the business to survive if a sale is delayed.

An essential part of the planning for the sale of a troubled business must be disclosure and explanation of the problems to the potential buyers. While optimism is essential, nondisclosure of material problems is not a realistic option under modern legal standards. The objective in selling a troubled business is to be rid of its problems for a price that can be kept. Thus, the seller of a troubled business should seek buyers who have the skill and resources to achieve a turnaround. The seller should then take steps to assure that the material problems are disclosed and the buyer acknowledges the disclosures. Otherwise, the seller may inadvertently sell the business on terms which give the buyer the rewards if a turnaround is achieved and an option to sue for return of the price if the business fails.

SCREENING POTENTIAL BUYERS

Screening potential buyers is specially important in the sale of a business. Extended negotiations that do not result in a sale lose time, effort and expense. Other potential bidders may be lost. Although less common, adverse effects on the business may be experienced such as loss of customers and key personnel. Least likely, but nevertheless important, an unscrupulous bidder might use the opportunity to gain business knowhow or competitive advantage.

A business cannot realistically be sold unless the seller can trust the buyer and its representatives through preliminary negotiations, "due diligence" activities, preparation and approval of an acquisition contract, cooperation to obtain government and other consents and a closing. While the relationship is adversary, the buyer and seller must also cooperate successfully.

The authors suggest the following screening methods:

- Check the reputations of the bidder and its representatives handling the transaction. In addition to competence and integrity, what is their reputation for effectiveness and how much authority does each have?
- Question the buyer in detail about its financing arrangements. During early discussions, it is understandable that a potential buyer will have taken only preliminary steps. However, if time passes and the buyer does not produce a commitment from a bank or other financing sources, together with active "due diligence" efforts by them, something is amiss.
- When dealing with a large organization, inquire what levels of approval will be needed. In general, approval by corporate management is required for acquisitions including resolutions of the board of directors. Sponsorship by respected division or subsidiary managers may carry considerable weight, but approval at corporate level is never automatic.
- If the bidder is working only with its internal staff, inquire when professionals such as accountants and lawyers will commence work. If buyer representatives do not produce the usual professionals, they may be "shopping" or lack authority.
- If the bidder is foreign-owned, approval from home country management will almost always be required as well as approval of government agencies regulating foreign investment and the central bank. The bidder should be asked to outline the necessary steps and the time and any uncertainties involved. If the bidder's representatives state that no approvals are needed, they should be asked to confirm their statements specifically in writing. On most occasions,

they will result in local representatives checking with home country management and learning the necessary steps which can then be evaluated.

• Inquire about the buyer's business plans including continuity of products, operations and employees. Many buyers will respond with general conversation to the effect that seller's business will be continued with few changes. However, even reputable buyers are less than open about these matters because they believe the seller should not "interfere" in future operations. if some elements of future operations are important to the seller, it can request that buyer commit to enter into supply contracts, leases, employment contracts and other contracts consistent with its promises. While no buyer will give unqualified guarantees tying its hands indefinitely, a buyer that refuses to make reasonable contractual commitments may well be planning to "clean house."

• Inquire about the price including the amount and the medium and timing of payment. Obviously, the buyer cannot make a final commitment on price and terms until it has done its "due diligence" work, but it can almost always provide a target price or price range. If the buyer plans to pay anything other than the full price in cash at the closing, it should furnish copies of its financial statements and agree to undergo a "due diligence" review of reasonable scope to confirm its ability to perform.

2

Financing and Structuring Acquisitions: Definitions of Some Technical Terms

FINANCING SOURCES

Financing for acquisitions is available from a variety of sources:

- *Insurers.* Life insurers are a major source of long term loans. Casualty and liability insurers also provide long and intermediate term loans.
- *Banks.* Commercial and savings banks and savings and loan associations provide intermediate and short term loans. Through subsidiaries, some banks can buy stock subject to a 4.9% limit on voting stock, a 24.9% limit on nonvoting stock and other restrictions.
- *Commercial Lenders.* Commercial lenders, such as Heller Financial, Inc., provide interim and short term financing secured by collateral assets having readily realizable liquidation values. They may also make loans based on cash-flow or going business value loans, but will require mortgage and security interests in the available tangible and intangible assets.
- *Pension and Other Employee Benefit Funds.* Employee benefit funds provide long, intermediate and short term loans. They may buy stock under special circumstances. For an example, see the later discussion of Employee Stock Ownership Plans.
- *Small Business Investment Companies.* SBICs provide intermediate term loans by purchasing convertible debentures.
- *Venture Capital Funds.* Venture capital funds and pools provide intermediate and short term loans. They also buy preferred stock and common stock.
- *Wealthy Individuals.* Wealthy individuals sometimes extend intermediate and short term loans. More often, they buy stock of companies in business ventures they believe to be promising.

• *Sellers.* Sellers sometimes accept part of the acquisition price in installment payments over a period of years. They may also accept preferred stock, usually with dividend and mandatory redemption features. Sellers often seek employment or consulting contracts and are more likely to be reasonable about the price and terms of payment if their wishes are accommodated.

The Directory of LBO Financing Services published by Business Publications, San Diego, California, provides information about a large number of companies which finance acquisitions and their addresses throughout the United States.

FINANCIAL INTERMEDIARIES

Investment banking firms, brokerage firms, financial consulting firms and finders provide services to companies seeking financing. Through their contacts and experience, they locate sources likely to be interested in financing an acquisition. They often advise on terms of the financing and assist in negotiations. With some exceptions, these firms do not usually invest their own funds in acquisitions, although they often manage funds which provide financing and may have officers or partners who make selective investments.

During the 1980s, financial intermediaries became a major force in the M&A markets. An article in *Mergers & Acquisitions,* January/February, 1990 reports that over $1.2 billion was paid in advisory fees during the first nine months of 1989 to firms such as Morgan Stanley & Co., Goldman Sachs & Co., Credit Suisse First Boston, Alex Brown & Sons, Merrill Lynch, Paine Webber, Bear Stearns and Salomon Brothers. *The Directory of Intermediaries,* Business Publications, San Diego, California, provides information about many financial intermediaries including their addresses throughout the United States.

Even experienced businessmen sometimes misunderstand the role of financial intermediaries. They will review a proposed project or acquisition with an investment banking firm and, if they receive a favorable reaction, assume that financing will be available as soon as paperwork is prepared. They are surprised to encounter delay and the need to present the proposal again to insurers, banks or other financial sources. Financial intermediaries may contribute to this misunderstanding by failing to explain their role. Eager to market their services and maintain confidentiality of their source contacts, they sometimes overstate and even overplay their role. Highly professional and experienced investment bankers and other financial intermediaries clearly explain their role and also explain the value of their contacts and reputation among financial sources.

Complicating the picture, some firms act both as intermediaries and as financing sources. For example, some investment banking firms and financial consulting firms have sponsored related investment funds which are sources of capital. Many banks have established M&A consulting departments which advise on financing including loans and equity investment available from other sources. These multifaceted organizations, however, customarily maintain separation between their service personnel and those making credit and investment decisions.

For many years, financing has also been found throughout the United States through informal intermediaries including business acquaintances. Recommendations and introductions by business acquaintances were generally provided without compensation, except the expectation of a possible returned favor. However, finder's fees were sometimes asked, leading to the legal questions described in Chapter 3.

Accounting firms and law firms also frequently make informal recommendations and introductions to financing sources. These firms traditionally treated their efforts as done for client good will, expecting only to provide services related to the transactions. In recent years, however, many accounting firms have established consulting departments which have separate fee arrangements for financial and acquisition advice. A limited number of law firms have recently introduced imaginative fee arrangements based on financial results achieved. The authors recommend that any such fee arrangements be reviewed carefully to assure that they will not impair the law firm's ability to provide disinterested advice.

FINANCIAL INSTRUMENTS

Financing is provided through two broad categories of instruments: debt and equity.

Debt instruments take many forms from the simple promissory note to complex obligations containing many contractual commitments (covenants) and secured by a variety of collateral devices. Some examples are as follows:

- *First mortgage bonds* are promissory notes secured by mortgages and security interests in property such as an electric utility power station or a factory.
- *Revenue bonds* are promissory notes secured by a stream of revenues such as turnpike toll revenues or lease rentals from a new plant facility.
- *Sinking fund debentures* are generally unsecured promissory notes requiring the issuer to make periodic payments of principal to an indenture trustee to retire the bonds.
- *Convertible debentures* are unsecured promissory notes entitling the holder to convert the principal amount into shares of common stock of the issuer. Convertible debentures are usually also subordinated.
- *Subordinated debentures* are generally unsecured promissory notes which contain provisions subordinating the rights of their holders to receive principal and interest to the rights of specified other classes of creditors upon bankruptcy, liquidation and other events. Convertible debentures are usually also subordinated. A corporation can issue several tiers of subordinated debt instruments. Subordinated debentures and junior subordinated debentures are frequently called "junk bonds."
- *Zero Coupon Notes* are generally unsecured promissory notes which require payment of principal, but not interest. They are sold to investors who do not need periodic cash income at a discount from their face amount providing a return to maturity equivalent to prevailing interest rates. They are sometimes also subordinated. Internal Revenue Code §1273 provides that original issue

discount (OID) be included in the income of the holder. Code Section 163 governs deductions by the issuer.

• *Interest Holiday Notes* are promissory notes which permit the issuer to pay no interest for a specified time period, followed by interest payments at a specified or determinable rate. Like zero coupon notes, interest holiday notes are subject to the OID provisions of the Internal Revenue Code §1273.

• *Increasing Rate Notes* are promissory notes which provide for payment of principal over, or at the end of, an intermediate term. However, interest increases annually or semi-annually if the notes are not redeemed prior to maturity. These notes were issued in leveraged buyouts which the sponsor based on a divestiture strategy. The increasing rate serves as an incentive to the sponsor to maintain the divestiture schedule and compensates the holders for risk if the sponsor does not perform.

• *Reset Rate Notes* are notes calling for the interest rate to be reset at specified times. While attractive to investors, they can make it difficult for issuers to restructure financing. See Internal Revenue Code §1275 and IRS Notice 88-90, 1988-1 C.B. 496.

• *Notes with Premium "Put" Rights* are notes which entitle the holder to require their repurchase at a premium at a specified time or event. Events may include a change of control of the issuer; a purchase of stock of the issuer by the issuer or an outsider in excess of specified percentages; a merger or sale of substantially all of the issuer's assets, or an extraordinary distribution of money or assets by the issuer.

• *Pay in Kind (PIK) Notes* are promissory notes which require payment of principal in cash, but permit the issuer to pay interest by issuing further notes of the same kind. The notes issued in lieu of cash payments of interest (called "baby bonds") may create OID problems.

Debt instruments which are convertible or subordinated, or both, may be regarded as the equivalent of equity for some purposes.

Some examples of equity securities are as follows:

• *Preferred stock* is a class of stock whose holders are entitled to preferential rights over other shareholders in specified events stated in the issuer's certificate of incorporation. The preferential rights almost always include a right to be paid a stated amount plus accrued and unpaid dividends in bankruptcy or other liquidation before common stockholders receive any payments. Preferred stockholders are often also granted preferential dividend and voting rights. They are sometimes granted rights to convert into common stock. The issuer may also commit to redeem preferred stock and may retain optional redemption rights. When a preferred stock has very favorable preferential and mandatory redemption rights, it may become the equivalent of debt. A corporation can issue several classes of preferred stock which have different preferential rights. For example, a senior preferred stock may be entitled to payment upon liquidation before junior preferred stock.

• *Common Stock* is a class of stock whose holders are customarily entitled to vote, to receive such dividends as may be declared by the board of directors, and to receive upon bankruptcy or other liquidation such distributions of net corporate assets as may remain after all obligations to creditors and preferred stockholders are fulfilled.

• *Special Stocks.* Corporations can also issue a wide variety of special classes of stock including stock with mixed characteristics of preferred stock and common stock. The most common example is common stock issued in several classes, each of which is entitled to elect a specified number of directors. Another example is participating preferred stock which, in addition to a liquidation preference, also shares with common stock in distributions of net remaining assets. Still another example is a special stock entitling the holders to receive dividends equal to a percentage of the earnings of an acquired subsidiary with eventual conversion into the regular common stock of the issuer based on a formula related to the market values of the special stock and the common stock prior to conversion. The Class E Stock issued by General Motors to shareholders of Electronic Data Systems is the best known example of such a special stock.

• *Options, Warrants, Rights.* Corporations also issue a variety of instruments called options, warrants or rights which entitle their holders to purchase common stock and sometimes other securities for a specified price for a specified time period. These securities usually include so-called antidilution provisions which automatically adjust the price and number of shares if the corporation makes changes in its capital structure such as stock splits, stock dividends or reclassifications or enters into a merger or business sale transaction.

• *Transfers of Investment Securities.* Transfers of investment securities are governed by Article 8 of the Uniform Commercial Code as well as the rules of the Securities and Exchange Commission and any stock exchanges where they may be listed for trading. Securities traded in the over-the-counter market are governed by rules of the National Association of Securities Dealers, Inc. *NOTE:* These laws and rules govern contractual and property rights of security holders and the responsibilities of third parties such as transfer agents, registrars and signature guarantors. They are separate from the corporation laws and the securities laws designed to protect investors as described in Chapters 8 and 9.

• *Recharacterizing Stock or Debt Instruments for Tax Purposes.* For many years, the Internal Revenue Service (IRS) has questioned whether particular instruments should be treated as stock or debt based on the essential characteristics of the instrument and related factors. When the IRS recharacterizes an instrument, the nature of payments made with respect to the instrument will change together with the tax consequences. Payments described as principal may become interest. Payments described as principal and interest may become dividends. Payments described as dividends may become interest or principal. Code Section 385 authorizes the IRS to adopt regulations setting forth factors to be taken into account in determining whether a debtor-creditor or corporation-shareholder relationship exists, including the following factors:

(1) Whether there is a written unconditional promise to pay on demand or on a specified date a sum certain in money in return for an adequate consideration in money or money's worth, and to pay a fixed rate of interest,

(2) whether there is agreement to or preference over any indebtedness of the corporation,

(3) the ratio of debt to equity of the corporation,

(4) whether there is convertibility into stock of the corporation, and

(5) the relationship between holdings of stock in the corporation and holdings of interest in question.

The IRS has not yet adopted regulations under Code Section 385, but continues its challenges under other Code sections including Sections 163, 279 and 1059. See also Revenue Ruling 85-106, 1985-2 CB 116 prescribing dividend treatment of certain redemptions of preferred stock held by owners of a large portion of the common stock of a corporation.

PRESENTATIONS TO LENDERS AND INVESTORS

(A) Lenders

The first step toward a successful presentation to a lender is to understand that a lender, as such, is not an investor. Even the most experienced businessmen sometimes fail to understand that basic concept. A lender, as such, does not benefit from risk and properly does not wish to undertake risk. The lender's function is to enable the borrower to fill a time gap so that a business opportunity can be undertaken when available rather than risk its loss due to delay. Lenders earn interest for the use of money during the time gap.

The tendency to misunderstand results, of course, because loans always involve some degree of risk. Lenders seek higher interest rates as well as more collateral security when they perceive greater risk. Further, many characteristics of a business transaction which evidence a good investment also demonstrate a good loan. However, there are also some characteristics of a good investment which provide little or no support for a loan.

What information should be presented to lenders in support of acquisition financing? While the emphasis will vary with the type of lender, the following information is basic:

• Audited financial statements for your own company and the company or business to be acquired. If audited financial statements are unavailable and cannot reasonably be obtained, many lenders will accept well-prepared unaudited financial statements.

• Business plans for your company and the acquired company.

- Cash flow projections, based on the business plans, showing ability to meet the interest and principal payments and also to comply comfortably with loan covenants such as an interest coverage ratio, a current ratio, an earnings to fixed charges ratio and a limit on capital expenditures.
- Appraisals showing the net realizable value of the assets of your company and the acquired company. In these appraisals, the lender is primarily interested in the liquidation value of the assets in a prompt, orderly sale rather than replacement or going business value.
- Resumes of officers and directors.
- Credit history of the company.

When reviewing the information, the lender will focus on liquidity, realizable net worth and reliability of cash-generating revenue sources. Adjustments from GAAP financial condition and earnings will be made because loans cannot be repaid from capitalized "good will" or product development costs. On the other hand, lenders will not reduce earnings by depreciation or amortization charges and will recognize the income tax savings resulting from deductibility of interest on the loan.

As long term lenders, insurers tend to limit their loans to well-established companies in stable industries with strong net worth and reliable cash flow generating businesses. If a borrower can demonstrate ability to meet net worth, current ratio, interest coverage, debt to equity and other conservative standards maintained by insurers, the reward will be a low cost loan which can be repaid comfortably over a lengthy time period. The reason is that insurers, especially life insurers, have a relatively low cost of funds and can forecast their cash needs well into the future.

Banks emphasize cash flow reliability although they may also require asset collateral. Banks evaluate a loan somewhat more quickly and tend to charge lower rates than finance companies and other short and intermediate term lenders. Finance companies emphasize asset-based lending, although they also review cash flow projections carefully. Finance companies may undertake a loan requiring more extensive evaluation and administration than would be acceptable to banks, but will require a premium interest rate and perhaps other incentives to do so. Finance companies necessarily require higher loan rates than banks because finance companies derive their funds from sale of commercial paper while banks obtain funds from lower cost deposits.

SBICs evaluate an investment like a venture capital investor. They are privately owned, but licensed by the Small Business Administration (SBA) to provide long term funds to small business concerns which do not exceed size tests based on net worth, earnings and numbers of employees. They obtain funds by borrowing from the Federal Financing Bank for a term up to ten years and can charge interest rates up to 6% in excess of the borrowing rate for a loan which meets equity criteria. The resulting rate, although relatively high, can be a bargain in the risk capital market. SBICs are not permitted to control their portfolio companies. They cannot invest more than 20% of capital in any one investment. Thus, typical investments have been in 3 to 7 year debentures or preferred stock convertible into common stock or accompanied by warrants to purchase common stock. SBICs seek to achieve a return on invested capital in the 30% range. Thus, like venture capital funds, SBICs focus on high-technology and other companies whose business plans offer potential for an IPO or sale to a large company.

Those accustomed to dealing with lenders should be aware of several basic realties:

- *First,* lenders perform "due diligence" work and obtain committee approvals before loan commitments are issued or loans are made. If these steps have not been taken, a new loan applicant should not think that the loan is going forward without them. It probably means that the loan application has not yet progressed to the stage of serious evaluation.

- *Second,* it is customary for lenders to require borrowers to reimburse some amount of their costs for "due diligence" work as well as their legal and other expenses. The amounts can and should be negotiated, but work may not begin until agreement is reached.

- *Third,* lenders frequently issue commitment letters with attached term sheets summarizing the major loan terms and conditions. While commitment letters are often bypassed for direct preparation of loan agreements, no commitment exists until a commitment letter or loan agreement is signed.

- *Fourth,* lenders require "equity kickers" with growing frequency when asked to finance a large part of the price paid for an acquisition. The "equity kickers" may consist of an immediate allocation of common stock at nominal cost or warrants to purchase common stock for a nominal exercise price.

(B) Sellers as Lenders

Some sellers will sell a business only if the entire price is paid when the sale is closed. Some sellers will even accept a reduced amount in order to take the whole price to the bank on the closing date.

Other sellers feel differently, especially after they become acquainted with a serious and substantial buyer. These sellers may be willing to accept payment of part of the price in installments over a period of years. Installment sales are common when owners sell to a management or employee group. (Chapter 11 describes the tax effects of installment sales).

Sellers who are willing to accept installment payments sometimes change their mind if the buyer must also borrow part of the price from a bank or commercial lender. The lender will usually require a first mortgage on the acquired assets. The lender will also require the seller to subordinate the installment payments to its loan. Some sellers find these arrangements unacceptable. However, other sellers agree, especially when they are financing an amount of the price which they see as a premium.

Other sellers will agree to a price which is partially contingent on future profits or net cash flow. A contingent purchase price is helpful in resolving differences in price negotiations. The buyer will not have to pay unless the business actually achieves the profitability levels anticipated by the seller. If carefully defined and related to excess cash flow, a contingent price should also not interfere with financing by a bank or commercial lender.

An indirect form of seller financing is commonly achieved through employment and consulting contracts. These contracts can mean more than the money they represent to sellers who want to continue to participate in the business. The compensation payments, if reasonably related to the value of the services rendered, are tax deductible. Each contract must be carefully negotiated, however, to assure that the authority and responsibility assigned to sellers will not be inconsistent with the buyer's plans for future management of the acquired business.

(C) Equity Investors

A presentation to equity investors can begin with the documents presented to lenders. However, the emphasis must be different. Like lenders, equity investors are interested in asset values and the adequacy of cash flow to pay debt. However, equity investors will focus closely on—

- The business plan
- Ownership and management structure
- Income and related tax benefits, if applicable
- Capital appreciation potential
- Arrangements to realize on their investment

Equity investors who will be active in management as officers or managers think differently on these subjects than venture capital investors. Management investors are likely to accept a relatively long-term business plan. They focus closely on management structure and commitments to assure present and future income from their employment. They tend to be optimistic about capital appreciation potential. Unless their investments are large, they often ask little about realization on their investment, although most will ask for some buyout commitment upon death or termination of employment.

Venture capital investors want a relatively short-term business plan, typically 3 to 5 years. They will focus carefully on equity ownership allocation and management control at the board and shareholder level. They do not usually want to manage the daily operations, but they want to control, or veto, major investments and policy decisions and to be able to change management if severe problems develop. Income from consulting fees or interest on convertible debentures is important to some venture capital investors, but others do not seek income. Capital appreciation and feasible plans and commitments to realize upon their investment are major factors for all venture capital investors.

There are two classic methods to achieve and realize the capital appreciation sought by equity investors:

1. The true growth business (telecommunications, biotechnology, entertainment, etc.) can be developed and then sold to a large company or can "go public." Even if the investors do not sell in the initial public offering (IPO), a public market can enable them to realize on their investment.

2. A stable business can be bought with modest equity investment in a skillfully planned leveraged buyout. Once the borrowings obtained to pay the acquisition price are repaid from the business cash flow, the entire business will belong to the shareholders. If the business has enduring values, it can then be operated to support expansion or sold to realize a capital gain.

Venture capital investors typically seek a return of 30% to 40% on their money. They seek 80% to 90% of the equity ownership if management can provide only modest capital and its skills and experience. To entrepreneurs seeking to raise equity funds, these terms seem high. However, venture capitalists must realize enough from successful ventures to cover their losses in failing ventures. Negotiations between management entrepreneurs and venture capitalists about their relative investment, ownership shares, management control, compensation and other issues are often fierce and prolonged. They do not always reach agreement. However, devices such as options, voting agreements, contingent compensation and buyout obligations are used to achieve compromises. The final structure for each transaction is usually unique.

STRUCTURING ACQUISITIONS

(A) Corporations

A corporation is a fictional legal person created by filing a certificate of incorporation with a state or federal government department or agency. Its organization is then completed by meetings at which a board of directors is elected, by-laws are adopted, stock is issued, officers are elected and other steps are taken. Corporate existence is maintained by filing annual reports and paying annual franchise taxes. Corporate advantages include: (1) continuity of existence regardless of changes of directors, officers and shareholders; (2) limited liability of directors, officers and shareholders; (3) centralized management and (4) free transferability of the shares of stock which represent ownership interests. Corporations own and operate their assets and businesses separately from the shareholders who own them.

In the United States, most business corporations are organized in the State of Delaware because of its stable General Corporation Law and knowledgeable courts. However, many corporations are organized under the laws of other states, especially large states such as New York and California. Except for banks, federally chartered corporations are seldom used.

Some other reasons why Delaware corporations are widely preferred are as follows: (1) rapid and inexpensive incorporation procedures, (2) modest annual taxes if the corporation does not do business in Delaware, (3) enabling provisions in the Delaware General Corporation Law under which a wide variety of sophisticated transactions can be accomplished by relatively clear and simple procedures, (4) ability to grant broad indemnification and exculpation to directors, officers and employees and (5) experienced and knowledgeable courts which can promptly handle and resolve complex cases. For example, the Delaware General Corporation Law allows actions by directors and shareholders to be taken by written consent. "Triangular" and "short form" mergers are authorized. "Blank check" preferred stock and other special securities can be developed to meet financing needs. Mergers between domestic and foreign corporations can be accomplished with relative ease.

(B) Basic Acquisition Structures

There are three basic methods to acquire a corporate business:

- Statutory merger
- Acquisition of stock
- Acquisition of assets

A *statutory merger* is a combination of two corporations pursuant to procedures in the corporation laws of the state or states where the corporations exist. A merger is accomplished by preparing a merger agreement which is signed by the corporate officers and approved by the boards of directors and usually also the shareholders of both corporations. Upon filing a certificate of merger with the proper state agencies, the corporate existence of one corporation is merged into the other corporation which becomes the surviving corporation. The corporation laws provide that, upon the filing, the surviving corporation automatically succeeds to the assets, liabilities, rights and obligations of the other corporation. In legal theory, the two corporations become one and there is no need for real estate deeds, bills of sale and contract assignments to transfer the assets and business to the surviving corporation.

An *acquisition of stock* is a purchase of all or part of the stock of a corporation from its shareholders. The acquirer becomes the owner of the stock which may or may not be sufficient to provide voting control. A stock acquisition does not usually require consent of the directors or officers of the acquired corporation and is sometimes accomplished even when they oppose the acquisition. After the acquisition, the acquired corporation continues in existence and to own and operate its assets and business. If a corporation purchases all or a majority of the stock of another corporation, the acquired corporation will be called a subsidiary.

An *acquisition of assets* is a purchase of all or part of the assets and usually also the related business from a seller. The purchase is accomplished by preparing an acquisition agreement which is signed by officers and usually also approved by the boards of directors of both corporations. The agreement is usually also approved by seller's shareholders if substantially all its assets are being sold. It is not usually approved by buyer's shareholders. The assets must be transferred by deeds, bills of sale and assignments. If the buyers have agreed, liabilities and obligations may also be transferred. Consents of third parties are frequently necessary before the transfers can validly be made.

For each of the three methods, the corporation laws permit the price to be paid with cash, stock, debt or combinations of them. However, tax laws, accounting rules and other considerations may restrict or provide incentives affecting the choice.

ADVANTAGES AND DISADVANTAGES
OF THE BASIC STRUCTURES

Statutory Merger—Advantages. Some of the advantages of a statutory merger are the following:

(1) *Simplicity of title transfers.* In a statutory merger, transfer of title to the assets of the seller takes place by operation of law. The filing of the merger certificate with the Secretary of State of the state of incorporation of the continuing corporation effects an automatic transfer of title to the assets of the seller. The numerous documents transferring titles which are required in an asset acquisition—i.e., deeds to real estate, bills of sale, assignments of patents, assignments of leases, assignments of licenses, franchises and miscellaneous contracts, etc.—need not be prepared and separately delivered.

(2) *Flexibility in the type of securities issued.* In a tax-free acquisition, a statutory merger permits the issuance of preferred stock and even, under some circumstances, debt securities without affecting the tax-free nature of the transaction; whereas in both an asset transaction and a stock transaction, with minor exceptions, only voting stock may be issued if the transaction is to qualify as tax-free.

(3) *Elimination of minority interests.* Under merger statutes, minority stockholders who object to a transaction generally have a right to dissent and have their shares purchased for cash at fair value, but they are bound by the vote. The result is 100 percent ownership of the seller by the buyer.

(4) *Opportunity for charter amendment.* Since meetings of the stockholders of both corporations are generally required in a statutory merger, dual meetings provide an opportunity to amend the corporate charter and adapt it to the needs of the continuing enterprise.

(5) *Reverse merger.* In a statutory merger, if the seller has valuable assets, such as franchises, which are not transferable even by operation of law, a reverse merger procedure may be instituted in which the seller becomes the surviving corporation.

Statutory Merger—Disadvantages. Some of the disadvantages of a statutory merger are the following:

(1) *Assumption of liabilities.* The continuing corporation remains liable for all of the liabilities and obligations of the combined enterprise, including all of the liabilities and obligations of the selling corporation, whether disclosed, known or unknown, contingent or otherwise. This assumption of obligations and liabilities occurs through operation of law.

(2) *Stockholders' meetings.* Two stockholders' meetings, of both the buyer and seller, are generally required to approve the transaction. Normally a two-thirds favorable vote of the stockholders of each corporation is required, and each corporation must go through the expense of preparing proxy material and

holding meetings. Since the adoption of Rule 145 by the Securities and Exchange Commission, registration of securities issued in a merger is required where the seller has "public" shareholders even though the merger is accomplished by vote of shareholders and operation of law and does not involve a "sale" in the customary sense. To save time, however, the SEC permits proxy materials to be used as part of the registration statement.

(3) *Dissenters' rights.* Generally, stockholders of both corporations have the right to dissent from the transaction and be paid in cash an amount equal to the fair value of their shares. They are entitled to an appraisal proceeding if they do not agree with the amount offered by the corporation. A large number of dissents may result in a substantial cash drain on the combined entity.

(4) *Timing.* Notice requirements to stockholders with respect to stockholders' meetings may cause delay in consummating the statutory merger.

(5) *State merger statutes.* Peculiarities of state merger statutes may limit types of transactions which may qualify for statutory mergers.

Asset Acquisition—Advantages. Some of the advantages of an asset acquisition are the following:

(1) *Elimination of minority interests.* A buyer obtains 100 percent control of a seller's business in an asset transaction. A minority stockholder generally has no right beyond the right to dissent and be paid the fair value of his or her shares in cash.

(2) *One stockholders' meeting.* Only one stockholders' meeting is normally required, namely the meeting of the stockholders of the seller, although circumstances may exist in which a meeting of the stockholders of the buyer may also be required.

(3) *No right of appraisal in Delaware.* Under Delaware law, the right of appraisal of a seller's stockholders is limited to a statutory merger transaction. A stockholder in a corporation which sells substantially all of its assets may vote against the transaction, but if the transaction is approved by a sufficient vote of stockholders, the stockholder opposing the transaction is bound by the vote and has no statutory right to be paid the fair value of his shares in cash.

(4) *Limiting liabilities.* The liabilities to be assumed by the buyer may be designated in the contract, and the buyer may, subject to exceptions under special circumstances, avoid the assumption of undisclosed liabilities.

(5) *Allocation of purchase price.* From an income tax point of view, the buyer and seller may allocate the purchase price to specific assets in the acquisition agreement where such allocation has significant tax consequences. In an arm's length transaction between a buyer and seller where the allocation is reasonable and supported by an appraisal or other adequate evidence, the allocation may still be given some weight by the Internal Revenue Service although Section 1060 of the Internal Revenue Code does not require it.

Asset Acquisition—Disadvantages. Some of the disadvantages of an asset acquisition are the following:

(1) *Complexity.* Of the three basic types of acquisition, the asset acquisition is the most complex from the viewpoint of the preparation of documents for the transfer of titles to assets. In asset transactions, separate instruments of assignment must be prepared, and then executed and delivered at the closing to transfer title to real property, personal property, leases, contracts, franchises, and intangible assets, such as patents and copyrights. Preparation and filing of such title documents is time-consuming and expensive.

(2) *De facto merger.* Asset acquisitions, where the consideration involves securities of a buyer, may be construed as de facto mergers by courts long after the transaction has closed. In such instances, a buyer may have assumed liabilities of a seller as though a statutory merger had actually occurred.

(3) *Consents to transfers.* Consents may be required with respect to nonassignable contracts such as real property leases, license agreements, and franchises. Often, consents of third parties may be difficult or expensive to obtain.

(4) *Bulk sales laws.* In order to avoid liability to creditors of the seller, it may be necessary to comply with the bulk sales laws of the jurisdictions in which the seller's assets are located. Such compliance may be disruptive of the seller's business or expensive.

(5) *Loan agreement restrictions.* Long-term debt obligations of the seller, as set forth in loan agreements, may contain restrictions against sale and be accelerated by the sale.

(6) *Stockholder meetings.* As in the case of a statutory merger, a meeting of stockholders must often be held, with possible expense and delay.

(7) *Securities registration.* Since the adoption of Rule 145 by the SEC, registration of securities issued in an assets acquisition is required where the seller plans to liquidate and distribute the securities to public shareholders even though the sale and liquidation are accomplished by votes of shareholders and operation of law and do not involve a "sale" in the customary sense. To save time, however, the SEC permits proxy materials to be used as part of the registration statement.

(8) *ERISA.* The assumption, bonding or escrow, and secondary liability requirements of the Employee Retirement Income Security Act of 1974 including the Multiemployer Pension Plan Amendments Act of 1980.

(9) *Successor liability.* Under some circumstances, the courts may impose product, labor, environmental and other obligations on a buyer who did not assume, and even contractually disclaimed, such liabilities.

Stock Acquisition—Advantages. Some of the advantages of a stock acquisition are the following:

(1) *Simplicity.* Where the seller is a nonpublic corporation with comparatively few stockholders, the stock acquisition may be the simplest form of acquisition to consummate. From the seller's point of view, the only documents required to be delivered to effectively transfer title are the certificates representing the outstanding shares of the seller's stock, properly endorsed.

(2) *No assignability problems.* Since in a stock transaction the corporate

structure of the seller continues intact and the conduct of the seller's business is not affected by the transfer of stock ownership, no problems usually arise with respect to the assignability of lease or other contracts requiring the consents of third parties to their assignment.

(3) *Speed.* Because of the simplicity of the transfer of the certificates representing shares of the seller's stock, unless the stock acquisition is contingent upon the receipt of rulings from governmental agencies, it may be accomplished in a short period of time. Since normally there is no requirement for holding stockholders' meetings in a stock transaction, the delay involved in giving notices or having proxy material cleared by the Securities and Exchange Commission is avoided.

(4) *Unwilling management.* In a stock transaction, no approval of the board of directors of the seller is required. As a consequence, in those instances where a seller's management is opposed to an acquisition, the buyer may complete the acquisition in the form of a takeover by acquiring a controlling stock interest directly from the seller's stockholders. Management can use a variety of methods to delay or defeat the takeover, but cannot "just say no."

(5) *Seller's liabilities.* In a stock acquisition, where the seller remains a separate corporate entity from the buyer, the seller's liabilities are not assumed directly by the buyer. The acquired corporate entity remains liable for such liabilities and obligations, and the buyer does not become directly obligated with respect to such liabilities.

Stock Acquisition—Disadvantages. Some of the disadvantages of a stock acquisition are the following:

(1) *Liabilities.* The business and assets of the seller owned by the corporation whose shares are being sold remain subject to all liabilities including unknown liabilities, since the corporate structure and business of the seller are not affected by the transfer of stock ownership. If a buyer does not want particular assets or liabilities, it must arrange for the selling stockholders to strip them out of the corporation prior to the sale.

(2) *Minority interests.* If any of the stockholders of the seller refuse to sell their stock interests, they remain an outstanding minority with a continuing interest in the seller's business.

(3) *Allocation of purchase price.* Where stock is acquired, from an income tax point of view, the buyer does not obtain a stepped-up basis in the assets of the acquired corporation unless it makes an election under Section 338 of the Internal Revenue Code and pays the related income tax.

(4) *Depreciation recapture.* Where a buyer acquires a seller's stock, from an income tax point of view, any payment with respect to depreciation recapture or investment credit recapture on the seller's assets is shifted to the buyer. The buyer may become liable for the payment of such recapture items should the buyer liquidate the seller after having acquired the seller's stock.

(5) *Securities law requirements.* If the seller has "public" stockholders, a purchase for cash may be accomplished only in compliance with the tender offer

requirements of the Securities Exchange Act of 1934 and any applicable state securities laws. The issuance or transfer of securities by the buyer in a stock acquisition will have to be registered with the Securities and Exchange Commission. Since the adoption of Rule 145 by the SEC, however, registration of securities issued in mergers and asset acquisitions is also required where the seller has "public" stockholders.

(6) *Fiduciary* obligations of controlling stockholders. The controlling stockholders of the seller may have a fiduciary obligation to the minority stockholders to see that the minority are offered the same price per share as the controlling stockholders.

STRUCTURING TO ACHIEVE SPECIAL RESULTS

Acquisitions can be structured as two-party, three-party or multiparty transactions. The structure may also include one or more subsidiary corporations existing only for a brief duration as an acquisition vehicle.

(A) Two-Party Transactions

In a two-party transaction, the buyers organize a corporation (or other entity) and make the acquisition as an assets purchase, stock purchase or merger. Even within a two-party structure, many variations can be used to achieve business, financial or tax objectives. For example, a transaction may be planned for tax reasons as a complete redemption by the seller corporation of one group of its shareholders and a sale of stock to the buyer by the remaining shareholders.

(B) Three-Party Transactions

For many reasons which are explained in Chapter 16, leveraged buyouts are most commonly structured as three-party or multiparty transactions.

In a three-party transaction, the buyers organize a corporation (or other entity) as a holding company. The holding company then organizes a corporation (or other entity) to be an operating subsidiary. The operating subsidiary then makes the acquisition as an assets purchase, stock purchase or merger. Numerous variations are possible within a three-party structure. For example, capital contributions and loans can be obtained by the holding company and all or part contributed or loaned to the operating subsidiary. As an alternative, financing can be advanced directly to the operating subsidiary, often with a guaranty by the holding company. Financing may also be advanced initially to the acquired corporation and assumed after the acquisition by the operating subsidiary and guaranteed by the holding company.

An illustration of a three-party transaction is shown in Exhibit 2-1.

(C) Triangular Mergers

In two-party, three-party and multiparty transactions, the buyer often organizes another corporation as a subsidiary, sometimes called an acquisition subsidiary, for use in accomplishing a "reverse" or a "forward" triangular merger.

A "reverse" triangular merger is used in transactions where it is important to preserve the seller corporation as a corporate entity in order to eliminate the need to sell assets which are subject to transfer restrictions or to retain its tax or other characteristics. During its short life, the transitory subsidiary receives all or part of the purchase price, usually as a capital contribution from its parent which is a holding or operating corporation organized by the buyers. The transitory subsidiary is then merged into the seller corporation which distributes the purchase price to its shareholders in redemption of their stock except for shares owned by the parent of the transitory subsidiary. The result is that the seller corporation continues in existence and becomes a subsidiary of the holding or operating corporation organized by the buyers. An illustration of "reverse" merger is shown in Exhibit 2-2.

A "forward" triangular merger is less common. The steps are the same as those taken in a "reverse" merger, except that the seller corporation is merged into the newly organized subsidiary.

STRUCTURES FOR ESOP ACQUISITIONS

Acquisitions financed through Employee Stock Ownership Plans (ESOPs) are discussed in Chapter 12. A simplified example of an acquisition structure financed through an ESOP trust is shown in Exhibit 2-3.

Experience has shown that an ESOP trust seldom acquires a business alone. While the ESOP provides valuable tax benefits, the employee beneficiaries of the ESOP do not have the business management skills and financial resources to provide the necessary assurances to sellers and lenders that the transaction will be viable.

Most acquisitions funded through ESOP trusts have been made by an acquisition corporation owned by several interests: (1) a management group providing operating reputation and skills, (2) a venture capital group providing risk capital in reliance on the skills of the management group, (3) a lender group who have bargained for equity interests and (4) the ESOP trust. In this structure, the acquisition corporation creates the ESOP in order to fund a purchase of 100% of ABC Inc. The acquisition corporation adopts the ESOP and the ESOP trust together with the obligation to make contributions to fund loan payments (principal and interest) and to repurchase shares from employee and beneficiaries who exercise their "put" option rights.

FACTORS IN SELECTING
A LEVERAGED BUYOUT STRUCTURE

Numerous factors must be considered in selecting a leveraged buyout structure. Those motivated primarily by tax, creditors' rights and subjects considered in other sections will be discussed in those sections. However, there are several structuring considerations which result from the nature of corporations and the laws governing them.

- *"Freezeout" Effect of mergers and asset purchases.*

If a buyer wishes to acquire 100% ownership of a business, the stock purchase method can be used only if all shareholders are willing to sell. However, a merger or assets sale can achieve 100% ownership, provided that the requisite vote of shareholders is obtained, even though some shareholders are opposed. This effect is a major reason for the use of triangular mergers.

- *"Bypass" effect of stock purchases.*

If a buyer wishes to acquire control, but does not initially need 100% ownership, the buyer can bypass a hostile corporate management by making a stock purchase offer directly to shareholders.

- *Access to assets.*

If a buyer needs access to the assets of a seller or target corporation to secure or repay acquisition debt, the access cannot be assured solely by a stock purchase, even if control is obtained. For this reason leveraged buyouts are planned as two-step transactions; i.e., a stock purchase to gain control followed by a "freezeout" merger. As described later, the second step must be carefully planned because the buyer, as a controlling shareholder, and its representatives on the board of directors of the controlled corporation, will have a conflicting interest in the merger transaction and must be prepared to show that the price and terms of the merger are "fair" to the minority shareholders.

Exhibit 2-1

THREE-PARTY TRANSACTION

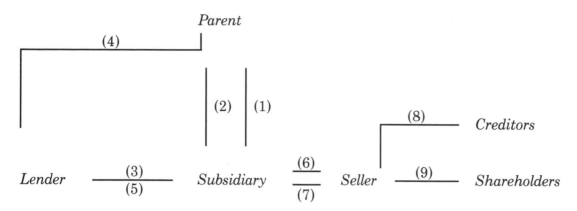

(1) Parent contributes $1.0 million capital to subsidiary.
(2) Subsidiary issues shares to parent.
(3) Subsidiary issues $2.0 guaranty to Lender
(4) Parent issues $2.0 guaranty to Lender
(5) Lender loans $2.0 to subsidiary
(6) Subsidiary pays $2.5 million to Seller
(7) Seller transfers assets to Subsidiary
(8) Seller begins performing plan of liquidation by paying taxes on the sale and other debts
(9) Seller completes plan of liquidation by distributing the remaining price to its shareholders

NOTE: The transaction shown is based on the parent's credit supported by its guaranty. Use of the subsidiary will shield the parent from liabilities of the acquired business except the guaranteed loan. Steps (7) and (8) are omitted if the seller is divesting only part of its assets. If the parent files a consolidated return including the subsidiary, the parent can deduct the interest on the loan from its income.

Exhibit 2-2

REVERSE MERGER

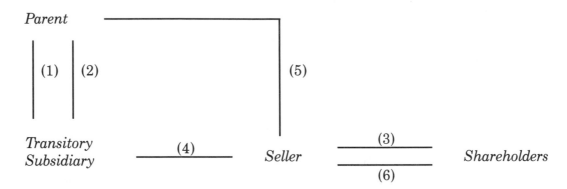

(1) Parent contributes $1.0 million to subsidiary's capital
(2) Subsidiary issues shares to parent
(3) Seller's shareholders approve the merger
(4) Transitory subsidiary merges into seller which continues in existence and succeeds to the assets and liabilities of the transitory subsidiary including the $1.0 capital contribution
(5) At the effective time of the merger, seller issues 10 shares to parent
(6) At the effective time of the merger, seller's previously outstanding shares are automatically canceled. The $1.0 million price is distributed to seller's shareholders upon surrender of their stock certificates

NOTE: In effect, a reverse merger accomplishes a purchase of all the outstanding stock of the seller. Even if some shareholders do not wish to sell, they will be bound if the merger is approved by the legally required percentage of the shareholders. The seller continues to operate its business, so it is not necessary to transfer assets and liabilities and assign contracts.

Exhibit 2-3

SIMPLIFIED ESOP ACQUISITION STRUCTURE

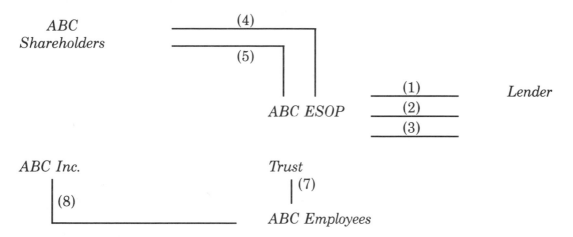

(1) Loan proceeds.
(2) Promissory Note.
(3) Pledge of shares of ABC Inc.
(4) Purchase Price.
(5) Delivery of shares of ABC Inc.
(6) Tax deductible contributions to fund the loan payments.
(7) Distribution of shares to ABC employees.
(8) Repurchase of shares by ABC Inc. from employees who exercise "put" option rights.

3

Investment Bankers, M&A Consultants, Brokers and Finders

Many acquisitions and divestitures are initiated by firms or individuals. Investment banking firms and securities brokerage firms have traditionally acted as a finder or broker for acquisitions and divestitures, frequently also acting as a financial adviser to the buyer or seller. Business consulting firms, specialized departments of banks, and a variety of other firms and individuals also are active as finders or brokers.

As described in Chapter 2, many acquisitions are developed from sources already close to the buyer or seller or at least within its own industry. However, particularly when a seller reaches a decision that all or part of its business must be sold promptly, the services of a broker or finder may be needed to locate interested buyers. Of course, an investment banking or business consulting firm may simultaneously be able to search for a buyer while also exploring other alternatives such as raising capital or reorganizing the business to become more competitive.

INVESTMENT BANKING FIRMS

The array of services offered by investment banking firms is impressive:

Knowledge of businesses available for sale
Knowledge of buyers seeking acquisitions
Knowledge of terms of recent transactions
Knowledge of the availability and terms of acquisition financing
Ability to raise financing by underwriting public offerings or acting as agent for
　　private placements
Ability to provide or arrange bridge loans for some acquisitions

Financial analysis of acquisition candidates
Business analysis of acquisition candidates
Advice in structuring acquisitions including introductions to legal, accounting
    and tax experts
Knowledge of developing government policies
Conducting divestiture "auctions"
Fairness opinions
Advice on negotiating strategies and conducting negotiations, when requested

A relatively recent activity which illustrates the role and skills of investment
banking firms is the private divestiture auction. Traditionally, sellers avoid public
knowledge that a business is for sale for fear of adverse effects on the morale of employees, customers and others. During negotiations, they will often tell potential
buyers they are undecided about the sale and that only a very attractive offer is
likely to be accepted. While this secrecy has some advantages, it limits the numbers
of buyers who learn of the acquisition opportunity and who will undertake a vigorous effort to buy.

During the 1980s, many companies adopted publicly announced divestiture
programs. Some followed leveraged buyouts and were undertaken to repay acquisition debt. Others were part of restructuring programs by public companies seeking
to avoid takeovers. To overcome the disadvantages of public knowledge, many companies place their divestiture program in the hands of an investment banker who
structures attractive business units for sale. They prepare "confidential" sale memoranda, including business descriptions and financial statements, and send them to
a relatively large number of selected potential buyers with instructions to submit
preliminary, *nonbinding* bids. At this stage, limited "due diligence" visits to plant facilities and document reviews are permitted. The bidders are told that those who
submit the most attractive offers will participate in a second round of negotiations
where more detailed "due diligence" will be permitted. The bidders are also told that
offers will be evaluated for price and also for certainty of financing and absence of
contract provisions disadvantageous to the seller.

This "private auction" technique, conducted skillfully, can be amazingly effective. After reassurance that first round bids really are nonbinding, many companies submit bids although their interest was originally marginal. Further, since
the bids are nonbinding, the bidders tend to make high offers with relatively few
of the conditions they would include in one-on-one negotiations. During the second round, the bidders hope to use additional "due diligence" to cut the bid and
seek additional protection. However, they usually find that the first round "due
diligence" disclosures covered the major items and further items are not easily
found. Communications are conducted through investment banker personnel
who question the necessity for information requests and emphasize that a bidder
who wastes time or reneges on its bid must be dropped. The bidders often become
infected by a competitive spirit and, in the final stages, two or more companies
will make final offers far higher than any of them would have offered in one-on-
one negotiations.

An example of a letter from an investment banking firm to potential bidders inviting them to participate in the second round is shown on page 52.

M&A CONSULTANTS

The field of M&A consulting is relatively new and includes a variety of organizations. For example, firms such as The Blackstone Group and Wasserstein Perella & Co. have roots in investment banking, venture capital and financial analysis. They put deals together and lean on their skills as strategists. Firms such as Kelso & Co. and Houlihan, Lokey, Howard & Zukin rely on special expertise in Employee Stock Ownership Plans. Firms such as Duff & Phelps, Arthur D. Little Valuation, Inc. and Houlihan, Lokey, Howard & Zukin cultivate a reputation for expertise in financial analysis.

The M&A departments of banks resulted from staff added by banks to evaluate loans to finance acquisitions. In many situations, bank personnel found themselves acting as informal and uncompensated advisers to customers. During the 1980s, as traditional loan markets thinned due to competition from commercial paper and foreign competitors, bank activity sought new sources of income. M&A departments were established to improve quality and derive revenue from services previously performed without compensation. In addition, they enabled the banks to reach out for new loan business where much higher interest rates could be charged together with equity sweeteners.

The M&A departments of accounting firms had a somewhat similar origin. For many years, the accounting firms gave advice on the accounting and tax aspects of acquisitions. While doing so, they inevitably included a wide variety of advice on business, financial and legal aspects of the transactions. Because of their multiple offices, they often found themselves introducing potential buyers, sellers and lenders. They were often asked to provide financial officers and staff for new companies acquired in leveraged buyouts. During the 1980s, accounting firms reviewed financial projections for leveraged buyouts and wrote solvency letters until the AICPA adopted a rule prohibiting its members from doing so. (See "The Accountants' Substitute for LBO Solvency Letters" *Mergers & Acquisitions,* September/October, 1989.) By combining M&A activities into specialized departments, the accounting firms were able to offer an attractive new service with greater coordination and expertise.

CLANTON BROTHERS, HOLIDAY & CO.
200 Wall Street
New York, New York 10075

Mr. William H. Bonney
Senior Vice-President
Acme Industries, Inc.
123 Main Street
Detroit, Michigan 48285

Dear Mr. Bonney:

We are pleased to advise you that, based on your letter dated June 15, 1991, your company has been selected to participate in the "due diligence" reviews of the numerically controlled machine tool business (the "Machine Tool Business") of Nationwide Automation Corporation ("Nationwide").

Please call the undersigned (212/456-7890) to arrange review by your representatives of the due diligence documents at the offices of Nationwide and to visit the satellite plants of the Machine Tool Business not included in your earlier review.

We enclose a draft Assets Purchase Agreement for the Machine Tool Business. We will be prepared to discuss the Assets Purchase Agreement with you and your counsel, accountants and financial advisers. Nationwide's Legal Department and Finance Department will also be available to discuss the Agreement.

The following procedures should be followed in submitting your offer:

1. Your offer must be to buy the assets of the Machine Tool Business for a lump sum in cash payable in full at the closing of the Assets Purchase Agreement.

2. Your offer should be made by a letter signed by an executive officer. The letter must explain the sources of financing for your offer. If you plan to raise financing from external sources, you must explain clearly the status and provide written copies of definitive financing commitments.

3. Your offer must be received at our office by 5:00 P.M., Tuesday, November 10, 1991, addressed to Nationwide, care of our firm, attention of the undersigned.

4. Your offer must be accompanied by a copy of the enclosed form of Assets Purchase Agreement. Any changes must be clearly marked on the draft Agreement and explained in your offer letter. Please do not submit your own form of agreement. Your changes in the Agreement will be considered by our firm and Nationwide in evaluating your offer.

5. Your letter must state that your offer will be binding for ten business days after November 10, 1991 and that your company is prepared to sign the Assets Purchase Agreement in the form submitted. Your letter must also state that, if your company is selected as the final offeror, your offer will remain in effect for an additional ten business days or until a definitive Assets Purchase Agreement is signed, whichever is earlier.

6. Nationwide will review and evaluate the offers submitted as soon as practicable after and decide which offer, if any, it will select for further negotiations. Nationwide and its advisers reserve the right to discuss with any offeror at any time the terms of its offer to seek clarification.

7. An offer will be accepted only when and if a definitive Assets Purchase Agreement is signed and delivered by Nationwide. Prior to acceptance, Nationwide shall have no obligation of any nature to any offeror or other prospective purchaser.

8. Nationwide reserves the right to evaluate each offer by any methods it chooses and to reject any or all offers in its sole discretion and without need to explain or justify its reasons. Nationwide further reserves the right, without liability and for any reason, to amend or withdraw offering procedures described in this letter and to negotiate and sell all or part of the Machine Tool Business to any person by any methods it selects.

If you have any questions on the offering procedures, please call the undersigned. We look forward to seeing you again during your due diligence visits.

Very truly yours,

Mr. P. J. Garrett
Managing Director

BROKERS AND FINDERS

Firms regularly engaged as finders or brokers maintain extensive data on industries and businesses and the prices, terms and background of recent acquisitions and mergers. Insofar as possible, they maintain widespread personal contact with business executives, particularly those known to be interested in acquisitions or divestitures. Since they are continually obtaining and arranging introductions, the great majority of their efforts are uncompensated, except on those occasions when a buyer or seller provides a retainer. This is why the fees of finders and brokers are quite high for successful acquisitions and mergers, although most firms will negotiate fees if asked to do so in advance.

Because many firms and individual consultants engaged in finding and brokerage activities also have other roles, it is not always clear when they are acting as a finder or broker. The introductions or proposals that they make are sometimes arranged during a brief time period. The subsequent negotiations and contracts that lead to acquisitions and mergers are lengthy and may be interrupted and resumed on one or more occasions. For these reasons and the high customary fees charged, there have been frequent misunderstandings about finder's and broker's fees. These misunderstandings have often resulted in claims and even lawsuits. This chapter explores the legal status of finders and brokers and the rights and obligations that buyers and sellers have in relation to them.

The time for settling questions of finder's or broker's fees is at the beginning of a negotiation, not after a price has been agreed upon and both buyer and seller will be reluctant to pay an unexpected commission.

Early in any meetings between a prospective buyer and seller, the parties should attempt to determine whether a finder's fee or broker's commission will be payable and to whom. If the seller has been offered through a broker, the buyer will know that a broker is in the picture. On the other hand, if the buyer has approached the seller directly without the intervention of any third party, he should find out from the seller whether or not the seller has entered into any arrangement with a broker or finder.

The possible existence of a brokerage arrangement should be investigated to determine (1) whether a broker may have been employed by the buyer or seller; (2) which party, the buyer or seller, may legally become responsible for the payment of the brokerage commission; (3) under what circumstances the commission will be payable and (4) what the amount of the commission will be. If in their early discussions of brokerage the parties determine there may be a broker involved in the transaction and the terms of the foregoing elements of the arrangement with the broker have not been settled, the parties should take immediate steps to formalize the brokerage arrangement by a written agreement with the broker.

The answer to each of the four questions in the preceding paragraph, if not incorporated in a written agreement, may rest in the legal rules surrounding arrangement with brokers and finders as those rules have been developed in decided cases. Differences exist in the laws of the fifty states of the United States, but certain principles of law may be generally applicable, and will serve as guides for developing an approach to and protection against brokerage problems. Although the general principles discussed below are helpful in developing an approach to brokerage, in specific instances brokerage problems will require research into the law of a specific state.

From the broker's viewpoint, knowledge of the general principles involved will help the broker collect a commission and formalizing the contract will minimize the need for a lawsuit to bring about the collection. Certainly, the broker or finder is in a better position where a contract establishes which of the two (buyer or seller) will pay the commission, the circumstances under which it is payable, and the amount of the commission. A typical finder's commission schedule is shown on page 62.

We will first discuss some legal principles applicable to business finders and brokers, and then offer a general approach and suggested methods for coping with brokerage problems, including suggested forms which may be utilized to meet the needs of specific situations.

LEGAL PRINCIPLES

Finder Versus Broker. A distinction is made in law between a business finder and a broker. A business finder is one who finds, interests, introduces, and brings parties together for a transaction that they themselves negotiate and consummate. A finder is an intermediary or middleman who is not necessarily involved in negotiating any of the terms of the transaction.

On the other hand, a broker, within the accepted meaning of the term, is an agent who has the duty of bringing the parties to agreement in accordance with the terms imposed upon him by his employer, his principal. Normally, in order to bring the parties to agreement on the terms set forth by his principal, the broker is required to take some part in the negotiations, even if the part is limited to a presentation of the terms upon which a particular sale or purchase of a business is offered.

The legal distinction between a business finder and a broker is generally not of importance in fixing the amount of fees and commissions agreed to be paid to the finder or broker. The distinction may have an effect, however, in determining whether a broker or finder may legally enforce a claim for a fee in a state which may require a written brokerage agreement or even a real estate broker's license. Under some circumstances, a finder may recover a fee from both a buyer and seller, regardless of the fact that the parties, do not know that a double fee is being paid. Generally, a broker may not recover a double fee without the knowledge of both parties because a broker has a fiduciary relationship to his principal. Some excerpts from opinions in decided legal cases may help highlight the distinctions made between business brokers and business finders.

Finder Versus Broker—Court Opinions. In a lawsuit brought in the courts of the State of New York by a plaintiff to recover for services rendered in connection with the sale of the defendant's brewery (*Knauss* v. *Krueger Brewing Company,* 142 N.Y. 70), the court held that the plaintiff was not a broker "in the strict sense of the word." The court held that the plaintiff was a finder and not a broker, and stated as follows:

The record shows there was evidence of the employment of the plaintiff for the mere purpose of bringing the possible buyer and seller together, and with the understanding that if a sale were to result the plaintiff was to have some compensation from the defendant for his services. The plaintiff testified that he was to have nothing to do with fixing the price or the terms of the sale; the principals were to do that part of the business; all he had to do was bring them together, and if through their subsequent negotiations a sale should result, the plaintiff was to be entitled to some compensation.

In another case (*Seckendorff v. Halsey, Sturat & Co., Inc.,* 254 N.Y. Supp. 250), a "finder" was defined as follows:

Plaintiff was in nowise a broker. He merely was a finder of this piece of business. He was to receive his compensation for finding the business and bringing the same to the attention of Rogers Caldwell & Company and its associates. He claimed his compensation solely upon the ground that he was the originator of the business and had disclosed to Rogers Caldwell & Company and its associates the opportunity to engage in this financing.

From the foregoing quotations, it is clear that if a business finder is employed, and if he introduces two parties who then negotiate a transaction which closes (except where special statutory requirements are not met), the business finder is entitled to compensation, in spite of the fact that the finder takes no part in the negotiations or assists in any other way in bringing about the transaction—other than making the introduction. For example, a finder whose complaint sought recovery for negotiating services was denied recovery in *Kilbane* v. *Dyas* 337 N.E. 2d 217 (Illinois, 1975).

To summarize, in law a business finder is a person who introduces two parties who subsequently negotiate and close a transaction, whereas a business broker is a person who not only introduces the parties but also assists in the negotiations to bring the parties to agreement and close the transaction. A business finder is entitled to a commission if his introduction results in a transaction. A business broker is entitled to a commission only if a transaction is closed in accordance with the terms set forth by his employer. As mentioned in the introduction to this chapter, variations exist in the law of brokerage within the different states. Not all states will necessarily make a distinction between a business finder and a business broker. However, in those states in which a distinction in law is made between a finder and a broker, the distinction may have the effect of permitting the recovery of a claimed commission, or denying such recovery depending upon whether a claimant is categorized as a business finder or a business broker. The effect of the distinction is further developed below.

Statutes of Frauds. It is the law of some states that any contract to pay compensation for services rendered in negotiating the purchase or sale of any business or a majority of the stock in a corporation is *void,* unless the contract or a memorandum thereof is in writing and is signed by the party who is charged with the payment of the commission. Statutes of this nature are generally referred to as "statutes of frauds." The underlying purpose of such statutes is to minimize the risk of unfounded claims for finders' fees or brokerage commissions in connection with sales or acquisitions of businesses.

New York State, a leading state in developing the law of business finders and brokers, has seen fit to enact a statute of frauds [N.Y. General Obligations Law § 5-701 (10)] which provides as follows:

> Every agreement, promise or undertaking is void, unless it or some note or memorandum thereof be in writing, and subscribed by the party to be charged therewith, or by his lawful agent, if such agreement, promise or undertaking . . .
>
> 10. Is a contract to pay compensation for services rendered in negotiating a loan, or in negotiating the purchase, sale, exchange, renting, or leasing of any real estate or interest therein, or of a business opportunity, business, its good will, inventory, fixtures or any interest therein, including a majority of the voting stock interest in a corporation and including the creating of a partnership interest. "Negotiating" includes procuring an introduction to a party to the transaction or assisting in the negotiation or consummation of the transaction. This provision shall apply to a contract implied in fact or in law to pay reasonable compensation but shall not apply to a contract to pay compensation to an auctioneer, an attorney at law, or a duly licensed real estate broker or real estate salesman.

Under the New York statute, then, the agreement to pay a finder's or broker's fee in connection with the sale of a business is void, unless there is a writing evidencing the agreement, which is subscribed by the party against whom the finder's fee or brokerage commission is claimed. *Haskins* v. *Loeb Rhoades & Co.*, 52 N.Y. 2d 523 (1981). Recovery for the reasonable value of services as a business broker or finder if also barred by § 5-701 in the absence of the necessary writing. *Minichiello v. Royal Business Funds Corp.* 18 N.Y. 2d 521 (1966).

The Writing. Generally, statutes of fraud will be satisfied by writings which establish the fact of the employment of a broker or finder by a buyer or seller to render the alleged services; however, the writing must be subscribed by the person to be charged with the payment of the commission or such person's lawful agent. The note or memorandum must be such that, standing alone, it completely represents an acknowledgement or admission on the part of the buyer or seller of the existence of a promise by the buyer or seller to pay the commission. In a New York case (*Morris Cohon & Company* v. *Russell*, 23 N.Y. 2d 569), an acquisition contract contained a representation by the sellers that they had not dealt with any person other than the broker named in the contract as well as an indemnification of the buyers by the sellers against any claim for brokerage or finder's fees by the plaintiff-broker. No other written memorandum of the brokerage arrangement, subscribed by the defendant, had ever been made. Although the acquisition contract clause did not contain a statement of the amount of the fee to be paid, the clause was held to be sufficient evidence of the fact of the plaintiff's employment by the defendant to render the alleged services, and a sufficient writing to meet the requirements of the statute of frauds. The writing was held to be sufficient to evidence the obligation of the defendant to pay *reasonable compensation* for the services rendered. In such an action, as opposed to a contract action, the court would have the obligation to determine the reasonable value of the brokerage services, since the value or fee had not been specified in the writing. Similar results were reached in other court decisions. *Flammia* v. *Mite Corporation,* 401 F.Supp. 1121 (1975); affirmed 553 F.2d 93; *Eaton* v. *Highland* 81 App. Div. 2d 603 (N.Y., 1981); *Bottomley* v. *Coffin,* 399 A.2d 485 (R.I., 1979).

On the other hand, a letter written by a broker to a buyer or seller, purporting to confirm a telephone understanding with respect to the payment of a fee, is not a sufficient writing if the broker is the only person who signs the letter. In order for the writing to meet the requirements of the statute of frauds, it must be signed by the party to be charged—i.e., the buyer or seller against whom the claim for a commission or fee is made, *Ames* v. *Ideal Cement Company,* 235 N.Y. Supp. 2d 622 (1962). In addition, the writing upon which a broker or finder relies must describe the transaction which actually occurred, and not a different transaction involving different parties, *Intercontinental Planning Limited* v. *Daystrom,* 24 N.Y. 2d 372 (1969).

Licensing Requirements. Many jurisdictions require that real estate brokers be licensed. In such jurisdictions, where the assets of a business include real estate, a requirement may exist that a business broker or finder be licensed as a real estate broker. The terms of the particular statute as well as the interpretation of the particular statute by the courts, will determine whether or not the business broker or finder is required to be licensed as a real estate broker before he may legally recover his brokerage commission or finder's fee. In Pennsylvania, an unlicensed broker was prohibited from recovering a stipulated commission for the sale of a manufacturing plant with land valued at about $9,000 and buildings with a going business thereon valued at $355,000, *Schultz* v. *Palmer Welloct Tool Corporation,* 207 F. 2d 652. In New Jersey, a person employed to find a buyer for a milk company where about one-third of the company's assets consisted of real estate, was held to be a real estate broker requiring a real estate broker's license, *Kenney* v. *Paterson Milk & Cream Company,* 110 N.J. Law 141, 164 A. 274. In California, a consultant was found within the finder's exception to the real estate brokers law where his services were limited to bringing together a construction firm and a financing firm, *Tyrone* v. *Kelley,* 9 Cal. 3d 1, 507 P.2d 65 (1973).

In the state of Washington (*Grammer* v. *Skagit Valley Lumber Company,* 162 Wash. 677) a person employed by a seller of a lumber company which owned real and personal property, although the contract of employment restricted employees to negotiating and obtaining offers, was also held to be a real estate broker. Therefore, in any situation in which a broker is requested to sell the assets of a business which includes real estate, the broker should determine whether or not he will be required to have a real estate broker's license in the particular jurisdiction, to have a legally enforceable claim to his commission.

Business Opportunity Publishers. Other types of individual state statutes may affect the rights of business brokers and finders. In New York State, a person may not act as a publisher of business opportunity advertisements unless he has filed with the Secretary of State of New York, in the form of an affidavit, a detailed statement as required in the statute. If a person acts as a business opportunity publisher without filing the necessary statement, the person may be guilty of a misdemeanor, and all third parties who have paid the business publisher fees may sue for the return of such fees, or if the fees have not been paid, may refuse to pay.

Conflict of Laws. The foregoing sections have indicated that in some jurisdictions a business broker or finder may require a real estate broker's license as a condition to a valid claim to a commission or fee, and in some jurisdictions, a broker or finder may not recover a commission or fee unless the agreement to pay the fee is in writing, subscribed by the party to be charged. Where different state laws may affect the enforceability of a claim for a commission, it may become important to determine which state law governs a particular brokerage agreement.

Assume a seller is incorporated under the laws of the state of Delaware and has offices and factories in New Jersey; the buyer is incorporated under the laws of the state of California and has offices and properties scattered throughout many western states. The broker who has brought the parties together has an office in New York, and negotiations have taken place in New York, New Jersey and California. Should the laws of New York, where the broker is located, the laws of New Jersey, where the seller has its factories, the laws of California, where the buyer has its main office, or the laws of Delaware where the seller is incorporated, determine the law which governs the transaction?

The answer to this question lies in the application of principles of law grouped under the topic "conflict of laws." Generally speaking, the law of the state in which the brokerage arrangement was made or the state which has the most significant contacts with the brokerage arrangement will be applicable in construing the validity of the brokerage contract. The place where the acquisition contract is made or the location of the properties, business, or headquarters of either the buyer or the seller will not normally determine the state law which governs and determines the validity of the broker's or finder's contract.

Contract of Employment. The legal relationship between a buyer or seller and a broker or finder is founded in contract law. In order for a broker to earn a fee, a contract must exist under which the buyer or seller, acting as principal, has employed the broker or finder as an agent.

Contract—Express and Implied. The contract of employment necessary to establish the relationship of agency between a broker and his principal, as those terms are used above, is governed by the law applicable to ordinary contracts. The contract need not be a formal one; it may either be express or implied. A written agreement defining the brokerage or finder's arrangement between the parties is an express contract and its terms will, of course, govern the rights of the parties. However, since no particular form is required for the contract, it may arise through correspondence, oral communications or conduct of the parties. In such situations the contract may be an implied one and the terms may be left to implication.

Contract—Implied. For an implied contract to exist, the broker or finder need only act with the consent of the principal, whether such consent is given in writing, orally, or by implication from the conduct of the parties. For example, assume a person known to you to be engaged in a general brokerage business approaches you and says he might have a buyer for your business "if you're interested." You need only tell him to bring the prospective buyer around because you "might sell if the price is right." An ultimate sale to the buyer as a result of the introduction furnished by the broker may entitle the broker to a commission on the theory that an implied contract of employment existed between you and the broker, although the contract may be void in a jurisdiction that requires that it be in writing.

Accordingly, a seller or buyer should think carefully before accepting disclosure of an acquisition opportunity from a broker or someone who may be a finder. The disclosure may foreclose the opportunity to make contact directly without paying compensation to the broker or finder. Of course, if the opportunity disclosed is already known, the broker or finder should be advised promptly. This can sometimes be difficult, particularly when seller or buyer is a large organization in which several officers or managers are involved in business development activities. Thus, some businesses do not accept disclosures without a prior agreement designed to protect against mistaken claims for commissions.

The earlier example illustrates the implied brokerage contract in its simplest form. The principal (buyer or seller) gives its consent to a certain course of action to be taken by the finder or broker, knowing he is engaged in the brokerage business, and the broker acts upon such consent or agrees to act upon such consent. Under contract law, an implied contract exists. The principal may be bound to pay the broker some compensation if the broker successfully completes the course of action undertaken.

Contract—Ratification. A contract of employment of a broker or finder may also arise where a finder has completely performed his services and the buyer or seller subsequently ratifies his actions. Legally, the ratification of the finder's acts has the same general effect as the buyer or seller initially employing the broker to perform the services, and upon ratification the buyer or seller, as the case may be, may become liable to pay a commission to the broker. To illustrate, assume a broker comes to you, an owner, and says that he has signed a contract as agent for an undisclosed principal (you) to sell your business to a buyer for $1,000,000. In spite of the fact that you never intended to sell your business and never employed the broker, if you ratify the broker's acts by selling your business to the buyer in accordance with the contract, you may owe the broker a commission.

Whose Agent Is the Broker? The principal may be either the buyer or seller, and the broker or finder may be an agent to sell or buy, or for both purposes. Stated differently, the broker may be the agent of either the buyer, the seller or of both. Where no express contract exists and the circumstances, correspondence, or conduct of the parties do not clearly establish whose agent the broker is, he is generally considered the agent of the one who first contacted him.

A broker's or finder's voluntary offer to become the agent for a buyer or seller, without any consent on the buyer's or seller's part, will not create an implied contract. But, if as a result of prior dealings between the principal and a finder, a finder could reasonably believe that by his silence the principal consents to such employment, an implied contract could exist. Assume, for example, that a friend of yours who knows you have your business for sale asks you how much you want for it. If this is the only communication you have with your friend concerning the sale of the business, and he sends a buyer to you to whom you sell, you probably will not owe your friend a commission. He is a volunteer, and you did not hire him to sell your business. But if you and your friend have had past dealings in which he has attempted to sell your business for an agreed commission, a sale to a buyer sent by your friend could result in a legal obligation to pay the commission. By course of past conduct, an implied brokerage contract may exist between you and your friend.

Time of Earning Commission. When has the broker earned his commission? The answer to this question again depends upon the terms of the agreement between the broker and the buyer or seller. If the agreement is an express contract, its terms will provide the answer. But if the agreement has risen as an implied contract, then the broker or finder earns his commission when he has done the work for which he was hired. Generally speaking, however, in a business brokerage or business finder situation, a commission is not earned until the transaction actually closes.

In real estate brokerage, different rules may apply. In a real estate situation, an implied contract may take one of two forms: (1) where the owner has given the broker full and complete terms upon which he is willing to sell his property; or (2) where the owner is willing to sell but has not fixed the terms of the sale, except perhaps, the sale price. In the first case, a broker is entitled to his commission when he produces a customer "ready, willing, and able" to fulfill all the terms fixed by the owner. In the second case, the broker does not earn his commission until the buyer and seller reach agreement upon the price and the terms upon which a sale may be made, or, as often stated, the broker does not earn his commission until he has brought about a "meeting of the minds" between the buyer and seller. These rules are succinctly stated in a leading New York State real estate brokerage case decided in 1911, *Arnold v. Schmeidler,* 144 App. Div. 420, 129 N.Y. Supp. 408 at page 413:

> In the absence of a special agreement, the services rendered by a broker to an owner of real estate generally fall into one of two categories:
> (1) Where the owner has given the broker the full and complete terms upon which he is willing to sell his property, and not merely the asking price thereof;
> (2) Where the owner has his property for sale, and may or may not have set an asking price thereon, but does not fix the terms of the transaction leaving them to be determined thereafter.
> In the first case the broker's duty is fulfilled, and his commissions are earned when he produces a customer ready, willing, and able to comply with all the terms fixed by the owner. Should the latter then desire to add to the terms already imposed, the additional conditions must be germane to the original ones, if they are to furnish a sufficient reason for the refusal to pay the broker in case of the customer's refusal to agree to any modification of the original terms. In the second case the broker's commissions are not earned until the customer produced by him reaches an agreement with the

owner upon the price and terms upon which a sale can be made. This, of course, does not mean that a contract in writing must be signed by the parties, but that their minds must meet not only upon the price, but upon the essential terms of an agreement to purchase.

Amount of Commissions or Fees. The size of the commissions payable to a business broker or finder may vary greatly, depending upon the terms which have been negotiated with his principal. No two situations are alike. Fees have ranged from as much as 10 percent or more of the total value of a transaction to less than 1 percent. Sometimes, fees paid to brokers or business finders appear exorbitant and may lead to private litigation, or even investigation by administrative agencies. On other occasions, finders have accepted fees substantially below those which the transaction could have warranted.

Although the amount of broker's commissions or finder's fees may vary greatly from situation to situation, a formula has developed that is often suggested as the formula for determining brokerage and finder's fees in a transaction which closes. This formula is as follows:

If the Amount of Consideration Paid Is:

Over	But Not Over	Commission or Fee
$ 0	$ 1,000,000	5% of consideration
$ 1,000,000	$ 2,000,000	$ 50,000 plus 4% of excess over $ 1,000,000
$ 2,000,000	$ 3,000,000	$ 90,000 plus 3% of excess over $ 2,000,000
$ 3,000,000	$ 4,000,000	$120,000 plus 2% of excess over $ 3,000,000
$ 4,000,000	$10,000,000	$140,000 plus 1% of excess over $ 4,000,000
$10,000,000		$200,000 plus 0.5% of excess over $10,000,000

The formula set forth above may be mentioned in fixing brokerage commissions, but is not necessarily followed. Often, in sizable transactions, the amount of the brokerage commission or finder's fees may be stated as a flat percentage of between 1 percent and 2 percent of the consideration paid.

Since the rights of the buyer or seller and the broker are determined by the contract terms, after the broker has carried out his obligations, he will be entitled to whatever commission was agreed upon. But where the contract is an implied one, the amount of his fees may not have been fixed. The contract may nevertheless be valid, and where the parties have not fixed the amount of commission payable, reasonable compensation will be implied. So many factors may enter into a determination of reasonable compensation in any particular acquisition that no general rule can be stated to fix such compensation in all cases. But as an indication of how the implied commission may be fixed, the general principle is that the commission should be sufficient to pay the broker or finder a commission or fee which (1) is commensurate with standard fees for such brokers, fixed by custom or otherwise, (2) is stated in the statutes of the state whose law governs where such statutes fix the commission or (3) is the broker's or finder's usual fee, if such usual fee is reasonable.

Duration of Contract. Once a contract between a buyer or seller and finder exists, the duration of the agreement depends upon the intention of the parties as expressed in the written contract or implied from the terms of the implied contract. Where the period of employment is not fixed by the terms of the contract, differing circumstances and a number of differing events can cause its legal termination. Thus, the contract will terminate after a reasonable time, or after the broker or finder accomplishes the purpose for which he was hired, or definitely and finally fails to accomplish such purpose, or if the contract is otherwise modified or revoked. As an example of termination of a brokerage contract, assume you, as a prospective buyer, have hired a broker to negotiate the purchase of the Split-Second Outboard Motor Company. If at some time after the broker has been hired and begins his work you learn from your morning newspaper that the Split-Second Outboard Motor Company was acquired by your competitor at a much higher price than you were willing to pay, you may assume that your arrangement with your broker has terminated.

Revoking the Contract. Unless the contract has a fixed duration, generally a buyer or seller always has the power to revoke the agency at any time and for any reason. Whether this right to terminate relations with a broker may be exercised without liability on the part of the buyer or seller depends upon the contract and the good faith of the buyer and seller. Although a principal may have the power to revoke a broker's or finder's agency, he may not breach the contract; and if he breaches the contract by terminating the relationship, he may be liable to pay damages. If a buyer or seller acts in good faith, he has the right to terminate the agency at any time before the commission has been earned. Generally, he may not, however, revoke in bad faith in order to avoid payment of a commission where the broker or finder has substantially accomplished his mission. Where a buyer hires a finder to find a company for the buyer to acquire and the finder finds a company acceptable to the buyer, the buyer may not, without incurring liability to the finder, revoke the agency and then buy the company.

Annotation. For further information, see the annotation titled "Validity, Construction and Enforcement of Business Opportunities" or "Finder's Fee Contracts," 24ALR3d 1160.

WORKING WITH BROKERS AND FINDERS

How should you approach brokerage situations? In general, to avoid uncertainties, all brokerage arrangements should be reduced to writing and should contain details of the understanding between the principal and the broker or finder of each of the major terms of the contract. To illustrate, assume that you are an officer of a corporation. A broker arrives at your office and says: "I know you people are interested in acquiring companies in the electronics field. Dyne-O-Space Electronics Company is for sale. Are you interested?" You have some familiarity with Dyne-O-Space and might be interested in buying the company. How do you answer the broker?

Your answer to the broker should first question whether or not the broker has authority to offer Dyne-O-Space for sale. Determining the broker's authority to act at the outset will avoid possible subsequent disagreement between you and the seller as to the employer of the broker. You might say to the broker: "Of course you have written authority to offer Dyne-O-Space for sale. May I see it?"

If the broker has such written authority, the written authority may contain an agreement on the part of the seller to pay the broker his commission upon the completion of the sale, or it may provide that the broker must collect his commission from the buyer. At least the written authority will give you a concrete starting point.

Even if the broker has no written evidence of authority to act, it may be that you will feel that the broker could be helpful and you would be willing to pay the broker a commission if he could bring about a purchase of Dyne-O-Space. You may feel that he can put you in direct touch with the proper officials of Dyne-O-Space or that he has developed detailed financial information of the company and projections of earnings in its field which could be helpful. In any event, whether you will pay the commission or whether the seller will pay the commission, the terms of the brokerage arrangement should be fixed in advance, in detail, in a written contract for the protection of both the principal and the broker. Certain of the aspects of brokerage arrangements mentioned in this chapter should be discussed with the broker with particular emphasis on the major elements: (1) Whose agent is the broker—i.e., who pays him? (2) What are the terms and conditions to be fulfilled? (3) What will the amount of commission be? (4) When will the commission be earned? (5) How long will the brokerage contract remain in effect?

Before you agree to move forward with the broker, the details of the arrangement should be reduced to writing and signed by the buyer and broker, or seller and broker, as the case may be. Written brokerage agreements often take the form of a letter signed by both the broker and the party who agrees to pay the commission. A more elaborate contract is not necessary, provided the letter agreement details the major understanding.

As an example of a general form of brokerage letter agreement, printed below is a form of agreement the broker showed you when you asked him whether he had the authority to represent Dyne-O-Space:

DYNE-O-SPACE ELECTRONICS COMPANY
(Seller Corporation)

June   , 19____

Dear Mr. Broker:

We are writing to confirm the brokerage agreement arrived at between us concerning the sale of our company, Dyne-O-Space Electronics Company. We hereby employ you as our broker to bring about the sale of our company in accordance with the terms and conditions expressed in this letter.

The purchase price of our company must be satisfactory to us in amount and must be paid in the capital stock of a company listed on a National Stock Exchange; the sale must be made as a "tax-free" reorganization under the U.S. tax laws, and the buyer and the terms and conditions of the Agreement and Plan or Reorganization must be satisfactory to us.

Should you bring about the sale of our company, we will pay you a commission of $20,000. This commission will be payable to you only as if, and when, the transfer of substantially all of the assets or the stock of the company has been completed and the stock of the buyer has been received by our company or its stockholders. If the transaction is not consummated, no commission will be payable to you regardless of whether the failure to close is due to any action or failure to act on our part, or due to any action or failure to act on the part of a prospective buyer.

You warrant to us that you have no arrangement or understanding of any kind with any other person or firm who may claim a commission from us as a result of such arrangement or understanding and you agree to hold us harmless against any such claims. You also agree that you will not seek any commission or remuneration of any kind from any buyer of our company, and that our payment of $20,000 to you upon fulfillment of the conditions contained in this letter will be in complete discharge of any and all obligations to you in connection with the sale of our company.

This agency will automatically terminate 180 days from the date you sign this agreement, unless our company terminates the agency sooner by 10 days written notice to you.

If this letter sets forth the understanding arrived at between us, will you please sign and date the carbon copy of this letter below under the word "Agreed" and return the signed carbon to us.

Very truly yours,
DYNE-O-SPACE ELECTRONICS COMPANY

_____
/s/ John Jones
Vice President

Agreed:
Date: June   , 19____

_____
/s/ Jack Smith
Broker

You will note that Dyne-O-Space Electronics Company proposes to pay the $20,000 commission. This means that the assets of the company will be reduced by that amount, and that you as the buyer should take this fact into account in negotiating the price you are willing to pay. Sometimes, where the seller is a closely held corporation, a buyer will insist that any brokerage commissions or finder's fees be paid by the seller's shareholders individually. But under the circumstances, a buyer may expect that the seller's shareholders will, in turn, take their agreement to pay commissions into account in negotiating a sales price.

If when the broker approached you with Dyne-O-Space Electronics Company, you were employed by a company that had specified conditions under which it would accept offerings of companies, you might say to the broker: "Our company imposes strict conditions under which it will accept information concerning proposed acquisitions. Before I talk to you about Dyne-O-Space, I would like you to read these conditions and see if you agree." With that you might hand the broker a document which might read as follows:

Conditions for Submission of Companies to the Buyer for Consideration as Acquisitions

Buyer is a company which has grown by combination of internal expansion and the acquisition of related businesses. While buyer is anxious to take every opportunity to add profitable related businesses to its current product lines, it has found that certain precautions are required to protect the interests of itself, prospective sellers and their designated intermediaries. This is particularly true since buyer solicits suggestions for potential acquisitions from many sources, its employees, bankers, outside directors and others, and actively pursues these prospects though various business contacts and direct overtures to principals. Buyer, therefore, will only accept submissions which conform to the following conditions:

(1) Buyer must see an executed copy and be provided with a copy of the agreement between the seller and the intermediary, which includes: (a) The amount of the fee; (b) Who is responsible for payment; (c) The conditions under which payment becomes due; (d) The period of the agreement's effectiveness; (e) A statement indicating whether this particular agreement is exclusive for the period indicated.

(2) Any submission made to the buyer must be with the understanding that the buyer assumes no obligation to do more than consider such submission to the extent, in the buyer's sole judgment, the submission merits consideration, and to indicate to the intermediary the buyer's interest or lack thereof.

(3) Unless specifically requested in writing and agreed to by the buyer in writing, the buyer will not ordinarily return financial or other data submitted to it for analysis of the proposed acquisition.

(4) Although the buyer will treat the submission with care and discretion, it will not, however, agree to hold a submission in confidence. In making its analysis, the buyer must reveal the information submitted to various employees. Al-

though these employees have instructions to keep the information confidential, the buyer is unwilling to assume responsibility that no disclosure of information will be made. It is understood, therefore, that no confidential relationship or agreement to compensate is entered into by reason of buyer considering the submission.

(5) No submissions will be accepted without an asking price for the business in question. The asking price will enable the buyer to inform the intermediary more quickly of whether or not the buyer has any interest in the proposed acquisition.

(6) The buyer is to be provided with complete and detailed operating statements, balance sheets, records of ownership, sales and product data, reasons for selling, and other information which the buyer may reasonably request for initial analysis.

Having read and understood the foregoing conditions, I hereby agree to comply with them, and I herewith submit Dyne-O-Space Electronics Company for your consideration on the conditions set forth above.

Signed this _____ day of _____, 19____.

Signature of Intermediary

Signature of Buyer Executive

Types of Brokerage Agreements. Some broker's or finder's arrangements consist of concise letters, while others are more elaborate and detailed. An example is reproduced below, with the parties' names fictionalized.

November   , 19____

Mr. Robert Searcher, President
Excellent Finders & Company, Inc.
100000 Broadway
New York, New York

Dear Mr. Searcher:

I am writing to confirm the understanding we have reached concerning the proposed sale of the business or stock of Seller Factories, Inc. ("Seller"). You are hereby employed as a broker to bring about the sale of the assets or stock of Seller, subject to the terms and conditions expressed in this letter.

The brokerage arrangement is nonexclusive.

We expressly reserve the right to reject any proposed purchaser you submit to us. On your part you agree that you will submit the name of any proposed pur-

chaser to us in writing, and our written approval noted in each submission will be a prerequisite, before you may reveal our name to any prospective purchaser.

You will be entitled to the commission mentioned below only if a prospective purchaser has been submitted to us and approved by us in writing, and an acquisition by such purchaser is actually consummated—i.e., the acquisition has closed —and we have received the full consideration specified in the contract of sale.

Should the Seller's business or the stock of Seller be acquired by a purchaser introduced by you and approved by us in accordance with this agreement, on behalf of Seller and myself and the other stockholders of Seller, we agree to pay to you a commission of 5% of the sale price for the business or stock of Seller.

Should the sales transaction take the form of an exchange of stock then, in such event, Seller or its stockholders will deliver to you 5% of the stock received by Seller or its stockholders after delivery to us.

Should the transaction take the form of a sale of assets, the 5% commission will be based upon the total purchase price paid by the buyer plus any cash or other assets that might have been retained by the Seller in the transaction, minus any liabilities retained by the Seller (not including any income tax due solely as the result of the sale of assets).

If the entire consideration is received by the Seller in stock or cash at the closing, the entire commission will be payable at the closing. If the consideration for the acquisition of the business or stock is paid in installments, any commission payable hereunder shall also be payable in installments at the time the installments are received from the purchaser, and each installment payment of commission will be equal to 5% of each installment as received.

If the transaction is not actually closed with a purchaser submitted by you to us in writing and approved by us in writing, no commission will be payable to you regardless of whether the failure to close is due to any action or failure to act on Seller's part or on the part of Seller's stockholders, or due to any action or failure to act on the part of the prospective purchaser submitted by you.

You agree that no charge will be made to us for any expense incurred by you in your efforts and activities to effect the sale of the Seller's business or the stock of the Seller. You warrant that you do not have and will not enter into any arrangement of co-brokerage, and you agree to pay any third parties retained by you in connection with this agreement and to hold Seller and its stockholders harmless against any claims by such persons. You also agree that you will not seek any commission or remuneration of any kind from any buyer of Seller's business or stock and that Seller's payment of the commission to you in accordance with the terms contained in this letter will be in complete discharge of any and all obligations to you in connection with the sale of Seller's business or stock.

This agency will automatically terminate 180 days from the date you sign this agreement.

It is hereby understood and agreed that, should you have introduced us to a prospective purchaser approved by us as herein provided and a transaction is not actually closed with such purchaser prior to the expiration of this agency, should we continue, resume or reinstate negotiations with such prospective purchaser which ripen into a transaction which is actually closed within 18 months after the date of termination of this agency, we will pay you a commission with respect to such transaction as herein provided. You agree to furnish to us a written list of all prospective purchasers introduced to us within 30 days after the termination of this agreement including the date and place of the introduction and the person in our company to whom the introduction was made. We will not be obligated to pay commission for a sale to any person not included on such list together with accurate information describing the introduction.

If this letter sets forth the understanding arrived at between us will you please sign and date the carbon copy of this letter below under the word "Agreed" and return the signed copy to us.

SELLER FACTORIES, INC.

By   */s/ Bill Greatfellow*
President

Agreed:
Dated: _____

EXCELLENT FINDERS & COMPANY, INC.

_____*/s/ Robert Searcher*_____
President

In summary, where a broker or finder is involved in the transaction, the buyer and seller should establish the responsibility for payment of commission between each other and with the broker or finder as soon as possible. The terms of the arrangement should be set down in a written contract before the principals have progressed to a point in the negotiations where they may be in substantial agreement. Without a written brokerage contract, the vague principles of implied contract may lead to future disputes between the parties or with the broker or finder, which can hinder and even ruin negotiations that would otherwise mature smoothly into an acquisition satisfactory to both parties.

4

Determining
the Purchase Price:
Negotiation and
Valuation Methods

THE PRIMARY FACTOR: NEGOTIATION

The purchase price for an acquisition is determined by negotiation. When first considering the sale of a business, sellers are often uncertain about an asking price, even though they are closely familiar with every asset and operation. Buyers are often more uncertain because they are initially unfamiliar with the business being sold.

There are a variety of valuation experts and methods to which buyers and sellers can turn for help in making price decisions. However, in acquisitions, the methods and experts can only help sellers and buyers to make informed judgments. If they are unable or unwilling to reach agreement through negotiation, there will be no acquisition.

VALUATION EXPERTS

Services for valuing businesses are available from investment banking and brokerage firms, banks, appraisal firms, financial consulting firms and the consulting departments of accounting firms. Large companies having active acquisition and divestiture programs often employ one or more financial analysts skilled in valuing acquisitions and divestitures.

In acquisitions involving public shareholders or beneficiaries of employee benefit plans owning stock of the company being sold, it is increasingly common to obtain a "fairness opinion" from an investment banking firm or other expert as a basis for the judgment of management, particularly when management may have conflicting interests or loyalties. A typical "fairness opinion" is shown at the end of this chapter.

Appraisal firms were originally known for their valuation of tangible assets for such purposes as estate and inheritance taxes and eminent domain proceedings. In acquisitions, appraisal firms have traditionally valued tangible assets to support the allocation of the purchase price among assets acquired. However, in recent years, appraisal firms also value intangible assets, closely held businesses, and stock of public and private companies.

CONSIDERATIONS BEFORE VALUATION

Fair Market Value. Fair market value is commonly defined as the price a willing seller would accept and a willing buyer would pay for a property, where both are equally well informed and under no compulsion to sell or buy.

Value vs. Price. Whatever valuation methods are used, the value of a business depends importantly on the present and potential uses by its owner. Even when a seller and buyer have the same data and use the same methods, they may reach widely divergent values and price terms. If value to the seller is higher than value to the buyer, it may not be possible to negotiate a transaction unless a compromise can be negotiated. On the other hand, if value to the buyer is equal to or greater than value to the seller, it usually should be possible to negotiate a transaction if there is a mutual desire to do so. However, even in the latter situation, negotiations may not be easy. A seller who perceives that its business has greater value to the buyer than the value in its present use will often attempt to negotiate a price based on the potential value to the buyer. The buyer usually will resist this attempt and an acquisition will take place only if buyer or seller yields or a compromise is negotiated.

Going Concern Basis vs. Liquidation Basis. Businesses are ordinarily valued on a "going concern" basis that attributes greater value to the business than to the liquidation value of its assets. However, when ability to continue is in doubt or the liquidation value of assets is greater than the value obtained as a going concern, liquidation value should be used. A typical example of the latter situation is a small restaurant business that owns a corner lot in a city where the buyer wishes to build a large office building. The land often will be more valuable than the going concern value of the restaurant business.

Overall Costs and Benefits. When considering price, both seller and buyer should consider the true overall costs and benefits of the transaction, not only the price that will be paid directly from buyer to seller at the closing. The seller should consider such factors as debt assumed and contracts for employment or consulting services by seller personnel as price increases and taxes that reduce net proceeds as price decreases. The seller also should consider the effects of the sale on its retained businesses, if any. The buyer should consider its overall cost including debt assumed; employment contracts and other obligations undertaken; tax effects; loan financing; installation of new or upgraded facilities; additional working capital if programs to increase sales are successful; closing of unneeded facilities including severance pay and integrating the organizational structure and personnel. However, the buyer can subtract from its cost such items as readily disposable unneeded assets, duplicate facilities, and personnel; undervalued assets; access to new customers for its own unused manufacturing capacity and entry to new markets without the need for extensive development effort and cost.

THE BUSINESS JUDGMENT RULE

Directors and other members of management of corporations have long been protected in stockholder lawsuits by the "business judgment rule." In essence, this rule says that management is not liable for mistakes which result in losses if made in the good faith exercise of business judgment and free of elements such as conflict of interest or violation of law. This rule usually protects judgments made by management in acquisition transactions. *Treadway* v. *Care Corp.,* 638 F.2d 357 (2 Cir., 1980). Traditionally the initial burden of proof that a transaction was outside the "business judgment" rule was placed on the party challenging an action by corporate management.

In a landmark decision in 1985, the Delaware Supreme Court ruled that the directors of Trans Union Corporation had failed to meet the minimum standards required by the business judgment rule and breached their fiduciary duties to its 10,000 stockholders in a sale of the company for $688 million, or $55 per share, to Marmon Corporation. In their defense, the directors showed that the shares of Trans Union were trading at $37 just before the Marmon offer and had traded in the $25 to $35 range during the previous five years. However, the Court found that the directors approved the sale in only two hours and did not make any study of the intrinsic or inherent worth of the company. While not imposing a "fairness opinion" as a requirement of law, the Court said that a board must actively seek information, take the time and get expert advice, if needed, in order to make an informed decision.

When directors and officers of a corporation act on a matter involving conflicts of interest, such as frequently happens during a management buyout, they do not have the protection of the "business judgment" rule and must bear the burden of proof that the transaction is "fair" or "fair and reasonable." In order to retain the benefit of the "business judgment" rule, it has become common for boards of directors to designate committees of independent directors to evaluate and decide on the issues involved in management buyouts and to authorize these committees to retain independent counsel, investment advisers and other resources. The courts have likened the duties of a board of directors (or independent committee) which has decided to sell in a management buyout or to a "White Knight" as those of an "auctioneer" whose duty is to consider all bids and obtain the best terms for the shareholders. *Revlon Inc.* v. *MacAndrews & Forbes Holdings,* 506 A.2d 173 (Del., 1986); *Edelman* v. *Fruehauf Corporation* 798 F.2d 882, CCH Fed. Sec. L. Rep. §92,863; *Hanson Trust PLC* v. *MLSCM Acquisition, Inc.,* 781 F.2d 264 (2 Cir., 1986). The "auction" duties do not require the board to sell a company that is not for sale or forego properly adopted business plans in favor of a hostile tender offer. *Paramount Communications, Inc. v. Time Incorporated,* Del. Sup. Ct., CCH Fed. Sec. L. Rep. §94,938 (1990). "Auction" duties also do not require the board to accept the highest offer if it is a two-tier debt obligation and financial experts advise that a lower all cash offer is more favorable. *Citron v. Fairchild Camera and Instrument Corp.* Del. Sup. Ct., CCH Fed. Sec. L. Rep. §94,860 (1990). It has become customary to make available the same information to all known bidders including hostile bidders. It has also become customary to obtain "fairness" opinions from an independent investment banking firm or other firm expert in financial analysis.

VALUATION METHODS

A wide variety of methods are used by buyers and sellers and their expert advisers in valuing businesses as part of the negotiating process in acquisitions. Although certain methods are generally recognized as more applicable to particular industries and types and sizes of businesses than other methods, neither seller nor buyer is required to recognize any particular method. On the contrary, sellers and buyers often choose methods that favor their respective negotiating positions and argue that their chosen method is most applicable or at least entitled to weight in the price negotiations.

While other groupings are possible, our discussion of valuation will be under the following categories:

> Market value
> Financial statement values
> Nonfinancial statement values
> Effects of method of payment

MARKET VALUE

Before discussing the effect of market values on the negotiation of acquisition prices, it is best to review briefly stock market mechanisms and the significance of the prices reported as a result of trading on the stock exchanges and the bid and asked prices quoted in the over-the-counter market.

The large companies whose shares are traded on the stock exchanges and through the NASDAQ system in the over-the-counter market have millions of outstanding shares. Even the smaller companies whose shares are thinly traded in the over-the-counter market generally have hundreds of thousands of outstanding shares. Many of these shares are held by founders, parent companies, management and other long term investors who rarely sell or buy. Thus, the "float" shares available for trading are usually only a small percentage of the total outstanding shares. Of the "float" shares, only a small percentage will actually be traded during a given day, week, or month unless an unusual event occurs.

At the stock exchanges, the "market maker" is a specialist firm which maintains a "book" of buy and sell orders for the stock of each company assigned to it. The stock exchanges hold their specialist firms responsible to maintain orderly and ethical markets and to provide depth to the market by using their own capital to buy or sell when there is a temporary imbalance between buy and sell orders. If the exchange believes that the imbalance may result from a need for further disclosure about the company's business or other activities, it can contact the company and take other steps to obtain disclosure. The exchange also can stop trading if it regards disclosure as inadequate. However, the stock exchanges are free markets. If all required disclosures have been made and public enthusiasm leads to a buying wave, the trading price of a stock may rise to levels well above the value determinable by conventional valuation methods. If public investors are disenchanted with a company or industry, market prices may decline to values well below those determinable by other methods. This is especially likely to happen to lightly traded stocks of smaller companies. Of course, over a period of years, financial analysts can be expected to identify and make recommendations on stocks for which the market prices do not reflect values determinable by other methods, and arbitrageurs may move even more quickly if they anticipate a counter trend. In recent years, some arbitrageurs have created their own trends by large block investments and takeover or proxy activities. Nevertheless, stocks sometimes remain overpriced or underpriced for lengthy time periods before corrections occur.

In the over-the-counter market, the "market makers" are investment banking firms trading for their own account, subject to regulation by the National Association of Securities Dealers, Inc., and the Securities and Exchange Commission. The decision by each firm to submit bid and asked prices to the NASDAQ system or the "pink sheets" is voluntary. With some exceptions, the companies whose shares are traded in the over-the-counter market are smaller than the companies whose shares are listed on the stock exchanges. Thus, depth of trading in the over-the-counter market depends importantly on the degree of interest that particular investment banking firms have in the company and their desire to maintain its goodwill and the goodwill of their customers who have invested in the stock. Thus, prices in the over-the-counter market tend to be more volatile than those on the stock exchanges.

In spite of their known imperfections, the stock markets achieve remarkably realistic valuations over a period of time, utilizing the disclosure system sponsored by the Securities and Exchange Commission and the self-regulatory agencies. "Insider trading" restrictions and electronic reports of trading and business and financial events have improved the access of the public to timely information. In forums where judgments are at the risk of real money, the stock markets have often been right when experts have been wrong. For public shareholders, they are the primary source of liquidity. Thus, stock market prices carry considerable weight in the valuation of companies whose shares are publicly traded.

When market values are used in valuing a company and its business, two extrinsic factors also must be considered: "blockage" and the effects of the restrictions imposed by the securities laws on stock owned by controlling persons and persons who receive unregistered stock in acquisitions, privately placed financings and other exempt transactions. The reality of the discounts in valuation for securities law restrictions has been recognized by the Internal Revenue Service in Revenue Ruling 77-287 (1977-2 C.B. 319) and can range from 1 percent for the shares of large companies traded on The New York Stock Exchange to over 50 percent for shares of small companies traded in the over-the-counter market.

Even in the valuation of businesses not having publicly traded shares, market prices of shares of similar companies having publicly traded shares are an important factor in comparison studies. They also are important in determining price/earnings ratios. These techniques are described later in this chapter.

FINANCIAL STATEMENT VALUES

Financial Statement Analysis. Before making judgments about an acquisition price based on financial statements furnished by the seller, the buyer should analyze and adjust seller's financial statements to reflect the effects of the accounting policies it has adopted within the variations allowed by generally accepted accounting principles. Some of the more common areas in which variations exist are—

- Basic accounting methods—Standard cost, percentage of completion, etc.
- Timing of income and expense recognition
- Inventories—FIFO, LIFO, and writedown and writeoff policies
- Receivables—Allowances for doubtful accounts and other reserves
- Values assigned to purchased intangibles and treatment of internal costs for development of intangible assets
- Depreciation and depletion methods
- Investment tax credit treatment
- Tax loss carrybacks and carryforwards
- Treatment of leases as operating leases or as financing leases capitalized as assets and related debt
- Treatment of minority interests in affiliated companies
- Contingent liabilities and assets
- Treatment of management compensation, particularly stock incentive compensation
- Asset valuation methods
- Treatment of extraordinary and nonrecurring items
- Accrual of obligations for retiree medical and death benefits
- Computation of book value and earnings per share to reflect dilution

An example of the effects of the use of different accounting policies permitted by generally accepted accounting principles is shown on pages 110 and 111 under "Accounting Magic."

Another important adjustment resulting from differences in management policy rather than accounting policy should be made to reflect the use of debt to finance businesses being compared. Debt provides leverage that can be used, successfully or not, to increase sales and earnings, but it also has a substantial interest cost. To achieve comparability, the financial analyst should adjust the earnings results of the businesses being compared to a "debt-free" basis.

Dividend Value. Historical and projected dividends are of interest in valuing portfolio securities, especially for foundations, pension trusts, retirees and others needing income from investments. However, dividends as such are rarely relevant in valuing an acquisition of all, or a controlling interest in, a business since the buyer ordinarily will be in a position to determine policy on earnings distributions after the acquisition.

Book Value. Book value of the seller's business, generally the net value shown on the seller's balance sheet including the capital stock account, may be considered in negotiating the acquisition price. However, for most industrial enterprises, book value of a business tends to be understated. For example, accelerated depreciation, LIFO or FIFO inventory treatment, or methods of accruing liabilities may inflate or deflate book value. Furthermore, whether book value of an industrial corporation is high or low will seldom affect its earnings, which are vital to its ability to compete and to provide a return on investment to its owners.

On the other hand, in an acquisition of a bank, investment company or other business consisting primarily of liquid assets, book value may have great relevance to price. Book value may also have some relevance in acquiring a public utility, or railroad or other business which is subject to rate fixing by governmental agencies. Such agencies often fix their rates on the basis of invested capital and, therefore, book value may be important in determining price because of its effect on earnings.

Liquidation Value. The financial statements of the great majority of businesses are prepared on a "going concern" basis in accordance with generally accepted accounting principles. However, when business can no longer conduct business as a "going concern"—i.e., the business is in bankruptcy, insolvency or other reorganization proceedings, its financial statements will be prepared on a liquidation basis. Assets will be valued at the amount they would bring in an "auction"-type sale. However, even for businesses which are "going concerns," the liquidation value of assets may be essential to the availability of secured financing of the acquisition price and, therefore, may indirectly affect the negotiations by limiting available financing. Liquidation value is discussed further under "Shareholder Value Analysis" and "Nonfinancial Statement Values" in this chapter and under Chapter 15—Leveraged Buyouts.

Replacement Cost. To an active business, the replacement cost of its assets such as property, plant, and equipment may seem to be interesting but academic information except when applying for insurance against property damage. However, many acquisitions result from a scenario that has grown increasingly common for more than a decade. A company decides that there is a market opportunity to sell a significant volume of a product. It has the necessary sales organization and manufacturing knowhow, but finds that the capital cost of new property, plant and equipment and the related government permits is prohibitive. It begins a search for existing plant facilities designed or readily modifiable to manufacture the product. For such a buyer, older plant facilities that have existing government permits or are exempt under "grandfather" clauses may be much more valuable than their depreciated book value.

Regulation S-X of the Securities and Exchange Commission, the regulation which prescribes the content of financial statements prepared for the stockholders of larger public companies, requires that the current replacement cost of assets be disclosed in a footnote.

During negotiations, the seller may know or learn of buyer's plans for use of the property, plant and equipment. The seller will argue for a price higher than book value or a typical liquidation value because buyer is saving the cost of new facilities. However, buyer will want a substantial bargain because savings are its primary motive for the acquisition.

Asset-Oriented Values—Generally. While it is often and correctly stated that book value and other asset-oriented valuation methods are not usually best for valuing ongoing industrial businesses, they cannot be ignored because they act as an anchor in the buyer's decision whether to develop internally or acquire. As an acquisition price rises based on earnings-oriented valuation methods, it becomes more practical for potential buyers to enter the business through internal investment. Further, high earnings, even those which withstand the closest scrutiny by financial analysts, tend to encounter business competition—particularly where capital investment in assets is a relatively low entry barrier in relation to potential revenues and earnings.

Capitalization of Gross Revenues. A valuation technique commonly used for service businesses is capitalization of gross revenues. Examples of service businesses are insurance agencies, advertising agencies, public relations firms, employment and talent agencies, publishing firms with an established circulation and advertising base but limited facilities and equipment, medical clinics with limited investment in facilities and equipment and professional firms such as accounting, engineering and law firms. These are "people-oriented" businesses whose value exists in their management, employees and customers.

Asset valuation techniques are seldom useful in valuing service businesses that usually generate revenues and earnings well in excess of amounts attributable to their assets. Earnings techniques can be used, but historical earnings of service businesses may be distorted by discretionary expenses incurred by existing owners that need not be continued by the buyer. The reverse may also be true where the seller has managed costs with unusual strictness which could not be continued without risking loss of employees and customers. Rather than attempt to debate the seller's expense policies, it often is simpler and more palatable to both seller and buyer to value on the basis of gross revenues. The assumption is that buyer will pay a fair price for a revenue stream and will be responsible for its own future expense policies.

When valuing based on gross revenues, the quality and continuity of the revenues should be determined and adjustments made, if necessary. If seller has a substantial volume of business "bought" by unusual rebates, discounts or other disadvantageous arrangements, adjustments should be made either to the gross revenues or the valuation multiplier to reflect that fact. If revenues are cyclical and appear to be temporarily inflated or deflated by a "popular" trend, adjustments also should be made.

Because service businesses are "people-oriented," revenues also should be weighed in light of the personal relations between seller's management and key employees and customers. Unlike asset ownership which is permanent, the value of service businesses depends on voluntary or contractual relations. If the "due diligence" review reveals that certain customers or employees who control customer accounts may not continue after the business is sold, revenues should be adjusted to reflect their loss. If seller has recently obtained an important new customer whose revenues are not yet reflected in historical gross revenues, projections of increased revenues can be used. Of course, gain and loss of revenues is a business risk and efforts to protect against that risk should not be limited to valuation and price negotiation. Buyer should attempt during negotiations to make arrangements that will assure continuity of key employees and customers and, if risk of their loss is excessive, should decline to buy.

Techniques for selecting revenue periods, multipliers and discount rates used in valuation by capitalization of gross revenues are similar to those described later for valuation based on earnings and cash flow. For service businesses that are frequently sold, such as insurance agencies, customary criteria for the industry may exist that provide a starting point for valuation and negotiations.

Capitalization of Historical Earnings. Among the most commonly used techniques for valuing businesses, especially manufacturing businesses, are those based on earnings—i.e., capitalization of historical earnings, price/earnings ratios and discounting future earnings.

Capitalization of historical earnings requires careful determination of two elements: (1) the seller's earnings after analysis and weighting for trends and (2) the appropriate capitalization rate.

To determine seller's earnings, the analyst must select a time period (such as two, three, five or ten years) judged to be relevant to present value. The techniques of financial analysis described earlier should then be used to determine valid and comparable earnings. The adjusted earnings should then be averaged or weighted, according to the judgment of the analyst, to reflect earnings patterns (such as the cyclical nature of seller's business) or trends. Similar adjustments and weighting should be applied to the earnings of companies used for comparisons.

To select a capitalization rate, the analyst could use a variety of factors, including long-term interest rates, rates of return on preferred stocks, and buyer's own borrowing costs. In each case, the rate should be adjusted upward to reflect the greater risk of equity investment, taking into account buyer's objectives for return on investment. Another source of data that can be considered in determining the capitalization rate or as a separate valuation method are the price/earnings ratios of selected comparable companies whose shares are traded in the market or were recently sold and of the seller's industry. The capitalization rate is the reciprocal of the price/earnings ratio after adjustment for the elements of opportunity and risk. As discussed in the next section, the analyst should keep in mind that price/earnings ratios for particular publicly traded or recently sold companies reflect not only the monetary value of its historical earnings, but also anticipation of future earnings.

A weakness of capitalization of historical earnings as a valuation method for acquisitions is its backward-looking orientation. Another weakness is that the method bases value on earnings determined according to generally accepted accounting principles (GAAP) rather than cash flow. Buyers concerned about cash management, especially those borrowing to finance the acquisition price, will also be interested in methods that link value to cash.

Price/Earnings Ratios. One of the most popular methods to determine an acquisition price, especially among businessmen, is the use of the price/earnings ratios of other comparable companies and the industry. The method has an appealing simplicity and is earnings rather than assets-oriented, but it can be misleading unless careful analysis is performed.

The ratio itself is simply a price divided by some recent period of historical earnings. Once the ratio is determined for comparable companies or an industry, it is applied as a multiplier to the earnings of the business to be acquired.

The initial effort required for valid use of price/earnings ratios is the selection of truly comparable companies, public and private. To the extent possible, non-comparable factors, such as subsidiaries and divisions in other lines of business, should be eliminated. If an industry ratio is to be used, a determination of the competitive standing in that industry of the business to be acquired should be made.

When using the market prices of publicly traded shares, the analyst should recognize that the prices were paid or quoted for minority interests and are subject to the limitations previously described under "Market Values" in this chapter. On the other hand, as described later in this section, market prices are future-oriented since the public invests not only based on historical earnings record but the expectation of future earnings.

In determining earnings, the financial analyst should use the financial analysis techniques described earlier under "Financial Statement Analysis." Both the earnings of the business to be acquired and those of the comparable companies should be adjusted to the same basis. Where the comparable companies have publicly traded shares, information for this purpose is often available in their annual and periodic reports sent to shareholders and filed with the SEC. If a division or subsidiary of a public company is used for comparison, the reports often include a lesser, but significant, amount of information because the SEC requires partial separate reporting for business "segments" of public companies. If available, data for privately owned businesses recently sold also should be used, but it is more difficult to obtain. It may also be less reliable and require more financial analysis than public company data. The reason is that private businesses generally (1) make substantial amounts of owner-directed discretionary expenditures, (2) prepare financial statements on a tax-oriented basis and (3) provide less disclosure in their financial statements than public companies.

Price/earnings ratios for publicly traded shares (and sometimes recently sold businesses) reflect not only the monetary value of historical earnings, but also anticipation of future earnings. For example, when a stock trades in the market at fifteen times earnings, it does not mean that the shareholders seek only a 6.7 percent rate of return on investment (calculated as a simple reciprocal), but that they expect earnings to improve to provide a better return. Thus, the elements of opportunity and risk are inherent in price/earnings ratios for publicly traded shares. The same is also true for industry price/earnings ratios, although the base is broader. This future orientation gives price/earnings ratios one element of advantage over asset-oriented and historical methods in valuing manufacturing and other industrial businesses.

Buyer management should realize that any price/earnings multiple (or capitalization rate) can be roughly equated to the number of years over which an acquisition can be expected to pay for itself. Thus, when a buyer pays a price equal to ten times earnings, the assumption is that the acquisition will pay for itself over ten years at the earnings level used in determining the ratio. Of course, as described earlier, higher price/earnings multiples reflect anticipation that earnings will increase, thus repaying the investment sooner.

Knowledgeable buyers do not rely only on capitalization of historical earnings and price/earnings ratios but also determine value by the discounted future earnings and cash flow methods described later in this chapter.

Cash Flow Multiples. For several years, cash flow multiples have been replacing earnings multiples in acquisition transactions. Earnings before income tax, depreciation and amortization (EBITDA) are determined and a multiplier obtained by analyzing comparable businesses is applied. The calculation is performed for historical and projected cash flows during valuation and price negotiations.

As described in the discussion of the discounted cash flow method later in this chapter, there are several components which can be included or excluded when projecting EBITDA. For example, amounts to be spent for capital expenditures and the proceeds of planned sales of assets are judgmental. As a practical matter, financial analysts can prepare valuations using several different assumptions based on information obtained from operating managers. A volatility factor can be expressly stated or included as an implied element in selecting a multiplier. The financial analyst should identify the methods and assumptions used and their effects to enable senior management to use the valuation report effectively in acquisition decisions and negotiations.

It is worth commenting at this point that EBITDA, carefully negotiated and defined, is also commonly used in loan agreements for acquisition financing. It is used in compliance covenants and also in covenants restricting funds which the buyer/borrower can use for purposes such as discretionary capital expenditures, employee bonuses and dividends.

The parallel uses illustrate the close link between valuation and financing. Financial managers will point out that even when an acquisition price is paid entirely from internal corporate funds, there is in reality a financing cost. Thus, it makes practical sense to link valuation and price negotiations to that cost.

Discounted Present Value of Future Earnings. To value a business by discounting future earnings, it is first necessary to prepare projections of future earnings. Forecasting future earnings is difficult and is necessarily based on assumptions. However, all substantial businesses prepare operating and capital budgets, sales forecasts, debt repayment schedules and many other future-oriented financial plans. Many companies prepare five-year plans, being fully aware that they must annually be updated and corrected, because they are valuable tools that cause management to think beyond current needs. To the extent that management enlists broad "bottom up" participation from all parts of the business, the need for assumptions and the margins of error are reduced.

Buyers can independently, but better with the cooperation of seller's management, prepare projections of future earnings for some years in the future. Projections of earnings should, of course, begin with projections of sales or revenues, considering such factors as the markets for seller's products and changes in technology, and proceed with projections of costs, expenses and taxes in a consistent manner. The number of years projected is determined by the judgment of buyer's financial analyst. After the discounted value of the earnings for a selected period is determined, a residual value for the business must be added unless the period is very lengthy or indefinite.

Selection of the discount rate also depends on the judgment of the financial analyst. The choice should be made carefully because modestly different rates result in significantly different valuations. Reference can be made to long-term interest rates, rates of return on equity for publicly traded preferred stocks or the buyer's own borrowing costs. These rates should then be adjusted upward to reflect the greater risk of equity investment, taking into account also buyer's objectives for return on equity investment. The return-on-investment objectives of buyer's management also should be considered.

Formulae and calculations for discounting to present value are shown later in this chapter under "Discounted Cash Flow Valuation."

Finally, from the present value of the sum of the future projected after-tax earnings plus the present value of the residual value of the business, the buyer should subtract the amount of cash which the buyer will be required to advance to the business at the time of acquisition to pay off debt of the seller or for similar reasons. The resulting figure should then indicate what may be a fair price for the seller's business.

As an example, in a situation in which a ten-year earn-out period is utilized, during which it is estimated (1) that total after-tax earnings of the seller's business for the ten-year period will amount to $8,550,000, (2) that the business will have a residual value at the end of the ten years equal to $4,000,000 and (3) that the buyer must advance cash in the amount of $1,000,000 to satisfy debt, the total of the estimated earnings and residual value, less the cash advance, would amount to $11,550,000. The present value of such total estimated earnings and residual value discounted at 10%, 15% or 20%, respectively, would result in fixing a purchase price of the seller amounting to $5,462,000, $3,927,000 or $2,885,000, depending upon the discount ratio which is chosen as indicated in the table below:

Ten Future Years	(Thousands of dollars) Estimated Earnings Stream (After Tax)	Present Value at Discount		
		10%	15%	20%
1st	$ 680	$ 618	$ 592	$ 566
2nd	720	595	544	500
3rd	750	563	494	434
4th	790	540	452	381
5th	830	515	413	334
6th	870	491	376	291

7th	910	467	342	254
8th	950	444	311	221
9th	1,000	424	284	194
10th	1,050	405	259	170
Subtotal	$ 8,550	$ 5,062	$ 4,067	$ 3,345
Plus assumed residual value	$ 4,000	$ 1,400	$ 860	$ 540
Subtotal	$12,550	$ 6,462	$ 4,927	$ 3,885
Less cash advance	$ 1,000	$ 1,000	$ 1,000	$ 1,000
Total	$11,550	$ 5,462	$ 3,927	$ 2,885

Because of the inherent uncertainties involved in the projection of future earnings and determination of a discount rate, some analysts tend to be conservative in valuing a business by the discounted future earnings method. This tendency is especially serious at public companies where pressure to show ever-increasing earnings causes management to focus on short-term "bottom line" earnings rather than long-term opportunity. Thus, the method could be subjected to criticisms similar to those leveled against the discounted cash-flow method by Professors Robert H. Hayes and David A. Garvin of Harvard Business School. These criticisms are described on page 87.

Discounted Cash Flow Valuation. It has been common for many years to value real estate companies and investments by cash-flow techniques. This was done because real estate enterprises typically generate depreciation charges, particularly in early years, which absorb earnings and often generate losses. Thus, they could be valued more realistically by cash earnings than earnings after noncash charges.

In recent years, discounted cash-flow (DCF) valuation methods have increasingly been used for valuation of manufacturing and other industrial businesses. In 1978, an article entitled "The Cash Flow Takeover Formula" appearing in *Business Week* said that approximately half the major acquisition-minded companies were using discounted cash-flow methods. Since then, DCF valuation methods have continued to grow for several reasons:

1. DCF valuation methods can be readily used to value acquisitions and internal capital expenditures in a comparable manner including the cost of interest on acquisition indebtedness and additional investment in the acquired business.

2. Investments are evaluated net of depreciation and other non-cash charges to GAAP earnings, thus avoiding adverse comparison with older investments. The policy variations allowable within GAAP in determining net earnings are also eliminated.

3. DCF valuation methods are future-oriented, but deflate projections of future earnings and other cash flow items to present value.

4. DCF valuation methods are compatible with cash flow projections pre-

pared for prospective lenders. For example, when planning leveraged buyouts, the predominant concern is the adequacy of cash flow to repay acquisition debt including mezzanine financing. Thus, the use of a valuation method consistent with projections developed for payment of acquisition financing is a realistic step.

"Cash flow" can be defined in several ways depending on the purpose of the definition. A familiar definition is net earnings after income tax, plus noncash charges such as depreciation, amortization and depletion, plus deferred taxes. This definition can then be adjusted for working capital changes—i.e., increases and decreases of amounts used to carry inventories and receivables. It can also be adjusted for principal amounts of borrowings and repayments. It can also be adjusted for capital expenditures and amounts realized from sales of capital assets. Planners of a leveraged buyout or takeover will, however, start with pre-tax earnings, because the deductibility of interest will shelter them, and will include only those capital expenditures necessary to maintain operations. They will also include the proceeds of planned divestitures of businesses (net of disposition and tax costs) on a schedule which should allow enough time to avoid pressure during negotiations.

DCF valuation methods include a variety of techniques. For example, cash flow for the current or the most recent fiscal year may be presumed to continue indefinitely and be discounted to present value. More commonly, the analyst develops cash-flow projections for such number of future years as reasonably reliable information is available.

Discount rates are typically determined based on (1) a risk free rate plus an equity premium based on a standard such as the S & P 500 Index, (2) buyer's own weighted average cost of capital or (3) buyer's own internal borrowing costs. However, the discount rate may be adjusted to take into account buyer's objectives for return on equity investment.

The discount rate is adjusted by a beta factor designed to reflect the volatility of the investment. Betas for comparable investments can be found in standard investment publications such as Value Line. The beta for a company or industry with average market volatility is 1.0. A stock with a beta of 1.1 would be expected to rise or fall at a rate 10% greater than a stock with a 1.0 beta. For example, the stock would be expected to rise or fall 11% with each 10% rise or fall in the general market. In determining an appropriate beta multiplier, the analyst may adjust to a beta reflecting only business volatility unrelated to capital structure since reported betas reflect both business and financial volatility. The adjusted beta can then be further adjusted to reflect the capital structure for the proposed acquisition. This adjustment would, of course, be greater for a leveraged buyout structure than for a conventional acquisition structure.

A formula showing cost of equity (COE) determined with a beta adjustment is as follows:

$$\text{COE} = \frac{\text{10-year treasury}}{\text{bond rate}} + \text{Beta} \left(\frac{\text{S \& P 500}}{\text{return}} - \frac{\text{10-year treasury}}{\text{bond rate}} \right)$$

When a smaller company is being valued, an index for equity return on smaller companies should be used.

A formula for determining weighted average cost of capital is as follows:

$$\text{WACOC} = \text{COE (\%equity)} + \text{MIR (1--MIR) (\% debt)}$$

In the above formula WACOC is the weighted average cost of capital, COE is the buyer's cost of equity, and MIR is the buyer's marginal interest rate on debt.

A buyer's own internal "hurdle rate" can be computed by a variety of methods and then adjusted in accordance with management policies which are discretionary in nature. For example, management of a company having some businesses earning a high return on investment may set high hurdle rates for approval of discretionary capital expenditures by other businesses. The objective is to force all the businesses to compete with the more successful businesses when seeking to use corporate capital.

The discount rate (or rates) are applied to determine the present value of the projected cash flows for the years chosen. A residual value of the business is then calculated and added to the sum of the cash-flow values and the result is the present value of the business. Residual value, particularly after a long period of projected cash flow, will usually be calculated on a conservative basis through asset-oriented methods or by discounting perpetual cash flows. Finally, excess cash in the business should be added and liabilities expected to remain outstanding at the end of the project period should be deducted from present value.

A basic formula for discounting future value (FV) to present value (PV) by a determined discount rate (R) is as follows:

$$\text{PV} = \frac{\text{FV}}{(1 + \text{R})^n}$$

n is the number of years in the future when the cash flow FV will accrue.

A simple calculation of the present value of projected cash flows over a three-year period at a 15 percent discount rate is as follows:

$$\text{PV} = \frac{\overset{1985}{\$100,000}}{(1 + 0.15)^1} \quad \frac{\overset{1986}{\$150,000}}{(1 + 0.15)^2} \quad \frac{\overset{1987}{\$200,000}}{(1 + 0.15)^3}$$

$$\text{PV} = \$331,881$$

A simple DCF valuation calculation can be expressed as follows:

$$\frac{\text{PV of}}{\text{Acquisition}} = \frac{\text{PV of Cash Flows}}{\text{for \_\_\_\_ years}} + \text{Residual Value} + \text{Excess Cash}$$

A formula for determining residual value by discounting cash flows to perpetuity follows:

$$\frac{\text{Residual Value}}{\text{Multiplier}} = \frac{1}{\text{DR}} \quad \frac{+ \quad \text{GR}}{- \quad \text{GR}}$$

In the above formula, DR is the discount rate and GR is the average rate of growth of cash flows during the period selected for projections. The multiplier is then applied to cash flows for the last year of the projected period and then discounted to present value dollars.

As an alternative to measuring risk by using cost of equity capital as a discount rate, some financial analysts use an interest-based discount rate to obtain "risk-free" valuation based on cost of funds employed. Separate calculations are then made to quantify risk elements. Multipliers are then developed and applied to the discount rate. Another alternative is to use an interest-based discount rate to obtain a "risk-free" valuation and compare the valuation result to an investment of comparable risk such as the cost of the same business developed internally rather than through an acquisition.

Experts do not always agree on the methods for discounted cash flow valuation. For example, some will suggest that cash flow be projected for a definite period such as five years or seven years. Others recommend the longest period for which meaningful forecasts can be made. Some recommend the marginal cost of borrowing as a discount rate. Others recommend the weighted average cost of capital or cost of equity. Some experts recommend use of a cost of capital for seller's business and others suggest use of buyer's cost of capital. Even less agreement exists among business executives who will urge low discount rates and optimistic projections for acquisitions they favor and high discount rates and conservative projections for acquisitions they oppose.

In the authors' experience, it is not necessary to resolve these differences. The high-speed modeling capability furnished by personal computers enables financial analysts to make multiple calculations using alternate methods. Examination of the particular acquisition and the results of calculations using different methods will enable the analyst to select those which best reflect sound value. In reports, the analyst can also present alternative reasonable calculations with explanations of the different methods used and how they affected the results.

Nevertheless, it is proper to observe that discounted cash flow valuation using borrowing cost as the discount rate will produce higher value than calculation using equity in whole or part. This results from the assumption that interest cost is less than equity cost because of the deductibility of interest. Since all businesses require an equity base, the authors suggest that weighted average cost of capital is likely to produce realistic valuation results for a typical opportunistic, nonspeculative acquisition. Borrowing cost is likely to be appropriate for an acquisition made as an alternative to an otherwise essential capital expansion if business risk is low because of protected markets or similar factors. Cost of equity with a fully leveraged beta and a financial risk premium may be appropriate for a discretionary, leveraged acquisition.

Most important, the authors recommend that the financial analyst be alert to business realities and human factors during the valuation process. Apparently solid asset values and cash flows can melt away if technological or competitive obsolescence is occurring without recognition by operating or financial personnel. On the other hand, an acquisition with borderline asset values and cash flows may nevertheless be successful if it includes capable personnel and technological improvements needed to maintain stability.

Excellent articles illustrating DCF methods appear in the *Handbook of Acquisitions, Mergers, and Buyouts,* Lee and Colman, Prentice-Hall, Inc, 1981. The first of these articles is "Determining the Right Price to Pay" by Ralph A. Harris. The second is "Strategic Analysis for More Profitable Acquisitions" by Alfred Rappaport, an article that originally appeared in the *Harvard Business Review,* July-August, 1979.

More recent articles on DCF and other valuation methods appear in *Financial Valuation: Business and Business Interests,* James H. Zukin, Maxwell Macmillan/ Rosenfeld Launer Publication, 1990; *Employee Stock Ownership Plans,* Robert W. Smiley, Jr. and Ronald J. Gilbert Maxwell Macmillan/Rosenfeld Launer Publication, 1980; "The Debt-Free DCF Model," Daniel W. Bielinski, *Mergers and Acquisitions,* September/October 1989; "Business Value Lending in a Leverage Acquisition", Mitchell Vernick, *Mergers & Acquisitions,* November/December 1987 and "Chapter 6—Principles of Valuation," *Mergers, Restructuring and Corporate Control,* Weston, Chung & Hoag, Prentice-Hall, Inc., 1990.

As use of DCF methods has grown, however, its limitations have been identified. Projections of sales (revenues), capital and operating expenditures, residual values, excess cash and the appropriate discount rate involve the exercise of judgment and inherent uncertainties. In an article entitled "Managing as if Tomorrow Mattered" (*Harvard Business Review,* May-June 1982), Professors Robert H. Hayes and David A. Garvin submit that DCF methods inhibit needed long-term capital investment in favor of short-term profits. They comment that "Present value calculations support a decision to operate on the goose and remove some of its eggs prematurely, even though doing so impairs its future egg-laying ability." The article blames four factors: (1) the seeming precision of complex DCF calculations that are actually based on uncertain assumptions, (2) the tendency of company managements to require such high rates of return on investment that realistically presented projects cannot qualify for approval, (3) inability of present value methods to measure less obvious benefits such as increased worker skills, new products and a different cost structure and (4) management failure to recognize that a decision to forego investment in needed plant and equipment not financially attractive at a point in time cannot always be reversed at a later date. Professor Hayes notes that "Managers can all too easily hide behind the apparent rationality of such financial analyses while sidestepping the hard decisions necessary to keep their companies competitive."

Most interesting in relation to acquisitions and mergers, Professors Hayes and Garvin conclude that DCF methods tend to favor acquisitions over internal investment:

> Systematic adjustments for risk are quite appropriate when computing present values but many of the hurdle rates that we have seen contain unreasonably high risk components. Moreover, using such rates as a motivational tool undermines their worth in evaluating investment opportunities. For one thing, they often discourage investment in existing businesses

whose risks are known and direct it toward businesses whose risks are less understood.

Such behavior also reflects a growing preference among managers for acquisitions over internal investments. Despite considerable evidence to the contrary, American managers appear to believe that aggressive acquisition programs make possible both higher long term growth rates and greater profitability. Many are so firmly convinced that the grass is greener in almost any industry other than their own that they are far less tough-minded in evaluating acquisition candidates than they are in assessing internal investment proposals.

The management attitudes criticized by Professors Hayes and Garvin can be partially explained by the fact that internal expansion inevitably takes time and faces a growing array of government regulatory barriers. Thus, the benefits of internal expansion must be discounted for time and uncertainty. An article, "Conglomerate Mergers, Allocative Efficiency, and Section 7 of the Clayton Act," Mantell, *Texas Law Review,* 1981, contains a discussion of benefits of acquisitions not similarly realizable through internal expansion.

DCF Valuation in the Courts. The Delaware Supreme Court in *Weinberger* v. *UOP Inc.,* 457 A. 2d 701 (1983) ruled that the proceedings for the valuation of stock of shareholders who dissent from a merger should no longer be limited to the traditional "Delaware Block" method, a weighted-average method based on book value, market value, earnings and other traditional factors. The Delaware Supreme Court ruled that all generally accepted valuation techniques used in the financial community should be considered, including DCF methods which had previously been rejected by the Delaware Chancery Court. The Supreme Court held that valuation based on future projections (as required by the DCF method) is not prohibited by language of the Delaware appraisal statute that requires exclusion of any element of value arising from the accomplishment or expectation of the merger. The Supreme Court ruled that only pro forma data and projections of a speculative variety are excluded.

Subsequent decisions illustrating valuation methods and their strengths and weaknesses are *Kahn* v. *United States Sugar Corp.* (Del. Ch., 1985) 11 Del. Journal of Corporate Law 908;*Sarrouf* v. *The New England Patriots Football Club, Inc.* 494 N.E. 2d 1122 (1986);*Sussman v. Lincoln American Corp.,* 578 F. Supp. 1041 (N.D. Ill., 1984);*Rosenblatt v. Getty Oil Company,* 493 A. 2d 929 (Del., 1985); *Herskowitz* v. *Nutri/System, Inc.,* 857 F. 2d 179 (3 Cir., 1988).

Weighting Techniques. Within each valuation method, the analyst may perform the calculations using various assumptions and present the different results in the valuation report. It also is common for financial analysts to calculate values by several methods and present each result. For businesses whose values are effectively measured by more than one method, the analyst also may assign weight to the value obtained by each method and calculate a weighted value.

A brief article "Valuing the Closely Held Business," Faris, Holman and Martinelli (*Mergers & Acquisitions,* 1983), provides an interesting method for calculating the weighted composite value of small businesses. Three factors are suggested: (1) Effective Liquidation Value (ELV), (2) Gross Revenue Capitalization Value (GRCV) and (3) Buyer's Discretionary Cash Value (BDCV). Tables for determining Relative Weights and Factor Weights for ELV, GRCV and BDCV are provided. The three factors were selected because data to calculate them is likely to be available for small businesses while data for more elaborate valuation methods may not be available. While the authors of the article freely describe the limitations of the techniques suggested, the author of this chapter has found that they provide a useful tool for introducing the owner of a small business to the concepts that should be considered in pricing a small business for sale.

Shareholder Value Analysis ("Bust Up" Analysis). Sophisticated analysts have for several years been developing new methods of analysis which led to many highly successful transactions and to several highly publicized failures in the late 1980s.

Critics, often the managements of companies which are tender offer targets, call these methods "bust up analysis." Those who developed and use the methods say they recognize, measure and help to realize shareholder values.

Despite the controversy, the methods of shareholder value analysis are, like other analytical tools, essentially neutral. They invite study, not only because they can lead to successful acquisitions, but also because they have caused changes in corporate management and financial policies throughout the United States.

For years, the primary measures of corporate and management performance have been earnings per share (EPS), return on investment (ROI) and return on equity (ROE) based on generally accepted accounting principles. Stocks have been sold and acquisitions negotiated based on multiples of GAAP earnings. However, GAAP methods were developed by the FASB and SEC primarily to protect from buying equity securities at inflated prices. They do not effectively measure a variety of other factors:

1. Undervalued assets
2. Restructurable businesses
3. Cash flow, present and potential
4. Investment requirements, short and long term
5. Effective use of debt in relation to investment opportunities, tax benefits and cash flow obligations
6. Corporate performance measured by net return of capital appreciation and income to equity investors
7. Opportunity and risk in relation to the time-adjusted value of money

As a result, EPS, ROI and ROE often do not measure management performance effectively, even without use of the many alternate policies permissible within GAAP to "manage" earnings. Thus, many investors have discovered in recent years that their shares were worth considerably more than market value to a management buyout group, a corporate raider or a "White Knight." When active bidding developed, the shareholders frequently benefited from competitive price increases, but the GAAP-oriented financial reporting system has not been directly helpful.

Originated as part of the analysis for conventional leveraged buyouts (LBO's), shareholders value analysis is primarily based on cash flow. However, both the definition of cash flow and the sources from which cash flow may be derived are much expanded beyond traditional concepts.

Cash flow is traditionally considered to be net income plus noncash charges such as depreciation, amortization and deferred taxes. However, many companies also adjust for changes in working capital accounts; i.e., inventories, receivables and payables. They may also subtract capital expenditures. The shareholder value analyst is more likely to work with pretax income and subtract only nondiscretionary capital expenditures, since this reveals more accurately the business potential to produce cash for a new owner to use for payment of acquisition debt and to build equity.

Once determined, cash flow is compared to the market value plus debt of the company to be acquired. Cash flow projections are prepared using numerous alternative assumptions for the eventual acquisition terms and the subsequent restructuring of the company.

The analyst will also use as sources of cash a variety of assets, and increased values of assets, at liquidation values not reflected in the financial statements. These assets may include readily salable subsidiaries and divisions, excess real estate and recapturable surpluses in pension plans. It may also include the closing of businesses creating heavy drains on cash. The analyst typically assigns conservative values to these nonfinancial statement items and also makes conservative assumptions about the times when they can be converted to cash. However, the recognition of such asset values as valid supplements to cash flow can make such a dramatic difference compared to conventional analysis that the analyst can afford to be conservative, at least until competition arises during acquisition negotiations or a tender offer contest.

The liquidations of businesses and assets described in the last paragraph are, of course, the reason why the name "bust up analysis" has been used by critics. On the other hand, shareholder advocates have long urged that managements should run corporate businesses to realize shareholder values in stock appreciation and dividends, not for other objectives including their own desire to build or maintain "empires." Alert managements have increasingly been using shareholder value analysis themselves to restructure their businesses, realizing that failure to do so may mean a hostile tender offer by a stranger who will restructure more quickly, harshly and less skillfully than they can do themselves.

The substitution of debt, particularly high yielding securities, for equity provides leverage creating increased opportunity for capital appreciation and risk. Thus, the accuracy of the analysis is critical. In the late 1980s, planners of several leveraged buyouts greatly overestimated cash flows, including the timing and prices obtainable from business divestitures, leading to severe problems and bankruptcies. Examples were the acquisition of Jim Walter Corporation by Hillsborough Holdings, Inc., a vehicle sponsored by Kohlberg, Kravis and Campeau Corporation's acquisitions of Allied Stores and Federated Department Stores. The difficulties experienced after buyouts of Dart Drug, Revco, Fruehauf and several other highly leveraged transactions have received widespread publicity.

For further information, the authors recommend that the reader review *Creat-*

ing Shareholder Value, Rappaport, Free Press/Macmillan, Inc.,1986. See also, *Corporate Restructuring: A Guide to Creating the Premium Valued Company,* Rock, McGraw-Hill, 1990.

Operating Ratios and Other Data. While not purporting to be complete valuation methods, there are numerous operating ratios and other data that are useful in valuing a business. Some examples are the following:

- Current ratio and "quick" ratio
- Inventory turnover
- Backlog
- Inventory and accounts receivable aging
- Return on investment, return on equity and return on total capital
- Return on sales (gross profit)
- Break-even analysis under various assumptions
- Ratios of various expenses to sales, assets, etc.
- Market value to book value ratio
- Premiums (positive or negative) paid for comparable acquisitions for control or minority ownership

Tax Valuation Methods. While they are applicable to the valuation of stock of closely held corporations for estate tax purposes, analysts should be aware of the valuation methods prescribed by Revenue Ruling 59-60 of the Internal Revenue Service found at 1959-1 C.B. 237, as well as subsequent modifications in Revenue Ruling 65-192 (1965-2 C.B. 27), Revenue Ruling 65-193 (1965-2 C.B. 370), Revenue Ruling 68-609 (1968-2 C.B. 237), Revenue Ruling 77-287 (1977-2 C.B. 319) and Revenue Ruling 80-213 (1980-2 C.B. 101).

The reason for interest in these rulings and related valuation decisions by the Tax Court and the federal courts is that they constitute one of the largest sources of valuation data available to analysts. The *Federal Tax Valuation Digest,* published annually by Warren, Gorham & Lamont annotates court decisions under thirty valuation factors.

At first glance, Revenue Ruling 59-60 prescribes an asset-oriented approach to valuation. However, in addition to the values of tangible business assets, the ruling requires valuation of intangible assets. The most controversial of the intangible values are "goodwill" or "going concern value," which reflect excess earning capacity over a fair return attributable to tangible assets. In valuing these intangibles, earnings-oriented methods and discounted cash flow methods are valid. An unusually lucid article entitled "Valuation of Goodwill and Going Concern Value" (*Mergers & Acquisitions,* Spring 1979) provides helpful suggestions on these subjects.

Revenue Ruling 77-287 is of special interest because it recognizes that valuation discounts may be appropriate for restricted securities issued without registration pursuant to the private offering exemption in the Securities Act of 1933. The growing use of the so-called Section 4(1½) exemption described in Chapter 8 may have improved the value of restricted securities to some extent. The subsequent amendments to Rule 144 and the adoption of Rule 144A should also improve the value of some restricted securities.

NON-FINANCIAL STATEMENT VALUES

Market values and financial statement values are important in valuing and pricing an acquisition. However, it is not possible to make a complete and sound valuation based on these values alone. There are many elements of a business that are (1) unknown or underappreciated by the markets and (2) not reflected in financial statements, even those prepared in great detail and fully in accordance with generally accepted accounting principles. These elements are often more important than those that can be measured by market data and financial statement valuation techniques. In fact, a major reason for the difficulties experienced by many conglomerates resulted from acquisitions of unfamiliar businesses based entirely or primarily on market and financial statement values.

Among the assets of a business not directly appearing in its financial statements and sometimes, but not always, reflected in market value are the following:

- Reputation including quality, service, customer and government relations and respect of competitors
- People including organization, skills and motivation; good employee relations
- Intellectual properties including patents, trade secrets, trademarks and copyrights
- Undervalued land, buildings, equipment and leases
- Products that are well-designed and suitable and safe in their uses
- Leading market shares
- Established distribution system
- Relative freedom from competition due to such factors as high entry cost or government regulatory restrictions
- Franchise or distributorship agreements
- Government permits and approvals; demonstrated capability to meet government, industry and customer standards and specifications
- Customer and supply contracts
- Access to raw materials and energy and transportation facilities and services
- Well-funded pension and other employee benefit plans
- Unneeded assets readily salable for cash or usable as loan collateral
- Terminable expenses such as management "perquisites" and unpromising discretionary projects
- "Synergies" such as expansion opportunities through combining technologies or market entry of one company with manufacturing capacity of the other and cost-saving opportunities such as eliminating duplicate facilities and personnel. (In the experience of the author of this chapter, synergies consisting of expansion opportunities tend to be more successful than cost-savings opportunities that are often resisted by personnel.)

Businesses also have liabilities not necessarily appearing in their financial statements or reflected in market value. Many consist of an absence or weakness in the assets described above. For example, management itself may be unaware of the gradual onset of obsolescence of products or equipment or the quiet entry of indirect competition from substitute products. In recent years, many companies had to make difficult adjustments when raw materials and energy sources, long taken for granted, became unavailable or much more costly. Many companies, after complaining for years about the restraints of government regulation, found it difficult to compete when "deregulation" opened their industries to new entrants and freedom to compete at lower prices.

All of these "business" factors must be considered in valuing an acquisition and negotiating the price. It may be possible to quantify the potential effects of some of them in financial terms by cooperation between experienced businessmen and the financial analyst. Others must be left to the judgment of management and the processes of negotiation.

EFFECTS OF METHOD OF PAYMENT

Different possible media and methods of payment of the purchase price may also permit adjustment in the initially conceived price, and since available media and methods of payment are as many and varied as the imagination of the parties and the circumstances of the transaction will permit, parties unable to agree on price should consider changes in how payment is to be made to arrive at a mutually satisfactory solution. Two extremes in the media of payment are (1) an acquisition solely for stock, and (2) an acquisition solely for cash. Between these extremes innumerable combinations and methods for paying a purchase price are available.

Stock vs. cash. Assume, as is often the case, that a stockholder of a closely held business has a low tax basis for his stock; he would presumably wish to sell the business in a tax-free transaction to avoid payment of a substantial capital gains tax at the time of sale. As is explained in Chapter 10, a tax-free transaction will require payment in stock. Assuming the selling stockholder has indicated he is willing to accept $1,000,000 for the business without immediately incurring liability for payment of income taxes, $1,000,000 in the stock of the buyer, received tax-free, would satisfy the stockholder. However, if the buyer for reasons of its own wants to pay in cash, the cash payment would be taxable to the selling stockholder. Assume the seller's stock had a tax cost to him of $100,000. If the stock were bought for $1,000,000 in cash the stockholder would realize a taxable capital gain of $900,000 and would be liable to pay capital gains tax. Therefore, if the buyer insists on paying cash, the seller may insist upon an upward adjustment in price to compensate for payment of taxes.

Stock vs. convertible debentures. In a transaction between listed companies, originally conceived as an acquisition for stock, a substantial discrepancy exists between dividends paid on the buyer's and seller's stock. The seller's stock had over the years consistently maintained a trading price of $50 per share, and the seller had consistently paid a $2.50 dividend to its shareholders. As a consequence, the seller's stockholders had gradually, as a group, become older investors in the nature of retired individuals interested primarily in price stability and income realized on the shares. Furthermore, the price of the seller's stock had consistently remained at approximately $50 per share for many years. A study of the stock ledger revealed that by far the greatest portion of the shares had exchanged hands during these years, and presumably would have a tax cost in that area, thus minimizing the effect of a taxable transaction where the purchase price would be in the $50 per share range.

At the time of the negotiations, the buyer's stock also sold at approximately $50 a share, but the buyer was paying a dividend of only $1.25 per share. The parties reasoned that the seller's stockholders would not approve the transaction on a share-for-share basis because of the resultant substantial loss in dividend income. The buyer therefore offered to give convertible debentures for the seller's business, offering for each two shares of the seller one $100 5½ percent debenture, convertible into two shares of the buyer's stock at a price somewhat above the market price of the buyer's shares. As a net result, a selling stockholder's income from each $100 5½ percent convertible debenture would be $5.50 annually as opposed to the $5 annual dividend the stockholder would receive on his two shares given in exchange; furthermore, through the conversion feature in the debentures, the selling stockholders would have an opportunity to share in the prospective growth of the buyer.

Inventory purchase. In one situation a buyer wished to acquire the seller's machinery and equipment which the buyer intended to dismantle and reassemble in the buyer's own factory in a distant city. Since the machinery and equipment were massive, the buyer estimated that it would take three months to complete the dismantling, shipping and reassembling. Therefore, to supply customers during the three-month period and as a part of the purchase price, the buyer ordered a three-month estimated inventory from the seller for delivery at the closing of the transaction. This order for inventory and the profit the seller would realize from the order was taken into consideration as part of the payment of the purchase price for the machinery and equipment.

Loans. Situations arise in which a seller is in financial difficulties, and a buyer, not prepared to buy immediately, may lend the seller working capital in return for an option to buy and the temporary right to place someone on the seller's management team. From the seller's point of view two things are accomplished. The seller's immediate financial difficulties are solved, and if the option price is right, the seller may in the future be able to sell a business which, because of financial difficulties, could not be sold for a reasonable price at the time of the transaction. From the buyer's point of view, it gains an opportunity to study and perhaps acquire a business it desires, risking as its total possible loss the funds loaned to the seller. Each of the varying elements in such a transaction will affect ultimate price.

Installment payments. Installment payments should normally result in an increase in purchase price. Obviously, except for unique income tax situations, an immediate payment of the full purchase price to the seller is worth more to it than a promise to pay in future installments. Installment payments may be made either in stock or cash or other assets.

Contingent purchase price. Where a buyer and seller are unable to agree upon a purchase price because of different projections of estimated future earnings, a contingent price determined under a formula that fixes the price, payable in contingent future installments, as a function of the earnings actually realized in future years may bring the parties to agreement. Such arrangements for contingent price payments also may be effective where a buyer wishes to retain a seller's management and give the management an incentive to maximize future earnings.

In arrangements involving a contingent purchase price based upon future earnings, three basic elements should be considered:

(1) What portion of the purchase price should be contingent upon future earnings? Most generally the contingent portion of the price may range between 20 percent and 40 percent, although lower percentages and also higher percentages up to 100 percent of the price have been utilized;

(2) Over what period should the contingent price payments be determined? —Most generally this period will range between one and three years;

(3) On what basis should the amount of contingent payments be determined?—Most often the payments are determined by earnings of the seller's business above a specified level of base earnings, sometimes combined with a minimum market value for the buyer's stock to determine the number of the buyer's shares to be delivered.

The contingent price based upon future earnings is an appropriate tool when the buyer and seller are far apart on price, because the seller projects future earnings increases that the buyer does not believe attainable. In such a situation, the buyer may say, "All right, I'll pay you $2,500,000 plus an additional $1,000,000 in installments provided the business earns $300,000 net after taxes the first year, $350,000 the next and $400,000 the third as you've said it will."

To meet the objectives of the parties, the purchase price of a business may be paid in an unlimited number of ways: common stock, preferred stock, convertible securities, warrants, notes, cash, property of all kinds and varying combinations of all of the foregoing. The parties should be aware that the method of payment may affect the ultimate price, and may make possible agreement on price where initially it appears that no agreement can be reached.

VALUE CONTRIBUTED BY BUYER

In order to develop a systematic, objective approach to price, the foregoing discussion has taken no account of increases in future earnings of the seller's business as a result of integration with the buyer's business. Needless to say, a seller's business may have more value to one buyer than to another. One may need what the seller has to offer more than another. Deliberately, the foregoing discussion of price is based upon a theory that the seller's business will be operated as an isolated unit. But if the acquisition is well-conceived, the acquired business will often complement and be complemented by the buyer's business organization, and should earn more than if the seller continued on its own.

Once having determined a price for a seller's business, treating that business as an isolated unit, a buyer should determine what improvement in the seller's projected earnings may result from integration of the two businesses. If the integration will apparently increase expected future earnings, the buyer has the flexibility of offering a premium over the price based upon isolated projected earnings of the seller. In this connection, any and all of the possible objectives for acquiring a going business may give added value to the seller's business when operated by the buyer.

To state a few examples, the buyer may expect to increase earnings (1) through economies effected by combining sales organizations or manufacturing facilities, (2) by utilizing the seller's established sales outlet in a geographical area of the country in which the buyer has no outlets or (3) by utilizing the seller's heavy equipment or seller's personnel. If the buyer is acquiring the seller solely to obtain a new product line in order to avoid the loss of time and expense required in tooling up for the line and putting the line in production, the buyer may wish to take into account the savings in time and money as possible "plus factors" to the purchase price. Since plus factors may be added, in essence, because of the added value brought to the business by the buyer's operation of that business, the added value of the business theoretically should not accrue to the seller's sole benefit. However, a buyer may wish to consider increasing the price in the course of negotiation because of the added value which the seller's business may have when operated by the buyer.

LIMITS ON MAXIMUM PRICE

We have indicated that the price of a going business is largely a matter of judgment. Only future events will confirm or deny that the price paid was justified. Two fundamental tests exist by means of which a buyer may, at least theoretically, determine what the maximum price should be, unless the acquisition represents an unusual long term investment opportunity.

Dilution of earnings per share. First, if the acquisition is to be made for stock, the buyer should satisfy itself that the earnings acquired from the seller divided by the shares used to pay the price, result in per share earnings in excess of the per share earnings of the buyer, taking no account of the possible acquisition. In other words, the earnings per share of the buyer should be upgraded by the acquisition. The upgrading need not necessarily take place on the basis of earnings of the seller at the time of acquisition. But at some time in the reasonably predictable future, it should appear that the earnings per share from the acquired business on the purchase price shares should exceed the earnings per share of the remaining outstanding shares of the buyer, taking no account of the earnings acquired from the seller.

For example, assume that the seller's business will show earnings per share on the buyer's shares used to buy the business, and the buyer's other outstanding shares (without regard to the seller's business) will show earnings per share, as follows:

Future Years	*Projected Earnings per Buyer Share Exchanged from Seller's business*	*Projected Earnings per Buyer Share from Buyer's Other Business*
1st year	$1.00	$1.20
2nd year	1.25	1.32
3rd year	1.50	1.46
4th year	1.80	1.60
5th year	2.16	1.78

In the foregoing example, the seller's earnings are expected to upgrade earnings slightly per share of the buyer's exchanged stock by the end of the third year and to upgrade by an amount in excess of 20 percent in the fifth year. In view of the possible future upgrading, a buyer may decide that the price on which the forecast was based is acceptable. On the other hand, if the projected per share earnings of the seller's business should indicate a continual dilution of the buyer's future earnings per share, the price would appear excessive and the buyer should not agree to pay it without overriding considerations present in the situation. As a general rule, to justify the price in a stock transaction the earnings acquired per share of stock paid should be greater than the per share earnings of the buyer's outstanding stock—either at the time of the closing or within the reasonably foreseeable future.

Return on Investment. In a second basic type of transaction, a cash transaction, the buyer should determine what the after-tax return on its investment will be. As in the case of a stock transaction, this determination may be based upon earnings at the time of the negotiations as well as projected earnings. If the after-tax return on the buyer's own invested capital, realized from the conduct of the buyer's own business amounts to, let us say, 10 percent, the buyer should think twice before investing in a seller's business in which the after-tax return is less than 10 percent. Each acquisition should upgrade the buyer's earnings, if not immediately then over a foreseeable period for long term investments.

High Technology Investments. The foregoing limits, and indeed most conventional criteria, may not apply to an acquisition of a business which has established a bona fide lead in a newly developing high technology field. For example, acquisitions in fields such as biotechnology, fiber optics, telecommunications or special materials may be priced in a manner similar to the methods used in determining its research budget. Major considerations will be the capital and operating needs of the business and incentives for the key scientific personnel. A buyer wishing to gain entry to a high technology field may, accordingly, decide to subsidize the acquisition cost by the risk standards associated with research programs, subject also to the future evaluation controls used for such programs.

The Board of Directors
ABC Corporation
New York, New York

Gentlemen.

You have requested our opinion as to the fairness, from a financial point of view, to the shareholders of ABC Corporation ("ABC") of the consideration to be received by them in connection with the acquisition by merger of ABC by XYZ Incorporated ("XYZ") pursuant to an Agreement and Plan of Reorganization dated _____, 199____ (the "Agreement").

We have acted as financial advisor to ABC and participated in the planning and negotiation of the terms and conditions of the transaction. As is more fully described in the Agreement, each outstanding share of XYZ Common Stock will be exchanged for 1.5 shares of ABC Common Stock in a manner intended by the managements of ABC and XYZ to qualify for treatment as a tax-free reorganization under applicable provisions of the Internal Revenue Code.

In rendering this opinion we have, among other things, (i) reviewed the financial terms of the Agreement and the proposed amendment to the Certificate of Incorporation of ABC authorizing the issuance of ABC Common Stock; (ii) reviewed the Proxy Statements sent to shareholders of ABC and XYZ including the financial statements included therein; (iii) reviewed and analyzed the financial position and performance of ABC and XYZ as reflected in certain information provided to us for this purpose by their respective managements and outside representatives; (iv) reviewed and studied business and financial forecasts and generally familiarized ourselves with the prospects for ABC; (v) reviewed the historical stock prices and reported trading volume of the ABC Common Stock; (vi) reviewed the historical stock prices and reported trading volume of the XYZ Common Stock; (vii) reviewed publicly available information and made a general financial and statistical comparison of ABC and XYZ with certain other companies whose business or businesses we believe to be comparable. We have also conducted discussions with members of senior management of ABC and XYZ and conducted such other financial studies, analyses and investigations as we deemed appropriate.

In our review, we have assumed without independent verification the accuracy and completeness of the financial and other information provided to us or publicly available and have not independently verified such information.

Based upon our analysis of the foregoing and upon such other factors as we deem relevant, including our assessment of general economic, market and monetary conditions, it is our opinion that the consideration to be received in the proposed transaction is fair to the shareholders of ABC from a financial point of view.

Very truly yours,

ABLE, BAKER, & CHARLES

5

Conducting
the Negotiation and
Coordinating the Investigation

After the buyer and seller reach agreement in principle, they should next turn to the task of negotiating a detailed acquisition contract, during which the buyer may undertake a more detailed investigation of the seller's business. In practice, reaching agreement in principle, negotiating the detailed contract and conducting the investigation cannot be approached as isolated functions. They are closely interrelated and dependent upon one another. For example, reaching agreement in principle will fix some of the major provisions of the detailed contract, and the investigation of the seller's business will uncover knowledge of additional facts and problems which will affect contract provisions.

Bearing in mind that these aspects of an acquisition are interrelated, discussing the conduct of the negotiation and coordination of the investigation as separate subjects, nevertheless, serves to highlight and clarify the major elements involved in each topic. Remember, however, that in the ordinary situation, the investigation of the seller's business by the buyer and the negotiation of the detailed contract proceed apace. As the contract is being negotiated, the seller ordinarily makes available to the buyer additional information about the seller's books of account, its tangible properties such as plant and equipment and its intangible properties such as contracts and patents, and grants the buyer access to the seller's plant to observe the seller's business in operation.

Under those unusual circumstances where a seller has the bargaining power to insist that a detailed contract be signed prior to permitting the buyer to conduct its investigation, the buyer may still protect itself by exercising care to cover all imaginable contingencies in the contract as conditions precedent to the buyer's legal obligation to close, thus permitting buyer to refuse to make the purchase where subsequent investigation reveals a material defect in the seller's business.

THE NEGOTIATION

Successful negotiating tactics involve interpersonal relations as well as business, technical, and financial knowledge. For example, a few years ago a major company was negotiating the sale of a large division to a medium-sized manufacturer. The latter demanded a significant reduction of the high asking price to a level that would have been typical for an acquisition in the industry. The chief executive officer of the seller was interviewed a few days later by the press. He commented that he doubted the division would be sold because it appeared that the only active buyer was too small to finance the price. This public comment so affected the pride of the buyer's management that it was diverted from its objective to reduce the price and devoted its efforts to raise financing for the priced asked by the seller.

Prior to each negotiating session, however, both the buyer and seller should consider carefully and decide who should be present—and who should be the major spokesman. Naturally, no fixed rule can be stated which will cover all circumstances, including who should participate and how the negotiation should be conducted, but general observations may be helpful.

The Negotiating Team. The first meeting, which may be called the "probing session," normally may not require attendance by the lawyer, accountant or financial adviser for either side. The person who has the responsibility for conducting the negotiation on behalf of the buyer (whether he be an officer of the buyer, a director of planning or an acquisitions group executive) should meet with either the controlling stockholder or principal officer of the seller, as the case may be. If the initial meeting proves successful, and the buyer and seller feel there may be mutual advantages in consummating an acquisition, the parties should not delay in bringing in their respective lawyers, accountants and financial advisers.

When the buyer's investment banking firm or other financial advisors have originated the transaction, they will be involved from the beginning and will play a leading role. In other transactions, management will wish to consult with them on valuation, structure, financing sources and methods—and perhaps negotiating strategies.

The lawyer should participate in the earlier stages of serious negotiation to develop knowledge of the facts and problems needed to draft a satisfactory acquisition agreement. Some businessmen tend to delay too long in bringing lawyers into the negotiation sessions. Perhaps, the delay results from fear that the lawyer may adversely affect negotiations by raising unimportant technicalities. Such a fear is unfounded in the case of the great majority of lawyers practicing commercial law today. In fact, lawyers experienced in the acquisition field are often helpful in steering negotiations in the right direction and bringing negotiations to a satisfactory conclusion.

The negotiation should be conducted not only with a view to determine price and to decide whether or not the acquisition should be made but also to develop the acquisition contract. If a buyer buys or a seller sells, the contract fixes the deal for both. The sooner the lawyer is brought into the picture the sooner he may begin to outline the transaction and begin preparation of a draft of an acquisition contract. Such a draft will help point up areas still open for further negotiation between businessmen. Depending on the circumstances of each transaction, if the lawyer becomes involved in the negotiations at the earlier stages, he will also have an opportunity to help to structure the transaction. When lawyers are invited belatedly to participate, they may discover legal, tax or other reasons why the transaction should have been structured differently. The result can be serious delay and cost while the restructuring is done. If it is too late to restructure, the buyer or seller may suffer loss.

The buyer's accounting firm should also be consulted on the investigation of the finances of the seller's business including a review of its financial statements and perhaps an audit as of the closing date.

Negotiating Objective. Obviously, one of the basic negotiating objectives of both the buyer and seller is to fix a satisfactory price. However, both parties should bear in mind that normally they are not legally bound until the acquisition contract is signed, and the negotiating sessions give both parties an opportunity to test the general conclusion, previously reached, that the acquisition would be advantageous to each.

Obviously, from the buyer's point of view, its objective in conducting the negotiation should be to develop as many facts as possible about the operation of the seller's business and to ferret out trouble areas. In conducting the negotiation, the buyer should constantly strive to determine the actual reason motivating the seller to sell its business. When asked, the seller will give a plausible reason. The seller's principal stockholder may state that he faces possible estate tax problems, that the seller needs research facilities that the buyer may make available to it, that the rapid growth of seller's business has made financing difficult, or any one or more of the other numerous reasons for selling businesses. Although the reason given by the seller may be accurate, a Harvard Business School study conducted by interviewing executives engaged in acquisitions, indicated that in a great majority of instances, the seller did not reveal its actual reason for selling—fear; fear that the competition was growing too strong; fear that a product was becoming obsolete; fear that substantial capital outlays would be required to remain competitive; fear that a basic patent might be proved invalid. In very few of these instances did the seller tell the buyer the actual motivating force for selling its business.

The importance of determining the seller's true motive for selling cannot be stressed too strongly. Assume the buyer is negotiating to buy a business in which an engineer is an essential to the strength of the business. This engineer has invented all the new processes of the business and each advance of the business is largely the result of his genius, but the seller knows that this engineer intends to resign and compete with the seller. If, in the course of its investigation, the buyer does not uncover first, that this engineer is the mainstay of the business and second, that he intends to resign, the buyer may pay a substantial amount for a business worth a great deal less.

Often the seller should also try to determine the buyer's reason for buying. In those instances where a seller is not just selling out for cash with the intent of retiring, the seller should also attempt to establish to its satisfaction the objectives motivating the buyer in making the purchase. For example, if some of the seller's owners, or key executives expect to remain in the employ of the buyer and continue to conduct the seller's business, their objectives will not be met if it is the buyer's intention to substitute its own management or to liquidate the seller's business and utilize the assets for strengthening the buyer's business. Or, if the seller intends to retain the buyer's stock for retirement dividend income, the seller will have a rude awakening if the buyer cuts its dividend and needs the seller's assets to satisfy creditors.

The Desire for Secrecy. In an acquisition, a seller will often stress that it wishes to keep the negotiations secret. Generally, the seller will believe, and rightly, that rumors of an impending sale of the business may have adverse effects on employee morale or customer and supplier relationships. The buyer should also give consideration to the importance of continuing the smooth operation of the seller's business. Where secrecy is important, both parties should take all reasonable steps to satisfy that end. In this regard, negotiation meetings may generally be held away from the seller's and the buyer's places of business, in hotel rooms, or other neutral places. If the attorneys for buyer and seller maintain offices outside the parties' places of business, all correspondence may be addressed to the attorneys' offices. If the seller employs independent certified public accountants, the buyer's accountants may concentrate the major portion of the audit function in the offices of the seller's accountants. Any physical inspection of the seller's plant may be made on weekends or evenings after proper preparation of the seller's employees—the purpose of the inspection relates to fire insurance or some similar matter. The buyer and seller may cooperate in many ways to keep their negotiations from becoming public knowledge. But unfortunately, experience has shown that in spite of all precautions, rumors of negotiations for the sale of the seller's business often begin to circulate. In most instances, the buyer and seller should be prepared to accept this fact—should be prepared to take the steps dictated by the circumstances to cope with the situation, not permitting strong feelings on the part of either to cause a breakdown in negotiations.

People. No business is made up exclusively of plant and equipment, of inventory, of customers and suppliers. Every business includes as a major element the human beings who operate the business and cause it to function. And just this element, since it involves the uncertainties of human emotions, may become the biggest threat to the successful sale or purchase of a business. The seller's key executives, with big mortgages on their houses, may begin to worry about being replaced by the buyer's counterparts. The factory workers may begin to worry about their privileges gained under a boss they feel free to address by first name—a boss who started the business in a garage and gradually built his work force over the years. The authors are aware of acquisitions that failed within a year or so because of departures of key employees. Other acquisitions have succeeded when employees became more successful and productive working with the buyer. Both the buyer and seller should constantly be aware of the worries that an acquisition may spawn in the human beings involved and should be prepared to quickly dispel any unfounded fears.

Certainly, the negotiating teams for both parties should never fail to maintain their equilibrium. A show of sternness or even anger—if deliberately thought out—may be appropriate on occasion. But, rudeness never. If the accountants conducting the investigation of the seller's books decide they are messy, this fact should not be announced in the seller's bookkeeping department, unless to convey a predetermined effect. If the buyer's lawyer finds a lease that could have been drawn better by the youngest associate on his staff, let him keep this thought from the seller's attorney and make it known only to the buyer—if the thought is at all material to the negotiation. During negotiations, emotions often become taxed, but they should never be permitted to interfere with the fundamental objectives of the negotiation.

THE BUSINESS INVESTIGATION

Regardless of the specific tactics employed in the investigation, the buyer should observe the fundamental principle that the investigation of the seller's business be a team effort. The investigation should proceed in three separate areas. But the investigation of these areas should be coordinated. The seller's business should be investigated from (1) the business point of view; (2) the legal point of view and (3) the accounting and financial point of view. Although the three areas of investigation are largely autonomous, the results should be coordinated. The tendency exists to conduct the investigation of the seller, in each of the areas mentioned, as isolated separate investigations. The business team tends to forget the legal and accounting aspects; the lawyer tends to become engrossed in the legal problems and the accountant and financial adviser tend to concentrate on their specialties to the exclusion of the other aspects of the seller's business. For an investigation to be successful, this tendency should be overcome, and the investigators should coordinate their efforts. Why this is so is developed in greater detail in this and subsequent chapters.

Coordination of Effort. Each investigator should endeavor to keep the other investigators informed as to problems that might arise in their area. For example, the business team, in conducting an investigation of the customers of the seller may find unusual pricing structures or unusual arrangements with distributors. They should immediately bring such matters to the attention of the lawyer. The lawyer may then assess whether there has been a violation of the antitrust laws and may be able to provide necessary indemnification or guard against liability for violations in the acquisition contract.

On the other hand, the lawyer in reviewing the seller's contracts may find antitrust pricing violations. Although the lawyer may guard the buyer against the assumption of liability for these violations in the contract, he should nevertheless call the violations to the attention of the business team. The profitability of the seller's business may depend upon the pricing violations. If the pricing structure must be amended to avoid violations of law, the business team may decide that the buyer should not make the acquisition.

The accountant, as he reviews the financial data, may uncover possible sizable income tax deficiencies of the seller for past years. The lawyer and business team should be given immediate knowledge of this fact. The lawyer may protect the buyer by contract against the assumption of any obligations with regard to the taxes, by escrow or otherwise, and the business team will assess the effect of the tax deficiencies on the going business.

Coordination of the Business Team. When planning a "due diligence" investigation, management should select the members of the business team carefully to be sure that all aspects of the seller's business will be covered. For example, one or more team members should be qualified to review sales, marketing, advertising, research and development, purchasing, accounting, treasury, credit, insurance, real estate, transportation, personnel and labor relations, tax manufacturing, quality control, engineering, public, and government relations to the extent they exist in the seller's business.

Even though many members of the business investigation team work regularly for or with the buyer, they may not work with each other in daily activities and may not fully understand each other's interests and responsibilities. This is specially common in large companies. Thus, the team should meet and plan their work to assure that it is performed in a coordinated manner.

Senior management should select members of the business team who have the capability and persistence to obtain essential information while remaining courteous at all times. The team members should never lose sight of the fact that they are guests at the seller's facilities and that seller personnel will judge the buyer organization based partially on their conduct.

Each of the investigators should keep sight of the objective that all collected information should be interchanged and correlated with the others.

Using the Information in the Acquisition Contract. Businessmen and accountants are often of the opinion that an acquisition contract is a document made up of "boiler plate" provisions. Their attitude is that, if they thoroughly perform their areas of the investigation, the acquisition contract is of little importance. Nothing could be further from the truth or more dangerous to the success of an acquisition.

The acquisition contract should contain provisions stating clearly the agreement between buyer and seller on every significant aspect of the business being sold. To the extent that the acquisition contract is silent, inaccurate or vague, someone may be hurt. For example, the seller may not transfer all assets expected by the buyer. The buyer may not assume all the liabilities expected by seller. Seller's equipment may be found to be defective or some its inventories to be obsolete after the sale without any remedy available to buyer. Employees may not receive promised employment contracts or benefits. Seller's products or manufacturing processes may infringe patents without a remedy for the buyer. The seller may not have adequate insurance to cover accidents which have occurred but are not yet known. The seller might decide to start a competitive business shortly after the sale and to hire key employees of the business sold to the buyer. Numerous additional examples could easily be given.

Buyer and seller representatives should discuss each element of the transaction and decide how it will be handled and also allocate the risk of any contingencies between them. Experienced lawyers can often assist them by describing customary methods to reach agreement and sometimes by suggesting imaginative solutions. The lawyers should then state each agreement clearly in the acquisition contract.

Since the contract embodies the transaction in its entirety, the clearing house for information developed in the course of the negotiation should be the lawyer's office. The reason is that lawyers are accustomed to handling confidential information and acting as coordinators during the negotiation of contracts. The safest procedure to follow is to have both the business team and the accountant send to the lawyer all important information as developed, regardless of whether or not they believe the information will have any effect upon the contract. On his part, the lawyer should keep both the businessman and the accountant informed of information he develops independently.

Nature of Business. The nature of the seller's business should also alert the buyer to the aspects of the business which should receive the most emphatic investigation. For example, if the buyer is acquiring a manufacturing business utilizing costly, heavy or intricate manufacturing machinery and equipment, the buyer should obviously have its engineers make a careful evaluation of the condition of the machinery and equipment. Similarly, if a patent structure is the major asset of the business, the buyer's patent attorneys should make a careful search and evaluation of all patents to determine whether they might infringe on other patents or whether patent litigation involving the patents may exist. If a personal service business is being acquired, such as a public relations or advertising firm, the investigation should concentrate on the personnel and their willingness to remain with the business. Stated generally, the buyer should bear in mind the type of business it is acquiring to indicate where it should place the major emphasis in the investigation.

The Investigation—Business. If the planning for the proposed acquisition has been properly conducted, a general investigation of the seller's industry and the seller's business will have been completed prior to reaching agreement in principle with the seller. The buyer should have sufficient general knowledge of the seller and its industry to make the acquisition appear worthwhile on the surface. The further business investigation should be directed at developing specific facts of the seller's business and industry which the buyer may not normally develop from public knowledge and financial publications. Specifically, if the buyer is acquiring a manufacturing business, it should obtain access for its engineers to the factory buildings of the seller. On-the-spot observation of the seller's business operation will give the buyer's engineers an opportunity to assess whether the buildings, machinery, equipment and processes are efficient, or whether they are in need of substantial overhaul. It is not extraordinary to make substantial capital outlays in the form of new factory buildings or expensive equipment after an acquisition. Such capital outlays, if necessary, may convert an otherwise profitable acquisition into one of dwindling profits in the face of required additional cash investments on the part of the buyer.

Most investigations from a business viewpoint should also include field investigation of customers and distributors to determine product acceptance and pricing methods. Direct contact with customers and distributors may reveal weaknesses in the seller's business in the form of excessive product rejects or weaknesses in servicing customer complaints and problems.

An important aspect of the business investigation should be the employees and personnel of the seller. As indicated above, an important ingredient in every business is people. People constitute an intangible asset in the form of know-how, developed often over many years of experience, customer contact and a general knowledge of the business which buyers cannot normally hope to develop successfully without the goodwill of the seller's employees.

For example, the authors know of two occasions where the buyer of a division being divested by a large conglomerate learned that the division's plant facilities had suffered serious technical difficulties during startup of new manufacturing facilities including equipment breakdowns and poor product quality. Buyer personnel visiting the plants learned from local engineers and operators that demonstrable solutions to the technical problems had been developed, but had not been implemented because the conglomerate had become discouraged and was unwilling to commit funds to a plant that had not met profit projections. After verifying the technical data, the buyer used the information on both occasions to negotiate a successful acquisition on favorable terms.

On the other hand, the investigation may reveal negative information that saves the buyer from a bad acquisition or enables buyer to negotiate more favorable terms. On one occasion, an author learned from a financial officer of a business that a significant part of the sales booked during the current financial quarter had actually been shipped on consignment to customers. On another occasion, an author learned that a seller's plant included a landfill containing drums of hazardous waste materials that were leaching into nearby wells and streams. Both discoveries resulted in termination of negotiations.

Acquiring the employees of a business together with their goodwill is a delicate maneuver. When employees learn that a business is being sold, human nature comes into play and the employees worry about the effect the acquisition will have upon their personal lives. Worry is the general rule. If it is a buyer's intention to keep the personnel structure of the seller intact and to keep the business intact, the buyer should take all reasonable steps to mollify any unfounded fears. Furthermore, where the buyer will be dependent upon the continued employment of key executives and employees of the seller to carry on the business, the buyer should obtain assurance that the key people will remain with the seller's organization and perhaps negotiate employment contracts with such personnel.

The Investigation—Legal. The nature of the seller's business will affect upon the lawyer's choice of the areas of investigation he should emphasize. The structure of the acquisition will also affect the investigation. Will the transaction be a merger, stock sale or assets sale? Will the buyer use stock, notes or cash to make the acquisition? The answers to these questions have a direct bearing on the areas of the investigation requiring major emphasis.

The lawyer must keep these differences in mind in his own investigation, but, of equal importance, he must call to the attention of the businessmen and accountant the effect the forms of the transaction have on their investigation.

For example, stock of the seller is being acquired, the lawyer should carefully check the minute books and stock books of the corporation. He should satisfy himself that the stock of the seller, when acquired, will be fully paid, nonassessable and not subject to any liens or encumbrances. The lawyer should be certain that each seller of stock has good legal title to deliver. For example, if the shares of stock have at any time passed through an estate, the lawyer should satisfy himself that the distribution of the stock from the estate has been made properly and is not subject to any outstanding estate tax liens or subject to possible invalidation of the transfer of the stock by disgruntled relatives of the decedent.

In every type of transaction, when real estate or other tangible assets are involved, the lawyer should satisfy himself as to the title to such assets. For real estate, a title report and commitment for title insurance should be obtained from a reputable and financially stable title insurer together with an updated survey meeting ALTA standards. The lawyer should review each title exception, including any outstanding liens and easements, and either arrange for them to be removed or advise the buyer on the effects of accepting them. For personal property, the lawyer should arrange a search for security interests, tax liens and other encumbrances by Infosearch, local counsel or others who can rapidly review the records of secretaries of state, county recorders and courts.

A further necessary function of the lawyer is to review all major contracts, including leases to real property. These should be reviewed with the primary objective of determining whether any unusual terms exist which should be brought to the attention of the businessman or the accountant, and whether any arrangements might be illegal. Also, as part of this review, if assets are being acquired, the lawyer should be certain that all important contracts, license agreements and franchises are assignable by the seller. If any are not assignable, provisions should be made in the contract for the seller to obtain the consent to the assignment of the contract.

To obtain information, representations and warranties made by the seller in the acquisition contract are helpful. Instead, the acquisition contract may serve as one of the basic tools for developing the necessary information for a thorough investigation of the seller's business. When an experienced lawyer senses that a seller or buyer is being vague about information during a "due diligence" review, he may add to the next draft of the acquisition contract a provision representing and warranting that the facts are consistent with the interpretation of the information furnished that is most favorable to the lawyer's client. This technique often compels a buyer or seller to be more candid.

The Investigation—Accounting. The accounting investigation should be addressed to two fundamentals. First, do the profit and loss statements and the balance sheets supplied by the seller fairly present the income of the seller and fairly present the financial position of the seller? Second, what differences exist between the seller's accounting methods and the buyer's accounting methods?

The second objective of the accounting investigation is an important factor in helping the businessman to determine the desirability of the acquisition and the price. Generally accepted accounting principles, because of the number of different principles applicable to each specific financial situation and the judgment factors involved in the ultimate selection of the principles, provide such a broad range of possible different profit and loss and balance sheet results, in the same business, that a change in the particular generally accepted accounting principles may, on paper, cause a low profit business to appear highly profitable.

For example, on pages 00, 00 are imaginary Profit and Loss Statements of Company "A" and Company "B" first printed as pages 178 and 179 in the book *Management Problems of Corporate Acquisitions* published by the Harvard University Press, and reproduced here through the courtesy of the Harvard University Press and Leonard Spacek, managing partner of Arthur Anderson & Company, who prepared the statements. Company "A" and Company "B" do an identical amount of business. But note from these Profit and Loss Statements that the application of different accounting principles, all of which are generally accepted accounting principles, change the net profits reported by the same business from $1,076,000 to $480,000.

The profit and loss statements make it abundantly clear that the accountant, in his investigation, should note any differences in the seller's accounting methods from those of the buyer, and should reconstruct the seller's income by applying the buyer's accounting methods to the seller's business. The accountant should make certain that the businessman understands the accounting differences and the effect these differences may have on reported earnings. Assume the buyer finds out only after he acquired Company "B" that a change in Company B's accounting methods to conform them to the buyer's will reduce Company B's reported earnings from $1,076,000 to $480,000. The result is an unhappy buyer.

A specific accounting problem, the valuation of inventory, is often difficult to resolve. In many situations where inventory forms an important part of the seller's business, the problem of valuing inventory becomes a matter for detailed negotiation. If inventory constitutes an important part of the seller's business, the buyer should insist on the right to take a physical inventory as a condition to the acquisition. The buyer may not be willing to accept "obsolete" or "slow-moving" inventory as part of the acquired inventory. Under these circumstances, the buyer and seller may be faced with the difficult problem of defining what is meant by "obsolete" or "slow-moving" inventory. Where an attempt is made to define such inventory terms in the acquisition agreement, provisions relating to the definitions may run on for many pages.

In certain instances, the accounting investigation may be as thorough as a complete audit of the seller's business by certified public accountants. If a business is closely held and has not been audited regularly by certified public accountants, the accounting investigation should be much more thorough and perhaps consist of a complete audit. In other instances, and more generally the case, the investigation will not be quite as extensive. If the company being acquired has been regularly audited by independent certified public accountants and has certified annual financial statements, the investigation by the buyer's accountants may be limited to a verification of the financials from the worksheets of the certified public accountants of the seller.

The procedure utilized in each investigation (that of the businessperson, the lawyer, and the accountant) will differ under the varying circumstances of the acquisition, and no investigation should be conducted in a purely mechanical manner. As already indicated, different circumstances will vary the emphasis placed on investigating different areas of the seller's business. Judgment and thought should be the keynotes. However, checklists may help as final references to assure a buyer that no area of the investigation has been overlooked.

ACCOUNTING
All "In conformity with generally
Company B's Profits

	Company A Col. 1	Use of FIFO in Pricing Inventory Col. 2	Use of Straight-line Depreciation Col. 3
Sales in units	100,000 units		
Sales in dollars	$100 each		
	$10,000,000		
Costs and expenses—			
Costs of goods sold	$ 6,000,000		
Selling, general and administrative	1,500,000		
LIFO inventory reserve	400,000	$(400,000)	
Depreciation	400,000		$(100,000)
Research costs	100,000		
Pension costs	200,000		
Officers' compensation:			
Base salaries	200,000		
Bonuses	200,000		
Total costs and expenses	$ 9,000,000	$(400,000)	$(100,000)
Profit before income taxes	$ 1,000,000	$ 400,000	$ 100,000
Income taxes	520,000	$ 208,000	$ 52,000
	480,000	$ 192,000	$ 48,000
Gain on sale of property (net of income tax)	—	—	—
Net profit reported	$ 480,000	$ 192,000	$ 48,000
Per share on 600,000 shares	0.80	$ 0.32	$ 0.08
Market value at:			
10 times earnings	$ 8.00	$3.20	$0.80
12 times earnings	9.60	3.84	0.96
15 times earnings	12.00	4.80	1.20

( ) Denotes deduction.

Accounting Magic
Explanation of Columns 2 to 7, inclusive

Column	Company A	Company B
2.	Uses LIFO (last in, first out) for pricing inventory	Uses FIFO (first in, first out)
3.	Uses accelerated depreciation for book and tax purposes	Uses straight-line
4.	Charges for product development costs to expense currently	Capitalizes and amortizes over five-year period

(If product development costs remain at same level, the difference disappears
after five years. The difference of $80,000 in the chart
is in the first year, where A expenses $100,000, and B capitalizes
the $100,000 but amortizes 1/5.)

MAGIC
accepted accounting principles"
Are Higher Because of

Deferring Costs over Five Years Col. 4	Funding Only the Pensions Vested Col. 5	Use of stock Options for Incentive Col. 6	Including Capital Gain in Income Col. 7	Company B Col. 8
				100,000 units
				$100 each
				$10,000,000
				6,000,000
				1,500,000
				—
				300,000
$(80,000)				20,000
	$(150,000)			50,000
				200,000
		$(200,000)		—
$(80,000)	$(150,000)	$(200,000)	—	$ 8,070,000
$ 80,000	$ 150,000	$ 200,000	—	$ 1,930,000
$ 42,000	$ 78,000	$ 104,000	—	$ 1,004,000
$ 38,000	$ 72,000	$ 96,000	—	$ 926,000
—	—	—	$150,000	$ 150,000
$ 38,000	$ 72,000	$ 96,000	$150,000	$ 1,076,000
$ 0.06	$ 0.12	$ 0.16	$ 0.25	$ 1.79
$0.60	$1.20	$1.60	$2.50	$17.90
0.72	1.44	1.92	3.00	21.48
0.90	1.80	2.40	3.75	26.85

Column	Company A	Company B
5.	Funds the current pension costs—i.e., current service plus amortization of past service and interest at the maximum deduction levels allowed by the Internal Revenue Code	Funds at the minimum rates required by ERISA.

(Difference in pension charges might also arise where management decides that current contribution can be reduced or omitted because of excess funding in prior years and/or increased earnings of the fund or the rise in the market value of the investments.)

Column	Company A	Company B
6.	Pays incentive bonuses to officers in cash.	Grants stock options instead of paying
7.	Credits gains (net of tax thereon) directly to earned surplus (or treats them as special credits below net income)	Includes such gains (net of income tax thereon) in income

AN ACQUISITION TIMETABLE

After the buyer and seller have reached agreement in principle, and have commenced negotiations to agree upon a detailed acquisition agreement, the lawyers should begin preparation of a timetable for the transaction.

If the transaction involves approvals or rulings by administrative agencies, such as the Securities and Exchange Commission or the Internal Revenue Service, or involves meetings of stockholders of a publicly held buyer or seller, the timetable should take into consideration the time involved in dealing with such administrative agencies and notice requirements to stockholders with respect to meetings. The timetable should include a feasible closing date for the transaction, establish the order of priorities of the steps required to close the transaction and indicate the delegation of responsibility to the various parties involved for the preparation of the documents and fulfillment of the tasks required to close.

The tentative timetable set forth below was prepared in connection with the proposed acquisition of the assets of a seller, whose stock was traded in the over-the-counter market, in exchange for stock of a buyer, whose stock was listed on the New York Stock Exchange. This tentative time schedule illustrates in outline form the action that must normally be taken by a buyer and seller in a transaction of the nature indicated.

ACQUISITION OF ASSETS OF SELLER
FOR STOCK OF BUYER

TENTATIVE TIME SCHEDULE

		Responsibility
June 28 *(Friday)*	Meeting of board of directors of buyer to approve proposed acquisition of seller.	buyer
July 1 *(Monday)*	Meeting of board of directors of seller to approve acquisition by buyer.	seller
	Press release.	buyer and seller
July 2 *(Tuesday)*	Meeting of buyer and seller officers with counsel to review terms of acquisition and to assign drafting responsibility.	buyer and seller
	"Due diligence" reviews scheduled.	
July 12 *(Friday)*	First draft of agreement distributed.	buyer's counsel

July 19 *(Friday)*	Preliminary "due diligence" reports reviewed by officers and advisers.	buyer and seller
July 24 *(Wednesday)*	Meeting of buyer and seller officers with counsel to review first draft of agreement.	buyer and seller
July 25 *(Thursday)*	Draft of proxy materials for special meeting of the stockholders of seller and revised draft of agreement distributed for review.	buyer's and seller's counsel
	Draft of listing application for NYSE prepared.	buyer's counsel
July 26 *(Friday)*	Final "due diligence" reports reviewed by officers and advisers.	buyer and seller
July 29 *(Monday)*	Meeting of buyer and seller officers with counsel to review agreement and draft of proxy materials.	buyer and seller
July 30 *(Tuesday)*	Special meeting of board of directors of seller for the purpose of: (a) approving agreement. (b) calling special meeting of stockholders to be held on September 25, to adopt the agreement, and setting record date therefor. (c) approving proxy material and appointing proxies.	seller
	Special meeting of the board of directors of buyer for the purpose of: (a) approving agreement. (b) approving application for listing additional shares on the NYSE. (c) extending authority of the transfer agent and registrar to cover shares issuable in connection with the acquisition.	buyer
July 31 *(Wednesday)*	Execute agreement.	buyer and seller

August 2 *(Friday)*	File preliminary proxy materials with SEC.	seller's counsel
	File HSR notification and report with DOJ and FTC.	
	Mail joint letter from counsel for buyer and seller to the Commissioner of Internal Revenue requesting tax ruling with respect to tax aspects of the proposed acquisition.	buyer's and seller's counsel
August 23 *(Friday)*	Obtain SEC comments on proxy material.	seller's counsel
	Receive early termination of HSR waiting period from DOJ or FTC.	
August 27 *(Tuesday)*	Commence printing definitive copies of proxy material.	seller's counsel

August 30
(Friday)
	Mail proxy material to:
	  (a) all holders of record of seller.
	  (b) SEC and NYSE.
		seller

	File listing application and supporting documents with NYSE.	buyer's counsel
September 16 *(Monday)*	Mail any follow-up letters deemed advisable in order to solicit further proxies of stockholders of seller.	seller's counsel

September 25
(Wednesday)
	Special meeting of stockholders of seller at which the following action is to be taken:
	  (a) approve and adopt the agreement.
	  (b) authorize such other matters as may be deemed advisable in connection with the acquisition.
		seller

	Notify NYSE of stockholder approval.	seller's counsel
September 30 *(Monday)*	Board of Governors approves listing application pending notice of issuance.	
October 23 *(Wednesday)*	Receive favorable tax ruling from IRS.	seller's counsel

October 31
(Wednesday)   Closing in New York.
                      Press release, Form 8-K
                      Balance sheet audit by buyer's accountants   buyer and seller

Not only should the lawyers prepare a timetable similar to that printed above, but after the first draft of the acquisition agreement is prepared and the acquisition details begin to take shape, the lawyers should begin the preparation of a form of detailed closing memorandum. Preparing a draft of the closing memorandum will further highlight the documents required for the closing and will provide added protection against overlooking any details or preparations required for the closing.

THE BUSINESS INVESTIGATION CHECKLIST

A business investigation checklist includes the major considerations in the financial area that should be checked by accountants for the buyer. As indicated above, the accountant should not only investigate the financial aspects of the seller's business as set forth in the checklist, but should summarize for the buyer the differences in accounting principles utilized by the seller and the buyer, and should indicate to the buyer the significance and effect of these differences on future earnings of the seller's business.

The investigation of the seller's business should not be conducted solely through the use of such a checklist. However, a checklist of this nature is a handy tool for a buyer to assure itself that it has not overlooked some possible problem area involving the seller's business.

BUSINESS INVESTIGATION CHECKLIST

GENERAL DATA

> Name, headquarters address and phone number
> General description of the business
> Type of entity: corporation, partnership, other
> Ownership and control if not wholly owned by one person
> CEO and senior management
> Subsidiaries and affiliates
> Divisions and major departments
> Annual reports to shareholders
> If a public corporation, 10-K, 10-Q and 8-K reports and proxy statements and other SEC filings
> Reports on the company or its industry by brokerage forms and research firms
> Recent stock trading activity (stock exchange, NASDAQ, OTC)
> Acquisition and divestiture history

Reputation as perceived by industry, government, the financial community, shareholders, employees and the public

Professional advisers: Accounting firm, investment banking firm, bank, law firm

STRATEGIC ISSUES

Why is the business being sold?

What synergies exist between the acquiring and acquired businesses, particularly in technology?

Does the seller's business present major opportunities or risks? Will the acquisition improve or worsen them?

Is the acquired business self-sufficient or will it require management and investment?

Is the acquired business protected by technology leadership or entry barriers such as high capital cost?

Has the seller been candid and realistic in its disclosures? For example, has the business been operated for short term profit before it was offered for sale?

Are cash flows steady or cyclical?

How realistic is the seller's business plan and how does it fit with buyer's business plan?

Can economies be achieved by eliminating perquisites, selling surplus assets or eliminating duplication of facilities and personnel?

Does the business have excess manufacturing, sales or other capabilities?

Will the business provide entry to a new field which can lead to further expansion?

Will the acquisition place the company or the acquired business in competition or conflict with customers or other valued relationships?

How should information gathered during the "due diligence" review be assembled and analyzed?

MANAGEMENT

Positions and responsibilities of management
Experience, education and ages of management
Structure of management (formal and real)
Management information systems
Presence of founders
Management style:

Attitude toward risks
Attitude toward delegation
Attitude toward speed in decision-making

Attitude toward wide participation in planning and the persons
whose participation or approval are needed for decisions
Attitude on accountability for results

Recent and planned changes in management
Experience and skills at middle and junior management levels and
opportunities for advancement
Key employees on whom important elements of the business depend
Known alliances and rivalries among management
Evidence of understaffing or overstaffing
Compensation levels in relation to industry and to achievements
in growth and profitability
Extent to which management and compensation policies are
incentive-oriented and effective

SALES AND MARKETING

Major product lines
Gross sales by product line
Gross profits by product line
Market shares: national, regional, local
Export sales
Sales by foreign subsidiaries
Nature of products: high-technology, middle technology, commodity
Horizontal integration of product lines
Vertical integration and value added to products
Major customers, volume and profitability
Market trends
Market strategies and research
Sales forecasts and "product mix" effects
Major competitors
Competitive position and critical factors such as technology
leadership, capital intensive products, control of essential
raw materials, etc.
Sales and marketing staff and structure
Customer technical service
Sales and technical literature
Distributors and agents
Design and packaging
Trademarks, brand names, copyrights
Advertising: internal staff and agency
Public relations
Price history and sensitivities
Price discounts and credit terms
Price in relation to quality, volume and competitors' prices

Returns policy; consignment sales

Customer deposits or progress payments

Backlog of orders

Inventory turnover

Product substitutes

Seasonality

Long term contracts

Dependency on patents, licenses, etc.

Government business: availability of funding, authority of contracting officer; possible termination for the convenience of the government; audits of cost reimbursement contracts; security classifications, title to technology developed

Franchise agreements

Tariffs, taxes, government controls

Quality control and safety

Product warranties

Claims history

Product liability history and use of product specifications, instructions, warnings, MSDS sheets, labels, etc.

Methods used in price estimating

MANUFACTURING

Plants, locations and facilities

Access to customers, suppliers, transportation facilities, public utilities, labor, etc.

Production cycles: continuous or batch; number of work shifts

Order processing and scheduling; lead time for orders; inventory management and records

Processes and yields; comparison to state of the art

Production equipment: age, manufacturers, capacities and maintenance history

Components and raw materials (substitutes)

Important suppliers and their sources

Salaried, union or nonunion work forces

Subcontractors

Possible raw material storages

Intracorporate transfer pricing, if applicable

Electricity, fuel oil, natural gas, water and other utilities

Inbound freight: ship, barge, rail, truck

Inplant materials handling

Outbound freight: rail, truck, customer pick-up

Offsite warehouses: owned, leased, public

Scrap and waste

Shutdown and lost time history

Quality control programs

Safety and environmental (See separate list)
Fixed and variable costs
Proposed capital expenditures
Recycle or sale of containers, scrap and waste

TRANSPORTATION

Loading and unloading facilities and methods
Weigh scales
Ships, barges, railcars and trucks (owned or leased)
Tariffs and rate agreements
Charters and leases
Permits and licenses
Private carriage arrangements
Common carrier agreements/mileage credits
Customer pickup arrangements
Offsite warehouses and terminals
Association and conference memberships
Insurance and contractual indemnities
Transfer points (FOB) for risk of loss, damage and liability
Safety and environmental

PURCHASING

Relative responsibilities of central and local purchasing
Policy on long and short term contracts
Use of bidding procedures and negotiation
Coordination with manufacturing to establish quality specifications and inspection procedures and to monitor supplier performance
Coordination with transportation personnel to monitor materials in transit
Coordination with research and development to be aware of new or substitute materials
Policy on carrying inventories including use of "just in time" systems
Use of credit terms of suppliers to conserve corporate cash
Ability to monitor inventory levels
Use of purchase order forms to verify purchase terms
Business trends and economic conditions in supplier industries
Procedures to authorize emergency orders at special prices
Programs to evaluate internal manufacture of materials used in high volumes
Use of "base load" contracts, "toll" manufacture contracts, facility sharing, customer pickup and other cooperative arrangements to save supplier costs
Programs to recycle waste or scrap materials or to sell them to recycle and scrap contractors

PROPERTY (TANGIBLE)

Land owned:

Original cost and present appraised value
Title policies and descriptions
Legal surveys and photographs
Easements, rights of way, etc.
Zoning and code restrictions
Buildings, facilities and improvements
Mortgages
Leases
Areas to be used for expansion
Surplus land: potential for sale or lease
Nearby properties
Demographics
Environmental
Assessed values and taxes

Land leased:

Lease terms and restrictions
Relevant items listed above

Buildings and facilities:

Description: use, size, materials of construction, utilities, access to other facilities, suitability for uses

Equipment: age, size, capacity, manufacturers, performance characteristics and reliability, operating and maintenance cost, fair market value replacement cost, state of the art, safety and environmental

Tools, dies, maintenance inventories

Idle facilities: potential for startup or sale; demolition and removal costs

RESEARCH AND DEVELOPMENT

Educational background and experience of R&D management and staff
Long term research programs: objectives, status and viability
Development programs: objectives, status and viability
History of successful programs
Customer technical support programs
Allocation of resources between product and process programs
Extent of services to sales, marketability, manufacturing, quality control, safety, environmental, legal and other functions

Resources: laboratory, equipment, library, data bases

Laboratory notebooks

Patents and patent applications

Trade secrets and systems for their protection including secrecy agreements

Research sponsored at universities and other university affiliations

Government sponsored research programs

Customer and supplier sponsored research

Ownership rights to research funded or performed by government, universities and others

Patent and other rights of competitors; research to develop products and processes outside their claims

INTELLECTUAL PROPERTIES

Patents and applications

Trademarks and registration applications

Trade secrets and systems for their protection including secrecy agreements

Copyrights

Corporate names, trade names, brand names

Franchise agreements including services

Distributorship agreements

License agreements

Long term contracts

Corporate reputation and reputation of founders, executives, research personnel and others associated with the business

Membership in trade associations

Permits from government agencies

Listing as an approved supplier by major customer

Certifications by rating organizations that products or processes meet their standards: Underwriters Laboratories, Good Housekeeping, ANSI/ASTM, Factory Mutual, Kosher, etc.

Laboratory notebooks

Customer lists including product specifications, delivery schedules, contact personnel, special process needs, etc.

Business opportunity files

FINANCIAL

Financial statements and audit reports (5 years)

Accounting policies and their effects on reported revenues and income

Management letters from accountants

Internal financial controls

Internal audit reports

Internal financial statements by subsidiary, division, region, plant, etc.

Business plans (3 years)

Operating budgets

Cost system (standard cost, etc.)

Capital budgets

Capital appropriation requests, whether or not approved

Electronic data processing equipment, reports and staff

Credit terms, collection policies and experience

Lines of credit

Revolving credit agreements

Intermediate and long term loan agreements

Securities outstanding: debt, preferred stock and common stock, options and warrants

Inventories, raw materials, work-in-process and finished goods: age, quality

Receivables: age, collectibility

Prepaid expenses and deferred charges

Depreciation and amortization policies

Short term investments

Accounts payable (discount policy)

Goodwill (sources, possible writeoff)

Extraordinary gains or losses affecting reported income

Defaults in debt payments and covenants

Contingent liabilities:

> Guarantees and letters of audit
>
> Contractual indemnities
>
> Purchase commitments
>
> Commitments to fund or pay employee and retiree pension, medical, vacation, severance and death benefits (actuarial reports)
>
> Tax audits
>
> Claims
>
> Lawsuits
>
> Economic changes

Tax returns and schedules (5 years):

> Federal, state and local
>
> Audit reports; open and closed years
>
> Deficiency assessments
>
> Aggressive deductions and other treatment
>
> Loss carryovers
>
> Depreciation history
>
> Potential for stepped-up bases

        Appraisals of assets
        Effects of taxes on future cash flow
        Payroll taxes

Accounting treatment of the acquisition:

        Purchase
        Pooling of interests
        Emerging issues relating to leveraged buyout and ESOP transactions
        Issues relating to the particular acquisition such as the future impact of SFAS No. 106 if the seller has retiree health care programs

Analysis:

        Trends in revenues, costs and profits
        Return on investment
        Return on assets
        Gross margins
        Potential revenue increases/decreases
        Potential cost increases/decreases
        Break-even points

Cash flow projections:

        Define cash flow (See Chapter 4)
        SFAS No. 95
        Match with cash obligations including provision for contingent liabilities
        Allow for unexpected expansion/construction

INSURANCE

Property coverage:

        Reputability of carriers
        Fire, windstorm, freeze, flood and other events covered
        Limits and deductibles
        Basis for reimbursement: replacement value, depreciated value, etc.
        Limits compared to present values; coinsurance
        Coverage of products and raw materials in transit
        Premiums

Liability coverage:

        Primary and excess carriers
        General liability
        Product liability

Environmental liability, if any

Policy forms

Occurrence coverage

Claims made coverage and late notice rights, if any

Limits, aggregate and per occurrence

Exclusions

Deductibles

Self-insured retentions

Policy applications (disclosures)

Excess carriers: following form or separate policies, limits, etc.

Premiums: fixed, retrospective

Extent to which old policies were retained and have unused aggregate coverage

Special coverage: ERISA, fidelity, D&O

Automobile liability

Marine insurance: ships, barges, cargo

"Key man" policies

See *Human Resources* for life, disability, hospital, medical, workers compensation and other policies maintained as part of personnel programs

ENVIRONMENTAL AND SAFETY

Clean air permits: construction permits and operating permits; emissions of pollutants and toxics, additional permits needed; compliance with permits

Clean water permits: NPDES permits; effluent components, additional permits needed; compliance with permits; spill control plans; discharge to POTW and pretreatment requirements

Hazardous waste management system permits: generator; transporter; on-site treatment, storage and disposal; insurance and closure plans; use of licensed transportation and disposal contractors; use of manifest system; small generator regulations

Cost and performance of emission, effluent and waste control facilities and equipment

Plans to install new facilities or equipment or to remediate existing conditions

Contamination of soil, groundwater and surface water

Community right to know compliance; community complaints

Toxic Substances Control Act: Inventory; premanufacturing notices; significant new uses; products selected for testing; Section 8(e) notices; PCB transformers, capacitors and other uses of PCB fluids and leaks and spills

Asbestos: State or local laws and possible future federal laws mandating removal or remediation; potential claims and lawsuits by employees who are heavy smokers or have other respiratory health problems; OSHA and EPA rules

Storage tanks: Secondary containment, leak prevention and monitoring; removal, cleanup and other requirements

"Superfund" Cleanup Liability: PRP status at NPL or state cleanup sites, § 104 letters, historical disposal practices

State transfer laws: New Jersey Environmental Cleanup Responsibility Act; Illinois Responsible Property Transfer Act; Connecticut Transfer Act

State superliens and CERCLA lien

Permit transfers and reissues

Contracts with federal and state agencies and copies of inspection reports

OSHA 200 Log

Workers compensation claim history

OSHA state inspection reports

Insurer inspection reports

Safety committee recommendations

Workplace air emissions and noise

Use of personal protective equipment

Engineering controls of workplace hazards: past and future needs and costs

Potential chronic health problems not yet manifested

LEGAL

Organization, qualification and good standing

Certificate of incorporation

By-Laws

Minute book

Authorized and outstanding capital structure including debt, stock, options, warrants, rights and convertible or exchangeable securities

"Supermajority" classified or other special voting arrangements

Stock book and ledger; certificates

Preemptive rights

Shareholder agreements and restrictions

Subsidiaries and affiliates

Real estate titles, easements and restrictions

Title insurance UCC-1 search

Insurance; scope and limitations of coverage

Employee benefit plans, trusts and other agreements

Claims, lawsuits and administrative proceedings

Permits and licenses

Compliance with regulatory laws; i.e., antitrust, environmental, safety, securities, equal employment opportunity, foreign corrupt practices, political contributions

Product liability exposure

Other contingent liabilities; i.e., guarantees, contractual indemnities, warranties, on-site contractors and subcontractors

Patents, trade secrets, trademarks, copyrights

Important contracts:

> Employment and consulting agreements
>
> Sale and purchase agreements including "blanket" purchase orders
>
> Leases of real estate and equipment
>
> Franchise and distributorship agreements
>
> License agreements
>
> Collective bargaining contracts
>
> Agreements with suppliers of utilities: electricity, oil, gas, water, rail, truck, etc.
>
> Loan agreements, mortgages, indentures

Procedures for corporate approval of the acquisition including corporate governance issues, if any

Government approvals and clearances needed for the acquisition and the procedures, time and possible difficulties to obtain them

Antitrust evaluation

Tax rulings needed or desirable and procedures, time and possible difficulties

Consents of customers, suppliers and others to assign contracts

Registration and listing of securities

Compliance with Regulation D and Rule 144

Bulk transfer requirements

Escrow agreements; depository and exchange agreements

Need for fairness opinions or solvency letters

Legal opinions

Transactions with officers, directors, shareholders and other related persons including officer loans

"Control premium" issues

Arrangements to protect insider and confidential information

Validity of noncompetition agreements

Liability to brokers, finders, etc.

Sales/use taxes; transfer taxes

HUMAN RESOURCES

> Organization structure
>
> Descriptions of responsibilities
>
> Key officers and managers

Policies and procedures on hiring, compensation changes, promotions, transfers and terminations

Compensation levels in relation to industry norms

Employee productivity and morale

Employee turnover, causes and effects

Area employment pool of qualified workers

Community living conditions and costs

Competition by other companies for qualified employees

Employment contracts, if used

Training programs

Labor unions representing hourly paid employees

Collective bargaining contracts: term, reopeners, wage and benefit scales, reserved management rights, restrictive practices and their effects

Decertification campaigns

Unfair labor practice changes

Grievances and arbitrations

Strikes and work stoppages or slowdowns

Accident and sickness frequency, lost time accidents, OSHA 200 Log

Charges under equal employment opportunity laws based on race, religion, color, national origin, age, sex, disabilities, military service and other groups entitled to preferential status as remedies for historical discrimination

EEO-1 reports; affirmative action compliance

Alcohol and drug testing programs; no smoking programs

Stock purchase and stock option plans

Pension plans (defined benefit): See separate checklist

401(k) plans and profit sharing plans

Other deferred compensation programs

Hospital, medical, disability and death plans

Health Maintenance Organizations

Life insurance programs

Vacation and sick pay policies, formal and informal

Severance pay policies, formal and informal

Retiree medical and death benefits

Employee expense reimbursement policies, automobiles, entertainment, etc.

PENSION PLANS (DEFINED BENEFITS)

The applicable laws are the Internal Revenue Code, Employee Retirement Income Security Act of 1974, the Single Employer Pension Plan Amendments Act of 1986 (SEPPAA), the Multiemployer Pension Plan Amendments Act (MEPPAA), the Omnibus Budget Reconciliation Act of

1987 (OBRA), the Technical and Miscellaneous Revenue Act of 1988 (TAMRA) and the Revenue Reconciliation Act of 1989 (RRA).

Documents to be reviewed:

Plan documents including amendments, trust agreements, group annuity contracts, pension commitments in collective bargaining or other agreements, summary plan descriptions and plan booklets.

Financial statements of each plan and any related audit reports with special attention to the quality of assets and their liquidity in relation to cash flow obligations for benefits and expenses.

Investment management contracts and the record of performance of the investment managers.

Actuarial reports including the actuarial method and assumptions and any recent and proposed changes. Determine the amount of all benefit liabilities (not only vested benefits) and how they compare to plan assets.

Tax returns, reports, determination letters and other forms and communications to and from the Internal Revenue Service, Department of Labor and Pension Benefit Guaranty Corporation (PBGC) including Form 5500, Annual Return/Report of Employee Benefit Plan. Identify any reportable event, accumulated funding deficiency, prohibited transaction or potential for recapture of surplus.

Major issues to be evaluated:

• The financial status of the plan, including minimum funding obligations and deficiencies. See I.R.C. Secs. 412 and 4971 and ERISA, Part 3. See IRS Reg. § 1.412(i)-1 exempting certain individual and group annuity contract plans.

• Choices for continuing, freezing, merging and terminating plans.

• Controlled group liabilities for failures to meet minimum funding standards and other obligations.

• Liability for failure to notify participants of failures to meet minimum funding standards. ERISA Sec. 502(c).

• Coverage and other anti-discrimination requirements and limitations. See I.R.C. Secs. 401(a)(26), 410, 415 and 416.

• Vesting upon termination or partial termination. See I.R.C. Secs. 411 and 412(c) and ERISA Secs. 4041 and 4062.

• Credit for service with predecessor employers. See I.R.C. Secs. 411 and 414.

• Reportable events. See ERISA Sec. 4043(a) and PBGC Regulation §§ 2615.1-to 23 for single employer plans.

- Fiduciary obligations. See ERISA Secs. 3(21), 404, 405, 406, 407, 409 and 410, and I.R.C. Sec. 4975.
- Termination liability for single-employer plans under SEPPAA. See ERISA Secs. 4041, 4062, 4068, 4069 and 4070. See also IRS/PBGC Forms 500, 501 and EA-S.
- Withdrawal liability for multiemployer plans under MEPPAA. See ERISA Secs. 4001(a)(3), 4201, 4203, 4204, 4205, 4211 and 4218. A sale of assets of a business is a withdrawal unless certain conditions are met. ERISA Sec. 4204.
- Excise tax liens applicable to controlled group members for unpaid minimum contributions. I.R.C. Secs. 412 and 4971.
- Possible recapture of a funding surplus after a termination or spinoff termination of defined benefit plans and the related tax under I.R.C. Sec. 4980. See ERISA Secs. 4041 and 4044(d). See PBCG Regulations 2618.30 et seq. See also *Pollock v. Castrovanci,* 476 F.Supp. 606 (S.D.N.Y. 1979), aff'd 622 F.2d 575 (2 Cir. 1980); *Washington-Baltimore Newspaper Guild Local 35 v. Washington Star Co.,* 555 F.Supp. 257, aff'd 729 F.2d 863 (D.C. Cir. 1984); *Wilson v. Bluefield Supply Co.,* 819 F.2d 487 (4 Cir. 1987); *Chait v. Bernstein,* 835 F.2d 1017 (3 Cir. 1987); *Fechter v. HMW Industries, Inc.,* 879 F.2d 1111 (3 Cir. 1989), *Payonk v. HMW Industries, Inc.* 883 F.2d 221 (3 Cir. 1989).
- Choices for continuing, freezing, merging and terminating plans.

NOTE: This Business Investigation Checklist appears in Chapter 1 of *The Acquisition Yearbook—1991*, Shea, The New York Institute of Finance (Simon & Schuster), 1991.

6

Antitrust and Other
Initial Legal Considerations

Once a buyer and seller begin to negotiate the details of an acquisition, they should consider not only the business arrangements but also legal, accounting and tax aspects which may affect the substance, structure or procedures of the acquisition.

At times, major opportunities or problems may be identified. Occasionally, a problem can be so severe as to prevent an acquisition entirely or to require that the acquisition be renegotiated and restructured. Most commonly, however, the problems are minor or can be solved by effort and negotiation. Whether major or minor, it is best to identify problems early because considerable time may be needed to resolve them, especially if government clearances are needed.

This chapter discusses several threshold legal problems:

- Antitrust—Clayton Act § 7 and Hart-Scott-Rodino Federal Trade Commission Improvements Act
- Unintended assumption of seller liabilities by the buyer, i.e. successor liability
- Stock exchange and NASDAQ requirements
- State securities laws
- Insiders and insider information
- Confidential proprietary information
- Sale of control
- State Corporation Laws
- Disclosure obligations in stock acquisitions
- Unusual charter provisions
- Pension and profit-sharing plans
- Employee stock options
- Nonassignability of contracts
- Loan Agreement Restrictions
- Bulk transfers

- Restricted securities
- Sales and use taxes
- Liabilities to employees
- Environmental, worker safety, and product liability

Accounting treatment of acquisitions is discussed in Chapter 7. Federal securities laws are discussed in Chapters 8 and 9. Federal tax laws are discussed in Chapters 10 and 11. Creditors rights laws, including the Bankruptcy Code, are discussed in Chapter 15. In addition to the discussion in this Chapter, the state corporation laws are also discussed in Chapters 2, 4, 5, 9 and 15.

ANTITRUST—CLAYTON ACT § 7

General. Three aspects of the antitrust laws should be considered in an acquisition: (1) Will the buyer inherit liability for any past violations of the antitrust laws on the part of the seller? (2) Will the acquisition in and of itself constitute a violation of the antitrust laws? (3) Will the intended future conduct of the business by the buyer result in any violations of the antitrust laws?

Obviously, a complete discussion of the antitrust laws is beyond the scope of this book. Volumes have been written concerning individual statutes which make up just a portion of the body of laws which are generally considered in their entirety as our antitrust laws. This entire body of laws must be taken into consideration to determine whether any past violations by the seller exist and whether future conduct of the business will result in violations. This determination requires such a thorough knowledge of the seller's business methods, contracts and relationship to his industry that the buyer's lawyers can only form an opinion of the broader antitrust aspects as the investigation proceeds and knowledge is developed. But one antitrust statute, Section 7 of the Clayton Act, specifically addresses itself to acquisitions. This is the section of the antitrust laws which the lawyer must consider initially in any acquisition. He must ascertain initially at least, sufficient facts to estimate the risk, if any, of possible violation of Section 7 of the Clayton Act.

To place Section 7 of the Clayton Act in its proper context, briefly consider the broad scope of our antitrust laws. There are three other federal acts which, read together with the Clayton Act, make up the major body of these laws. All of these are familiar by name.

The first is the Sherman Act, which provides that "every contract, combination in the form of trust or otherwise, or conspiracy, in restraint of trade or commerce . . . is declared to be illegal," and further that "every person who shall monopolize, or attempt to monopolize, or . . . conspire . . . to monopolize any part of . . . commerce" shall violate the act. Note that the Sherman Act provides the contract or combination must *be* in restraint of trade, and further the monopoly or attempt to monopolize must actually be found. This act, the first of the trust-busting statutes, prohibits among other things price-fixing, boycotts and allocations of territories through concert of action by competitors. It is also designed to curb the power and activities of corporations with monopoly or near-monopoly positions.

The second major act is the Federal Trade Commission Act, which provides that "unfair methods of competition in commerce, and unfair or deceptive acts or practices in commerce" are "declared unlawful." This act prohibits, in addition to false advertising, unfair methods of competition which, if permitted to grow unchecked, might enable a company to achieve a monopolistic position.

The third act which is grouped among the antitrust laws is the Robinson-Patman Act. Although this act is an amendment to the Clayton Act, it is generally referred to by its own name. This act prohibits discrimination in the price charged to customers for products of like kind and quality where the probable consequences of such discriminations would be either a substantial lessening of competition or a tendency to create a monopoly or to injure competition between third parties and the person granting or receiving a discrimination. Exceptions are permitted where the price discrimination is done in good faith to meet a competitive price or the sale arrangements result in an actual, non-incremental cost saving to the seller.

Section 7 of the Clayton Act provides that the act is violated where a corporation acquires assets or stock in another corporation and the effect of the acquisition *may be* substantially to lessen competition, or to *tend* to create a monopoly. In other words, it need not actually be demonstrated that the acquisition *has* or will definitely lessen competition. The statute by the use of the words "may be" only requires that there be a reasonable probability that the undesirable effects on competition will result.

Although very different in approach, and although very different in the practices at which they are aimed, these acts have one fundamental objective common to all. That objectives is to maintain a competitive business economy.

The acts also have one important additional element in common. Each one affords wide discretion to the Department of Justice, Federal Trade Commission and the courts to interpret their meaning. In this sense, the acts are like the Constitution of the United States—a document with broad general provisions, the meanings of which have developed with the years through interpretation by the courts of the general provisions as these provisions are applied to specific fact situations. In interpreting the antitrust laws, it is therefore not sufficient to refer only to the statutory language. One must try to determine the meaning given to the words of the statutes by government agencies and the courts.

Clayton Act, Section 7. With this background, consider pertinent language of Section 7 of the Clayton Act blocked out and enumerated to highlight its four basic elements:

> No corporation . . . shall
> [1] *acquire,* . . . the whole or any part of the stock, or . . . the whole or any part of the assets of another corporation . . . where in any
> [2] *line of commerce* in any
> [3] *section of the country,* the effect of such acquisition
> [4] MAY BE *substantially to lessen competition, or to* TEND *to create a monopoly.*

As indicated by the statutory language, four basic elements must be considered to determine whether a violation of Section 7 may occur. These are:

Clayton Act, Section 7—"Acquisition." The presence of this element is obviously the easiest to establish. There must simply be an acquisition of all or a part of the assets or stock of another corporation. The acquisition may be made directly or indirectly by the acquiring company.

Clayton Act, Section 7—"Line of Commerce." The lessening of competition under the statute may take place in "any line of commerce." The statute does not refer to a lessening of competition in an *industry*. This language has given the enforcement agencies an opportunity to restrict and broaden relative product lines to attempt to prove possible lessening of competition. Generally, however, the courts and administrative agencies have now reached a conclusion that the line of commerce in each particular instance should be determined by means of the characteristics and end use of the product. For example:

In ordering E. I. duPont to divest itself of its stock interest in General Motors, the Supreme Court held that the line of commerce was automotive finishes and fabrics, not paint and upholstery material in general. The Court felt that the invention of "DUCO" for use on automobiles in preference to varnish set the automotive finish market apart from the market for paints in general and that the pricing policies in the automotive fabrics market differentiated that market from the market for other fabrics where an established price prevailed. By restricting the line of commerce and thus reducing the size of the market under consideration, the Court laid the groundwork for finding the necessary tendency to the substantial lessening of competition or creation of a monopoly in a restricted line of commerce, i.e. a submarket. To quote the language of the Court:

> However, within this broad market, well-defined submarkets may exist, which, in themselves, constitute product markets for antitrust purposes.

In *Brown Shoe Co. v. U.S.*, 370 U.S. 294 (1962), the Supreme Court went on to identify several "practical indicia" which may help determine the boundaries of a submarket: (1) industry or public recognition of the submarket as a separate economic entity; (2) the product's peculiar characteristics and uses; (3) unique production facilities; (4) distinct customers; (5) distinct prices; (6) sensitivity to price changes and (7) specialized vendors. These criteria are not exclusive and not all of them need be proven to establish relevant markets or submarkets.

The Federal Trade Commission also narrowed the concept of a line of commerce when it ordered the Reynolds Metals Company to divest itself of Arrow Brands, Inc., a small manufacturer of aluminum foil. The commission found the aluminum foil for sale to the florist trade was a separate line of commerce from aluminum foil for general household purposes. Foil for the florist trade was sold only to florists, was used only to decorate and wrap flowers, and its price fluctuated independently of the prices of household aluminum foil. Again, aluminum foil for the florist trade was not a large line of commerce, amounting to only $1.5 to $2 million annually, compared to many millions annually expended on aluminum foil for all purposes.

As the reader will see, the identification of the market or submarket relevant to an acquisition can be quite difficult. Almost every product faces direct or indirect competition from one or more alternate products. Whether a product and its substitutes are so interchangeable in use and there is such cross-elasticity of demand for them as to include them in the same market or submarket are difficult questions. However, analysis of the antitrust status of any acquisition under Section 7 must begin with the most realistic identification possible of the relevant markets or submarkets. Only then can the potential effects on competition be estimated.

Clayton Act, Section 7—"Section of Country." The tendency of lessening competition need occur only in "any section of the country," not the country as a whole. But the government agencies have the leeway of attempting to prove possible lessening of competition throughout the country or in localized sections, or both. In determining the area meant by "any section of the country" the courts have decided that there may be areas within areas. In other words, the area of competition may be the entire United States as one area. Within this area there may localized areas of competition where smaller companies are engaged in localized activities, and such smaller companies may be less competitive where their competitor in the localized area is acquired by a large corporation. For example:

In the Bethlehem Steel case involving Youngstown Tube, the Supreme Court found the section of the country within which competition had been lessened to be the United States as a whole, because Bethlehem and Youngstown competed nationwide, and also found five separate regional areas, each of which was centered around a particular mill and was segregated from adjoining areas by the barrier of differing freight rates.

An extreme instance of a narrowing of the relevant geographic market to a small area occurred in a proceeding involving Erie Sand and Gravel Company where the Federal Trade Commission confined the section of the country within which competition between two gravel companies had been affected to the South Shore area of Lake Erie in the states of New York, Pennsylvania and Ohio. This was the so-called "area of effective competition" since it was in this area that buyers from the merged companies were located.

In recent acquisitions in the cement, brewing, and other industries, buyers have voluntarily agreed to divest plants and operations in one market area in order to avoid opposition by the Department of Justice or FTC to a larger acquisition with only modest effects on competition when measured nationally and in other market areas.

An interesting case in which a U.S. Court of Appeals reversed a finding of a national market by the FTC and found that regional markets existed is *Jim Walter Corp. v. Federal Trade Commission,* (5 Cir. 1980) 1980-2 CCH Fed. Trade Reg. Rep. § 63,535.

Clayton Act, Section 7—"Tendency to Lessen Competition." The acquisition must be one the effect of which "*may* be substantially to lessen competition, or to *tend* to create a monopoly." The effect on competition need therefore not be immediate. The words of the statute have been held by the courts to mean that a "reasonable probability" of a substantial lessening of competition is all that is required to violate the statute.

Decisions have also made it clear that a buyer does not have to buy a competitor to come within Section 7. Of course, buying a competitor will in and of itself lessen competition, and in such an acquisition the only remaining question relating to competition is whether the acquisition tends *substantially* to lessen competition or to create a monopoly. Where a buyer acquires a seller who is not a competitor, the courts have considered many factors to determine whether the competitive effect prohibited by the statute may occur. Among these are (1) the market shares of the companies, (2) the degree of concentration of business in a limited number of companies in the industry, (3) the ease of entry into the business from the standpoint of capital required, (4) the number of remaining competitors after the acquisition, (5) the industry trends and the number of previous mergers, (6) the anticipated or actual behavior of the merged company after the merger and (7) the foreclosure of a potential market to others.

To quote the Court in the *Bethlehem Steel* case, the lessening of competition may occur when an acquisition "(1) substantially increases concentration, (2) eliminates a substantial factor in competition, (3) eliminates a substantial source of supply or (4) results in the establishment of relationships between buyers and sellers which deprive their rivals of a fair opportunity to compete."

Each of the foregoing elements must be considered in the confines of the limited lines of commerce and geographical areas involved in the particular acquisition under consideration.

FEDERAL MERGER GUIDELINES

1968 Merger Guidelines. In 1968, the United States Department of Justice published guidelines for use by its own staff and by industry in evaluating the potential competitive effects of acquisitions under Section 7. The guidelines also were used by the Federal Trade Commission. The guidelines for horizontal acquisitions were quite strict. For vertical transactions, they were more lenient because vertical transactions were perceived as less likely to affect competition adversely.

The guidelines for horizontal acquisitions indicated a challenge could ordinarily be expected if the market shares of the parties were as follows:

Market	Acquiring Company	Acquired Company
Highly concentrated	4%	4% or more
	10%	2% or more
	15%	1% or more
Less highly concentrated	5%	5% or more
	10%	4% or more
	15%	3% or more
	20%	2% or more
	25% or more	1% or more

A highly concentrated market was defined as one in which the four largest firms held 75 percent or more of the market.

Changing Enforcement Patterns. For many years, the federal courts consistently ruled in favor of government enforcement agencies in acquisition challenges. Strict divestiture decrees were issued which required disposition of acquired companies or assets in a manner designed to restore competition, even though the disposition was at a considerable loss. However, particularly after adoption of the 1968 merger guidelines, enforcement tended to become mechanistic. The Department of Justice and FTC relied heavily on the percentage tests of the guidelines and regarded broader economic analyses of competitive effects by companies as arguments entitled to little weight. For some years, the courts took the same viewpoint.

In *United States v. General Dynamics Corp.,* 415 U.S. 486 (1974), the United States Supreme Court ruled that a *prima facie* case of illegality based on statistical evidence could be rebutted by evidence of fundamental changes that limited the acquired firm's ability to compete, even though it was not actually a failing business. Following this signal, the federal courts, particularly the Circuit Court of Appeals for the Seventh Circuit, began to consider broader evidence of the potential competitive effects of acquisitions than those revealed by statistical analysis of market shares. For example, in *FTC v. Great Lakes Chemical Corporation,* 528 Fed. Supp. 84 (1981), a leading manufacturer of fire retardant additive products was allowed to acquire the other leading manufacturer whose commitments to research and development in a rapidly developing field had become noncompetitive. A history of cases allowing a "General Dynamics" defense is found in *Kaiser Aluminum & Chemical Corporation v. FTC,* 652 Fed.2d 1324 (7th Cir., 1981).

1982 Merger Guidelines. In 1982, after sponsorship by William Baxter, the first lawyer to head the Antitrust Division of the Department of Justice who was also an economist, new merger guidelines were published. More sophisticated measurement was based on the Herfindahl-Hirschman Index (HHI) developed by Orris C. C. Herfindahl and Albert Hirschman. Under the 1982 guidelines, challenge of an acquisition is described as follows:

Market	HHI Increase	Challenge
Highly concentrated	Under 50	Unlikely
	50 to 100	Possible
	Over 100	Likely
Moderately concentrated	Under 100	Unlikely
	Over 100	More likely than not
Unconcentrated	—	Unlikely

A market is highly concentrated if the HHI will be greater than 1,800 after an acquisition. It is moderately concentrated if the HHI will be greater than 1,000 after the acquisition. It is unconcentrated if the HHI will be less than 1,000 after the acquisition.

The HHI is calculated by adding the squares of the market shares of the companies in the relevant market. For example, if there are ten companies in the relevant market, each with a 10 percent share, the HHI is calculated as follows: $10 \times 10^2 =$ 1,000. The HHI increase can be quickly calculated by multiplying the merging companies' market shares and multiplying again by 2. For example, if a company with a 7 percent market share acquires a company with a 4 percent market share the HHI increase is 65. Such an acquisition would be subject to possible challenge if it occurred in a highly concentrated market, but challenge is unlikely in a less concentrated market.

The 1982 guidelines contain a proviso that the Department of Justice is likely to challenge any acquisition by a leading firm in a market if (1) the firm has a market share of at least 35 percent, (2) the firm is at least twice as large as the second largest firm in the market and (3) the acquired company has at least 1 percent of the market.

It is too early to predict the future patterns of enforcement. It is clear that the HHI, which includes all companies in the market and squares their market shares, is a more comprehensive and sensitive working tool than the previous four company concentration ratio. Analysts of the 1982 merger guidelines indicate they are likely to apply as strictly to mergers of companies with relatively large market shares as the previous guidelines. They are expected to be more permissive to mergers of companies having small market shares.

Finally, the 1982 guidelines include for the first time descriptions of principles to be used in defining relevant markets. The likelihood of challenge to nonhorizontal (vertical) mergers is reduced from the already more lenient standards of the 1968 guidelines, again because of economic perception that vertical acquisitions often create economic and competitive benefits counterbalancing potential adverse effects.

For example, in recent years difficulties in meeting the merger guidelines have tended to focus on regional competition which can be more difficult to analyze than national competition. United States Steel cancelled its proposed acquisition of Republic Steel after the United States Department of Justice objected on grounds that regional competition would be adversely affected by the proximity of certain production facilities of the two companies. In the Schlitz-Heilman acquisition, concentration in a Southeast region was reported at 2531 level measured by the Herfindahl-Hirschman Index. Excessive regional concentration can sometimes be solved by exclusion of one of the competing plants from the transaction or a commitment by the buyer to the Department of Justice or Federal Trade Commission to divest the plant within a specified time period. However, if the two plants are essential to the acquisition plan, the seller and buyer must either cancel the acquisition or risk challenge by the government.

1984 Merger Guidelines. On June 14, 1984, the U.S. Department of Justice revised the 1982 Merger Guidelines in light of its first two years of experience in applying them and republished them as the 1984 Merger Guidelines. The revisions principally address: (1) Market definition and measurement, (2) factors that may affect the significance of concentration and market share data in evaluating horizontal mergers, (3) the treatment of foreign competition, (4) the treatment of efficiencies and (5) the treatment of failing divisions of healthy firms.

Most important, the 1984 Guidelines restructured again the factors which the DOJ will consider in analyzing an acquisition. Market concentration and shares became one of four major standards together with ease of entry, other factors and pro-competitive efficiencies. Further, a new standard was added listing factors which might limit the significance of market concentration and share data: (1) changing market conditions, (2) financial condition of firms in the relevant market and (3) special factors affecting foreign firms.

The introduction of procompetitive efficiencies as a standard was a major and controversial element of the 1984 Guidelines. The DOJ indicated that it would consider clear and convincing evidence of efficiencies such as economies of scale, integration of production facilities, lower transportation costs and reductions in general selling, administrative and overhead costs. However, if the same or similar efficiencies can be achieved independently, they will not be considered. Further, the more significant the competitive risks, the greater the level of efficiencies which must be established to outweigh them.

In market definition, a key principle is the so-called "five percent test." Markets are delineated by postulating a "small but significant and nontransitory" price increase—generally five percent for one year—for each product of each merging firm at that firms's location and examining the likely reactions of buyers, sellers of other products, and sellers in other areas. The 1984 Guidelines clarify that the "five percent test" is not inflexible, but is an analytical tool.

In evaluating market concentration and market share data, the 1984 Guidelines clarify that the Department of Justice does not regard the HHI Index as a set of strict mathematical rules without regard to qualitative factors. Of special interest among the qualitative factors, financial condition of a merging firm or any other firm in the relevant market which reflects chronic financial weakness may indicate that its current market share may overstate its future competitive significance.

In general, standards relating to definition of markets and calculation of market shares apply equally to foreign and domestic firms, even where sales of a foreign firm are subject to market quotas. Efficiencies which will be considered include economies of scale, better integration of production facilities, plant specialization, and lower transportation costs. While indicating that the Department did not relax the failing firm defense or create a declining industries defense, the 1984 Guidelines indicate that the Department will consider the financial condition of firms in evaluating the competitive significance of their market shares and any significant increases of efficiency resulting from the acquisition. Under limited circumstances, the Department will also consider appropriate cases involving a "failing division" of an otherwise healthy firm.

Enforcement Trends Under the New Guidelines. The willingness of the DOJ and FTC to consider a wider range of factors in acquisition analysis contributed to the growth of merger and acquisition activity in the 1980s. The courts also considered a wider range of factors. For example, changing technology was considered in sustaining acquisition in the oilfield drilling services business. *Gearhart Industries, Inc. v. Smith International, Inc.* After the DOJ's definition of the market for plastic pump sprayers and dispensers was rejected in *U.S. v. Calmar, Inc.* 612 F.S. 1298 (D., N.J. 1985), ease of entry and availability of alternative products became the basis for denial of a preliminary injunction. Ease of entry was also considered in a decision upholding a acquisition in the waste collection market. *U.S. v. Waste Management, Inc.,* 743 F. 2d 976 (2 Cir. 1984).

Another development limiting enforcement has been decisions denying standing to initiate private antitrust lawsuits to a takeover target company and to competitors. *Carter-Hawley Hale Stores Inc. v. Limited, Inc.,* 587 F.S. 246 (C.D. Cal. 1984); *Cargill, Inc. v. Monfort of Colorado, Inc.,* 761 F.2d 570 (10 Cir. 1985), cert. granted.

Examples of acquisitions blocked or ordered divested by the Department of Justice, Federal Trade Commission, or the courts in recent years include *FTC v. Bass Brothers Enterprises, Inc.,* 1984-1 CCH Trade Cases § 66,041 (carbon black); *Christian Schmidt Brewing Co., Inc. v. G. Heileman Brewing Co., Inc.,* 753 F. 2d 1354 (6 Cir. 1985) (C.D. Cal. 1985) (beer brewing), and *FTC v. PPG Industries Inc.,* 1986-2 CCH Trade Cases, § 67,235 (D.C., 1986) (glass and acrylic transparencies for aircraft). *FTC v. Elders Grain,* 868 F. 2d 901 (1989) (industrial dry corn); *Owens-Illinois, Inc.,* CCH Trade Reg. Rep. § 22,731 (FTC 1989) (glass containers); *Emerson Electric Co.,* CCH Trade Reg. Rep. § 22,786 (FTC 1989) (mounted ball bearings); *Imo Industries, Inc.,* CCH Trade Reg. Rep. § 22,795 (FTC, 1990) (25 millimeter image intensifier tubes); *Rhone-Poulenc S.A.,* CCH Trade Reg. Rep. § 22,796 (FTC, 1990) (dairy culture products); *U.S. v. Pacific Dunlop Holdings, Inc.,* 1990-1 CCH Trade Cases § 69,087 (E.D., Pa. 1990) (industrial gloves) and *Promedes, S.A.,* 1990-1 CCH Trade Reg. Rep. § 22,800 (FTC, 1990) (grocery stores).

Pre-Acquisition Notification and Reporting Requirements. On September 30, 1976, The Hart-Scott-Rodino Antitrust Improvements Act of 1976 became law and added Section 7A to the Clayton Act. Federal Trade Commission Rules to implement the new Section 7A became effective on September 5, 1978, and have since been amended.

Section 7A of the Clayton Act does not change the substantive aspects of the antitrust laws by which the legality of acquisitions is determined. However, Section 7A and the rules to implement it impose responsibilities upon acquiring companies, and selling companies, to provide pre-acquisition notification and reports to the Federal Trade Commission and to the Justice Department, and impose a waiting period after the notification and report is filed before an acquisition may be consummated.

Requirements for Filing. The filing requirements, and waiting period, come into play if an acquisition of voting securities or assets meets the following tests:

1. The commerce test. If either the acquirer or the seller of stock or assets "is engaged in commerce or in any activity affecting commerce" this test is met.
2. The size of the parties test. This test is met if either of the parties has sales or assets of $100 million or more and the other party to the transaction has sales or assets of $10 million or more.
3. The size of the transaction test. This test is met if as a result of the transaction the acquiring company will hold 15 percent or more of the voting securities or assets of the acquired company, or in excess of $15 million of the voting securities and assets of the acquired company. However, by § 802.20(b) Federal Trade Commission rules, an acquisition of not more than $15 million in voting securities which does not confer control of a company which, to-

gether with all entities which it controls, has annual sales or total assets of $25 million or more. "Control" means (1) holding 50 percent or more of the outstanding voting securities of a company or (2) having the contractual power presently to designate a majority of its board of directors. Where the acquisition is of voting stock, this rule transforms the size of the transaction test so that a buyer may acquire any amount of voting stock up to $15 million without an obligation to file unless it obtains control of the company.

Exemptions. In Section 7A(c), the act specifies numerous types of transactions exempt from the filing requirements. Some of these exemptions include:

1. Acquisitions of goods or realty transferred in ordinary course of business;
2. Acquisitions of bonds, mortgages, deeds of trust, or other obligations which are not voting securities;
3. Acquisitions of voting securities of a company, at least 50 percent of the voting securities of which are owned by the acquiring person prior to such acquisition;
4. Transactions exempted from the Antitrust Laws or transactions requiring approval and information filing with other federal agencies, if copies of the information filed with other federal agencies are contemporaneously filed with the Federal Trade Commission and the Assistant Attorney General;
5. Acquisitions of voting securities solely for the purpose of investment if as a result of such acquisition, the securities acquired or held do not exceed 10 percent of the outstanding voting securities of the company,
6. Acquisitions by foreign persons of (a) assets located outside of the United States; (b) less than $10 million of assets (other than investment assets) in the United States; (c) a foreign person with less than specified amounts of sales and assets in the United States and (d) voting securities of foreign persons which will not confer control of certain assets or companies in the United States; and
7. Such other transactions as may be, from time to time exempted by the Federal Trade Commission with the concurrence of the Assistant Attorney General.

In 1986, new exemptions were adopted which are specially useful in leveraged buyouts. In effect, they exempt the typical management buyout using a "shell" corporation as the buyer and the typical employee buyout financed through an Employee Stock Option Plan. These exemptions recognize that the typical management buyout or ESOP transaction leaves the competitive situation essentially unchanged.

Responsibility for filing and method of filing. In a negotiated transaction, both parties to the transaction must file the notification and reports. On the other hand, in a tender offer, only the acquiring person must file the notification. Section 801.30(b) of the rules requires that the target company file a notification and report on the fifteenth day after the date of the receipt by the FTC and Antitrust Division of the acquiring person's filing, except in the case of a cash tender offer, the target company must file its notification by the tenth day. The notification form must be filed with both the Federal Trade Commission and the Assistant Attorney General in charge of the Antitrust Division of the Department of Justice. The waiting period mentioned below only begins to run after the notification and report form has been filed with both agencies. Specifically, the form provides that two notarized copies of the notice and one set of attachments must be filed with the Pre-Merger Notification Office, Bureau of Competition, Room 3013, Federal Trade Commission, Washington, D.C. 20580, and three notarized copies with one set of documentary attachments must be filed with the Director of Operations, Antitrust Division, Room 3218, Department of Justice, Washington, D.C. 20530. A filing fee of $20,000 must be paid by each reporting person. See 54 Fed. Reg. § 48726, November 24, 1989.

The notification and report form. Pursuant to authority granted to it in the act, the Federal Trade Commission has developed the form of notification that is to be filed. The form is entitled "Antitrust Improvements Act Notification and Report Form." The form consists of some twenty-two sheets of requested information and instructions, and requires the submission of detailed information of the parties' business. In general, the form requires the parties to the transaction to provide information describing the transaction and their business operations. In addition, the form requires other documents to be submitted to the Federal Trade Commission and the Department of Justice, including such items as the acquisition contract, agreement in principle, or a letter of intent, SEC filings and accounting records and documents prepared to evaluate the transaction with respect to market shares, competition and competitors. The form contemplates that a complete answer will be given to each item on the form. In any circumstance, where a complete response may not be supplied, the party filing the form must give its reasons for noncompliance.

The waiting period. The waiting period required under Section 7 before an acquisition may be consummated begins on the date of receipt by the Federal Trade Commission and the Department of Justice of the completed notification from both the acquirer and the acquired person, or in the case of a tender offer from the acquiring person. The waiting period ends on the thirtieth day thereafter or on the fifteenth day in the case of a cash tender offer, unless earlier terminated by the Federal Trade Commission and the Assistant Attorney General, or extended as a result of a request for additional information or documentary material. Under the law, prior to the expiration of the thirty-day waiting period or in the case of a cash tender offer, the fifteen-day waiting period, the Federal Trade Commission or the Assistant Attorney General may require the submission of additional information or documentary material relevant to the proposed transaction and usually does so if serious issues appear to be presented. The Federal Trade Commission, or the Department of Justice, may extend the thirty-day waiting period or in the case of a cash tender offer, the fifteen-day waiting period, for an additional period of not more than twenty days (or in the case of a cash tender offer, ten days) after the date on which the Federal Trade Commission or the Department of Justice receives all of the information and documentary material required to be submitted pursuant to such request. Such additional period may only be further extended by the United States District Court upon an application by the Federal Trade Commission or the Department of Justice.

As a practical matter, when the Federal Trade Commission or Department of Justice identify a potentially serious problem, their request for additional information is sometimes so broad that it would take many weeks for the seller and buyer to respond fully. They usually reach an informal understanding under which a smaller volume of relevant information is furnished for review. The result is that the government obtains ample time for review and the buyer and seller are spared burdensome document production. Under 16 CFR, § 801 10, seller and buyer can file a statement of reasons for not furnishing requested information, thus starting the waiting periods. However, few buyers or sellers choose to confront the government since the resulting disputes would further add to delay and would also create friction.

When satisfied that no serious antitrust problems exist, the DOJ or FTC will grant termination of the waiting period, sometimes prior to the original 30-day period.

Penalties for noncompliance. Any person or any officer, director or partner of a person who fails to comply with the notification, reporting and related requirements is liable for a civil penalty of not more than $10,000 for each day during which such person is in violation of the section. The penalty may be recovered in a civil action brought by the United States. In addition, if any officer, director, partner, agent or employee of a person fails to comply substantially with the notification requirement, or any request for additional information within the waiting periods provided, the United States District Court may extend the waiting period specified until there has been substantial compliance.

Past antitrust violations. As indicated, a discussion of the impact of the antitrust laws in the broadest sense is beyond the scope of this book. Nevertheless, as the investigation proceeds, the lawyer for the buyer should be constantly vigilant to check all of the seller's contracts and pricing arrangements to uncover any possible past antitrust violations. Of course, past violations may be eliminated by changing methods of doing business after the seller is acquired. Such a change in methods, however, may have considerable effect upon the profits of the seller's business. Contrary to the adage that "crime does not pay," undetected illegal activities carried on by sellers have on occasion produced substantial profits.

For example, assume that a major portion of a seller's business is done with one large customer under a contract which violates the Robinson-Patman Act. This contract may result in lower profits per unit sold to the major customer, rather than other customers, but may nevertheless be the basic reason for a major portion of the seller's profits. Should the price discrimination in favor of the major customer be corrected, this customer may seek a new supplier with a resultant loss of substantial profits in the seller's business.

Future antitrust violations. The lawyer for the buyer should be alert not only to possible past antitrust violations but should also consider the impact which the acquisition may have on future competition. The acquisition need not have an immediate effect upon competition to result in a violation of Section 7 of the Clayton Act. If the long range effect of integrating the companies may be to substantially lessen competition a violation may occur. As indicated by the E. I. duPont case, where duPont was ordered to divest itself of its stock interest in General Motors more than a generation after its acquisition, an acquisition may not be illegal at the time of closing, but may become so because of the method of operating the acquired business.

As an example of circumstances a lawyer should consider in appraising the possible long range effect of an acquisition on competition, assume that the buyer is a large distributor of household products who commands substantial shelf space in retail outlets. Should the buyer acquire a product completely unrelated to the buyer's own products, the acquisition at the time it is consummated may not be considered a violation of the Clayton Act. But if the buyer uses his powerful distribution system and shelf space to drive other manufacturers of the seller's product out of business, the buyer may be charged with violation of Section 7 of the Clayton Act as a result of his subsequent conduct of the acquired business.

State Antitrust Enforcement. The merger guidelines of the U.S. Department of Justice and Federal Trade Commission have been opposed by a variety of groups. They include attorneys who had been active in enforcement and defense work and economists whose views differ from the "Chicago School" analysis used in developing the guidelines.

In 1987, the National Association of Attorneys General (NAAG), a group of state law enforcement attorneys, issued "Horizontal Merger Guidelines" to be used in enforcing state antitrust laws which had been dormant. They also adopted pre-clearance procedures.

The state enforcement policies seek to return to simpler industry or market concentration tests to measure legality of acquisitions. They reject defenses based on efficiencies and give lesser weight to factors such as ease of entry. Not surprisingly, they emphasize protection of regional and local businesses.

During the 1980s, several lawsuits were commenced by state attorneys general against parties to large acquisitions. Some of these cases were settled by consent orders to divest parts of the acquired company. Such divestitures may not have been too difficult to negotiate since many high-priced leveraged buyouts were made in contemplation of divestitures to repay acquisition debt.

There has been serious concern about fragmentation of antitrust enforcement. Antitrust policies formed to protect small business from competition are perceived by many business and government leaders as preventing the formation of companies able to compete with giant foreign companies in world markets. The visible success of large foreign manufacturers in exporting automobiles, electronic equipment and other products to the United States has reinforced this concern, although it is not clear that size was essential to the success.

In April, 1990, the U.S. Supreme Court ruled that state governments (and other private parties) had standing to seek divestiture of businesses acquired in violation of Section 7 of the Clayton Act. Unlike the Department of Justice and Federal Trade Commission, they must show threatened loss or damage to their own interests. They are also subject to equitable defenses such as undue delay or unclean hands. *California v. American Stores Co.,* 1990-1 CCH Trade Cases § 69,003 (1990).

Enforcement by Competitors and Targets of Tender Offers. During the 1980s, the federal courts rendered important decisions denying standing to initiate private antitrust lawsuits to a takeover target company and to competitors, *Carter Hawley Hale Stores Inc. v. The Limited, Inc.,* 587 F.2d 246 (CD Col. 1984); *Cargill, Inc. v. Monfort of Colorado, Inc.* 479 U.S. 104 (1986). These decisions reflected concern that takeover targets companies and competitors might well seek to frustrate lawful acquisitions by involving them in litigation too lengthy to permit financing and other vital steps.

However, when a private competitor showed that an acquisition would result in an 84% share of the herbal tea market, a market share that the court found might be "decisive" and much higher than the market shares in *Cargill,* the Court of Appeals for the Second Circuit ruled that the competitor had standing to obtain a preliminary injunction. *R.C. Bigelow, Inc. v. Unilever N.V.,* 867 F.2d 102 (2 Cir. 1989). The same Court also granted standing to a tender offer target company *Consolidated Gold Fields PLC v. Minorco, S.A.,* 871 F.2d 252 (2 Cir. 1989).

The decision in *American Stores* will provide important impetus for further lawsuits by state attorneys general. Readers interested in further information about the economic aspects should refer to "Challenges to the Chicago School Approach," 40 *Antitrust Law Journal* 629 (1989). An article describing the progress of state antitrust law enforcement is "Why the States are Stepping Up Attacks on Large Mergers," *Mergers and Acquisitions,* Lewis, July/August, 1990.

UNINTENDED ASSUMPTION OF SELLER'S LIABILITIES—A BUYER PROBLEM

The acquisition of a seller may take the form of either a merger, a purchase of stock from stockholders or a purchase of the assets of the business. In a merger, all liabilities of buyer and seller are continued by operation of law. Where stock is bought, since the seller continues as a going business and the same corporate entity continues to exist, all liabilities of the seller will continue. A change in stock ownership will not have any effect on the outstanding liabilities of the seller. This is not the appropriate place, but we will discuss below how a buyer may obtain contract or other protection when it uses a merger or buys the seller's stock.

When the assets of a corporation are bought as a going business as opposed to buying stock, the buyer normally has greater freedom to select assets and liabilities and to avoid assuming disclosed and undisclosed liabilities of the seller. This is especially true where the buyer buys assets for cash in an arm's-length transaction.

With the exception of obligations specifically assumed by the buyer in the purchase contract, in a purchase of assets for cash the buyer normally assumes no obligations for undisclosed liabilities of the seller, and creditors must continue to look to the seller for payment. There are two major exceptions to this rule: (1) If the buyer acquires a going business for cash and pays the cash directly to the stockholders of the seller rather than to the corporation, the buyer may find itself liable to satisfy undisclosed creditors of the seller; (2) if the requirements of the applicable bulk sales law are not met, undisclosed creditors may be in a position to enforce their claims against the assets bought by the buyer. In a later chapter bulk sales requirements are discussed in greater detail.

Buying assets for cash, where the corporation receives payment and bulk sales law requirements are met, will generally eliminate assumption of undisclosed liabilities by the buyer, but buying assets of a going business for stock may result in the assumption of undisclosed liabilities by the buyer through operation of law. Where assets are bought for stock, a buyer may become liable to satisfy undisclosed liabilities of the seller even where the purchase contract specifically sets forth that the buyer does not assume any undisclosed liabilities. The courts invoke a number of theories to hold a buyer that pays with stock liable for obligations not assumed in the purchase.

Trust Fund Theory. One theory applied by the courts is that of the trust fund doctrine. Under this doctrine, some courts have held that where a buyer buys all of the assets of a selling corporation in exchange for the buyer's stock and the stock is then distributed to the selling corporation's stockholders, creditors of the seller may assert claims against the buyer. The courts have reasoned that the buyer knew at the time the transaction was consummated, by the nature of the purchase, that its stock was to be distributed among stockholders of the seller, and by permitting this stock, the last remaining asset of the seller, to be distributed the buyer should be liable to creditors of the seller. The buyer, these courts have held, received the assets of the seller in trust for the benefit of creditors of the seller. Under these circumstances, creditors of the seller may look to the buyer for payment of claims to the extent of the assets bought by the buyer. One judge has stated the trust doctrine as follows:

It follows that when this purchasing corporation took over in exchange for its own stock and bonds the assets of the other, and permitted these securities which it had substituted for the visible tangible property of the selling corporation to be distributed among the shareholders of the latter, without provision for the creditors of the latter, it thereby became a party, with full notice, to the diversion of a trust fund. As such, the purchasing corporation holds the property so acquired impressed with the same trust with which said property was originally charged, and the purchasing corporation is liable to the creditors of the selling corporation to the extent of the property thus obtained.

De Facto Merger. A second theory under which unexpected liabilities are imposed on a buyer is that the purchase of assets for stock was in effect a merger or consolidation—sometime referred to as a de facto merger. In this connection, courts have disregarded the actual transaction to which the parties have agreed and have treated the transaction as a merger or a consolidation under the state statutes. The usual effect of state merger or consolidation statutes is that the continuing company remains liable for all outstanding obligations of both of the corporations that were parties to the statutory merger or consolidation. By treating the transaction as a merger or consolidation, courts have concluded that the buyer assumed all of the obligations of the seller, regardless of the limitation of the assumption of obligations in the contract of sale.

Creditor Protection. A third theory under which a buyer of assets for stock is held liable for the obligations of the seller provides that a state should protect its creditors. Under this theory the courts reason that a seller which has sufficient tangible assets in the state to satisfy creditors before a sale may have no assets left after the seller distributes the buyer's stock to the seller's stockholders. The courts further reason that the creditors of the seller should not be forced to pursue the stock received by the seller's stockholders into foreign jurisdictions, but should rather be permitted to pursue the tangible assets left in the jurisdiction although owned by the buyer.

Under any of the theories mentioned, a buyer may find that he has taken the seller's property subject to unknown and unexpected rights of seller's creditors. If the lawyer for the buyer determines that applicable state law may result in assumption of obligations in addition to those assumed in the contract, he should take steps in the early stages of negotiation to protect his client. One method to obtain protection is an indemnification by the seller and a form of escrow agreement under which sufficient property or cash is pledged to protect the buyer against unassumed liabilities. The indemnity and escrow may be provided by all the seller's stockholders or the major stockholders involved in the transaction.

Successor Liability. When the original editions of this book were written the National Labor Relations Board (NLRB) and some courts had ruled that a buyer of assets might become liable for performance of the seller's collective bargaining agreement even though the buyer did not wish to hire seller's union employees and did not agree to assume the collective bargaining agreement in the acquisition contract. This concern was subsequently put to rest by a decision of the United States Supreme Court in *Howard Johnson Co. v. Detroit Local Joint Executive Board*, 417 U.S. 249 (1974). See also *Russom v. Sears, Roebuck & Co.*, 558 Fed.2d 439. (8 Cir. 1977). However, if the buyer hires all or most of seller's union-represented employees and continues essentially the same business, the buyer must recognize and bargain with the union which represented the seller's employees, although it is not bound by the seller's collective bargaining agreement. See *NLRB v. Burns International Security Services, Inc.*, 406 U.S. 272 (1972) *Fall River Dyeing & Finishing Corp. v. NLRB*, 109 S. Ct. 2225 (1987). Recognition of a union may also be ordered if the buyer discriminates in hiring on the basis of union membership. *Sherwood Trucking Company*, 270 NLRB No. 82 (1984); *NLRB v. Babach et al.*, 785 F. 2d 46 (2 Cir. 1986); *NLRB v. Jarm Enterprises, Inc.*, 785 F. 2d 195 (7 Cir. 1986). However, where the buyer has legitimate business reasons for declining to hire former union employees, it is free to do so. *Jim's Big M*, 264 NLRB 1124 (1982); *Inland Container Corporation*, 267 NLRB No. 92 (1983). Further, the buyer has some freedom to determine in good faith whether the employees continue to wish to be represented by a union before recognizing the union. *Sofco, Inc.*, 268 NLRB No. 15, October 25, 1983, 114 LRRM 1233.

As described above, the obligation of a buyer, as a successor, to recognize and bargain in good faith as required by the National Labor Relations Act with a union representing a majority of its employees does not mean it must accept the terms of the previous collective bargaining agreement. *New England Mechanical, Inc. v. Local 294*, 134 LRRM 3048 (9 Cir. 1990). However, an employer which is a mere *alter ego* of the seller may be bound by the collective bargaining agreement.

As a practical matter, it is not easy for a buyer to avoid recognizing the union representing the seller's workforce unless it has business plans for significantly changed operations or is willing to accept some interruption in operation of the business. If the buyer hires an initial workforce consisting primarily of union members in order to maintain business continuity, the union can be expected to demand recognition, even though the buyer plans to hire a much larger workforce which later consists primarily of nonunion workers. *NLRB v. Jeffries Lithograph Co.*, 752 F. 2d 459 (9 Cir. 1985).

Successor liability has now risen in three other areas: product liability, environmental pollution and employment practices. They are discussed later in this chapter.

STOCK EXCHANGE REQUIREMENTS

Where the stock of the buyer or seller is listed on a securities exchange, the rules of the exchange must be considered in all acquisitions. Even where cash is employed, a stock exchange rule may require the taking of action by the buyer or seller, which would not be necessary under the laws of the state of incorporation or under the provisions of the corporate charter. For example, companies listed on the New York Stock Exchange are required to keep studies of major acquisitions confidential when circumstances indicated in the following exist. The New York Stock Exchange Company Manual contains the following provision relating to predisclosure handling of important corporate matters:

Internal Handling of Confidential Corporate Matters

Unusual market activity or a substantial price change has on occasion occurred in a company's securities shortly before the announcement of an important corporate action or development. Such incidents are extremely embarrassing and damaging to both the company and the Exchange since the public may quickly conclude that someone acted on the basis of inside information.

Negotiations leading to mergers and acquisitions [emphasis supplied], stock splits, the making of arrangements preparatory to an exchange or tender offer, changes in dividend rates or earnings, calls for redemption, new contracts, products or discoveries, are the type of developments where the risk of untimely and inadvertent disclosure of corporate plans is most likely to occur. Frequently, these matters require discussion and study by corporate officials before final decisions can be made. Accordingly, extreme care must be used in order to keep the information on a confidential basis.

WHERE IT IS POSSIBLE TO CONFINE FORMAL OR INFORMAL DISCUSSIONS TO A SMALL GROUP OF THE TOP MANAGEMENT OF THE COMPANY OR COMPANIES INVOLVED, AND THEIR INDIVIDUAL CONFIDENTIAL ADVISORS WHERE ADEQUATE SECURITY CAN BE MAINTAINED, PREMATURE PUBLIC ANNOUNCEMENT MAY PROPERLY BE AVOIDED (emphasis supplied). In this regard, the market action of a company's securities should be closely watched at a time when consideration is being given to important corporate matters. If unusual market activity should arise, the company should be prepared to make an immediate public announcement of the matter.

At some point it usually becomes necessary to involve other persons to conduct preliminary studies or assist in other preparations for contemplated transactions—e.g., business appraisals, tentative financing arrangements, attitude of large outside holders, availability of major blocks of stock, engineering studies, market analyses and surveys and so on. Experience has shown that maintaining security at this point is virtually impossible. Accordingly, fairness requires that the company make an immediate public announcement as soon as confidential disclosures relating to such important matters are made to outsiders.

The extent of the disclosures will depend upon the stage of discussion, studies, or negotiations. So far as possible, public statements should be definite as to price, ratio, timing and/or any other pertinent information necessary to permit a reasonable evaluation of the matter. As a minimum, they should include those disclosures made to outsiders. Where an initial announcement cannot be specific or complete, it will need to be supplemented from time to time as more definitive or different terms are discussed or determined.

Corporate employees, as well as directors and officers, should be regularly reminded as a matter of policy that they must not disclose confidential information they may receive in the course of their duties and must not attempt to take advantage of such information themselves.

In view of the importance of this matter and the potential difficulties involved, the Exchange suggests that a periodic review be made by each company of the manner in which confidential information is being handled within its own organization. A reminder notice of the company's policy to those in sensitive areas might also be helpful.

A sound corporate disclosure policy is essential to the maintenance of a fair and orderly securities market. It should minimize the occasions where the Exchange finds it necessary to temporarily halt trading in a security due to information leaks or rumors in connection with significant corporate transaction.

While the procedures are directed primarily at situations involving two or more companies, they are equally applicable to major corporate developments involving a single company.

The manual also contains the following statement with regard to timely disclosures:

Timely Disclosure of Material News Developments

A listed company is expected to release quickly to the public any news or information that might reasonably be expected to affect the market materially for its securities. This is one of the most important and fundamental purposes of the listing agreement that each company enters into with the Exchange.

A corporation should also act promptly to dispel unfounded rumors that result in unusual market activity or price variations.

STOCK EXCHANGE MARKET SURVEILLANCE

The New York Stock Exchange maintains a continuous market surveillance program through its Market Surveillance and Evaluation Division. An "on-line" computer system has been developed that monitors the price movement of every listed stock—on a trade-to-trade basis—throughout the trading session. The program is designed to review the markets closely in those securities in which unusual price and volume changes occur or where there is a large, unexplained influx of buy or sell orders. If the price movement of the stock exceeds a predetermined guidelines, it is immediately "flagged" and review of the situation is undertaken to seek the causes of the exceptional activity. Under such circumstances, the company may be called by its Exchange representative to inquire about any company developments that have not been publicly announced but that could be responsible for unusual market activity. Where the market appears to be reflecting undisclosed information, the company normally will be requested to make it public immediately. Occasionally, it may be necessary to carry out a review of the trading after the fact, and the Exchange may request such information from the company as may be necessary to complete the inquiry.

The listing agreement provides that a company furnish the Exchange with such information concerning the company as the Exchange may reasonably require.

Subsequent sections of the manual provide detailed procedures for public release of information and annual and interim reporting requirements.

Furthermore, under state statute and corporate charter a buyer may generally acquire a seller in exchange for the buyer's stock without having to obtain approval of the buyer's stockholders. However, where the buyer is listed on a stock exchange, the stock exchange may require the buyer to seek approval of the acquisition by the buyer's stockholders—in spite of state corporation laws and the buyer's corporate charter. As a prerequisite for listing additional securities, a buyer listed on the New York Stock Exchange is required to obtain the approval of its stockholders of an acquisition where the directors, officers or substantial security holders of the buyer have an interest in the seller, or where the relative size of the seller is substantial in relationship to the buyer. The rule as expressed in the New York Stock Exchange Company Manual is as follows:

Stockholder Approval—Exchange Policy

Stockholders' interest and participation in the corporate affairs of the companies which they own has greatly increased. Management has responded by providing more extensive and frequent reports on matters of interest to investors. In addition, an increasing number of important corporate decisions are being referred to stockholders for their approval. This is especially true of transactions involving the issuance of additional securities.

Good business practice is frequently the controlling factor in the determination of management to submit a matter to stockholders for approval even though neither the law nor the company's charter makes such approval necessary. The Exchange encourages this growth in corporate democracy.

Stockholder approval is a prerequisite to listing securities to be issued for or in connection with the following:

1. Options granted to or special remuneration plans for directors, officers or employees.
2. Actions resulting in a change in the control of a company.
3. The acquisition,* direct or indirect, of a business, a company, tangible or intangible assets or property or securities representing any such interests:
    (a) From a director, officer or substantial security holder of the company (including its subsidiaries and affiliates) or from any company or party in which one of such person has a direct or indirect interest;
    (b) Where the present or potential issuance of common stock or securities convertible into common stock could result in an increase in outstanding** common shares approximating 18½ percent or more; or
    (c) Where the present or potential issuance of common stock and any other consideration has a combined fair value approximating 18½ percent or more of the market value of the outstanding** common shares.

Shareholder approval would also be a prerequisite of listing warrants where the aggregate of common shares purchasable upon exercise of those warrants exceeds 18½ percent of the outstanding common shares outstanding at the time of issuance of such warrants.

Companies are urged to discuss questions relating to this subject with their Exchange representative sufficiently in advance of filing a listing application to allow time for the calling of a stockholders' meeting and the solicitation of proxies where this may be involved. All relevant factors will be taken into consideration in applying the above policy and the Exchange will advise whether stockholder approval will be required in a particular case.

Listing authorization subject to stockholder action: Under certain circumstances, the Exchange will act upon a listing application, relating to a matter on which shareholders are to take action prior to the time such action is taken. In such cases it is the practice of the Exchange to make its listing authorization subject to the action subsequently taken by stockholders on such matter, so that such authorization does not become final until the shareholders have acted. Where this procedure is followed the ap-

---

* A series of closely related transactions may be regarded as one transaction for the purpose of this policy.
** Only those shares actually issued and outstanding (excluding treasury shares or shares held by a subsidiary) are to be used in making this calculation. Unissued shares reserved for issuance upon conversion of securities, exercise of options or warrants for any other purpose will not be regarded as outstanding.

plication is not released for public distribution, nor is public announcement of the Exchange's action made, until advice of stockholder approval is received. By this procedure, early admission of the securities involved and, perhaps, early consummation of the transaction in which they are to be issued may be expedited, while any possible influence that the prior announcement of the Exchange's listing authorization might have upon the outcome of stockholder's action is avoided.

STATE "BLUE SKY" LAWS

Although a buyer is not required to register its securities with the Securities and Exchange Commission, because the proposed acquisition falls within one of the exemptions, discussed in some detail in Chapter 8, below, state law may nevertheless require registration of the buyer's stock and/or broker-dealer registration with a state securities commission or similar authority or at least notice to such an organization. Although many state laws have exemptions similar to the federal exemptions, including broad exemptions for listed securities or securities meeting certain financial tests, other states may require registration or notice despite a federal exemption being involved. To avoid violating state "blue sky" laws, a buyer should therefore carefully check the blue sky laws of any states involved in an acquisition to determine the existence of any requirements for registration or giving notices.

Uniform Securities Act. The Uniform Securities Act, or portions of the Uniform Act are in effect as part of the blue sky law in a majority of the United States. Uniform forms for the registration of broker-dealers, investment advisors and issuer-dealers, as well as for application for a salesman certificate, are in effect under the securities laws of many of the jurisdictions involved. In spite of the general acceptance of the Uniform Securities Act, many differences exist in the securities laws of the various states. For example, California has an unusually strict and a comprehensive securities law which must be given careful consideration in any acquisition involivng the issuance of stock to a California corporation or resident. As a result of differences in state law, each acquisition involving the issuance of securities in more than one jurisdiction, may involve consideration of the securities laws of each jurisdiction affected.

Effect of noncompliance. Although some states attempt to enforce their blue sky laws strictly, others lack necessary enforcement personnel, and therefore failure to comply with state blue sky laws often may not be serious from the point of view of action the state authorities may take. However, many state blue sky laws provide that a shareholder of a seller who receives securities of a buyer, which should have been registered with the state and were not, may void the transaction. He may sue to have the consideration paid returned by the buyer, often plus interest. Obviously, a selling shareholder who has received a buyer's stock will not sue if the buyer's stock increases in price. But if the buyer's stock declines in price, the selling shareholder may very likely be tempted to bring a law suit.

INSIDERS AND INSIDER INFORMATION

To what extent may insiders such as officers, directors or controlling shareholders of a seller take advantage of inside information for their own benefit in connection with an acquisition? Underlying this question is the problem of what fiduciary obligations, if any, the insiders have to minority shareholders. To explore this problem consider a typical acquisition situation.

A family corporation is operated and controlled by a father, John Jones, and two sons, Bill and Ed, who own in the aggregate 55 percent of the outstanding stock, and the remaining shares are held by approximately 200 outside shareholders. The stock is traded in the over-the-counter market, and in infrequent sales over the past year has commanded a price of $13 per share. In the course of negotiations with John, Bill and Ed, a prospective buyer has offered to buy all of the assets and business of the family corporation at a price equivalent to $20 per share. Armed with this knowledge, may the insiders solicit shares from minority shareholders at $13 per share, or do the insiders owe some fiduciary duty to the minority shareholders to disclose their inside information?

Under common law different jurisdictions came to different conclusions. At one extreme, courts held that insiders owed a fiduciary duty to disclose all information to minority shareholders. At the other extreme, they held that although an insider, such as an officer or director, owed a fiduciary duty to his corporation, he owed no such duty to outside shareholders and he could deal in the corporation's stock with such outsiders without disclosing important inside information. Other courts found a compromise solution, holding that an insider owed a duty to reveal unusual factors affecting the value of a stock in dealing in the corporation's stock with outside shareholders. Although common law remedies are still available, in a situation such as outlined above, regulations of the Securities and Exchange Commission provide outsiders with tailor-made remedies. Rule 10b-5 of the General Rules and Regulations adopted to implement Section 10(b) of the Securities Exchange Act of 1934 is particularly applicable:

> It shall be unlawful for any person, directly or indirectly, by the use of any means or instrumentality of interstate commerce, or of the mails, or of any facility of any national securities exchange,
> 1. to employ any device, scheme, or artifice to defraud,
> 2. to make any untrue statement of a material fact or omit to state a material fact necessary in order to make the statements made, in the light of the circumstances under which they were made, not misleading, or
> 3. to engage in any act, practice, or course of business which operates or would operate as a fraud or deceit upon any person,
> in connection with the purchase or sale of any security.

Note that the rule makes it unlawful for *any person to omit to state* a material fact necessary in order to make statements made not misleading in connection with the purchase or sale of any security. If the rule is applicable, John and his sons Bill and Ed would be hard pressed to solicit stock at $13 a share and not violate the rule.

For federal jurisdiction to apply, a transaction must involve some element of interstate commerce or the use of the mails. But the deception itself need not be accomplished through the use of interstate facilities, as long as the facilities are incidentally used in connection with a transaction. For example, sending a confirmation slip through the mails is sufficient for federal jurisdiction to apply. Therefore, although no national securities exchange would be involved, let us assume that an attempt to solicit sales of stock from a substantial portion of the 200 outside shareholders would involve the use of the mails or some other instrumentality of interstate commerce. Therefore the rule would be applicable. In other words, John, Bill or Ed need not buy the stock from a seller using a national securities exchange, or a recognized over-the-counter market. A private purchase is subject to the rule, provided some incidental use of interstate facilities is involved.

Rule 10b-5 uses the term "any person." There is no doubt that insiders such as the Joneses are included. Court decisions have indicated that other persons, including "tippees," who obtain inside information may also be covered by the rule, even if such a person is not an officer, director or large stockholder. Thus the rule will ordinarily apply to a lawyer working on the matter or an employee doing research in a corporation planning division (Insider Trading Sanctions Act of 1984).

The Securities and Exchange Commission, as the overseer of the national securities markets, is authorized to bring an action seeking civil penalties against anyone who has traded securities, on or through a national securities exchange or from or through a securities broker or dealer, on the basis of material nonpublic information. Furthermore, such actions may be brought against those who aid or abet another person in such trading. The civil penalty can amount to three times the profit gained or the loss avoided as the result of such trading and the penalty is payable into the United States Treasury (Insider Trading Sanctions Act of 1984).

Recent decisions by the United States Supreme Court have indicated that there are limits to the persons who are restricted by Rule 10b-5. In *Chiarella v. United States,* 445 U.S. 222 (1980), an employee of a financial printing firm who had obtained information about his employer's customers in the course of his work, but was not "tipped" by any insider, was exonerated from charges of trading before the information became publicly known. In *Dirks v. Securities and Exchange Commission, U.S.,* 103 S. Ct. 3255 (1983), an investment analyst received information from a corporate insider about a major fraud that had overstated the corporation's assets and income. The insider revealed the information as part of efforts to expose the fraud and received no monetary or personal benefit for doing so. Neither the analyst nor his firm traded stock of the corporation. The analyst attempted unsuccessfully to persuade *The Wall Street Journal* to publish the insider's charges. Before notifying the SEC, the analyst revealed the charges to several of his firm's customers who sold millions of dollars of stock before trading was halted. After news of the fraud was revealed, the stock was recognized as worthless. The Supreme Court, divided 6 to 3, ruled that the analyst could not be held liable to a finding of violation and censure by the SEC.

Nevertheless, the Supreme Court made it clear in both the *Chiarella* and *Dirks* decisions that corporate insiders and "tippees" who misuse corporate information for personal gain will continue to be liable. In a footnote to the *Dirks* decision, the Supreme Court indicated that underwriters, accountants, lawyers and consultants working for a corporation may sometimes be subject to fiduciary responsibility for corporate information:

> Under certain circumstances, such as where corporate information is revealed legitimately to an underwriter, accountant, lawyer, or consultant working for the corporation, these outsiders may become fiduciaries of the shareholders. The basis for recognizing this fiduciary duty is not simply that such persons acquired nonpublic corporate information, but rather that they have entered into a special confidential relationship in the conduct of the business of the enterprise and are given access to information solely for corporate purposes. See *SEC v. Monarch Fund*, 608 F. 2d 938, 942 (CA2 1979); *In re Investors Management Co.*, 44 SEC 633, 645 (1971); *In re Van Alstyne, Noel & Co.*, 43 SEC 1080, 1084-1085 (1969); *In re Merrill Lynch, Pierce, Fenner & Smith, Inc.*, 43 SEC 933, 937 (1968); *Cady, Roberts & Co.*, 40 SEC at 912. In a case where such a person breaches his fiduciary relationship, he may be treated more properly as a tipper than a tippee. See *Shapiro v. Merrill Lynch, Pierce, Fenner & Smith, Inc.*, 495 F.2d 228, 237 (CA2 1974) (investment banker had access to material information when working on a proposed public offering for the corporation). For such a duty to be imposed, however, the corporation must expect the outsider to keep the disclosed nonpublic information confidential and the relationship at least must imply such a duty.

During the middle 1980s, the SEC strengthened its enforcement efforts against misuse of insider information. Convictions and civil damages were imposed on senior officers of investment banking firms, a famous risk arbitrageur, the founder of a major discount brokerage firm and even a former Secretary of Defense. An usually complex case involved a financial reporter who was accused of revealing to friends the content of articles he had written prior to their publication. As a result, both Congress and the SEC were urged to develop a clearer definition of "inside information."

In August, 1987, the SEC recommended the following definition of "insider trading" for inclusion in the proposed Insider Trading Act of 1987:

> "It shall be unlawful for any person, directly or indirectly, to purchase, sell, or cause the purchase or sale of, any security while in possession of material nonpublic information concerning the issuer of its securities, if such person knows or recklessly disregards that such information has been obtained wrongfully or that such purchase or sale would constitute a wrongful use of such information.
>
> For purposes of this section, information is obtained or used wrongfully if, directly or indirectly, it has been obtained by, or as a result of, or its use would constitute theft, bribery, misrepresentation, or espionage

through electronic or other means, or a breach of duty to maintain such information in confidence or to refrain from purchasing, selling or causing the purchase or sale of, the security, which duty arises from any fiduciary, contractual, employment, personal or other relationships with:

    a. the issuer of the security or its security holders;

    b. any person planning or engaged in an acquisition or disposition of the issuer's securities or assets:

    c. any government or a political subdivision, agency or instrumentality of a government;

    d. any person or any self-regulatory organization registered or required to be registered with the commission;

    e. any person engaged in the market for securities or the financial conditions of issuers;

    f. any person that is a member of a class that the commission designates by rule or regulation where the commission finds that the activities of the members of such a class have a regular nexus to the operation of the nation's securities markets and that such designation is necessary or appropriate to effectuate the purposes of this section; or

    g. any other person who obtains such information as a result of a direct or indirect confidential relationship with any persons or entities referred to in paragraphs a–f above."

Multiservice investment banking firms, banks and other financial institutions have adopted Chinese Wall, restricted list and watch list procedures to prevent disclosure and misuse of insider information. The Securities Exchange Commission and other government agencies have encouraged the use of these procedures. For example, see Commission Rule 14e-3. For an example of the difficulties encountered by large firms in administering these procedures, see SEC v. The First Boston Corporation, 86 Civ. 3524 (S.D. N.Y., 1986) in which information was allegedly transmitted from the corporate finance department to an analyst who relayed the information to a trader who used it to trade in CIGNA securities. Without admission, First Boston consented to an injunction including improvement of its information procedures.

When Congress adopted the Insider Trading and Securities Fraud Enforcement Act of 1988 ("ITSFEA"), it intentionally refrained from defining "insider information." However, the House Report supported the "misappropriation" theory adopted in *U.S. v. Carpenter,* 791 F.2d 1024 (2 Cir. 1986); affirmed on securities law counts, 484 U.S. 19 (1987). Under this theory, a violation can consist of a breach of fiduciary duty to an employer (such as *The Wall Street Journal* or *Business Week*) or to shareholders or some other person not to misappropriate material nonpublic information.

The ITSFEA took several steps to control insider information and impose criminal and civil sanctions on those who fail to do so. Civil penalties can be as high as the greater of an unlawful sale, purchase or communication. The ITSFEA created new liability to contemporaneous traders who are harmed by trading affected by the misuse of insider information, even though they did not deal with persons involved in the wrongdoing. Most important, the ITSFEA imposes civil penalties on controlling persons, and, in effect, holds them responsible for failures to supervise controlled persons. The ITSFEA also authorizes private actions against controlling persons.

For further information, see "Inside the New Insider Trading Act," Shea, *The Practical Lawyer,* Sept. 1989 and the report by the SEC Division of Market Regulation titled "Broker-Dealer Policies and Procedures Designed to Segment the Flow and Prevent the Misuse of Material Non-Public Information," March 1990, Executive Summary reproduced in CCH Fed. Sec. L. Rep. § 84,520.

CONFIDENTIAL PROPRIETARY INFORMATION

During the preparations for acquisition transactions, sellers, buyers, investment bankers, lenders, competitive bidders and others obtain and use information which one of the parties regards as its confidential proprietary information. Confidential information is, for example, often furnished by a seller to a prospective buyer during "due diligence" investigation. The same information may also be furnished to the investment banking firm or lenders who are considering loans to finance the acquisition. Of course, a seller expects that confidential information will be used solely for the transaction, but what happens if it is used for other purposes such as the organization of a competitive business?

Problems involving arguably confidential information arise frequently in hostile takeover campaigns. To obtain information about a target company, a takeover bidder may consult with former key employees of the target company. Lenders asked to finance the bid may review files accumulated to evaluate loans previously made to the target company.

The protection of confidential proprietary information is part of the intellectual property law. The law protects intellectual property from theft or misappropriation by persons who have a fiduciary or contractual obligation to the owner. However, if the owner discloses the information to persons who have no contractual or fiduciary obligation, the property rights are lost. *Walton v. Morgan Stanley & Co.* (2 Cir. 1980) 623 F.2d 796; *Washington Steel Corporation v. TW Corporation* (3 Cir. 1979) 602 F.2d 594. *American Medicorp v. Continental Illinois Nat. Bk. & Trust Co.* 475 F.Supp. 5 (N.D. Ill. 1977). On the other hand, a tender offer for Burlington Industries was enjoined on grounds which included consultation with a former senior officer of Burlington who provided confidential information which the court treated as "insider" information. *Burlington Industries, Inc. v. Edelman, CCH Fed.* Sec. L. Rep. § 93,338.

The practical way to protect confidential information is to enter into a written secrecy agreement with persons to whom such information will be entrusted. The agreement must be carefully negotiated because it should not only protect the person providing information from wrongful disclosure and use, but also protect the recipient from excessive obligations. Key elements of a secrecy agreement are as follows:

1. Identify the protected information or provide means to do so without including information which is not both confidential and proprietary.

2. Prohibit disclosure of the protected information to persons not having a "need to know" who are subject to individual secrecy agreements. In addition, prohibit use of the information for any purpose other than the project for which the disclosure was made.

3. Provide clarifying exceptions for information in the public domain, information already known to the receiver when received, information lawfully obtained from a third party entitled to provide it and information independently developed by personnel of the receiving organization who had no access to the confidential information.

4. Provide a cutoff date or dates for the secrecy obligations based on the anticipated life and value of the information furnished balanced with the needs of the recipient to carry on competitive business free of restrictions.

SALE OF CONTROL

Assume that the buyer who approached John Jones and his sons in the example discussed in the foregoing section offered to buy their 55 percent controlling interest in the corporation for $20 a share, rather than all the assets and business of the corporation. The $7 a share premium over market price of $13 a share could look attractive to the Joneses. Could acceptance of the offer cause the Joneses legal difficulties or loss of the profits resulting from the sale? Although logic would dictate that a person may sell his own property for any price he is able to realize and that shares representing a controlling interest may have more value to a buyer than small minority blocks, the Joneses must give careful consideration to the legal consequences resulting from a sale of their controlling interest.

Although the courts generally state that a sale of a controlling block of shares will not in and of itself subject the sellers to legal liability for any premium received, courts often find that other circumstances are present in addition to the sale of control which may subject the sellers to liability. For example, where the sellers resign from management as a condition to the sale, the courts may find that some or all of the premium was paid for the corporation's offices. Such a sale of corporate offices would be a violation of fiduciary duty to the corporation. Or, if the sellers lie to minority holders by concealing a premium and stating that all of the stockholders are being offered the same price, or the corporation is looted after exchange of control, or the buyer uses corporate control to the buyer's own advantage rather than to the corporation's advantage, the sellers may be charged with legal liability for the premium they received for their controlling share interest.

An interesting case in this area of the law is *Perlman v. Feldmann*, 219 F.2d 173 (2nd Cir. 1955). This involved a steel company of which holders of a 37 percent controlling block sold their shares at $20 a share when the stock was selling at $12 a share in the open market. At the time of the sale, a severe shortage of steel existed. The buyer was a user of steel and obviously bought control of the seller to use the seller's steel in the buyer's business. Minority shareholders sued the sellers of the controlling interest, alleging that the sale of control would deprive the corporation of an opportunity to increase its goodwill by allocating steel to customers in a geographical area where the corporation could operate most profitably, and also of a further opportunity to expand the business by obtaining interest-free loans from other customers. The court held that the controlling shareholders would be required to account for the premium paid to them if the corporation ultimately was harmed as the minority shareholders alleged.

In the course of its opinion, the court stated some of the applicable rules as follows:

> In Indiana, then, as elsewhere, the responsibility of the fiduciary is not limited to a proper regard for the tangible balance sheet assets of the corporation, but includes the dedication of his uncorrupted business judgment for the sole benefit of the corporation, in any dealings which may adversely affect it. . . . Although the Indiana case is particularly relevant to Feldmann as a director, the same rule should apply to his fiduciary duties as majority stockholder, for in that capacity he chooses and controls the directors, and thus is held to have assumed their liability. . . . This, therefore, is the standard to which Feldmann was by law required to conform in his activities here under scrutiny.
>
> It is true, as defendants have been at pains to point out, that this is not the ordinary case of breach of fiduciary duty. We have here no fraud, no misuse of confidential information, no outright looting of a helpless corporation. But on the other hand, we do not find compliance with that high standard which we have just stated and which we and other courts have come to expect and demand of corporate fiduciaries. In the often-quoted words of Judge Cardozo: "Many forms of conduct permissible in a workaday world for those acting at arm's length, are forbidden to those bound by fiduciary ties. A trustee is held to something stricter than the morals of the market place. Not honesty alone, but the punctilio of an honor the most sensitive, is then the standard of behavior. As to this there has developed a tradition that is unbending and inveterate. Uncompromising rigidity has been the attitude of courts of equity when petitioned to undermine the rule of undivided loyalty by the 'disintegrating erosion' of particular exceptions,". . . . The actions of defendants in siphoning off for personal gain corporate advantages to be derived from a favorable market situation do not betoken the necessary undivided loyalty owned by the fiduciary to his principal.
>
> The corporate opportunities of whose misappropriation the minority stockholders complain need not have been an absolute certainty in order to support this action against Feldmann.

In the light of the above discussion, John, Bill and Ed Jones should investigate before accepting the buyer's offer of $20 a share for their controlling block. Does the corporation have substantial liquid assets that may entice a buyer to undertake some gentle looting? Does the buyer have a reputation for acquiring corporations primarily for the purpose of siphoning off liquid assets for use in other ventures?

Concern about the decision in *Perlman v. Feldmann* was narrowed somewhat when the same court later ruled that there is no impropriety in sale of 28 percent of the stock of a public corporation for a modest premium where the sellers also agreed to resign and elect the buyer's representatives to a majority of the seats on the board of directors. In this decision, *Essex Universal Corporation v. Yates*, 305 F.2d 572 (2 Cir., 1962), the court distinguished its earlier decision by noting the absence of any suggestion that transfer of control to the buyer, Essex, carried any threat to the interests of the corporation or its other shareholders.

A lawyer advising the Joneses on the possible sale of their interest should consider all of the foregoing possibilities, and in advising the course of action to be followed may find that the only safe course for John, Bill and Ed Jones to follow would be to insist that the buyer make the same $20 a share purchase offer to all of the corporation's shareholders.

To summarize, in addition to Federal Securities Laws and income tax problems, many other legal and technical problems may affect the substance, form or mechanics of an acquisition. Initially, from a buyer's point of view, certain legal problems involving possible unintended assumption of a seller's liabilities, antitrust laws, special stock exchange requirements and state securities law must be considered. The seller and buyer should also consider legal problems with respect to the use of insider information by officers, directors or others participating in an acquisition, as well as any rights of minority shareholders where a sale of control of the seller takes place.

DISCLOSURE OBLIGATIONS IN STOCK ACQUISITIONS

Remedies for breach of warranties and covenants and for misrepresentation and other kinds of fraud in the sale of a business have traditionally been governed by state law. The courts applied the "sale of business" doctrine to deny remedies under the federal securities laws even when the transaction is accomplished by a sale of stock.

The U.S. Supreme Court recently reexamined the "sale of business" doctrine in *Landreth Timber Company v. Landreth*, 471 U.S.681, 105 S.Ct. 2297, 85 L. 2d 692 and *Ruefenacht v. O'Halloran*, 737 F. 2d 320 (3 Cir., 1984), aff'd sub nom *Gould v. Ruefenacht*. 471 U.S. 701, 105 S.Ct. 2308, 85 L.Ed. 2d 708. In those decisions, the remedies of the federal securities laws were made available for lawsuits involving businesses acquired by the sale of stock method. The practical effect is to impose seller liability for misrepresentations, including failure to disclose material information, without need to prove intent to defraud.

While the federal securities laws are not presently available for lawsuits involving privately negotiated mergers and sales of assets, the courts may soon consider lawsuits seeking to expand the *Landreth and Ruefenacht* precedents.

Full and accurate disclosure about the business being sold must now be a seller concern as well as a buyer concern. As a practical matter, sellers should cooperate more readily and fully with "due diligence" investigations by buyers and should keep records of the information furnished to rebut possible later nondisclosure claims, especially when the stock sale method is used.

STATE CORPORATION LAWS

In each acquisition, the corporation statutes of the states of incorporation of the buyer and seller must be studied to determine the effect they may have upon the proposed form of the transaction. Most states have fairly liberal corporation laws on their books. But some states still restrict certain types of acquisitions. For example, some statutes may provide that mergers between corporations may take place only if both corporations are engaged in "business of the same or similar nature." Therefore, in an acquisition involving a corporation incorporated under the laws of a state with such a statute, where the buyer and seller are in different businesses, a route other than statutory merger must be chosen—for example, a stock-for-stock acquisition.

In addition, where a seller is selling assets, the laws of the seller's state of incorporation must be examined to determine the percentage of shareholders that must approve the sale and the rights of dissenting shareholders, if any. For example, in Delaware the vote of only a favorable majority of shareholders is required to sell assets and there are no dissenter's rights, whereas in many states a vote of at least two-thirds of the shareholders is required and dissenters may demand the fair value of their stock in cash. Further, under Delaware law, in a statutory merger rather than an acquisition of assets a favorable vote of a majority only of the shareholders is required, but dissenters may have a right to cash. In general, the laws of the states of incorporation must be studied to find any unusual provisions affecting the proposed acquisition.

UNUSUAL CHARTER PROVISIONS

In a merger, to determine which corporation should survive, the certificates of incorporation of both the buyer and seller should be studied to determine whether one certificate is more favorable than another. For example, if a New York corporation engaged in engineering is to be merged with another engineering firm, the corporate name provided in the certificate of incorporation may even determine which corporation should survive. Generally, since April 15, 1935, no corporation may be formed in New York with the word *engineering* as part of its corporate title. Therefore, if one of the corporations has the word *engineering* in its title, permissible because of its formation prior to April 15, 1935, this may be the corporation that should survive. One certificate of incorporation may have cumulative voting for directors and the other not. One may have unfavorable restrictions on the payment of dividends.

See Chapter 9 for a description of supermajority, disproportionate voting and "poison pill" provisions which many publicly owned companies have added to their certificates of incorporation as a defense against hostile tender offers.

PENSION AND PROFIT-SHARING PLANS

As soon as possible in the process of negotiating a detailed acquisition contract, the relationship between pension, profit-sharing, stock option and other fringe-benefit plans of the buyer and seller (if any) should be given careful consideration. Such plans involve not only possible grave business, legal and financial problems, but always involve human elements. The seller's business consists not only of tangible and intangible assets but also of human beings who in some instances may cause the difference between a success and a failure of the seller's business.

Pension and Profit Sharing Fundamentals. Retirement benefits are provided to employees by a variety of methods. The simplest method is continuation of all or part of the salary or wages of employees after retirement without any funding arrangements. However, most companies provide retirement benefits by establishing pension or profit sharing plans.

Pension plans are adopted by companies and funded either by payment of premiums to an insurer under a contract providing for annuity payments by the insurer to retired employees or by contributions to a trust (usually with a bank) in amounts sufficient to permit the trustee to make periodic payments to retired employees. Some pension plans require or permit modest amounts of employee contributions.

A pension plan either defines the contributions or defines the benefits. Under a defined contribution plan, the company contributes definite amounts which are allocated to employee accounts and the employees receives after retirement the accumulated contributions and net earnings in periodic payments. Under a defined benefit plan, the company makes a commitment in the plan to provide retirement payments in definite amounts (such as a percentage of salary multiplied by years of employment) and contributes amounts calculated by an actuary to be sufficient to fund the payments when they eventually become due. The actuary calculates the necessary contributions by adopting a basic method (such as entry age normal or unit credit) and applying assumptions as to mortality, turnover, retirement, disability, compensation increases, investment return and administrative expenses.

Profit sharing plans are adopted by companies and funded by contributions to a trust, usually with a bank. The contributions are credited by the trustee to an account for each participating employee and accumulate with earnings until they are distributed to the employee after retirement. A wide variety of formulae are used by companies in determining their profit sharing contributions and it is also common to require or permit employee contributions. For example, a company may contribute 5% of pre-tax profits in excess of a fixed dollar amount or agree to match employee contributions dollar for dollar. A wide variety of investments are also made by profit sharing trusts. For example, many trusts invest conservatively in balanced portfolios or bank investment funds. However, profit sharing trusts are also the vehicles for stock purchase plans including the Employee Stock Ownership Plans described in Chapter 15.

Billions of dollars of retirement funds have accumulated with insurers and in bank trusts since World War II and have become a major factor in the investment world.

Accounting for pension plans in the financial statements of the sponsoring companies is governed by Accounting Principles Board Opinion No. 8 and Financial Accounting Standards Board Statements No. 35, No. 87 and No. 88.

The funding of pension plans, whether by group annuity and newer contracts offered by insurers or by trust funds administered by banks and other trustees, has long been entitled to special tax status under the Internal Revenue Code, provided that plans meet the standards for qualification under Section 401 and related sections of the Code. The standards were made considerably stricter and more detailed by the Employee Retirement Income Security Act of 1974 (known as "ERISA") which created the Pension Benefit Guaranty Corporation ("PBGC"). PBGC insures accrued benefits in the event of termination of a plan and is funded by mandatory contributions supported by companies maintaining qualified pension plans.

Among other changes, ERISA adopted a new Section 412 of the Code that establishes minimum funding standards for qualified defined benefit pension plans. Briefly, the standards call for payment each plan year of the normal cost for the year plus the amounts necessary to amortize in equal annual installments the unfunded past service liability over a forty-year period (pre-1974 plans) or a thirty-year period (plans coming into existence after January 1, 1974). Payments are also required to meet liabilities created by plan amendments, net experience losses and changes in actuarial methods and assumptions. The value of a plan's assets must be determined by reasonable actuarial valuation methods. All costs, liabilities, rates of interests and other factors must also be determined by actuarial assumptions and methods which are reasonable. Failure to provide adequate funding results in an "accumulated funding deficiency."

The Multiemployer Pension Plan Amendments Act of 1980 ("MEPPA") added amendments to ERISA that create a withdrawal liability for a share of the plan's unfunded vested benefits. This liability is not contingent and must be paid after withdrawal, whether partial or complete, by any company that is a member of multi-employer pension plan. The payment must be made even though the plan is not being terminated and the withdrawing employer previously met its commitments. This withdrawal liability is further described below.

The Single Employer Pension Plan Amendments Act of 1986 ("SEPPAA") added amendments to ERISA that create a termination liability for the sponsoring employer (and any member of its controlled group) upon the termination of a defined benefit pension plan. SEPPAA also provides that a defined benefit pension plan cannot be voluntarily terminated unless the plan assets are sufficient to meet all benefit commitments except in bankruptcy or insolvency proceedings or certain narrowly defined hardship situations. A plan cannot be terminated in violation of an existing collective bargaining agreement. The termination liability is further described below.

Contrary to the general trend toward stricter regulation, the federal government and the courts have, since the adoption of ERISA, permitted companies to "terminate" defined benefit pension plans by changing the funding method from a trust to an annuity contract in order to recapture trust assets in excess of the premium cost of the annuity contract. The opportunity to recapture millions of dollars from a pension trust has been an important incentive for some acquisitions. Recapture of "surplus" pension funds is discussed further below.

"Due Diligence" Reviews and Planning Alternatives. In view of the numerous restrictions created by ERISA, as amended by MEPPAA and SEPPAA, it is increasingly important to perform "due diligence" review and carefully prepare to handle pension and profit sharing plan decisions prior to an acquisition.

The buyer should review all plan documents, annuity contracts, trust agreements, financial statements, actuarial reports, tax returns including Forms 5500, investment managers contracts and related agreements such as collective bargaining agreements. The review should also include other employee benefit plans. The review should identify, among other things, any surplus or accumulated funding deficiency, any prohibited transactions or other fiduciary violations and any weaknesses in the actuarial method or assumptions. The buyer should also review the plan and composition of employee participants for possible adverse effects on its own plans such as the creation of discrimination prohibited by ERISA or the Internal Revenue Code. If the buyer does not wish to continue a defined benefit pension plan, it must also consider possible termination liability or withdrawal liability.

The seller must consider potential termination liability or withdrawal liability if the buyer does not wish to adopt seller's pension plans. If the seller will retain and continue to operate other businesses with qualified pension or profit sharing plans, it should determine whether the transactions will adversely affect the qualification of its retained plans. Finally, seller will wish to protect itself, to the extent possible against contingent liability for the plans assumed by the buyer.

Planning for the future of pension and profit sharing plans after an acquisition is affected by the form of the transactions. In a merger, the buyer succeeds by operation of law to all rights and obligations of the seller and will automatically succeed to seller's plans unless otherwise arranged. In a stock purchase, the acquired company will continue its plans unless otherwise arranged, but buyer will not be directly responsible for them except for the liability imposed by ERISA on members of a consolidated group. In an assets purchase, the seller will transfer and buyer will assume pension and profit sharing plans only to the extent agreed and as provided by ERISA.

The most common alternatives for pension and profit sharing plans in acquisition transactions are as follows:

> Buyer continues seller's plans without change.
> Buyer continues seller's plans, but modifies them—most often to conform them to, or merge them with, buyer's own plans.

Buyer continues seller's plans, but later "freezes" or terminates them.
Buyer declines seller's plans and seller "freezes" or terminates them.

Where the seller is divesting a division or subsidiary, the employees of the business sold may participate in plans which also cover employees of retained businesses. In this situation, if the buyer is to continue the plan, seller can arrange to split-off the assets and liabilities of the plan relating to the business being sold and transfer them to a plan and trust established by the buyer. For defined contribution pension plans and profit sharing plans, the allocation is readily accomplished, but actuarial advice is needed to allocate the assets of a defined benefit pension plan. Code Sections 412(a) and 414(e) and ERISA Section 208 require that each participating employee and their beneficiaries be entitled immediately after the transfer to a benefit which would, if the plan were then terminated, be at least equal to their benefit if the plan were terminated immediately before the transfer.

If buyer continues a plan, Code Section 414 requires that it treat service for the seller as credited service for the buyer for eligibility purposes. Regulation Section 1.411(a)-5(b)(3)(2) requires the same treatment for vesting purposes. Letter rulings issued by the Internal Revenue Service confirm that a company can deduct the cost of contributions to fund such credited service under Section 404.

If seller and buyer do not agree on adoption and continuation of the plan by buyer, it is possible to "freeze" the plan rather than terminate it. To "freeze" a defined benefit pension or profit sharing plan, the company amends the plan to discontinue future contributions, but vesting, distributions and other provisions of the plan continue. To "freeze" a defined benefit pension plan, the company amends the plan to discontinue accrual of benefits on and after the amendment date, but continues to make contributions to fund benefit commitments accrued prior to the amendment date including amounts owed for funding deficiencies. See Code Section 411.

If seller or buyer completely discontinue contributions to a plan, the rights of participating employees, to the extent then funded, must become vested. See Code Section 411 (d) (3). In addition, termination liability under SEPPAA and withdrawal liability under MEPPAA must be considered.

Termination of a Single Employer Pension Plan. Under ERISA, as amended by SEPPAA, an employer can terminate a defined benefit pension plan only by a standard termination or a distress termination. Notice must be sent to the Pension Benefit Guaranty Corporation (PBGC), all participants and their beneficiaries and any union or other person representing them.

ERISA Section 4041 (b) permits a standard termination only if the plan assets are sufficient to meet all benefit liabilities accrued through the termination date. If so, the plan administrator must distribute the plan assets by purchasing irrevocable commitments from an insurer or otherwise provide for all benefit commitments in accordance with the plan and PBGC regulations. A distress termination is permitted only if the employer is in bankruptcy or insolvency proceedings or meets a hardship test. If permitted, a distress termination is handled as an involuntary termination by the PBGC.

In an involuntary termination, each company contributing to the plan and each member of their controlled groups is jointly and severally liable to the PBGC under Section 4062 (b) for all unfunded benefit liabilities to participants and beneficiaries of the plan.

ERISA Section 4068 creates a lien securing amounts payable under Section 4062 and other provisions of ERISA. The liability of controlled group members imposed by ERISA Section 4062 means that the usual insulation from direct liability in an acquisition by stock purchase is not available to the buyer. In addition, Section 4069 (b) provides that the successor corporation in a merger and the parent corporation into which a subsidiary is liquidated will be treated as the corporation subject to ERISA.

Section 4069 (a) imposes termination liability on any person and its controlled group (determined as of the termination date) if such person entered into any transaction within five years before the termination, a principal purpose of which was to evade its liability under the Act. This provision creates potential seller liability whether a merger, stock sale or assets sale is made.

Multiemployer Pension Plan Withdrawal Liability. Section 4201 of ERISA, as amended by MEPPAA, imposes withdrawal liability on any employer which withdraws from a multiemployer plan in a complete withdrawal or partial withdrawal. The withdrawing employer is required, subject to certain limits, to continue contributions to fund a proportionate share of the plan's unfunded vested benefits. A multiemployer plan is a plan to which more the one employer is required to contribute, which is maintained pursuant to one or more collective bargaining agreements between one or more employee organizations and more than one employer, and which satisfies and other requirements prescribed in regulations of the Department of Labor.

The amount of the withdrawal liability can be calculated under Section 4211 by several methods including a presumptive method, a rolling-5-year method, a direct allocation method and alternative methods adopted under PBGC regulations. The amount calculated is adjusted for permitted reductions and limitations.

Section 4225 (a) limits the liability of an employer which sells all or substantially all its assets on a *bonafide* arm's length transaction to an unrelated third party to an amount not exceeding the greater of

(A) A portion of the liquidation or dissolution value of the employer determined after the sale or exchange of such assets, or

(B) The unfunded vested benefits attributable to employees of the employer.

The portion described in subparagraph (A) is prescribed in a table which begins at 30% of the value where it is not more than $2 million and increases gradually. For a value more than $10 million, the portion is $4,350,000 plus 80% of the amount in excess of $10,000,000.

ERISA Section 4204 provides that withdrawal liability will not be imposed in an arm's length sale of assets to an unrelated third party if the buyer assumes the plan at substantially the same contribution levels as the seller, surety bond or escrow requirements are met by the buyer and the seller contractually agrees to retain secondary liable for its obligations to the plan if buyer does not pay them. If the seller wishes to liquidate or distribute assets during the five year period, it must also meet bond or escrow requirements. The PBGC regulations provide for waivers of the bond/escrow requirements and can be obtained if certain conditions are met.

Reversion of Surplus Assets Upon Termination. ERISA Sections 403 (d) and 4044 (d) provide for the allocation of assets upon termination of a plan. Any residual assets of a single employer plan may be distributed to the employer if (A) all liabilities of the plan to participants and their beneficiaries have been satisfied, (B) the distribution does not contravene any provision of law and (C) the plan provides for a distribution in such circumstances.

The requirements for voluntary termination of a plan are contained in ERISA Section 4041 including the requirement that the employer purchase irrevocable commitments from an insurer or otherwise fully provide for all benefit commitments. See also PBGC Regulations 2618.30 et seq. which include allocation of assets attributable to employer contributions. See also RR 83-52, 1983-13 IRB 7.

In 1984, the PBGC, IRS and DOL adopted Guidelines on Asset Reversions. The Guidelines require participants be provided fully vested rights in their accrued benefits and that annuities be obtained from an insurer to provide such benefits. Spin-off terminations in which a plan is divided into two plans—one to continue and one to be terminated with a recapturable surplus—were subjected to special requirements including full vesting, purchase of irrevocable annuities for accrued benefits and advance notice to all employees covered by the original plan.

Leading court decisions permitting reversion of actuarial surplus to a sponsoring employer include *Inre C.D. Moyer Co. Trust Fund* (E.D., Pa., 1977) 441 F. Supp. 1128, aff'd (3 Cir. 1978) 582 F. 2d 1273; *Pollock v. Castrovinci* (S.D., N.Y., 1979) 476 F. Supp 606, aff'd (2 Cir. 1980) 622 F. 2d 575; *Audio Fidelity v. Pension Benefit Guaranty Corporation* (4 Cir., 1980) 624 F. 2d 513; *Washington-Baltimore Newspaper Guild Local 35 v. Washington Star Co.* (D.D.C., 1983) 555 F. Supp. 257; *International Union, United Automobile v. Dyneer* (6 Cir., 1984) 747 F. 2d 337 and *Wilson v. Bluefield Supply Co.* (S.D., W. Va 1986) 650 F. Supp. 578. In recent cases, some courts have found reasons to prevent a reversion to an employer. A reversion upon termination of a plan originally established as a defined contribution plan was denied in *Del Grosso v. Spang and Company* (3 Cir. 1985) 769 F. 2d 928, cert. den. 106 S.C. 2246. The court found contract language in a pension agreement preventing reversion in *Bryant v. International Fruit Co.* (6 Cir. 1986) 793 F. 2d 118, cert. den. 107 S.C. 576. The decision in *Bryant* was followed in *Unitis v. JFC Acquisition Corp.* (N.D. Ill. 1986) 643 F. Supp. 454.

Section 4069 (a) imposed termination liability on any person and its controlled group (determined as of the termination date) if such person entered into any transaction within five years before the termination, a principal purpose which was to evade its liability under the Act. This provision creates potential seller liability whether a merger, stock sale or assets sale is made.

Section 4980A of the Internal Revenue Code imposes a 20% excise tax on the amount of a reversion. This tax is payable by the employer in addition to the income tax on the reversion.

EMPLOYEE STOCK OPTIONS

Employee stock options may cause similar problems. The mechanics of converting options held by the seller's employees to options on the buyer's stock are provided for in the Internal Revenue Code of 1954, as amended, and if the requirements of Section 425 of the code are met (basically that the employee be in no better financial position as a result of the conversion), the conversion may be made without tax consequences to the employee. Where the buyer has no options outstanding, however, it must assess the effect upon its employees of substituting options on its stock for options held by the seller's employees.

Even where the buyer has options outstanding, it must consider the difference of relative prices between the seller's options and those of the buyer's employees. Relative differences between the stock option prices of the seller's and buyer's options may cause discontent in one or the other group of employees. Other fringe benefits such as group life insurance, hospitalization and major medical plans may, to a lesser degree, cause difficulties.

In view of all of the problems that may arise from employee benefit plans, the directors of personnel and the actuaries, where necessary, of both the buyer and seller, should meet early in the negotiations to seek out possible problems and find solutions.

NONASSIGNABILITY OF CONTRACTS

With a few exceptions such as government contracts, law throughout the United States provides that contracts are assignable unless they contain provisions restricting or prohibiting assignment. However, it is very common for leases, formal contracts and even printed purchase orders to include restrictions or prohibitions on assignment. Some of these provisions may not only apply to assignment, but also to a merger or change of control resulting from a stock sale.

If the "due diligence" review reveals that important leases, license agreements, customer and supply agreements or other contracts are not freely assignable to the buyer, the lawyer should include a covenant in the acquisition contract requiring the seller to obtain consents from the other parties to the nonassignable contracts. Conditions excusing the buyer and seller if the consents cannot be obtained should also be included.

LOAN AGREEMENT RESTRICTIONS

If the seller has outstanding bank loan agreements containing restrictions which the buyer is unwilling to assume, the buyer may be required to make some provision to refinance outstanding loans. Conversely, the buyer's bank loan agreements may not permit the seller's loan to remain outstanding, and thus require refinancing.

BULK TRANSFERS

For many years, most states had so-called "bulk sales" laws on their books, intended to protect creditors against a seller selling his business and absconding with the proceeds. The bulk sales laws were codified in the Uniform Commercial Code in Article 6 entitled "Bulk Transfers." Under Article 6, if a major part of the materials, supplies, merchandise or other inventory of a business is transferred in bulk and not in the ordinary course of business, specific procedures must be followed or the transfer is ineffective against any creditor of the transferor. The procedures require preparation of a sworn list of creditors and a schedule of the property being transferred. Ten days' notice must be sent to all creditors giving the time and place of the transfer; the location of the property; the place where the list of creditors and schedule of property can be inspected; whether the transferor will pay debts in full and other matters. The notices should be sent by registered or certified mail.

If the procedures are followed, a buyer to whom a bulk transfer subject to Article 6 is made is then free of further duties. The creditors who receive the notices must help themselves by arrangements with the seller or legal remedies. The buyer is not responsible for errors or omissions by seller in preparing the creditors' list unless buyer is shown to have had knowledge of them.

When notice to creditors is not feasible, the buyer may protect itself by requiring an escrow from the seller in the acquisition contract. When a buyer is buying assets and agrees to assume all liabilities of the seller, contingent or otherwise, the buyer will generally waive compliance with the bulk sales law, since it must pay the seller's creditors in any event.

RESTRICTED SECURITIES

If a seller proposes to pay for an acquisition with stock or other securities which will not be registered under the Securities Act of 1933 and applicable Blue Sky Laws, the seller must recognize that payment will consist of "restricted securities." The seller will be required to make representations in the acquisition contract or an investment and without any view to public resale. A restrictive legend will be endorsed on the face of the securities to prevent their sale except upon further compliance with the securities laws. The nature of these restrictions is discussed further in Chapter 8 and their economic effects are discussed in Chapter 4.

If a seller does not wish to assume the risk of restricted securities, seller should negotiate for a cash price or for redemption or registration of securities paid as the acquisition price.

SALES AND USE TAXES

In some jurisdictions, sales and use taxes apply to the sale of tangible assets in connection with an acquisition of a business. In such jurisdictions, the tax may not be avoided by closing the transaction outside of the particular state or jurisdiction, since, at least in theory, the tangible assets transferred will be subject to the use tax since they are physically located in the taxing jurisdiction. In some instances where such a sales or use tax would be sizable in amount, the buyer and seller may consider an acquisition of stock rather than assets to avoid the imposition of the tax. However, in other states, the sales tax does not apply to "casual" sales or one-time bulk sales of business assets. Because sales taxes, even at low rates, can be a major cost in an acquisition, seller and buyer should check on their applicability at an early time and consider who will pay them as part of the negotiation of the price and other contract terms.

LIABILITIES TO EMPLOYEES

In addition to ERISA and other liabilities already described, a variety of other potential liabilities to employees must be evaluated as part of an acquisition transaction. They include the Worker Adjustment and Retraining Notification Act (WARNA), 29 U.S.C. § 2101 to § 2109., severance and vacation pay, retiree medical and death benefits, limitations on the traditional doctrine that employment is "at will," equal employment opportunity laws and the Older Workers Benefit Protection Act (OWBPA). Further information on these potential liabilities and methods to evaluate and limit them can be found in an article titled "Emerging Liabilities to Employees," Edward E. Shea, *The Acquisition Yearbook: 1991,* New York Institute of Finance (Simon & Schuster), 1991.

ENVIRONMENTAL, WORKER SAFETY AND PRODUCT LIABILITY

In recent years, potential liability under federal and state laws governing the environment, worker safety and product liability has become a major concern for buyers. It has also become a major concern for lenders financing acquisition transactions, not only because these liabilities affect the credit standing of the borrower but also because the courts have imposed environmental liability directly on several lenders that exercised rights to foreclose on contaminated property or to participate in borrower decisions during loan workout situations. Equity investors share these concerns, particularly since several courts have pierced the corporate veil and held stockholders liable for environmental cleanup costs and liabilities. It is customary that at least a first phase environmental audit be performed before loans are extended and an acquisition contract is closed.

The authors recommend that potential liability (under state workers compensation laws) for worker injuries and illnesses be reviewed and that compliance with the federal Occupational Safety and Health Act, Hazardous Materials Transportation Act and corresponding state laws also be reviewed.

The seller's past and present products and its claims and lawsuit records should be reviewed to identify and evaluate potential product liability.

Key court decisions and statutory references relating to these potential liabilities are as follows:

- *Purchaser Liability. NJDEP v. Ventron Corp.,* 468 A.2d 150 (1983); *Smith Land & Improvement Corp. v. Celotex Corp.,* 851 F.2d 86 (3 Cir. 1988); *Philadelphia Electric Co. v. Hercules,* 762 F.2d 303 (3 Cir. 1985); *In re Acushnet River and New Bedford Harbor Proceedings,* 712 F. Supp. 1010 (DC, Mass. 1989) and *Anspec Co. v. Johnson Controls,* 30 ERC 1672 (ED, Mich. 1989).

- *Lender Liability: U.S. v. Mirabile,* 15 ELR 20,992 (ED, Pa. 1985); *U.S. v. Maryland Bank & Trust Co.,* 632 F.Supp. 573 (D.Md. 1986); *U.S. v. Fleet Factors,* 901 F.2d 1550 (11 Cir. 1990); *Guidice v. BFG Electroplating,* 30 ERC 1665 (WD, Pa. 1989) and *In re Bergsoe Metal Corp.* 31 ERC 1785 (9 Cir. 1990). See the rule proposed by the U.S. Environmental Protection Agency interpreting Section 101(20) of the Comprehensive Environmental Response, Compensation and Liability Act.

- *Stockholder Liability. State of New York v. Shore Realty,* 759 F.2d 1032 (2 Cir. 1985); *Idaho v. Bunker Hill Co.,* 635 F.Supp. 665 (DC Idaho 1986); *U.S. v. Mottolo,* 695 F. Supp. 615 (DC, NH 1988); *U.S. v. Kayser-Roth Corp.,* 724 F.Supp. 15 (DC, RI 1987) and *Joslyn Manufacturing Corp. v. T.L. James & Co.,* 893 F.2d 80 (5 Cir. 1990).

- *"Innocent Purchaser" Defense. State of New York v. Shore Realty,* supra; *U.S. v. Bliss,* 667 F. Supp. 1298 (ED, Mo. 1987); *In re Sterling Steel Treating, Inc.,* 94 B.R. 924 (Bkptcy, ED, Mich. 1989); *Kelley v. Thomas Solvent,* 714 F. Supp. 1439 (WD, Mich. 1989); *U.S. v. Marisol, Inc.,* 725 F. Supp. 833 (MD, Pa. 1989).

- *Key Federal and State Cleanup Laws.* The Comprehensive Environmental Response, Compensation and Liability Act (ERCLA) is found at 42 USCA § 9601 et seq. The Resource Conservation and Recovery Act (RCRA) is found at 42, U.S.C. § 6901 et seq. The New Jersey Environmental Cleanup Responsibility Act is found at 13 NJSA § 13:1K-56 et seq. The Connecticut Transfer Act is found at CGSA § 22a-134 et seq. The Illinois Responsible Property Transfer Act is found at Ill. Rev. Stat. Ch. 30, Section 903.

- *Examples of Environmental Liens and Superliens.* The lien securing cleanup costs incurred by the U.S. Environmental Protection Agency is found at 42 USCA § 9607. Superliens imposed in Connecticut and New Jersey are found at CGSA § 22a-452a and NJSA § 58: 10-23.11(f).

- *Key Federal Worker Safety Laws.* The Occupational Safety and Health Act (OSHA) is found at 29 USCA § 654 et seq. The Hazardous Materials Transportation Act (HMTA) is found at 49 USCA § 1801 et seq.

- *Successor Liability for Defective Products.* A recent decision on successor liability for products sold by a seller prior to an assets acquisition in which the buyer did not assume the seller's product liability is *Niccum v. Hydro Tool Corp.,* 438 N.W. 2d 96 (Minn. 1989). The *Niccum* decision cites and discusses the earlier decisions adopting and rejecting successor liability based on continuation of a product line.

For further information, see the articles titled "Evaluation of Environmental Liability," "Evaluating Product Liability and Workplace Liability in M&A Transactions" and "Emerging Liabilities to Employees in M&A Transactions," Edward E. Shea, *The Acquisition Yearbook: 1991,* New York Institute of Finance (Simon & Schuster), 1991. See also "Better Insurance and Contractual Protection from Product Liability," *The Practical Lawyer* (Shea, 1983) and *The Preventive Law Reporter* (Shea, 1983).

7

Accounting
for Acquisitions

SOME BASIC ACCOUNTING CONCEPTS

Generally Accepted Accounting Principles (GAAP). These are principles adopted and published by the Financial Accounting Standards Board (FASB) together with those Accounting Research Bulletins and Opinions of the Accounting Principles Board of the American Institute of Certified Public Accountants that are not superseded by action of FASB. Under Rule 203 of the Rules of Conduct of the AICPA Code of Professional Ethics, member accountants shall not express an opinion that financial statements are presented in accordance with GAAP if such statements contain any departure from an accounting principle promulgated by the FASB.

Differences between Accounting for Shareholders and Accounting for Tax Purposes. The objective of accounting for shareholders is to present fairly the financial condition and results of operations of businesses in accordance with generally accepted accounting principles consistently applied. This permits shareholders (as well as management, potential investors and others) to make certain judgments about the business insofar as the measurement tools of the accounting profession can reflect them. Accounting for tax purposes is a matter of compliance with the U.S. Internal Revenue Code or other applicable tax statutes that, for the most part, prescribe their own accounting rules. These rules frequently differ from GAAP, so that the balance sheet and determination of taxable income in a business tax return typically differs considerably from a balance sheet and statement of income prepared in accordance with GAAP for the same business.

METHODS OF ACCOUNTING FOR ACQUISITIONS

For accounting purposes, an acquisition may be treated by either of two methods: the "purchase" method or the "pooling of interests" method. These methods are purely accounting concepts that have no effect upon the actual cash position or cash earnings of the business a buyer has acquired from a seller. But whether or not an acquisition may be treated as a "pooling of interests" rather than a "purchase" may have a profound effect upon the future per share earnings which a buyer reports to its stockholders in its annual report and other aspects of the buyer's financial statements.

"Purchase"—Goodwill. The choice of accounting method assumes major importance primarily where a buyer pays more for a seller than the book value of the assets shown on the seller's books. In such a situation, where the price paid exceeds the book value of the seller's assets, if the transaction is treated as a "purchase," generally accepted accounting principles will require that the assets acquired by the buyer be recorded at their cost on the buyer's books and any excess which cannot be allocated to specific tangible and intangible assets be set up on the buyer's books as an item of goodwill. The cost is determined by allocating the present value of the amounts paid (consisting of cash, properties and assumption of obligation) among the assets purchased. Assets acquired by issuing shares of stock of the buyer are recorded at the fair value of the assets received.

The cost thus determined must be allocated to the individual assets which make up the seller's business. The total cost of the assets acquired is assigned to the individual assets on the basis of the fair market value of each, generally on the basis of an expert appraisal. The difference between the sum of the fair values of the tangible and identifiable intangible assets acquired, less liabilities assumed, and the total cost of all assets acquired constitute, unspecified intangible values—normally referred to as goodwill. Goodwill should then be amortized and charged against income, based upon a reasonable estimate of the useful life of the goodwill. The period of amortization should not, however, exceed forty years.

Such amortization write-offs may substantially reduce reported book earnings and since the write-off of goodwill is against after-tax earnings and is not deductible for income tax purposes, the reported earnings of the buyer are reduced and the buyer does not receive any offsetting tax benefit.

Note: A choice of "purchase" accounting treatment does not inevitably result in lower profits. The acquisition of Delta Steamship Lines, Inc., by Tco Industries, Inc., was a good example of the effect of "negative goodwill." An excess of equity of $17,541,425 in the underlying assets over investment in Delta at the date of acquisition was recorded as a deferred credit and was amortized over a fifteen-year period by credits to earnings of the acquisition company in amounts of over $1 million per year.

"Pooling of Interests"—No goodwill. Under the "pooling of interests" accounting treatment, the respective book values of the assets of the buyer and seller, the liabilities and the surpluses or deficits are added together (pooled) in the balance sheet of the successor business. New stock issued to acquire the seller is added on the liability side of the balance sheet. Any excess par value or stated value of the capital stock account of the buyer, after the issuance of stock by the buyer and cancellation of the stock of the seller, over the sum of the individual capital stock accounts of the buyer and seller prior to the acquisition is charged to the additional paid-in capital. If capital surplus is insufficient, earned surplus is charged to the extent necessary. And reduction in the capital stock account resulting from the acquisition is credited to capital surplus. Since a "pooling of interests" essentially involves only an adding together of items on two separate balance sheets, no new item of goodwill is originated on the buyer's books, and no amortization or write-off need be made against the buyer's reported after-tax earnings. Although the difference in accounting treatment has other effects on the buyer's books, the effect on reported book earnings is most immediately of concern and will be discussed in the following examples.

The "purchase"—An example. Assume that the buyer pays $3 million in market value of preferred stock and debentures for the seller, and the seller's assets have a book value of $500,000. The excess purchase price (excess market value of stock and debentures paid over the book value of the assets of the seller) is therefore $2.5 million ($3 million paid, less the net book value of assets—i.e., $500,000). If the acquisition is treated as a "purchase," generally accepted accounting principles require that if the excess purchase price may not be allocated to other identifiable assets, an additional asset of $2.5 million usually designated as goodwill, be set up on the buyer's balance sheet. Accounting principles require that the $2.5 million be amortized over a period of years, not exceeding forty years, from after-tax earnings of the buyer. The amortization or write-off does not in any way affect actual net cash earnings, cash flow or income taxes. But the effect that the amortization or write-off may have on the earnings the buyer reports to its shareholders in the buyer's annual report may be substantial.

Assume that the seller had annual after-tax earnings of $300,000 and that it is the buyer's accounting determination to write off goodwill over ten years. As a result of the "purchase," the $2.5 million written off over ten years will cause an annual reduction of $250,000 for ten years in the book earnings of the buyer—the earnings the buyer reports to its shareholders. The annual reduction of $250,000 must be made against after-tax income. Therefore, if the seller's rate of after-tax annual income is maintained by the buyer at $300,000, the buyer may report an annual income of only $50,000 from the seller's business to the buyer's shareholders over the ten-year amortization period ($300,000 annual net after-tax income less $250,000 annual goodwill amortization).

Expressed in outline form, the effect of the "purchase" by the buyer of the seller's original $300,000 annual after-tax net income on the reported book earnings of the buyer is as follows:

(1) Purchase price paid in the buyer's stock:	$3,000,000
(2) Book value of the seller's assets:	$500,000
(3) Excess purchase price over the book value of the seller's assets:	$2,500,000
(4) Goodwill in a "purchase":	$2,500,000
(5) Annual amortization over a ten-year period:	$250,000

(6) Annual after-tax net income from seller's business
(before goodwill amortization): $300,000
(7) Annual book income reported by buyer from seller's
business ($300,000 income less $250,000 goodwill
amortization): $50,000
(8) Total book earnings from the seller's business reportable
by buyer to its shareholders over ten years: $500,000

As a result of treating the acquisition as a "purchase," the buyer must report to its shareholders total after-tax earnings of $500,000 over a ten-year period from a business which the buyer brought for $3 million. The actual after-tax net earnings realized by the buyer from the seller's business total $3 million, and the buyer has fully recovered its original investment in the seller's business over the ten-year period. But as a result of treating the transaction as a "purchase," the buyer, through its reported book earnings, has, in effect, reported to its shareholders that over the ten-year period it has recouped only 16.6 percent of its original investment.

"Pooling of interests"—Same example. Assume that the same transaction reviewed in the preceding example as a "purchase" receives a "pooling of interests" accounting treatment. Stressing only the effect on reported earnings, if the same acquisition is treated as a "pooling of interests," the buyer may report earnings to its shareholders of $300,000 annually—500 percent more than the $50,000, of annual earnings it may report under a "purchase" accounting treatment. Remember, if the acquisition is treated as a "pooling of interests," no goodwill need be placed upon the buyer's books. After-tax net earnings need not be reduced by goodwill amortization or write-off. Now note, by following the outline of the previous example of a "purchase" transaction, how a "pooling of interests" changes the reported book earnings realized by a buyer from the seller's business:

(1) Purchase price paid in the buyer's stock: $3,000,000
(2) Book value of the seller's assets: $500,000
(3) Excess of the purchase price over the book value of
the seller's assets: $2,500,000
(4) Goodwill in a "pooling of interests": $000
(5) Annual amortization over a ten-year period: $000
(6) Annual after-tax net income from the seller's business
(without goodwill amortization): $300,000
(7) Annual book income reported by the buyer from the
seller's business ($300,000 net income, without
amortization): $300,000
(8) Total book earnings from the seller's business reportable
by the buyer to its shareholders over ten years: $3,000,000

As a result of treating the acquisition as a "pooling of interests," the buyer reports to its shareholders total after-tax earnings of $3 million over a ten-year period from a business that the buyer bought for $3 million. Thus, by treating the acquisition as a "pooling of interests" the buyer reports to its shareholders that the earnings from the seller's business over a ten-year period have fully paid the purchase price of the business.

ACCOUNTING CRITERIA FOR "POOLING OF INTERESTS"

Since the difference between treating an acquisition as a "pooling of interests" or a "purchase" for accounting purposes may have such a profound effect upon a buyer's financial statements, it would appear that a buyer should choose the accounting treatment, in each acquisition, producing the best financial results to the buyer. However, certain criteria must be met before an acquisition may be treated as a "pooling of interests." Furthermore, if an acquisition meets the accounting criteria for a "pooling of interests," it *must* so be treated for accounting purposes. All acquisitions not meeting the "pooling" criteria *must* be treated as "purchases."

"Pooling Criteria"—Historical Background. In 1957, Accounting Research Bulletin No. 48 was issued by the Committee on Accounting Procedure of the American Institute of Certified Accountants. In this bulletin, the committee set forth the criteria to determine whether an acquisition could be treated as a "pooling of interests" under generally accepted accounting principles. If an acquisition met the criteria, the bulletin permitted, but did not require, that the acquisition be treated as a "pooling of interests" for accounting purposes. In other words, although an acquisition met the requirements for treatment as a "pooling of interests," the acquisition could, nevertheless, at the option of the buyer and its accountants, be treated as a "purchase."

Bulletin No. 48 set forth certain general criteria to qualify an acquisition for "pooling of interests" accounting treatment. The four basic criteria were (1) a continuity of equity ownership by the seller's stockholders in the buyer's business after the acquisition, (2) a continuation of the business of both the buyer and seller, (3) a continuity of management and (4) the relative size of the buyer and seller. The first requirement contained in the bulletin, a continuity of equity ownership, contemplated that the basic consideration paid for a seller should consist of common stock of a buyer. Where cash or other property was paid for a seller, or a major portion of the price was paid in cash or other property, the bulletin contemplated that the "pooling of interests" accounting treatment would not be available. With the passage of time, the requirement of payment in common stock was eroded and transactions involving miscellaneous types of securities including preferred stocks and substantial amounts of cash were treated as qualifying for "pooling of interests" accounting treatment. In addition, concepts involving part "purchase" and part "pooling of interests" accounting treatment were applied.

The relative size between the buyer and seller required for the "pooling of interests" accounting treatment to be available was also stated in general terms in the bulletin. However, the bulletin contained a presumption that if the seller received only 10 percent or less of the buyer's voting interest, the acquisition should be treated as a purchase. Again, however, with the passage of time, determinations made by accountants and the SEC permitted the test of the relative size between the buyer and seller to be eroded to a point of almost nonexistence. Poolings were approved where the size of the seller was less than one percent of the buyer's size.

The relaxation of the basic conditions for treating an acquisition as a "pooling of interests" permitted the use of the "pooling of interests" accounting treatment to report the results of more and more acquisitions. During the 1960s, when the cost (based on the market value of securities issued) of the great majority of acquisitions was far in excess of the book value of the assets of the sellers, treatment of such acquisitions as "pooling of interests" permitted buyers to ignore the element of goodwill involved in the transactions in reporting the buyer's subsequent earnings. Frequent use was also made of other advantages of accounting for acquisitions as "pooling of interests," such as a subsequent sale of a seller's assets for a price substantially in excess of the seller's book value and the consequent increase in reported earnings of a buyer. Companies under pressure from the marketplace to report higher earnings per share, made use of the "pooling of interests" accounting treatment to continue reporting increases in earnings per share.

In a speech given during debate on these issues, Emanuel Cohen, who was then chairman of the Securities and Exchange Commission, commented that companies had formerly made acquisitions because their businesses fit well together, but had recently been making acquisitions because their financial statements fit well together.

Administrative agencies, financial writers, security analysts and the accounting profession began to question the soundness of the "pooling of interests" accounting treatment as applied in many acquisitions. As a consequence, the entire area was reviewed by the Accounting Principles Board of the American Institute of Certified Public Accountants resulting in an exposure draft of a proposed Accounting Principles Board Opinion on Business Combinations and Intangible Assets, distributed under date of February 23, 1970. The result of the distribution of this exposure draft was the issuance of separate opinions, No. 16 "Business Combinations" and No. 17 "Intangible Assets," by the Accounting Principles Board setting forth new "pooling of interests" criteria, and rules for amortization of goodwill. The opinions were made to apply to all business combinations entered into after October 31, 1970.

Pooling of interests—current general conditions. Under present accounting criteria, if an acquisition meets the conditions of a "pooling of interests," the buyer may no longer at its option determine whether it will treat the acquisition as a "pooling of interests" or a "purchase." If an acquisition meets the pooling conditions, accounting practice now *requires* that the buyer account for the acquisition as a "pooling of interests." The general conditions set forth in the accounting opinion of the Accounting Principles Board for a "pooling of interests" are classified by (1) attributes of the buyer and seller, (2) the manner of effecting the acquisition and (3) the absence of certain planned transactions.

Attributes of the buyer and seller—two conditions. With respect to attributes of the buyer and seller, the following two conditions must be met:

1. Each company, buyer and seller, must have been an active independent company for at least two years before the plan for the acquisition is initiated.

This condition requires that none of the corporations involved in the acquisition has been a subsidiary or division of another corporation within the preceding two years.

2. The second condition requires that each of the combining companies be independent of the other combining companies. This condition means that, subject to certain exceptions from the date the plan of acquisition is initiated through consummation, the combining companies hold as intercorporate investments no more than 10 percent in total of the outstanding voting common stock of any combining company.

It is interesting to note that any requirements with respect to the relative sizes of the buyer and seller were eliminated from the criteria with respect to a "pooling of interests."

Manner of effecting the acquisition—eight conditions. With respect to the manner of effecting the acquisition, the following eight conditions must be met:

1. The acquisition should be effected in a single transaction or must be completed, pursuant to a plan, within one year after the acquisition is initiated. (The one year limit may be extended in the event of governmental intervention or litigation.)

2. The buyer may issue only common stock with rights identical to those of the majority of the buyer's outstanding voting common stock, in exchange for substantially all of the voting common stock interest of the seller. Generally, the acquisition of substantially all of the voting common stock of the seller by the buyer means the acquisition of 90 percent or more of the outstanding common stock of the seller. Also, generally, the stock to be issued by the buyer must be all common stock unless both preferred and common stock of the seller are outstanding, in which case the buyer may issue common stock and preferred stock in the same proportions as the outstanding common and preferred stock of the seller.

3. Neither the buyer nor the seller "changes" the equity interest of its voting common stock in contemplation of effecting the acquisition, either within two years before the plan of acquisition is initiated or between the dates the acquisition is initiated and closed. Distributions to stockholders which are no greater than normal dividends are not "changes" within the meaning of this condition.

4. The buyer and seller reacquire shares of voting common stock only for purposes other than purposes related to the acquisition, and neither company may reacquire more than a "normal number" of its shares between the dates the plan of acquisition is initiated and consummated. Under this condition, treasury stock may be acquired for stock options and compensation plans and for recurring distributions, provided a systematic pattern of reacquisitions was established at least two years before the plan of acquisition was initiated.

5. The relative interest of individual common stockholders in the buyer and seller may not be realigned by the exchange of securities in the acquisition. Under this condition each individual common stockholder of the buyer and

seller must receive a voting common stock interest exactly in proportion to his relative common stock interest before the acquisition.

6. The voting rights to which the common stock ownership interests of the stockholders in the continuing combined corporation are entitled must be exercisable by the stockholders; the stockholders may neither be deprived nor restricted in exercising these voting rights for a period of time. Under this condition, for example, shares of common stock issued to consummate the acquisition may not be transferred to a voting trust.

7. The seller may distribute no more than normal dividends, and may not reacquire more than a normal number of shares of the seller's common stock after the plan for the acquisition is initiated.

8. The acquisition must be completed at the time of closing, and no provisions in the plan of acquisition may relate to future issues of securities or other consideration. Under this condition, the continuing corporation may not agree to contingently issue additional shares of stock or distribute other consideration at a later date to former stockholders of the seller, nor may the buyer issue common stock to an escrow agent or issue other consideration to the escrow agent which is either to be transferred to the common stockholders of the seller or returned to the buyer, depending upon the resolution of contingencies.

Absence of Planned Transactions—Three Conditions. The following three conditions as to future transactions involving a buyer and seller must be met:

1. The buyer may not agree, directly or indirectly, to retire or reacquire all or part of the common stock issued to consummate the acquisition.

2. The buyer may not enter into other financial arrangements for the benefit of the seller's stockholders, such as a guarantee on loans secured by stock issued in the acquisition, which may have the effect of negating the exchange of equity securities.

3. The buyer may not plan to dispose of a significant part of the combined assets of the buyer and seller within two years after the acquisition, except to eliminate duplicate facilities or excess capacity, as well as those assets which would have been disposed of in the ordinary course of business of the buyer.

AICPA opinions No. 16 and No. 17 have been carried forward and are part of the Accounting Standards published by the Financial Accounting Standards Board (50.143-407).

"Pooling" Versus "Purchase"—A Summary. The examples given earlier illustrate dramatically the possible effects on financial position and book earnings which can result from the differences between "purchase" and "pooling of interests" treatment of an acquisition. In a typical "purchase" transaction, of course, the buyer will allocate most, and perhaps all, of the purchase price among the assets acquired on the basis of fair market value, usually supported by an appraisal, and only the balance, if any, will be recorded as goodwill. The assets will be entered on buyer's balance sheet at fair market value and depreciated over their remaining useful lives.

Only future earnings of buyer are affected by the adjusted depreciation, and the amortization of goodwill.

In order to preserve comparability, the "pooling of interests" method requires the buyer to restate earnings retroactively on a "pooled" basis for up to five years. Thus, if buyer acquires a business that has a substantial earnings capacity and history, the history of the combined businesses is shown without any implication that earnings suddenly increased in the year of the acquisition because of a fundamental improvement of business. The restatement requires costly and time-consuming effort.

Under the "purchase" method, when buyer acquires for a bargain price less than seller's book value, the allocation of the purchase price on the basis of fair market values of assets may result in "negative goodwill." This is amortized by credits to earnings. Under FASB accounting standards (B50.160 and 161), the use of this method must be disclosed and the amortization period must be not greater than forty years.

The acquisition of Delta Steamship Lines, Inc. by Tco Industries, Inc. was a good example of the effect of "negative goodwill." An excess of equity of $17,541,425 in the underlying assets over investment in Delta at the date of acquisition was recorded as a deferred credit and was amortized over a 15-year period by credits to earnings of the acquisition company in amounts over $1 million per year.

In a corresponding requirement applicable to the "purchase" method APB Opinion No. 16 requires a buyer to disclose pro forma results of operations for the preceding two years.

SEGMENT REPORTING

A related accounting improvement, segment reporting, was adopted by the SEC in 1975 and made a major contribution to the process of informing investors about the effects of acquisitions and mergers. Once publicly owned companies were required to report earnings of each of their material business segments, concern that conglomerates could mislead investors by "buying earnings" and pooling them with its results was greatly reduced.

ACCOUNTING FOR LEVERAGED BUYOUTS

In general, the purchase method is used to account for leveraged buyouts. However, some leveraged buyouts result in retention of significant equity interests by prior shareholders who also continue as part of management. When the degree of retained equity and control is high, the leveraged buyout becomes little more than a restructuring transaction involving (1) a large borrowing secured by assets of the corporation, (2) a distribution of the loan proceeds to shareholders and (3) a sale of shares to outside investors. Related management, customer and supplier agreements may further demonstrate that the essence of the transaction is a restructuring.

If a leveraged buyout has many characteristics of a restructuring transaction, several issues arise. First, should a public company be entitled to treat a leveraged buyout as a divestiture if it will continue to control and have many of the benefits and risks of the corporate business sold? Second, should the buyer step up the book value of its assets to fair market value and thereafter use the stepped-up values in calculating earnings? Debate has reopened on the question whether acquisition transactions should be treated partially by the purchase method and partially by the pooling of interests methods.

Accounting for leveraged buyouts has not attracted widespread public attention because most of the resulting companies are privately owned. Further, leveraged buyouts focus on cash flow, taxable income and divestiture values of assets. Nevertheless, accounting for leveraged buyouts can become important when an LBO vehicle decides to make a public offering of stock. Accounting is also important if loan agreement covenants contain tests based on GAAP financial statements.

Interested readers will benefit from reading "How Accounting Rules Shook Up LBO Dealmaking," *Mergers & Acquisitions,* Jerry Gorman, MLR Publishing, July/August 1990. The article is an informative discussion of EITF Consensus No. 88-16, entitled "Basis in Leverage Buyout Transactions," reached in May, 1989 by the Emerging Issues Task Force. The article provides examples of balance sheets and earnings statements using the historical accounting basis before a leveraged buyout, recapitalization accounting, fair value accounting and the LBO accounting required by EITF Consensus No. 88-16. Subsequent articles include "Challenges to Accountants in State of the Art LBOs," *Mergers & Acquisitions,* Jerry Gorman, MLR Publishing, November/December 1990 and "Accounting for Leveraged Buyouts," *The Acquisition Yearbook—1991,* Jerry Gorman, New York Institute of Finance (Simon & Schuster), 1991.

8

Securities and Exchange Commission Problems— Acquisitions

THE LAW AND SEC RULES

Securities law problems in acquisitions may involve many areas of the law. For example, if a seller requires the approval of its stockholders to sell its business, the seller may be required to prepare and file with the Securities and Exchange Commission proxy material to hold its stockholders' meeting. The work involved in the preparation of the proxy material for approval of the sale is more involved than preparing such material for a regular annual meeting. Moreover, as a further example, some of the stockholders of a seller, because of their relationship to the seller, may become subject to the restrictions on short-swing profits under Section 16(b) of the Securities Exchange Act of 1934. Securities law problems of this nature normally do not threaten the successful consummation of an acquisition.

On the other hand, where a buyer intends to buy a seller for stock or securities, a basic problem may arise under the Securities Act of 1933 that may cause collapse of negotiations and failure of the proposed acquisition, unless the buyer and seller find a solution satisfactory to each. This basic problem involves the registration requirements under the Securities Act of 1933, which, in turn, may involve the fundamental aims of the Act. These aims, as stated in the Act, are:

> to provide full and fair disclosure of the character of securities sold in interstate and foreign commerce and through the mails, and to prevent frauds in the sale thereof . . .

Pursuant to these objectives, the Act and rules promulgated by the Securities and Exchange Commission under the Act seek (1) to inhibit the sale and trading in public markets of securities of issuers which have not disclosed material information about themselves in appropriate filings with the SEC, and (2) to permit by exemptions the issuance of securities in private transactions to institutional and other sophisticated investors who do not need the information disclosed in filings with the SEC, and (3) to permit the resale in ordinary trading transactions of limited quantities of the securities of issuers that are making such filings by investors who acquired the securities in private transactions.

Accordingly, this chapter examines the effects of the securities laws on acquisitions and mergers under the following topics:

- The registration process under the integrated disclosure system adopted in 1982 by the SEC including "shelf registration."
- Rule 145 of the SEC which treats acquisitions of assets and mergers as "sales" even though those transactions are accomplished by votes of stockholders rather than by traditional "sale" mechanisms.
- The private offering exemption by which securities are often issued in acquisitions and mergers without registration under the Act.
- The "safe harbor" provisions of Regulation D governing the issuance of unregistered securities in private transactions.
- The restrictions on resale of unregistered securities issued in acquisitions and mergers because the sellers who receive them may be "underwriters" as defined by the Act.
- Rules 144 and 144A which permit limited resales of unregistered securities by their holders.
- Regulation S which permits limited sales and resales of unregistered securities in offshore transactions.

THE REGISTRATION PROCESS UNDER THE INTEGRATED DISCLOSURE SYSTEM

In 1982, after a 16-year period of gestation, the Securities and Exchange Commission took a giant stride toward achieving a single disclosure system in an effort to eliminate overlapping and unnecessary disclosure. Through the adoption of extensive revisions to the rules and forms under the reporting system of the Securities Exchange Act of 1934 and the Securities Act of 1933, the two systems, which had for the most part operated independently of each other, were integrated into a single disclosure system (the "Integrated Disclosure System").

An Overview. Anyone involved with a securities offering must first make a threshold determination whether or not the particular offering is exempt from the registration requirements of Section 5 of the Securities Act of 1933. If it is determined that the offering is not exempt from registration a decision must be made as to how the required registration is to be accomplished.

Under the Integrated Disclosure System, guidance for the preparation of the appropriate registration statement of report should first be sought from a review of the Securities and Exchange Commission's array of registration and reporting forms. This review will identify the proper form to file in order to accomplish the necessary registration. Each registration form has specified disclosure requirements and these requirements are identified by references to Securities and Exchange Commission Regulation S-K. Procedural requirements for preparing and filing the registration statement are contained in Securities and Exchange Commission Regulation C.

Securities registration requires the filing of a registration statement with the Securities and Exchange Commission in order to assure the investing public adequate information upon which a prospective investor may base his or her investment decision. The registration statement is reviewed by the commission's staff and depending upon such factors as the staff's workload, the form of registration statements and the nature of the issuer involved, this review may require anywhere from ten days to several months to complete. After completing the review process, the staff will issue its comments. As a result of the staff's comments one or more amendment to the registration statement may have to be filed. If the review process is lengthy, it will more likely than not be necessary to file an amendment to reflect changes in the issuer's business that will have taken place during this process. It is only after the registration statement (with any necessary amendments) is declared effective that the issuer can accept offers to purchase its securities.

As the cornerstone for registration statements under the Integrated Disclosure System, the Securities and Exchange Commission implemented a three-tier approach to the registration of securities and adopted new Forms S-1, S-2 and S-3. Basically, the nature of the issuer determines which registration form can be utilized within this three-tier system. Each registration form requires disclosure of the same basic information. The registration forms are differentiated by the manner in which such information is delivered—fully set forth in the prospectus (S-1), incorporated by reference in a document attached to the prospectus (S-2) or incorporated by reference from a document filed under the Securities Exchange Act of 1934 that is not attached to the prospectus (S-3).

The SEC has also adopted other special purpose registration forms including Forms S-4, S-8, S-11 and S-18 and Forms F-1, F-2, F-3 and F-4 used by foreign issuers.

The major component of any registration statement is the prospectus. A great deal of the time and effort that are required to prepare a registration statement for filing with the Securities and Exchange Commission is devoted to the prospectus. The term *prospectus* is defined in Section 2(10) of the Securities Act of 1933 to include:

> any prospectus, notice, circular, advertisement, letter or communication, written or by radio or television, which offers any security for sale or confirms the sale of any security; except that (a) a communication sent or given after the effective date of the registration statement (other than a prospectus permitted under subsection (b) of section (10) shall not be deemed a prospectus if it is proved that prior to or at the same time with such communication a written prospectus meeting the requirements of subsection (a) of section (10) at the time of such communication was sent

or given to the person to whom the communication was made, and (b) a notice, circular, advertisement, letter, or communication in respect of a security shall not be deemed to be a prospectus if it states from whom a written prospectus meeting the requirements of section (10) may be obtained and, in addition, does no more than identify the security, state the price thereof, state by whom orders will be executed, and contain such other information as the Commission, by rules or regulations deemed necessary or appropriate in the public interest and for the protection of investors, and subject to such terms and conditions as may be prescribed therein, may permit.

The eligibility criteria for determining the tier in which an issuer belongs and, therefore, which form of registration statement (within the three-tier system) the issuer may utilize to register its securities is, as stated in Securities Act Release No. 6235 (September 2, 1980), based upon the theory that the operation of the securities trading markets:

> is such that investors are protected by the market's analysis of information about certain companies which is widely-available, both from the Commission's files and other sources, and that such analysis is reflected in the price of the securities offered. Therefore, with companies whose shares are actively traded, disclosure to potential investors in a prospectus may be strictly limited to essential matters concerning the issuer and the offering without loss of investor protection or market efficiency. However, even though the registration statement is abbreviated, it should incorporate by reference the issuer's Exchange Act information which otherwise would be included in the prospectus to ensure that the information previously furnished is accurate in all material respects. Thus, the system operates in an effective manner: interested investors have access to the detailed Exchange Act reports which generally confirm or supplement information previously in the market and all investors are presented with short, readable prospectuses.

Under this "efficient market theory," the Securities and Exchange Commission has established separate eligibility requirements for each tier of the three-tier system.

Form S-1 is the registration form that must be used by issuers that are not eligible to use any other registration form. Form S-1 may, however, be used by other issuers who choose to make use of it except foreign governments and their political subdivisions. Generally, Form S-1 is used by issuers that have not been reporting companies under the Securities Exchange Act of 1934 for three years or more (e.g., a new issuer). All information that is disclosed in Form S-1 must be set out in its entirety without incorporating by reference any document that may have been filed under the Securities Exchange Act of 1934.

Form S-2 is available to issuers that have been reporting companies under the Securities Exchange Act of 1934 for not less than three years (and have for the year preceding the filing of the registration statement filed all such reports in a timely manner) but about which corporate information is not broadly disseminated because such issuers are not widely followed by investors and professional analysts. In addition, several other conditions must be met, if applicable.

The availability of Form S-3 is limited to a more select group of issuers and can be utilized for the registration of both primary and secondary offerings (offerings by the issuer and by security holders of outstanding securities, respectively) and is limited to offerings for cash. Form S-3, more than any other registration form, evidences the Securities and Exchange Commission's belief in and reliance upon the "efficient market theory." An issuer will qualify to use Form S-3 if, in addition to meeting certain "registrant requirements", a minimum "float" requirement is met or the securities being registered are "investment grade," nonconvertible debt or preferred securities. In addition to the "investment grade" exception, there are several other types of offerings that need not meet the "float" requirements.

Forms S-1, S-2 and S-3 and Regulations S-K and S-X. The three registration forms that represent the nucleus of the registration process under the Securities and Exchange Commission Integrated Disclosure System (Registration Forms S-1, S-2 and S-3) all require certain specified information to be included in the prospectus. This standardization is accomplished through the requirement that specific Regulation S-K items are to be included in each form. These standard items include the content of the cover, inside front cover and outside back cover page, a summary of the information contained in the prospectus (where the length or complexity of the prospectus makes a summary appropriate), a discussion of the ratio of earnings to fixed charges and the principal purpose(s) for which the proceeds of the offering are intended to be used. Other standard information requirements include a description of the securities, disclosure of the various factors considered in determining the offering price, disclosure of any substantial disparity between the public offering price and the price paid by officers, directors and promoters of the issuer (dilution), and a description of the plan of distribution of the securities being offered. These standard items, as well as disclosure of the interests of certain experts employed in connection with the offering, are contained in Items 1–10 and 12 of Forms S-1. Items 1–10 of Form S-1 correspond to identically numbered items on Forms S-2 and S-3. Item 12 of Form S-1 corresponds to Item 13 of Forms S-2 and S-3.

The form and content of the financial statements contained in a registration statement is governed by Regulation S-X. One or more years of financial statements prepared in accordance with generally accepted accounting principles are typically required. Certain additional information is regarded by the Securities and Exchange Commission as essential to all investors—be they prospective or current investors. This information includes selected financial information (five-year comparative financial data presented in columnar form) the disclosure of which is designed to show trends in the issuer's financial condition. Among the items requiring disclosure are net sales or operating revenues, income (loss) from continuing operations, income (loss) from continuing operations shown on a per common share basis, long-term obligations and redeemable preferred stock, and cash dividends declared per common share. In addition to requiring the disclosure of this financial data, any factor bearing upon the comparability of such financial data must be disclosed. Factors that may affect the comparability of the financial data include changes in accounting methods, business combinations, or divestitures.

Another item of disclosure that the Securities and Exchange Commission deems essential to all investors is "Management Discussion and Analysis" of the registrant's financial condition and results of operations. The purpose of this discussion and analysis is to provide information relevant to the assessment of the financial condition and results of operations by evaluating cash flow from operations and outside sources. In fulfilling this disclosure requirement, information need only include that which is available without "undue effort and expense" and which does not clearly appear in the financial statements. The discussion and analysis should focus on material events and uncertainties that are known to management that would cause the reported financial information not to be necessarily indicative of future operating results or future financial condition including (1) matters that would have an impact on future operations and have not had an impact in the past and (2) matters that may have had an impact on reported operations and are not expected to have an impact upon future operations.

To the extent that a line item in the financial statements shows a material change from year to year, it must be discussed to the extent necessary for an understanding of the registrant's business. Although not required to do so, the Securities and Exchange Commission encourages registrants to include "forward-looking information." Examples of such forward-looking information include (1) a statement containing a projection of revenue, income (loss), earnings (loss) per share, capital expenditures, dividends, capital structure or other financial items; (2) a statement of management's plans and objectives for future operations; (3) a statement of future economic performance; (4) statements of assumption underlying or relating to (1), (2) or (3). This forward-looking information is expressly brought into the safe harbor rule relating to projections as contained in Rule 175 under the Securities Act of 1933. Rule 175 provides that a forward-looking statement shall not be deemed a fraudulent statement unless such statement was made or reaffirmed without a reasonable basis or was disclosed other than in good faith.

The foregoing are examples of information the Securities and Exchange Commission regards as essential to all investors and for this reason is found in Forms S-1, S-2, and S-3 as well as in the Annual Report to Shareholders and the Annual Report on Form 10-K. Because of this redundancy and in keeping with the objectives of the Integrated Disclosure System, such information is presented differently in the forms that represent the nucleus of this system.

In Form S-1, this essential information must appear in its entirety because incorporation by reference is not permitted in Form S-1. However, in Forms S-2 and S-3, where incorporation by reference is permitted, such information would be incorporated by reference from the last Annual Report to Shareholders (which must be sent with the prospectus) and from Form 10-K, respectively.

Shelf-Registration—Rule 415. As part of the Integrated Disclosure System the Securities and Exchange Commission adopted Rule 415 on an experimental basis. Although originally scheduled to end on December 10, 1982, following substantial debate subsequent action by the Commission first extended the life of the Rule to December 31, 1983, and later gave it permanent status.

Rule 415 permits the registration of equity or debt securities in a manner that enables some or all of these securities to be offered for sale on very short notice ("shelf registration"). The availability of shelf registration tends to negate some of the objections a potential bidder might have in structuring an exchange offer as the means to bring about a corporate combination. However, in view of limitations imposed upon the use of Form S-2 ("not in connection with an exchange offer for securities of another person") and Form S-3 (offerings for cash only), a shelf registration that is part of an acquisition program will be required to be on Form S-1.

The amount of securities that can be registered for the shelf is limited to the amount of securities that can reasonably be expected to be offered and sold within two years of the effective date of the registration. A registrant preparing a registration statement for an offering pursuant to Rule 415 may use any form of registration statement that it is otherwise eligible to use. There is no registration statement that applies exclusively to a Rule 415 registration. The fact that a particular registration form is utilized to register securities being offered on a continuous or delayed basis does not alter the eligibility requirements for that registration form nor does it alter the disclosure requirements for said form.

Three basic conditions must be met before securities may be registered for the shelf:

1. the seller has a bona fide intention to offer and sell the securities being registered;
2. accurate current information is available during the "life" of the registration statement; and
3. investors receive the full benefit and protection of liability coverage afforded by the Securities Act of 1933.

The obvious benefit that a shelf registration offers to a registrant is that it affords a much greater degree of flexibility in responding to ever changing market conditions. Shelf registration is available for primary and secondary distributions and for securities offered under employee benefit plans and dividend reinvestment plans.

Rule 415 requires the filing of "post-effective" amendments during any such offering to keep the registration statement current with respect to (1) financial statement updates; (2) fundamental changes in information contained in the registration statement as filed and (3) new information with respect to the plan of distribution for the offering.

REGISTRATION BY FOREIGN ISSUERS

The SEC adopted Forms F-1, F-2, F-3 and F-4 to encourage registration by foreign issuers. These Forms are relatively brief and are designed to permit foreign issuers to adapt disclosure materials used in their own nations and to incorporate by reference from reports, such as Forms 20-F and 6-K, filed under the Securities Exchange Act of 1934. One important difficulty encountered by foreign issuers in meeting registration requirements is the adaptation of financial statements to generally accepted accounting principles and other requirements of Regulation S-X.

THE PRIVATE OFFERING EXEMPTION

A basic securities law problem in the acquisition area involves registration requirements under the Securities Act of 1933 affecting stock or securities paid by a buyer to make an acquisition. Section 5 of the Securities Act of 1933 provides that "unless a registration statement is in effect as to a security, it shall be unlawful for any person . . . to sell . . . or to offer to sell . . . such security . . ."

Under the Securities Act of 1933, the requirement that a registration statement be in effect to permit a lawful sale of a security, applies only to an issuer, underwriter or dealer. In this connection, Section 4(1) of the act provides that Section 5 (the section that makes it unlawful to sell unregistered stock) "shall not apply to transactions by any person other than an issuer, underwriter or dealer." In acquisitions, the term *dealer*, as used in the Act, does not normally present any special problems. However, in acquisitions where a buyer pays its stock or securities for a seller, the acquisition involves an "issuer" and also will often involve an "underwriter."

The Buyer-Issuer. A buyer that utilizes its stock or securities to acquire either the assets or stock of a seller is an "issuer" within the meaning of the Act. The buyer is an issuer whether it transfers its treasury stock or transfers its authorized and newly issued stock to the seller or its stockholders. In addition, in a statutory merger where stock or securities of the continuing corporation are transferred to the stockholders of the disappearing corporation, the continuing corporation (the buyer) is also an "issuer" within the meaning of the Act. Since the buyer or the continuing corporation, as the case may be, is an "issuer" within the meaning of the Act, a transfer of its stock to the seller or the stockholders of the seller will be lawful only if a registration statement is in effect, or if an exemption to the registration requirements is available in the particular acquisition.

The Seller's Stockholders—Underwriters. Under certain circumstances, a stockholder of a seller may be an "underwriter" and, therefore, may not lawfully sell securities of the buyer unless a registration statement is in effect with regard to the sales transaction. Under Section 2(11) of the Securities Act of 1933, "The term 'underwriter' means any person who has purchased from an issuer with a view to, or offers or sells for an issuer in connection with, the distribution of any security, or participates or has a direct or indirect participation in any such undertaking . . .". Under the foregoing definition of an "underwriter" a seller's stockholders who receive stock of a buyer in connection with an acquisition and subsequently sell the stock, may be "underwriters" within the meaning of the Act. The stockholders may be "underwriters" if they are considered as links in a chain of transactions through which the stock moves from the buyer to the public. The sale of the buyer's stock by the seller's stockholder, where the stockholder is an underwriter, would be unlawful, unless a registration statement was in effect at the time of the sale, or an exemption from registration existed with respect to the transaction.

The Practical Problem. The practical problem involving registration of securities under the Securities Act of 1933, arises where a buyer is unwilling to register the securities offered to make the acquisition, and the seller or its stockholders are unwilling to accept unregistered securities because such securities may not be salable.

You may ask, why is the buyer not willing to register its stock? A buyer may be unwilling to register for numerous reasons, among which may be any one or more of the following:

1. Registration is expensive;
2. Registration is time-consuming and disruptive of the conduct of the buyer's ordinary business, since the buyer's executives are required to devote substantial portions of their normal working time to the preparation of the registration statement;
3. Registration may impede the conduct of the buyer's business, since the buyer may be hindered from taking important action with regard to its business which could require an amendment to the registration statement and a delay in its effectiveness; and
4. Registration may be inconvenient at the time, because the buyer does not wish to reveal, either to the public or to a competitor, financial or other information which could at that time adversely affect the buyer's business.

Whatever the reason, if the buyer is unwilling to register, and yet wishes to acquire the seller's business for stock or other securities, a form of transaction should be negotiated which permits the buyer to pay with its stock or securities and does not require the filing of a registration statement.

From the seller's point of view, the stockholders of the seller should be willing to accept the buyer's stock or securities only if the stock or securities may be lawfully sold in the open market, or if the stockholders have reasonable assurance that the stock will be lawfully saleable at some definite time in the future. The assurance of salability may be derived either under the Securities Act of 1933, regulations thereunder, or contractual obligations to register stock or repurchase the same assumed by the buyer. Certainly, any stock or securities of a buyer received by a seller's stockholders that are not saleable in the open market may have a substantially reduced value.

Therefore, in the negotiated stock acquisition, where a buyer is unwilling to register its stock, and where selling stockholders will accept stock in payment for their business only if the stock is saleable, the parties should seek to negotiate a form of acquisition which qualifies for an exemption under the Securities Act of 1933 to permit the transfer by the buyer of unregistered stock and the subsequent sale of such stock, or mutually satisfactory contract provisions respecting registration or sale. Failure to negotiate such terms may cause abandonment of the proposed acquisition.

Nonpublic Offering Exemption. An exemption which may be available to a buyer where the seller's stockholders are comparatively few in number is the nonpublic offering exemption. This exemption, contained in Section 4(2) of the Securities Act of 1933, states that the "provisions of Section 5 shall not apply to . . . transactions by an issuer not involving any public offering." Therefore, under this exemption, where the transfer by the buyer of its stock or securities does not involve any public offering, the prohibition contained in Section 5 of the Act does not apply.

Whether a transfer of securities by a buyer qualifies as a transaction not involving any public offering, however, frequently may not be decided with certainty. Shortly after the effective date of the Securities Act of 1933, in Release No. 33-285, January 24, 1935, the General Counsel of the Securities and Exchange Commission stated:

> the determination of what constitutes a public offering is essentially a question of fact, in which all surrounding circumstances are of moment. In no sense is the question to be determined exclusively by the number of prospective offerees.

Since that time, where the exemption is sought, issuers have been faced with the problem of determining whether, under the circumstances of each distribution of stock or securities, the particular distribution qualifies as a transaction not involving any public offering. Due to the factual nature of the problem, the SEC has, from time to time, issued guidelines to determine the availability of the exemption. Relevant considerations in the guidelines are (1) the number and identity of offerees, (2) the number of units offered, (3) the size of the offering, (4) the manner of the offering, (5) investment intent, (6) period of retention and (7) change of circumstances. *It should always be remembered that the person claiming the exemption has the burden of proving it.*

Acquiring Privately Owned Businesses. Acquisition of privately owned businesses—businesses owned by relatively few shareholders—that are financed through the issuance of the buyer's securities may be accomplished through the private offering exemption and thus escape the registration requirements of the Securities Act of 1933. The indispensable prerequisite to a private offering exemption is assurance that the security owners of the acquired corporation will not resell the securities that they receive in exchange for their securities in the acquired corporation. If such a resale were to take place, it would cause the original offering to be a public offering requiring registration.

Apparent at first blush in the private offering scheme is the fact that issuers of securities can violate the registration requirements of the Securities Act of 1933 by the post-issuance conduct of its offeree. As precarious and at risk as the issuer's position might seem under the private offering exemption, there are measures that the issuer can and should always take to avoid the possibility of participating in an unregistered public offering.

The issuer can insist that the offerees in such private offerings execute and deliver what is commonly known as an "investment letter" in which the offeree acknowledges that he has acquired the securities without registration and that he is purchasing the securities for investment and not with a view to their distribution or sale. Such a letter will acknowledge the offeree's awareness that the shares will be "legended," and "stop transfer" instructions will be issued to the transfer agent. Legending and stop transfer instructions are the other preventive measures that are available to an issuer that issues unregistered securities. Of course, an "investment letter" may be dispensed with if the matters covered in such a letter are addressed in the acquisition agreement. Typically, shares issued in a private placement will bear the following legend:

> These shares have not been registered under the Securities Act of 1933. They may not be sold or transferred in the absence of an effective registration statement under that Act or an opinion from counsel satisfactory to the company that registration is not required.

RULE 145 AND FORM S-4

Rule 145. Prior to 1973, SEC Rule 133 provided that where a business combination took the form of a statutory merger or consolidation or where the buyer acquired the assets of the seller, no "sale," "offer," "offer to sell" or "offer for sale" was deemed to have been made within the meaning of Section 5 of the Securities Act of 1933. Effective January 1, 1973, Rule 145 rescinded this "no sale" theory.

Securities issued in connection with certain business combinations are deemed to involve a "sale," "offer," "offer to sell" or "offer for sale" under Section 5 and therefore the issuance of such securities must be registered, or qualify under a specific registration exemption, to be issued lawfully.

Transactions under Rule 145. The business combinations that are subject to Rule 145, if a plan or agreement is submitted to security holders for approval, are:

a) Reclassifications of securities other than a stock split, reverse split or change in par value involving the substitution of one security for another, or

b) Mergers, consolidations or similar acquisition plans in which the securities of the corporation or other person will be exchanged for securities of any other persons, other than a transaction whose sole purpose is to change the issuer's domicile; or

c) Transfers of assets for securities if:

  i) the plan or agreement provides for dissolution of the corporation whose security holders are voting on the plan or agreement; or

  ii) the plan or agreement provides for a pro rata or similar distribution of the securities to the security holders who are voting on the plan or agreement; or

  iii) the board of directors of the corporation whose security holders are voting on the plan or agreement adopt resolutions relative to i) or ii) within one year after the vote of the security holders, or

  iv) the transfer of assets is a part of a preexisting plan for the distribution of the securities, notwithstanding i), ii) or iii).

Form S-4. As part of its overhaul of the basic registration forms in connection with the adoption of the Integrated Disclosure System, the Securities and Exchange Commission amended Forms S-14 and S-15 to bring them into conformity with the system. Both forms related to securities issued in transactions involving corporate combinations. These forms were then consolidated into a new form, Form S-4.

Form S-4 Registration-Rule 145 Transactions. The registration of the securities acquired in connection with the above-described business combinations may be accomplished by means of Form S-4, which permits registration under the Securities Act of 1933 through compliance with the less burdensome requirements of Regulation 14A of the Securities Exchange Act of 1934 (the proxy rules). The information that is required by Form S-4 is identified by references to Regulation S-K and Schedule 14A and includes most of the standard items of information that are found in Forms S-1, S-2 and S-3. Information requiring detailed disclosure in an S-4 registration statement, by virtue of the nature of the transaction that gives rise to the need to register the securities, centers around the corporation fusion process (merger, consolidation, assets for securities, etc.). In that regard, Schedule 14A requires that the proxy-prospectus set forth the reasons for the combination and the rights of dissenting stockholders (appraisal rights). Of course, standard financials must be presented for the constituent corporations both separately and on a pro forma basis. Generally speaking, the method for disclosing the information presented in an S-4 proxy-prospectus centers on not only the parts (the individual constituent corporations) but the sum of the parts as well (the combined operation).

In an S-4 registration, the prospectus (which began as a proxy statement) should be delivered 20 days prior to the vote of the security holders voting on the combination. If no meeting is held, the prospectus should be delivered 20 days prior to the date on which the combination is effectuated. However, if the law of the applicable jurisdiction permits the furnishing of a notice of meeting or other action within less than 20 days, Form S-4 may nevertheless be utilized if there is compliance with such jurisdiction's notice requirements.

Form S-1 may be used to register securities issued in a Rule 145 transaction, but Form S-4 will permit registration through the use of a form of proxy statement that would, more likely than not, be required to be sent to stockholders for approval of the proposed combination. The use of Form S-4 permits one document to become both a proxy statement and a prospectus.

Other Transactions. Form S-4 can also be used to register securities offered in a merger in which the applicable state law does not require solicitation of the votes or consents of the security holders of the company being acquired and securities offered in an exchange offer for securities of the issuer or another entity.

Control Persons-Underwriters. Form S-4 also may be utilized to register a public offering (actually a re-offering) of securities acquired by persons in a Rule 145 transactions, who, by virtue of the rule, are deemed to be "underwriters." For such persons to be able to avail themselves of Form S-4, the prospectus must disclose certain additional information relating to the persons on whose behalf the securities are to be offered, and certain information relating to the underwriter and distribution of such securities. For the purpose of Rule 145, an affiliate or control person of the acquired entity is deemed to be an underwriter. A registration of securities to be offered by persons deemed to be underwriters under Rule 145 permits such persons to offer their securities to the public in excess of the volume limitations imposed by Rule 145 (d). These volume limitations are incorporated from Rule 144, which is discussed below.

Noncontrol persons. All persons acquiring securities in a Rule 145 transaction other than persons deemed to be underwriters and affiliates of the parties to a Rule 145 transaction may immediately dispose of, at public sale, the shares they receive in such a transaction. Rule 145 underwriters and affiliates of the parties to a Rule 145 transaction are permitted to make limited sales of the shares they receive in such a transaction provided the requirements of Rule 144 are met, except that such persons need not meet the holding period and notice requirements of Rule 144. The details of Rule 144 are discussed later.

RULE 144

The Rule. On January 11, 1972, in Release No. 5223, the Securities and Exchange Commission announced the adoption of Rule 144 under the Securities Act of 1933. Rule 144 applies to the resale of securities acquired directly from an issuer in transactions "not involving any public offering." With the adoption of Rule 144, the Securities and Exchange Commission provided a nonexclusive means to sell limited amounts of "control" and "restricted" securities acquired after April 15, 1972, the effective date of the rule. The stated rationale for the rule is to implement the fundamental purpose of the Securities Act of 1933:

> To provide full and fair disclosure of the character of the securities sold in interstate commerce and through the mails, and to prevent fraud in the sale thereof . . . .

Control Securities— "Control" securities are securities held by an "affiliate" of an issuer. Rule 144 defines an "affiliate" as "a person that directly or indirectly through one or more intermediaries, controls, or is controlled by, or is under common control with, such issuer," Rule 144 permits a holder of control securities, as well as a broker for such holder, to sell such securities without filing a registration statement and without complying with the private placement requirements of Section 4(2) of the Securities Act of 1933, if each of the following prerequisites is met:

1. There is available certain current public information concerning the issuer;
2. The limitation on the amount of securities sold in three months preceding the proposed sale has not been exceeded;
3. The shareholder sends notice of the proposed sale to the SEC; and
4. The sale is made through a "brokers' transaction."

Restricted Securities— "Restricted securities" are, generally speaking, securities acquired directly or indirectly from the issuer thereof, or from an affiliate of such issuer, in a transaction or chain of transactions not involving any public offering (e.g., a Regulation D offering). The holders of restricted securities, as well as brokers for such holders, may sell restricted securities in reliance upon Rule 144 without the necessity of registration or complying with the requirements of a "private placement" if each of the four prerequisites listed above in connection with "control securities" is present and the securities have been held for a specified period of time.

Current Public Information— For Rule 144 to apply, adequate public information concerning the issuer must be available. Adequate public information is deemed available if the issuer has been subject to the reporting requirements of Section 13 or 15(d) of the Securities Exchange Act of 1934 for not less than 90 days immediately preceding the sale, and has filed all reports required to be filed during the 12-month period (or for such shorter period that the issuer was required to file such reports) preceding the sale. Unless the person selling the restricted or control securities knows or has reason to know that the issuer has not complied with the above reporting requirements, such person may rely upon a written statement from the issuer that it has complied with such reporting requirements.

Although the great majority of issuers whose securities are involved in Rule 144, transactions are subject to Section 13 or 15(d) of the 1934 Act, recognizing that not all issuers are subject to these sections, the rule provides that adequate public information will also be deemed available if other information detailed in Rule 15(e)2-11 or, in the case of insurance companies, Section 12(g)(2)(G)(i) of the 1934 Act is publicly available.

Limitation on Amount of Sales. The provisions of Rule 144 limiting the amount of securities that may be sold are similar to the limitations that were contained in Rule 133, the predecessor to Rule 144.

The amount of securities not listed on a national securities exchange that may be sold under Rule 144 during any three-month period is 1 percent of the outstanding shares, whereas the corresponding limitation for securities traded on a national securities exchange is the greater of (1) 1 percent of the outstanding shares or (2) the average weekly reported volume of trading in such securities on all securities exchanges or NASDA during the four calendar weeks prior to the filing of Form 144. A determination of the 1 percent limitation may be based upon the number of shares outstanding as shown on the issuer's most recent report or statement that has been filed with the Securities and Exchange Commission. However, a person who is a nonaffiliate for at least 90 days may sell securities under Rule 144 without regard to the rule's volume limitations if such securities have been held for at least three years.

"Persons"— An understanding of the definition of "person" as used in Rule 144 is necessary to determine the amount of securities that can be sold. In determining the number of shares sold by a "person," the rule's definition of "person" mandates the inclusion of securities sold by (1) relatives living in the seller's home, (2) any trust or estate in which such person owns a 10 percent or greater beneficial interest or in which such person serves as trustee, executor or similar capacity and (3) any corporation in which such person owns a 10 percent interest.

Affiliates— In determining the volume limitation for affiliates, sales of both restricted and nonrestricted securities are combined, whereas in connection with nonaffiliates the volume limitation applies only to restricted securities. Both affiliates and nonaffiliates may, for the purpose of Rule 144 volume limitations, ignore sales made pursuant to a registration statement, a Section 4(2) exemption, or a Regulation A exemption. There is no volume limitation with respect to restricted securities held by an estate if neither the estate nor the beneficiary of the estate is an affiliate. The rule allows for sales within successive three-month periods, but no accumulation is permitted.

Notice of Proposed Sale. Rule 144 provides that a seller must file three copies of a Notice of Proposed Sale on Form 144 (a copy of which appears as Appendix 8-2) with the Securities and Exchange Commission, one of which must be manually signed. In addition, if the security is traded on a national securities exchange, one copy must be sent to such exchange. No notice need be filed if the sale involves not more than 500 shares and the sale price is not more than $10,000. The person filing the notice must have a bona fide intention to sell the securities referred to in the notice within a reasonable time of filing the notice. If within 90 days of filing the notice, all of the securities referred to in the notice are not sold and thereafter further sales are made, an amended notice must be filed with the commencement of the further sales.

Brokers' Transactions. Except in the case of sales by nonaffiliates who have held their restricted securities for at least three years, all sales made in reliance of Rule 144 must be made through a "brokers' transaction," and the person selling the securities may not solicit or arrange for the solicitation of buy orders nor can such person make any payment to anyone in connection with the sale except that such person may pay the broker his usual and customary commission. The rule imposes the obligation of "reasonable inquiry" upon brokers for the purpose of determining if the seller is engaged in a distribution. To aid the broker in meeting this obligation, the rule sets forth certain matters that should be investigated by the broker.

Holding Period. If restricted securities are to be sold under Rule 144, they must have been fully paid for and held for a period of at least two years. Although an affiliate selling nonrestricted securities (those acquired in open market purchases) is subject to the rule, such an affiliate with nonrestricted securities is not required to meet the holding period provision of the rule. The holding period commences to run with the assumption of economic risk of ownership by the acquiring person. If the consideration given for the shares includes a promissory note or other obligation to pay the purchase price, such consideration is not deemed full payment unless the note, obligation, or contract:

1. provides for full recourse against the acquiring person;
2. is secured by collateral, other than the securities purchased, having a fair market value at least equal to the purchase price of the securities purchased; and
3. is discharged by payment in full prior to the sale of the securities.

The Securities and Exchange Commission staff has indicated that the economic interest assumed by the purchaser of restricted securities must be a continuing interest, and therefore, the holding period is tolled for the period during which the value of any collateral securing the note, obligation, or contract falls below the outstanding value of the debt. Should the value of the collateral appreciate, any collateral in excess of the outstanding value of the debt may be withdrawn.

Date of Acquisition. Under Rule 144, the date of acquisition of shares acquired from stock dividends, splits and recapitalizations or upon the conversion of convertible securities is deemed to be the date on which the primary securities were acquired. The date on which the purchase price of securities acquired under a stock option is mailed or personally delivered to the company is deemed the date on which such securities were acquired.

Estates—Restricted Stock. Although Rule 144 is applicable to restricted securities held by an estate or acquired by the beneficiary of an estate, such securities are deemed to have been acquired when they were acquired by the decedent. In addition, there is no holding period requirement or limitation on the amount of securities sold if neither the estate nor the beneficiary of the estate is an affiliate of the issuer.

REGULATION D

In an effort to open up the capital markets to small businesses and to clarify certain exemptions that are available under the Securities Act of 1933, the Securities and Exchange Commission on March 3, 1982, issued Securities Act Release No. 6389 entitled "Regulation D—Revision of Certain Exemptions from Registration under the Securities Act of 1933 from Transactions Involving Limited Offers and Sales." The Release, representing the culmination of the Commission's efforts to establish guidelines for determining the availability of exemptions from the registration requirements of the Securities Act of 1933, placed several major exemptions that are available to prospective issuer-offerors under the umbrella of a single regulation. Former rules containing limited offering exemptions have been replaced with a series of eight rules (Rules 501–508, hereinafter "Regulation D").

The exemptions from the registration requirements of Section 5 of the Securities Act of 1933 contained in Regulation D are based on Sections 3(b), 4(2) and 4(6) of the Act. These exemptions are available to the issuer of the securities and may not be available to affiliates of the issuer or for resales of the issuer's securities.

Rule 501 defines the terms that are used throughout the Regulation including "accredited investor," "affiliate," "aggregate offering price" and "issuer."

Rule 501(a) states:

(a) *Accredited investor.* "Accredited investor" shall mean any person who comes within any of the following categories, or who the issuer reasonably believes comes within any of the following categories, at the time of the sale of the securities to that person:

(1) Any bank as defined in section 3(a)(2) of the Act whether acting in its individual or fiduciary capacity; insurance company as defined in section 2(13) of the Act; investment company registered under the Investment Company Act of 1940 or a business development company as defined in section 2(a)(48) of that Act; Small Business Investment Company licensed

by the U.S. Small Business Administration under section 301(c) or (d) of the Small Business Investment Act of 1958; employee benefit plan within the meaning of Title I of the Employee Retirement Income Security Act of 1974, if the investment decision is made by a plan fiduciary, as defined in section 3(21) of such Act, which is either a bank, insurance company, or registered investment adviser, or if the employee benefit plan has total assets in excess of $5,000,000; employee benefit plan within the meaning of the Employee Retirement Income Security Act of 1974 if the investment decision is made by a plan fiduciary, as defined in section 3(21) of such Act, which is either a bank, savings and loan association, insurance company or registered investment adviser, or if the employee benefit plan has total assets in excess of $5,000,000, if a self-directed plan, with investment decisions made solely by persons that are accredited investors;

(2) Any private business development company as defined in section 202(a)(22) of the Investment Advisers Act of 1940;

(3) Any organization described in Section 501(c)(3) of the Internal Revenue code corporation, Massachusetts or similar business trust, or partnership not formed for the specific purpose of acquiring the securities offered, with total assets in excess of $5,000,000;

(4) Any director, executive officer, or general partner of the issuer of the securities being offered or sold, or any director, executive officer, or general partner of a general partner of that issuer;

(5) Any natural person whose individual net worth, or joint net worth with that person's spouse, at the time of his purchase exceeds $1,000,000;

(6) Any natural person who had an individual income in excess of $200,000 in each of the two most recent years or joint income with that person's spouse in excess of $300,000 in each of those years and has a reasonable expectation of reaching the same income level in the current year; and

(7) Any trust, with total assets in excess of $5,000,000, not formed for the specific purpose of acquiring the securities offered, whose purchase is directed by a sophisticated person as described in § 230.506(b)(2)(ii); and

(8) Any entity in which all of the equity owners are accredited investors.

The general conditions applicable to all exempted offerings under Regulation D are set forth in Rule 502. These general conditions include:

1. Guidelines for determining whether separate offerings constitute part of the same offering under the integration principal;
2. Disclosure requirements for Regulation D offerings;
3. Restrictions on how a Regulation D offering can be conducted; and
4. Limitations on the resale of securities acquired in a Regulation D offering.

Integration. All sales that are part of the same offering under Regulation D must be integrated. Whether or not integration is required turns on a question of fact to be decided after considering five factors:

1. Whether the sales are part of a single plan of financing;
2. Whether the sales involved are the issuance of the same class of securities;
3. Whether the sales have been made at or about the same time;
4. Whether the same type of consideration is received; and
5. Whether the sales are made for the same general purpose.

These factors notwithstanding, a safe harbor provision in Rule 502(a) allows an issuer to exclude from integration all offers and sales that took place at least six months prior to the start of or six months following the completion of a Regulation D offering, if there are no offers or sales of the same securities (excluding offers and sales to employee benefit plans) within either of the two six-month periods.

Disclosure. Whether an issuer is required to furnish information to prospective purchasers in connection with a Regulation D offering depends upon the nature or classification of the persons who purchase securities in such an offering. As discussed below, the information requirements of Rule 502(b) do not apply to offerings that are exempt from registration by virtue of Rule 504 (offerings up to $1,000,000 by issuers not subject to the reporting requirements of the Securities Exchange Act of 1934). If an issuer sells securities to accredited investors and only accredited investors, no specific information is required to be furnished to such investors. Therefore, if an issuer sells its securities in reliance on Rules 505 and 506 to any investor who is not an accredited investor, Rule 502(b) requires that specific information be delivered to *all* investors.

Where Regulation D requires the furnishing of information, the type of information that is called for depends upon the size of the offering and the nature of the issuer. In the case of a nonreporting company, the disclosure requirements are keyed to the size of the offering.

For offerings up to $2.0 million, a nonreporting issuer must furnish the same information as required in Part II of Form 1-A, except that the issuer's balance sheet must be audited and dated within 120 days of the start of the offering.

In offerings up to $7,500,000, a nonreporting issuer must provide the same type of information that would be required in Part I of a registration statement on Form S-18. Such information includes two years of financial statements but only the most recent year must be audited. These information requirements are subject to further relaxation for issuers, other than limited partnerships, which cannot obtain the necessary financial statements without unreasonable effort or expense. Such issuers need only provide an audited balance sheet within 120 days of the offering.

A nonreporting issuer for offerings in excess of $7.5 million is required to furnish the same type of information that would be required in Part I of whatever registration form such issuer would be entitled to use for the offering if it was being registered.

An issuer that is a reporting company must fulfill the disclosure requirements of Regulation D, furnishing its most recent materials filed under the Securities Act of 1933 or Securities Exchange Act of 1934 as described in Rule 502(b)(ii)(A) through (D).

Manner of Offering. Except in the case of a Rule 504 exemption made in accordance with certain State Blue Sky requirements, a Regulation D offering cannot avail itself of general solicitation or general advertising.

Limitation on Resale. Securities acquired in a Regulation D offering have the status of securities exempt from registration under Section 4(2) of the Securities Act of 1933. As a consequence of this status, securities acquired in a Regulation D offering cannot be resold without registration under the Act or pursuant to an exemption therefrom except for securities exempt under Rule 504(b)(1). Again, a Regulation D exemption is available only to the issuer of the securities.

Notice. Pursuant to Rule 503, an issuer that makes an offering under Regulation D must file five copies of a notice of sale with the Securities and Exchange Commission. Compliance with Rule 503 is accomplished by furnishing the information on Form D as set forth in Appendix 8-3. The initial Form D is due not later than 15 days after the first sale in a Regulation D offering.

The Exemptions. Rule 504 and Rule 505 exemptions (both of which are exemptions under Section 3(b) of the Securities Act of 1933 and which replaced Rules 240 and 242, respectively) are available for offerings that do not exceed $1,000,000 and $5 million, respectively. The dollar limitations that are applicable to both exemptions are calculated during a floating 12-month period. This period must be carefully examined and monitored; that is, within 12 months before the start of the offering *and* during the offering of securities under Rules 504 and 505. In calculating dollar limitations applicable to Rule 505 and Rule 506 offerings, all securities sold within this 12-month period in reliance of any exemption under Section 3(b) of the Securities Act of 1933 (including Rule 504 and Rule 505 exemptions) or in violation of Section 5(a) of the Act must be taken into consideration.

Rule 504. To qualify for a Rule 504 exemption, the issuer cannot be subject to the reporting requirements of the Securities Exchange Act of 1934, nor can the issuer be an investment company. There is a $1,000,000 limitation on the aggregate offering price (as defined at Rule 501(c)) and the general guidelines contained in Rules 501 through 503 must be complied with before this exemption is available. However, if the Rule 504 offering is made in one or more states, each of which provides for the registration of the securities and requires the delivery of a disclosure document prior to sale and if the offering is made in accordance with such state provisions (State Blue Sky requirements), the restrictions on the manner of offering [Rule 502(c)] and the restrictions on resales of securities (Rule 502(d)) will not apply.

The operation of the floating 12-month period that must be focused upon in calculating the limitation on the aggregate offering price in a Rule 504 offering is illustrated in Note 1 to Rule 504(b)(2):

Example 1. If an issuer sells $500,000 worth of securities pursuant to state registration on January 1, 1988 under this § 230.504, it would be able to sell an additional $500,000 worth of securities either pursuant to state registration or without state registration during the ensuing twelve month period, pursuant to this § 230.504.

Example 2. If an issuer sold $900,000 pursuant to state registration on

June 1, 1987 under this § 230.504 and an additional $4,100,000 on December 1, 1987 under § 230.505, the issuer could not sell any of its securities under this § 230.504 until December 1, 1988. Until then the issuer must count the December 1, 1987 sale towards the $1,000,000 limit within the preceding twelve months.

Rule 505. The general terms and conditions of Rules 501 and 502 must be satisfied in order for the issuer to qualify for an exemption under Rule 505. Notwithstanding Rule 508, the authors recommend that an issuer wishing to claim a Rule 505 exemption be ready to establish that:

1. All sales that are part of the same Regulation D offering meet all of the terms and conditions of Regulation D;
2. The required information has been furnished to all offerees who are entitled to receive same;
3. The offering did not employ any form of general advertising or general solicitation, including any advertisement, article or other communication published in newspapers, magazines or similar media, or broadcast over television or radio or through any seminar or meeting at which there was any general solicitation or advertising;
4. The restrictions on transferability and re-sale of the securities have been disclosed to the offerees with a restrictive legend affixed to the securities that indicate this fact; and
5. The timely filing of Form D pursuant to Rule 503.

In addition, Rule 505 provides that an issuer must satisfy three specific conditions before its exemption is available. These specific conditions are (1) that the aggregate offering price does not exceed $5 million, (2) that there are no more, or the issuer reasonably believes that there are no more than 35 nonaccredited investors and (3) that the issuer is not disqualified as a consequence of certain acts or omissions by the issuer or certain persons affiliated with the issuer.

The $5 million limitation on the aggregate offering price in a Rule 505 offering is determined in the same manner that is used to determine the offering limitation under Rule 504. Again, a floating 12-month period is relevant to this determination and is illustrated in the rule as follows:

> Example 1. If an issuer sold $2,000,000 of its securities on June 1, 1982 under § 230.505 and an additional $1,000,000 on September 1, 1982, the issuer would be permitted to sell only $2,000,000 more under this § 230.505 until June 1, 1983. Until that date the issuer must count both prior sales towards the $5,000,000 limit. However, if the issuer made its third sale on June 1, 1983, the issuer could then sell $4,000,000 of its securities because the June 1, 1982 sale would not be within the preceding 12 months.
>
> Example 2. If an issuer sold $500,000 of its securities on June 1, 1982 under § 230.504 and an additional $4,500,000 on December 1, 1982 under this § 230.505, then the issuer could not sell any of its securities under this

§ 230.505 until June 1, 1983. At that time it could sell an additional $500,000 of its securities.

A Rule 505 offering may be made to no more than 35 nonaccredited investors or to an unlimited number of accredited investors. The nonaccredited investors taking part in a Rule 505 offering, unlike those in a Rule 506 offering, are not specifically required to be persons having knowledge or experience in financial and business matters sufficient to render such persons capable of evaluating the merits and risks of the prospective offering.

The final specific condition to a Rule 505 offering, other than that under no circumstances is this exemption available to an investment company, is that the issuer cannot be disqualified due to certain conduct of the issuer or persons who maintain a special position with respect to the issuer. The acts or omissions that give rise to disqualification are incorporated by reference from § 230.252(c), (d), (e) and (f) of Regulation A. In general, these disqualifications stem from administrative or judicial inquiries or findings relating to securities law violations by the issuer, its predecessors, affiliates, directors, officers, 10 percent beneficial owners or underwriters.

Rule 506. The last of the Regulation D exemptions is contained in Rule 506, the rule that replaced Rule 146. It is available for limited offers and sales of securities without regard to the aggregate offering price and is available in connection with securities relating to business combinations. An offer and sale of securities that complies with Rule 506 will be deemed to be exempt from registration pursuant to Section 4(2) of the Securities Act of 1933—transactions not involving any public offering.

As is generally the case in Rule 504 exemptions and in the case of a Rule 505 exemption, the conditions and terms of Rules 501 and 502 are applicable to a Rule 506 exemption. These general conditions and terms were discussed previously in connection with Rule 505. Rule 506 allows sales to be made to no more than 35 nonaccredited investors and an unlimited number of accredited investors. However, prior to any sale to a nonaccredited investor, the issuer must reasonably believe that each nonaccredited investor, either alone or with his purchaser representative (as defined in Rule 501(h)), has sufficient knowledge of and experience in financial and business matters so that he is capable of evaluating the merits and risks of the prospective investment.

Rule 507. If an issuer or its predecessors or affiliates have been subject to any order, judgement or decree of any court of competent jurisdiction enjoining such person for failure to comply with Rule 103, exemption under Rules 504, 505 or 506 is not available unless the SEC determines otherwise upon a showing of good cause.

Rule 508. Failure to comply with Regulation D will not result in loss of the exemption for a sale to a particular individual or entity if the person claiming the exemption shows that (1) the failure did not pertain to a term, condition or requirement directly intended to protect that particular individual or entity; (2) the failure was insignificant in relation to the offering as a whole and (3) a good faith and reasonable attempt to comply was made.

Valuation Discounts. The restrictions on resale of securities resulting from their issuance without registration under Sections 4 (2) and 4 (6) of the Securities Act of 1933 result in discounted values which have been recognized by securities analysts and the Internal Revenue Service. See the discussion of Revenue Ruling 59-60 and subsequent Revenue Rulings in Chapter 4.

RULE 144A AND REGULATIONS

The Section 4 (1 ½) Exemption. Securities issued without registration pursuant to Sections 4 (2) and 4 (6) exemptions can be resold upon registration or, as previously described, in compliance with Rule 144. Restricted securities can also be resold to other investors who meet the standards for those exemptions and assume the same restrictions on sale to the public. The rationale permitting these sales, which are commonly made to institutional investors, is based on analysis of the purposes of Sections 4 (1) and 4 (2). Thus, attorneys will sometimes say that these sales are based on a Section 4 (1 ½) exemption. While that imaginative term is humorous, the resales, if handled properly, are consistent with protection of the public and provide reduced risk and liquidity for holders of restricted securities.

Rule 144A and Regulation S. In April 1990, the SEC adopted a "safe harbor" Rule 144A creating new freedom to make private placements with certain large institutional investors and for those investors to resell securities acquired in private placements.

Rule 144A permits issuers to sell securities not traded on a national securities exchange or NASDAQ to qualified institutional buyers (QIBs) such as insurers, banks, investment companies, investment advisers and broker-dealers that own at least $100 million of securities. To be eligible, banks and savings and loan associations must also have a net worth of $25 million. Investment banking firms engaging in distributions must own at least $10 million of securities. The issuer need not take steps to restrict trading in the securities in the manner required by Regulation D. QIBs can freely resell the securities to other QIBs without the restrictions required by Regulation D and Rule 144. Any resale to a person who is not a QIB can be made only pursuant to registration or one of the traditional exemptions.

The National Association of Securities Dealers, Inc. has developed a new computerized trading capability, called PORTAL, to facilitate institutional trading in unregistered securities sold pursuant to Rule 144A. During its initial months, activity in the PORTAL market was very light.

Together with Rule 144A, the SEC also adopted a new "safe harbor" rule called Regulation S to clarify the application of the registration requirements of the Securities Act of 1933 to sales of securities in "offshore transactions" outside the United States. Regulation S also contains cautious provisions relating to resales of securities sold in "offshore transactions" by persons not involved in their distribution.

Rule 144A and Regulation S should facilitate efforts to raise acquisition financing from QIBs in the United States and from a wide range of sources outside the United States.

Regulation S allows greater freedom for U.S. companies to acquire foreign businesses because the sellers will have a clearer understanding when and how the securities can be resold. Similarly, Regulation S allows greater freedom for foreign companies to use securities traded in foreign markets to acquire businesses in the United States because sellers of businesses will have a clearer understanding when and how the securities can be resold in offshore transactions.

CONCLUSION

Whether or not an acquisition for stock or securities requires the filing of a registration statement with the Securities and Exchange Commission, and, if one is required, what type of registration statement should be filed, may be of fundamental importance in a particular acquisition. The answer depends upon the rules of the Securities and Exchange Commission, which change with the changing attitudes of the Commission. Because of the complexities involved in this area of the law, in any acquisition involving the use of stock or securities to pay the purchase price, where the question of registration may be involved, both the buyer, as the issuer, and the stockholders of the seller, as possible underwriters, should obtain advice from a qualified source attempting to establish and negotiate the mechanics of the acquisition. The buyer should receive assurance that it will not violate the registration requirements of the Securities Act of 1933 under the form of the transaction as proposed, and the seller's stockholders should receive assurance of the applicable rules and conditions under which they will be lawfully permitted to sell the stock or securities they receive in the transaction.

Appendix 8-1

SECURITIES AND EXCHANGE COMMISSION

FORM S-1

REGISTRATION STATEMENT UNDER
THE SECURITIES ACT OF 1933

_____

(Exact name of registrant as specified in its charter)

| (State or other jurisdiction of incorporation or organization) | (Primary Standard Industrial Classification Code Number) | (I.R.S. Employer Identification No.) |

(Address, including zip code, and telephone number, including
area code, of registrant's principal executive offices)

(Name, address, including zip code, and telephone number,
including area code, of agent for service)

Approximate date of commencement of proposed sale to the public

_____

If any of the securities being registered on this form are to be offered on a delayed or continuous basis pursuant to Rule 415 under the Securities Act of 1933, check the following box. ☐

CALCULATION OF REGISTRATION FEE

Title of each class of securities to be registered	Amount to be registered	Proposed maximum offering price per unit	Proposed maximum aggregate offering price	Amount of registration fee

GENERAL INSTRUCTIONS

I. Eligibility Requirements for Use of Form S-1.

This Form shall be used for the registration under the Securities Act of 1933 ("Securities Act") of securities of all registrants for which no other form is authorized or prescribed, except that this Form shall not be used for securities of foreign governments or political sub-divisions thereof.

II. Application of General Rules and Regulations.

A. Attention is directed to the General Rules and Regulations under the Securities Act, particularly those comprising Regulation C thereunder. That Regulation contains general requirements regarding the preparation and filing of the registration statement.

B. Attention is directed to Regulation S-K for the requirements applicable to the content of the non-financial statement portions of registration statements under the Securities Act. Where this Form directs the registrant to furnish information required by Regulation S-K and the item of Regulation S-K so provides, information need only be furnished to the extent appropriate.

III. Exchange Offers.

If any of the securities being registered are to be offered in exchange for securities of any other issuer the prospectus shall also include the information which would be required by Item 11 if the securities of such other issuer were registered on this Form. There shall also be included the information concerning such securities of such other issuer which would be called for by Item 9 if such securities were being registered. In connection with this instruction, reference is made to Rule 409.

PART I. INFORMATION REQUIRED IN PROSPECTUS

Item 1. Forepart of the Registration Statement and Outside Front Cover Page of Prospectus.

Set forth in the forepart of the registration statement and the outside front cover page of the prospectus the information required by Item 501 of Regulation S-K.

Item 2. Inside Front and Outside Back Cover Pages of Prospectus.

Set forth on the inside front cover page of the prospectus or, where permitted, on the outside back cover page, the information required by Item 502 of Regulation S-K.

Item 3. Summary Information, Risk Factors and Ratio of Earnings to Fixed Charges.

Furnish the information required by Item 503 of Regulation S-K.

Item 4. Use of Proceeds.

Furnish the information required by Item 504 of Regulation S-K.

Item 5. Determination of Offering Price.

Furnish the information required by Item 505 of Regulation S-K.

Item 6. Dilution.

Furnish the information required by Item 506 of Regulation S-K.

Item 7. Selling Security Holders.

Furnish the information required by Item 507 of Regulation S-K.

Item 8. Plan of Distribution.

Furnish the information required by Item 508 of Regulation S-K.

Item 9. Description of Securities to Be Registered.

Furnish the information required by Item 202 of Regulation S-K.

Item 10. Interests of Named Experts and Counsel.

Furnish the information required by Item 509 of Regulation S-K.

Item 11. Information with Respect to the Registrant.

Furnish the following information with respect to the registrant:

(a) Information required by Item 101 of Regulation S-K, description of business;

(b) Information required by Item 102 of Regulation S-K, description of property;

(c) Information required by Item 103 of Regulation S-K, legal proceedings;

(d) Where common equity securities are being offered, information required by Item 201 of Regulation S-K, market price of and dividends on the registrant's common equity and related stockholder matters;

(e) Financial statements meeting the requirements of Regulation S-X (Schedules required under Regulation S-X shall be filed as "Financial Statement Schedules" pursuant to Item 16, Exhibits and Financial Statement Schedules, of this Form), as well as any information required by Rule 3-05 and Article 11 of Regulation S-X;

(f) Information required by Item 301 of Regulation S-K, selected financial data;

(g) Information required by Item 302 of Regulation S-K, supplementary financial information;

(h) Information required by Item 303 of Regulation S-K, management's discussion and analysis of financial condition and results of operations;

(i) Information required by Item 304 of Regulation S-K, disagreements with accountants on accounting and financial disclosure;

(j) Information required by Item 401 of Regulation S-K, directors and executive officers;

(k) Information required by Item 402 of Regulation S-K, executive compensation;

(l) Information required by Item 403 of Regulation S-K, security ownership of certain beneficial owners and management; and

(m) Information required by Item 404 of Regulation S-K, certain relationships and related transactions.

Item 12. Disclosure of Commission Position on Indemnification for Securities Act Liabilities.
Furnish the information required by Item 510 of Regulation S-K.

PART II. INFORMATION NOT REQUIRED IN PROSPECTUS

Item 13. Other Expenses of Issuance and Distribution.
Furnish the information required by Item 511 of Regulation S-K.

Item 14. Indemnification of Directors and Officers.
Furnish the information required by Item 702 of Regulation S-K.

Item 15. Recent Sales of Unregistered Securities.
Furnish the information required by Item 701 of Regulation S-K.

Item 16. Exhibits and Financial Statement Schedules.
(a) Subject to the rules regarding incorporation by reference, furnish the exhibits as required by Item 601 of Regulation S-K.

(b) Furnish the financial statement schedules required by Regulation S-X and Item 11(e) of this Form. These schedules shall be lettered or numbered in the manner described for exhibits in paragraph (a).

Item 17. Undertakings.
Furnish the undertakings required by Item 512 of Regulation S-K.

SIGNATURES

Pursuant to the requirements of the Securities Act of 1933, the registrant has duly caused this registration statement to be signed on its behalf by the undersigned, thereunto duly authorized, in the City of ....

State of ...., on ...., 19.....
(Registrant) ....
By (Signature and Title) ....

Pursuant to the requirements of the Securities Act of 1933, this registration statement has been signed by the following persons in the capacities and on the dates indicated.
(Signature) ....
(Title) ....
(Date) ....

Instructions.

1. The registration statement shall be signed by the registrant, its principal executive officer or officers, its principal financial officer, its controller or principal accounting officer and by at least a majority of the board of directors or persons performing similar functions. If the registrant is a foreign person, the registration statement shall also be signed by its authorized representative in the United States. Where the registrant is a limited partnership, the registration statement shall be signed by a majority of the board of directors of any corporate general partner signing the registration statement.

2. The name of each person who signs the registration statement shall be typed or printed beneath his signature. Any person who occupies more than one of the specified positions shall indicate each capacity in which he signs the registration statement. Attention is directed to Rule 402 concerning manual signatures and to Item 601 of Regulation S-K concerning signatures pursuant to powers of attorney.

INSTRUCTIONS AS TO SUMMARY PROSPECTUSES

1. A summary prospectus used pursuant to Rule 431 shall at the time of its use contain such of the information specified below as is then included in the registration statement. All other information and documents contained in the registration statement may be omitted.

(a) As to Item 1, the aggregate offering price to the public, the aggregate underwriting discounts and commissions and the offering price per unit to the public;

(b) As to Item 4, a brief statement of the principal purposes for which the proceeds are to be used;

(c) As to Item 7, a statement as to the amount of the offering, if any, to be made for the account of security holders;

(d) As to Item 8, the name of the managing underwriter or underwriters and a brief statement as to the nature of the underwriter's obligation to take the securities; if any securities to be registered are to be offered otherwise than through underwriters, a brief statement as to the manner of distribution; and, if securities are to be offered otherwise than for cash, a brief statement as to the general purposes of the distribution, the basis upon which the securities are to be offered, the amount of compensation and other expenses of distribution, and by whom they are to be borne;

(e) As to Item 9, a brief statement as to dividend rights, voting rights, conversion rights, interest, maturity;

(f) As to Item 11, a brief statement of the general character of the business done and intended to be done, the selected financial data (Item 301 of Regulation S-K), and a brief statement of the nature and present status of any material pending legal proceedings; and

(g) A tabular presentation of notes payable, long-term debt, deferred credits, minority interests, if material, and the equity section of the latest balance sheet filed, as may be appropriate.

2. The summary prospectus shall not contain a summary or condensation of any other required financial information except as provided above.

3. Where securities being registered are to be offered in exchange for securities of any other issuer, the summary prospectus also shall contain that information as to Items 9 and 11 specified in paragraphs (e) and (f) above which would be required if the securities of such other issuer were registered on this Form.

4. The Commission may, upon the request of the registrant, and where consistent with the protection of investors, permit the omission of any of the information herein required or the furnishing in substitution therefor of appropriate information of comparable character. The Commission may also require the inclusion of other information in addition to, or in substitution for, the information herein required in any case where such information is necessary or appropriate for the protection of investors.

Appendix 8-2

FORM 144

U.S. SECURITIES AND EXCHANGE COMMISSION
WASHINGTON, D.C. 20549

NOTICE OF PROPOSED SALE OF SECURITIES
Pursuant to Rule 144 under the Securities Act of 1933

ATTENTION: *Transmit for filing 3 copies of this form concurrently with either placing an order with a broker to execute a sale or executing a sale directly with a market maker.*

SEC USE ONLY
DOCUMENT SEQUENCE NO.
CUSIP NUMBER
WORK LOCATION

1(a) NAME OF ISSUER | (b) IRS IDENT. NO. | (c) S.E.C. FILE NO.

1(d) ADDRESS OF ISSUER — STREET | CITY | STATE | ZIP CODE

2(a) NAME OF PERSON FOR WHOSE ACCOUNT THE SECURITIES ARE TO BE SOLD | (b) SOCIAL SECURITY NO. OR IRS IDENT. NO. | (c) RELATIONSHIP TO ISSUER | (d) ADDRESS — STREET | CITY | STATE | ZIP CODE

(e) TELEPHONE NO. AREA CODE — NUMBER

INSTRUCTION: *The person filing this notice should contact the issuer to obtain the I.R.S. Identification Number and the S.E.C. File Number.*

3(a) Title of the Class of Securities To Be Sold	(b) Name and Address of Each Broker Through Whom the Securities are to be Offered or Each Market Maker who is Acquiring the Securities	(c) Number of Shares or Other Units To Be Sold (See instr. 3(c))	(d) Aggregate Market Value (See instr. 3(d))	(e) Number of Shares or Other Units Outstanding (See instr. 3(e))	(f) Approximate Date of Sale (See instr. 3(f)) (MO. DAY YR.)	(g) Name of Each Securities Exchange (See instr. 3(g))
	SEC USE ONLY — Broker-Dealer File Number					

INSTRUCTIONS:

1. (a) Name of issuer
    (b) Issuer's I.R.S. Identification Number
    (c) Issuer's S.E.C. file number, if any
    (d) Issuer's address, including zip code
    (e) Issuer's telephone number, including area code

2. (a) Name of person for whose account the securities are to be sold
    (b) Such person's Social Security or I.R.S. identification number
    (c) Such person's relationship to the issuer (e.g., officer, director, 10% stockholder, or member of immediate family of any of the foregoing)
    (d) Such person's address, including zip code

3. (a) Title of the class of securities to be sold
    (b) Name and address of each broker through whom the securities are intended to be sold
    (c) Number of shares or other units to be sold (if debt securities, give the aggregate face amount)
    (d) Aggregate market value of the securities to be sold as of a specified date within 10 days prior to the filing of this notice
    (e) Number of shares or other units of the class outstanding, of if debt securities the face amount thereof outstanding, as shown by the most recent report or statement published by the issuer
    (f) Approximate date on which the securities are to be sold
    (g) Name of each securities exchange, if any, on which the securities are intended to be sold

SEC 1147 (11-78)

TABLE I - SECURITIES TO BE SOLD

Furnish the following information with respect to the acquisition of the securities to be sold and with respect to the payment of all or any part of the purchase price or other consideration therefor:

Title of the Class	Date You Acquired	Nature of Acquisition Transaction	Name of Person from Whom Acquired (If gift, also give date donor acquired)	Amount of Securities Acquired	Date of Payment	Nature of Payment

INSTRUCTIONS

1. If the securities were purchased and full payment therefore was not made in cash at the time of purchase, explain in the table or in a note thereto the nature of the consideration given. If the consideration consisted of any note or other obligation, or if payment was made in installments describe the arrangement and state when the note or other obligation was discharged in full or the last installment paid.

2. If within two years after the acquisition of the securities the person for whose account they are to be sold had any short positions, put or other option to dispose of securities referred to in paragraph (d)(3) of Rule 144, furnish full information with respect thereto.

TABLE II - SECURITIES SOLD DURING THE PAST 3 MONTHS

Furnish the following information as to all securities of the issuer sold during the past 3 months by the person for whose account the securities are to be sold.

Name and Address of Seller	Title of Securities Sold	Date of Sale	Amount of Securities Sold	Gross Proceeds

REMARKS:

INSTRUCTIONS:
See the definition of "person" in paragraph (a) of Rule 144. Information is to be given not only as to the person for whose account the securities are to be sold but also as to all other persons included in that definition. In addition, information shall be given as to sales by all persons whose sales are required by paragraph (e) of Rule 144 to be aggregated with sales for the account of the person filing this notice.

ATTENTION:
The Person for whose account the securities to which this notice relates are to be sold hereby represents by signing this notice that he does not know any material adverse information in regard to the current and prospective operations of the Issuer of the securities to be sold which has not been publicly disclosed.

DATE OF NOTICE

_____

The notice shall be signed by the person for whose account the securities are to be sold. At least one copy of the notice shall be manually signed. Any copies not manually signed shall bear typed or printed signatures.

_____
(SIGNATURE)

ATTENTION: Intentional misstatements or omission of facts constitute Federal Criminal Violations (See 18 U.S.C. 1001).

Appendix 8-3

FORM D

U. S. SECURITIES AND EXCHANGE COMMISSION
Washington, D. C. 20549

OMB Approval
OMB 3235-0076
Expires December 31, 1984

SEC USE ONLY

NOTICE OF SALES OF SECURITIES
PURSUANT TO REGULATION D OR SECTION 4(6)

SEC USE ONLY
SERIAL

21-   -

Nature of this filing with respect to this offering.

INSTRUCTION: Please check the box(es) corresponding to the exemptive provision applicable to this offering.

Rule 504 ☐   Rule 505 ☐   Rule 506 ☐   Section 4(6) ☐

INSTRUCTION: Circle "N" for a new filing or "A" for an amended filing.

ORIGINAL 1 $\frac{N}{A}$ COMBINED ORIGINAL AND FINAL 2 $\frac{N}{A}$ SIX-MONTH UPDATE 3 $\frac{N}{A}$ FINAL 4 $\frac{N}{A}$

INSTRUCTIONS: The issuer shall file with the Commission five copies of this notice at the following times: (a) no later than 15 days after the first sale of securities in an offering under Regulation D or Section 4(6); (b) every six months after the first sale of securities in an offering under Regulation D or Section 4(6), unless a final notice has been filed; and (c) no later than 30 days after the last sale of securities in an offering under Regulation D or Section 4(6), *except that if the offering is completed within the 15-day period described in "(a)" above, and if the notice is filed no later than the end of that period but after the completion of the offering, then only one notice need be filed*. If more than one notice for an offering is required to be filed, notices after the first notice need only report the issuer's name, information in response to Part C and any material changes from the facts previously reported in Parts A and B. This notice shall be deemed to be filed with the Commission for purposes of the rule as of the date on which the notice is received by the Commission, or if delivered to the Commission after the date on which it is due, as of the date on which it is mailed by means of United States registered or certified mail to the Office of Small Business Policy, Division of Corporation Finance, U.S. Securities and Exchange Commission, Washington, D.C. 20549.

A. Basic Identification of Issuer.

INSTRUCTION: State the address of the issuer's executive offices and, if different, the address at which the issuer's principal business operations are conducted or proposed to be conducted.

NAME			
ADDRESS OF EXECUTIVE OFFICES			
CITY		STATE	ZIP
AREA CODE	TELEPHONE NUMBER		
ADDRESS OF PRINCIPAL BUSINESS OPERATIONS			
CITY		STATE	ZIP
AREA CODE	TELEPHONE NUMBER		

INSTRUCTION: Please list the full name and address of the following persons: each promoter of the issuer involved in the offering of securities as to which sales pursuant to Regulation D or Section 4(6) are reported on this notice, the issuer's chief executive officer, and each of the issuer's affiliates. Indicate the status of each person named by placing an "X" in the applicable box(es) opposite such person's name. The term "promoter" includes . . .

(a)   Any person who, acting alone or in conjunction with one or more other persons, directly or indirectly takes the initiative in founding and organizing the business or enterprise of an issuer; or

(b)   Any person who, in connection with the founding or organizing of the business or enterprise of an issuer, directly or indirectly receives in consideration of services or property, or both services and property, 10 percent or more of any class of securities of the issuer or 10 percent or more of the proceeds from the sale of any class of securities. However, a person who receives such securities or proceeds either solely as brokerage commissions or solely in consideration of property shall not be deemed a promoter within the meaning of this paragraph if such person does not otherwise take part in founding and organizing the enterprise.

SEC 1972 (3-82)

FORM D	NOTICE OF SALES OF SECURITIES PURSUANT TO REGULATION D OR SECTION 4(6)	Page 2

			CEO	Aff	Pro

NAME

ADDRESS	CITY	STATE	ZIP

			CEO	Aff	Pro

NAME

ADDRESS	CITY	STATE	ZIP

1. Has the issuer filed any periodic reports pursuant to Section 13 or 15(d) of the Securities Exchange Act of 1934?   YES ☐   NO ☐

   If yes, please indicate the file number of the docket in which the periodic reports are filed. _____

2. Please indicate the issuer's IRS employer identification number. If an application for such number is pending, please enter "00-0000000."

3. Please briefly describe the issuer's business.

   _____

   _____

   _____

4. Please indicate the issuer's type of business organization.
   a. corporation   b. partnership   c. business trust   d. other, *please specify* _____

5. Please indicate the issuer's Standard Industrial Classification (SIC) at the 3 or 4 digit level. If the issuer has more than one SIC, please enter the issuer's primary SIC. If a 3 digit SIC is given, enter "X" in the left-most box.

6. In what year was the issuer incorporated or organized?

7. In what state is the issuer incorporated or organized? Please enter the standard two letter U.S. Postal Service abbreviation. Enter "CN" if the issuer is incorporated or organized in Canada; "FN" if the issuer is incorporated or organized in another foreign jurisdiction.

8. Has the issuer been assigned a CUSIP number for its securities?   YES ☐   NO ☐

   If yes, please specify the first six (6) digits. If no, please enter "000000."

9. Please check the appropriate box for each exchange or market, if any, where the issuer's securities are traded.
   American Stock Exchange . . . . a. ☐
   New York Stock Exchange . . . . b. ☐
   Other National Securities Exchanges . . . . c. ☐
   Over-the-Counter (including
      National Association of Securities Dealers Automated Quotations System) . . d. ☐
   Other   *Please Specify* . . . . e. ☐

SEC USE ONLY		

   _____

   _____

   None. . . . . f. ☐

| FORM D | NOTICE OF SALES OF SECURITIES PURSUANT TO REGULATION D OR SECTION 4(6) | Page 3 |

B. Statistical Information About the Issuer

INSTRUCTION: Please enter the letter for the appropriate response to each item in Part B in the box indicated. If the issuer's first fiscal year has not yet ended, furnish the requested information as of a date, or as to a period ending on a date, no more than 90 days prior to the first sale of securities in this offering.

1. What were the issuer's gross revenues for its most recently ended fiscal year?　□

   a. $500,000 or less　　b. $500,001 – $1,000,000　　c. $1,000,001 – $3,000,000
   d. $3,000,001 – $5,000,000　　e. $5,000,001 – $25,000,000　　f. $25,000,001 – $100,000,000
   g. Over $100,000,000

2. What were the issuer's total consolidated assets as of the end of its latest fiscal year?　□

   a. $500,000 or less　　b. $500,001 – $1,000,000　　c. $1,000,001 – $3,000,000
   d. $3,000,001 – $5,000,000　　e. $5,000,001 – $25,000,000　　f. $25,000,001 – $100,000,000
   g. Over $100,000,000

3. What was the issuer's net income, or income before partners' compensation, for its most recently ended fiscal year?　□

   a. None or net loss　　b. $1 – $50,000　　c. $50,001 – $250,000　　d. $250,001 – $1,000,000
   e. $1,000,001 – $5,000,000　　f. Over $5,000,000

4. What was the issuer's shareholders' or partners' equity at the end of its latest fiscal year?　□

   a. Negative　　b. $1 – $50,000　　c. $50,001 – $250,000　　d. $250,001 – $1,000,000
   e. $1,000,001 – $3,000,000　　f. $3,000,001 – $10,000,000　　g. Over $10,000,000

5. How many shareholders or partners did the issuer have at the end of its latest fiscal year?　□

   a. 0 – 4　　b. 5 – 9　　c. 10 – 24　　d. 25 – 99　　e. 100 – 299
   f. 300 – 499　　g. 500 or more

6. What percentage of shares outstanding were held by non-affiliated shareholders at the end of the issuer's latest fiscal year? 1/　□

   a. None　　b. Less than 5.0%　　c. 5.0% – 9.9%　　d. 10.0% – 24.9%
   e. 25.0% – 49.9%　　f. 50.0% – 74.9%　　g. 75.0% or more　　h. Not applicable

7. How many shares were outstanding at the end of the issuer's latest fiscal year?　□

   a. 500,000 or less　　b. 500,001 – 1,500,000　　c. 1,500,001 – 2,500,000
   d. 2,500,001 – 3,500,000　　e. 3,500,001 – 5,000,000　　f. Over 5,000,000　　g. Not applicable

8. How many full-time equivalent employees did the issuer have at the end of its latest fiscal year? 2/　□

   a. None　　b. 1 – 5　　c. 6 – 10　　d. 11 – 20　　e. 21 – 50　　f. 51 – 100
   g. 101 – 500　　h. 500 or more

1/　A non-affiliated person is defined to be anyone other than a person that directly or indirectly, through one or more intermediaries, controls or is controlled by the issuer or is under common control with such person.

2/　Full-time equivalent employees is defined to equal the sum of the number of full-time employees plus the number of part-time employees working 25 or more hours per typical work week.

FORM D	NOTICE OF SALES OF SECURITIES PURSUANT TO REGULATION D OR SECTION 4(6)	Page 4

C. Section 3(b) or 4(6) Sales Limit and Other Information About the Offering

INSTRUCTION: If a response to any item is "none" or "zero," please enter zero ("0") in the corresponding space.

1. Type and aggregate offering price of securities intended to be sold pursuant to Regulation D or Section 4(6) in this offering.

    a. Debt . . . . $ _____ .

    b. Equity . . . . $ _____ .

    c. Convertible . . . . $ _____ .

2. Number of accredited and non-accredited investors who have purchased securities in this offering in reliance on Rules 505 or 506 and aggregate dollar amounts of their purchases to date. For sales in reliance on Rule 504 or Section 4(6), please enter the number of persons who have purchased securities and aggregate dollar amounts of their purchases to date on the accredited investor lines.

	Number of Investors (A)	Aggregate Dollar Amount (B)
Accredited investors	_____	$ _____ .
Non-accredited investors	_____	_____ .
Total	_____	$ _____ .

3. If this offering is being made pursuant to Rule 504 or 505, report by exemption and type of security (i.e., debt, equity, convertible) the dollar amount of all Section 3(b) sales of securities (other than sales reported in Item C.2 above) occurring from twelve (12) months prior to the first sale of securities in this offering to date.

	Type (A)	Dollar Amount (B)
Rule 505	_____	$ _____ .
Regulation A	_____	_____
Rule 504	_____	_____
Total		$ _____ .

4. Please list the full name and address of each person who has been or will be paid or given directly or indirectly any commission or similar remuneration for solicitation of purchasers in connection with sales of securities in this offering pursuant to Regulation D or Section 4(6). If a person to be listed is an associated person of a broker or dealer registered with the Commission and/or with a state or states, then please also list the name of that broker or dealer. If more than five (5) persons to be listed are associated persons of a broker or dealer registered with the Commission and/or a state or states, then the issuer may list the name and address of only such broker or dealer. Please also list, using the standard two-letter Postal Service abbreviation the state or states in which each person, or if an associated broker or dealer is listed, each such broker or dealer, intends to or is offering securities in this offering; if all states, enter "all."

NAME				SEC USE ONLY
ADDRESS	CITY	STATE	ZIP	8-
NAME OF ASSOCIATED BROKER OR DEALER				
STATES				

NAME				SEC USE ONLY
ADDRESS	CITY	STATE	ZIP	8-
NAME OF ASSOCIATED BROKER OR DEALER				
STATES				

FORM D

NOTICE OF SALES OF SECURITIES
PURSUANT TO REGULATION D OR SECTION 4(6)

Page 5

5. a.   Aggregate offering price of securities, from C.1 above $ ☐ _____

    b.   Furnish a reasonably itemized statement of all expenses in connection with the issuance and distribution of the securities being offered in this offering. Please exclude any amounts relating solely to the organizational expenses of the issuer. Insofar as practicable, give amounts for the categories listed below. The information may be given as subject to future contingencies. If the expenditure in any category is not known, furnish an estimate and place an "X" in the box to the left of the amount given.

       a.   Blue Sky Fees and Expenses . . . . $ ☐ _____
       b.   Transfer Agents' Fees . . . .   ☐ _____
       c.   Printing and Engraving Costs . . . .   ☐ _____
       d.   Legal Fees . . . .   ☐ _____
       e.   Accounting Fees . . . .   ☐ _____
       f.   Engineering Fees . . . .   ☐ _____
       g.   Sales Commissions *(including Finders' Fees)* . . . .   ☐ _____
       h.   Other Expenses *(Identify)*

       _____   ☐ _____
       _____   ☐ _____

           Total $ ☐ _____

    c.   Enter the difference between the aggregate offering price in 5.a. and total costs in 5.b. This difference is the "adjusted gross proceeds to the issuer." $ ☐ _____

6.   Indicate below the amount of the adjusted gross proceeds to the issuer *(other than amounts specified in Item 5.b. above)* proposed to be used or used for each of the purposes listed below. If the amount to be used for any purpose is not known, furnish an estimate and place an "X" in the box to the left of the amount given.

		Payments to officers, directors and affiliates (A)	Payments to others (B)
a.	Salaries and fees	$ ☐ _____	$ ☐ _____
b.	Purchase of real estate	☐ _____	☐ _____
c.	Purchase, rental or leasing and installation of machinery and equipment	☐ _____	☐ _____
d.	Construction or leasing of plant building and facilities	☐ _____	☐ _____
e.	Development expense *(product development, research, patent costs, etc.)*	☐ _____	☐ _____
f.	Purchase of raw materials, inventories, supplies, etc.	☐ _____	☐ _____
g.	Selling, advertising, and other sales promotion	☐ _____	☐ _____
h.	Acquisition of other businesses *(including the value of securities involved in this offering which may be used in exchange for the assets or securities of another issuer pursuant to a merger)*	☐ _____	☐ _____
i.	Repayment of loans	☐ _____	☐ _____
	Other – *please specify*		
j.	_____	☐ _____	☐ _____
k.	_____	☐ _____	☐ _____
l.	_____	☐ _____	☐ _____
m.	_____	☐ _____	☐ _____
	Total	$ ☐ _____	$ ☐ _____

NOTICE OF SALES OF SECURITIES
PURSUANT TO REGULATION D OR SECTION 4(6)

Page 6

D. Undertaking by issuers filing pursuant to Rule 505.

The undersigned issuer hereby undertakes to furnish to the Securities and Exchange Commission, upon the written request of its staff, the information furnished by the issuer to any non-accredited person pursuant to paragraph (b)(2) of Rule 502.

ISSUER _____

SIGNATURE _____

NAME _____

TITLE _____

E. The issuer has duly caused this notice to be signed on its behalf by the undersigned duly authorized person.

DATE OF NOTICE:

_____

ISSUER _____

SIGNATURE _____

NAME _____

TITLE _____

INSTRUCTION: Print the name and title of the signing representative under his signature. One copy of every notice on Form D shall be manually signed. Any copies not manually signed shall bear typed or printed signatures.

─ATTENTION─

Intentional misstatements or omissions of fact constitute Federal Criminal Violations (See 18 U.S.C. 1001).

FORM D Continuation Sheet	NOTICE OF SALES OF SECURITIES PURSUANT TO REGULATION D OR SECTION 4(6)	Page 7
Item of Form (identify)	Answer	

| FORM D Continuation Sheet | NOTICE OF SALES OF SECURITIES PURSUANT TO REGULATION D OR SECTION 4(6) | Page 8 |

Item of Form
(identify)   Answer

9

Tender Offers and Defenses
Issuer Repurchases and
"Going Private" Proxy Contests

Takeover Bids. A takeover bid is an offer to buy securities of a corporation made directly to the shareholders of the corporation for the purpose of gaining control of the corporation. The offer may be made for cash or securities of the offeror, and it may be made with or without the approval of the management of the target company. Normally the target company is a publicly held company, since if the target company had absolute voting control concentrated in a few shareholders, the negotiations to acquire control would take place directly between the acquiring corporation and the controlling shareholders personally.

The takeover bid includes two fundamentally different types of offers. If the offer to buy the stock is made for cash, the takeover bid is called a tender offer. If the offer to buy the stock is made for securities, the takeover bid is called a registered exchange offer. A tender offer is made for cash; a registered exchange offer is made for securities.

A vocabulary has evolved that is found in not only technical, legal and financial publications but in general-circulation newspapers and periodicals, and news telecasts on national radio and television as well. Although not yet found in the dictionary, an excellent overview of the jargon has been compiled by a leading authority on securities regulation:

> "Beautiful maiden" or "sleeping beauty" (a ripe target); "casual pass" or "Teddy bear pat" (a notification to the target that a business combination is desired); "bear hug" (an ultimatum out of the blue, with or without a public announcement, in which a formal acquisition or merger proposal is made to target management with the hope of avoiding the necessity for a tender offer); "clamp" (an aggressive form of "bear hug" in which a firm

223

offer is made without significant preconditions); "reverse bear hug" (a target's willingness to negotiate a friendly acquisition but at a far higher price); "sandbag" (a target's agreeing to negotiate after a "bear hug" but with the intention of delaying a tender offer as long as possible); "blitz-krieg" or "Saturday night special" (an unnegotiated, surprise tender offer of short duration); "low ball" (a tender offer at a bargain price); "godfather offer" (one the directors can't afford to refuse); "front-end loaded" or "two-tier" deal (a partial cash offer followed by an offer of securities, valued at less than the cash consideration and sometimes issued by the company to survive a merger, for the rest); "trading stamp" (a security offered in an exchange offer); "toehold" or "creeping" acquisition (a gradual accumulation not involving a statutory "tender offer"); "white knight" or "Prince Charming" or "sweetheart" (a third company that the target persuades to merge with it or to make a competing offer that it hopes will lead to a combination more to its liking); "grey knight" (a competing tender offeror no more acceptable to target management than the original offeror); "black knight" (a third company that comes in to spoil an offer that the target favors); "black book" or "Pearl Harbor file" (a combination of defensive materials and procedures); "shark repellent" or "porcupine" provisions (defensive steps such as amendment of the target's articles in an attempt to ward off potential offers by going over to staggered boards or adopting super-majority voting requirements for mergers and the like); "iron maiden" (a resolute target management); "scorched earth" (no-holds-barred defense tactics); "stopper" or "show stopper" (an impediment, such as an antitrust defense, that effectively halts a tender offer); "golden parachute" (a special employment agreement with a target officer affording certain financial assurance in the event of a change in control).[1]

The Tender Offer. The tender offer has long been available as a means of acquiring stock, or control, of a corporation in which the acquiror is interested. Since the enactment of the Williams Act on July 29, 1968, the tender offer has been subject to regulation by the Securities and Exchange Commission, although it was free from such regulation prior to that time. The Securities Act of 1933 requires the registration of securities offered to the public; however, since the tender offer is an offer to buy for cash (as opposed to an exchange offer where the consideration used is securities), it is not subject to the registration requirements of the Securities Act of 1933. Interestingly, the Williams Act that governs tender offers does not define the term *tender offer* nor is the term defined by rules promulgated under the Act.

Although the Securities and Exchange Commission has steadfastly refused to define the term *tender offer* because of its apparent belief that to do so would give the term a rigid meaning which, in the Commission's opinion, would be contrary to congressional intent that the term remain flexible, it has expressed the view that the regulation of tender offers is not limited to the conventional type. Furthermore, in

---

[1]Louis Loss. *Fundamentals of Securities Regulation* (1983). Pgs. 569–570.

several court cases where the Securities and Exchange Commission has taken a position and filed briefs, the Commission has suggested the examination of eight factors to determine whether or not particular conduct constitutes a tender offer. The eight factors are:

1. Whether there is active and widespread solicitation of the issuer's public shareholders;
2. Whether there is an attempt being made to acquire a substantial percentage of the issuer's stock;
3. Whether a premium is offered over the market price;
4. Whether the terms of the offer are fixed rather than negotiable;
5. Whether the offer is contingent upon the acquisition of a minimum number of shares;
6. Whether the offer is for a limited period of time;
7. Whether the offerees are under pressure to sell their stock; and
8. Whether a public announcement is made concerning the purchasing program.

In the absence of a definition of "tender offer" in the Williams Act or the regulations thereunder, the task of defining the term has been left to the courts. In a leading case on the subject, *Kennecott Copper Corp.* v. *Curtis-Wright Corp.*, 449 F. Supp. 957 (1978), defendant Curtis-Wright purchased slightly less than 10 percent of Kennecott's outstanding shares. The purchases were made in the open market. The court rejected the plaintiffs argument that "off the floor" solicitation by brokers for Curtis-Wright securities to 50 Kennecott shareholders and a dozen institutional shareholders constituted a tender offer. The court's opinion in the *Kennecott* case acknowledged that the Williams Act does not define the term *tender offer* but found that the characteristics of a "conventional tender offer" as well settled. As recognized by the court in *Kennecott,* a conventional tender offer involves: (1) a premium above the market price, (2) a tendering of shares and (3) an obligation to purchase all or a specified number of shares conditioned upon a specified number of shares being tendered.

Subsequent to the decision in the *Kennecott* case, a court in *Brascan Ltd.* v. *Edper Equities Ltd.,* 477 F. Supp. 773 (1979) refused to apply the Williams Act to a situation in which the defendant had acquired approximately 25 percent of the plaintiff's outstanding shares over a two-day period through open market purchases on the American Stock Exchange and privately negotiated block trades. The court in *Brascan* considered the Securities and Exchange Commission's eight factors and went on to reject the applicability of the Williams Act to stock acquisitions other than through conventional tender offers.

Another leading case in which a court grappled with the term *tender offer* in the context of the Securities and Exchange Commission's eight factors was *Wellman* v. *Dickinson,* 475 F. Supp. 784 (1979). The only factor that the *Wellman* court found lacking was a public announcement concerning the purchase program. In view of the finding of a tender offer in the *Wellman* case and no such finding in either *Brascan* or *Kennecott,* total reliance upon the Commission's eight factors does not seem possible. More recently, both a Federal District Court and a Federal Court of Appeals rejected efforts by the Securities and Exchange Commission to invalidate the purchase by Carter Hawley Hale Stores of almost 18 million of its shares in an effort to thwart an unwanted takeover by The Limited, Inc. The purchases were made in brokerage transactions executed on the New York Stock Exchange. The Commission took the position that the purchase constituted an issuer tender offer which, in the absence of the filing of an appropriate schedule 14D-1, was unlawful. Notwithstanding the fact that Carter Hawley purchased in excess of 50 percent of its outstanding shares over a six-day period requiring shareholders to make what the Commission characterized as "precipitous decisions," the trial court found the conduct complained of met but two of the eight factors. The pressure that may have been felt by Carter Hawley's shareholders to take advantage of the Carter-Hawley's defensive tactic was not sufficient to warrant deviation from the eight-factor test.

Other cases in which the courts found that a tender offer had been made were *S-G Securities, Inc.* v. *Fuqua Investment Co.* (D. Mass. 1978) 466 F.S. 1114, where 28% of the stock was acquired by open market and privately negotiated purchases and *Hoover Company* v. *Fuqua Industries, Inc.* (N.D., Ohio, 1979) 1979 CCH Fed. Sec. L. Rep. § 96,882, where 41% was acquired from over 100 members of the Hoover family.

However, the Hanson Trust terminated a tender offer and promptly then purchased over 30% of the shares of SCM Corporation in open market and privately negotiated purchases. A challenge to this tactic was denied in *Hanson Trust PLC* v. *SCM Corporation* 744 F. 2d 47 (2 Cir., 1985) 17 SRLR 1705.

The "Creeping Tender Offer." A prospective tender offeror may take a position in an issuer's security through open market or substantial block purchases (even at a premium over market price) unencumbered by the Williams Act provided such prospective tender offeror does not own (or as a consequence of such market or block purchases become the owner of) 5 percent of a class of the issuer's outstanding shares. Obviously, this "gap" in the tender offer regulatory scheme can be used by the prospective offeror to gain an advantage before formally commencing its tender offer by gradually increasing its holdings in the target to just below the threshold figure of 5 percent ownership. Any person acquiring 5 percent of an issuer's outstanding securities (whether or not a tender offer is contemplated) must, within ten days of reaching the threshold percentage, file a Schedule 13D with the Securities and Exchange Commission and send a copy of same to the issuer whose shares have been acquired with copies to each exchange on which the issuer's securities are traded.

It should be noted that there is no prohibition against additional purchases of securities once the reporting threshold is reached. Therefore, during the ten-day period following a 5 percent acquisition the purchaser may continue its purchases without making the required disclosure. This area of possible exploitation has been addressed by a recommendation of a Securities and Exchange Commission Advisory Committee on Tender Offers that would prohibit continued accumulation once a purchaser obtains 5 percent of an issuer's securities until 48 hours following the filing of Schedule 13D with the Securities and Exchange Commission. Legislation has also been introduced to shorten the 10-day filing period, but not enacted.

Schedule 13D. The disclosure required by Schedule 13D includes:

1. Identification of the security to which the filing relates and the address of the principal executive office of the issuer of such security;

2. The name, place of organization, and principal place of business if the acquiror (the person filing Schedule 13D) is a corporation, partnership syndicate or other group and whether or not such acquiror has been convicted of any crime during the last five-year period preceding the filing and whether or not during such five-year period the acquiror has been a party to any civil proceeding involving federal or state securities laws. If the acquiror is an individual, in addition to the information relating to criminal convictions and civil securities law proceedings the 13D filed by an individual must disclose the individual's name, residence or business address, principal occupation, name and address of employment and the individual's citizenship;

3. The source of funds for the purchases, and if the securities were acquired other than by purchase, the method of acquisition must be described;

4. The purpose for which the securities were acquired, including plans which may result in:
   a. the acquisition of additional or the disposition of securities of the issuer;
   b. a merger, reorganization, liquidation, etc., of the issuer or its subsidiaries;
   c. a disposition of a subsidiary or a material portion of the issuer's assets;
   d. a change in the issuer's management;
   e. a material change in the capitalization or dividend policy of the issuer;
   f. any material change in the issuer's business or corporate structure;
   g. changes in the issuer's charter, bylaws, etc.; or
   h. any action that would result in the issuer's securities being delisted from a national exchange or quotation system on which it is traded or quoted or an action which would result in the issuer becoming a nonreporting company ("a going private" transaction).

5. The number of shares of the issuer's securities owned and the percentage of the issuer's outstanding securities these shares represent (based on the issuer's most recently available filing with the Securities and Exchange Commission), the date on which the person filing Schedule 13D acquired more than 5 percent of the issuer's securities and a description of any transactions during the 60-day period preceding the filing or since the filing of the most recent Schedule 13D (whichever is less) including the identity of the person effecting the transactions, the date of the transaction, the amount of securities and price per share and where and how the transaction was effected ("off the floor," negotiated block trades, etc).

6. A description of any contract arrangement, understanding or relationship among the persons whose acquisition triggered the filing of Schedule 13D including the transfer or voting of the subject securities, finder's fees, joint ventures, loan arrangements, guarantees of profits, division of profits or loss or the giving or withholding of proxies.

Pre-Williams Act Tender Offers. Prior to the enactment of the Williams Act, the tender offer was often conducted in the following manner:

1. The offeror made an offer to buy stock for cash to the shareholders of the target company either by newspaper advertisement, or, if the offeror had a stock list of the target company, by letter addressed to the individual shareholders of the target company.
2. The offer was limited to a fixed period of time, perhaps 30 days, although the offeror often retained the right to extend the fixed period.
3. The offer was for a fixed amount of cash, and generally included an agreement on the part of the offeror to pay all brokerage commissions.
4. If the offer was not to acquire all the stock of the target company, the offeror often reserved the right not to buy shares tendered after the full number of shares offered to be purchased had been tendered.
5. The offeror often reserved the right to withdraw the offer if any materially adverse change took place in the financial position of the target company, and the newspaper advertisement or letter to shareholders contained with it a letter of transmittal with additional terms of the agreement to be signed by the shareholder of the target company.

The Williams Act. The Williams Act, Sections 14(d) and 14(e) of the Securities Exchange Act of 1934, codified the procedure to be followed in making a tender offer by requiring the filing of certain information with the Securities and Exchange Commission *prior* to making a tender offer. Section 14(d) and all regulations promulgated thereunder (14D regulations) are applicable to offers that utilize the mails or other instrumentalities of interstate commerce if the prescribed ownership level is met and the securities sought are registered equity securities or equity securities of certain insurance or closed end investment companies. Section 14(e) and regulations with the prefix 14E are applicable to all tender offers. Therefore, a tender offer regulated by Section 14(d) is also subject to the regulatory parameters of Section 14(e).

It is noteworthy that tender offers require a *pre*-transaction filing (Schedule 14D-1) while significant open market and block purchases require a *post*-transaction filing (Schedule 13D). Under Section 14(d)(1) of the Securities Exchange Act of 1934, added by the Williams Act, it is unlawful for any person to make a tender offer for any class of security that may result in the acquisition of more than 5 percent of a class of registered securities unless such person has filed with the Securities and Exchange Commission in Washington, D.C., a statement containing information prescribed by the Commission (Schedule 14D-1). Securities and Exchange Commission Rule 14d-2 deems a tender offer to have commenced upon the announcement of a proposed offer that identifies the target and makes reference to the price or the number of shares sought. Given such an announcement, the required Schedule 14D-1 must be filed notwithstanding the fact that the actual offer will be made at a later time.

Although the enactment of the Williams Act was an attempt to address perceived abuses in the context of a hostile tender offer, a friendly tender offer must be conducted under the regulatory scheme of the Williams Act as well. However, as illustrated in the recent court decisions discussed above, not all accumulations of an issuer's securities are tender offers. See Appendix 9-1 for a form of announcement of a friendly tender offer.

Schedule 14D-1. In addition to much of the same information contained in Schedule 13D, Schedule 14D-1 requires financial information about the bidder or the entity controlling the bidder where such information is material to shareholders in deciding whether or not to accept the bidder's offer. Additional information, material to shareholders in deciding whether or not to tender his shares, concerning the possible effect of antitrust laws and any material pending litigation relating to the tender offer must also be disclosed. Schedule 14D-1 appears as Appendix 9-2.

PROCEDURAL SAFEGUARDS

Withdrawal of Tendered Shares. In addition to the mechanical requirements of filing the information required by Schedule 14D-1 and the form that the tender offer must take, the Williams Act provides certain substantive safeguards for the security holders of the target company. Section 14(d)(5) of the Securities Exchange Act of 1934, added by the Williams Act, provides that any security holder who tenders shares shall have the right to withdraw the shares at any time until the expiration of seven days from the date the tender offer is first published or given to security holders, and also after 60 days from the date of the original tender offer.

The statutory safeguards relating to withdrawal rights of tendered (deposited with the offeror) shares have been extended by the Securities and Exchange Commission. By regulation, the withdrawal rights of a tendering shareholder extend to the expiration of 15 business days from the commencement of the tender offer and to the expiration of ten business days following the date of a competing tender offer provided (1) the bidder (to whom the shares have been tendered) has received notice or has knowledge of the competing offer and (2) the tendered securities have not been accepted for payment (in the manner set forth in the bidder's tender offer) prior to commencement of the competing offer.

The time periods with respect to the extended withdrawal rights afforded tendering shareholders through the Commission's exercise of its regulatory powers are concurrent; that is, a competing bid that is commenced on business day 11 of the initial tender offer and pursuant to which initial offer the shareholder has tendered his shares, extends the withdrawal period of the initial offer through its twenty-first business day which would be the tenth business day of the competing tender offer. Subject to the imposition of any additional reasonable requirements that may be set by the bidder, notice of withdrawal will be made in a timely fashion if it is in writing and received by the bidder's depository within the applicable time period provided it specifies the name of the tendering shareholder, the amount of securities being withdrawn and the name of the registered owner (if different from that of the tendering shareholder).

Pro Rata Acceptance. Section 14(d)(6) of the Securities Exchange Act of

1934 provides that if the person making the tender offer seeks less than all of the outstanding equity securities of a class, and if a greater number of shares than those sought by or acceptable to the offeror are deposited within the first ten days after the offer has first been published, the offeror must take the shares deposited on a pro rata basis.

As in the case of the statutory withdrawal rights of Section 14(d)(5) of the Securities Exchange Act of 1934, the statutory proration period of the 1934 Act has been extended by Securities and Exchange Commission Rule 14(d)(8). Pursuant to the rule an offeror in an oversubscribed partial tender offer must accept tendered securities on a pro rata basis during the period the offer remains open.

Price Increases. Finally, Section 14(d)(7) of the 1934 Act provides that any increase in the offering price prior to the expiration of the tender offer must also be paid to those security holders of the target company who tendered their securities prior to the price increase.

Open Period. Originally, the Williams Act contained no requirement as to the length of time during which a tender offer must remain open. However, with the adoption of Regulation 14E the Securities and Exchange Commission fixed the minimum period for which a tender offer must remain open at 20 business days and for at least ten business days from notice of an increased offering price. Again, Regulation 14E—which is, generally speaking, an antifraud regulation—is applicable to all tender offers whereas Regulation 14D is applicable only to nonissuer tender offers for securities registered under Section 12 of the Securities Exchange Act of 1934 and to securities of certain closed-end investment companies and insurance companies that result in the offeror acquiring more than 5 percent of any class of the target's securities. Accordingly, if the tender offer is subject to Regulation 14D, then it is also subject to Regulation 14E. In addition to the federal securities laws governing the conduct of a tender offer, the New York Stock Exchange, pursuant to its rules has established criteria that must be met in connection with a tender offer for a security registered on that exchange.

The Securities and Exchange Commission has interpreted the expiration of the 20-day minimum offering period to mean 12 midnight eastern time on the twentieth business day. Therefore, if a bidder wishes to limit its offer to "the close of business" the offer must remain open until the day following the twentieth business day.

Announcement and Delivery of Documents. A bidder who announces an all cash tender offer (or one that offers securities exempt from the registration requirements of the Securities Act of 1933) is deemed to commence same on the latter of (1) the bidder's public announcement of its offer by means of press release, etc., provided the public announcement identifies the bidder and the target and discloses the amount of the securities that are sought by the offer as well as the price being offered or (2) within five business days of its public announcement if the filing and disclosure requirements of the tender offer have been complied with, in which case the cash tender offer is deemed to commence on the date the required disclosure is disseminated to security holders. The rule allows for a flexible definition of the "commencement" of the tender offer and affords a bidder an opportunity to rethink its position. If during the five-day period following its public announcement the bidder, for whatever reason, makes a subsequent public announcement that it has determined not to continue with the tender offer, the initial public announcement will not be deemed to have commenced a tender offer.

Rule 14(d)3 requires the bidder, *prior* to commencing its tender offer to (1) file ten copies of a Tender Offer Statement on Schedule 14D-1 with the Securities and Exchange Commission, (2) hand deliver a copy of the schedule to the target company at its principal office (and if there is a competing bidder who has filed a Schedule 14D-1, to the competing bidder as well) and (3) give telephonic notice to each national securities exchange on which the target's securities are traded and to NASD if the target's securities are quoted in the NASDAQ system.

Certain Disclosures. Rule 14(d)6 sets forth the various disclosure and dissemination requirements that must be complied with in a tender offer. As one would expect, the information that is required to be disclosed includes the identities of the bidder and the target, the amount of securities sought and the type and amount of consideration offered, the expiration date of the offer as well as information concerning the possible extension of the offer, the dates applicable to the exercise of withdrawal rights by tendering shareholders, and an explanation of the operation of proration if the bidder has not obligated itself to accept all tendered shares.

Equal Treatment of Securityholders. Rule 14d-10 provides that no bidder shall make a tender offer unless: (1) the tender offer is open to all securityholders of the class of securities subject to the tender offer and (2) the consideration paid to any securityholder pursuant to the tender offer is the highest consideration paid to any other securityholder during such tender offer. The Rule contains certain exceptions, including a right to exclude securityholders in a state where the bidder cannot obtain clearance by administrative or judicial action to make the tender offer.

Tender Offer—Tax Consequences. A cash tender offer may affect adversely the possibility of obtaining "tax-free" treatment for a subsequent reorganization involving the offeror and the target corporation. If the purchase of the securities of the target company for cash and the subsequent attempt to combine the offeror and the target company are treated as parts of the integrated plan, the tax-free nature of the subsequent reorganization may be destroyed because of the prior cash payment to the shareholders of the target company. In a subsequent statutory merger, the requisite continuity of interest may not be present because of the previous buy out of certain of the target company's shareholders. A subsequent attempt to acquire the remaining outstanding shares of the target company in exchange for the offeror's stock, a "stock-for-stock" tax-free reorganization, or an attempt to acquire substantially all of the assets of the target company in exchange for the stock of the offeror, an "assets-for-stock" tax-free reorganization, may be taxable as not meeting the statutory requirement that the stock or the assets of the target company be acquired for "solely voting stock."

Under some circumstances, it should be noted, the offeror may not be deterred from making the cash tender offer merely because a subsequent reorganization would not qualify as tax-free. When the offeror pays more for the stock that is tendered than the tax basis of the assets of the target company, as is often the case, a subsequent taxable rather than "tax-free" reorganization may be to the offeror's advantage. Upon the consummation of the taxable reorganization, the offeror may be in a position to write up the underlying assets for tax purposes and obtain substantial tax benefits in the form of increased depreciation or amortization deductions from such a write-up. These matters are dealt with in greater detail in Chapter 11, which deals with the "tax-free" aspects of acquisitions and mergers.

Rule 10b-5. Prior to the enactment of the Williams Act, attacks upon cash tender offers under Rule 10b-5 (described in Chapter 6) of the General Rules and Regulations under the Securities Exchange Act of 1934, were generally unsuccessful. To cause the offeror's conduct to be unlawful, the rule required that the conduct "would operate as a fraud or deceit upon any person, in connection with the purchase or sale of any security." Since the plaintiff, who was attacking the tender offer, would not make a purchase or sale of a security, the plaintiff normally had no standing under Rule 10b-5. Section 14(e) of the Securities Exchange Act of 1934, added by the Williams Act, has eliminated this impediment to a nontendering shareholder invoking his rights under Rule 10b-5. Under Section 14(e), the prohibited conduct is made unlawful if engaged in by any person making a tender offer, regardless of whether a purchase or sale of a security takes place. The United States Supreme Court has refused to apply Rule 10b-5 in an attack by minority shareholders against the adequacy of the cash payment they received in a cash-out merger.

Rule 14e-3 makes it illegal for *anyone* to engage in the trading of the securities of an issuer with respect to which a tender offer has commenced (or substantial steps toward such commencement have been taken) if such person possesses material nonpublic information about the tender offer. This trading bar remains in effect until after the information has been disclosed to the public. The Rule also makes it illegal for officers, directors, employees or advisors of either the bidder or the target or persons acting on their behalf to disclose nonpublic information where it is foreseeable that such disclosure will result in a violation of Rule 14e-3. Of course, good faith disclosures that are made to persons connected with the planning, financing, preparation, and so on, of the tender offer are beyond the reach of the rule.

In addition, prior to the Williams Act the acquiring company was not an insider, and therefore was under no obligation to make disclosure of pertinent facts in connection with the tender offer. Since the Williams Act, of course, the acquiring corporation must file Schedule 14D-1, and has the obligation to make fair and truthful disclosures of the information required in the schedule. The requirement that the acquiring company make known its plans for future major changes in the business where control is being acquired, may present nontendering shareholders with opportunities to bring successful lawsuits, if the plans are not carried out in the future as set forth in Schedule 14D-1.

Open Market Purchases. Offerors frequently make purchases of securities of the target company in the open market before a tender offer is commenced. Such open market purchases are not disclosed to the public in Schedule 13D and in the Schedule 14D-1 filed when the tender offer begins. However, open market purchases must cease during the tender offer. In Release No. 34—8712, October 8, 1969, the Securities and Exchange Commission adopted Rule 10b-13 that prohibits any person who makes a tender offer from purchasing the same securities in the open market during the period that tendered securities may be accepted or rejected under the offer. After tender offer is terminated, open market purchase may resume. Hanson Trust PLC v. SCM Corporation 774 F. 2d 47 (2 Cir. 1985).

Section 16(b). Often it has appeared that the initial offeror making a cash tender offer could not lose. If, after having acquired some of the stock of the target company as a result of the tender offer, the offeror is outbid by a third party's tender offer, the initial offeror will have a built-in profit in the stock of the target company, acquired prior to the defeat of its tender offer. Should the initial offeror be in a position to sell securities obtained in a tender offer, at a profit, the offeror should consider the effect of Section 16(b) of the Securities Exchange Act of 1934 before realizing the profit. This section provides that the profits "from any purchase and sale, or any sale and purchase, of any equity security ... within any period of less than six months," by a 10 percent shareholder inure to and are recoverable by the issuer. Therefore, if an offeror acquires more than 10 percent of the stock of a target company but is outbid by a second offeror, any profit realized by the first offeror from a sale within six months of the acquisition of equity securities obtained in the tender offer, would be recoverable by the issuer. The first offeror should, therefore, avoid such a resale within the six-month period. However, if the successful second offeror brings about a statutory merger between the issuer and the second offeror within the six-month period, it may be beyond the control of the unsuccessful first offeror to avoid a sale within the six-month period.

Because of Section 16 (b) and the antitrust notification and reporting requirements described in Chapter 5, a company accumulating shares will often stop at 9.9% and buy no more shares until it is ready to make a tender offer for control. However, if a company accumulates shares in excess of 10% and is defeated by a "White Knight" or management buyout, it can sell voluntarily enough shares to reduce its holding to less than 10%. While these sales will result in Section 16 (b) liability, a subsequent and separate sale of the remaining 9.9% should not be subject to such liability.

State Statutory Regulation of Tender Offers. Many states have enacted tender offer legislation. Generally these state laws appear to be aimed at discouraging "outsiders" from displacing local corporate control and offer managements a haven within which to operate if they choose to locate or organize in states that have enacted such statutes, commonly referred to as "anti-takeover" statutes.

One such statute was the Illinois Business Take-Over Act. Under the Illinois act, any takeover attempt for an issuer that (1) had 10 percent of any class of stock owned by Illinois residents or (2) met any two of the following conditions: (a) had its principal office in Illinois, (b) was incorporated in Illinois or (c) had 10 percent of its stated capital and paid in surplus located in illinois, had to be registered with the Illinois Secretary of State. An offer became registered 20 days after the filing of a registration statement with the Illinois Secretary of State unless the Secretary called a hearing. If the Secretary of State determined it necessary to protect the target's shareholders, he was empowered to call a hearing during the 20-day waiting period to determine the fairness of the offer and he was statutorily obligated to conduct such a hearing if requested to do so by a majority of the target's outside directors or by Illinois shareholders owning 10 percent of the target's securities. Furthermore, if after holding a hearing the Secretary of State found that the offer "fails to provide full and fair disclosure to offerees of all material information concerning the takeover offer or that the takeover offer is inequitable or would tend to work a fraud or deceit upon the offerees" the Secretary had to deny registration to the offer.

The United States Supreme Court struck down the Illinois Business Take-Over Act in the case of *Edgar* v. *Mite Corporation,* 102 S. Ct. 2629 (1982) finding the statute violated the Commerce Clause of the United States Constitution and finding that it unduly burdened interstate commerce. After the decision in *Edgar,* the federal courts repeatedly enjoined enforcement of state antitakeover laws for several years.

In 1987, another split (6 to 3) decision by the U.S. Supreme Court gave new life to state antitakeover laws which are carefully drafted to remain within constitutional boundaries and free of conflict with the Williams Act. In *CTS Corporation v. Dynamics Corporation of America* (1987) 55 LW 4478, CCH Fed. Sec. L. Rep. § 83,213, the Supreme Court upheld the Control Share Acquisitions Chapter (the "Indiana Act") of the Indiana Business Corporation Law. The Indiana Act applies only to a corporation incorporated in Indiana that has 100 or more shareholders; its principal place of business, principal office or substantial assets within Indiana and either (A) more than 10% of shareholders resident in Indiana, (B) more than 10% of its shares owned by Indiana residents or (C) 10,000 shareholders resident in Indiana. If an entity acquires shares that, but for the operation of the Indiana Act, would bring its voting power to or above any of three thresholds—20%, 33⅓% or 50%—the entity gains voting rights for its shares only to the extent that a majority of the disinterested shareholders of the corporation approve a resolution granting such rights. The acquiring entity can file an acquiring person statement and request that a shareholders meeting be held at its expense within 50 days. If the acquiring entity does not file the statement or the shareholders do not restore its voting rights, the corporation can, but is not required, to redeem the control shares at fair value. The Supreme Court ruled that the Indiana Act is neither unconstitutional nor preempted by the Williams Act because, unlike the Illinois Act, it places investors on equal footing with takeover bidders and does not give management an advantage in communicating with shareholders, impose an indefinite delay on tender, or allow the state government to interpose its views of fairness between willing buyers and sellers.

While the Indiana Act does not prevent tender offers, it creates an important delay factor and also weakens the threat of a proxy contest which is an alternative weapon available to shareholders seeking to force management to realize shareholder values. As a result, management groups urged legislatures across the nation to adopt laws regulating takeovers. Most states now have some form of law which restricts tender offers and other steps used to achieve takeovers. These laws carefully avoid conflict with the Williams Act, but each is designed to provide advantages to incumbent management in contested takeovers.

Business Combination Laws. For example, Section 203 of the Delaware General Corporation Law, adopted in 1988, prohibits a bidder acquiring over 15% of the stock of a Delaware corporation to engage in a business combination (i.e., merge) with the corporation for three years unless the bidder acquires 85% of its outstanding shares in the transaction by which it exceeds 15%. To preserve an appearance of neutrality, Section 203 provides that management shares are not counted in the 85% calculation. However, shares held by an ESOP are counted if the participating employees can direct that their shares be tendered confidentially. In 1989, Polaroid Corporation used Section 203, an ESOP and sales of shares to a friendly institutional investor to defeat a tender offer.

In New York, Section 912 of the Business Corporation Law prohibits a bidder who requires 20% or more of a New york company from engaging in a merger or other business combination with the company for five years thereafter unless its board of directors approved the business combination before the 20% acquisition limit was crossed.

In Wisconsin, the takeover law prohibits a bidder who acquires 10% or more of the stock of a Wisconsin corporation from merging, dissolving or selling any assets of the corporation without approval of the pre-existing board. The law does not limit the number or percentage of shares which can be acquired. Universal Foods successfully used the Wisconsin law to defend a takeover attempt by Amanda Acquisition.

Supporters of state takeover statutes emphasize their objective to block leveraged takeovers based on "breakup" values of business operations which can be sold to reduce acquisition debt. However, the prohibition of a merger also denies access to the regular cash flow of the acquired corporation. Few businesses would be bought even in friendly transactions if the buyer could not have access to the cash flow of the acquired business.

Other Laws. The laws adopted in Delaware, New York and Wisconsin are commonly called "business combination" statutes. They have been adopted in several states.

Over 20 states have adopted another type of device to frustrate, but not entirely prohibit, takeovers by tender offers and also by proxy contests. These laws provide that any shareholder who acquires more than a specified percentage (i.e., 30%) of shares without the approval of the incumbent board of directors cannot vote the share until a shareholders meeting is held and the disinterested shareholders vote on the question whether the so-called "control shares" will be entitled to vote.

Approximately 20 states have adopted so-called "fair price" statutes. These statutes mandate that a bidder pay a price in a second step merger at least equal to the highest price paid during the first step acquisition of control, unless a lower price is approved by the board and a high percentage of the shareholders.

Some states have extended dissenters' appraisal rights to entitle shareholders to demand payment in cash of the fair market value of their shares from any person who acquires a specified percentage (20–30%) of the outstanding shares.

Other state takeover laws expressly permit (or require) directors responding to a takeover bid to consider other constituencies than the shareholders to whom they owe fiduciary obligations. The primary constituencies are employees and bondholders who purchased bonds not containing the familiar restrictions against incurring additional debt. These laws are controversial because they shift value from shareholders, who have no cohesive representation in most corporations, to groups which have bargaining power but sometimes choose to bargain for benefits other than those they belatedly want when a change of management occurs.

REGISTERED EXCHANGE OFFER

A registered exchange offer differs from a tender offer in that the consideration offered for the stock of the target corporation consists of securities of the offeror rather than cash. The offer to buy for securities is subject to different regulatory provisions than the cash offer, resulting in substantial differences in the time factors involved and in the mechanics for making the offer. Generally speaking, the registered exchange offer is a more cumbersome vehicle than the cash tender offer, and certainly, if the element of surprise or speed is considered important to success, should be employed only where overriding considerations dictate its use. For example, it may not be possible for the offeror to raise sufficient cash to make a cash tender offer, and under such circumstances a registered exchange offer may be required.

Registration Statement. A registered exchange offer, by definition, involves an offering of securities to the public. As such, prior to making the offering, a registration statement must be in effect with regard to the securities under the Securities Act of 1933. The preparation and filing of the registration statement, and the lapse of time until the registration statements is cleared by the Securities and Exchange Commission eliminate the surprise element, which an offeror could have achieved in a tender offer. On July 8, 1983, the Advisory Committee on Tender Offers established by the Securities and Exchange Commission recommended that the registered exchange offer should be placed on equal footing with the cash tender offer by permitting an exchange offer to commence upon the filing of a registration statement. Nevertheless, prior to the announcement of the registered exchange offer, the offeror's problem generally remains the maintenance of initial secrecy. The offeror will wish to achieve as much surprise as possible, in order to allow management of the target company as little time as possible to take defensive action. The difficulty in maintaining initial secrecy in a registered exchange offer, prior to the actual announcement of the offer, arises from the inescapable circumstance that the offeror must normally deal with many persons outside its own organization. Among such persons are investment bankers, brokers, banks, the SEC staff, lawyers and accountants and public relations and proxy soliciting firms.

Open Market Stock Purchases. In addition, at the outset, the management of the offeror must determine whether or not it wishes to acquire stock of the target company in the open market, and if so, how many shares. A prior acquisition of stock, of course, gives an offeror a head start, and may provide an ultimate profit in the acquired stock if the offer fails due to a competing bid by a third party or defensive action take taken by management. On the other hand, the prior acquisition of securities of the target company may lead to information leaks, may cause an increase in the cost of the offer, and may alert a watchful management of a target company that a takeover bid may be forthcoming.

Rule 135 Statement. Under Rule 135 of the General Rules and Regulations under the Securities Act of 1933, a statement may be made in the form of a notice of the prospective registered exchange offer to security holders of the target company. The notice may contain only the information outlined in Rule 135. Rule 135 provides in part as follows:

> Reg. § 230.135 (a) For the purpose only of Section 5 of the Act, a notice given by an issuer that it proposes to make a public offering of securities to be registered under the Act shall not be deemed to offer any securities for sale if such notice states that the offering will be made only by means of a prospectus and contains not more than the following additional information:
>
> (1) The name of the issuer;
> (2) The title, amount and basic terms of the securities proposed to be offered, the amount of the offering, if any, to be made by selling security holders, the anticipated time of the offering and a brief statement of the manner and purpose of the offering without naming the underwriters;
>
> * * *
>
> (4) In the case of an offering of securities in exchange for other securities of the issuer or of another issuer, the name of the issuer and the title of the securities to be surrendered in exchange for the securities to be offered, the basis upon which the exchange may be made, or any of the foregoing;
>
> * * *
>
> (6) Any statement or legend required by State law or administrative authority.
> (b) Any notice contemplated by this rule may take the form of a news release or a written communication directed to security holders or employees, as the case may be, or other published statement.

If a preliminary announcement is made containing the above information, it should be amended to include any material changes which may occur in the proposed offer during the pre-offering period.

Target Company Information. In addition to the normal problems encountered in preparation of a registration statement, namely the accurate presentation of information concerning the history, business and finances of the offering company, the offeror is required to include in the registration statement information concerning the history, business and financial information of the target company. A request for such information from the target company may result in a refusal, or, on the other hand, the submission of so much information to the offeror, that delay could be encountered in preparing the registration statement. One of the defensive measures that may be taken by a target company in connection with a registered exchange offer, is to deluge the offeror with information, making the preparation of the registration statement a difficult and time-consuming task. On the other hand, where an offeror is unable to obtain information from the target company, the Securities and Exchange Commission permits the use of such available information as the offeror is able to obtain. Such information may include prior years' annual reports and registration statements of the target company, as well as proxy statement and various periodic forms under the Securities Exchange Act of 1934 such as Forms 10-Q, 8-K, 9-K and 10-K.

Percentages of Ownership. Practical considerations, such as ownership of shares by unfriendly shareholders, may limit the percentage of the target company securities the offeror may be able to acquire. While on the other hand, corporate law, tax rules or accounting rules may require acquisition of greater percentages of the stock to attain desired legal, tax or accounting goals. From the viewpoint of corporate law, in many states to effect a statutory merger of two corporations, the merger agreement must be approved by a vote of at least two-thirds of the shareholders of each of the corporations. Therefore, under certain circumstances where the offeror plans a subsequent merger of the target company, the offeror may determine to seek to obtain at least 66⅔ percent of the target company's stock. As discussed in greater detail in Chapter 11, tax rules provide that a stock-for-stock acquisition does not qualify as a "tax-free" reorganization, unless the acquiring company obtains at least 80 percent of the voting power and 80 percent of all other classes of stock of the target company. From an accounting point of view, to report the earnings of the two corporations on a consolidated basis, normally one corporation must own a specified percentage of the voting equity of the other. These factors may come into play in determining the number of shares of the target company which the offeror offers to purchase in connection with the registered exchange offer.

Advantage of Registered Exchange Offer. A basic advantage of the registered exchange offer is that an offeror, with limited cash resources may attempt a takeover bid with hope of success, since such exchange offers have been successful where the offeror was many times smaller than the target company and had minimum resources in comparison to the target company.

Disadvantages of Registered Exchange Offers. However, registered exchange offers involve disadvantages not present in cash tender offers. As mentioned above, a registration statement must be filed with the Securities and Exchange Commission with respect to the offeror's securities, since the exchange offer constitutes an "offer to sell" within the meaning of the Securities Act of 1933. At the present time, the preparation of the registration statement and its clearance through the Securities and Exchange Commission causes delay before an exchange offer becomes effective. This delay and the intricacy and detail of the information required to be included in a registration statement make the registered exchange offer vulnerable to attack by court action on the part of the target company.

ISSUER TENDER OFFERS, STOCK REPURCHASES AND "GOING PRIVATE" TRANSACTIONS

Issuer Tender Offers. Tender offers by an issuer to the holders of its own equity securities require the filing with the SEC of a Schedule 13E-4 Issuer Tender

Offer Statement. The information required is similar to that required by Schedule 14D-1, except for items irrelevant to an offer by an issuer such as identity and background and applicability of the antitrust laws. The tender must be made in compliance with Rule 13E-4 which prescribes time periods withdrawal rights, provisions and other rules similar to those required of hostile bidders by Rule 14(d).

Issuer Stock Repurchases. Issuers can repurchase their own shares without making a tender offer if they plan and make the purchases carefully. *Vaughan v. Teledyne, Inc.,* 628 F. 2d 1214 (98 Cir. 1980); *SEC v. Carter Hawley Hale Stores Inc.,* 760 F. 2nd 945 (9 Cir. 1985); *Hanson Trust PLC v. SCM Corporation,* 774 F. 2d 47 (2 Cir. 1985).

In 1982, the SEC adopted a "safe harbor" Rule 10b-18 providing guidelines for issuer repurchases after discontinuing efforts to adopt a more ambitious mandatory Rule 13e-2 for several years. On its face, Rule 10b-18 is procedural. For example, it prescribes timing, price and volume conditions. The issuer may make purchases from or through not more than one broker/dealer on any one day. Exceptions are made for employee and shareholder plans meeting specified requirements. Nevertheless, Rule 13b-3 affords important protections for shareholders.

"Going Private." In 1979, the SEC adopted Rule 13e-3 governing "going private" transactions by issuers and persons affiliated with them. Rule 13b-3 represents a remarkable effort to use disclosure techniques to deal with a variety of transactions in which the interests of management or other controlling persons are or may be wholly or partially in conflict with those of public shareholders. Rule 13e-3 applies to (A) repurchases by issuers and affiliates, (B) tender offers by issuers and affiliates and (C) proxy solicitations by issuers and affiliates for mergers, sales of substantially all assets and recapitalizations if the effect is likely or for the purpose of causing any class of equity securities to be deregistered or delisted. Rule 13e-3 requires filing with the SEC and dissemination of a Schedule 13E-3 Transaction Statement. Schedule 13E-3 requires a variety of information, but the heart of the disclosure is found in *Item 8—Fairness of the Transaction* and *Item 9—Reports, Opinions, Appraisals and Certain Negotiations.*

Under Item 8, the issuer or affiliate (often a management group) filing a Schedule 13E-3 Issuer Transaction Statement must (1) state whether they reasonably believe that the transaction is fair or unfair to unaffiliated shareholders, (2) discuss in reasonable detail the material factors in which the belief is based and the weight assigned to each factor, (3) state whether the transaction is structured so that approach of at least a majority of the unaffiliated shareholders is required, (4) state whether a majority of the issuer's nonemployee directors has retained an unaffiliated representative to act solely in behalf of unaffiliated security holders in negotiating the transaction and/or preparing a report in its fairness, (5) state whether the transaction was approved by a majority of the issuer's nonemployee directors and (6) state and describe any offers made by any unaffiliated person during the preceding 18 months for a merger, an acquisition of all or a substantial part of the issuer's assets or an acquisition of securities which would enable the holder to exercise control.

Under Item 9, the issuer or affiliate must describe any report, opinion or appraisal (including any "fairness opinion") from an outside party related to the transaction. It must also describe the outside party including identity, qualifications, method of selection and relationships to the issuer and its affiliates. If the report, opinion or appraisal relates to the fairness of the consideration for the transaction, it must state who determined the consideration and whether the outside party recommended the consideration to be paid. Finally, a summary of the report, opinion or appraisal must be furnished together with a statement of its availability for inspection and copying by shareholder or their representatives. Such information must also be provided for negotiations conducted or reports arranged by independent nonemployee directors.

The discussion of fairness must include analysis and conclusory statements are not considered sufficient disclosure. The instructions recognize that the factors important to fairness and the weight to be given to them will vary. Item 8 contains a list of factors normally considered in determining fairness of the price offered to unaffiliated shareholders: (i) current market prices, (ii) historical market prices, (iii) net book value, (iv) going concern value, (v) liquidation value, (vi) the price paid for recent purchases of the issuer's securities, (vii) any report, opinion or appraisal described in Item 9 and (viii) firm offers made by unaffiliated persons within the preceding 18 months.

In effect, the Section 13E-3 Issuer Transaction Statement serves as a "roadmap" showing how management and/or controlling persons of a public corporation are performing their fiduciary obligations to public shareholders in "going private" transactions. Rule 13e-3 does not, of course, require that independent directors evaluate or negotiate the transaction or that they determine the acquisition price based on a sound and fully supported "fairness opinion" from an independent firm with expert qualifications in financial analysis. The Rule does not require that offers from unwelcome bidders be evaluated seriously. However, if management does not take these steps, the required disclosures may expose them to lawsuits under state law for failure to meet the "business judgment" or "entire fairness" standards described in Chapter 4 and later in this chapter.

Indeed, lawsuits are routinely filed during "going private" transactions, sometimes within a few days (or hours) after public information is disseminated. The complaints usually allege breach of fiduciary duties under the corporation law. They also allege misleading statements and failures to provide adequate disclosure in materials filed with the SEC. Thus, any failure to disclose and describe all steps taken and omitted in the planning and negotiation of a management leveraged buyout will risk liability under the Securities Exchange Act of 1934. Some of these lawsuits have been highly successful. *Edelman v. Fruehauf Corporation,* 798 F. 2d 882 (6 Cir. 1986). Lawsuits challenging the right of directors to rely on fairness opinions and other financial advice rendered by experts who lacked independence or whose methods were subject to criticism have also been wholly or partially successful. *Edelman v. Fruehauf,* supra; *Weinberger v. UOP, Inc.,* 426 A. 2d 1333 (Del. Ch. 1981); *Mills Acquisition Co. v. McMillan Inc.,* CCH Fed. Sec. L. Rep. § 94,401 (Del. 1989); *Grand Metropolitan Public Limited Company v. The Pillsbury Co.,* 588 A. 2d 1049 (1988).

A strict standard was applied to a fairness opinion in *Hershkowitz v. Nutri-*

System, Inc., 857 Fed. 2d 179 (3 Circ. 1988). In that case, dissenting shareholders challenged a fairness opinion used by independent directors to evaluate a $7.16 per share price paid in a management leveraged buyout of Nutri-System, Inc. Among the issues raised was the use of the existing 46% federal income tax rate in preparing a discounted cash flow valuation which became the primary basis for the opinion. An expert witness for the shareholders testified that it was generally recognized by knowledgeable people in the field of financial analysis in July 1976 that tax reform legislation reducing the rate to between 33% and 36% was virtually certain to become law. He also testified that use of the lower rate would have resulted in a range of values from $7.58 to $10.35. A majority of the Court of Appeals ruled that this was a valid issue and the shareholders were entitled to a jury trial on it. One judge dissented stating that use of the 46% rate was reasonable because the tax reform law had not been passed by Congress or signed by the President. Further, the cash flow projections used in preparing the fairness opinion extended for five years and it was widely publicized that the tax reform would be "revenue neutral." Regardless of the opposing points of view, the greatest significance of the *Hershowitz* decision is the growing scrutiny of the methods used by management in dealing with minority shareholders.

Short Form Mergers. The corporation laws of many states contain a provision that a shareholder who acquires 90% or 95% of the outstanding stock of a corporation can cause it to be merged into another corporation without the customary vote of shareholders. The merger is accomplished simply by filing a certificate with the secretary of state or corporation commission. Subject to appraisal rights, the shares held by the minority shareholders are cancelled without any need to solicit proxies or hold a meeting. An attempt to impose liability under Rule 10b-5 failed in *Santa Fe Industries, Inc. v. Green,* 430 U.S. 462 (1977).

While plaintiff attorneys would prefer the leverage of a broader range of remedies, modern valuation methods permitted in statutory appraisal proceedings under the Delaware General Corporation Law provide a meaningful remedy. *Weinberger v. UOP, Inc.,* 457 A 2d 702 (1983). Unfortunately, the courts in some states continue to use outmoded valuation methods. See "Modern Business Valuation Methods," *The Practical Lawyer,* Shea, 1988.

PREPARING FOR TAKEOVER BIDS

Theoretically, every publicly held company may be a prospective target for a takeover bid.

Price of Stock. Among elements which may indicate that a corporation is a candidate for a takeover bid is a decline in the price of the corporation's stock. Where such a decline in the price of stock results in a low price earnings multiple or in a price near or below book value of a corporation's assets, management should become more alert to the possibility that the corporation may become a target for a takeover bid. A continued decline in profits usually couples with it a decline in the price of the corporation's stock. If the market value of the stock has decreased over a period of time, or if the price of the stock has not risen in an extended period of general market buoyancy, a prospective offeror may conclude that stockholder unrest will make it likely that a takeover bid will succeed.

Nature of Assets. If the assets of a corporation consist to a large degree of liquid assets—i.e., that the cash, marketable securities and receivables are high in relationship to the total assets employed in the business, such a circumstance may increase the possibility that a third party may attempt a takeover bid for the corporation. On the other hand, a corporation may have hidden values in its assets that may appeal to a possible takeover bidder. Most often such values may be reflected in properties similar to real estate that have been held for a long period of time, and are largely depreciated on the books, or were bought at earlier bargain prices. A prospective takeover bidder, if successful, may plan to realize the value on such properties by liquidating them and utilizing the cash in other areas of the bidder's business.

Substantive Business Steps. While there are numerous financial and legal steps that can be taken to reduce the likelihood of a successful tender offer, the most important and effective protection is skillful business management. Managements must invest in the hope of capital appreciation or dividends, and usually both. Except for traders and arbitrageurs, stockholders are notably patient, so long as management performs and communicates reasonably well. Thus, before turning to financial and legal stratagems, management can take some or all of the following steps:

- Keep cash fully invested in worthwhile business projects, so that cash does not attract bidders.
- Use borrowing power effectively, so that corporate borrowing power cannot be used to finance a tender offer.
- Use assets effectively in the business, so that they cannot easily be sold to finance a tender offer.
- Upgrade facilities and equipment, so that older undervalued assets do not dominate the balance sheet.
- Direct the business into fields using "hands on" management and employee skills. Avoid businesses that can be operated by passive management, because these businesses can be managed as well and sometimes better by outsiders.
- Sponsor research and development for long-term growth and communicate to shareholders the objectives and potential values of the research programs. Many managements adopt very conservative policies in shareholder communications because it seems to be an easy way to comply with SEC requirements. Only when threatened with a tender offer, do they begin to inform shareholders of values perceived by the bidder, but not by shareholders. This belated disclosure often has too little credibility and comes too late.
- Keep management compensation in line with companies of similar size and achievements in the industry in which the business competes and in industry generally.
- Pay dividends, including special dividends, when cash accumulates. If dividends are reduced or cannot be increased, treat management compensation in a consistent manner.

• Structure and restructure to realize shareholder values by such means as divestitures of unused or unprofitable assets and businesses to companies who can use and manage them successfully. Use debt within cash flow limits to provide leverage.

THE TARGET'S INITIAL RESPONSES

Having received the blood-curdling hand-delivered notice from the bidder as required by Rule 14(d)-3, the target's management is faced with the task of deciding whether to embrace the offer, reject it or remain neutral. The target's board of directors must put aside their own future (which may include the prospect of unemployment if the tender offer were to be successful) because they owe a fiduciary duty to shareholders. This fiduciary duty requires that the directors apply sound business judgment and make a good faith effort to assess the soundness of the offer. If the target's management were to disregard their fiduciary duty, they would subject themselves to shareholders' liability the likelihood of which generally increases proportionately with the size of any premium over the market price that the bidder may be offering. The rules governing the approach taken by management in assessing the fairness of a tender offer are contained in the law of the target's state or incorporation and not in federal securities laws. See the discussion later in this chapter of directors' duties in evaluating a takeover bid and defensive steps which can be taken before and after a bid is made.

Rule 14e-2 imposes a federal securities law obligation upon the target's management to state its position concerning the tender offer and to recommend (1) acceptance; (2) rejection; (3) remain neutral or (4) express its inability to take a position. Management must express its position no later than ten business days from the first publication of the tender offer. Whatever statement of management's position is forthcoming, the reasons for taking the position must also be disclosed.

Schedule 14D-9. Any solicitation or recommendation to shareholders of a target company to accept or reject the tender offer requires a contemporaneous filing of Schedule 14D-9 with the Securities and Exchange Commission. If the person filing Schedule 14D-9 is the target company, the schedule must be hand delivered to the bidder with telephone notification to each exchange on which the subject securities are listed or quoted. If the filer is not the target company, copies of Schedule 14D-9 must be mailed to the bidder and the target at their respective principal places of business.

In addition to the identity and background of the person filing Schedule 14D-9, the schedule requires the identity of the target company and the tender offer to which the filing is responsive. Further disclosure is required with respect to the solicitation or recommendation, persons employed in connection with the solicitation or recommendation, any transactions involving the subject security within 60 days of the filing by the person making the filing and a description of any merger or reorganization of the target company or the disposition of its material assets that may be contemplated. Any change in material information subsequent to the filing of

Schedule 14D-9 requires the filing of an amended schedule with its dissemination as in the case of the initial schedule. It should be noted that the statement of the target management's position required by Rule 14e-2 requires the filing of Schedule 14D-9.

PRELIMINARY DEFENSIVE STEPS

Procedural Safeguards. Since any publicly held company may become the target of a takeover bid, management may wish to establish certain routine safeguards in an attempt to obtain information of a prospective takeover bid as early as possible. Certainly, if management has any reason to believe it likely that the corporation may become the target of a takeover bid, management should establish procedural safeguards to alert itself of any initial stirrings of a takeover bid. A daily check should be maintained on the volume of trading of the corporation's securities as well as on the list of security holders of the corporation to ascertain any unusual purchases and the accumulation of any large blocks.

Charter Amendments. As a defensive tactic, management may also consider amending the certificate of incorporation to make it more difficult for an offeror to gain control of the target company. Such charter amendments, sometimes referred to as "shark repellant" provisions, may include various types of restrictions. The board of directors may be staggered—i.e., one-third of the board of directors may be elected at each annual meeting of shareholders for a three-year term. An amendment to the charter may require a greater percentage of shareholder votes to permit a merger of the corporation with another corporation, than is required by the statutes of the state of incorporation. A charter amendment requiring that nontendering shareholders in a two-tier merger receive the same premium offered to tendering shareholders could have the effect of making the takeover more costly and thus act as a deterrent.

Defensive Merger Candidate. Management should also consider the possibility of finding a friendly prospective merger candidate. An effective means of countering an unwelcomed takeover bid is to offer shareholders an opportunity to participate in a merger, or to have the corporation acquired by a friendly acquisition partner, whereupon a shareholder may receive greater after-tax market value of securities in a "tax-free" exchange than upon a sale of stock to the takeover bidder.

Directors' Duties in Evaluating a Hostile Bid

Directors confronted by an unwanted tender offer or other takeover bid are not free to engage in unlimited warfare. It has long been settled that directors of corporations have fiduciary duties to the shareholders, particularly public shareholders who may welcome an opportunity to sell their shares at a premium over recent market levels.

As described in Chapter 4, directors are usually protected by the "business judgment" rule in their decisions. Only a failure to meet minimum standards for business judgment will result in liability in relation to a business sale. *Smith v. Van Gorkom,*

488 A.2d 858 (Del. 1985). However, in any situation involving a threatened change of control, the Delaware courts will make an initial review before applying the business judgment rule because of the omnipresent specter that the board may be acting primarily in its own interest. *Unocal Corp. v. Mesa Petroleum Co.* 493 A.2d 946 (Del. 1985). In this review, the board must show that its decisions are not made to entrench existing management, but to respond to a real threat to corporate effectiveness such as an inadequate or coercive tender offer. To demonstrate inadequacy or coerciveness requires good faith and reasonable investigation of the bid and alternatives, based on independent expert advice. The board must also demonstrate that its response is a reasonable response to the threat. Similar results have been reached by courts sitting in other jurisdictions. *Hanson Trust PLC v. ML SCM Acquisition, Inc.* 781 F.2d 264 (2 Cir. 1986); *Terrydale Liquidation Trust v. Barness,* 642 F. Supp. 917 (S.D., N.Y. 1986).

Stricter standards apply in two situations. If management cannot meet the scrutiny of the *Unocal* standard or its response to a takeover bid involves conflicting interests such as those involved in a management buyout, the courts will apply a standard of "entire fairness." For example, when directors responded with a partial self-tender offer found to be coercive in structure and timing, the Delaware Chancery Court issued an injunction even though it found the directors had no conflict of interest. *AC Acquisitions Corp. v. Anderson, Clayton, & Co.,* 519 A.2d 103 (Del. Ch. 1986). When directors responded with a restructuring plan found to be "financially chaotic," the court enjoined the plan. *Grand Metropolitan Public Limited Company v. Pillsbury Co.,* 588 A.2d 1049 (1988). If the board decides to sell to management or to a "white knight" or if the bidding progresses to a "range of fairness" where a sale becomes inevitable, "auction obligations" apply. These obligations require the board to cease defending the corporate bastion and to use all reasonable efforts to obtain the best bid for the shareholders. *MacAndrews & Forbes Holdings, Inc. v. Revlon, Inc.* 506 A.2d 173 (Del. 1985); *Edelman v. Fruehauf Corporation,* 795 F.2d 882 (6 Cir. 1986). The "auction obligations" typically require the board to afford to a hostile bidder the same information as it makes available to friendly bidders about corporate business and financial affairs. They must also refrain from conduct which places a disfavored bidder at a disadvantage. For example, when officers favored one bidder with extra information including the amount of a competitive bid, an injunction was granted. *Mills Acquisition Co. v. McMillan Inc.,* CCH Fed. Sec. L. Rep. § 94,401 (Del. 1989).

"Auction obligations" do not apply, however, simply because a takeover bid is made. The directors are free to respond with a sound restructuring plan in response to a bid found to be inadequate on the basis of expert financial advice. *Ivanhoe Partners v. Newmont Mining Corporation,* 535 A.2d 1334 (Del. 1987); *Gelco Corporation v. Coniston Partners,* 652 F. Supp. 829 (D. Minn. 1986); affirmed 811 F.2d 414 (8 Cir. 1986). Even after expressing several doubts, the Delaware Chancery Court permitted Interco Inc. to proceed with a restructuring plan. *City Capital Associates Limited Partnership v. Interco Inc.,* 551 A.2d 787 (Del. Ch. 1988). The courts have also allowed directors to respond by selling shares to an ESOP which had previously been planned, even though the ESOP was implemented and expanded after the takeover bid. *Danaher Corporation v. Chicago Pneumatic Tool Company* 635 F. Supp. 246 (S.D.,

N.Y. 1986); *Shamrock Holdings Inc. v. Polaroid Corporation.* 599 A.2d 278 (Del. Ch. 1989). A corporation has also been allowed to proceed with a previous plan for a major corporate merger, even though compelled by the takeover bid to change the planned transaction to a two-step tender offer and "cash out" merger. *Paramount Communications, Inc. v. Time Inc.,* CCH Fed. Sec. L. Rep. § 94,514 (Del. Ch. 1989).

In order to retain the "business judgment" standard, most boards of directors delegate authority to deal with takeovers and management buyouts to a committee consisting of independent outside directors. In turn, the independent committee retains its own financial and legal advisers. The courts will scrutinize the independence of committees and advisers and have criticized investment banking firms who compromised their independence by accepting fee arrangements including a bonus for achieving results favorable to management. However, if actual independence exists, the committee's decisions should be measured by the "business judgment" rule.

DEFENSIVE MANEUVERS TO A TAKEOVER BID

Schedule 14D-9. Management of the target company is prohibited from making any recommendation to its security holders either to accept or reject a tender offer unless management has previously filed with the Securities and Exchange Commission certain information specified in Schedule 14D-9. Therefore, the management of the target company should prepare and file with the Securities and Exchange Commission the form of Schedule 14D-9 as promptly as possible. The information required to be filed pursuant of Schedule 14D-9 is set forth in this chapter.

Possible Defensive Litigation. The target company should consider bringing litigation to prohibit or hinder the takeover. A number of areas of law may form the foundation of such litigation. Some of these areas are the following:

1. If the proposed takeover has antitrust overtones, the target company may bring an injunctive action against the aggressor, subject to the limits described in Chapter 5.
2. If the takeover bid is a registered exchange offer, the target company may bring an injunctive action, based upon a claim that the prospectus is faulty;
3. If the takeover bid is a tender offer, the target company may claim that the tender offer violates the disclosure or other requirements of the Williams Act and base its injunctive action on such a claim;
4. Additionally, the target company may claim that the margin requirements under Section 7 of the 1934 Securities and Exchange Act or Regulations T, U, and G promulgated by the Board of Governors of the Federal Reserve Board are being violated by the aggressor, although the courts ordinarily rule that a target company lacks standing to raise these issues.
5. If the aggressor requests a shareholder list from the target company, the target company may refuse to supply such a list and thereby put the issue into litigation, although the courts usually direct that the list be furnished.
6. The target company may attempt to convince state securities authorities

that state antitakeover and securities laws may be violated by the proposed takeover bid of the aggressor.

While usually successful in gaining time, defensive litigation has only occasionally been successful in deterring a well-planned and financed tender offer. For example, the courts have been skeptical about antitrust claims hurriedly presented by target companies raising issues which the Department of Justice or Federal Trade Commission chose not to pursue. The courts have repeatedly ruled that target companies have no private remedy for alleged violations of the margin regulations. Tender offerors usually file successful lawsuits to require production of the shareholder list.

Publicity and Communications. The target company should consider the advisability of communications with its shareholders, employees and principal customers and suppliers, both through written communication and newspaper advertisements. In addition, the target company may communicate with investment bankers, brokers and mutual funds which have a position or interest in the target company's securities to convince such institutions and funds that the takeover bid of the aggressor company will be unsuccessful. If the aggressor has conditioned its takeover bid upon obtaining a minimum percentage of the target company's securities, securities brokers and funds will not be willing to take positions in the target company's securities, unless such institutions are satisfied that the takeover bid will be successful. Should the bid be unsuccessful, the market price of the target company's stock should presumably recede to its price prior to the time of the takeover bid.

Defensive Merger. If the target company has taken proper precautions to guard against a possible takeover bid, the target company may have had discussions with a prospective acceptable acquirer prior to the takeover bid. Under such circumstances, the target company may be in a position to consummate a merger or acquisition with a more friendly larger corporation (a "white knight") and thus block the possible takeover bid. Even if discussions of a possible merger or acquisition have not been previously held, the target company may find a sympathetic hearing from a friendly buyer.

Counter-takeover Bid. An interesting possibility involves a possible counter-takeover bid for the aggressor. This tactic has come to be known as the "Pac-Man" defense and was recently employed in the Bendix-Martin Marietta takeover battle. If the aggressor's takeover bid is in the form of a registered exchange offer, presumably the target company will have substantially all of the information it would require in order to register its own registered exchange offer. If the counter-takeover bid should be made in the form of a tender offer, the target company need only meet the requirements set forth in the Williams Act, which it would presumably be able to do in a relatively short period of time.

"Greenmail." The elimination of a block of the target company's shares from the hands of an unfriendly company ("greenmail") may be possible through the purchase of these shares at a premium over the market price. Of course, employing this tactic must be viewed in the context of possible 16(b) problems to the unfriendly shareholder. Although the implementation of the greenmail defense usually requires the payment of a premium over market value Avco was able to acquire slightly less than 11 percent of its shares that were in the hands of Leucadia International at a price that was slightly less than the market price for the shares. Walt Disney Productions' use of greenmail to wrest a significant block of its shares from Saul Steinberg and thereby thwart his efforts to gain control of the company brought cries of discontent from many within the business and financial community. In Delaware, directors who authorized payment of a premium price to repurchase shares from a hostile shareholder have been protected by the "business judgment" rule. *Polk v. Good*, 507 A. 2d 531 (1986); *Grobow v. Perot*, 539 A. 2d 180 (Del. 1988); *In re General Motors Class E Stock Buyout Securities Litigation*, 694 F. Supp. 1119 (D.Del. 1988); cf. *Heckmann v. Ahmanson*, 168 Cal. App. 3d 119, 204 Cal. Rep. 177 (1985). However, a number of corporations have included anti-greenmail provisions in their charters.

Section 5881 of the Internal Revenue Code imposes a nondeductible 50% excise tax on any gain realized on the receipt of "greenmail." In summary, Section 5881 defines "greenmail" as a consideration paid by a corporation to acquire its stock from a shareholder who held the stock less than two years before agreeing to make the transfer *if* the shareholder (or persons with whom the shareholder acted in concert or was related) made or threatened during such period to make a public tender offer *and if* the acquisition of stock is pursuant to an offer not made on the same terms to all shareholders. The language of Section 5881 is quite vague and there is concern that the excise tax might be imposed on persons who act as a "White Knight" or "White Squire."

Discussions of the economic effects of "greenmail" payments are presented in *Mergers, Restructuring and Corporate Control*, Weston, Chung and Hoag, Prentice-Hall, 1990.

Employee Benefit Plans. Employee benefit plans may be utilized as a defensive measure by instructing the plan's investment managers not to tender the company's shares that are in the plan's portfolio or instructing the managers to actively purchase the company's shares and thus deny the bidder access to these shares. Extreme caution is required when utilizing an employee benefit plan to advance the interests of the company. The plan's investment managers are governed by federal regulation of employee benefit plans. They owe a fiduciary duty to the plan's beneficiaries and are subject to liability for a breach of this duty. However, an accumulation of a company's securities by an employee stock ownership plan ("ESOP") prior to the commencement of a tender offer seems less likely to run afoul of the fiduciary requirements and federal regulations. An example of an employee benefit plan being used to prevent a takeover and the dilemma that faces the plan's fiduciaries in such instances can be found in the litigation that was an outgrowth of LTV Corporation's attempt to acquire Grumman Corporation [see *Donovan v. Bierwirth*, 680 F. 2d 263 (1982)].

Golden Parachutes. The "golden parachute" is a contract providing special compensation and benefits to corporate executives in the event of a change of corporate control. There is considerable variety among these contracts. In general, they are designed to compensate executives for services which may include the risk and uncertainty of a takeover campaign. Some "golden parachute" contracts promise enormous rewards which have been excused by the claim that their burden serves as a takeover deterrent. Shareholders have challenged "golden parachute" contracts in court with little success because they are usually approved by "independent" directors. "Golden parachutes" have been among the favorite items used by takeover bidders to challenge corporate management and discredit claims that they are dedicated to the long-term best interests of shareholders.

Some corporations have also granted "silver parachutes" and "tin parachutes", i.e. contracts calling for more modest benefits, to wider groups of management and salaried employees.

Section 280G of the Internal Revenue Code denies deductions for "excess parachute payments" as defined therein. Section 4999 of the Code imposes a nondeductible 20% excise tax on corporate executives or any other person who receives excess parachute payments.

Extreme Measures. Some of the most extreme responses to an unwanted takeover bid that a target's management may unleash include self-tenders, liquidation (partial or total), the sale of attractive corporate assets commonly referred to as "crown jewels," "lock ups," "poison pills" and spinoffs. It is noteworthy that the regulatory scheme of tender offers allows the target company an advantage over a competing offeror in the context of a self-tender in that the proration period for a self-tender is limited to ten business days as opposed to length of the offer for the competing bidder.

"Lockups" are option agreements given to a friendly third party to acquire stock or assets of a target company. While not held illegal as such, lockups have not generally fared well in the courts. There is a split of authority whether they may violate the Williams Act. *Mobil Corp. v. Marathon Oil Co.* (6 Cir., 1981) 669 F. 2d 366; *Buffalo Forge v. Ogden* (2 Cir., 1983) 717 F. 2d 757; *Data Probe Acquisition Corp. v. Datatab Inc.* (2 Cir., 1983) 722 F. 2d 1. They clearly cannot be used to avoid the fiduciary duty of a board of directors to obtain the best price for shareholders when a corporation or its assets are to be sold. *Revlon, Inc. v. MacAndrews & Forbes Holding, Inc.* (Del. Sup. Ct., 1986) 506 A. 2d 173; *Hanson Trust PLC v. ML SCM Corporation* (2 Cir., 1986) 781 F. 2d 264; *Edelman v. Fruehauf* (6 Cir., 1986) 798 F. 2d 882.

"Poison pills" are structured as "flip-in," "flip-over" and "voting rights" devices designed to give shareholders extremely favorable bargain purchase or voting rights in the event of a hostile tender offer opposed by management. The typical "poison pill" provides expressly that it will not be triggered by a friendly transaction approved by the board of directors of the target company.

Some "poison pill" devices have been rejected and others upheld by the courts. The principal grounds for upholding them has been their effect in countering two-step takeovers in which a tender offer is made at an attractive price to acquire sufficient shares to permit the tender offeror to implement a "squeeze out" merger at a lower price. In *Moran v. Household International, Inc.*, 500 A. 2d 1346 (Del., 1985), the Delaware Supreme Court made it clear that its decision upholding a preferred stock rights dividend plan of the "flip-over" type was limited to a device which would not act as a "show stopper" for all tender offers. The Court also emphasized that the conduct of boards of directors in using a "poison pill" to resist a tender offer would be subject to scrutiny in light of their fiduciary obligations to the corporation and its shareholders.

A "poison pill" can be used to oppose a leveraged takeover, but is unlikely to be effective against a carefully planned and attractively priced offer to purchase all outstanding shares together with all option, voting and other rights resulting from the "pill" device. In addition, an offeror can place management of the target company under pressure by making an attractive tender offer conditioned upon action by the target company management to take whatever actions may be necessary to redeem the "pill" rights or otherwise nullify the effects of the "poison pill." If the tender offer appears to be made at a fair price and management can find no equal or better alternative, the board of directors must evaluate it in light of its fiduciary obligations to shareholders. Management assumes considerable risks of liability if it turns to a "greenmail" payment or "scorched earth" tactics to defeat an offer which is in the range of fair value. *Heckmann v. Ahmanson,* 168 Cal. App. 3d 119 (1985). In this connection, the Office of the Chief Economist of the Securities and Exchange Commission concluded that "poison pills" decrease shareholder wealth on the basis of a study of 245 provisions adopted between 1983 and 1986.

Some recent Court decisions involving "poison pills" are as follows: *Moran v. Household Finance International, Inc.,* 500 A. 2d 1346 (Del., 1985); *MacAndrews & Forbes Holdings, Inc. v. Revlon, Inc.,* 506 A. 2d 173 (Del., 1976); *Hanson Trust PLC v. ML SCM Acquisition, Inc.,* 781 F. 2d 264 (2 Cir., 1986); *CTS Corporation v. Dynamics Corporation of America* (1987) 55 USLW 4478, CCH Fed. Sec. L. Rep., § 93,213; *Edelman v. Fruehauf Corporation,* (6 Cir., 1986) 798 F. 2d 882; *Hurwitz v. Southwest Forest Ind.,* 604 FS 1130 (1985) *Unilever v. Richardson-Vicks,* 618 FS 407 (1985) *Minstar v. AMF Inc.,* 621 FS 1252 (1985) *Packer v. Yampol,* No. 8432 (Del. Ch. 1986). Several of the cases cited elsewhere in this chapter also involve "poison pills."

THE FUTURE OF TAKEOVERS

As the 1990s progress, it seems clear that the leveraged takeover phenomenon of the 1980s has ended. There were several contributing factors.

- Once the U.S. Supreme Court allowed the states to adopt statutes regulating takeovers, state legislatures rushed to adopt restrictions to inhibit takeovers by out-of-state investors who might disregard local interests in maintaining control of management, employment and commercial benefits of corporate businesses.
- "Insider trading," "parking" and other convictions of several famous financial executives (Levine, Boesky, Siegel, Jefferies, Freeman and Milken) who had leading roles in takeover activities created a negative image for campaigns which had prospered under the banner of shareholder democracy advocated by T. Boone Pickens and others.
- Prices for leveraged buyouts and debt burdens rose so high in the late 1980s

that the buyers of several companies could not accomplish the restructuring and divestitures planned to provide essential cash flows. Bankruptcies followed for companies such as Hillsborough Holdings, which had acquired Jim Walter, and for Campeau Corporation, Revco and others.

- The bankruptcy of Drexel Burnham Lambert and government pressure on banks to divest high yielding securities ("junk bonds") interrupted a major source of takeover financing.
- With some exceptions, takeovers are perceived as primarily benefitting a narrow range of interests in the financial community while threatening broader interests of corporate management, employment and the industrial and financial community. While efforts were made by T. Boone Pickens, Drexel Burnham Lambert and others to demonstrate public benefit from the realization of shareholder values and improved financial management, federal and state governments and the public were not convinced.

The tender offer remains a lawful, though highly regulated, acquisition method. As time passes, acquisition prices will return to reasonable levels and markets for debt securities will stabilize. Thus, friendly tender offers and some hostile tender offers will continue to occur such as AT&T's offer for NCR Corporation.

PROXY CONTESTS

Although not widely perceived, major support for takeovers in the 1980s came from large financial institutions such as insurers, mutual funds, pension funds and other investment funds. These institutions have accumulated enormous portfolios of corporate investments. When dissatisfied with corporate management, they found the proxy process inadequate to achieve changes because management controls the solicitation process. Thus, they welcomed the opportunity to provide capital to colorful takeover strategists who forced companies to restructure or bought and restructured them.

As impediments to unwelcome tender offers were erected, institutional and other shareholders have turned again to proxy contests as a means of changing policies or control of the management of publicly owned companies. Among the issues fought are management recommendations or actions to adopt antitakeover devices such as "poison pill" rights plans or other devices authorized by state antitakeover laws. Other contests seek board seats for dissident shareholders or to oust the existing board members.

Solicitation of proxies by management and by dissident shareholders is governed by Regulation 14A under the Securities Exchange Act of 1934. Even for routine annual meetings, a proxy statement containing information required by Schedule 14A must be filed with the SEC prior to its distribution to shareholders together with the corporation's annual report. The SEC staff may furnish comments on the proxy statement in a manner similar to the comments furnished on a registration statement for the sale of securities. Regulation 14A contains numerous other requirements including procedures for shareholder proposals, specifications for the form of proxies, methods which can be used in solicitation and the filing with the other solicitation material including newspaper ads and radio and television materials.

Rule 14a-11 contains special provisions applicable to election contests. Dissident shareholders must file information required by Schedule 14B with the SEC. They must also file their proxy statement, proxy and solicitation materials with the SEC prior to use and respond to comments by the SEC staff. The regulations require that public companies mail the proxy materials of dissident shareholders at their expense, but most dissidents prefer to obtain a court order directing management to deliver a copy of the stockholder list so they can handle the mailing and solicitation themselves. Regulation 14B requires that brokers, clearing services and other nominees distribute proxy materials promptly to beneficial owners.

An elaborate system to improve the proxy solicitation process and facilitate direct mailings and communications was created by the Shareholder Communications Act of 1985. Interested readers can obtain information from the American Society of Corporate Secretaries, Inc., 1270 Avenue of the Americas, New York, New York, including its Manual for the Solicitation of Proxies, Proxy Contact List and Nominee List. Information is also published by the Depository Trust Company (Cede & Co.) and the Independent Election Corporation of America, Lake Success, New York.

While not relaxing its substantive standards, the SEC allows plain, colorful and even insulting language to be used in solicitation materials. They recognize that it would be difficult to overcome shareholder inertia and inform them of the conflicting positions of the contestants if management and the dissidents were limited to the prosaic language used in prospectuses. Nevertheless, statements out of context, statements unsupported by fact and opinions presented as fact are not allowed. Projections and valuations must also be supported by factual data, must disclose limitations and qualifications, and must be prepared in compliance with recognized standards of financial analysis. See Rule 14a-9 and SEC Release No. 34-16833 (May 23, 1980).

Proxy contests require a major and costly effort requiring a team of lawyers, investment bankers, accountants, public relations consultants, proxy solicitors and a financial printer. Lawsuits are inevitably filed. Proxies are revocable, so the campaigns surge back and forth for weeks and through the morning of the shareholders meeting. While the regulations attempt to keep the contest on a level playing field, incumbent management has major advantages even when corporate performance has long been disappointing. Among the advantages are timing, familiarity to the shareholders, ability to use corporate funds and resources in the contest and the opportunity to shift policies if needed to win key votes. In recent years, management also benefits from antitakeover laws which they persuaded legislatures to adopt in many states. For example, some of these laws provide that a person or group acquiring more than a specified percentage (20%–30%) of the outstanding shares without approval of incumbent management cannot vote their shares unless the voting rights are restored by vote of the independent shareholders. Other antitakeover laws create appraisal rights against a person or group who acquires in excess of a specified percentage of the outstanding shares.

Because of the advantages held by incumbent management, dissident shareholders are seldom wholly successful in ousting management, but they may achieve changes in management policy or other concessions such as board seats for dissident candidates. For example, proxy campaigns recently obtained at least some objectives at Allegheny Corporation, Amdura Corp., American General, Avon Products, Datapoint Corp., Great Northern Nekoosa, Lockheed Corporation, Norton Company and Xtra Corp.

While not outweighing management advantages, a proxy contest has some advantages for a sponsoring shareholder. The sponsoring shareholder often acquired his investment at approximately the depressed price levels which created shareholder dissatisfaction. There is no need to pay a premium or raise high risk financing as happens in tender offer/merger takeovers. Thus, the sponsoring shareholder may gain control with a minor investment in terms of dollars and percentage of the total outstanding equity. Third, the corporation will continue to be a registered and listed public corporation, thus providing an "exit" not always available in hostile takeovers using the tender offer/merger strategy.

Proxy contests are real battles, not academic debates about corporate governance, although both sides may argue their positions in those terms. Proxies are revocable and often shift during a proxy contest as issues and positions change. The victor cannot be determined until the polls close at the shareholders meeting and the actual result is usually not known until lawsuits are resolved much later.

A rare example of a successful proxy contest by a dissident shareholder who began with only 6% of the outstanding stock was the 1983 campaign by Samuel Heyman to achieve the election of an entirely new slate of directors of GAF Corporation. The campaign cost well over $1.0 million and pending litigation maintained the incumbent management in office for almost eight months after the annual meeting when 58% of the shares were voted for the Heyman nominees. Once in office, however, Mr. Heyman led a rapid turnaround of GAF's operations, resulting in a major increase in the market value of its shares.

Institutional shareholders have urged that the SEC adopt regulations to reduce the one-sided control of management over the proxy process by such methods as confidential voting, greater freedom to place proposals on the agenda for annual meetings and easier access to shareholders lists. If reforms are not achieved, tender offers with institutional investor support may be resumed as the only means to change management policies and membership.

Readers interested in a broad ranging overview of proxy contests and their effects can refer to a series of articles which appeared in 1988 and 1989 in the *Journal of Financial Economics*. Of special interest is an article titled "Proxy Contests and the Governance of Publicly Held Corporations," 12 *Journal of Financial Economics* 29, H. and L. DeAngelo, University of Michigan, 1989.

Finally, a discussion of the proxy process and shareholder democracy would not be complete without mention of the tireless campaigners, Lewis and John Gilbert. To the best of the authors' knowledge, the Gilberts have never waged a proxy contest. Rather, they submitted for decades a variety of proposals they believed to be in the best interests of shareholders. Some later became law or accepted corporate practice. Over the decades, they have won respect, although certainly not the affection, of corporate managements who suffered their criticism. This respect for a capable opponent is not shared with those who use corporate proxy materials to advance narrow personal interests.

"One Share, One Vote" Controversy. Publicly owned corporations have traditionally issued common stock following a "one share, one vote" principle. Corporations occasionally issued shares with reduced voting rights for trading in the over-the-counter market. However, the New York Stock Exchange refused to list for trading any common stock not entitled to one vote per share, thus acting as a bastion for the "one share, one vote" principle.

As previously described, managements of some publicly owned corporations have recently subdivided their common stock into two classes. One class is granted multiple votes per share, counterbalanced with lower dividend and liquidation rights and perhaps also some transfer restrictions. The other class remains essentially the same except as affected by the rights granted to the other class.

Faced with competition from the growing NASDAQ technology of the over-the-counter market and from the American Stock Exchange, the New York Stock Exchange revised its policy in 1986 and proposed to allow the listing of dual classes of common stock with unequal voting rights subject to specified conditions. After widespread public debate, the SEC adopted a new Rule 19e-4 in 1988 requiring the stock exchanges to adopt rules denying listing of equity securities to companies which take any corporate action to nullify, restrict or disparately reduce the per share voting rights of an outstanding class or class of registered common stock. Rule 19e-4 also requires the NASD to adopt rules denying NASDAQ quotation and/or reporting facilities for the same reasons. Rule 19c-4 contains exceptions for shares issued in an initial public offering and mergers and acquisitions.

In June 1990, the U.S. Court of Appeals for the District of Columbia ruled that the SEC had exceeded its authority under the 1934 Act in adopting Rule 19e-4 and enjoined its enforcement. Indeed, the New York Stock Exchange has listed shares of several dozen companies which have disproportionate voting rights including General Motors whose issuance reduced voting shares to acquire EDS Corporation and sparked the original controversy.

Thus, the Court of Appeals decision on Rule 19c-4 gave managements another powerful weapon to maintain their control and prevent tender offers to public shareholders.

Appendix 9-1

ANNOUNCEMENT OF A FRIENDLY TENDER OFFER

This announcement is neither an offer to purchase nor a solicitation of an offer to sell any Shares. The Offer is made solely by the Offer to Purchase and the related Letter of Transmittal and is not being made to, nor will any tender be accepted from or on behalf of, holders of Shares in any jurisdiction in which the making or acceptance thereof would not be in compliance with the securities, blue sky or other laws of such jurisdiction.

NOTICE OF AMENDED OFFER TO PURCHASE FOR CASH
UP TO 1,000,000 SHARES OF COMMON STOCK

of

UNITED TARGET CORPORATION

at

$50 NET PER SHARE

by

WHITE KNIGHT, INCORPORATED

WHITE KNIGHT, INCORPORATED, a corporation organized under the laws of the State of Delaware ("WKI"), is offering to purchase up to 1,000,000 shares of Common Stock, par value $1 per share (the "Shares"), of UNITED TAR-GET CORPORATION, a corporation organized under the laws of the State of Michigan ("UTC"), at $50 per Share, net to the seller in cash, upon the terms and subject to the conditions set forth in the Amended Offer to Purchase dated October 20, 199____ (the "Offer to Purchase") and in the related Letter of Transmittal (the "Letter of Transmittal" and collectively, the "Offer"). The Offer to Purchase and the Letter of Transmittal contain important information which should be read before any decision is made with respect to the Offer.

THE OFFER EXPIRES ON WEDNESDAY, NOVEMBER 20, 199____ at 5:00 P.M., NEW YORK CITY TIME, UNLESS EXTENDED. SHARES MAY BE WITHDRAWN AT ANY TIME PRIOR TO PURCHASE. THE OFFER IS NOT CONDITIONED UPON ANY MINIMUM NUMBER OF SHARES BEING TENDERED.

The purpose of the Offer is to acquire Shares which would constitute control of UTC and entitle WKI to elect at least a majority of the Board of Directors of UTC.

THE BOARD OF DIRECTORS OF UTC RECOMMENDS THAT HOLD-ERS OF SHARES WHO WISH TO RECEIVE CASH FOR AT LEAST A POR-TION OF THEIR SHARES ACCEPT THE OFFER.

The Offer will expire on the Expiration Date. The term "Expiration Date" means 5:00 P.M., New York City Time, on Wednesday, November 20, 199____, un-less WKI extends the period of time for which the Offer is open, in which event the term "Expiration Date" means the latest time and date to which the Offer is ex-tended. WKI reserves the right (i) to extend the Offer and the Expiration Date from time to time by giving oral or written notice to First Trust Company of New York in its capacity as depositary (the "Depositary") and making a public announcement or release to the Dow Jones News Service prior to 9:00 A.M., New York City Time, on the business day following the previously scheduled Expiration Date and (ii) to amend the Offer at any time.

If at the Expiration Date, more than 1,000,000 Shares have been properly tendered and not withdrawn, WKI will, upon the terms and subject to the conditions set forth in the Offer, purchase 1,000,000 Shares on a pro rata basis with appropriate adjustments to avoid the purchase of fractional shares. WKI reserves the right, but shall not be obligated, to purchase a nominal number of Shares tendered in excess of 1,000,000 in the event that such nominal number of Shares purchased would avoid proration. If 1,000,000 or fewer Shares have been properly tendered and not withdrawn, WKI will, upon the terms and subject to the conditions set forth in the Offer, purchase all such Shares.

WKI will be deemed to have purchased tendered Shares as, if and when WKI gives oral or written notice to the Depositary of its election to purchase such Shares. Payment for Shares purchased pursuant to the Offer will be made by deposit of the purchase price therefor with the Depositary, which will act as agent for the tendering stockholders for the purpose of receiving payment from WKI and transmitting payment to tendering stockholders.

All Shares tendered pursuant to the Offer may be withdrawn at any time prior to their purchase by WKI. To be effective, a written, telegraphic, telex, or facsimile notice of withdrawal must be received by the Depositary at the appropriate address specified in the Offer prior to such purchase and must specify the names of the tendering and registered holders of, and the serial numbers of certificates evidencing, the Shares to be withdrawn.

The information required to be disclosed by Rule 14d-6(e)(1)(vii) of the General Rules and Regulations under the Securities Exchange Act of 1934, as amended, is contained in the Offer to Purchase and is incorporated herein by reference.

Requests for copies of the Offer to Purchase and the Letter of Transmittal may be directed to First Trust Company of New York, 850 Wall Street, New York, New York 10015, (212) 555-6151 (Call Collect). Copies will be furnished promptly at WKI's expense.

The Dealer Manager for the Offer is:

ABLE, BAKER & CHARLES, INCORPORATED

October 21, 199____

Appendix 9-2

SECURITIES AND EXCHANGE COMMISSION
Washington, D.C. 20549

SCHEDULE 14D-1

Tender Offer Statement Pursuant to Section 14(d)(1) of the Securities Exchange Act of 1934 (Amendment No. ...)*

. . . .

(Name of Subject company [Issuer])

. . . .

(Bidder)

. . . .

(Title of Class of Securities)

. . . .

(CUSIP Number of Class of Securities)

(Name, Address, and Telephone Number of Person Authorized to
Receive Notices and Communications on Behalf of Bidder)

Note: The remainder of this cover page is only to be completed if this Schedule 14D-1 (or amendment thereto) is being filed, inter alia, to satisfy the reporting requirements of Section 13(d) of the Securities Exchange Act of 1934. See General Instructions D, E and F to Schedule 14D-1.

*The remainder of this cover page shall be filled out for a reporting person's initial filing on this form with respect to the subject class of securities, and for any subsequent amendment containing information which would alter the disclosure provided in a prior cover page.

The information required in the remainder of this cover page shall not be deemed to be "filed" for the purpose of Section 18 of the Securities Exchange Act of 1934 ("Act") or otherwise subject to the liabilities of that section of the Act but shall be subject to all other provisions of the Act (however, see the Notes).

CUSIP No. . . . .

Calculation of Filing Fee

Transaction valuation*	Amount of filing fee

*Set forth the amount on which the filing fee is calculated and state how it was determined.

☐ Check box if any part of the fee is offset as provided by Rule 0-11(a)(2) and identify the filing with which the offsetting fee was previously paid. Identify the previous filing by registration statement number, or the form or schedule and the date of its filing.

Amount Previously Paid: _____Filing Party: _____

Form or Registration No.: _____Date Filed: _____

---

1) Name of Reporting Persons S.S. or I.R.S. Identification No. of Above Person ....
   ....

---

2) Check the Appropriate Box if a Member of a Group

   (a) ....

   (b) ....

---

3) SEC Use Only ....

---

4) Sources of Funds ....

---

5) Check Box if Disclosure of Legal Proceedings is Required Pursuant to Items 2(e) or 2(f) ....

---

6) Citizenship or Place of Organization ....

---

7) Aggregate Amount Beneficially Owned by Each Reporting Person.................................

---

8) Check if the Aggregate Amount in Row (7) Excludes Certain Shares ....

---

9) Percent of Class Represented by Amount in Row (7) ....

---

10) Type of Reporting Person ....

Instructions for Cover Page

(1) *Names and Social Security Numbers of Reporting Persons*—Furnish the full legal name of each person for whom the report is filed—i.e., each person required to sign the schedule itself—including each member of a group. Do not include the name of a person required to be identified in the report but who is not a reporting person. Reporting persons are also requested to furnish their Social Security or I.R.S. identification numbers, although disclosure of such numbers is voluntary, not mandatory (see "SPECIAL INSTRUCTIONS FOR COMPLYING WITH SCHEDULE 14D-1", below).

(2) If any of the shares beneficially owned by a reporting person are held as a member of a group and such membership is expressly affirmed, please check row 2(a). If the membership in a group is disclaimed or the reporting person describes a relationship with other persons but does not affirm the existence of a group, please check row 2(b) [unless a joint filing pursuant to Rule 13d-1(f)(1) in which case it may not be necessary to check row 2(b)].

(3) The third column is for SEC internal use, please leave blank.

(4) *Source of Funds*—Classify the source of funds or other consideration to be used in making purchases as required to be disclosed pursuant to Item 4 of the schedule and insert the appropriate symbol (or symbols if more than one is necessary) in row (4):

Category of Source	Symbol
Subject Company (company whose securities are being acquired)	SC
Bank	BK
Affiliate (of reporting person)	AF
Working Capital (of reporting person)	WC
Personal Funds (of reporting person)	PF
Other	OO

(5) If disclosure of legal proceedings or actions is required pursuant to either Items 2(e) or 2(f) of Schedule 14D-1, row 5 should be checked.

(6) *Citizenship or Place of Organization*—Furnish citizenship if the named reporting person is a natural person. Otherwise, furnish the place of organization. (see Item 2 of Schedule 14D-1.)

(7),(9) *Aggregate Amount Beneficially Owned by Each Reporting Person, etc.*— Columns (7) and (9) are to be completed in accordance with the Instructions to Item 6 of Schedule 14D-1. All percentages are to be rounded off to nearest tenth (one place after decimal point).

(8) Check if the aggregate amount reported as beneficially owned in row (7) does not include shares as to which beneficial ownership is disclaimed.

(10) *Type of Reporting Person*—Please classify each "reporting person" according to

the following breakdown and place the appropriate symbol (or symbols, i.e., if more than one is applicable, insert all applicable symbols) on the form:

Category	Symbol
Broker Dealer	BD
Bank	BK
Insurance Company	IC
Investment Company	IV
Investment Adviser	IA
Employee Benefit Plan, Pension Fund, or Endowment Fund	EP
Parent Holding Company	HC
Group Member	GM
Corporation	CO
Partnership	PN
Individual	IN
Other	OO

Notes:

Attach as many copies of the second part of the cover page as are needed, one reporting person per page.

Filing persons may, in order to avoid unnecessary duplication, answer items on the schedules (Schedules 13D, 13G or 14D-1) by appropriate cross-references to an item or items on the cover page(s). This approach may be used only where the cover page item or items provide all the disclosure required by the schedule item. Moreover, such a use of a cover page item will result in the item becoming a part of the schedule and accordingly being considered as "filed" for purposes of Section 18 of the Securities Exchange Act or otherwise subject to the liabilities of that section of the Act.

Reporting persons may comply with their cover page filing requirements by filing either completed copies of the blank forms available from the Commission, printed or typed facsimiles, or computer printed facsimiles, provided the documents filed have identical formats to the forms prescribed in the Commission's regulations and meet existing Securities Exchange Act rules as to such matters as clarity and size.

SPECIAL INSTRUCTIONS FOR COMPLYING WITH SCHEDULE 14D-1

Under Sections 14(d) and 23 of the Securities Exchange Act of 1934 and the rules and regulations thereunder, the Commission is authorized to solicit the information required to be supplied by this schedule by certain security holders of certain issuers.

Disclosure of the information specified in this schedule is mandatory, except for Social Security or I.R.S. identification numbers, disclosure of which is voluntary. The information will be used for the primary purpose of determining and disclosing the holdings of certain beneficial owners of certain equity securities. This statement will be made a matter of public record. Therefore, any information given will be available for inspection by any member of the public.

Because of the public nature of the information, the Commission can utilize it for a variety of purposes, including referral to other governmental authorities or securities self-regulatory organizations for investigatory purposes or in connection with litigation involving the Federal securities laws or other civil, criminal, or regulatory statutes or provisions. Social Security or I.R.S. identification numbers, if furnished, will assist the Commission in identifying security holders and, therefore, in promptly processing statements of beneficial ownership of securities.

Failure to disclose the information requested by this schedule, except for Social Security or I.R.S. identification numbers, may result in civil or criminal action against the persons involved for violation of the Federal securities laws and rules promulgated thereunder.

Filing Instructions and Fees: 1. Eight copies of this statement, including all exhibits, and two additional copies of this statement, including only the exhibits described in Item 11(a) of this statement, should be filed with the Commission.

2. This statement shall be accompanied by a fee payable to the Commission as required by Rule 0-11.

General Instructions. A. The item numbers and captions of the items shall be included but the text of the items is to be omitted. The answers to the items shall be so prepared as to indicate clearly the coverage of the items without referring to the text of the items. Answer every item. If an item is inapplicable or the answer is in the negative, so state.

B. Information contained in exhibits to the statement may be incorporated by reference in answer or partial answer to any item or sub-item of the statement unless it would render such answer misleading, incomplete, unclear or confusing. Material incorporated by reference shall be clearly identified in the reference by page, paragraph, caption or otherwise. An express statement that the specified matter is incorporated by reference shall be made at the particular place in the statement where the information is required. A copy of any information or a copy of the pertinent pages of a document containing such information which is incorporated by reference shall be submitted with this statement as an exhibit and shall be deemed to be filed with the Commission for all purposes of the Act.

C. If the statement is filed by a partnership, limited partnership, syndicate or other group, the information called for by Items 2-7, inclusive, shall be given with respect to: (i) each partner of such partnership; (ii) each partner who is denominated as a general partner or who functions as a general partner of such limited partnership; (iii) each member of such syndicate or group; and (iv) each person controlling such partner or member. If the statement is filed by a corporation, or if a person referred to in (i) (ii), (iii), or (iv) of this instruction is a corporation, the information called for by the above mentioned items shall be given with respect to: (a) each executive officer and director of such corporation; (b) each person controlling such corporation; and (c) each executive officer and director of any corporation ultimately in control of such corporation. A response to an item in the statement is required with respect to the bidder and to all other persons referred to in this instruction unless such item specifies to the contrary.

D. Upon termination of the tender offer, the bidder shall promptly file a final amendment to Schedule 14D-1 disclosing all material changes in the items of that Schedule and stating that the tender offer has terminated, the date of such termination, and the results of such tender offer.

E. If the bidder, before filing this statement, has filed a Schedule 13D with respect to the acquisition of securities of the same class referred to in Item 1(a) of this statement, the bidder shall amend such Schedule 13D and may do so by means of this statement and amendments thereto, including the final amendment required to be filed by Instruction D: *provided* that the bidder indicates on the cover sheet of this statement that it is amending its Schedule 13D by means of this statement.

F. The final amendment required to be filed by Instruction D shall be deemed to satisfy the reporting requirements of section 13(d) of the Act with respect to all securities acquired by the bidder pursuant to the tender offer as reported in such final amendment.

G. For purposes of this statement, the following definitions shall apply:

(i) The term "bidder" means any person on whose behalf a tender offer is made; and

(ii) The term "subject company" means any issuer whose securities are sought by a bidder pursuant to a tender offer.

Item 1. Security and Subject Company.

(a) State the name of the subject company and the address of its principal executive offices;

(b) State the exact title and the number of shares outstanding of the class of equity securities being sought (which may be based upon information contained in the most recently available filing with the Commission by the subject company unless the bidder has reason to believe such information is not current), the exact amount of such securities being sought and the consideration being offered therefor; and

(c) Identify the principal market in which such securities are traded and state the high and low sales prices for such securities in such principal market (or, in the absence thereof, the range of high and low bid quotations) for each quarterly period during the past two years.

Item 2. Identity and Background.

If the person filing this statement or any person enumerated in Instruction C of this statement is a corporation, partnership, limited partnership, syndicate or other group of persons, state its name, the state or other place of its organization, its principal business, the address of its principal office and the information required by (e) and (f) of this Item. If the person filing this statement or any person enumerated in Instruction C is a natural person, provide the information specified in (a) through (g) of this Item with respect to such person(s).

(a) Name;

(b) Residence or business address;

(c) Present principal occupation or employment and the name, principal business and address of any occupation or other organization in which such employment or occupation is conducted;

(d) Material occupations, positions, offices or employments during the last 5 years, giving the starting and ending dates of each and the name, principal business and address of any business corporation or other organization in which such occupation, position, office or employment was carried on;

Instruction. If a person has held various positions with the same organization, or if a person holds comparable positions with multiple related organizations, each and every position need not be specifically disclosed.

(e) Whether or not, during the last 5 years, such person has been convicted in a criminal proceeding (excluding traffic violations or similar misdemeanors) and, if so, give the dates, nature of conviction, name and location of court, and penalty imposed, or other disposition of the case;

Instruction. While a negative answer to this sub-item is required in this schedule, it need not be furnished to security holders.

(f) Whether or not, during the last 5 years, such person was a party to a civil proceeding of a judicial or administrative body of competent jurisdiction and as a result of such proceeding was or is subject to a judgment, decree or final order enjoining future violations of, or prohibiting activities subject to, federal or state securities laws or finding any violation of such laws; and, if so, identify and describe such proceeding and summarize the terms of such judgment, decree or final order; and

Instruction. While a negative answer to this sub-item is required in this schedule, it need not be furnished to security holders.

(g) Citizenship(s).

Item 3. Past Contacts, Transactions or Negotiations with the Subject Company.

(a) Briefly state the nature and approximate amount (in dollars) of any transaction, other than those described in Item 3(b) of this schedule, which has occurred since the commencement of the subject company's third full fiscal year preceding the date of this schedule, between the person filing this schedule (including those persons enumerated in Instruction C of this schedule) and:

(1) the subject company or any of its affiliates which are corporations: *provided, however,* that no disclosure need be made with respect to any transaction if the aggregate amount involved in such transaction was less than one percent of the subject company's consolidated revenues (which may be based upon information contained in the most recently available filing with the Commission by the subject company,

unless the bidder has reason to believe otherwise) (i) for the fiscal year in which such transaction occurred or, (ii) for the portion of the current fiscal year which has occurred, if the transaction occurred in such year; and

(2) the executive officers, directors or affiliates of the subject company which are not corporations if the aggregate amount involved in such transaction or in a series of similar transactions, including all periodic installments in the case of any lease or other agreement providing for periodic payments or installments, exceeds $40,000.

(b) Describe any contacts, negotiations or transactions which have occurred since the commencement of the subject company's third full fiscal year preceding the date of this schedule between the bidder or its subsidiaries (including those persons enumerated in Instruction C of this schedule) and the subject company or its affiliates concerning: a merger, consolidation or acquisition; a tender offer or other acquisition of securities; an election of directors; or a sale or other transfer of a material amount of assets.

Item 4. Source and Amount of Funds or Other Consideration.

(a) State the source and the total amount of funds or the consideration for the purchase of the maximum number of securities for which the tender offer is being made.

(b) If all or part of such funds or other consideration are or are expected to be, directly or indirectly, borrowed for the purpose of the tender offer:

(1) Provide a summary of each loan agreement or arrangement containing the identity of the parties, the term, the collateral, the stated and effective interest rates, and other material terms or conditions relative to such loan agreement; and

(2) Briefly describe any plans or arrangements to finance or repay such borrowings, or if no such plans or arrangements have been made, make a statement to that effect.

(c) If the source of all or any part of the funds to be used in the tender offer is a loan made in the ordinary course of business by a bank as defined by Section 3(a)(6) of the Act, the name of such bank shall not be made available to the public if the person filing the statement so requests in writing and files such request, naming such bank, with the Secretary of the Commission.

Item 5. Purpose of the Tender Offer and Plans or Proposals of the Bidder.

State the purpose or purposes of the tender offer for the subject company's securities. Describe any plans or proposals which relate to or would result in:

(a) An extraordinary corporate transaction, such as a merger, reorganization or liquidation, involving the subject company or any of its subsidiaries;

(b) A sale or transfer of a material amount of assets of the subject company or any of its subsidiaries;

(c) Any change in the present board of directors or management of the subject company including but not limited to, any plans or proposals to change the number or the term of directors or to fill any existing vacancies on the board;

(d) Any material change in the present capitalization or dividend policy of the subject company;

(e) Any other material change in the subject company's corporate structure or business, including, if the subject company is a registered closed-end investment company, any plans or proposals to make any changes in its investment policy for which a vote would be required by Section 13 of the Investment Company Act of 1940;

(f) Causing a class of securities of the subject company to be delisted from a national securities exchange or to cease to be authorized to be quoted in an inter-dealer quotation system of a registered national securities association; or

(g) A class of equity securities of the subject company becoming eligible for termination of registration pursuant to Section 12(g)(4) of the Act.

Item 6. Interest in Securities of the Subject Company.

(a) State the aggregate number and percentage of the class represented by such shares (which may be based on the number of shares outstanding as contained in the most recently available filing with the Commission by the subject company unless the bidder has reason to believe such information is not current), beneficially owned (identifying those shares for which there is a right to acquire) by each person named in Item 2 of this schedule and by each associate and majority-owned subsidiary of such person giving the name and address of any such associate or subsidiary.

(b) Describe any transaction in the class of securities reported on that was effected during the past 60 days by the persons named in response to paragraph (a) of this item or by any executive officer, director or subsidiary of such person.

Instructions. 1. The description of a transaction required by Item 6(b) shall include, but not necessarily be limited to: 1) the identity of the person covered by Item 6(b) who effected the transactions; 2) the date of the transaction; 3) the amount of securities involved; 4) the price per share; and 5) where and how the transaction was effected.

2. If the information required by Item 6(b) of this schedule is available to the bidder at the time this statement is initially filed with the Commission pursuant to Rule 14d-3(a)(1), such information should be included in such initial filing. However, if such information is not available to the bidder at the time of such initial filing, it shall be filed with the Commission promptly but in no event later than two business days after the date of such filing and, if material, shall be disclosed in a manner reasonably designed to inform security holders. The procedure specified by this instruction is provided for the purpose of maintaining the confidentiality of the tender offer in order to avoid possible misuse of inside information.

Item 7. Contracts, Arrangements, Understandings or Relationships with Respect to the Subject Company's Securities.

Describe any contract, arrangement, understanding or relationship (whether or not legally enforceable) between the bidder (including those persons enumerated in

Instruction C to this schedule) and any person with respect to any securities of the subject company (including, but not limited to, any contract, arrangement, understanding or relationship concerning the transfer or the voting of any of such securities, joint ventures, loan or option arrangements, puts or calls, guaranties of loans, guaranties against loss, or the giving or withholding of proxies) naming the persons with whom such contracts, arrangements, understandings or relationships have been entered into and giving the material provisions thereof. Include such information for any of such securities that are pledged or otherwise subject to a contingency, the occurrence of which would give another person the power to direct the voting or disposition of such securities, except that disclosure of standard default and similar provisions contained in loan agreements need not be included.

Item 8. *Persons Retained, Employed or to be Compensated.*

Identify all persons and classes of persons employed, retained or to be compensated by the bidder, or by any person on the bidder's behalf, to make solicitations or recommendations in connection with the tender offer and describe briefly the terms of such employment, retainer or arrangement for compensation.

Item 9. *Financial Statements of Certain Bidders.*

Where the bidder is other than a natural person and the bidder's financial condition is material to a decision by a security holder of the subject company whether to sell, tender or hold securities being sought in the tender offer, furnish current, adequate financial information concerning the bidder *provided* that if the bidder is controlled by another entity which is not a natural person and has been formed for the purpose of making the tender offer, furnish current, adequate financial information concerning such parent.

Instructions. 1. The facts and circumstances concerning the tender offer, particularly the terms of the tender offer, may influence a determination as to whether disclosure of financial information is material. However, once the materiality requirement is applicable, the adequacy of the financial information will depend primarily on the nature of the bidder.

In order to provide guidance in making this determination, the following types of financial information will be deemed adequate for the purposes of this item for the type of bidder specified: (a) financial statements prepared in compliance with Form 10 as amended for a domestic bidder which is otherwise eligible to use such form; and (b) Financial statements prepared in accordance with Item 17 of Form 20-F for a foreign bidder that is otherwise eligible to use such form.

2. If the bidder is subject to the periodic reporting requirements of Sections 13(a) or 15(d) of the Act, financial statements contained in any document filed with the Commission may be incorporated by reference in this schedule solely for the purposes of this schedule *provided* that such financial statements substantially meet the requirements of this item; an express statement is made that such financial statements are incorporated by reference; the matter incorporated by reference is

clearly identified by page, paragraph, caption or otherwise; and an indication is made where such information may be inspected and copies obtained. Financial statements which are required to be presented in comparative form for two or more fiscal years or periods shall not be incorporated by reference unless the material incorporated by reference includes the entire period for which the comparative data is required to be given.

3. If the bidder is not subject to the periodic reporting requirements of the Act, the financial statements required by this item need not be audited if such audited financial statements are not available or obtainable without unreasonable cost or expense and a statement is made to that effect disclosing the reasons therefor.

Item 10. Additional Information.

If material to a decision by a security holder whether to sell, tender or hold securities being sought in the tender offer, furnish information as the following:

(a) Any present or proposed material contracts, arrangements, understandings or relationships between the bidder or any of its executive officers, directors, controlling persons or subsidiaries and the subject company or any of its executive officers, directors, controlling persons or subsidiaries (other than any contract, arrangement or understanding required to be disclosed pursuant to Items 3 or 7 or this schedule);

(b) To the extent known by the bidder after reasonable investigation, the applicable regulatory requirements which must be complied with or approvals which must be obtained in connection with the tender offer;

(c) The applicability of anti-trust laws;

(d) The applicability of the margin requirements of Section 7 of the Act and the regulations promulgated thereunder;

(e) Any material pending legal proceedings relating to the tender offer including the name and location of the court or agency in which the proceedings are pending, the date instituted, the principal parties thereto and a brief summary of the proceedings; and

Instruction. In connection with this sub-item, a copy of any document relating to a major development (such as pleadings, an answer, complaint, temporary restraining order, injunction, opinion, judgment or order) in a material pending legal proceeding should be promptly furnished to the Commission on a supplemental basis.

(f) Such additional material information, if any, as may be necessary to make the required statements, in light of the circumstances under which they are made, not materially misleading.

Item 11. Material to be Filed as Exhibits.

Furnish a copy of:

(a) Tender offer material which is published, sent or given to security holders by or on behalf of the bidder in connection with the tender offer;

(b) Any loan agreement referred to in Item 4 of this schedule,

Instruction. The identity of any bank which is a party to a loan agreement need not be disclosed if the person filing the statement has requested that the identity of such bank not be made available to the public pursuant to Item 4 of this schedule.

(c) Any document setting forth the terms of any contracts, arrangements, understandings or relationships referred to in Item 7 or 10(a) of this schedule;

(d) Any written opinion prepared by legal counsel at the bidder's request and communicated to the bidder pertaining to the tax consequences of the tender offer;

(e) In an exchange offer where securities of the bidder have been or are to be registered under the Securities Act of 1933, the prospectus containing the information to be included therein by Rule 432 of that Act.

(f) If any oral solicitation of security holders is to be made by or on behalf of the bidder, any written instruction, form, or other material which is furnished to the persons making the actual oral solicitation for their use, directly or indirectly, in connection with the tender offer.

Signature. After due inquiry and to the best of my knowledge and belief, I certify that the information set forth in this statement is true, complete and correct.

. . . .
              (Date)   (Signature)

                                    . . . .
                                    (Name and Title)

The original statement shall be signed by each person on whose behalf the statement is filed or by his authorized representative. If the statement is signed on behalf of a person by his authorized representative (other than an executive officer or general partner of the bidder), evidence of the representative's authority to sign on behalf of such person shall be filed with the statement. The name and any title of each person who signs the statement shall be typed or printed beneath his signature.

10

Taxable Acquisitions
and General Concepts

This chapter discusses taxable acquisitions. Like Chapter 11, the discussion is presented in sufficient detail to present the problems and offer solutions to the more usual situations. However, in actual transactions, there is no substitute for careful thought and research into existing qualifications, exceptions and refinements to the general tax principles described.

As a practical matter, all tax problems must concern both the buyer and seller because either party may refuse to proceed unless the other party cooperates in finding solutions to them. For example, a seller who seeks to pay only a single tax by structuring a transaction taxable as a stock sale will probably have to negotiate a price reflecting the loss to the buyer of a stepped up basis in the corporate assets or the tax cost of an election to obtain such basis.

Throughout Chapters 10 and 11, the discussion presumes that each seller and buyer is a corporation taxable under Subchapter C of the Internal Revenue Code. Different methods and affects apply to acquisitions involving partnerships and Subchapter S corporations.

BASIC PRINCIPLES

The simplest taxable acquisition is a sale of stock for cash. The seller realizes gain or loss on the sale taxable at the rates applicable to the sale of a capital asset.[*] The buyer obtains a basis in the stock equal to the purchase price and other acquisition costs. Neither the buyer nor the corporation sold obtains any increased basis in its assets unless an election is made under Code Section 338 as described later. Thus, the acquired corporation will continue to take depreciation deductions using the

---

[*]Corporations filing a consolidated return may not claim a *loss* on a sale of stock of its consolidated subsidiaries.

same bases as it used prior to the acquisition. The buyer cannot claim any deduction for its basis in the stock until it resells the stock. The result is satisfactory to the seller, but disadvantageous to a buyer who pays a premium acquisition price.

A corporation can also sell its assets for cash. Even though the seller and buyer agree on a lump sum price, the Code treats the transaction as a sale of each of the numerous assets transferred. The seller must allocate the lump sum price among the assets as required by Code Section 1060. The kind of gain realized by the seller depends on the nature of each asset sold as do other consequences such as recapture of depreciation. The buyer obtains a basis in each asset (or asset group) equal to the cost obtained through the allocation process. The new asset bases are used in calculating future depreciation (modified ACRS) deductions. If the seller corporation is liquidated and distributes to its shareholders the price remaining after payment of taxes and other debts, each shareholder will pay another tax on the gain, if any, equal to the excess of the amount received in liquidation over the basis in his or her stock.

Transactions accomplished by mergers, including triangular mergers, for a cash price follow the same concepts. As described later, the reverse triangular merger is treated as an acquisition of stock and the forward triangular merger is treated as an acquisition of assets.

The simple principles described have created controversy for many years because corporate income is taxed twice. It is taxed when the corporation earns it. It is taxed again when distributed to shareholders as dividends or in liquidation. The corporation cannot claim any deduction against its income for these distributions as it can for interest and other business expenses.

The double taxation is especially visible in corporate acquisitions because each tax can be very large. Further, much of the gain results from inflation rather than intrinsic increase in value. Thus, over the years, corporations and shareholders have made numerous efforts, successful and unsuccessful, to eliminate or minimize the double tax effects. *General Utilities and Operating Co. v. Helvering*, 296 U.S. 200 (1935); *Commissioner v. Court Holding Co.*, 324 U.S. 331 (1945); *Kimbell-Diamond Milling Co. v. Commissioner*, 14 T.C. 74, affirmed 187 F.2d 718 (5 Cir. 195), cert. den. 342 U.S. 827 (1951).

Congress has reacted periodically to court decisions by amending the Code in ways which upheld, modified or nullified the taxpayer efforts and the court decisions.

PRE-1987 ACQUISITIONS

Prior to the adoption of the Internal Revenue Code of 1986, the Code contained several provisions which provided relief from double taxation of income in taxable acquisitions.

Code Section 336(a) provided that no gain or loss be recognized to a corporation on the distribution of property (other than LIFO inventory) in complete liquidation. This provision, based on the so-called *General Utilities* doctrine, meant that a corporation could distribute its assets in liquidation without taxation of the corporation on unrealized appreciation of property distributed.

Code Section 331(a) provided, as it does today, that amounts received by a shareholder in a distribution in complete liquidation of a corporation shall be treated as full payment in exchange for the stock, subject to an exception for gain on LIFO inventory. Section 334(a) provided, as it does today, that the basis of the property in the hands of the shareholders is its fair market value on the date of distribution. The combined effect of Code Section 336(a), 331(a) and 334(a) meant that corporate assets could be distributed in complete liquidation to the shareholders and sold by them concurrently at the cost of a single capital gains tax on the difference between the shareholder's basis in their stock and the fair market value of the corporate assets on the date of the liquidation distribution. *U.S. v. Cumberland Public Service Co.*, 338 U.S. 431 (1950). Until 1982, this treatment was also available for partial liquidations of corporate assets.

In most situations, however, Code Section 337 made unnecessary the cumbersome task of liquidation and sale of the corporate assets by the shareholders. Code Section 337 allowed a corporation to adopt a plan of complete liquidation, file a form 966 with the IRS within 30 days, and then distribute all its assets (less amounts retained to meet claims) in complete liquidation within a 12 month period. This allowed the corporation to sell its assets directly to a buyer and distribute the purchase price (less amounts retained for claims) to its shareholders. Under Code Sections 331(a) and 336(a), the cost was again a single capital gains tax on the difference between the shareholders' basis in their stock and the fair market value of the purchase price. If the purchase price was paid in cash, the calculation of gain was simple. If a noncash price was paid, valuation was required and the shareholders obtained a basis in the property equal to fair market value under Code Section 334(a).

Until 1982, Code Section 334(b)(2) allowed a corporation to buy the stock (at least 80%) of another corporation and to distribute its assets in liquidation within two years. If it did so, the corporation obtained a basis in the assets equal to its adjusted basis in the stock. Complex requirements governed the purchases and their timing. However, the effect was that shareholders could sell their stock at the cost of a single capital gains tax and the buyer corporation could obtain a stepped up basis in the assets for depreciation purposes without paying a tax.

The IRS challenged these double tax relief provisions for many years, primarily to limit efforts of corporations and shareholders to expand their application by imaginative structuring of acquisitions. For example, the IRS opposed taxpayer efforts to use the one-year liquidation period allowed by Section 337 to shelter income. The IRS also challenged self-serving allocations of the acquisition price among assets pursuant to Section 334(b)(2). These challenges became more important as the Code was amended to allow accelerated depreciation deductions and investment tax credits together with provisions for their recapture upon a sale of assets.

POST-1987 ACQUISITIONS

The President and Congress who took office in 1982 had campaigned on a platform which included tax simplification and reduction. To redeem their promises in spite of rapidly growing federal government expenses, they combined visible rate reductions with elimination or modification of many exclusions, deductions and credits which had previously sheltered some income. The objective was to reduce rates without reducing corporate tax revenues.

Congress concentrated specially on the taxation of acquisitions. This became politically popular because of a growing number of controversial acquisitions such as hostile takeovers, tax-driven leveraged buyouts and acquisitions by foreign companies. Congressional committees expressed concern that Code provisions made a corporate business potentially more valuable to buyers than in the hands of its existing owners and management. Taken alone, this idea was a considerable oversimplification, but it provided a rationale to eliminate Code provisions providing relief against double taxation of income in connection with corporate acquisitions.

The first "reform" was the repeal of Section 334(b)(2) and its replacement in 1982 with a new Section 338 described later in this chapter. The effect was to allow a corporation to acquire the stock of another corporation and elect a stepped up basis in its assets, as had been permitted by Section 334(b)(2), but only at the cost of a tax imposed on a hypothetical sale of the assets at fair market value in a single transaction. Section 338(b)(5) authorized the IRS to adopt regulations governing the allocation of the acquiring corporation's basis in the purchased stock among the assets. The IRS adopted the strict four tier "residual" method described later in this chapter. The result is that elections under Section 338 are rarely made except when the acquired corporation has a net operating loss carry forward in an amount sufficient to cover the gain and in situations governed by Section 338(h)(10) which is also described later.

Section 336(a) was amended to provide that gain or loss shall be recognized to a liquidating corporation on the distribution of property in complete liquidation as if the property were sold to the distributee at fair market value. A few exceptions were allowed, most significantly for transactions governed by a revised Section 337.

Section 337 was amended to limit nonrecognition of gain or loss by a liquidating corporation to complete liquidations in which the distributions are made to "80-Percent Distributee" meeting the requirements of Section 332(b). The requirements of Section 332 include a requirement that the corporation liquidated and the corporation receiving the distributions are, at all relevant times, members of an "affiliated group" as defined in Code Section 1504(a)(2). Thus, since 1989 when transitional provisions expired, Section 337 has not been available to corporations owned primarily by individuals or a mix of individuals and unrelated corporations.

In 1987, Congress further amended Section 337 to define an "80-Percent Distributee" in a manner designed to prevent its use for "mirror" subsidiary liquidations which had been used frequently in hostile leveraged takeovers.

The result is a general rule that two taxes must be paid upon the sale of a corporation or its assets unless the buyer is willing to forego a stepped up basis in the assets acquired. The advantage to a buyer of an election under Code Section 338(h)(10) is a significant benefit to the buyer of a subsidiary which has been a member of a selling consolidated group (or an affiliated group), but will be agreeable to the seller group only when it has essentially the same basis in the assets as it has in the subsidiary's stock.

Congress reinforced the effectiveness of its imposition of the second tax by adopting a new Code Section 1060 effective in May, 1986. Code Section 1060 authorizes the IRS to adopt regulations applicable to asset acquisitions for the purposes of determining (1) the transferee's basis in the assets and (2) the gain or loss of the transferor with respect to the acquisition. As described later in this chapter, the IRS adopted strict regulations based on the four tier, residual method it had used in the regulations under Code Section 338.

ALLOCATION OF BASIS

As previously mentioned, Code Section 1060 was adopted effective for acquisitions after May 6, 1988. It requires that the consideration for assets be allocated among them for purposes of determining both the buyer's basis and the transferor's gain or loss in the same manner as amounts are allocated to assets under Code Section 338(b)(5).

Code Section 1060 also requires that the seller and buyer furnish to the IRS the amount of the consideration allocated to good will or going concern value and any modifications of such amount. They must also provide any other information with respect to the assets transferred as the IRS finds necessary.

The regulations require allocation among assets by a "residual" method under which the assets are divided into four classes. Class I consists of cash, demand deposits and similar items. Class II consists of certificates of deposit, U.S. government securities, readily marketable stock or securities, foreign currency and similar items. Class III consists of all assets other than Class I, II and IV assets. Class IV assets are intangible assets in the nature of good will and going concern value.

The essence of the "residual" method is that basis is allocated to assets at face value in Class I and then at fair market values in Classes II and III. Any excess over such values is then allocated entirely to class IV. Allocation within classes is proportional.

The IRS has issued a Form 8594 to implement the reporting requirements. It must be filed by both seller and buyer with their tax returns for the taxable years in which the acquisition occurred. Form 8594 requires the names and identification numbers of both seller and buyer. It requires information as to the total acquisition price and its allocation among the four asset classes. It asks whether the sales price was allocated in the acquisition contract or in another written document signed by both parties and whether the allocations shown in the Form 8594 correspond to such contract. It also requires that payments for intangible amortizable assets (i.e., licenses, covenants not to compete, leases, employment contracts, management contracts and other such arrangements) be identified.

A copy of Form 8594 is shown as Exhibit 10-1 on pages 276 and 277.

Some articles on Section 1060 have stated that it requires the seller and buyer to agree on the allocation of the price. Indeed, Section 1060 and the temporary regulations adopted by the IRS in 1988 make it desirable to do so. However, nothing in Section 1060 or the regulations require that a seller and buyer agree. They simply require that certain documents be disclosed to the IRS.

One important difference between the regulations under Section 1060 and those under Section 338 is that the regulations under Section 1060 include covenants not to compete in Class III assets.

The regulations contain provisions governing reallocation of the price in the event of subsequent increases, such as contingent formula payments, and decreases, such as refunds for audit adjustments and breaches of representations and warranties.

The regulations contain helpful examples. Examples (1) and (4) are reproduced below:

Example (1). (i) On January 1, 1987, S, a sole proprietor, sells to P, a corporation, a group of assets which constitute a trade or business under paragraph (b)(2) of this section. P pays S $2,000 in cash and assumes $1,000 in liabilities. Thus, the total consideration is $3,000.

(ii) Assume that P acquires no Class I assets and that on the purchase date, the fair market values of the Class II and III assets S sold to P are as follows:

Asset Class	Asset	Fair market value		III		
II	Portfolio of marketable securities	$ 400			Furniture and fixtures	800
	Total Class II	400			Building	800
					Land	200
					Equipment	400
					Accounts receivable	100
					Covenant not to compete	100
					Total Class III	$2,400

(iii) Under paragraph (d)(1) and (2) of this section, the amount of consideration allocable to the Class II, III, and IV assets is the total consideration reduced by the amount of any Class I assets. Since P acquired no Class I assets, the total consideration of $3,000 is next allocated first to Class II and then to Class III assets. Since the fair market value of the Class II asset is $400, $400 of consideration is allocated to the Class II asset. Since the remaining amount of consideration is $2,600 (*i.e.*, $3,000–$400), an amount which exceeds the sum of the fair market values of the Class III assets ($2,400), the amount allocated to each Class III asset is its fair market value. Thus, the total amount allocated to Class III assets is $2,400.

(iv) The amount allocated to the Class IV assets (assets in the nature of goodwill and going concern value) is $200 (*i.e.*, $2,600–$2,400).

Example (4). (i) On January 1, 1989, S, a sole proprietor, sells to P a group of assets which constitutes a trade or business under paragraph (b)(2) of this section. S, who plans to retire immediately, also executes a covenant not to compete in P's favor. P pays S $3,000 in cash and assumes $1,000 in liabilities. Thus, the total consideration is $4,000.

(ii) On the purchase date, P and S also execute a separate agreement that states that the fair market values of the Class II and III assets S sold to P are as follows:

Asset Class	Asset	Fair market value
II	Portfolio of marketable securities	$ 500
	Total Class II	500

III		
	Furniture and fixtures	800
	Building	800
	Land	200
	Equipment	400
	Construction contract	200
	Covenant not to compete	900
	Total Class III	3,300

(iii) P and S each allocate the consideration in the transaction among the assets transferred under paragraph (d) of this section in accordance with the agreed upon fair market values of the assets, so that $500 is allocated to Class II assets, $3,300 is allocated to Class III assets, and $200 ($4,000 total consideration less $3,800 allocated to asset classes I, II and III) is allocated to the Class IV assets (assets in the nature of goodwill and going concern value).

(iv) In connection with the examination of P's return, the District Director, in determining the fair market values of the assets transferred, may disregard the parties' agreement. Assume that the District Director correctly determines that the fair market value of the covenant not to compete was $100. Since the allocation of consideration among Class I, II, and III assets results in allocation up to the fair market value limitation, the $800 of unallocated consideration resulting from the District Director's redetermination of the value of the covenant not to compete is allocated to Class IV assets.

Most interesting, the regulations contain no real guidance about the determination of the fair market value of Class III assets. This is surprising because the major questions relating to allocation have for many years been centered on the assets grouped by the regulations in Class III. For example, there is no description of the methods to be used in determining fair market value. There is no requirement of appraisals or that the appraisers be independent. The result is that buyer and seller have considerable freedom in determining fair market values of Class III assets and the IRS has considerable freedom in challenging their values.

Form **8594**	**Asset Acquisition Statement**	OMB No. 1545-1021
(July 1988)	**Under Section 1060**	Expires: 09-30-90
Department of the Treasury Internal Revenue Service	► **Attach to Your Federal Income Tax Return.**	Attachment Sequence No. 61

Name as shown on return	Identification number as shown on tax return

Part I　To Be Completed by All Filers

1　Name of buyer	Buyer's identification number as shown on tax return

Address (number and street)

City, state, and ZIP code

2　Name of seller	Seller's identification number as shown on tax return

Address (number and street)

City, state, and ZIP code

3　Date of sale	4　Total sales price

Part II　Assets Transferred—To be completed by all filers of an original statement

1　Assets	Aggregate Fair Market Value (Actual Amount for Class I)	Allocation of Sales Price
Class I	$	$
Class II	$	$
Class III	$	$
Class IV	////////////	$
Total	////////////	$

2　Did the buyer and seller provide for an allocation of the sales price in the sales contract or in another written document signed by both parties? . . . . Yes ☐ No ☐

If "Yes," are the aggregate fair market values listed for each of asset Classes I, II, and III the amounts agreed upon in your sales contract or in a separate written document? . . . . Yes ☐ No ☐

3　To be completed by buyer only: In connection with the purchase of the group of assets, did you also purchase a license or a covenant not to compete, or enter into a lease agreement, employment contract, management contract, or similar arrangement with the seller (or managers, directors, owners, or employees of the seller)? . . . . Yes ☐ No ☐

If "Yes," specify (a) the type of agreement, and (b) the maximum amount of consideration (not including interest) paid or to be paid under the agreement. (Attach additional sheets if more space is needed.)

Part III　Class III, Intangible Amortizable Assets Only—Complete if applicable. The amounts shown below also must be included under Class III assets in Part II. (Attach additional sheets if more space is needed.)

Assets	Fair Market Value	Useful Life	Allocation of Sales Price
	$		$
	$		$
	$		$

Part IV　Supplemental Statement—To be completed only if amending an original statement or previously filed supplemental statement because of an increase or decrease in consideration.

1　Assets	Allocation of Sales Price as Previously Reported	Increase or (Decrease)	Redetermined Allocation of Sales Price
Class I	$	$	$
Class II	$	$	$
Class III	$	$	$
Class IV	$	$	$
Total	$	////////////	$

2　Reason(s) for increase or decrease (Attach additional sheets if more space is needed.)

3　Tax year and tax return form number with which the original Form 8594 and any supplemental statements were filed

For Paperwork Reduction Act Notice, see instructions.　　　　　　　　　　　　　　　　Form **8594** (7-88)

Form 8594 (7-88)

Instructions

(Section references are to the Internal Revenue Code, unless otherwise noted.)

Paperwork Reduction Act Notice.—We ask for this information to carry out the Internal Revenue laws of the United States. We need it to ensure that taxpayers are complying with these laws and to allow us to figure and collect the right amount of tax. You are required to give us this information.

The estimated average time needed to complete this form, depending on individual circumstances, is 1.1 hours. If you have comments concerning the accuracy of this time estimate or suggestions for making this form more simple, we would be happy to hear from you. You can write either IRS or the Office of Management and Budget at the addresses listed in the instructions of the tax return with which this form is filed.

Purpose of Form.—For acquisitions after May 6, 1986, the seller and buyer of a group of assets constituting a trade or business must report to IRS on Form 8594 if goodwill or a going concern value attaches, or could attach, to such assets and if the buyer's basis in the assets is determined only by the amount paid for the assets ("applicable asset acquisition," defined below).

Who Must File.—Both the buyer and the seller of the assets must prepare and attach Form 8594 to their Federal income tax returns (Forms 1040, 1041, 1065, 1120, 1120S, etc.).

Exceptions.—You are not required to file Form 8594 if any of the following apply:

(1) The acquisition is not an applicable asset acquisition.

(2) The asset acquisition occurs pursuant to a binding contract in effect on May 6, 1986, and at all times thereafter.

(3) A group of assets that constitutes a trade or business is exchanged for like-kind property in a transaction to which section 1031 applies. However, if section 1031 does not apply to all the assets transferred, Form 8594 is required for the part of the group of assets to which section 1031 does not apply. For information about such a transaction, see Regulations section 1.1060-1T(b)(4).

(4) A partnership interest is transferred. See Regulations section 1.755-2T for special reporting requirements.

When To File.—Generally, attach Form 8594 to your Federal income tax return for the year in which the sale date occurred. If the amount allocated to any asset is increased or decreased after Form 8594 is filed, the seller and/or buyer (whoever is affected) must complete Part I and the supplemental statement in Part IV of a new Form 8594 and attach the form to the Federal tax return for the year in which the increase or decrease is taken into account.

Exception.—If the sale (or increase or decrease) is in a taxable year for which the due date (including extensions of time) of the return is before September 13, 1988, you need not file Form 8594 for that event. For example, if a reportable sale, or an increase or decrease, occurred in 1987 and you filed your 1987 Form 1040 by April 15, 1988, you need not file Form 8594 for that event. But if the due date of your 1987 Form 1040 is extended to September 15, 1988, Form 8594 must be attached to that return.

Definitions

Applicable asset acquisition means a transfer of a group of assets that constitutes a trade or business in which the buyer's basis in such assets is determined wholly by the amount paid for the assets. An applicable asset acquisition includes both a direct and indirect transfer of a group of assets, such as a sale of a business.

A group of assets constitutes a trade or business if goodwill or going concern value could under any circumstances attach to such assets. A group of assets could qualify as a trade or business whether or not they qualify as an active trade or business under section 355 (relating to controlled corporations). Factors to consider in making this determination include (a) any excess of the total paid for the assets over the aggregate book value

of the assets (other than goodwill and going concern value) as shown in the buyer's financial accounting books and records, or (b) a license, a lease agreement, a covenant not to compete, a management contract, an employment contract, or other similar agreements between buyer and seller (or managers, directors, owners, or employees of the seller).

The **buyer's consideration** is the cost of the assets. The **seller's consideration** is the amount realized.

Fair market value is the gross fair market value unreduced by mortgages, liens, pledges, or other liabilities. However, for determining the seller's gain or loss, generally, the fair market value of any property is not less than any nonrecourse debt to which the property is subject.

Class I assets are cash, demand deposits, and similar accounts in banks, savings and loan associations and other depository institutions, and other similar items that may be designated in the Internal Revenue Bulletin.

Class II assets are certificates of deposit, U.S. Government securities, readily marketable stock or securities, foreign currency, and other items that may be designated in the Internal Revenue Bulletin.

Class III assets are all tangible and intangible assets that are not Class I, II, or IV assets. Examples of Class III assets are furniture and fixtures, land, buildings, equipment, a covenant not to compete, and accounts receivable.

Class IV assets are intangible assets in the nature of goodwill and going concern value.

Allocation of Consideration

An allocation of the purchase price must be made to determine the buyer's basis in each acquired asset and the seller's gain or loss on the transfer of each asset. Use the residual method for the allocation of the sales price among the goodwill and other assets transferred. See Regulations section 1.1060-1T(d). The amount allocated to an asset, other than a Class IV asset, cannot exceed its fair market value on the purchase date. The amount you can allocate to an asset also is subject to any applicable limits under the Internal Revenue Code or general principles of tax law. For example, see section 1056 for the basis limitation for player contracts transferred in connection with the sale of a franchise.

First, reduce the consideration by the amount of Class I assets transferred. Next, allocate the remaining consideration to Class II assets in proportion to their fair market values on the purchase date, then to Class III assets in proportion to their fair market values on the purchase date, and finally to Class IV assets.

Reallocation After an Increase or Decrease in Consideration

If an increase or decrease in consideration that must be taken into account to redetermine the seller's amount realized on the sale or the buyer's cost basis in the assets occurs after the purchase date, the seller and/or buyer must allocate the increase or decrease among the assets. If the increase or decrease occurs in the same tax year as the purchase date, consider the increase or decrease to have occurred on the purchase date. If the increase or decrease occurs after the tax year of the purchase date, consider it in the tax year in which it occurs.

For an increase or decrease related to a patent, copyright, etc., follow the rules under *Specific allocation*, described below.

Allocation of Increase.—Allocate an increase in consideration as described above under *Allocation of Consideration*. If an asset has been disposed of, depreciated, amortized, or depleted by the buyer before the increase occurs, any amount allocated to such asset by the buyer must be properly taken into account under principles of tax law applicable when part of the cost of an asset (not previously reflected in its basis) is paid after the asset has been disposed of, depreciated, amortized, or depleted.

Allocation of Decrease.—Allocate a decrease in the following order: (1) reduce the amount previously allocated to Class IV assets, (2) reduce the amount previously allocated to Class III assets in proportion to their fair market values on the purchase date, and (3) reduce the amount previously allocated to Class II assets in proportion to their fair market values on the purchase date.

You cannot decrease the amount allocated to an asset below zero. If an asset has a basis of zero at the time the decrease is taken into account because it has been disposed of, depreciated, amortized, or depleted by the buyer, the decrease in consideration allocable to such asset must be properly taken into account under principles of tax law applicable when the cost of an asset (previously reflected in basis) is reduced after the asset has been disposed of, depreciated, amortized, or depleted. An asset is considered to have been disposed of to the extent the decrease allocated to it would reduce its basis below zero.

Patents, Copyrights, and Similar Property.—You must make a *specific allocation* if an increase or decrease is the result of a contingency that directly relates to income produced by a particular intangible asset, such as a patent, a secret process, or a copyright, and the increase or decrease is related only to such asset and not to other assets. If the specific allocation rule does not apply, make an allocation of any increase or decrease as you would for any other assets as described above under *Allocation of Increase* and *Allocation of Decrease*.

Specific allocation.—Limited to the fair market value of the asset, any increase or decrease is allocated first specifically to the patent, copyright, or similar property to which the increase or decrease relates, and then to the other assets in the order described above under *Allocation of Increase* and *Allocation of Decrease*. For purposes of applying the fair market value limit to the patent, copyright, or similar property, the fair market value of such asset is redetermined when the increase or decrease is taken into account by considering only the reasons for the increase or decrease. However, the fair market values of the other assets are not redetermined.

Specific Instructions

For an original statement, complete Parts I, II, and, if applicable, III. For a Supplemental Statement, complete Parts I and IV.

Part I, Identification number as shown on tax return.—You are required to provide your taxpayer identification number (TIN) and the TIN of the other person (buyer or seller) who entered into this transaction. For an individual or sole proprietor, enter the social security number. For a corporation, partnership, or other entity, enter the employer identification number.

Part I, Item 3.—Enter the date on which the sale of the assets occurs.

Part I, Item 4.—Enter the total consideration transferred for the assets.

Part II.—For a particular class of assets, enter the total fair market value of all the assets in the class and the total allocation of the sales price. For item 3, to determine the maximum consideration to be paid, assume that any contingencies specified in the agreement are met and that the consideration paid is the highest amount possible. If you cannot determine the maximum consideration, state how the consideration will be computed and the payment period.

Part III.—Enter in Part III only those Class III assets that are intangible and amortizable. Be sure to enter the total Class III assets in Part II.

Part IV.—Complete Part IV and file a new Form 8594 for each year that an increase or decrease in consideration occurs. Give the reason(s) for the increase or decrease in allocation. Also, enter the form number and tax year with which the original and any supplemental statements were filed. For example, enter "1987 Form 1040." If an original or supplemental Form 8594 was not required to be filed, so state.

EXAMPLE OF CONTRACTUAL
PRICE ALLOCATION

The following is an example of a contractual provision allocating a $1,500,000 cash purchase price among assets in which seller has an aggregate tax basis, net of depreciation and accruals for unsalable inventories and uncollectible reserves of $1,000,000.

Seller and buyer agree that the $1,500,000 purchase price is allocated to the assets purchased as follows:

Asset	Seller's Basis	Price
Inventories	$ 200,000	$ 225,000 (1)
Accounts receivable	250,000	250,000
Prepaid items	25,000	25,000
Land	25,000	100,000 (2)
Buildings and fixtures	100,000	200,000 (3)
Machinery, equipment and vehicles	400,000	500,000 (4)
Tools and parts	—	25,000 (5)
Patents	—	75,000 (6)
Covenant not to compete for three years	—	50,000 (7)
Goodwill	—	50,000 (8)
	$1,000,000	$1,500,000

(1) Ordinary income to seller. Increased basis to buyer, recoverable against sales.
(2) Capital gain to seller. Increased basis to buyer, but non-depreciable.
(3) Capital gain to seller, subject to § 1250 recapture. Increased basis to buyer for MACRS writeoff.
(4) § 1231 capital gain to seller, subject to § 1245 recapture. Increased basis to buyer for MACRS writeoff.
(5) Ordinary income to seller since previously expensed. Increased basis to buyer for expense writeoff.
(6) Capital gain to seller. Increased basis to buyer, amortizable over patent lives.
(7) Ordinary income to seller. $50,000 amortizable by buyer over three-year period.
(8) Capital gain to seller. Increased basis to buyer, but non-depreciable.

UNIFIED TAX RATES

Since 1986, the Internal Revenue Code has taxed income from the sale or exchange of capital assets at the same rates as income from other sources. Nevertheless, the Code retains most of the provisions which have historically related to capital gains and losses.

There are several situations in which capital gain or loss continue to be significant. First, capital losses can be deducted only from capital gains, except that individuals may deduct up to $3,000 of capital losses from other kinds of income. Second, various corporate transactions are taxed differently if they are characterized as capital gain or loss. A corporate transaction treated as a sale or exchange of a capital asset will result in gain or loss to the seller and a new basis to the buyer. If a corporate transaction is recharacterized and treated as payment of a dividend or of imputed interest, the tax consequences will change.

Because of unified tax rates, some issues have a different or lesser significance than they did when capital gain income and ordinary income were taxed at different rates. For example, sellers are less likely to be concerned about allocation of basis, imputed interest and depreciation recapture. On the other hand, sellers will be concerned about issues that accelerate income recognition (such as original issue discount) or which change its character. Buyers will continue to be concerned about issues such as allocation of the price and net operating loss carryovers.

The fact that the Code retains separate treatment of capital gains and losses means that Congress can readily restore different rates at such time as it may recognize the need to stimulate capital investment in U.S. businesses by domestic investors. While the issue is politically sensitive, taxation of risk investment at the same rates as other income diverts capital from investment or into investments perceived as having low risk or more favorable tax treatment. For example, since Congress first curtailed favorable capital gain rates in 1969, the economy experienced "stagflation" during the 1970s, high interest rates and "tax shelter" investment problems during the late 1970s and early 1980s, and the substitution of leveraged lending and "junk bonds" for scarce equity capital during the 1980s. Congress must eventually address the nation's capital formation needs and may reinstate reduced taxation of capital gains, perhaps linked to a relatively lengthy holding period or to gain reduced by an inflation index.

INSTALLMENT SALES—§ 453

In a proposed acquisition where the price is not to be paid in stock, a buyer may not be in a position to pay the entire purchase price in cash. To close a transaction, the seller may be required to accept a substantial portion of the purchase price in the form of promissory notes or other debt securities of the buyer. Under these circumstances, if the transaction is taxable, the seller may not realize sufficient cash to be willing to pay the entire income tax owed as a result of the acquisition in one year. The solution is to cast the transaction in such a form that not all of the income taxes are payable for the year in which the transaction is closed. If the transaction is cast to qualify for installment sale treatment under the Internal Revenue Code, income taxes will be payable by the seller only as the proceeds of sale are actually realized in cash—i.e., as the evidences of indebtedness delivered by the buyer mature and are paid off. The seller will, therefore, have sufficient cash to pay taxes as the taxes fall due.

Installment Sale—Requirements. Under Section 453 of the Internal Revenue Code, income from an "installment sale" is taxed under the "installment method," unless the taxpayer elects to the contrary on or before the due date of the tax return for the taxable year in which the sale occurs. An "installment sale" means a disposition of property in which at least one payment is to be received after the close of the taxable year in which the disposition occurs, except for transactions by dealers and sales of inventories.

Under the foregoing requirements, if a seller sells stock of a corporation for a consideration of $10,000 and if the consideration received consists of $2,000 in cash and $8,000 of indebtedness in the form of notes of the buyer, payable over a seven-year period, only the $2,000 will be taxed in the year of sale, subject to exceptions described later.

Installment Sale—Tax Treatment. The "installment method" taxes income from a disposition in the taxable year when each payment is received in the proportion which the gross profit (the profit which will be realized when all payments are completed) bears to the total contract price of the acquisition. To illustrate, assume that selling stockholders sell 100 percent of the stock of the seller to a buyer in an acquisition that qualifies under the installment sales provisions, in accordance with the terms indicated in the following tabulation:

(1)   Total contract price $100,000
(2)   Tax cost of selling stockholder's stock . . . .$ 90,000
(3)   Gross profit . . . .$ 10,000
(4)   Payment in year of closing . . . .$ 20,000, cash
(5)   Notes payable in years subsequent to closing
        $10,000 per taxable year in each of the 8
        succeeding taxable years after the closing . . . .$ 80,000

Under the foregoing example, the seller will receive a gross profit of $10,000 when all payments are completed. This gross profit represents 10 percent of the total contract price ($10,000 gross profit divided by $100,000 total contract price). Therefore, the seller must report 10 percent of the actual installment payment received in the taxable year in which the transaction closed as taxable gain—i.e., $2,000 (10 percent of the total installment payment of $20,000). In each of the subsequent eight years following the year of the closing, the seller will receive $10,000 of which 10 percent will represent the portion of the payment subject to tax. Therefore, in each of the eight subsequent taxable years after the taxable year in which the transaction is closed, the sellers will be required to report 10 percent of each $10,000 installment payment—i.e., $1,000 as taxable gain for income tax purposes.

Gain equal to the amount of depreciation recaptured under Code Sections 1245 and 1250 must be recognized as ordinary income in the year of sale, regardless of the amount of installment payments received in the year of sale. The adjusted basis of the property is increased by the amount of the recapture in determining the gross profit percentage used in computing gain to be recognized on receipt of the installment payments.

Evidences of Indebtedness—Exceptions. As was mentioned above, in determining the payments received in the taxable year of the sale, evidences of indebtedness of the buyer that are not payable on demand or readily marketable are excluded even if guaranteed by a third party. Instruments on which the buyer is the payor, including bonds, notes and debentures, qualify as evidences of indebtedness, with certain exceptions. Such evidences of indebtedness do not include bonds or other evidences of indebtedness which are payable on demand or which are issued by a corporation: (1) with interest coupons attached or in registered form (other than debt instruments in registered form which the taxpayer establishes will not be readily tradable in an established securities market) or (2) such bonds or other evidences of indebtedness in any form designed to render them readily tradable in an established securities market.

The Tax Reform Act of 1986 amended Code Section 453 to deny installment treatment of stock and securities traded in an established securities market. The Internal Revenue Service is also authorized to adopt regulations denying installment reporting to other property regularly traded in an established market. The benefits of installment reporting were also reduced for certain taxpayers who have outstanding indebtedness.

The amended Code Section 453 contains proportionate disallowance rules with respect to "allocable installment indebtedness" owed by the taxpayer to other creditors.

Since 1988, the benefit of Code Section 453 has been diluted by the adoption of Code Section 453A(c) which imposes an interest charge (payable as additional tax) on the amount of tax deferred by use of the installment method, but only to the extent that the deferral is attributable to dispositions exceeding $5,000,000 in a taxable year. In addition, if the taxpayer borrows money or otherwise incurs indebtedness secured by the installment obligation, Section 453A(d) treats the proceeds of the secured indebtedness as payment received on the obligation. This provision was adopted in 1988 in response to publicity relating to installment sales of department store operations by Campeau Corporation which used the installment obligations to secure loans obtained to meet cash needs.

IMPUTED INTEREST—§ 483

Code Section 483 treats as taxable interest a portion of each deferred payment to which the section applies, received under a contract for a sale of property which does not provide for the payment of interest, or does not provide for the payment of sufficient interest under the Code. The effect of Section 483 is to convert some portion of each payment which could be a capital gain into ordinary income.

Payments to which Section 483 Applies. The section applies to any payment on account of the sale of property which constitutes a part of the sales price and which is due more than six months after the date of the sale or exchange under a contract where (1) some or all of the payments under the contract are due more than one year after the date of the sale and (2) using a rate of interest provided by regulations, there is "total unstated interest:" Section 483 contains exceptions for a sale or exchange of property where the total sale price cannot exceed $3,000 and for sales of patents pursuant to Code Section 1235(a). Section 483 applies only to sales eligible for capital gain treatment, but whether or not a gain is actually realized.

Unstated Interest—Calculation. For the purposes of Section 483, the term *total unstated interest* with respect to a contract of sale means an amount equal to the excess of (1) the sum of payments to which Section 483 applies which are due under the contract over (2) the sum of the present values of such payments plus the present values of any interest payments under the contract. To determine whether there is any unstated interest, present value is determined by using a "safe harbor" discount rate equal to 110 percent of the applicable federal rate provided in Code Section 1274(b)(2). If the 110 percent test is not met, interest is imputed at 120 percent of the applicable federal rate under Code Section 1274(d). The total unstated interest is then allocated among the payments under the contract in the manner provided in Code Section 1272(a).

Under Code Section 1272, the applicable federal rate is determined twice each year with separate rates specified for short-term (3 years or less), mid-term (3 to 9 years) and long-term (over 9 years) periods.

Imputed Interest—Some Examples. Examples taken from the regulations illustrate the operation of the imputed interest sections of the Code:

Example (1). On December 31, 1963, A sells property to B under a contract that provides that B is to pay $3,000 on the date of sale, $1,000 on June 1, 1964, and $1,000 on December 26, 1964. No interest is provided for in the contract. Since none of the payments under the contract are due more than one year after the date of the sale, Section 483 does not apply to any payments due under the contract.

Example (2). The facts are the same as in example (1), except that there is an additional payment due on June 1, 1965.

Since, under the contract there is at least one payment due more than one year after the date of the sale, Section 483 applies to any definite payment under the contract which is due more than six months after the date of the sale. Thus, Section 483 applies to the $1,000 payments due on December 26, 1964, and June 1, 1965.

Example (3). On December 31, 1963, A sells property to B under a contract that provides that B is to make payments of $2,040 ($2,000 sales price plus $40 interest), $2,080 ($2,000 sales price plus $80 interest) and $2,120 ($2,000 sales price plus $120 interest), such payments being due, respectively, one, two and three years from the date of sale. Assume that both A and B are calendar year taxpayers, that Section 483 applies to each of the payments, and that the total unstated interest under the contract is $345.85. The portion of each $2,000 payment (sales price) which is treated as interest is $115.28

($2,000 $\times \dfrac{\$\ 345.85}{\$6,000.00}$). Thus, for 1964, the total amount to be treated as interest

by A and B with respect to the contract is $155.28 ($115.28 unstated interest plus $40 stated interest), for 1965 such total amount is $195.28 ($115.28 unstated interest plus $80 stated interest), and for 1966 such total amount is $235.28 ($115.28 unstated interest plus $120 stated interest).

In the foregoing example, the computations of the present values of the payments and interest due under the contract were made in accordance with the tables set forth in Regulation Section 1.483—1(g), mentioned above.

ORIGINAL ISSUE DISCOUNT—§ 1272

In addition to questions about installment reporting and imputed interest, a seller who accepts a debt instrument for all or part of the acquisition price must consider the application of the original issue discount rules contained in Code Sections 1271 through 1275.

The OID rules, which are not limited to acquisition transactions, were adopted to require and accelerate the reporting of interest income from zero coupon and other debt instruments providing for payment of a stated redemption price at maturity in excess of the issue price (OID) by more than a *de minimis* amount (i.e., less than one-fourth of one percent of the stated redemption price multiplied by the number of complete years to maturity). See Code Section 1273. The holder of a debt instrument having OID issued after July 1, 1982 must include in gross income an amount equal to the sum of the daily portions of the OID for each day during the taxable year on which the holder held the debt instrument. See Code Section 1272.

Code Section 1273 prescribes the methods to determine the amount of OID and Code Section 1272 prescribes the methods for allocating OID to daily portions. Special rules apply to publicly issued debt instruments not issued for property. See Code Section 1273(b).

A special rule also applies to the determination of the issue price of certain debt instruments issued for property. If a debt instrument issued for property has adequate stated interest, the issue price is the stated principal amount. If not, the issue price is an "imputed principal amount" equal to the sum of the present values of all payments due under the debt instrument determined by using a discount rate equal to the applicable federal rate, compounded semiannually. However, in any potentially abusive situation, the imputed principal amount is the fair market value of the property adjusted to take into account any other consideration involved in the transaction. The special rule contains several exceptions including certain sales of farms and principal residences; sales involving payments of $250,000 or less; certain debt instruments that are publicly traded or issued for publicly traded property; certain sales of patents and certain land transfers between related persons. See Code Section 1274.

Code Section 1274A authorizes a joint election by a borrower and certain lenders to use the cash method for certain cash method debt instruments not exceeding

$2,000,000 in principal amount, notwithstanding the provisions of Sections 483 and 1274. The instrument must, among other things, be a qualified debt instrument meeting certain characteristics including a stated principal amount not exceeding $2,800,000 and an interest rate of at least 9%, compounded semiannually.

Deductions of OID are governed by Code Section 163. See the later discussion under the caption "Interest on High Yield Discount Bonds" of the denial of a deduction under Code Section 163(e) of a "disqualified portion" of the interest on certain high yield instruments.

PREFERRED STOCK—§ 306 STOCK

Section 306 of the code was enacted to prevent the so-called "preferred stock bail-out." It was aimed at a situation where common stockholders of a corporation received preferred stock as a dividend on a tax-free basis. Subsequently, the preferred stock could be sold or redeemed and the gain realized from the sale could be reported as capital gain. In effect, prior to Section 306, stockholders of a corporation could convert what would normally have been ordinary dividend income into capital gain through the device of the issuance of stock dividends payable in preferred stock. Although the section was enacted to prohibit the use of the stock dividend payable in preferred stock as a tax avoidance device, the application of the section is much more far-reaching. It may come into play in any tax-free acquisition in which preferred stock forms a part of the consideration paid to the seller by the buyer.

Section 306 stock—Definition. For the purposes of considering tax problems involved in acquisitions, one definition of Section 306 stock is particularly applicable. Section 306 stock is stock received by a stockholder of a seller in pursuance of a plan of reorganization within the meaning of Section 368(a) of the code, which is not common stock, but only to the extent that the effect of the transaction was substantially the same as the receipt of a stock dividend.

Under this definition, Section 306 stock must be other than common stock. Therefore, the provisions of Section 306 will come into play in an acquisition only if preferred stock is utilized by the buyer to pay a portion of the price to the seller or the seller's stockholders. Furthermore, the preferred stock must be received in connection with a tax-free reorganization within the meaning of Section 368(a) of the Internal Revenue Code—i.e., a tax-free statutory merger, stock-for-stock acquisition or stock-for-assets acquisition described in Chapter 10. Finally, the effect of the receipt of such stock upon the seller's stockholders must be substantially the same as the receipt of a stock dividend.

Substantially the Same as Stock Dividend. In some situations, the determination of whether or not the receipt of preferred stock is substantially the same as the receipt of a stock dividend, is simple. For example, if a seller's stockholders receive 95 percent of the consideration for the sale of their business in the form of a buyer's common stock and 5 percent in the form of a buyer's preferred stock, the receipt of the preferred stock would be "substantially the same as the receipt of a stock dividend," and the preferred stock would be Section 306 stock. On the other hand, where 100 percent of the consideration received by a seller's stockholders consists of preferred stock of a buyer, the receipt of the preferred stock would not be "substantially the same as the receipt of a stock dividend," and the preferred stock would not constitute Section 306 stock. Further, if the buyer has no current or accumulated earnings and profits and a distribution of money would not be a dividend, then preferred stock issued at such a time generally will not be Section 306 stock.

The regulations contain the following examples:

Example (1). Corporation A, having only common stock outstanding, is merged in a statutory merger [qualifying as a reorganization under Section 368(a)] with Corporation B. Pursuant to such merger, the shareholders of Corporation A received both common and preferred stock in Corporation B. The preferred stock received by such shareholders is Section 306 stock.

Example (2). X and Y each own one-half of the 2,000 outstanding shares of preferred stock and one-half of the 2,000 outstanding shares of common stock of Corporation C. Pursuant to a reorganization within the meaning of Section (E) (recapitalization) each shareholder exchanges his preferred stock for preferred stock of a new issue which is not substantially different from the preferred stock previously held. Unless the preferred stock exchanged was itself Section 306 stock, the preferred stock received is not Section 306 stock.

Sale of Section 306 Stock—Tax Effect. Where a stockholder disposes of Section 306 stock the tax effect upon the stockholder may be the realization of ordinary income. If the Section 306 stock is sold, a portion or all of the proceeds of sale may be treated as if realized from the sale of a non-capital asset. If the issuing corporation redeems the Section 306 stock, a portion or all of the proceeds of redemption may be treated as if the stockholder has received a dividend.

Some Exceptions to Ordinary Income Tax Treatment. The ordinary income tax treatment will not be applicable to a redemption of Section 306 stock which is a complete redemption of all of the stock of the corporation owned by the stockholder. Also such treatment does not apply to a disposition of Section 306 stock where (1) the disposition results in the termination of a stockholder's interest, (2) the disposition is in connection with a liquidation of the issuing corporation, (3) the disposition is one involved in a transaction in which no gain or loss is recognized to a stockholder with regard to the disposition of the Section 306 stock and (4) if it is established to the satisfaction of the Internal Revenue Service that the distribution and the disposition or redemption of the Section 306 stock was not in pursuance of a plan having as one of its principal purposes the avoidance of federal income tax.

Section 306 Stock—Seller's Approach. Because of the far-reaching effect of the Section 306 provisions, in any acquisition in which a seller's stockholders are to receive preferred stock, they should carefully investigate the question whether the preferred stock will be Section 306 stock and, if circumstances are appropriate, should apply for a tax ruling to the effect that disposition of the Section 306 stock will not result in ordinary income.

COLLAPSIBLE CORPORATIONS—§ 341

Under Section 341 of the Internal Revenue Code a stockholder of a seller may find that gain from the sale of his stock will result in ordinary income instead of capital gain. If what the shareholder is selling is stock in a "collapsible corporation" (as that term is defined in the code), a seller, in a taxable transaction, will realize ordinary income instead of capital gain. Speaking generally, the code defines a "collapsible corporation" as a corporation formed or availed of principally for:

1. the manufacture, construction or production of property, or
2. the purchase of inventory, unrealized receivables or similar assets, or
3. the holding of stock in a corporation formed or availed of for such purposes,

with a view to the sale or exchange of the stock of the corporation, or the distribution of the corporation's assets to its stockholders, *before* the corporation has realized a substantial part of the income from such manufacture, construction, production, or purchase of property.

To appreciate the underlying purpose of the collapsible corporation provision, consider a method of converting ordinary income to capital gain utilized in the film industry a number of years ago. Under this tax plan, a corporation would be formed to produce a film. After the film was produced and before any income was realized by the corporation from the film, the corporation was liquidated and its stockholders received the rights to any income to which the corporation would be entitled from film royalties. Since the stockholders received the film royalties as liquidating dividends they were subject, at the time, to a maximum tax of 25 percent capital gain rates. On the other hand, if the corporation had been permitted to receive the film royalties, the royalties would have been taxed an initial rate of 52 percent on the corporation, and an additional tax would have been due from the stockholders upon distribution of the income from the corporation or upon liquidation of the corporation.

The collapsible corporation section of the Code may be broader in its ultimate application than may have been intended by the original draftsmen. The section is complicated with detailed presumptions as to when a corporation is a collapsible corporation as well as limitations and exceptions to the operation of its provisions. Where in a stock transaction, the prospective seller has substantial unrealized income or substantial increase in value of its assets that produce ordinary income (i.e., inventory property held for sale to customers, receivables or depreciable property not used for production), a review of Section 341 may be in order to determine its applicability.

The Deficit Reduction Act of 1984 amended Section 341 to provide that a corporation will be deemed to have realized a "substantial part" of the income only when it has realized two-thirds of the income to be realized from its collapsible assets.

NET OPERATING LOSS CARRYOVERS—§ 381 AND § 382

Under Code Section 381, after a tax-free statutory merger or acquisition of assets, numerous statutory items involving tax determinations on future returns are carried over from the seller to the buyer. These items are the great majority of the tax characteristics of the seller including its inventory and depreciation methods. Of these 29 items, the one that has probably the most significance in acquisitions is the net operating loss carryover. Under Section 381, where a seller has a net operating loss, the loss carries over to a buyer who acquires the assets of the seller in a tax-free transaction. Generally, the type of transaction which will qualify for the carryover of a seller's net operating loss to a buyer, will be a tax-free asset transaction under Section 368(a)(1)(C) or a tax-free statutory merger under Section 368(a)(1)(A).

Reduction in Loss Carryover. Although a net operating loss may be carried over from a seller to a buyer in a tax-free asset transaction, the amount of the loss which the buyer may utilize in the future may not equal the seller's total net operating loss. Under Code Section 382(b), the net operating loss which is carried over is disallowed entirely after an "ownership change" if the new loss corporation does not continue the business enterprise of the old loss corporation for at least two years. Further, if the business enterprise continuity requirement is met, the annual amount of taxable income which can be offset by pre-change net operating loss carryforwards is limited to an annual amount equal to (A) the value of the old loss corporation, multiplied by (B) the long-term tax exempt rate.

An "ownership change" may be triggered by either of two events:

1. An "owner shift involving a 5-percent stockholder" which means any change in the respective ownership of stock of a corporation affecting the percentage of stock owned by any person who is a 5-percent shareholder before or after such change, or
2. An "equity structure change" which means any tax free reorganization other than an "F" reorganization and certain "D" and "G" reorganizations.

After either of these events occurs, there is an "ownership change" if the percentage of stock of the new loss corporation owned by one or more 5-percent shareholders has increased by more than 50 percentage points over the lowest percentage of stock of the old loss corporation (or any predecessor) owned by such shareholders during a testing period which, with some exceptions, is three years.

Code Section 382(k) states that a new loss corporation means a corporation which (after an ownership change) is a loss corporation and that the same corporation may be both the old loss corporation and the new loss corporation. An important practical effect of this provision is that a corporation will lose the right to use all or part of its own net operating loss carryforwards after an acquisition of a percentage of its stock which amounts to an "ownership change."

The Section 382 limitation applies not only losses recognized by the loss corporation, but also to net unrealized built-in gain and loss. Special rules in Code Section 382(h) govern built-in gains and losses including gain recognized by reason of an election under Code Section 338.

Taxable Acquisitions—Net Operating Loss Carryovers. In a taxable *asset* transaction, any net operating loss which the seller may have, remains with the seller and may be taken into account by the seller in determining the ultimate tax effects of the sale of assets to the buyer. No portion of a seller's net operating loss carries over to the buyer in such a taxable acquisition of assets by a buyer.

When an acquisition is accomplished by a taxable sale of stock, the net operating loss carryforward remains with the acquired corporation and is not used by the buyer unless an election is made to file a consolidated return. However, a stock acquisition will, of course, be an ownership change which will trigger the Section 382 limitation on the right of the acquired corporation to use its own loss carryforward. The acquired corporation may also lose its carryforward entirely if the new owners do not assure that it continues its business enterprise for the required two year period.

Built-In Gains. If a corporation acquires control of another corporation or acquires the assets of another corporation in a tax free reorganization described in Code Sections 368(a)(1)(A), (C) or (D) and either has built-in gains, preacquisition losses of each corporation may be used only to offset income attributable to its own recognized built-in gains as defined in Section 382(h). See Section 384.

Section 269 Disallowance. Under Code Section 269, in any acquisition of control of a corporation or acquisition of assets of a corporation where basis of assets carries over to the buyer (normally a tax-free merger or acquisition of assets), the carryover of a net operating loss and other deductions, credits and allowances may be denied. If the principal purpose for making such acquisition was evasion or avoidance of federal income tax by securing the benefit of a deduction, credit or other allowance, which the buyer would not otherwise enjoy, such deduction, credit or allowance may be disallowed. Under this section, control is defined as ownership of stock possessing at least 50 percent of the total combined voting power of all classes of stock entitled to vote or at least 50 percent of the total value of shares of all classes of stock of the corporation.

The section applies to any acquisition of stock, taxable or tax-free, where such control is obtained. It also applies to all tax-free acquisitions of assets. Therefore, in any acquisition of control of a seller or assets of a seller, where the seller has a net operating loss, if the principal purpose of the acquisition is the evasion or avoidance of federal income tax, the deduction of the net operating loss in the future may be denied to either the seller or the buyer, as the case may be.

Even though a tax-free transaction appears to qualify for a net operating loss carryover under Section 382 described above, if the prohibition in Section 269 applies, the deduction of the net operating loss will be disallowed. Regulation Section 1.269-6 contains the following example of this principle:

Example: L Corporation has sustained heavy net operating losses for a number of years. In a merger under state law, P Corporation acquires all of the assets of L Corporation for the principal purpose of utilizing the net operating loss carryovers of L Corporation against the profits of P Corporation's business. As a result of the merger, the former stockholders of L Corporation own, immediately after the merger, 12 percent of the fair market value of the outstanding stock of P Corporation. If the merger qualifies as a reorganization to which Section 381(a) applies, the entire net operating loss carryovers will be disallowed under the provisions of Section 269(a) without regard to the application of Section 382.

Code Section 269(b) specifically authorizes the IRS to disallow deductions, credits and allowances if (1) a corporation makes a qualified stock purchase of another corporation, (2) an election is not made under Code Section 338 and (3) the acquired corporation is liquidated pursuant to a plan of liquidation adopted not more than two years after the acquisition date.

Corporate Equity Reductions. Code Section 172(m) imposes limits on net operating loss carryovers of a corporation which engages in a "corporate equity reduction transaction" or which has a "corporate equity reduction interest loss" for years ending after August 2, 1989. The limitations apply to a corporation which (1) acquires stock, or the stock of which is acquired, in a major stock acquisition or (2) makes distributions with respect to, or redeeming, its stock in connection with an excess distribution. A major stock acquisition involves 50% or more (by vote or value) of the stock of another corporation, but does not include a qualified stock purchase to which a Section 338 election applies or to certain acquisitions of stock among members of an affiliated group. An excess distribution is the excess of the aggregate distributions (including redemptions) during a taxable year over the greater of (1) 150% of the average distributions during the three previous taxable years or (2) 10% of the fair market value of the stock of the corporation at the beginning of the taxable year. Like many recent tax "reforms," Code Section 172(m) is intended to limit tax deductions to corporations adopting leveraged capital structures in connection with acquisitions or restructuring programs.

BUYING STOCK TO ACQUIRE ASSETS—§ 338

Where a purchase price exceeds the tax cost of assets in a seller's hands, a buyer may wish to acquire assets in a taxable transaction in order to obtain an increased tax basis for the assets. The seller may insist on selling stock. In such instances, a buyer may buy stock of a seller and still obtain an increased tax basis for the seller's assets, provided the buyer complies with Section 338 of the code.

Section 338 was adopted in 1982 when predecessor provisions in Code Section 334(b)(2) were repealed. Section 334(b)(2) provided that a buyer could obtain a "stepped up" tax basis provided the buyer received the assets of the seller in a complete liquidation of the seller, pursuant to a Plan of Liquidation adopted not more than two years after the date on which the buyer acquired the seller's stock in a taxable transaction or transactions. To be applicable, Section 334(b)(2) provided that the buyer must have acquired, in taxable transactions and during a twelve-month period, stock of the seller possessing at least 80 percent of the total combined voting power and at least 80 percent of the total number of shares of all other classes of stock.

Section 338 requires that the buyer file an election within nine months and 15 days (or such other period as may be provided by the IRS regulations) after it acquires 80 percent control of a subsidiary. The election allows the acquiring parent corporation to treat its subsidiary, called the "target corporation," as though it had sold and bought its own assets in a simple transaction on the acquisition date. The "deemed sale price" for the assets is fair market value which can be based on a formula contained in IRS regulations or on competent appraisals. The "deemed purchase price" used in determining the "stepped up" basis in the assets is the price, subject to certain adjustments, paid by the parent for the stock of the subsidiary.

The former requirement that the subsidiary be liquidated is no longer in effect. However, the subsidiary's taxable year must be closed on the date of acquisition of 80 percent control and a final income tax return prepared and filed. The subsidiary is then treated as a new corporation commencing on the day after the acquisition of control when it may become a member of its parent's affiliated group. Incident to the "stepped up" basis, no tax characteristics of the subsidiary prior to the acquisition of control are carried over. Recapture items are reported in the final return filed by the subsidiary as of the date of the acquisition of control.

Under the Tax Reform Act of 1986, Code Section 338 was amended so that a purchase of 80 percent of the value and voting rights of a corporation's stock must be accomplished within a 12 month period. "Stepped up basis", subject to recapture of depreciation and investment tax credits, continues to be available. The former non-recognition of gain or loss on the "deemed sale" of assets by the subsidiary has been eliminated. Allocation of the price among assets must be accomplished by the "residual" method under regulations which divide assets into four classes and require that any amount in excess of the fair market value of the assets in Classes I, II and III must be allocated to Class IV which is good will or going business value. These regulations were a model for the regulations under Code Section 1060 described earlier. As a result, there will be few situations in which a Section 338 election will be attractive in the future and many corporations will decide to file a protective carryover basis election within the time otherwise allowed for election of "stepped up" basis.

According to Code Section 338(h)(10) and the regulations adopted in 1986 by the IRS, a joint election may be made under which (1) the acquired corporation will recognize gain or loss as if it had sold all its assets in a single transaction and (2) a selling consolidated group (or affiliated group) will not recognize gain or loss on the stock sold in the transaction. The practical effect is that the transaction is treated as a sale of assets by the selling group and only a single corporate level tax is imposed. The election is made by filing Form 8023. The ability of the buyer and the selling group to agree on a joint election will depend on (A) the value to the buyer of having a stepped up basis in the assets of the acquired corporation and (B) a comparison by the selling group of the net tax effects of the election with those of a sale of the subsidiary's stock without the election. If the basis which the selling group has in the subsidiary's assets compares favorably with its basis in the subsidiary's stock, the selling group may agree to the election. A helpful article is entitled "The Joint Election under Section 338(h)(10)," 42 *Tax Lawyer* 235 (Winter 1989).

INTEREST ON ACQUISITION INDEBTEDNESS—§ 279

Under Code Section 279, no deduction is allowed for any interest paid or incurred by a corporation during a taxable year with respect to its "corporate acquisition indebtedness" to the extent that such interest exceeds a specified maximum amount. Under this rule, the maximum deduction permitted for interest paid or incurred during a taxable year with respect to "corporate acquisition indebtedness" is limited to $5 million. The $5 million maximum allowable interest deduction must be reduced by interest paid or incurred on obligations issued after December 31, 1967, to provide consideration for the acquisition of (1) stock in another corporation or (2) assets of another corporation pursuant to a plan under which at least two-thirds in value of all of the assets used in the trades and businesses of the seller are acquired.

Corporate Acquisition Indebtedness—Definition. The term *corporate acquisition indebtedness* means any obligation evidenced by a bond, debenture, note, or certificate or other evidence of indebtedness issued after October 9, 1969, by a corporation if such obligation is issued to provide consideration for the acquisition of (1) stock in another corporation or (2) assets of another corporation pursuant to a plan under which at least two-thirds in value of all of the assets (excluding money) used in trades and businesses carried on by such corporation are acquired. To constitute "corporate acquisition indebtedness" the obligation must also fulfill each of the additional conditions mentioned below:

(1) *Subordination condition.* The obligation must be (a) subordinated to the claims of trade creditors of the issuing corporation generally or (b) expressly subordinated in right of payment to the payment of any substantial amount of unsecured indebtedness of the issuing corporation.

(2) *Convertibility condition.* The bond or other evidence of indebtedness must either be (a) convertible directly into stock of the issuing corporation *or* (b) part of an investment unit or other arrangement that includes, in addition to such bond or other evidence of indebtedness, an option to acquire, directly or indirectly, stock of the issuing corporation.

(3) *Ratio of debt to equity or earnings condition.* As of the last day of the year in which the debt security was issued in connection with the acquisition, (a) the ratio of debt to equity of the buyer must exceed 2 to 1 *or* (b) the "projected earnings" of the buyer must not exceed three times the annual interest to be paid or incurred by the buyer.

Ratio of Debt to Equity—Explanation. The ratio of the buyer's debt to the buyer's equity is determined by subtracting the buyer's total indebtedness from the aggregate net value of all of its assets to determine the amount of the buyer's equity. For these purposes, total indebtedness includes short-term liabilities such as notes and accounts payable, and the aggregate net value of all of the assets includes cash and the value of all other property equal to the adjusted basis of such property for tax purposes. The debt is compared to equity, and if the debt is more than twice the equity, the test is met.

To illustrate the computation of the foregoing ratio, assume that on January 1, 1971, buyer issued debentures to purchase all of the stock of the seller. On December 31, 1971, buyer had total assets of $200 million and total indebtedness of $150 million. Buyer's equity is $50 million ($200 million assets less $150 million indebtedness). Its ratio of debt to equity is therefore 3 to 1 ($150 million indebtedness compared to $50 million equity). Since the ratio exceeds the statutory 2 to 1 limit, the debentures issued to purchase the seller meet the statutory ratio of debt to equity test.

Earnings Test—Explanation. Under the earnings test, the "projected earnings" of the buyer are compared with the "annual interest to be paid or accrued" on the buyer's total outstanding indebtedness. If the projected earnings do not exceed three times the annual interest cost, the earnings test is considered as having been met. Projected earnings for these purposes mean the "average annual earnings" for the three-year period ending on the last day of the year for which the determination is being made. For the purposes of the code, the buyer's earnings are computed without reduction for (1) any interest paid or incurred, (2) any depreciation or amortization deductions, (3) any federal tax liability and (4) any dividends paid (dividends paid by the seller to the buyer are not included in the buyer's earnings and profits). The buyer's annual interest cost is the buyer's interest paid or accrued on its total outstanding indebtedness.

If a buyer that issues "corporate acquisition indebtedness" does not meet either the ratio of debt to equity test or the projected earnings test for each of three consecutive taxable years after issuing such corporate acquisition indebtedness, the interest deduction limit imposed on such obligations terminates, beginning with the first taxable year after the end of the three consecutive taxable years.

Section 279 of the code contains many special rules in its treatment of acquisition indebtedness applicable to many different circumstances. Therefore, in any situation in which it appears that the section may apply to indebtedness incurred in making an acquisition, the buyer should carefully review the applicability of its detailed provisions to the proposed acquisition.

In October, 1987, the Ways and Means Committee of the U.S. House of Representatives drafted a new Section 279A as part of a proposed Revenue Act 1987. The new Section 279A would deny a deduction for interest in excess of $5 million per year incurred by a corporation with respect to debt supporting either (1) the acquisition of 50% or more of the stock of another corporation or (2) the redemption by a corporation of 50% or more of its own stock. The denial would not apply if the acquisition is a qualified stock purchase under section 338 and an election is made to treat the acquisition as an assets acquisition. The new Section 279A was not adopted, but may again be considered in the future.

INTEREST ON HIGH-YIELD DISCOUNT OBLIGATIONS

Code Section 163(e) denies an interest deduction for the "disqualified portion" of the original issue discount (OID) on certain high yield discount obligations. In addition, an interest deduction is not allowed for the remainder of the OID until it is paid. An applicable high yield discount obligation is one with (1) a maturity date more than five years from its issue date, (2) a yield to maturity at least equal to the applicable federal rate when issued plus 5% and (3) a significant OID. The definition of the "disqualified portion" allows an additional 1%, so the interest deduction denial applies only to the extent of the excess over the applicable federal rate plus 6%. Like many recent tax "reforms," Code Section 163(e) is intended to limit tax deductions to corporations adopting unusual debt burdens with a view to distributing corporate earnings on a tax deductible basis.

DEPRECIATION AND INVESTMENT CREDIT RECAPTURE

The tax provisions providing for depreciation and investment credit recapture have little immediate significance in tax-free acquisitions discussed in Chapter 11. In tax-free transactions, the significance of the recapture provisions may be limited to an understanding by a buyer that upon disposition of the seller's assets in the future, the recapture provisions may come into play at that time if the future disposition involves a taxable transaction. The recapture provisions of the Code, however, assume immediate importance to a buyer and seller in negotiating the terms of a taxable transaction.

Depreciation and the ADR, ACRS and MACRS Systems. For many years, businesses were allowed to recover their cost of investment in most kinds of facilities and equipment by depreciation deductions based on their estimated useful lives, less a reasonable salvage value. A variety of depreciation methods were permitted including straight-line, declining balance and sum-of-the-years digits methods. Faced with the need to compete with businesses manufacturing in foreign nations which allow very rapid methods for recovery of investment for tax purposes, businesses in the United States urged Congress and the Internal Revenue Service to implement faster investment recovery systems under the Internal Revenue Code.

The first step was the adoption of the Asset Depreciation Range (ADR) System applicable to assets first placed in service after 1970 and before 1981. Under this system, all tangible assets were assigned to classes with a class life (i.e., an "asset guideline period") for each of them. Each class was assigned a range of years (i.e., an "asset depreciation range") extending about 20 percent above and below the class life. Taxpayers were free to select a depreciation period within the allowable ranges, except that the class life was used for buildings and land improvements.

Under the Economic Recovery Act of 1981 (ERTA), later modified by the Tax Equity and Fiscal Responsibility Act of 1982 (TEFRA), a new system of investment cost recovery was adopted. The system adopted is called an accelerated cost recovery system (ACRS). The system plainly turned away from an effort to base recovery on estimated lives and salvage value. It assigned three, five, ten and fifteen-year recovery periods for specified classes of new and used property (without salvage value) commencing when the property is placed in service. In general, the three and five-year properties were vehicles, machinery, equipment and other personal property. In general, the fifteen-year properties were buildings and other improvements to real property. Statutory ACRS percentages assigned to each class determined the allowable deductions. The percentages were calculated using a 150 percent declining balance method with a switch to straight line at the time when that step optimizes a deduction. However, taxpayers are free to elect a straight-line method.

The Tax Reform Act of 1986 repealed the investment tax credit for tangible personal property placed in service after December 31, 1986. The Act also modified the ACRS system in several ways, generally to lengthen the times for cost recovery of specified classes of property. These steps were partially counterbalanced by allowing use of the 200% declining balance depreciation method for 3, 5, 7 and 10-year property which had previously been limited to the 150% method.

The Act reduced depreciation benefits for real property by allowing only use of the straight line method and lengthening the recovery period from 19 to 27.5 years for residential property and to 31.5 years for nonresidential property.

Taxable Transaction—Recapture Problems. Depreciation, accelerated cost recovery or investment credit recapture may make a substantial difference in the tax bill payable by a buyer or seller, depending upon the form of transaction as a sale of stock or sale of assets and the difference, if any, in the tax rates applicable to ordinary income and capital gain income.

Where a buyer buys the assets of a seller, the seller becomes liable for the payment of depreciation, accelerated cost recovery and investment credit recapture. This liability must be satisfied out of the assets of the seller before these assets are distributed to the stockholders of the seller. Therefore, in an asset transaction, the burden of the depreciation, accelerated cost recovery and investment credit recapture falls upon the seller and, indirectly, upon the seller's stockholders. On the other hand, where a buyer buys stock from the stockholders of the seller, the tax burden with respect to depreciation, accelerated cost recovery and investment credit recapture falls upon the buyer, if it elects to obtain a stepped-up tax basis of assets. Since the buyer will have paid the consideration to the stockholders of its new subsidiary, the burden of payment for depreciation, accelerated cost recovery and investment credit recapture falls upon the buyer due to the subsequent payment of the tax from the subsidiary's assets.

During times when capital gain income and ordinary income are taxed at the same rates, the tax amounts may not differ importantly. However, in negotiating the structure of any taxable transaction, a seller should be aware that the burden of the payment of depreciation and investment credit recapture falls upon the seller where the buyer acquires the assets. A buyer should be aware that the burden of such depreciation, accelerated recovery and investment credit recapture falls upon the buyer where the buyer acquires stock except when buyer and a selling consolidated or affiliated group agree to make a joint election under Code Section 338(h)(10).

Recaptures—Generally. Since ordinary income and capital gain income have been taxed at the same rates, the effects of the recapture provisions of the Code have been reduced. However, a brief discussion of recaptures is retained because of the other effects of characterization of income and the possibility that Congress may again grant reduced rates to capital gains.

Depreciation Recapture—Personal Property. Under Code Section 1245, the sale of personal property, "Section 1245 property," or "Section 1245 recovery property," generally property of a nature subject to the allowance for depreciation provided in Section 167, the allowances under the accelerated cost recovery system (ACRS) under Section 168, or to the allowances for amortization provided in several other sections of the code, may result in ordinary income rather than capital gain to a seller. If gain is realized, the gain will be taxed to the seller as ordinary income to the extent of depreciation, cost recovery or amortization deducted.

For example, assume a seller bought a color printing press at a cost of $150,000 on January 1, 1978, and the life of the press for depreciation purposes is 10 years. Assume further that the seller chose to claim straight-line depreciation of $15,000 per year without regard to ADR or ACRS methods and then sells the equipment on December 31, 1978. Due to the scarcity of such equipment at the time, the seller is paid its full original purchase price of $150,000 for the equipment. In determining the depreciation recapture to be taxed at ordinary income tax rates to the seller, the seller may make the following computations.

(1)	Original cost of equipment	$150,000
(2)	Depreciation deducted from January 1, 1969, to and including December 31, 1982, at $10,000 per year	130,000
(3)	Recomputed basis ($150,000 minus $130,000)	20,000
(4)	Amount of taxable gain ($150,000 sale price less $20,000 recomputed basis)	130,000
(5)	Depreciation recaptured	130,000

Of the total gain of $130,000 realized in the preceding example, $110,000 is therefore taxable as ordinary income in accordance with the depreciation recapture provisions of Section 1245 of the code.

The effect of Section 1245 is to "recapture" depreciation and allowance for cost recovery and amortization subject to the section, by including as ordinary income proceeds of sale in excess of tax basis to the extent of the Section 1245 depreciation.

Depreciation Recapture—Real Estate. Under Section 1250 of the code, upon sales of "Section 1250 property"—i.e., buildings, fixtures and other real estate improvements eligible for depreciation and accelerated cost recovery allowances—differing portions of prior depreciation and cost recovery may be recaptured, depending upon the dates after which the depreciation or cost recovery was deducted, the method of depreciation or cost recovery and the length of time during which the real estate was owned by the seller. As in the case of personal property, real estate recapture is limited to the amount of gain realized upon a sale. For "Section 1250 property," there is an important limitation on the amount of the recapture. The recapture applies only to the extent of depreciation and accelerated recovery allowances above the allowances which would have been available if the straight-line method had been used. However, if the property was held one year or less, the full amount of the allowances is captured.

Investment Credit Recapture. Under Sections 38 and 46 through 48 of the code, a taxpayer is allowed a variety of credits against income tax for expenses and investments related to job creation, alcohol fuels, increased research, low-income housing, enhanced oil recovery, rehabilitation, energy and reforestation. They formerly included a more general credit against income tax payable equal to 10 percent of certain qualified investments.

When the assets of a business are sold, or are treated as sold pursuant to an election of a stepped up basis under Section 338, investment credit and depreciation recapture must be considered by seller and buyer. In addition, they must consider the effects of recapture of amounts deducted for expensed tools and supplies and, if the LIFO method of inventory valuation is used by seller, an amount equal to any excess of the amount of the inventory valued by the FIFO method over the LIFO method [see Section 336(b)]. The price and other terms of the transaction should be negotiated to minimize the recapture, if possible, and to consider the effects on the party that will bear the recapture. See also Code Section 47.

STATE AND LOCAL TAXES

It is beyond the scope of this chapter to discuss the multitude of state and local taxes that may apply to acquisitions, particularly when accomplished by a sale of assets. These taxes may include income tax, sales or use tax, transfer taxes, reassessed property taxes and taxes imposed on filing mortgages and security interests. Some helpful comments are as follows:

- Planners should not assume that federal tax structures or concepts will be accepted by state or local tax authorities. For example, they may not allow consolidated tax returns or allow a step up in the basis of assets for state tax purposes after a Section 338(h)(10) election for federal income tax purposes.
- Some states have industrial sale or bulk sale exemptions that excuse a sale of corporate assets from sales/use tax. These are typically states seeking to encourage industry.
- Other states, such as New York, impose large transfer taxes on acquisition transactions including implied asset transfers when an acquisition is accomplished by a sale of stock or merger.
- Some states, such as New York, have large taxes payable upon recording a mortgage. Although filing a UCC-1 financing statement usually requires a modest filing fee, the State of Maryland imposes a major tax on filing a financing statement.
- Local real estate assessors customarily reassess the value of property whenever it is sold. When a buyer is obtaining an appraisal to support the price allocation under Code Sections 338 or 1060, the appraiser should perhaps also be asked to determine value by the standards used for property tax purposes.

OTHER TAX INFORMATION

Several other chapters contain information about the taxation of transactions involved in acquisitions, but relating to subjects more specific than those discussed in this chapter. For example, please see the following chapters:

Chapter 2—Hybrid Securities; Recharacterizing Stock or Debt Instruments for Tax Purposes

11

Tax Free Reorganizations

In this chapter, the tax-free acquisitions are discussed in some detail. Taxable acquisitions and other tax problems that may arise in acquisitions are discussed in Chapter 10.

TAX TREATMENT VERSUS ACCOUNTING TREATMENT

Bear in mind that an acquisition structured to achieve the best income tax results for a buyer may not achieve the best results for reporting earnings per share in the buyer's financial statements. A cash transaction that is treated as a "taxable" transaction for income tax purposes and a "purchase" for accounting purposes, may result in substantial income tax savings from increased depreciation deductions flowing from the write-up of the tax cost of assets acquired from the seller. The "taxable" transaction may increase cash flow substantially. However, "purchase" accounting treatment may reduce reported earnings per share due not only to increased depreciation deductions but also to amortization of goodwill to which a portion of the price paid may have been allocated in a "purchase" accounting transaction. Management of the buyer may therefore insist that the form of transaction be recast in accordance with criteria set forth in Chapter 7 to achieve "pooling of interests" accounting treatment to avoid the increased depreciation and goodwill amortization deductions.

Not only may conflict exist between the best tax results from either a "taxable" or "nontaxable" transaction and the best accounting results from either a "purchase" or a "pooling of interests," but the criteria for determining whether an acquisition is "tax-free" from a tax viewpoint or a "pooling of interests" from an accounting viewpoint, although similar in some respects, differ in significant details. As a result of the differences in the tax and accounting criteria, it has been possible to treat an acquisition as "taxable," to obtain the benefits of increased depreciation deductions and at the same time as a "pooling of interests" to avoid reduction in reported earnings per share due to amortization of goodwill.

This chapter and Chapter 10 limit discussion to the tax aspects of acquisitions, without regard to the accounting aspects discussed in Chapter 7.

Often the tax objectives of a buyer may be in conflict with the tax objectives of a seller. In this chapter, let us first explore what these differing objectives may be.

TAX OBJECTIVES OF SELLER

The basic tax objectives of the seller will generally depend upon the relationship between the purchase price being offered and the tax basis (cost) of the stock or assets in the hands of the seller. Where the purchase price exceeds the tax basis, a tax-free transaction will generally be advantageous to the seller. Where the purchase price is less than the tax basis, a taxable transaction will generally not be advantageous to the seller.

Tax-free Transaction—Seller's Objectives. As indicated, a seller may want a tax-free transaction if the purchase price exceeds the tax basis of the assets or stock in the hands of the seller. Consider a situation which occurs with relative frequency. The sellers started their closely held business a number of years ago with a minimum investment of $100,000 in capital. The sellers conducted the business successfully over the years, reinvesting earnings, and as a result sales have grown to $15 million and a buyer is willing to pay $10 million for the business. The average age of the sellers is now 66 and they wish to retire. Under these circumstances, the sellers may be willing to accept a tax-free transaction. Younger owners selling a new high—tech business may also be willing to accept a tax-free transaction because they hope to contribute to the future success of the buyer.

In a taxable transaction, since the tax basis of the business in the hands of the sellers is only $100,000, the sellers would realize a taxable gain of $9.9 million (the excess of the $10 million price over the $100,000 tax cost). Depending on the rates currently applicable, a tax in the range of $2,000,000 to $3,000,000 will be payable. On the other hand, if the transaction is tax-free, no tax will be payable as a result of the receipt of the buyer's stock, and substantially the entire capital gains tax may be avoided if the sellers retain substantially all of the buyer's stock as an investment. At the time of the death of the sellers, the stock of the buyer in the hands of the estates will obtain a so-called "stepped up" tax basis provided by Section 1014 of the Internal Revenue Code to its fair market value on the date of death or the alternate valuation date for estate tax purposes, and the capital gain tax will be avoided.

Taxable transaction—an objective of seller. A seller may want a taxable transaction if the purchase price is less than the tax cost of the assets or stock in the hands of the seller. In such a situation, where a seller sells assets, a seller may realize a capital loss and may also realize a net operating loss for tax purposes which may be carried back and result in refund of income taxes. In addition, if the loss is sizable enough, a seller may attempt to utilize additional unused tax loss carryforwards by acquiring profitable businesses.

TAX OBJECTIVES OF BUYER

As in the case of a seller, the basic tax objectives of a buyer will generally depend upon the relationship between the purchase price and the tax cost of the stock or assets being acquired from the seller. Especially when capital gains are taxed at a lower rate than ordinary income, the general tax objective of a buyer is often the opposite of that of the seller. Where the purchase price exceeds the tax cost of the stock or property in the hands of the seller, a taxable transaction will generally be advantageous to the buyer. On the other hand, where the purchase price is less than the tax cost of these properties—the buyer may prefer a tax-free transaction to take advantage of the continued higher tax basis of the seller's properties in the hands of the buyer.

"Tax-free" and taxable transactions—buyer's objective. As indicated, a buyer will often want a taxable transaction if the purchase price exceeds the tax cost of the assets or stock in the hands of the seller. Assume that the total tax cost of the assets of the seller's business amounts to $500,000. If the buyer is willing to pay $750,000 for the seller's business, the buyer may desire a taxable transaction in order to write the tax cost of the seller's assets up from $500,000 to $750,000. As described in Chapter 10, assuming that the entire purchase price is allocable to depreciable (cost recoverable) assets, the buyer, after a taxable transaction, could write off against pre-tax earnings cost recovery deductions based on a cost of $750,000. On the other hand, in a tax-free transaction, the buyer would be able to recover only $500,000 against pre-tax earnings, because the seller's tax cost would carry over into the hands of the buyer in a tax-free transaction.

SUBSEQUENT EFFECTS OF A "TAX-FREE" REORGANIZATION

Tax on Subsequent Sale. Describing a tax-free acquisition as one which has "no immediate tax effect" is more accurate than the term "tax free." A stockholder of a seller receives a buyer's stock in exchange for the stockholder's shares of the seller, and need not pay income tax due to the receipt of the buyer's shares. This does not mean that the stockholder will never have to pay tax. If the stockholder sells the buyer's stock for the same price as its fair market value when received, all of the gain will be taxed in the year of the sale. On sale, the full gain is taxed, because the basis of the stockholder in his shares of the seller becomes his basis in the stock received in exchange as provided in Code Section 358.

Stepped-Up Basis on Death. If the stockholder retains the buyer's stock until death, all or part of the gain may escape income taxation because Section 1014 of the Internal Revenue Code provides write-up of tax basis to fair market value as a result of the imposition of estate tax on that value upon death. On the other hand, where a buyer's stock is ultimately sold by the seller's stockholder, a tax-free receipt of stock means a postponement of tax rather than escape from tax.

As an example, assume a stockholder of a seller paid $100 for his stock of the seller. In a tax-free exchange, the stockholder receives stock of the buyer that has a value of $200. The $100 gain ($200 value received less $100 cost) is not taxed at the time the stockholder receives the buyer's stock. But the cost to the stockholder of the buyer's stock remains $100—the same as the cost of the shares the seller originally held. Therefore, $100 of gain will be recognized and taxed if the stockholder sells the buyer's stock for $200 ($200 cash from sale less the $100 carryover cost). Should the buyer's shares be valued in the stockholder's estate at $200, income tax may be avoided in its entirety. The $200 value placed on the buyer's share for estate tax purposes becomes the new tax cost of the shares. Therefore, if the shares are sold for $200 by the estate or a legatee no gain will result for income tax purposes ($200 received for stock with a new tax cost, or basis, of $200).

THE "TAX-FREE" ACQUISITION

General. Every corporate acquisition involves a receipt or exchange of stock or other property, and many acquisitions also involve distributions by corporations to shareholders. Where a corporation buys a business for stock, the stock may be used to buy the assets of the business or the stock of the seller's business; where a corporation buys a business for cash, the cash also may be given for assets or stock, as may any combinations of stock, cash or other properties, such as notes. Furthermore, where assets are sold, the selling corporation frequently distributes the consideration, whether it be stock, cash or other properties, to its stockholders. In these situations each acquisition involves a receipt or exchange and may involve a corporate distribution of property to shareholders.

Under our Internal Revenue Code the general rule is that each exchange of property and each receipt of property constitutes a taxable event, unless the transaction falls within one of the specific exemptions provided in the Code. Under the Internal Revenue Code gross income is defined as "all income from whatever source derived, including . . . gains derived from dealings in property." The law further provides that "on the sale or exchange of property the entire amount of the gain or loss . . . shall be recognized," which means that the gain or loss is taken into account in computing federal income taxes.

The foregoing general income tax rules are subject to exceptions which, under specific enumerated circumstances, permit a taxpayer to receive or exchange property without immediate tax consequences. As examples, the law excludes from gross income certain death benefits, gifts and inheritances, interest on state and municipal obligations, compensation for injuries or sickness, amounts received under accident and health plans, scholarship and fellowship grants, receipts of contributions to capital by corporations and meals or lodging furnished for the convenience of an employer.

Common Non-Taxable Exchanges. In addition to the enumerated receipts that are excluded from gross income, certain exchanges of property are treated as nontaxable. As examples, exchanges of property held for productive use or investment, with certain exceptions, are non-taxable under Code Section 1031; exchanges by a corporation of its stock for property are nontaxable to the corporation under Code Section 102; the involuntary conversion of property as a result of destruction or similar event into similar property is a nontaxable exchange under Code Section 1033; the sale or exchange of a residence, where a new residence is bought, may be treated as nontaxable under Sections 1034 and 121 and exchanges of certain types of insurance polices, stock for stock of the same corporation and certain exchanges of United States obligations are also treated as nontaxable exchanges.

With this background, let us address ourselves to the specific provisions of the Internal Revenue Code which exempt exchanges and distributions of property and stock in acquisitions from immediate income tax consequences. In order to be tax-free, any exchanges or distributions in acquisitions must be exchanges or distributions made in connection with a "reorganization" as defined in our tax law. Code Section 368 contains six definitions of such reorganizations. Since, however, only three of the definitions concern acquisition transactions, we will limit our discussion to these three—described generally as (1) a statutory merger or consolidation, (2) an acquisition of the *stock* of a corporation by another corporation for a part of its stock and (3) an acquisition of the *assets* of a corporation by another corporation for a part of its stock. (Under limited circumstances, tax-free acquisitions can also be accomplished using Section 351, but the techniques are quite specialized.)

MERGER OR CONSOLIDATION

The first definition contained in the Internal Revenue Code of a reorganization which will qualify for tax-free treatment is "a statutory merger or consolidation." This type of reorganization is often referred to as an "A" reorganization, because it is defined in Section 368(a)(1)(A) of the 1954 Internal Revenue Code.

A technical distinction between a merger and consolidation, often made in print, is that a merger involves combining two or more corporations into one of the *former* independent corporations as the continuing entity, whereas a consolidation involves combining two or more corporations into a *new* corporation organized to conduct the combined former businesses. The distinction is largely technical, and since the merger route is the more customary of the two, this discussion speaks generally in terms of mergers. Most comments concerning statutory mergers would, however, apply to consolidations.

The essential element to qualify a merger or consolidation for tax-free treatment is that it be statutory—i.e., that it be accomplished in accordance with the procedures set forth in the corporation laws of the state or states of incorporation of the merging companies. The result of a merger or consolidation is the same as the acquisition of the assets of one corporation by another corporation, whether for stock or cash, in the sense that after the merger or consolidation or acquisition, two businesses, formerly conducted separately, are continued as an integral part of one corporate entity. In spite of this similarity, corporation laws of the various states relating to mergers and consolidations cause important procedural differences between a merger as a method of acquisition as opposed to an acquisition of a corporation's assets for stock or cash.

Merger—procedure. In most states, the basic procedure prescribed for merger is that the boards of directors of the merging corporations must approve a plan or agreement of merger which sets forth the terms of the merger, and then submit the plan or agreement to the stockholders of each of the corporations for approval by the requisite statutory vote. For example, the New Jersey statutes provide that corporations may merge by having each board of directors adopt a plan of merger which must then be submitted to a vote of stockholders—a favorable vote of two-thirds of the stockholders may be required to effect the merger. In Delaware, an agreement of merger must be approved by the boards of directors of the merging corporations for submission to the stockholders for approval, but only a favorable vote of a majority of the stockholders, rather than a two-thirds vote, is required to complete the merger.

Both the New York and Delaware corporation laws contain another attribute common to many state merger statutes—i.e., that stockholders of a corporation who oppose the merger may dissent. The dissent is a statutory method whereby a dissenting stockholder may have the value of his stock appraised by a disinterested referee or other official and be paid its fair value in cash by the corporation.

Merger—controlled corporation. Under Section 368(a)(2)(D) of the Code, which applies to statutory mergers occurring after October 22, 1968, a merger of a seller into a subsidiary controlled by a buyer in exchange for stock of the buyer may qualify as an "A" type tax-free reorganization. Under this Section, a buyer may organize a new subsidiary into which a seller may be merged, and avoid the requirement for a meeting of the buyer's stockholders which would have been required if the seller were merged directly into the buyer. However, in order for this procedure to be available the state merger statutes must permit the issuance of stock of a third corporation (the buyer) where two other corporations, the buyer's controlled subsidiary and the seller are merged.

Under Code Section 368(a)(2)(C), a similar result can be obtained after an "A" reorganization if the surviving corporation transfers the assets in the merger to a controlled subsidiary. However, this method requires specific asset transfers which can be expensive and time-consuming.

Merger versus stock or asset acquisition. An acquisition by corporate statutory merger differs in an important fundamental from the acquisition of stock or assets of a seller in exchange for voting stock of a buyer. (Other types of tax-free acquisitions we will discuss below.) Unless the merger is a Section 368(a)(2)(D) merger of a seller into a subsidiary of a buyer (where the buyer's directors may approve the merger), a statutory merger is generally subject to the approval of the stockholders of both the buyer and seller. In other words, the stockholders of the buyer desiring to make the acquisition through the merger have the right to vote upon the acquisition. Lacking exceptional circumstances, the stockholders of a buyer which acquires, in exchange for its voting stock, the stock or assets of a seller have no such right to vote upon the acquisition except in states where the corporation law requires a shareholder vote for a sale of substantially all of the assets of a corporation and where a shareholder vote is required by policy of the New York Stock Exchange.

In one respect, however, an acquisition by statutory merger has a substantial advantage over the other types of tax-free acquisitions which we will discuss below. You will notice when we discuss the acquisition of assets or stock in exchange for the stock of the buyer, the buyer is limited, with only a very limited exception, to the use of its *voting stock* to pay for the acquisition. The Internal Revenue Code imposes no such restriction upon a statutory merger to attain tax-free status. Therefore, in a tax-free statutory merger the consideration for the acquisition may include such securities as nonvoting preferred stock, debentures, bonds and other classes of securities, limited only by the corporation statutes of the states involved. This flexibility from an income tax viewpoint in choosing the method of payment of the purchase price in an acquisition by merger may make possible a tax-free acquisition where circumstances require unique combinations of securities to satisfy the seller's stockholders or the buyer.

For example, assume a situation in which a buyer and seller, both listed companies, are traded at the same approximate price—$40 per share. The seller pays $2.00 in dividends annually and the buyer only pays $1.60 in dividends annually. The parties believe that the seller's shareholders would vote against a share for share exchange (in spite of the equal market values), because of the discrepancy in dividend payments. If the parties desire a tax-free transaction, and the buyer refuses to make up the dividend deficiency by offering more stock, the buyer could offer a package paying $2.10 for each share of seller's stock, consisting of 3/4 of a buyer's share plus $15 principal amount of 6 percent debentures ($1.20 in dividend income and $0.90 in interest income). If the package is offered through the statutory merger route, the acquisition will be tax-free (except to the extent of the debentures), but if offered for seller's assets, the acquisition generally (subject to some exceptions) will be taxable in its entirety, and if offered for seller's stock, the acquisition will be taxable in its entirety. Subject to refinements discussed below, to be tax-free, an acquisition of assets or stock must be made solely for the buyer's voting stock, whereas if the merger route is followed, the buyer has flexibility in its method of paying the purchase price and still maintaining the tax-free status of the merger.

Another advantage, a nontax advantage, of a statutory merger over an acquisition of assets, is that in a statutory merger, title to the seller's properties vests in the surviving corporation by operation of law. In other words, the numerous title documents involved in an asset acquisition are not required. The certificate of merger, filed with the proper authorities, effects the transfer of title to all of the seller's assets in a merger. However, where assets are acquired, deeds to real property must be delivered and recorded separately as well as assignments of leases, bills of sale of personalty, patent, trademark and contract assignments and separate instruments must often be executed involving assumptions of obligations. If the seller owns a number of parcels of real estate, expenses involved in preparing, executing and recording just the real estate deeds may be sizable.

In summary, to qualify as a tax-free reorganization, a merger or a consolidation (subject to a continuity of interest test discussed below) must only meet the specific requirement under the Internal Revenue Code that the transaction involved meet the statutory requirements and follow the statutory procedures contained in the corporation laws of states of incorporation. Although acquisition by merger may entail the complicating factor of requiring the approval of the acquiring company's stockholders, this type of tax-free acquisition has the tax advantage of substantial flexibility in the method of payment of purchase price and the non-tax advantage of transfer of title to assets by operation of law.

STOCK-FOR-STOCK ACQUISITIONS

The second definition of a tax-free reorganization contained in the Internal Revenue Code relates to the acquisition by one corporation (in exchange for some or all of its voting stock) of stock of another corporation, often called a "B" reorganization since the definition is contained in Section 368(a)(1)(B) of the 1954 Internal Revenue Code. The statutory language is that a tax-free reorganization includes "the acquisition by one corporation, in exchange solely for all or a part of its voting stock . . . of stock of another corporation, if, immediately after the acquisition, the acquiring corporation has control of such other corporation (whether or not such acquiring corporation had control immediately before the acquisition)."

You will notice that the two major elements contained in the definition of a tax-free, stock-for-stock acquisition are that (1) the buyer must exchange solely its voting stock for the stock of the seller and (2) the buyer must have control of the seller immediately after the exchange.

Stock-for-Stock Transaction—Solely Voting Stock. The requirement that the acquisition be made for solely voting stock should be considered inflexible. Although on occasion a court decision may indicate that consideration other than voting stock may be given in a stock-for-stock reorganization, such decision should not be trusted and the words "solely voting stock" should be construed to mean that nothing other than voting stock may be given by the buyer in the exchange. In other words, if the buyer gives its common stock and other property, such as non-voting preferred stock or cash, in payment for the stock of the seller, the entire acquisition exchange will generally be taxable. The stockholders of the seller will be required to pay income taxes on any gain they may have realized in the exchange. Conversely, if a selling stockholder suffers a loss on the exchange, this loss may be taken into account in his income tax return.

While the "solely voting stock" requirement is strictly interpreted, the Internal Revenue Service has ruled that various incidental agreements of a buyer will not prevent tax-free treatment of the acquisition and also will not be considered taxable themselves to the seller corporation. These agreements are discussed later under the heading "Receipt of Other Property."

The reader may also wonder whether a redemption for cash of part of its stock by the corporation to be sold in a "B" reorganization would violate the "solely voting stock" requirement. The Internal Revenue Service has ruled that such a redemption does not prevent tax-free treatment where less than 50 percent of the stock was redeemed and none of the redemption cash was advanced by buyer.

Stock-for-Stock Transaction—Control. In a stock-for-stock tax-free reorganization, in addition to the requirement that the buyer give solely voting stock for the stock of the seller, the buyer must be in control of the seller after the transaction. The tax law defines the word *control* to mean "the ownership of stock possessing at least 80 percent of the total combined voting power of all classes of stock entitled to vote and at least 80 percent of the total number of shares of all other classes of stock" of the seller. To satisfy the requirements of this definition, the buyer must acquire at least 80 percent of all classes of stock of the seller, or the transaction will not be tax-free. For example, if the buyer acquires 100 percent of the voting common stock of the seller but acquires only 79 percent of an issue of nonvoting preferred stock of the seller, the exchange will not meet the definition of control and the entire acquisition exchange will be taxable.

One interesting aspect of the control definition is that a buyer may acquire a portion of the stock of a seller in a taxable transaction, such as a purchase for cash, but may at some later date, in a separate transaction, acquire additional stock of the seller in a tax-free manner. Such a result may be achieved only where the subsequent acquisition of the seller's stock not only meets the requirements of the stock-for-stock reorganization definition contained in the code, but also is considered a separate transaction from the first purchase of stock for cash. For example, assume that the seller is a publicly held company with only common stock outstanding, in which the buyer owns a 30 percent stock interest which the buyer bought in the open market for cash. If the buyer subsequently acquires, in exchange solely for its voting stock, 50 percent or more of the outstanding stock of the seller, in a separate transaction, the second acquisition of the seller's stock will be tax-free, because, after this acquisition, the buyer will have the required 80 percent control of the seller. In our example, the original purchase of a 30 percent interest was taxable because the buyer paid cash for the stock, and the taxable nature of this purchase is not changed by the subsequent tax-free acquisition of the additional 50 percent of the seller's stock.

STOCK-FOR-STOCK REORGANIZATION: DIAGRAM

The following diagram shows elements of a stock-for-stock, tax-free reorganization and will help differentiate this type of reorganization from a stock-for-assets reorganization discussed later. As the fundamental difference between these types, you will note that in the stock-for-stock transaction the agreement and exchange is not between the buyer and seller but between the *buyer* and the *stockholders* of the seller.

Stock Acquisition—By Subsidiary. The definition of a tax-free, stock-for-stock reorganization includes "the acquisition by one corporation, in exchange solely for all or a part of its voting stock (*or* in exchange solely for all or a part of *the voting stock of a corporation* which is *in control of the acquiring corporation*), of the stock of another corporation. . . ." Under this portion of the definition, a subsidiary may acquire the stock of the seller in exchange for voting stock of the subsidiary's parent, provided the parent controls the subsidiary and the subsidiary controls the seller after the completion of the acquisition. "Control" for each of these purposes means the 80 percent stock ownership as defined above.

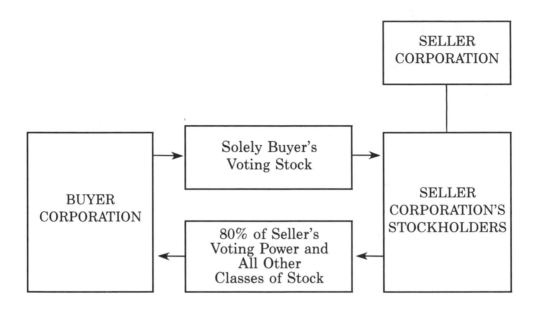

The steps typically involved are (1) a contribution by buyer of shares of its voting stock to a new subsidiary in exchange for all of the stock of the subsidiary and (2) delivery by the subsidiary of buyer's voting stock to the shareholders of the corporation being sold in exchange for stock meeting the 80 percent test. The result is that the corporation sold becomes a second-tier subsidiary of buyer.

Stock Acquisition—Merger of Subsidiary into Seller. An alternative method which can accomplish useful and practical results is the reverse subsidiary "B" reorganization. In some situations, buyer and seller agree that the corporation being sold should be a separate subsidiary, but the corporation has valuable permits, contracts and other assets that could not readily be transferred and a sale of stock is not practical because of a large number of shareholders or possible objection by a small number of shareholders. The solution is for buyer to (1) contribute shares of its voting stock to a new subsidiary and (2) merge the subsidiary into the corporation being sold under a merger plan which calls for the distribution of buyer's voting stock to the shareholders of the corporation being sold. The corporation becomes a subsidiary of buyer, but does not risk loss of valuable permits, contracts or assets because its corporate existence is maintained without change.

STOCK-FOR-ASSETS ACQUISITIONS

The third type of tax-free reorganization of importance in acquiring businesses involves the purchase of the assets of a seller for stock of a buyer. Section 368(a)(1)

(C) defines this type or reorganization as "the acquisition by one corporation, in exchange solely for all or a part of its voting stock . . . of substantially all of the properties of another corporation, but in determining whether the exchange is solely for the stock the assumption by the acquiring corporation of a liability of the other . . . shall be disregarded."

In the Deficit Reduction Act of 1984, Section 368(a)(2)(G) was added. This Section requires that the seller corporation must distribute to its creditors and shareholders, pursuant to the plan of reorganization, all of its assets (less those retained to meet claims), including the consideration received from the acquiring corporation. The liquidation requirement can be waived by the IRS. See Revenue Procedure 89-50, 1989-35 IRB 12.

As in a stock-for-stock tax-free reorganization, the stock-for-assets reorganization involves two major requirements for tax-free treatment. First, subject to qualifications that we will discuss below, the medium of payment for the assets must be voting stock of the buyer. Second, the buyer must acquire substantially all of the assets of the seller.

Asset Transaction—Solely Voting Stock. The requirement that the assets of the seller be bought "in exchange solely for all or a part of [the] voting stock" of the buyer is expressed in language identical to that contained in the stock-for-stock, tax-free reorganization, but in an asset transaction, as opposed to a stock-for-stock transaction, the tax law contains exceptions to the requirement that the buyer pay for the assets in solely voting stock. The first exception allows the assumption of seller's liabilities by buyer. As quoted above, Section 368(a)(1)(C) provides that "in determining whether the exchange is solely for stock the assumption by the [buyer] of a liability of the [seller]" should be disregarded. To illustrate, assume that the seller's balance sheet is as follows:

SELLER CORPORATION

Balance Sheet at December 31, 19____

Assets		Liabilities and Stockholder's Equity	
Cash	$ 1,000	Accounts Payable	$ 2,000
Accounts Receivable	2,000	Mortgage on Plant	3,000
Inventory	7,000	Capital Stock	15,000
Plant & Equipment	15,000	Earned Surplus	5,000
Total Assets	$25,000	Total Liabilities and Equity	$25,000

If the buyer acquires the assets of the seller for voting stock, and the buyer agrees to assume the payment of both the accounts payable of $2,000 and the mortgage of $3,000, the additional payment made by the buyer in assuming the obligation to pay the seller's debts is ignored for tax purposes. The transaction is treated as though the buyer had bought the assets of the seller "solely" for voting stock of the buyer.

The second exception to the requirement that the buyer pay "solely" voting stock for the seller's assets flatly permits the buyer to make part of the payment in the form of money or other property. Section 368(a)(2)(B) states that if an acquisition of assets for stock would qualify as a tax-free reorganization except that the buyer "exchanges money or other property in addition to voting stock," then if the buyer acquires "solely for voting stock," property of the seller "having a fair market value which is at least 80 percent of the fair market value of all of the property" of the seller, the acquisition of assets will qualify as a tax-free reorganization. This exception, permitting a buyer to use cash or property in addition to voting stock, is subject to a refinement in determining whether the buyer has obtained 80 percent of the seller's assets for solely voting stock of the buyer. Under this refinement, if the buyer assumes any liabilities of the seller or takes property of the seller subject to liabilities in addition to paying the seller cash or other property, the buyer must treat the total of the liabilities "as money paid for the property" of the seller to determine whether the buyer acquired 80 percent of the seller's property solely for the buyer's voting stock.

To illustrate the operation of this refinement, we will utilize the same balance sheet of a seller that appears on page 309. You will recall that if the buyer acquired the seller's assets for solely voting stock, then the assumption by the buyer of the $2,000 of the seller's accounts payable and the $3,000 mortgage did not affect the tax-free nature of the transaction. But under the refinement to the asset deal (assuming the fair market value of the seller's assets is equal to the balance sheet figures), if the buyer gives $1.00 in cash in addition to assuming the seller's accounts payable and taking the plant subject to a mortgage, the transaction will be disqualified as a tax-free transaction. Under our assumption, the fair market value of all of the seller's property as reflected on the seller's balance sheet is $25,000. If the buyer gives $1 in cash in addition to stock for the seller's property, the assumption of $2,000 of seller's accounts payable and the $3,000 mortgage on the plant must be treated as money paid for the seller's property. Therefore, $5,001 is treated as paid in money for $25,000 of fair market value of the seller's assets. Since $5,001 paid in money exceeds 20 percent of $25,000 (the fair market value of the seller's assets) less than 80 percent of the property of the seller was acquired for solely voting stock of the buyer, and the transaction will not qualify as a tax-free reorganization.

As a final observation on the type of consideration a buyer may pay in an asset-type of tax-free reorganization, corporations generally have outstanding liabilities in excess of 20 percent of the fair market value of their assets. Consequently, asset transactions in which a buyer assumes the seller's obligations and pays cash or other property in addition to the buyer's stock will, except in unique instances, be taxable rather than tax-free transactions.

Substantially all of the properties. The second broad requirement for a tax-free assets transaction is that the buyer acquire "substantially all of the properties" of the seller. Generally, in determining whether substantially all of the seller's properties were acquired, you must distinguish current assets such as cash, accounts receivable and inventories and fixed assets such as plant and equipment. Limited amounts of cash, receivables, and even inventory may be retained by the seller and nevertheless the buyer may acquire "substantially all of the properties" of the seller. However, retention of similar percentages of plant and equipment by the seller may disqualify the reorganization. The definition of "substantially all of the properties" is generally fluid, but the Internal Revenue Service may not rule favorably where a buyer acquires less than 90 percent of the seller's properties.

STOCK-FOR-ASSETS REORGANIZATION: DIAGRAM

The following diagram illustrates the elements of a stock-for-assets, tax-free reorganization where the buyer gives nothing but voting stock for the seller's assets. In such a transaction, the buyer *may assume the liabilities* of the seller and the transaction will qualify as a tax-free deal. Recall that in a stock-for-stock deal, diagrammed on page 308, the buyer could give *only* voting stock and could not assume any obligations of the selling stockholders or give any other consideration. The diagram below indicates that in an asset deal the contract is between the buyer and the seller rather than between the buyer and the seller's stockholders as would be the case in a stock-for-stock, tax-free reorganization:

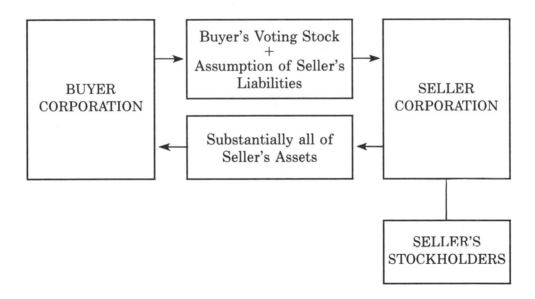

Of course, if the buyer in the above diagram gave money or other property as well as voting stock for the seller's assets, the liabilities assumed and to which the seller's property was subject would have to be treated as money to determine whether at least 80 percent of the seller's property was bought solely for voting stock. If less than 80 percent of the property was bought for solely voting stock, where the buyer gives money or other property in addition to voting stock, the transaction will not qualify as a tax-free, stock-for-assets reorganization.

Asset Acquisition—By Subsidiary. The definition of a tax-free stock-for-assets reorganization includes "the acquisition by one corporation, in exchange solely for all or a part of its voting stock (*or in exchange solely for all or a part of the voting stock of a corporation* which is *in control of the acquiring corporation*), of substantially all of the properties of another corporation. . . ." Under this portion of the definition, a subsidiary may acquire substantially all of the properties of the seller in exchange for voting stock of the subsidiary's parent, provided the parent controls within the meaning of the Code. "Control" for these purposes means the 80 percent stock ownership as defined above. Under Section 368(a)(1)(C), the acquisition of the assets of the seller corporation can be accomplished by transferring them item-by-item to buyer's subsidiary or by merging the seller corporation into buyer's subsidiary, thus transferring the assets by operation of law.

EFFECTS ON STOCKHOLDERS

Stated generally, and subject to the exceptions discussed below, stockholders who receive stock or securities in a statutory merger, stock-for-stock, or stock-for-assets tax-free reorganization neither realize taxable gain nor incur tax loss from the transaction. Code Section 354 reads that "*no gain or loss* shall be recognized if stock or securities in a corporation a party to a reorganization are, in pursuance of the plan of reorganization, exchanged solely for stock or securities in such corporation or in another corporation a party to the reorganization." For our purposes, the important part of the rule to remember is that "no gain or loss shall be recognized" when stock or securities are exchanged. In the usual statutory merger, stock-for-stock, or stock-for-assets transaction qualifying under a reorganization definition, the corporations involved will be parties to a reorganization, and generally the plan of reorganization will be provided in the acquisition agreement.

No gain or loss. What, then, do the words "no gain or loss shall be recognized" mean to the stockholders of a buyer or a seller exchanging stock in a tax-free reorganization? They do not mean that a tax will never be paid on gain. They do not mean that loss will never be deductible for income tax purposes. They mean that gain or loss will not be recognized from the exchange itself. But this nonrecognition carries with it other tax effects which may subject gain to tax in the future or permit loss to be deducted in the future.

The basic tax effect of an exchange of stock by a stockholder of a buyer or seller in a tax-free reorganization is that under Code Section 358 the basis of the stock received "shall be the same" as the basis of the stock given up in the exchange. In other words, the cost for tax purposes of the stock received is the same as the cost for tax purposes of the stock given up in the exchange.

To illustrate this basic principle, assume a tax-free, assets transaction in which the buyer acquires all of the seller's assets in exchange for the buyer's stock, and the seller distributes one share of the buyer's stock to the seller's stockholders in exchange for each of their shares. Assume further that at the time of the exchange the buyer's stock had a fair market value of $50 per share.

Seller's stockholder A, who paid $30 a share for his 100 shares of seller's stock—a total of $3,000 (100 shares × $30), receives 100 shares of buyer's stock worth $5,000 (100 shares × $50). Stockholder A has no tax to pay on the $2,000 gain. But his basis (cost for tax purposes) of the $5,000 worth of buyer's stock which A receives remains the same as A's cost for the stock of Seller which he has given up in exchange, namely $3,000. If A should sell his 100 shares of buyer's stock he received for $5,000, $2,000 of gain would be recognized for tax purposes at the time of the sale. The gain arises because the $3,000 A paid for his 100 shares of the seller carries over and becomes the cost, the tax basis, of the 100 shares of buyer that A received in the reorganization.

On the other hand, consider the situation of seller's stockholder B, who paid $70 a share for his 100 shares of seller's stock—a total of $7,000 (100 shares × $70). Although he suffers a loss in the sense that he receives only $5,000 worth of buyer's stock for his seller's stock which cost him $7,000, the loss is not recognized for tax purposes. However, should B sell the buyer's share he received and realize only $5,000, his $2,000 loss, the difference between his cost of $7,000 for his stock in the seller and the $5,000 proceeds from the sale of the buyer's stock, will be recognized for income tax purposes.

As a general observation applicable to both A and B, the holding period for tax purposes of the buyer's stock that they received in the reorganization will include the length of time they held the seller's stock at the time of the exchange. Under Code Section 1223 you simply add to the period the buyer's stock is held at the time of ultimate sale the length of time the seller's stock was held to the date of the reorganization exchange. If the total holding period to that time exceeds six months, A's gain or B's loss is treated as a long-term capital gain or loss for tax purposes. If held for less than six months, a short-term capital gain or loss results.

The carryover tax basis of A and B may be affected by an additional general tax rule. Under Code Section 1014 the tax basis of property forming the part of a decedent's estate is the fair market value of the property at the date of decedent's death or six months later. Thus, if A should die still holding Buyer's stock, the potential tax payable on the $2,000 inchoate gain resulting from the carryover of tax basis would be avoided. Since the stock has assumed a new tax basis from its inclusion in A's estate, the new tax cost will determine whether a sale of the stock after A's death will result in taxable gain or loss. For example, if the stock should have a value of $50 a share in A's estate and be sold for $50 a share soon after his death, no taxable gain would be realized. Eliminated from consideration is A's original cost of $3,000 for the seller's stock carried over to the buyer's stock; the $2,000 economic gain goes untaxed. B's estate, under the same circumstances as A's estate, would lose the right to deduct for tax purposes the economic loss B incurred.

Receipt of Other Property. The tax-free treatment of the recipient stockholders is subject to exceptions where other property or an excess amount of securities ("Boot") is received by the stockholder in addition to the stock which he is permitted to receive tax-free. In analyzing the treatment of stockholders who receive stock and securities in a tax-free acquisition the essential distinction between stock and securities in the tax law must be borne in mind. Stock under the tax law includes all types of stock, common—both voting and nonvoting—and preferred stocks of all classes. Securities consist of debt instruments, obligations of the buyer or seller which establish a creditor relationship with the stockholder, such as debentures (including convertible debentures) or bonds.

You will recall that of the pertinent three types of tax-free reorganizations: (1) statutory mergers, (2) stock-for-stock and (3) stock-for-assets, only the stock-for-stock transaction limited the buyer to the use of solely voting stock. On the other hand, in both statutory mergers and asset transactions other types of stock or securities as well as other property or cash may be used to pay a portion of the price, and the transaction may retain its fundamental characteristic as a tax-free reorganization. How, then, will receipt of securities or other property in addition to stock affect a stockholder of a corporation sold in an otherwise tax-free transaction? Let us consider each of the pertinent three types of reorganizations.

Amount of Gain. Where a stockholder receives other property or money in addition to stock or securities that may be received tax-free in an otherwise tax-free transaction, Code Section 356 provides that—gain if any, is recognized to the stockholder but not in excess of the money plus the fair market value of the other property. Where securities (debt obligations) of the buyer are received, the securities are treated as other property unless an equal or greater amount of securities is given in exchange by the stockholder. To the extent that the principal amount of securities received exceeds the principal amount of securities surrendered, gain will be recognized but not in excess of the fair market value of the excess principal amount of securities.

To illustrate these general principles whereby a portion of a distribution results in recognized gain to stockholders in an otherwise tax-free acquisition, consider first a statutory merger and second a stock-for-assets transaction. Assume that the surviving corporation in a merger—i.e., the buyer—distributes one share of its common stock, one share of preferred stock, one $10 debenture, and $10 in cash in exchange for each share of common stock of the merged company—i.e., the seller. The following table illustrates the package received by the selling stockholder, together with assumed fair market values, in exchange for the one share of seller's stock:

STOCKHOLDER RECEIVES

Item	Fair Market Value
1. One share buyer's common	$150
2. One share buyer's preferred	10
3. One $10 debenture	10
4. $10 in cash	10
Total fair market value received	$180

If we assume that the selling stockholder paid $100 for the share of seller's stock that he gives up in the exchange, he will have realized an economic gain of $80 in the exchange ($180 received in exchange for $100 cost). But for income tax purposes only $20 of the gain is recognized. In this "tax-free" statutory merger, gain is recognized but not in excess of the fair market value of the excess amount of securities received (the $10 value of the $10 debenture) plus the $10 in cash.

If the selling stockholder should receive the same package as the result of a stock-for-assets transaction that qualifies as a "tax-free" reorganization, rather than a statutory merger, the income tax effect would be the same.

"Boot"—Special Situations. Over the years, a question has arisen as to whether a variety of arrangements by buyer corporations might amount to the receipt of "boot" in a tax-free reorganization. The Internal Revenue Service has ruled that reasonable arrangements of the following kinds do not constitute "boot":

1. Employment agreements.
2. Reimbursement of legal, accounting, appraisal, advisory and other fees.
3. Substitution of employee stock options.
4. Agreements to register shares under federal and state securities laws.
5. Purchases of other assets from shareholders of the seller corporation for fair market value.
6. Payment of debt guaranteed by shareholders of the seller corporation.
7. Payment of a cash dividend by the seller corporation to its shareholders just prior to the reorganization, provided that it is paid out of funds of the seller corporation and not funds borrowed or indirectly advanced by buyer.
8. A right to receive contingent additional shares of stock if sales or earnings exceed agreed levels.

On the other hand, "put" and "call" and mandatory redemption rights have been ruled to be "boot." Rights to purchase additional common stock also have been ruled to be "boot."

In connection with the receipt of property or money by a stockholder in addition to stock in an otherwise tax-free transaction, Code Section 356(c) provides that no loss will be recognized for tax purposes. Although the receipt of property or money other than permissible stock or securities may subject a taxpayer to a taxable capital gain, receipt of the same property or money by the stockholder cannot result in a loss, deductible for income tax purposes. In other words, receipt of property other than stock in a tax-free merger or assets transaction may result in taxable gain but not in deductible loss.

Dividend Treatment. Finally, Code Section 356(a)(2) also provides that where the receipt of property or money results in recognized gain, the gain may be taxed as a dividend rather than a capital gain if the exchange "has the effect of a distribution of a dividend." Whether an exchange has the effect of a distribution of a dividend is often difficult to determine, but where the receipt of property or money in a "tax-free" exchange results in recognized gain, the parties should be aware that the gain may be taxed as a dividend and should investigate this possibility.

EFFECTS ON CORPORATIONS

The general tax effect of a tax-free reorganization on a corporation is that no gain or loss will be recognized to the corporation from the exchange of property for stock or securities of the other corporate party to the reorganization. This additional rule for tax-free exchange of property is necessary to provide for the tax-free exchange of properties in exchange for stock in an assets transaction. As in the case of a stockholder receiving other property or money, tax gain but not tax loss, will be recognized to a corporation which receives such property or money and does not distribute it to its shareholders as part of the "tax-free" reorganization.

When a corporation receives other property or money in addition to stock or securities which may be received tax-free in an otherwise tax-free transaction, Code Section 361(b)(2) provides that the corporation cannot deduct a loss incurred in the transaction. In this respect, a corporation is placed in the same position as a stockholder. In each case, whether a corporation or a stockholder, when a taxpayer receives other property or money in an otherwise tax-free transaction, gain may be recognized and taxed but loss will not be recognized and may not be deducted.

Another basic concept of the tax law is that the tax basis of the property transferred in a tax-free reorganization is the same in the hands of the transferee as it was in the hands of the transferor. In other words, where the buyer receives assets in a tax-free reorganization (in either a statutory merger or an asset transaction), Code Section 362(b) provides that the basis of the assets to the buyer remains the same as the depreciated tax cost of the assets to the seller, regardless of the value of the stock which the buyer may have given for the assets. This carryover of basis is often an important consideration in deciding whether the buyer should acquire assets in a tax-free or taxable transaction. In times of inflation and accelerated tax depreciation, the fair market value of assets will often far exceed depreciated tax cost. For example, assume that a seller's depreciable assets have a fair market value of $1 million, but a depreciated tax basis of only $500,000. If a buyer acquires the assets for $1 million worth of stock in a tax-free acquisition, the tax basis of the assets to the buyer will remain the tax basis in the hands of the seller—i.e., $500,000. Assuming a ten-year life of the assets and straight-line depreciation (cost recovery), the buyer may deduct only $50,000 per annum in depreciation for tax purposes. On the other hand, assume the same asset values and tax basis; but the buyer acquires the assets for $1 million in cash in a taxable transaction. Under these circumstances the $500,000 tax basis of the seller's assets does not carry over, but rather the tax basis to the buyer becomes the cost of the assets, $1 million. Now, if the buyer recovers its cost in the assets on a straight-line basis over a ten-year period, it may take an annual $100,000 deduction for income tax purposes. The depreciation deduction is doubled and the increase in this deduction means a substantial tax saving per year as a result of a taxable transaction rather than a tax-free transaction.

NONSTATUTORY PROBLEMS IN
TAX-FREE ACQUISITIONS

The foregoing discussion of tax-free reorganizations was limited to the basic statutory provisions with little consideration of court-imposed refinements or more detailed problems that may arise. Some of these are considered in outline fashion in this section:

1. *Business purpose.* To be treated as a tax-free reorganization, courts have held that an acquisition must not only meet the statutory requirements discussed above, but must in addition meet a court-imposed test that it have a "business purpose." Acquisitions involving publicly held companies engaged in the active conduct of businesses will have no difficulty in meeting the business purpose test, but an acquisition and transfer solely for the purpose of distributing marketable securities to shareholders may not meet the "business purpose" test and may be taxable.

2. *Step transaction.* The Internal Revenue Service and the courts have applied a "step transaction" doctrine to determine whether an acquisition in the form of a reorganization which meets the technical statutory requirements is actually tax-free. For example, if a buyer wishes to acquire a division of a seller which forms only a small part of the seller's assets, the buyer could not directly acquire this division from the seller for solely voting stock in a tax-free reorganization because the buyer would not be acquiring "substantially all of the properties" of the seller as the Internal Revenue Code requires. If the seller organizes a subsidiary and transfers to it all the assets and business of the division (which the seller can do tax-free) and the buyer acquires all of the assets and business of the subsidiary for solely voting stock, the technical requirement of the law is met, since the buyer acquired not only "substantially all of the properties" of the seller (the subsidiary corporation) but all of these properties. However, the courts would, in all likelihood, tie the separate steps of the transaction together and hold that the net effect of the two steps was the acquisition by the buyer of a small portion of the properties of the seller, and thus hold the transaction to be taxable.

Nevertheless, careful planning has sometimes led to successful tax-free reorganizations in spite of challenges by the IRS. *Litton Industries,* 89 TC 1986 (1987); *Esmark Inc.,* 90 TC 171 (1988); *Robert O. Anderson,* 92 TC 138 (1989); *Tandy Corporation* 92 TC 1165 (1989).

3. *Continuity of interest.* In addition, although the technical definition of a reorganization is met, an acquisition may still be taxable, where a so-called "continuity of interest" does not exist. Under this originally court-imposed concept the former stockholders of the seller must retain a substantial (50% under one IRS ruling) equity interest after the acquisition for some time period. In one decision by the Tax Court, a period of six months was held sufficient to establish continuity of interest. Obviously, if the selling stockholders received only bonds in exchange for their stock, they would become creditors, their equity interest would terminate and the transaction would be taxable. A recent decision of interest is *Penrod v. Commissioner,* 88 T.C. No. 79 (1987) in which a nine-month holding period was held insufficient. The Tax Court distinguished an earlier decision in *McDonald's Restaurants of Illinois v. Commissioner,* 688 F. 2d 520 (7 Cir., 1982).

DISSENTING STOCKHOLDERS

Dissenting stockholders may cause peripheral tax problems. As discussed in Chapter 6, where a buyer acquires assets of a seller, in many jurisdictions, the seller's stockholders have a right to dissent to the transaction. By dissenting, the seller's stockholders may receive cash for their stockholdings. The receipt of such cash by the dissenting stockholders may cause tax problems to arise, particularly in connection with tax-free acquisitions.

Substantially all of seller's assets—dissenting stockholders. Since, in many jurisdictions, successful dissenting stockholders may be required to be paid the fair value of their stock by the seller, to the extent that the seller utilizes its cash to pay dissenting stockholders, the buyer will not be acquiring the cash thus eliminated from the seller's corporate assets. You will recall that to qualify as a tax-free reorganization under Section 368(a)(1)(C) of the code, a buyer must acquire "substantially all" of the assets of the seller. If a large percentage of the seller's stockholders dissent and are paid off in cash, the cash drain could be so substantial that the buyer would not be acquiring "substantially all" of the assets of the seller. To protect against this possibility, acquisition contracts should be drafted to limit the percentage of dissenting stockholders, and provide a condition precedent to the buyer or seller's obligation to close the transaction that the percentage not be exceeded. If the limitation on the acceptable number of dissenting stockholders provided in the acquisition contract is sufficiently small, the problem of a buyer not acquiring "substantially all" of the assets of a seller may be avoided.

Solely voting stock test—dissenting stockholders. Generally, in both a tax-free acquisition of stock by a buyer and a tax-free acquisition of assets by a buyer, the consideration that a buyer may give to a seller is limited to "solely voting stock" of the buyer. In such tax-free acquisitions, where selling stockholders become entitled to be paid off in cash because of their dissent, the cash payments may not normally be made by the buyer or the buyer will not be acquiring the seller's stock or assets for "solely voting stock." To solve this tax problem, by the terms of the acquisition contract sellers are often permitted to retain sufficient cash to pay off dissenting stockholders. As a consequence, the seller, not the buyer, makes the cash payment to the dissenting stockholders.

Eighty percent control—dissenting stockholders. In order for a stock-for-stock acquisition to qualify as a tax-free reorganization under Section 368 of the Code, the buyer must acquire control of the seller. Control is defined as ownership of at least 80 percent of the total combined voting power of the seller as well as 80 percent of all other classes of stock. If, therefore, the parties desire a tax-free transaction, and question whether more than 20 percent of the seller's stockholders will refuse to sell their stock to the buyer, the acquisition contract may require, as a condition precedent to closing, that the buyer acquire at least 80 percent of the voting stock and all other classes of stock of the seller in the acquisition. Such a condition may also be provided in the offer to acquire stock in connection with a registered exchange offer, discussed in Chapter 9, where it is the intention to complete such a takeover as a tax-free reorganization. Where the buyer is unable to acquire a sufficient number of seller's shares to qualify under the control test, the parties may attempt to recast the acquisition as either a statutory merger or a stock-for-assets acquisition, if they intend to have the acquisition treated as tax-free.

TRIANGULAR MERGERS

Triangular mergers have become very common because they provide the "freezeout" effect of a merger while maintaining the separate corporate existence of the acquired corporation.

Section 368(a)(2)(D) permits the use of stock of a controlling corporation by a controlled subsidiary to accomplish a forward triangular merger to acquire substantially all the properties of another corporation in an "A" reorganization or a "G" reorganization, provided that stated conditions are met. The transaction must meet the "substantially all assets" and "solely for voting stock" requirements of Section 368(a)(1)(c).

Section 368(a)(2)(E) permits the use of stock of a controlling corporation by a controlled subsidiary to accomplish a reverse merger if (i) after the transaction, the surviving corporation holds substantially all of its properties and the properties of the merged corporation and (ii) in the transaction, former shareholders of the surviving corporation exchanged, for an amount of voting of the controlling corporation, an amount of stock in the surviving corporation which constitutes control of such corporation.

It is generally recognized that a forward triangular merger is equivalent to a purchase by the surviving corporation of the assets of the acquired corporation. *West Shore Fuel, Inc. v. United States,* 598 F,2d 1236 (2 Cir. 1979). A reverse triangular merger is equivalent to a purchase of stock of the acquired corporation by the parent corporation. Revenue Ruling 79-273, 1979-2C.B.125.

EFFECTS OF POISON PILLS

In an effort to prevent loss of control, management of many publicly owned corporations have caused the corporation to adopt so-called "poison pill" rights plans. Mere adoption of a plan is not a taxable event. However, if the plan is triggered and the rights become exercisable, a taxable event may occur. Further, "poison pill" rights may prevent a "B" reorganization. See articles at 41 *Tax Lawyer* 151 (1987) and 41 *Tax Lawyer* 457 (1988). See also 44 *Tax Notes* 137 (1989).

FOREIGN CORPORATIONS

Under Code Section 367, in the case of any exchange of securities in connection with a tax-free reorganization, a foreign corporation (one organized outside of the United States) is not considered as a corporation unless, before such exchange, it is established to the satisfaction of the Commissioner of Internal Revenue that the exchange is not in pursuance of a plan having as one of its principal purposes the avoidance of federal income taxes. Prior to 1985, when a foreign corporation was involved in a reorganization, Code Section 367 eliminated the tax-free treatment of exchanges of securities in connection with otherwise tax-free reorganizations, unless *prior to the exchange* a ruling was obtained from the Commissioner of Internal Revenue. Guidelines published by the Internal Revenue Service set forth the circumstances and the extent to which favorable rulings would be granted under this section.

The guidelines indicated that a favorable ruling would, generally speaking, only be granted where in one manner or another taxes will be collected by the United States to the fullest extent possible in connection with the transaction. For example, if the assets of a domestic corporation were being acquired by a foreign corporation, a favorable ruling would normally be granted only if the domestic corporation agreed to include in its income any unrealized appreciation attributable to certain types of assets such as inventory, copyrights, accounts receivable, installment obligations, investment securities, etc. Furthermore, where a domestic corporation acquired the assets of a foreign corporation, a favorable ruling would be granted only if United States shareholders of the foreign corporation agreed to report as ordinary income, upon the receipt of stock of the domestic corporation, an amount to reflect such shareholders' portion of the accumulated earnings of the foreign corporation.

Code Section 367 was restructured effective January 1, 1985, by the Deficit Reduction Act of 1984. The requirement that a ruling be obtained from the Internal Revenue Service for a tax-free transfer of assets to a foreign corporation was eliminated. Thus, United States persons are free to proceed based on substantive rules provided in Code Section 367. However, outbound transfers under Code Section 367(a) or (d) and liquidating distributions under Section 367(e) must be reported on an information return.

As restructured, Code Section 367(a) continues the fundamental principle that, if a United States person transfers property to a foreign corporation in connection with any exchange described in Code Sections 332, 351, 354, 355, 356, or 361, the foreign corporation will not be deemed a "corporation" within the meaning of those sections. Thus, tax-free treatment is not available for these "outbound transfers" and any gain on appreciated property must be recognized. (The tax imposed is sometimes called a "toll charge.")

There are two major exceptions to the "toll charge." First, Code Section 367(a)(2) continues to exempt from taxation outbound transfers of stock or securities of a foreign corporation which is a party to the exchange or reorganization. Second, Code Section 367(a)(3)(A) provides that, if property is transferred for use by the foreign corporation in connection with the active conduct of a trade or business outside the United States, tax-free treatment is available *except* for certain specific types of assets such as inventories: accounts receivable; patents, trade secrets, trademarks and copyrights; installment obligations; foreign currency and certain obligations payable in foreign currency and certain leased properties and other intangible properties. These assets are sometimes called "tainted assets."

Special rules apply to transfers to a foreign corporation of partnership interests, intangibles or the assets of a foreign branch of a United States person. Of particular interest, intangible property will generally be deemed sold for payments "contingent upon the productivity, use or disposition of such property" and the transferor must include constructive payments in income annually over the useful life of the intangible property. If a foreign branch which has operated at a loss is incorporated, the United States transferor must recognize ordinary income equal to the cumulative amount of prior losses.

As in the past, the objective of the restructured Code Section 367 is to permit tax-free treatment of transfers of property for the active conduct of a business outside the United States in transactions corresponding to domestic transactions eligible for tax-free treatment, but to prevent use of such transactions for the purpose of avoiding, reducing or changing the character of income otherwise taxable in the United States.

Code Section 367 provides that nonrecognition of gain or loss upon liquidating distributions (including debt payments) to 80-percent distributees is denied to distributees which are foreign corporations unless the Internal Revenue Service adopts regulations permitting nonrecognition in situations where appreciated property will remain subject to U.S. tax jurisdiction.

12

Leveraged Buyouts

INTRODUCTION

The leveraged buyout is essentially a means to create and build an equity ownership interest through the use of borrowing to be repaid from the cash flow of the acquired business.

Leveraged buyouts developed during the 1970s and early 1980s due to a combination of events. High capital gains taxes and other factors created a decade of "no growth" in the stock markets and retrenchment of investment banking and brokerage firms. With limited access to traditional equity markets, business turned to borrowing to meet funding needs. Pressed by increasing competition resulting from deregulation, increasing costs for their own funds and growing domestic and foreign competition, banks and other financial institutions were willing to provide loans that partially replaced the traditional role of equity. The additional risk was (1) compensated by higher lending rates and other forms of compensation such as direct equity participation and (2) minimized by careful use of modern cash flow analysis methods, security interests in business assets and "in-depth" understanding of the businesses being financed.

The decline of the traditional equity markets eventually resulted in the stocks of many established businesses selling at prices less than the net value of their assets, even though reasonably well-managed and profitable. Owners of privately owned businesses, who might have "gone public" in the 1950s and 1960s, were forced to realize that the public markets would value their companies at far less than their investment in its assets.

The leveraged buyout met many business needs. For management threatened with a tender offer for the undervalued stock of their company, it afforded an opportunity to "go private." For a conglomerate seeking to rationalize its businesses, it afforded an opportunity for divestitures. For the owners of private businesses established after World War II, it afforded an opportunity to sell for cash at acceptable prices and orderly management succession.

As the 1970s and 1980s progressed, banks, insurers and other financing institutions created departments and subsidiaries specializing in mergers and acquisitions staffed with management and personnel accustomed to structuring transactions using leverage. Many of them had practical "workout" experience. They were able to structure transactions which, although innovative in their concepts, were actually less risky than conventional loans providing lower investment return.

As the 1980s progressed, prices in the stock market increased dramatically. For example, the Dow Jones average, which remained less than 1,000 during the 1970s, rose to levels well in excess of 2,500 in spite of a sharp market break in October 1987. As acquisition prices and burdens of acquisition debt increased, the risks became real in the late 1980s and some buyers who used leveraged buyout methods failed. See "History."

ADVANTAGES TO SELLERS AND BUYERS

For sellers, leveraged buyouts present several advantages. A large corporation operating a division or subsidiary that earns a modest profit, but no longer fits its overall financial or business strategies, may prefer a sale to continued operation or a shutdown with its related problems. Business founders, nearing retirement, may prefer a sale to management employees for cash and notes rather than for stock of a public company, since the transaction fulfills moral obligations and also provides cash to meet retirement needs and estate tax obligations. It also may assure a more meaningful and congenial continuing role for the founders than would realistically be likely after a sale to a large unrelated company.

For buyers, leveraged buyouts present a unique opportunity to obtain whole or partial ownership of a business with limited equity investment. The new management-owners are expected, of course, to provide experience, skills and a high degree of dedication, but the chance to provide "sweat equity" in place of financial investment can be a lifetime opportunity for them.

An article which described with unusual clarity and brevity the needs, motivations, methods, opportunities and risks of leveraged buyouts is "When Power Investors Call the Shots," *Business Week*, June 20, 1988. Readers may also be interested in the study of leveraged buyouts between 1981 and 1988 by Professors Frank Lichtenberg of Columbia University and Donald Siegel of the State University of New York issued in 1989.

HISTORY

The combinations of techniques associated with leveraged buyouts were largely the result of work by two firms: Kohlberg, Kravis, Roberts & Co. and Kelso & Co. The Kohlberg firm has become famous as an owner of major businesses. The Kelso firm is known for the work of its founder, Louis Kelso, who sponsored enabling legislation for Employee Stock Ownership Plans (ESOPs) with authority to borrow to purchase stock of the sponsoring company. ESOPs are discussed in greater detail later in this chapter.

Originally, leveraged buyouts were used in relatively small transactions. However, as the field was entered by major investment banking firms, insurers, banks and venture capital funds, the size has grown. Later transactions involved hundreds of millions of dollars and then billions of dollars. Examples of transactions involving billions of dollars include such large leveraged buyouts as Esmark, City Investing, Metromedia, Revlon, NL Industries, Owens-Illinois, Beatrice, Macy's, Fruehauf, Safeway, Southland, Burlington Industries, Borg-Warner, Montgomery Ward, Fort Howard Paper, Jim Walter and RJR Nabisco. There have also been a number of transactions involving hundreds of millions such as Vista Chemicals the chemicals business of Conoco, Dr Pepper, Congoleum, Signode, Amstar and Bendix Forest Products. Major transactions funded by an ESOP include the Weirton Steel Division of National Steel Corporation, Raymond International, Inc., Dan River Mills, Inc. and Avis, Inc.

In general, leveraged buyouts have been successful—some, extremely so—and this fueled their growth. Some such as Gibson Greeting, have been followed by public sales of stock of the new company. Other successful LBOs included Georgia Gulf, Vista Chemical, Sterling Chemicals, Formica Corporation, American Can, National Cross and Beatrice Company. Among the reasons for success have been careful planning by sellers, buyers and lenders and dedicated effort by new management and employees. Other reasons are that some businesses can be operated more effectively when freed from corporate overhead and restrictions on management initiative; longstanding customs and practices imposed by founders and labor organizations and time-consuming and costly regulation imposed strictly by government on large companies but exempted or imposed leniently on small businesses.

During the late 1980s, LBOs became more difficult. After 1982, the stock market rose dramatically, as did acquisition prices and seller expectations. Gradually, friendly LBOs were eclipsed by the hostile leveraged takeover led by colorful entrepreneurs such as Boone Pickens, Carl Icahn, Ronald Perelman and Harold Simmons. Many of them were financed by Drexel Burnham Lambert Inc. Lobbying by threatened managements led to adoption by state legislatures of antitakeover laws designed to avoid the defects of earlier laws held invalid by the federal courts. New judges appointed to the federal courts by the Reagan Administration believed in judicial restraint. They upheld the new laws, although they openly questioned their economic wisdom. Insider trading scandals impaired public confidence. Eager for tax revenues, Congress seized the opportunity in 1986 to amend the Internal Revenue Code to repeal provisions which had provided relief against double taxation of corporate acquisitions. As described in Chapter 10, a variety of other amendments were adopted in 1987, 1988 and 1989 to deny tax benefits to leveraged buyouts and to corporate restructuring transactions which substitute debt for equity. Articles appeared in popular magazines predicting defaults in junk bonds and describing the aggressive tactics of LBO sponsors and advisers. An article capturing the atmosphere was "Bid 'em Up, Bruce," *Forbes,* 1989.

The high water mark was reached with the leveraged buyout of RJR Nabisco in

1989. Only the reputation of Kohlberg Kravis Roberts & Co. made it possible to complete the highly priced and leveraged transaction. (See "King Henry," *Business Week,* November 14, 1988.) Lenders were later to call on Kohlberg Kravis Roberts & Co. to provide $1.7 billion of capital as part of a restructuring plan to shore up RJR Nabisco.

The call to retreat came with the collapse of an effort to structure a leveraged buyout of UAL Corporation (United Air Lines). Bankruptcy reorganization petitions were filed by several LBO companies including Campeau Corporation (Allied, Federated, Bloomingdale's), Hillsborough Holdings (Jim Walter), Dart Drug Stores and Revco. The press reported severe financial strains at other companies such as Fruehauf, Macy's, Harcourt Brace, Tracor and Seaman Furniture.

For practical purposes, leveraged takeover activity ceased in 1989. Friendly leveraged buyouts continue on more conservative terms. *Mergers & Acquisitions* reported in its issues for May-June and for July/August 1990 that middle-market activity continued to be relatively strong.

For several years, some companies have followed a leveraged buyout with a public stock offering. This step was, of course, one of the "exit" alternatives for venture capitalists from the early development of leveraged buyouts. Recently, some companies have made initial public offerings of stock in order to raise capital and reduce risk. The market for these "Reverse LBOs" tends to be cautious because of the obvious possibility that the LBO sponsors may be seeking an exit. However, reinfusion of equity capital into businesses which benefited from the discipline of tight budgets could produce genuine growth.

Those seeking data on leveraged buyouts and leveraged takeovers can refer to *Leveraged Buyouts and the Pot of Gold: Trends, Public Policy and Case Studies,* a report prepared by the Economics Division of the Congressional Research Service, December, 1987; *Hostile Corporate Takeovers: Synopses of Thirty-Two Attempts,* prepared by the U.S. General Accounting Office, March 1988; and *Recent Developments in the High Yield Market,* a staff report prepared by the Securities and Exchange Commission and distributed in 1990.

PROFILE OF THE CANDIDATE BUSINESS

While marked by exceptions, several characteristics have been identified as having special importance for successful leveraged buyouts:

- Experienced management
- Stable business
- Sound business plan
- Minimal existing debt
- Strong and secure cash flow-projections with a significant depreciation component

Other valuable characteristics include: (1) historical profitability or a readily achievable turnaround program; (2) assets that can be sold to reduce or repay part of the purchase price; (3) physical assets that can serve as loan collateral because they have ready liquidation value; (4) assets that can be written up and depreciated to minimize taxes, particularly if the write-up will have a minimal recapture impact; (5) a diversified product and customer base that is minimally cyclical and (6) minimal need for capital improvements during the period while acquisition debt is to be repaid.

Technology-based and "people" businesses present more difficulty as leveraged buyouts because lenders tend to loan relatively modest amounts to businesses having primarily intangible assets and people. However, if such a business has sound management, marketable intangible assets and generates reliable cash flow, it also can be a leveraged buyout candidate. The buyout of Billboard Publications, Inc., a business based on talent and reputation, is an example of such a transaction.

FINANCIAL STRUCTURE

Although actual transactions are not so easily classified, the financing of leveraged buyouts can most easily be described under two headings:

Asset-based transactions: The financial structures of leveraged buyouts in which the loans are primarily based on assets that provide full security can be relatively simple and quickly arranged with banks or finance companies. For example, the buyer may arrange to borrow as follows:

Accounts receivable (high quality)	75–85%
Inventories (readily marketable)	35–50%
Plant, property and equipment (appraised liquidation value)	60–80%

The loan proceeds are used for the purchase price or a down payment, closing costs, and working capital in the business. The balance, if any, of the purchase price is paid to the seller by subordinated notes or installment payments that also may be entitled to a second priority security interest in the assets.

In asset-based buyouts, the management members arranging the transaction often receive all or most of the equity ownership. Thus, the leverage advantage for them is very high. The fully secured lender need not insist on an "equity cushion" diluting the equity available to management owners. Of course, deferral and subordination of part of the purchase price by the seller fills an equivalent role.

Cash-flow-based transactions: The financial structure of large cash-flow-based buyouts can be quite complex. It may consist of tiers of debt, "mezzanine" and equity cushion financing such as the following:

Long-term senior debt	Insurers, pension funds
Intermediate or revolving credit debt	Banks
Subordinated notes or preferred stock	Venture capital investors
Common stock	Lenders, investors, and management

While there are no absolutes, the tendency in cash flow-based transactions is for the buyout to be a larger and higher-priced transaction with all or much of the purchase price paid at the closing. These conditions create the need for additional financing at the "mezzanine" level (subordinated notes or preferred stock) or common stock level to provide an equity cushion supporting the senior debt and bank debt.

If a single lender finances a cash flow based buyout, the lender will require mortgages, security interests and other collateral as though the transaction were asset-based. However, when the transaction is financed by multiple lenders in several tiers, collateral becomes difficult to arrange.

When some of the lenders cannot be secured, it is common to arrange that none will be secured and that the buyer will include "negative covenants" in its loan agreements committing to maintain its assets free of mortgages, liens and security interests. Accordingly, these transactions are evaluated by lenders and investors on the basis of cash flow since collateral security is not provided. Lenders and investors will typically include a variety of other restrictions in their agreements that are designed to protect their loans or investments and the cash resources from which they will be paid.

In cash-flow-based transactions, management may receive a smaller percentage of the equity ownership because the lenders and "mezzanine" investors bargain for a share of the equity as incentive compensation for their risks. The initial equity ownership is often made subject to adjustments through the use of convertible securities, options or warrants. For example, lenders or "mezzanine" investors may bargain for the right to convert loans to common stock, especially in the event of a public stock offering. Management may bargain for options to acquire more stock if business or financial goals are achieved.

High Yield Securities ("Junk Bonds")

In traditional markets, an irony has existed and still exists. There is relatively active trading in high quality "blue chip" debt securities and also in equity securities. Markets for intermediate quality debt securities, even though of higher quality than stocks of the same companies, are sometimes thin and even nonexistent.

The public tendency has been to think of debt securities as worth par, plus a premium or minus a discount for changes in prevailing interest rates, or as worthless to anyone but speculators. Improved analysis, using methods similar to those used in shareholder value analysis, have become the foundation for markets in intermediate quality subordinated debt securities. These markets recognize that intermediate quality and especially subordinated debt securities have characteristics similar to stocks and other equity securities. Thus, they can be traded at market value reflecting credit risk, provided that adequate information and analysis is available to quantify value as it fluctuates with credit risk as well as with interest rate changes.

"Junk Bonds" are considered to be any debt securities which are nonrated or rated in the lowest categories by Moody's and by Standard & Poor's. Within that broad category and even within the bonds issued by a single company, they may present a wide range of characteristics. A single company may issue a variety of short and long term debt securities including secured debt, senior unsecured debt, subordinated unsecured debt and junior unsecured subordinated debt. Some of the debt securities may be convertible or be sold with attached warrants or as part of packages with other securities. Thus, the terms of each issue of "junk bonds" require careful evaluation, not only when bought but while they are held. This continuing evaluation is essential to permit the investor to take advantage of such market liquidity as is offered by dealers together with high yield as a substitute for "blue chip" quality.

It is generally recognized that at least the more subordinated issues of "junk bonds" are a substitute for stock, preferred or common, although carefully structured to avoid the penalties of Code Section 279. Corporations and sophisticated passive investors, such as institutions, prefer these instruments to stock because interest is deductible while dividends paid on stock are not. From the investor's point of view, the high yields and any related "equity kickers" are an ample substitute for the capital appreciation potential of common stock.

In 1989, several events combined to cause a sharp downturn in the "junk" bond market. Long pending criminal investigations against Drexel Burnham Lambert Inc. and Michael Milken finally resulted in indictments followed by negotiated guilty pleas to a few charges. In 1990, Drexel's parent and then Drexel filed bankruptcy reorganization proceedings. Drexel's role in the "junk" bond markets had been so extensive and aggressive that other firms were not ready or inclined to make strong markets in the face of heavy selling pressure. Many also complained that issuers were not supplying enough public information to allow informed trading.

Concurrently with these developments, selling pressures on "junk" bond holders were increasing. The Comptroller of the Currency, Federal Deposit Insurance Corporation and Federal Reserve Board adopted guidelines to be used by examiners in evaluating loans to finance highly leveraged transactions (HLTs). HLTs were defined primarily by a 75% total liabilities to total assets test. In late 1989, the SEC took the position that the bonds should be written down to market value. When adopting legislation to fund multibillion dollar potential obligations of the Federal Savings & Loan Insurance Corporation, Congress prohibited savings institutions from investing in "junk" bonds and required deinvestment over a five year period, creating selling pressure on a weakened market.

As disclosure improves and selling pressure eases, trading in sound "junk" bonds will stabilize. Firms such as Merrill Lynch, Donaldson Lufkin and Shearson

Lehman have long been active in "junk" bonds. There are numerous large funds specializing in "junk" bonds. These funds have been able to make bargain purchases during the past year. In the future, new issues of intermediate quality debt with relatively high yields will less often be identified with leveraged takeovers, but are likely to be used to finance a variety of venture capital needs.

Interested readers will find extensive information in a staff report titled "Recent Developments in the High Yield Market" issued in early 1990 by the Securities and Exchange Commission.

LEGAL STRUCTURE AND TRANSACTIONS

To provide a vehicle with limited liability, the management or entrepreneurs arranging a leveraged buyout organize a corporation to make the purchase arrangements. This corporation will usually later serve as a holding company.

After negotiating the buyout and related financing, the new corporation can acquire the seller's business by any of the usual methods: (1) assets purchase, (2) stock purchase or (3) merger. The assets-purchase method is commonly used for negotiated small and medium-size transactions, since it allows selection of assets and liabilities and readily accommodates the negotiations over price allocation and stepped-up basis which are important to the tax planning of the buyout.

A leveraged buyout can be accomplished as a stock purchase by organizing an acquisition which borrows the acquisition price from lenders and uses it to buy the acquired corporation from its shareholders. The acquisition subsidiary then causes its new subsidiary to guarantee the acquisition debt if such an "upstream" guarantee is valid under the applicable state corporation law. An alternative stock purchase method is to have the acquisition vehicle purchase some shares of the acquired corporation. The lenders then make secured loans directly to the acquired corporation which uses the proceeds to redeem all of its outstanding shares except those owned by the acquisition vehicle, provided that it can meet any restrictions on dividends and distributions under the applicable state corporation law. Triangular mergers, forward and reverse, are very commonly used as an LBO acquisition method. The lenders can make their loans initially either to the acquisition vehicle or the acquired corporation which became a single corporation upon the merger. The surviving corporation usually grants mortgages and security interests in its assets. Regardless of the method used, the courts may view the several steps as one transaction. *Wieboldt Stores, Inc. v. Schottenstein*, 94 Bkptcy. Rptr. 488, 502 (N.D. Ill. 1988).

If lenders will permit, there are accounting and tax advantages to the use of a holding company and operating company structure. For accounting purposes, the acquisition indebtedness owed by the holding company need not appear on the balance sheet of the operating subsidiary where it would create a "low" or negative net worth. The operating company will provide a guaranty and sometimes also securities interests in its assets to secure the acquisition indebtedness, but these are "off balance sheet" commitments that are disclosed but not charged directly to net worth. On the other hand, for tax purposes, the holding company can file a consolidated return including its subsidiary operating company, and deduct interest on the acquisition indebtness from income of the operating company.

A limited partnership can also be used as the buyer entity. The general partner will usually be a corporation.

For large acquisitions of publicly owned companies, more complex structures are used. The acquisition transaction can be accomplished by an immediate merger if negotiations are "friendly." It can also be accomplished by a two-step method by using a "front end" tender offer and a "back end" merger, whether the negotiations are friendly or not. The merger step is, of course, essential to permit the buyer to restructure the assets of the target company and use them to repay acquisition debt. For these transactions, it is common to use a holding company and a transitory acquisition subsidiary. The acquisition subsidiary is merged with or into the target company in a triangular merger.

CREDITOR'S RIGHTS

There are a number of creditor's rights questions in arranging the structures of leveraged buyouts, particularly if a holding company/operating company structure is used. Lenders must be confident that their loans are legally made and that promissory notes, guarantees and security interests are valid and enforceable against attacks under the U.S. Bankruptcy Code and state creditors' rights laws alleging invalidity of "upstream" guarantees of parent debt by the operating subsidiary, illegal dividend transfers from subsidiary to parent, preferential debt payments, fraudulent conveyances and debtor control to an extent calling for equitable subordination. The seller also must be concerned with these questions, particularly when part of the purchase price is deferred. Because of these concerns, lenders may insist that their loans be made to and repaid by a the acquired operating corporation.

The creditors rights laws of primary interest in leveraged buyout transactions are as follows:

1. The Uniform Fraudulent Conveyances Act ("UFCA"), the Uniform Fraudulent Transfers Act ("UFTA") and equivalent common law in states not having these statutes and Section 273-a of the New York Debtor and Creditor Law.
2. Sections 510(c), 544(b), 547, 548, 550 and 551 of the Bankruptcy Code.
3. Uncertainties about the enforceability of intercorporate guarantees, particularly "upstream" guarantees by subsidiaries.
4. Provisions of the corporate statutes restricting the sources from which dividends may be paid.
5. Court decisions holding lenders liable for inequitable conduct including dominance of a borrower during "workout" situations. Such conduct may also result in "equitable subordination" under Section 510(c) of the Bankruptcy Code.

A common theme of the creditors rights laws is to protect creditors of insolvent or inadequately capitalized companies against transfers of assets to shareholders or other persons without receiving fair consideration or reasonably equivalent value in return. In leveraged buyouts, the transaction, however structured, uses assets of the acquired corporation to pay (or to secure loans used to pay) the acquisition price. Thus, the acquired corporation never receives fair consideration or reasonably equivalent value. The acquired corporation may indeed receive intangible benefits, such as new management and business opportunities, but these intangibles are not considered fair consideration or reasonably equivalent value under the creditors rights laws. *U.S. v. Gleneagles,* supra; *Credit Managers Ass'n. v. Federal Co.,* 629 F.Supp. 175 (CD, Cal. 1985).

Since the acquired corporation does not receive fair value, if asset transfers involved in a leveraged buyout are made when the acquired corporation (or other resulting vehicle) is insolvent or lacks adequate capital, its creditors or a bankruptcy trustee can seek to recover them from the shareholders. They can also seek to nullify mortgages and security interests and to recover payments of acquisition debt made to lenders.

Creditors rights planning for leveraged buyout transactions involves careful financial analysis to assure that each corporation whose credit and cash flow will be committed to repay acquisition debt is solvent, has reasonably adequate capital and is able to meet its debts as they mature. Leading court decisions on creditors rights include *U.S. v. Gleneagles Investment Company, Inc.,* (M.D., Pa., 1983) 565 F.S. 556, affirmed sub nom; *U.S. v. Tabor Court Realty Corp.,* (3 Cir., 1986) 803 F.2d 1288; cert. denied sub nom. *McLellan Realty v. U.S.,* 107 S.Ct. 3229 (1987); *Rubin v. Manufacturers Hanover Trust Company,* (2 Cir., 1981) 661 F.2d 979; *Wells Fargo Bank v. Desert View Building Supplies,* (D.C., Nev., 1978) 475 F.S. 693 and *In the Matter of Process—Manz Press, Inc.,* (N.D., Ill., 1964) 236 F.S. 333.

If transfers involved in a leveraged buyout are challenged, a court cannot be limited to the closing date in determining solvency and capital adequacy. While the writer of a solvency letter may wish to limit a determination to that date, a court will examine a company's capital throughout a reasonable period of time surrounding the date of each challenged transfer *Barrett v. Continental Illinois Nat. Bank & Trust,* 882 F.2d 1 (1 Cir. 1989). Further, solvency and capital adequacy may also have to exist on the dates when subsequent payments of principal and interest are made on securities issued to pay the acquisition debt. *In re Flying Mailman Service, Inc.,* 402 F.Supp. 790 (SDNY 1975); affirmed 539 F.2d 866 (2 Cir. 1976), *In re Anderson Industries, Inc.,* 55 Bkptcy. Rptr. 922 (1985).

Because of concern about creditors rights, it has become customary for lenders to require borrowers in a leveraged buyout to deliver a "solvency letter" at the closing. Initially, the letters were written by accounting firms, but the American Institute of Certified Public Accountants (AICPA) decided that its members should not write such letters. Prior to the AICPA's decision, concern had been expressed about potential effects of solvency letters on accountants' independence and failure of the public to recognize the difference between future-oriented analytical services and the audit process involving the presentation of historical financial information in accordance with generally accepted accounting principles. Since the AICPA decision, solvency letters have been written by firms skilled in financial analysis, such as Houlihan Lokey Howard & Zukin and Duff & Phelps, as well as officers of the borrowers.

Standards for valuation have not been clearly defined in the UFCA or the Bankruptcy Code. Some courts have ruled that "present fair salable value" as used in the UFCA and "fair value" as used in the Bankruptcy Code mean orderly liquidation value. *In re Ohio Corrugating Co.,* 91 Bkptcy. Rptr. 430 (N.D. Ohio 1988); *Wieboldt Stores, Inc. v. Schottenstein, supra.* Other courts have held that "going business value" is a proper standard. *Kupetz v. Continental Illinois,* 77 Bkptcy. Rptr. 754 (C.D. cal. 1987); *In re Vadnais Lumber,* 100 Bkptcy. Rptr. 127 (D. Mass. 1989).

In 1989, institutional creditors holding bonds issued by RJR Nabisco, Inc. attempted a lawsuit against the corporation and its chief executive officer to recover a loss of market value which accompanied a leveraged buyout financed with high levels of bridge loans and high yielding securities. After finding that the bond indentures contained no prohibition against a leveraged buyout and that the bondholders were highly sophisticated, the court ruled that RJR Nabisco had no obligation to them to refrain from the leveraged buyout. *Metropolitan Life Insurance Company v. RJR Nabisco, Inc.,* 716 F. Supp. 1504 (S.D.N.Y., 1989).

Arguments have been made that the creditors rights laws should be amended to provide exemptions or clearer guidelines for leveraged buyouts. However, the consensus so far has been that the designers of the sophisticated transactions which increase debt and reduce the equity cushion providing a safety net to creditors should bear the burden of demonstrating solvency and capital adequacy.

The buyer, the seller and the lenders can take several practical steps to minimize creditors rights problems:

- Be prepared to demonstrate that the buyer, notwithstanding its debt obligation, is solvent and has reasonably adequate capital after the buyout and that detailed cash flow analysis (based on reasonable assumptions) shows ability to pay debts as they mature during the period over which the acquisition indebtedness will be repaid and a reasonable time thereafter.
- Remember that the confidence of suppliers and other trade creditors is important to the future success of the business.
- Be prepared to demonstrate that the buyout price and terms represent fair value and were negotiated at arm's length.

TAX CONSIDERATIONS

The tax principles applicable to leveraged buyouts are generally the same as those for acquisitions and mergers described in Chapters 10 and 11. The emphasis, of course, by planners must be on those tax considerations that generate and conserve cash, which is such an important element in leveraged buyouts.

In planning the debt-equity structure for the buyer, the Internal Revenue Code and the regulations thereunder must be considered, particularly if shareholders will hold debt or guarantee loans. Otherwise, the Internal Revenue Service may recharacterize payments of interest and even principal on acquisition debt as dividends to the shareholders, *Plantation Patterns, Inc. v. Commissioner,* 462 F.2d 712 (5 Cir. 1972). See "Recharacterizing Stock or Debt Instruments for Tax Purposes" in Chapter 2.

When assets are purchased and the price is higher than the seller's tax basis, it is important for the buyer to obtain a "stepped up" basis to use for depreciation (cost recovery). Negotiation between the buyer and the seller to allocate the price among the assets is done as described in Chapter 10.

If the tax basis is higher than the purchase price, the buyer may prefer a stock purchase, especially if there are also tax loss carryforwards available, although the faster ACRS writeoffs should be considered in making the decision. The seller may also prefer to sell stock or may prefer to sell assets and liquidate for its own business reasons. In either event, recapture of investment tax credits must be considered by the seller in a sale of assets.

When stock is purchased, assuming 80 percent control, the buyer can obtain a "stepped up" basis by making a timely election under Section 338 if the purchase price exceeds the tax basis of the assets held by the acquired corporation. Before doing so, the buyer must consider recapture effects including expensed items and LIFO recapture, if applicable, and the tax on the "deemed sale" of assets imposed by a the Tax Return Act of 1986. The buyer must also consider the effect of loss of tax loss carryforwards, if any. If the tax basis of the assets exceeds the purchase price, or if recapture, deemed sale of assets tax, or tax loss carryforward aspects are adverse, buyer will not elect a "stepped up" basis and will file a protective carryover basis election.

A meaningful benefit afforded by Section 338 is the election permitted by subsection (h) (10). It applies to the sale of a corporation which has been a member of a consolidated group. The buyer is permitted to cause the acquired corporation to elect to recognize gain or loss as though it sold or exchanged assets, but to be treated as a member of the selling consolidated group with respect to the sale. No gain or loss is recognized on the stock sold or exchanged by members of the selling consolidated group. When the selling consolidated group has approximately the same basis in the stock of the subsidiary to be sold, the selling consolidated group may be willing to agree to the election, even though it may want a sale of stock for non-tax reasons.

As described in Chapter 10, even the continuation of existence of the acquired corporation will not preserve the tax loss carryforward from restrictions if there is a "substantial ownership change" within the meaning of Section 382(b). See also the restrictions imposed by Code Section 172(m).

If a holding company and operating subsidiary structure is used and the subsidiary's earnings will be used to pay acquisition indebtedness incurred at the holding company level, the holding company and its subsidiary can file a consolidated income tax return. This allows the operating earnings of the subsidiary to be reduced by the interest paid by the holding company on its debt under Section 1502 of the Internal Revenue Code.

A limited partnership can also be used as the acquisition vehicle for a leveraged buyout. The primary advantage is that income earned by the limited partnership is subject to a single tax on the partners since the limited partnership, if organized carefully, will not be subject to income tax. However, a limited partnership with publicly traded limited partnership interests or having too many corporate characteristics will be taxed as a corporation. See Income Tax Regulation § 301.7701-2 and Code Section § 7704 added by the Revenue Act of 1987. See "Management Leveraged Buyouts as a Partnership," Clements and Haupt, *The Acquisition Yearbook—1991*, New York Institute of Finance (Simon & Schuster), 1991.

Similar advantages can also be obtained with careful planning by using a Subchapter S corporation as the acquisition vehicle for a leveraged buyout.

The acquisition indebtedness in a leveraged buyout should also be structured so as to avoid loss of the interest deduction in excess of $5 million per taxable year as described in Chapter 10. This is not a major problem for most leveraged buyouts because the $5 million threshold is relatively high. Further, the subordination or convertibility provisions of the acquisition indebtedness can be negotiated to fall outside the definition of "corporate acquisition indebtedness" contained in Section 379. See also the limitations imposed by Code Section 163(e) on certain high-yield discount obligations.

In many leveraged buyouts, the buyer plans to manage the business on a tight operating budget. Especially if the buyer plans that cost reductions may come from reduced pension costs, the buyer and seller must consider the obligations imposed by ERISA as described in Chapter 6. If assets are sold, even if the buyer wishes to continue the pension plans without change, the buyer and seller must consider the provisions of these laws relating to bonding and secondary liability of seller as described in Chapter 6.

Some special tax problems may arise in leveraged buyouts when shareholders of the seller corporation wish to become shareholders of the buyer corporation:

1. A purchase of assets for cash followed by distribution of the price to the seller corporation's shareholders might be recharacterized by the Internal Revenue Service as a "D" reorganization under Section 368(a)(1)(F) of the Internal Revenue Code, if substantially all the operating assets of seller are sold and, immediately after the transfer, one or more of the seller's shareholders are in control (80 percent) of the buyer corporation. If this happens, the price would be treated as "boot" and taxed as a dividend to the extent of the earnings and profits of the seller corporation. Where the buyer corporation is a "shell" corporation organized for the leveraged buyout, there is also risk that the Internal Revenue Service may attempt to recharacterize the transaction as an "F" reorganization if owners of a majority of the stock of the seller corporation become owners of a majority of the stock of the buyer corporation.

2. In a purchase of stock for cash and notes, it may seem pointless and costly for the buyer corporation to purchase the shares of the seller corporation owned by the members of its management who will become managers and shareholders of the buyer corporation, only to have them reinvest the after-tax proceeds in the buyer corporation. Can the managers contribute their shares to

the buyer corporation in a tax-free transaction under Section 351 of the Internal Revenue Code? In a 1978 letter ruling involving an acquisition of National Starch by a subsidiary of Unilever N.V., the Internal Revenue allowed tax-free treatment to continuing shareholders. However, in subsequent 1980 Revenue Rulings 80-284 and 80-285 the IRS retreated and refused to confirm tax-free treatment. A likely reason for the refusal was concern that buyer corporations might claim 100 percent step-up in basis of assets in spite of the partial tax-free treatment. Even in 1980, there was little reason for the IRS's caution where the exchanging management shareholders receive less than 20 percent of the stock and the buyer corporation claims stepped-up basis only in proportion to the taxable part of the transaction. Since the adoption of new Section 338 of the code, which limits the basis step-up to the asset value attributable to "purchased" stock, thereby excluding basis step-up attributable to the tax-free exchange element of the proposed transaction, there is no longer a need for the cautious position taken by the IRS in Revenue Rulings 80-284 and 80-285.

A helpful article on tax and related structuring issues is "Tax Considerations in Venture Capital Investments," *The Business Lawyer,* Vol. 45, Nov. 1989.

EMPLOYEE STOCK OWNERSHIP PLANS

For buyouts involving a broadly based management/employee group, tax advantages are available through the use of an Employee Stock Ownership Plan (ESOP). One of the largest leveraged buyouts of this type, the acquisition of the Weirton Steel Division of National Steel Corporation for $385 million, was recently funded through an ESOP. Adopted by the buyer corporation, the corporation and the ESOP must meet the requirements of Sections 409A, 44G, and other applicable sections of the Internal Revenue Code including minimum employee participation standards and voting rights for the participants. Once qualified, the ESOP trust purchases the stock of the buyer corporation, either issuing a promissory note in payment for the stock or borrowing the purchase price from a financial institution under a loan guaranteed by the buyer corporation. Contributions by the buyer corporation to the ESOT, which are used to repay both principal and interest of the loan, are deductible from the income of the buyer corporation within the limits of Section 404. Without the ESOP, of course, the buyer corporation can deduct only the interest on acquisition debt.

The deductions allowed to a corporation for contributions to an ESOT are important incentives:

1. For a stock bonus ESOP, up to 15% for the compensation otherwise paid or incurred to the beneficiaries. Code Section 404(a)(3).
2. For a stock bonus ESOP combined with one or more defined contribution and defined benefit plans, up to 25% of the compensation otherwise paid or accrued to the beneficiary, subject to various limits. Code Section 404(a)(7).
3. For a leveraged ESOP, up to 25% of compensation otherwise paid or accrued to the beneficiaries and used to pay the principal of a loan used to buy em-

ployer securities plus an unlimited amount to pay the loan interest. Code Section 404(a)(9).

For the limit on deductions when the corporation contributes one or more defined contribution plans, including one ESOP, and one or more defined benefit plans. See Code Section 404(a)(7).

Generous carryforward provisions are allowed by Code Section 404. Another important tax benefit is a deduction for cash dividends paid on employer stock held by an ESOT if the dividend is distributed to the ESOP participants. See Code Section 404(k). Financial institutions, including mutual funds, can exclude 50% of the interest received on loans to an ESOT to acquire employer securities if the loan is a "securities acquisition loan" meeting a number of requirements imposed by Code Section 133. In addition, an exemption from the excise tax imposed by Code Section 4980 on the reversion of excess assets remaining upon termination of a pension plan was provided if the surplus was transferred to an ESOT and used to purchase employer securities or to repay loans obtained to purchase employer securities. See Code Section 4980(c)(3).

Code Section 1042 allows sellers of shares of a closely held corporation to an ESOT to defer capital gains tax on the sale if the ESOT owns 30% of the corporation's stock after the sale and if they meet several conditions including a three-year holding period and reinvestment in Qualified Replacement Property of the sale proceeds within a specified time period ending twelve months after the sale. In 1989, Congress repealed Code provisions which formerly allowed an estate tax deduction of the value of shares sold to an ESOT and allowed an ESOT to assume estate tax liability with respect to employer securities transferred to an ESOT.

The ESOP was advocated to Congress by Louis Kelso, an Atlanta investment banker. Profit-sharing stock purchase plans previously had been used to fund purchases of stock of their sponsoring companies, occasionally achieving an unleveraged employee buyout over a period of years. However, the amendments to the Internal Revenue Code authorizing ESOPs expressly permitted borrowing. This created a vehicle usable for an immediate full buyout because the ESOT can borrow funds in excess of its existing resources to pay the purchase price.

In addition to the power to borrow and to repay both interest and principal from tax-creditable contributions, an ESOP has the usual benefits of profit-sharing stock purchase plans and their related trusts:

1. Contributions to the ESOT provide current deductions from the income of the sponsoring corporation.
2. Dividends and other earnings of the ESOT accumulate tax-free.
3. Employee beneficiaries are not taxed until they receive distributions from their accounts with the ESOT, usually upon retirement.

A considerable volume of literature has been written describing the potential of ESOPs as a vehicle for worker capitalism. Certainly, in such transactions as the buyout of Weirton Steel, there is an opportunity to demonstrate the ESOP as a practical device. Results at Weirton Steel have so far been encouraging.

An ESOT must pass on to employee participants the voting rights to shares allocated to their accounts if the shares are "registration type securities", i.e. publicly traded. If the shares are not publicly traded, only limited voting rights must be passed on to the participants. When an ESOT has borrowed to finance the purchase of shares, however, the shares are not allocated to the participants' accounts until the price is paid. The unpaid shares, whether or not pledged as collateral, are held in a suspense account and are voted by the trustee or a committee appointed by the employer. Since 1989, if the lender to the ESOT wishes to claim the interest exclusion under Code Section 133, full voting rights for allocated shares must be passed through regardless of whether they are publicly traded.

Distributions to employees upon retirement or in other events can be made in shares or cash. However, the participant must have the right to demand shares. The employer, not the ESOP, must also provide a commitment to repurchase shares from participants, at their option, unless the shares are readily tradeable in an established securities market. Under certain circumstances, an employer can have a right of first refusal to purchase shares which are not readily tradeable.

The Employee Retirement Income Security Act of 1974 ("ERISA") expressly allows the fiduciaries of an ESOP and ESOT to serve as officers or employees of corporation whose securities are purchased by the ESOT. Section 408 of ERISA contains conditional exemptions allowing an ESOT to obtain loans and to acquire employer securities in circumstances that would otherwise be prohibited transactions under Section 406. The fiduciaries responsible for an ESOP must, however, make a prudent investigation in purchasing securities of the sponsoring corporation. For example, in purchasing a minority interest, they cannot rely on an outdated appraisal of 100 percent of the stock where the appraisal projected sales and earnings increases that did not occur and did not consider the additional cost burden required to make contributions to fund the ESOP, *Donovan v. Cunningham*, 716 F.2d 1455 (5 Cir. 1983). See also *Eaves v. Penn*, 587 F.2d 453 (10 Cir. 1978).

ERISA Section 3(18) requires that an ESOP receive "adequate consideration" in transactions involving employer securities. Code Section 401(a)(28)(C) requires used of an independent appraiser for all valuations of employer securities which are not readily tradable in an established market. In 1989, the U.S. Department of Labor adopted regulations describing, among other things, valuation methods to be used in determining "adequate consideration" under ERISA Section 3(18).

As described in Chapter 9, a number of ESOPs have been established as part of programs to anticipate or defeat hostile tender officers. Where management demonstrated that it had fulfilled their duties of loyalty and due care, a decision to establish an ESOP was upheld in a lawsuit by a company which had made a tender offer and sought an injunction against issuance of shares to the ESOT. *Danaher Corporation v. Chicago Pneumatic Tool Company*, 633 F. Supp. 1066 (S.D., N.Y., 1986). See also *Shamrock Holdings, Inc. v. Polaroid Corporation*, 599 A.2d 278 (Del. Ch. 1989).

For further information on the establishment of an ESOP and valuation of employer stock in ESOP, see the following articles: "Financing Acquisitions Through Employee Stock Ownership Plans," and "Valuation of Securities in ESOP Transactions," Edward E. Shea, *The Acquisition Yearbook—1991*. For a survey of the effects of ESOPs on corporate performance, see *Employee Stock Ownership Plans,* a report by the U.S. General Accounting Office, December, 1987.

Chapter 2 contains a diagram (Exhibit 2-3) showing a simplified ESOP acquisition structure. The text explains how the structure is usually modified to include equity participation for management, venture capital investors and lenders.

FOUNDERS INVESTMENT AND STOCK OWNERSHIP

In structuring a leveraged buyout by a management group or other founders with limited financial resources, careful planning is needed to realize their equity ownership objectives. In a small asset-based buyout, where loans are fully secured, there may be little resistance to ownership by management of any amount up to 100 percent of the equity. In larger, higher-priced transactions where "mezzanine" or seller financing is used and senior lenders and venture capital investors want "equity sweeteners," the management group may be hard-pressed to negotiate for a major portion of the equity or even enough to assure control in all circumstances. However, it is widely recognized that a successful leveraged buyout depends on management dedication and entrepreneurial skills. Thus, lenders and outside investors want managers to commit whatever financial resources they have to investment in the buyer corporation. They usually also agree that management should have equity ownership considerably greater than would result if they invested on the same basis as other investors.

Once the management group negotiates its share of equity, the stock should be purchased in a manner that provides favorable tax consequences. In general, the objectives are to defer any significant amount of tax until eventual sale of the stock and then pay at capital gain rates. However, the Internal Revenue Service may scrutinize the stock purchase arrangements to determine whether all or part of any appreciation in value of the stock should be treated as compensation and taxed at ordinary income rates, even though this treatment allows a corresponding business expense deduction to the corporation.

There are several methods that are used by founders to buy stock at a relatively low price:

1. They can organize the buyer corporation and purchase stock for a modest price. As negotiations progress, shares can be sold to other investors at higher prices.

2. They can pay for part of its stock by promissory note.

3. The management group can be granted stock options (nonstatutory or incentive) with price, terms and numbers of shares keyed to performance goals.

4. They might consider "junior stock." This is a common stock that has proportionately reduced or subordinated voting, dividend and liquidation rights, but is convertible into the ordinary common stock upon the achievement of specified sales, earnings, or other goals by the corporation. After appraisal by an investment banking firm or other valuation expert, the junior stock usually

is sold to the management group at a small percentage of the value of the ordinary common stock because of its limited rights. The managers then elect to be taxed immediately under Section 83(b) of the Internal Revenue Code on the difference, if any, between the fair market value of the junior stock and the price they paid. There are a variety of valuation, tax and accounting questions that make risky the use of "junior stock", particularly if plans include a public offering and require careful planning if it is to be used.

5. They can negotiate with sellers or outside investors providing equity financing to accept nonconvertible subordinated notes or nonvoting preferred stock instead of common stock. Through these arrangements, the sellers and outside investors receive periodic income and preference if the business is unsuccessful, but do not share in voting control and future appreciation in value of the common stock. Most important for structuring purposes, of course, their acceptances of subordinated notes or preferred stock reduces the amount and price of the common stock needed by the founders to acquire a significant equity investment and achieve control.

CONFLICTS OF INTEREST

In planning a leveraged buyout, especially a management purchase or "going private" transaction, it is essential to (1) identify conflicting interests; (2) take objective steps to protect persons whose interests would otherwise depend on persons in a conflict situation and (3) document the support for decisions so that they can withstand later scrutiny.

In a management purchase, the founders who will be officers, directors and stockholders of the buyer corporation usually also hold responsible positions with the seller corporation. They are commonly officers and directors and sometimes also stockholders. They also may have special responsibilities such as trustees or committee members responsible for employee pension, profit-sharing or stock purchase plans. Some may have professional responsibilities as investment bankers or legal counsel.

The first and most difficult step in handling conflicts of interest is to recognize that they exist and that a unilateral decision that appears reasonable and even generous today can appear very different after time has passed. Whenever a business fails (or succeeds), the causes seem obvious by hindsight. A person who negotiates a leveraged buyout while in a conflict of interest can later claim that the price, terms, arrangements, and risks appeared reasonable at the time, but his accusers can easily claim that he was blinded to reality by self-interest.

Several steps can be taken to resolve conflicts of interest. Persons involved in a conflict of interest can sometimes resign from a conflicting position but, if that step is not feasible, they can refrain from participating in or influencing the decision process. Needless to say, a formal abstention from voting at a final meeting is not as significant as an earlier clearly communicated decision to act on only one side of the transaction.

It is widely recognized that independent advice should be obtained on financial, accounting, legal and other matters. It is equally important to recognize that the independent advisers should be selected by and report to the persons whose interests they represent and have adequate time and information to perform their work properly. As demonstrated in several lawsuits, little support for the fairness of a price can result from a belated hiring of the company's regular investment banking firm to perform a hasty study approving a price already predetermined by persons subject to conflicting interests.

For further information, readers should review Chapters 4 and 9, particularly the discussion under Issuer Tender Offers, Stock Repurchases and "Going Private" Transactions.

13

Foreign Company Acquisitions and Joint Ventures

FOREIGN INVESTMENT IN THE UNITED STATES

Before the 1970s, foreign investment in the United States was relatively modest. After the devaluation of the U.S. dollar in 1971, a growing inflow of foreign investment developed. By early 1983, total foreign direct investment in U.S. businesses exceeded $100 billion and total foreign holdings of all kinds exceeded $700 billion according to statistics maintained by the U.S. Department of Commerce. The most active investors have been companies from the United Kingdom, Canada, West Germany, France, the Netherlands and Japan.

Factors contributing to the growth of foreign investments were: (1) the lower cost of the U.S. dollar; (2) the desire of foreign companies to consolidate markets originally created by exports to the U.S.; (3) the decline of values in the U.S. stock markets, which resulted in lower acquisition prices; (4) advancement of foreign product and process technology together with gradual obsolescence of plant, equipment, and technology in many U.S. industries; (5) growing trade balance deficits between U.S. exports and imports that create investable funds in the hands of foreign investors and (6) perception of the U.S. as politically stable and distant from threats of war. Another important factor is that foreign investors are usually willing and have technology and financial resources to comply with rapidly growing U.S. environmental and safety laws. Uninvolved with the controversies over the laws which necessarily involve U.S. manufacturers, foreign companies evaluate the effort and cost of compliance and either buy or do not buy.

In 1984, foreign investment in the U.S. exceeded U.S. investment abroad for the first time since early in this century. During the years 1985 through 1989, foreign companies and investors made acquisitions of U.S. companies totalling over $200 billion dollars.

FEW DIRECT RESTRICTIONS ON FOREIGN INVESTMENT

In general, conditions in the United States are favorable to foreign investment. Currency is freely convertible. There are no restrictions on the repatriation of profits, dividends or royalties. Except for the activities discussed in this section, foreign investors are free to invest in the multitude of industries and businesses existing throughout the United States subject to the same laws and regulations that apply to domestic companies.

Important fields in which foreign ownership or investment is restricted are:

1. Coastal shipping (46 U.S.C.A., Secs. 802 and 883); towing and salvage (46 U.S.C.A., Sec. 316); fishing (46 U.S.C.A. Sec. 251); dredging (46 U.S.C.A. Sec. 292); vessel documentation and transfer (46 U.S.C.A. Secs. 835 and 12102).
2. Air transportation (49 U.S.C.A. Secs. 1371, 1372, 1378, 1401, and 1508).
3. Radio and television (47 U.S.C.A. Sec. 301 and 310); Communications Satellite Corporation (47 U.S.C.A. Sec. 734).
4. Government leasing of oil and gas, geothermal, coal and other mineral resources (30 U.S.C.A. Sec. 181, 185, and 352; 48 C.F.R. Sec. 3102.1(a), 3202.1, 3250.1-2, 3472.1-1 and 3502.1).
5. Nuclear energy (42 U.S.C.A. Secs. 2131–2134); geothermal energy (30 U.S.C.A. Secs. 1015 and 1522) and certain other energy programs.
6. Government subsidies for construction and operation of vessels used in foreign trade (46 U.S.C.A. Secs. 1151, 1171 et seq., 1204) and for fishing (16 U.S.C.A. Sec. 742); transport of government goods and personnel (46 U.S.C.A. Sec. 1241 et seq.).
7. Banking, including a requirement that a majority of the directors of national banks be U.S. citizens (12 U.S.C.A. Sec. 72) and denial of membership in the Federal Reserve System (12 U.S.C.A. Sec. 321). Otherwise, while subject to various regulatory restrictions, foreign banks have considerable freedom since the adoption of the International Banking Act of 1978.
8. Government contracting is generally open to foreign companies. However, companies bidding for national defense contracts or subcontracts may be ineligible if there is "foreign ownership, influence and control" in the absence of special procedures. The company and some of its personnel may be ineligible or require special procedures to obtain access to classified information and security clearances. (32 C.F.R. Sec. 155 et seq.; Industrial Security Manual for Safeguarding Classified Information).

Under Section 721 of the Defense Production Act, 50 U.S.C.A. § 2158 et seq., the President could suspend or prohibit any proposed or pending acquisition, merger or takeover by or with foreign persons so that such control will not threaten to impair the national security. Investigations and enforcement are conducted by the Committee on Foreign Investment in the United States (CFIUS). The law was intended to protect technologies considered critical to national defense by the Departments of Defense and Energy. In late 1990, Section 721 expired without reenactment by Congress, but CFIUS has announced that it will continue to review acquisitions submitted voluntarily and it is expected that Congress will reenact Section 721 in 1991.

ESTABLISHING OR ACQUIRING A BUSINESS

A business can be established directly by a foreign investor in the United States. The necessary steps include supplying and hiring management and employees, buying or leasing property and equipment, obtaining permits and the many other activities required of business proprietors. For smaller operations such as sales offices, a branch office is the choice frequently made.

For larger or more complex businesses, many foreign investors decide that it is wiser to acquire or participate in a business already in existence. This permits the foreign investor to provide for specific needs of the U.S. business such as capital, technology or raw materials which the foreign investor knows it is prepared to meet. Experienced U.S. management can then provide the remaining business needs.

Choice Between a Subsidiary or Direct Ownership and Operation. Before establishing or acquiring a business, a foreign company should evaluate whether it is best to do business directly or organize a subsidiary.

The organization of a subsidiary requires some cost and effort for the initial incorporation and for continuing administration. The cost includes legal fees for preparation of the certificate of incorporation, bylaws, minutes and stock certificates and franchise taxes and filing fees. In addition, the subsidiary is a separate taxable entity subject to U.S. income taxes at rates up to 34 percent on taxable income in excess of $100,000. Its costs and expenses are deducted from its own income and not that of its parent. Upon payment of dividends by the subsidiary, withholding tax at the rate of 30 percent (or a lower treaty rate) is required.

Nevertheless, the advantages of incorporation tend to favor the choice of a subsidiary:

1. Limitation of liability of the parent company for the risks and losses of the U.S. business to the capital invested in the subsidiary.
2. Ability to accumulate after-tax income in the U.S. to fund growth of business operations and other proper business purposes. There is a penalty tax on unreasonable accumulation of earnings in excess of $100,000 without need for their use in the corporate business, but this tax is rarely a problem for active businessmen.
3. Elimination of the need for the parent company to qualify to do business in one or more states of the U.S. at costs comparable to the cost of organizing and maintaining a subsidiary.
4. Elimination of the need for the parent company to submit to the jurisdiction of U.S. courts and government agencies including the possible need to submit parent company worldwide records to review by U.S. tax and other government agencies.
5. Ability to engage in certain activities prohibited to foreign companies and in-

dividuals, but permitted to domestic corporations without restriction based on foreign ownership.

6. Ability to offer stock options, stock purchase contracts or plans and similar benefits in businesses where such employee benefits are important incentives.

7. Continuity of existence, centralization and continuity of management, relatively simple evidence and transferability of ownership and other traditional corporate characteristics.

Domestic Holding Companies. In addition to a domestic subsidiary, many foreign companies decide to organize a corporation as a holding company. The parent owns the holding company which, in turn, owns the shares of operating subsidiaries engaging in active businesses. One reason for the organization of a domestic holding company is to have a vehicle to raise capital in the U.S. Companies from nations that restrict the outflow of capital often use a domestic subsidiary to obtain dollar loans guaranteed by the foreign parent. Assuming that the holding company repays out of business profits, no capital outflow from the foreign nation results.

The use of a holding company with subsidiaries for separate businesses is easily accomplished in the U.S. because corporations can be organized rapidly and at modest cost in states such as Delaware. The holding company can file consolidated federal income tax returns with its 80 percent-owned subsidiaries, other than foreign and certain other subsidiaries, thus permitting the set-off of income and deductions among the consolidated group of corporations, including the interest cost of borrowings by the holding company to supply the capital needs of its subsidiaries. Thus, separate corporate entities, each with liability limited to capital contributions, can be established for separate business risks without unduly burdensome increases of costs or federal income taxes.

A holding company cannot include in its consolidated tax return any subsidiaries that are less than 80 percent owned—i.e., 80% of the total voting power and value of the stock of each subsidiary. See Code Sections 1501 and 1504. If an operating business will be less than 80 percent owned, it is possible to obtain a business deduction for interest on borrowings by the holding company by establishing the business as a partnership and organizing a subsidiary corporation to become a general partner of the business. Since the partnership is not itself a taxable entity, its income is distributable to the corporate general partner which is actively engaged in a trade or business and can be included in the consolidated return of the holding company.

Methods Used in Acquiring Business. As described in earlier chapters, there are several methods by which a business or an interest in a business can be acquired in the United States:

> Purchase of assets
> Purchase of stock
> Merger (consolidation)

Early acquisitions in the United States by foreign companies are usually made for cash or a combination of cash and promissory notes or other deferred payments. One reason is that many foreign companies wish to invest cash in the U.S. where there is relative freedom from the political risks in their own nations. Another is that payment in stock or securities of the foreign company may not present a sufficiently attractive acquisition "currency" to U.S. sellers in the absence of registration with the SEC and listing or other arrangements for active trading in the United States. These steps are not easily or quickly accomplished. If the parent company does not wish to undertake them, once a holding company has been established in the United States with a successful business record and prospects, its shares and other securities can be registered, listed and used as acquisition "currency."

For the most part, the purchase of a business is the same for a foreign company or its U.S. holding company as for acquisitions made by U.S. companies. The preferred method is a purchase of assets. As described in Chapters 10 and 11, this method allows the buyer to negotiate to purchase only selected assets and to assume only selected liabilities except where the law imposes successor liability. It also permits the buyer to allocate the purchase price among the assets purchased and, if the purchase price exceeds the tax basis of the seller, to "step up" the basis of the purchased assets. This provides increased depreciation (MACRS) deductions and an earlier recovery of investment cost for tax purposes. When assets are purchased directly, the burden of depreciation and investment credit recapture is that of the seller.

The agreement to purchase assets or stock used by foreign companies or their U.S. subsidiaries can be similar to those used by domestic business buyers. However, the representations and warranties should be more comprehensive and more time and information should be devoted to financial or business review to allow for the limited familiarity of the buyer with U.S. business customs and distances that people and information must travel. For the foreign investor, the "due diligence" report of experienced counsel, accountants and other experts can be of special value.

The purchase agreement should condition the obligation of the buyer upon its liability to obtain within a reasonable time approval from government authorities of its own nation of the terms of the transaction including, if applicable, authorization to borrow on reasonable terms, to obtain U.S. funds and to transmit the purchase price to the U.S. for payment to the seller. In the authors' experience, foreign buyers may sometimes be more confident about the speed and terms of approval by their own government ministries than is realistic. This sometimes occurs because senior management has made a general presentation to senior government officials and received a preliminary favorable reaction. While preliminary clearance is valuable, it sometimes leads senior management to underestimate detail and delay inevitable when the formal application is submitted at lower government levels and the conditions and restrictions which may be imposed to fulfill legal requirements. Discussion with experienced counsel in the buyer's nation can be helpful on this subject.

It is not always possible for a buyer to negotiate for a direct purchase of assets. The sellers may insist on a sale of stock mainly because: (1) the sale can be quickly closed by delivery of stock certificates without need for time-consuming transfer of individual assets and obligations; (2) their entire profit is taxed at capital gain rates without need to allocate the price among the assets sold; (3) there is no recapture of depreciation (MACRS) deductions or investment tax credits; (4) there is no need for sellers to liquidate their corporation and provide for its taxes and residual obligations in order to distribute the purchase price. If time is an important factor and seller's business does not involve too many unwanted assets or liabilities, the buyer also may be inclined toward the speed and relative simplicity of a purchase of stock provided that the seller's price is attractive enough to overcome the tax disadvantages.

As described in Chapter 10, if the seller agrees to purchase stock and the price is significantly in excess of the basis of the acquired corporation in its assets, the buyer corporation, if it has purchased at least 80 percent of the voting and nonvoting stock, can make an election pursuant to Section 338 of the Internal Revenue Code to treat the transaction as a sale and purchase of assets in the manner and with the effects described in Chapter 11. The benefits of Section 338 are available only to the corporation that made the purchase of stock. If the foreign parent company made the purchase rather than a U.S. subsidiary, it is necessary to comply with regulations adopted by the Internal Revenue Service pursuant to Section 338(i) to coordinate the provisions of Section 338 with those pertaining to foreign corporations and their shareholders.

Government ministries sometimes impose a condition that companies in their nations wishing to make foreign acquisitions must raise part of the purchase price in the nation where the acquisition is being made by some other means that does not result in additional conversion of currency. Foreign companies often fulfill this requirement by borrowing from a bank or other institutional lender in the United States. However, if the seller wishes or is willing to defer part of the purchase price, the acquisition can be structured as an installment sale pursuant to Section 453 of the Internal Revenue Code.

Unless an exemption is available, acquisitions by foreign companies resulting in ownership of 10 percent or more of a U.S. enterprise must be reported as direct investments to the Bureau of Economic Analysis of the Department of Commerce under the International Investment Survey Act of 1976, 22 U.S.C.A. Sec. 3101 et seq. The initial report is on Form BE-13. Annual reports on Form BE-15 and quarterly reports on Form BE-605 must be filed thereafter. There also are a variety of reports that may be required of companies acquiring particular kinds of businesses such as banking.

TAXATION OF FOREIGN-OWNED BUSINESSES AND BUSINESSMEN

Foreign Corporations and Nonresident Aliens. *1. Income Effectively Connected to a Trade or Business in the United States.* Foreign corporations and nonresident aliens are subject to taxation under United States Internal Revenue Code on (1) all income from sources within the United States derived from engaging in a trade or business in the United States including all investment income from sources within the United States that is effectively connected to the trade or business and (2) these kinds of investment income from sources outside the United States if effectively connected to a place of business in the United States:

1. Rents and royalties from the active conduct of a leasing or licensing business,
2. Dividends (except from a controlled foreign corporation), interest, and gains from securities or debt obligations of a banking, financing or like business,
3. Income from sales of personal property if made through a United States office.

This income is taxable at the same rates which apply to domestic corporations:

Up to $50,000	15%
$50,001 to $75,000	25%
$75,001 to $100,000	34%
$100,000 and up	34% plus additional tax

An additional 5 percent tax is applied to taxable income, if any, in excess of $100,000, subject to a limit of $11,750 on the additional tax thus imposed.

The same rates apply to gain from the sale or exchange of capital assets. The usual deductions and credits are allowed against this income to the extent they are connected to income effectively connected within a United States trade or business including interest, ordinary and necessary business expenses, depreciation, calculated according to a modified accelerated cost recovery system (MACRS), state and local taxes, casualty losses and net operating loss carrybacks and carryforwards, the investment tax credit and the foreign tax credit.

Code Section 897 treats gain or loss from dispositions of U.S. real property interest and U.S. real property holding corporations as effectively connected with a U.S. trade or business and imposes a minimum tax rate of 20% on gain income.

2. Fixed or Determinable Periodical Income. Foreign corporations and nonresident aliens are also subject to taxation in the United States on fixed or determinable periodical income from U.S. sources that is not effectively connected with a U.S. trade or business. This income consists primarily of income from employment and passive investment income including salaries, wages, annuities, rents, royalties, dividends, interest other than bank deposit interest, premiums and other determinable or periodical gains, profits or income. This income is subject to a flat tax rate of 30 percent, which must be withheld at the source, except for interest on certain types of portfolio indebtedness owed by a U.S. borrower to foreign corporations and nonresident alien individuals. This rate has been reduced to lower rates by tax treaties existing between the United States and many other nations.

Section 861 of the Internal Revenue Code contains rules for determining the source of income:

A. *Interest.* The source is the place of residence of the person obligated for its payment, with certain exceptions for interest paid by domestic corporations earning at least 80% of their gross income from the active conduct of a foreign trade or business.

B. *Dividends.* A dividend from a domestic corporation is U.S. source income with certain exceptions for dividends paid by domestic international sales corporations, possessions corporations and domestic corporations earning at least 80% of their gross income from the active conduct of a foreign trade or business.

A dividend from a foreign corporation is foreign source income with certain exceptions for foreign corporations having 75 percent or more of their gross income effectively connected with a U.S. trade or business.

C. *Rents and Royalties.* The source is the place where the property is located. This includes intangible property such as patents, trade secrets and trademarks.

D. *Personal Services.* The source is the place where the services are physically performed except for certain services performed by nonresident alien individuals present in the United States for limited periods in the taxable year and receiving compensation not exceeding certain limits provided in Section 861(a)(3) or in applicable treaties.

E. *Sale of Property.* The source of gain from the sale of real property is the place where it is located. The source of gain from a sale of personal property is the place of sale and generally takes place where title passes from the seller to the buyer, subject to allocation in certain instances.

It should be noted, however, that special source and character of income rules apply to United States-owned foreign corporations.

With certain exceptions, Code Section 1445 imposes a withholding tax on dispositions of United States real property interests "by foreign persons in an amount equal to 10 percent of the sale price." The term "United States property interest" is defined broadly and the withholding requirement applies to disposition of stock of a "United States real property holding corporation" as defined in Section 1445.

3. Activities Not Taxed. In general, activities of nonresident aliens not included among those described in (1) and (2) are not subject to income taxation under the U.S. Internal Revenue Code. For example, profits from export sales to the United States by nonresident aliens and interest on certain portfolio investments are not subject to income tax, provided that the sales are not effectively connected to a trade or business in the United States except for gains on the disposition of United States real property interests. Gains from the sale or exchange of capital assets in the United States are also not subject to taxation unless effectively connected with a trade or business or realized by a nonresident alien—i.e., an alien who was not a lawful permanent resident (a "green card" holder) and did not meet a "substantial presence" test adopted by the Deficit Reduction Act of 1984.

4. Estate and Gift Taxes. Section 2101 of the U.S. Internal Revenue Code imposes a unified estate and gift tax on the taxable estates of nonresidents who are not citizens of the United States and who die after November 10, 1988 at the same rates as those applicable to U.S. citizens. The tax is imposed only on property situated in the United States at the time of death. Stock and debt obligations of U.S. domestic corporations are deemed situated in the United States regardless of where the instruments are kept. On the other hand, proceeds of insurance on the life of a nonresident noncitizen and certain bank accounts and debt obligations are exempt. Where an applicable treaty so permits, the estate is allowed to use the unified credit allowed to a U.S. citizen in proportion to the total gross estate located in the United States.

5. State and Local Taxes. All states and many cities, counties, school districts and other municipal authorities impose taxes which take a wide variety of forms. The most common are franchise taxes imposed on corporations for the privilege of doing local business; sales and use taxes, ad valorem taxes based on the value of real, personal and sometimes intangible property; income or business receipts taxes; estate or inheritance taxes and a variety of stamp and excise taxes. The value-added tax common in Europe is not used in the United States.

It is beyond the scope of this chapter to describe the great variety of local taxes. However, rates are generally much lower than those of the federal taxes. Further, U.S. and state constitutions require their apportionment to prevent (or at least minimize) duplication.

JOINT VENTURES WITH FOREIGN COMPANIES

Structure. Many foreign companies seek or welcome investment in a joint venture with an established U.S. company, particularly for early investments in the United States. Foreign companies are usually accustomed to doing business in the joint venture form in their own nations. When investing in the United States, it allows them to contribute capital, technology and special management skills while relying on the U.S. company for general management and the remaining elements needed for the business.

To establish the joint venture, an initial decision is made whether to use a simple cooperation agreement, a partnership or a corporation as the vehicle. Business, financial, tax and liability considerations are key factors in the decision.

Single-Purpose Joint Ventures and Cooperation Agreements. There are a variety of business arrangements that may be called joint ventures but do not necessarily require the organization of a partnership or corporation. These joint ventures develop from existing customer-supplier or even competitive relationships. They enable one or more companies to combine resources to accomplish limited objectives that could not be achieved alone and to share the benefits, profits, costs and risks.

Single-purpose joint ventures may be used for such purposes as construction projects, to develop natural resources or to underwrite a sale of securities. These ventures terminate upon completion of the project. Continuing cooperation agreements may be used, for example, to provide a raw material or energy source needed by two or more manufacturers or to develop and test new products.

Agreements for single purpose or continuing cooperation joint ventures are generally simple and focus on business and financial objectives. They typically will provide that no partnership or agency relation is intended and that neither party has any authority or liability beyond the express terms of the agreement. Reciprocal indemnities against liabilities incurred by either venture company outside of the scope of the venture will be included. Capital contributions, if any, will be limited. Properties, employees, and funds are often simply furnished by the parties as needed on a cost reimbursement basis, thus avoiding the transfers of assets and personnel involved in more formal joint ventures. Management of the venture may be delegated to a representative of one venture party or may be divided according to the roles of the parties. In either arrangement, authority usually will be limited and commitments in excess of specified levels and changes in the project will be subject to approval by both parties.

Although the joint venture agreement contains clear provisions limiting authority and liability, U.S. law generally does not give effect to such limitations to prevent claims by outsiders who were unaware of them. There are no central registries in the United States in which the authority of officers and managers of business entities can be enrolled. If a manager or representative of a joint venture is allowed to act with apparent authority for both joint venture parties, the law will hold both liable for their commitments to third parties who rely on the apparent authority, even though the commitments were actually unauthorized. Accordingly, a company considering a joint venture should satisfy itself as to the business and financial responsibility of the other company. During the progress of the venture, it should monitor the performance of the venture manager and representatives to assure that they are not creating an appearance of authority to act beyond their actual authorization. Finally, the company should arrange endorsements to its insurance policies, especially its liability policies, to assure that coverage extends to the joint venture because it is a virtual certainty that any personal injury or property damage caused by the joint venture will lead to claims against all companies participating in the venture.

Under Income Tax Regulation Section 301.7701-3, joint ventures are taxed as partnerships even though the agreements may expressly disclaim a legal partnership relation and even though the venture may be limited in time or purpose. Thus, the joint venture agreement should provide for partnership income tax returns. One of the partners should be designated as responsible for the preparation and filing of the returns and for dealings with the Internal Revenue Service upon audit.

Joint Ventures Organized as Partnerships. When a joint venture will involve a continuing business of substantial scope, immediate or potential, it is usually best to organize a partnership or corporation to serve as a vehicle. This is a fundamental business decision because it means recognition of the business as a separate entity, even though the companies may limit the personnel, properties and funds actually transferred to the venture and restrict the authority of its management.

A partnership is normally created by a written agreement. The agreement can be brief or lengthy as the partners wish. To the extent that the partners do not provide for their relationships in their agreement, they will be governed by the statutory law and court decisions of the state where the partnership is organized. Most states in the United States have adopted the Uniform Partnership Act ("UPA") to govern the formation of partnerships and relations between partners. Most states have also adopted the Uniform Limited Partnership Act, but limited partnerships are rarely used for business joint ventures since limited partners do not participate in corporate management and are essentially passive investors.

When preparing a partnership agreement, it is permissible to supplement and modify the provisions of the UPA by specific provisions in the agreement. In fact, it is important to do so because the objectives and relationships of each partnership are unique and will differ in many ways from the brief principles found in the UPA and the decisions made by courts about other partnerships.

It is beyond the scope of this chapter to describe the many items which can be included in joint venture partnership agreements. The most important subjects are (1) management, including rights of the minority partner or partners; (2) capital contributions, present and future, including adjustments for contributed properties in which the partners have differing tax bases; (3) sharing of profits and losses; (4) distribution of profits; (5) standards for dealings between the partnership and its partners; (6) liability, indemnities, and insurance; (7) preparation of financial statements and tax returns and (8) the events, including withdrawal of a partner, and effects of termination and the distribution of partnership properties upon a liquidation of the partnership business. An index for a joint venture partnership agreement is provided at the end of this chapter to show in somewhat more detail the coverage of such an agreement.

Under Section 701 of the Internal Revenue Code, partnerships are not subject to income tax. The partnership tax return (Form 1065) is an information return and the income of the partnership is treated under Section 702 as distributable to the partners, whether accumulated or actually distributed.

A foreign company which becomes a partner in a U.S. partnership must recognize that its partnership role will mean that it is engaged in the trade or business of the partnership in the United States. Thus, it will be taxed on its share of the partnership taxable income as though it were conducting its portion of the business through a directly operated branch. To avoid this result, it is common for foreign companies to organize a U.S. corporate subsidiary to serve as the joint venture partner. The subsidiary, rather than the foreign parent, will then be taxable on its distributive share of the income of the partnership. When the domestic subsidiary borrows to make capital contributions to the partnership business, it can deduct the interest cost against the distributive income from the partnership even though its partnership interest is less than the 80 percent that would be required for consolidation if the joint venture were conducted in corporate form. The same result occurs when a U.S. domestic holding company borrows the funds and contributes them to a consolidated domestic subsidiary for use as capital contributions to the partnership.

Each of the general partners of a partnership has actual authority to participate in its business and make binding commitments on behalf of the partnership, except as limited by the partnership agreement. Each of the general partners has unlimited liability for the debts and obligations of the partnership. Even when authority is limited in the partnership agreement, the partners may be liable to outsiders who rely on apparent authority of a partner to make a commitment. Accordingly, the precautions, monitoring and insurance coverage recommended under the discussion of single-purpose joint ventures and cooperation agreements also apply to partnership joint ventures.

Joint Ventures Organized as Corporations. There are a number of advantages and some disadvantages in the use of a corporation as a joint venture vehicle. A summary of the general advantages of incorporation was described earlier in this chapter. For a joint venture, limited liability, centralization and continuity of management and ability to accumulate income can be specially important factors in the decision to use a corporate vehicle.

On the other hand, certain corporate characteristics such as free transferability of ownership and the general powers exercisable by management, the board of directors and stockholders often require modification and limitation in order to allow the use of a corporation as a joint venture vehicle. This usually is accomplished through a shareholders' agreement signed by the companies sponsoring the joint venture and the corporation organized by them.

It is beyond the scope of this chapter to describe the many items that can be included in joint venture shareholders' agreements. The most important subjects are: (1) contents of the certificate of incorporation and bylaws; (2) subscriptions for the purchase of stock to provide capital contributions, present and future, including recognition of differences in basis if stock is issued for property; (3) management including membership of the board of directors and committees and the key officers; (4) policy on the declaration and distribution of dividends; (5) preparation of financial statements and tax returns; (6) restrictions on the transfer of shares and obligations or rights of the corporation or the other shareholders to purchase the stock of a shareholder in certain events such as management impasse, failure to make required capital contributions or a proposed sale of shares to an outsider; (7) voting arrangements including minority shareholder rights; (8) standards for dealings between the corporation and its shareholders and (9) the events and effects of termination and procedures for liquidation and dissolution of the corporation.

Restrictions on transfer of stock usually are achieved by endorsing a restrictive legend on the face of the stock certificates providing notice of the shareholders' agreement, thus protecting against sale or pledge of the stock for value to a person who might qualify as a holder in due course. Voting restrictions can be accomplished by a variety of methods, including the use of different classes or series of stock with different voting rights, a provision that certain actions cannot be taken without the vote of a percentage of shares which necessarily requires the favorable vote of the minority stockholder, a voting trust, an irrevocable proxy or a simple contractual provision on voting. Here, again, notice of the voting restrictions should appear on the stock certificates.

The principles of United States taxation of corporate income are described elsewhere in this chapter and other chapters. However, in view of the nondeductibility of dividends paid by the joint venture corporation, planning should include all arrangements by which the shareholder companies can properly receive income from the corporation in the form of management fees, rents, royalties, supply contracts and other arrangements that provide business expense deductions for the corporation. These arrangements will, of course, be subject to scrutiny upon audit of income tax returns on Form 1120 filed by the corporation, but will be accepted if they are shown to be equivalent to those made in arm's-length dealings between unrelated persons.

If the foreign company plans to finance its capital contributions by borrowing in its own nation, it may decide to invest directly in stock and securities of a joint venture corporation organized in the United States. However, if its home nation is one that restricts outflow of capital, it may be necessary to raise all or most of the capital here, using guarantees by the foreign parent company, if necessary. If so, a typical choice is to organize a corporation to serve as a U.S. holding company, as discussed earlier.

Antitrust Considerations. The domestic and international application of the U.S. antitrust and patent misuse laws should be considered. The U.S. Department of Justice published the *Antitrust Guide for International Operations* (1977) and the *Antitrust Guide Concerning Research Joint Ventures* (1980), which provide helpful, conservative guidelines. Joint ventures also may be subject to Section 7 of the Clayton Act and, if in corporate form, the reporting requirements of the Hart-Scott-Rodino Federal Trade Commission Improvements Act discussed in Chapter 6.

In November, 1988, the U.S. Department of Justice published new and more comprehensive *Antitrust Enforcement Guidelines for International Operations*. The *Guidelines* cover a wide range of topics. Of special interest are section 3.3 on Mergers and section 3.4 on Joint Ventures. The *Guidelines* contain illustrative cases including (1) a merger of a U.S. firm and a foreign firm, (2) merger analysis involving trade restraints, (3) acquisition of a foreign potential competitor and (4) a merger of two foreign firms with assets and sales in the United States. An illustrative case relating to a research and development joint venture is also provided. The *Guidelines* can be found at 4 CCH Trade Reg. Rep., § 13,109.

Joint Venture and Related Agreements. To establish a joint venture, either in partnership or corporate form, detailed joint venture agreements are prepared. Further, several additional agreements may be needed:

1. A license agreement for patents and other technology supplied by either company.
2. A services agreement which may include only general administration or may include all operations if the joint venture will not have independent personnel and facilities.
3. A raw material and energy supply agreement if either company will supply important raw materials or energy.
4. A distribution agreement if either or both of the companies will handle sales of products manufactured by the joint venture.
5. A lease agreement if the joint venture will lease its plant and facilities from either of the companies.
6. A sale and assumption agreement if the joint venture will purchase assets and liabilities from either of the companies.

Indexes showing typical contents of agreements for a corporate joint venture and a partnership joint venture and an agreement to provide technology, engineering services, equipment procurement and technical services for the construction and operations of a manufacturing plant follow:

JOINT VENTURE AGREEMENT (Corporate)
between DCF CORPORATION and XYZ, S.A.

INDEX

VI.   TERM, EVENTS OF DEFAULT, PURCHASE OPTIONS,
      FUTURE CAPITAL CONTRIBUTIONS, TERMINATION

VII. GENERAL PROVISIONS

EXHIBITS:

JOINT VENTURE AGREEMENT (Partnership)
between DCF CORPORATION and XYZ, S.A.

INDEX

AGREEMENT TO PROVIDE TECHNOLOGY,
ENGINEERING SERVICES, EQUIPMENT PROCUREMENT
AND TECHNICAL SERVICES FOR CONSTRUCTION
AND OPERATION OF A MANUFACTURING PLANT

INDEX

14

The Acquisition Contract Preliminary Agreements, Stock Purchase Agreements, and Acquisition Contract Checklist

The lawyers have the responsibility of preparing the acquisition contract. All parties involved in an acquisition should (but don't always) realize that the contract is the deal. Other aspects of the transaction such as requests for rulings from government agencies, securities registrations, stock listings and closing documents involve mechanical considerations and are drafted in accordance with terms dictated by the acquisition contract. Once signed, the contract fixes all the terms of the deal—the rights and obligations of the parties, one to another. Once signed, neither party can unilaterally change the terms of the acquisition. For this reason, the lawyer should know as much as possible about the concrete details of the transaction before completing the draft of the contract. After the contract is signed, sudden knowledge of circumstances that could have been provided for, but weren't, may be costly.

The lawyer, although responsible for the preparation of the contract, is dependent upon information supplied by both the business team and the accountant plus, of course, such information as he is given an opportunity to develop on his own. A successful acquisition generally evolves from a coordinated effort of businessmen, the lawyer and the accountant. Because of the numerous possible pitfalls in buying another's business, the buyer should approach the acquisition as though the entire purchase price could be sacrificed as a result of some oversight and the effort in drafting the contract should be coordinated to guard against all pitfalls from the business, accounting and legal viewpoints.

After businessmen have reached agreement in principle, they often wish to have a memorandum of understanding as soon as possible. The lawyers for both the buyer and seller should determine whether a letter of intent, option, restrictive agreement or detailed acquisition contract should be the first objective of the parties, and which would be most advantageous to either the buyer or seller—and acceptable to the other party.

OPTIONS, RESTRICTIVE AGREEMENTS AND LETTERS OF INTENT

After the buyer and seller have agreed upon a price, one or the other or both will sometimes want an immediate binding agreement. They may instruct their lawyers that a binding agreement should be signed that day. Any objection on the part of the lawyers on the grounds that an acquisition agreement should provide detailed coverage of many aspects of a going business may be met with the argument that the details should be ignored and a short form of agreement should be prepared detailing the major aspects of the transaction.

A number of different approaches to fulfilling the wish to "bind" the transaction promptly are feasible and sometimes helpful. One approach is the option. Another is a restrictive agreement that the seller will not seek or negotiate with another buyer while the present buyer is investigating the seller's business. Still another is a letter of intent that is nonbinding, but clarifies and records the status of the preliminary understandings and makes limited commitments on issues such as confidentiality, future steps to be taken and their costs.

The Option. In general, options are more advantageous to the buyer than to the seller. From the buyer's point of view, if it has bound the seller to an option contract, the buyer knows that should it, after investigation, decide to make the acquisition within the option period, the business will be available to the buyer. The buyer does not run the risk of losing an acquisition after an expensive investigation. On the other hand, from the seller's viewpoint an option has the disadvantage of prohibiting the seller from selling to a third party while the business is under option to the buyer, and the seller may lose an opportunity to sell its business to a third party for a higher price, because the buyer's option is outstanding.

Since an option is generally disadvantageous to the seller, under what circumstances should a seller grant an option? The answer to the question lies in the relative bargaining strength of the parties. An anxious buyer may offer a substantial price for the option. On the other hand, the seller may be in a position where it is most anxious to have the particular buyer make the acquisition. Many reasons could exist for this desire, such as the buyer's eminent position in the industry, excellent research facilities, promises of continued employment and pension coverage. The buyer wishes to make as thorough an investigation of the seller's business as is practicable, before making the acquisition. When a sizable business is investigated, the investigation, including attorney's and accountant's fees and time of the buyer's executives, can be quite expensive. Consequently, the buyer may refuse to proceed with negotiations and make its detailed investigation unless it has complete assurance, through an option, that the seller's business will be available should the buyer decide to buy. Under these or similar circumstances, a seller may be placed in a position where it grants an option.

Generally, for an option to be binding, consideration should pass from the buyer to the seller. In some instances, the sole consideration for an option has been a promise on the part of the buyer to conduct an investigation of the buyer's business and assets and perhaps to supply the seller with a copy of the report of the seller's business prepared by those conducting the investigation for the buyer. In other instances, a cash payment to the seller, which may or may not be applied against the purchase price is negotiated in return for the option.

The option is not necessarily a means of accelerating an agreement between the buyer and seller, and the buyer and seller should not mislead themselves into thinking it is. An option should not be unconditionally binding on either party unless it contains every term and condition of the acquisition or if a detailed acquisition agreement is attached to it. Otherwise the parties may have nothing more than an agreement to agree which may cause litigation.

Option—Acquisition Contract Attached. To bind the parties, both legally and with the least possibility of future litigation due to failure to specify terms, the option could be drafted to provide that the buyer will buy in accordance with the terms of a complete acquisition agreement attached to the option. Such an agreement should contain not only the purchase price and the assets being acquired, but also all the miscellaneous terms involved in an acquisition agreement such as lists of real estate, lists of important contracts, lists of patents, treatment of pension plans, employment contracts, bulk sales law and other numerous detailed questions which crop up in every acquisition. As a result of the need to attach an acquisition agreement to the option, the option agreement, as a practical matter, may not be executed in any shorter time than the execution of the acquisition agreement itself. Of course, once signed, the option agreement may give the buyer greater maneuverability, depending upon the conditions the buyer was able to negotiate permitting the buyer to refuse to exercise its option.

Conditional Option. The buyer and seller may agree upon an option subject to the negotiation of a detailed acquisition agreement and the approval by the board of directors of each party and their counsel. From the buyer's point of view, the buyer is free to exercise or not to exercise its option, and has the assurance that, during the option period, the seller will not sell to a third party. However, if the detailed terms of acquisition have not been agreed upon, should the seller receive a better offer from a third party, the seller may negotiate such difficult terms with the buyer that the buyer must refuse to make the acquisition. Then, after the option period the seller will be free to sell to the third party. In essence, an option without agreement as to the details of acquisition is often, as a legal and practical matter, no more binding on the parties than a verbal agreement.

Restrictive Agreements. Occasionally, circumstances of a proposed acquisition are such that a seller will agree not to negotiate with third parties for a fixed period of time while the buyer investigates the seller's business. Such an undertaking on the part of the seller may take the form of a letter addressed to the buyer. And the consideration for such a letter is the buyer's undertaking to investigate the seller's business in good faith. Where the buyer and seller agree to such an arrangement, the restrictive letter will usually contain few, if any, of the terms of the acquisition and may even omit reference to the purchase price or a description of the business and assets to be acquired. The restrictive letter buys time for the buyer and limits the seller's rights to negotiate with others, but neither party has any assurance that the transaction will be closed if the buyer's investigation proves satisfactory to it. A restrictive agreement is often included in a memorandum of understanding or letters of intent as described below.

Use of Options and Restrictive Agreements in Takeover Situations. The "lock-up," "leg-up," and "crown jewel" agreements described in Chapter 9 are option agreements used to facilitate or block tender offers. A "no shop" agreement is an example of a restrictive agreement. The "standstill" agreement is an example of a restrictive agreement by which a person owning shares in a potential target corporation agrees not to acquire shares beyond a specified limit in return for the commitment of corporation to take and/or refrain from specified actions.

Memorandum of Understanding or Letter of Intent. The signed or initiated memorandum of understanding or letter of intent constitutes another approach to the problem of promptly "formalizing" the parties after they have reached agreement in principle. Such a document should outline the major terms of the acquisition, such as price, a description of the business to be acquired and the major conditions to the acquisition—such as "tax-free" reorganization ruling, "pooling of interests" accounting treatment and antitrust clearance. The document should contain language to the effect that no contractual or other obligations will exist until negotiation, execution and delivery of a detailed written acquisition contract except for any obligations, such as secrecy, expressly stated to be binding in the memorandum of understanding or letter of intent. One need only remember the bankruptcy of Texaco Inc. to realize how easily the courts may impose unexpected contractual obligations, especially on "deep pocket" companies.

Nevertheless, memoranda of understanding and letters of intent serve several useful purposes. First, during their preparation, they identify major issues and determine whether the seller and buyer have a common understanding of their intentions about the acquisition. Second, they serve as a basis for further negotiations. Third, they can be used to commence the processes needed to obtain internal corporate approvals, loan and other financing, and some government clearances such as submission of notifications and reports under the Hart-Scott-Rodino Federal Trade Commission Improvements Act.

Customary Practices. Experience indicates that the acquisition contract is drafted frequently without any prior written options or other written understandings. In many cases, the investigation of the seller's business by the buyer and the preparation of a detailed acquisition contract proceed concurrently. As the investigation proceeds and problems become apparent, the acquisition agreement is tailored to reflect the understanding or compromises of the buyer and seller. Often, by the time both parties approve the acquisition contract and are ready to sign, the buyer will have substantially or fully completed its investigation of the seller's business. The acquisition contract generally will provide for a "closing"—actual transfer of legal title to the business—some time after the contract has been signed to enable the buyer to complete its investigation and to enable both parties to satisfy the conditions precedent to the closing contained in the contract. However, it is not unusual, even in sizable transactions, for the detailed acquisition agreement to be signed and the transaction closed, i.e. legal title passed, on the same day.

Conclusions. In conclusion, attempts to bind a buyer and seller fully and legally as soon as agreement in principle has been reached are impractical. Theoretically, from the buyer's viewpoint, a binding option with a completely negotiated, detailed acquisition contract attached is the most satisfactory approach to an acquisition; provided, of course, the price for the option is reasonable. From a practical point of view, since the detailed acquisition contract should be attached to such an option, the buyer often will have spent a good deal of money on the investigation before the option is signed, and a major portion of the advantage of the option to the buyer is thus lost before the option is signed. If the detailed option could be signed by the buyer without incurring any prior expense, the buyer would be in a position to investigate the seller during the option period and have a fixed transaction should it decide to buy.

Conditional options, restrictive letters and memoranda or letters of intent do not accomplish the result desired by the parties—if the parties are to be fully and legally bound. But memoranda or letters of intent which contain the major terms of the deal may be helpful as reminders to the buyer and seller of the major terms of the acquisition, as the details are negotiated.

Option Agreement—Form. A form of Option Agreement of a kind used in the defense of takeover contests is presented on pages 368 to 370. It can be readily modified for other kinds of acquisitions.

OPTION AGREEMENT

This OPTION AGREEMENT is made on _____, 199__ between ABC Corporation, a New York corporation ("ABC"), and XYZ, Inc., a Delaware corporation ("XYZ").

RECITALS:

ABC, XYZ and ABC Merger Corporation, a Delaware corporation and a wholly owned subsidiary of ABC ("Merger Corporation"), propose to enter into an Acquisition Agreement of even date (the "Acquisition Agreement") which provides that Merger Corporation, upon certain terms and subject to certain conditions will make a tender offer for _____ million of the outstanding shares of Common Stock, par value $1.00 per share, of XYZ ("XYZ Common Stock"); and

As an inducement for ABC to enter into the Acquisition Agreement, XYZ has agreed to grant to ABC an option to purchase shares of XYZ Common Stock.

AGREEMENTS:

NOW, THEREFORE, in consideration of the mutual covenants and agreements herein and in the Acquisition Agreement, the parties agree as follows:

1. The Option. XYZ hereby grants to ABC an irrevocable option (the "Option") to purchase up to _____ shares (the "Shares") of XYZ Common Stock at a price per Share of $_____.

2. Exercise. If (a) ABC has not received the Merger Cancellation Fee (as defined in the Acquisition Agreement), (b) all waiting periods under Hart-Scott-Rodino Federal Trade Commission Improvements Act applicable to the Option have expired or been terminated, (c) there is no preliminary or permanent injunction or other order by any court having valid jurisdiction prohibiting exercise of the Option, and (d) ABC is not then in material breach of its obligations under the Acquisition Agreement, ABC may exercise the Option, wholly or partially at any time or times, on or before the termination of the Acquisition Agreement in accordance with its terms, if any corporation, partnership, person, other entity or group (as defined in Section 13(d)(3) of the Securities Exchange Act of 1934, as amended (the "Exchange Act") (collectively, "Persons", and individually, a "Person")) other than XYZ or any of its affiliates, shall do any of the following actions ("Triggering Actions"):

(i) acquire beneficial ownership (as defined in Rule 13d-3 under the Exchange Act) of at least 20% of the then outstanding shares of the XYZ Common Stock;

(ii) if such person already has beneficial ownership (as defined in Rule 13d-3) of ____% or more of the XYZ Common Stock, acquire beneficial ownership (as defined in Rule 13d-3) of an additional .2% of the XYZ Common Stock;

(iii) commence a tender or exchange offer for at least 20% of the then out-standing shares of the XYZ Common Stock;

(iv) publicly propose any merger, consolidation or acquisition of all or substantially all of the assets of ABC or XYZ or other business combination involving XYZ, or publicly propose a transaction involving the transfer of beneficial ownership of securities presenting, of the right to acquire beneficial ownership of or to vote securities representing, more than 50% of the total voting power of XYZ; or

(v) solicit proxies, execute any written consent or become a "participant" in any "solicitation" (as such terms are defined in Regulation 14A under the Exchange Act, with respect to the XYZ Common Stock).

3. Payment and Delivery of Certificates. *At any closing hereunder, ABC will make payment to XYZ of the aggregate price for the Shares so purchased by delivery of immediately available funds to XYZ, and XYZ will deliver to ABC a certificate or certificates representing the Shares so purchased, registered in the name of ABC.*

4. Reserved Shares. *XYZ represents and warrants that it has taken all necessary corporate action to authorize and reserve and to permit it to issue, and at all times from the date hereof through the date of expiration of the Option will have reserved for issuance upon exercise of the Option, _____ Shares, all of which, upon issuance pursuant hereto, shall be duly authorized, validly issued, fully paid and nonassessable, and shall be delivered free and clear of all claims, liens, encumbrances and security interests and not subject to any preemptive rights.*

5. Investment Purpose. *ABC represents and warrants that it will acquire the Shares issued upon exercise of the Option for its own account and not with a view to any resale or distribution thereof, and will not sell or otherwise dispose of the Shares unless the Shares are registered under the Securities Act of 1933 or unless an exemption from registration is available.*

6. Registration and Listing. *As soon as practicable after exercise of the Option, XYZ shall prepare and file at its cost and expense with the Securities and Exchange Commission ("SEC") a registration statement under the Securities Act of 1933 (the "Securities Act") with respect to the Option Shares and shall file amendments and otherwise use its best efforts to cause such registration statement to become effective so as to permit ABC to sell or otherwise dispose of the Option Shares. XYZ will use its best efforts promptly to list the Shares for trading on The New York Stock Exchange, subject to official notice of issuance, including their registration under the Exchange Act.*

7. Adjustment Upon Changes in Capitalization. *If there shall be any change in the Shares by reason of stock dividends, split-ups, mergers, recapitalizations, combinations, conversions, exchanges of shares or the like, the number and kind of Shares subject to the Option and the purchase price per Share shall be appropriately adjusted.*

8. Consents. *ABC and XYZ each will use its best efforts to obtain consents of all third parties and governmental authorities necessary to the consummation of the transactions contemplated by this Agreement.*

9. Specific Performance. *The parties hereto acknowledge that damages would be an inadequate remedy for a breach of this Agreement and that the obligations of the parties hereto shall be specifically enforceable.*

10. Nonassignment. *Neither this Agreement nor any rights hereunder may be assigned directly or by operation of law by either party without the prior express written consent of the other parties and any attempt to make such an assignment shall be null and void.*

11. Entire Agreement; Assignment. *This Agreement and the Acquisition Agreement constitute the entire agreement among the parties with respect to the subject matter and supersede all other prior agreements and understandings, both written and oral, among the parties or any of them with respect to the subject matter.*

12. Notices. *All notices, requests, claims, demands and other communications hereunder shall be deemed to have been duly given when delivered in person, by cable, telegram or telex, or by registered or certified mail (postage prepaid, return receipt requested) to the respective parties as follows:*

If to ABC:

If to XYZ:

or to such other address as the person to whom notice is given may have previously furnished to the others in writing in the manner set forth above (provided that notice of any change of address shall be effective only upon receipt thereof).

13. Governing Law. *The validity, interpretation, performance and enforcement of this Agreement shall be governed by the laws of the State of Delaware, regardless of the laws that might otherwise govern under applicable principles of conflicts of laws.*

14. Parties in Interest. *This Agreement shall be binding upon and inure solely to the benefit of each party hereto, and nothing in this Agreement, express or implied, is intended to confer upon any other person any rights or remedies of any nature whatsoever under or by reason of this Agreement.*

ABC CORPORATION

By _____
    President

XYZ INC.

By _____
    President

Letter of Intent—Form. The following form of letter of intent illustrates how such a document may set forth the major terms of a proposed acquisition. Note that the detailed terms of the proposed acquisition are subject to the approval of the boards of directors of both the buyer and the seller. In this sense, the letter is not binding upon either party. Another form of letter of intent is provided later in this chapter.

BUYER
3000 Main St.
New York, N.Y.

November 30, 199_____

Mr. John Smith, President
SELLER
15 Green Street
Syracuse, New York

Dear Mr. Smith:

As a result of our discussions to date and a study of the information that you have furnished to us, it appears that it would be beneficial to both parties to consider an exchange of the common stock of Buyer for all of the outstanding and optioned capital stock of Seller on a "Pooling of Interests" basis, along the following lines:

1. Buyer will reserve 85,552 shares of its common stock out of the current authorized, but not issued, common stock for the sole purpose of exchange for Seller stock, as follows:

a) For the present 10,094 shares of Seller stock outstanding	*80,752 shares*
b) For seller options not yet exercised	*4,800 shares*
Total Reserved	*85,552 shares*

2. At the time of the Closing of such transaction (hereinafter called the Closing), Buyer will transfer to the then stockholders of Seller eight (8) shares of Buyer common stock for each outstanding share. Seller will not issue any additional shares except those that may result from exercise of options granted under the Seller Restricted Stock Option Plan.

3. Buyer, at the Closing, shall substitute for the stock options granted under the Seller's Nonqualified Stock Option Plan, to the extent that such options have not been exercised prior to the Closing, options to purchase shares of Buyer common stock in lieu of shares of Seller, on a basis which will have the same status under the Internal Revenue Code as the options now outstanding under Seller's Plan.

4. All shares of Buyer common stock issued under any of the conditions of this Agreement will be acquired for investment only, and not with a view of distribution, and your stockholders will be required to furnish Buyer with a Letter of Investment satisfactory to counsel.

5. It is Buyer's present intention that after the Closing the Seller's Profit Sharing Retirement Plan and Bonus Plan will be continued in full force and effect.

6. This Letter of Intent is subject to the owners of 100% of the outstanding shares of Seller agreeing to the sale.

7. Mr. John Smith and Mr. Robert Roe shall continue to be employed after the Closing to manage the affairs of Seller, subject to the discretion of the Board of Directors of Buyer.

8. This Letter of Intent is submitted subject to an independent audit and investigation, at Buyer's expense, by our accountants, market survey specialists, realty appraiser, and others, of your past and forecast future operations, and thereafter final approval by our Board of Directors. You agree to make available to our auditors, analysts, and others, such records and information as are needed for their independent investigation.

9. It is understood that this transaction was brought about by William W. Williams, and that no other agent or broker was authorized or instrumental in, or for, the negotiations of the transaction contemplated herein, and that Buyer will be solely responsible for any commissions due William W. Williams at the time of the Closing.

10. It is our understanding that you will warrant the Balance Sheet and the P&L Statement for the 9-month period ending September 30, 199___, and that you will further warrant that the business of Seller has been operated only in the ordinary course of business since that time, and that no dividends or unusual withdrawals or expenditures have been made.

11. You understand that the final Agreement and Plan of Reorganization will contain standard covenants, indemnities, conditions, and warranties required by Buyer, such as warranties as to litigation, inventories, receivables, real estate, trademarks, patents, tax liabilities, title to assets, and other related items.

12. This letter is not intended as a contract, but merely as a statement of the present intentions and understandings of the parties. The transaction will be binding upon the parties only in accordance with the terms contained in the final Agreement and Plan of Reorganization, if, as, and when such an Agreement has been executed by us and the Seller's stockholders.

13. If you are in agreement with the foregoing, please so indicate by having all of the stockholders of Seller sign and return the two copies of this letter which are enclosed herewith.

Very truly yours,

D. W. Jones, Vice President and Secretary

THE ACQUISITION CONTRACT

An acquisition contract performs the basic function of fixing the rights and obligations of the buyer and seller to each other. In addition, the contract may perform a second important substantial function of supplying a buyer with detailed information about a seller's business.

Structure and Contents. Acquisition contracts differ in many different ways. One basic structure difference results from the decision to structure the acquisition as a stock purchase, assets purchase or merger. Another basic structural difference results from the decision to pay the price in cash, in installments or by issuing securities. Once a basic structure is adopted, numerous special provisions are used to state the agreement on a wide variety of subjects covering all aspects of the business.

Nevertheless, acquisition contracts follow some common patterns. The subjects commonly covered can be grouped in broad categories:

- Parties
- Recitals
- Statement of the Transaction
- Representations and Warranties
- Covenants
- Conditions
- Closing Procedures, Documents and Payments
- Indemnities
- Termination and Default
- General Provisions
- Signatures
- Exhibits

The order and manner in which the subjects are presented varies greatly depending on the structure of the transaction, negotiations between the seller, buyer and others such as lenders, and the experience and style of lawyers. These variations are customary and also desirable because the acquisition contract should fully and accurately reflect the agreements of each buyer and seller for their own transaction. While they can benefit from ideas and provisions used in other transactions, no two businesses are identical and contracts for their sale cannot be identical.

Parties. All acquisition contracts must begin with an accurate identification of all persons whose role as a party is necessary to achieve the transaction. In addition to the buyer and seller, it is sometimes necessary or desirable to include other persons such as a corporate parent, a guarantor, a person whose vote or consent will be essential or a person who will provide financing. As an alternative, the buyer and seller may include a covenant to obtain the actions needed from these persons and a condition excusing one or both of them if the covenant is not fulfilled.

Recitals. Recitals provide an opportunity to state the background and overall objectives of the transaction in a simple manner which may not be evident in the subsequent detailed provisions. They can be important in the resolution of subsequent disputes, especially in court. They should be written carefully and readably.

Statement of the Transaction. An early article of the contract should state in detail what will be sold or merged and what will be paid in return. This article varies depending on the structure. A stock purchase contract must commit to sell shares in relation to an identified capital structure which assures the buyer of obtaining all or an agreed percentage of ownership in return for the purchase price which must also be clearly described. An asset purchase contract must commit to sell carefully defined assets in return for a purchase price and assumption, or disclaimer, of liabilities which must also be clearly described. The definitions of assets and liabilities must be comprehensive to assure that all intended items are included and limiting to assure that unintended items are not erroneously included. A merger contract must identify the surviving corporation and prescribe the terms on which stock and other securities will be exchanged for the purchase price to be paid by the surviving corporation or a parent or affiliated corporation. Among these provisions, the merger contract may also include the procedures for approval and implementation of the merger or they may be described later as covenants, conditions and closing events.

In asset purchase transactions, the contract will usually also contain a provision agreeing on the allocation of the purchase price among the assets sold.

Examples of transactional "buy-sell" commitments are contained in the forms of acquisition contracts in this chapter and Chapters 15 and 16.

Representations and Warranties. It would be possible to sell a going business "AS IS" and sellers sometimes begin negotiations with that objective. Businesses, even small ones, are far too complex to permit a sale without any representations and warranties for a fair price fairly reflecting their worth. Perceiving this, sellers sometimes offer a bargain price in the hope of avoiding representations and warranties, but this strategy is not persuasive and can be counterproductive because it makes the buyer fear that the seller is hiding something seriously adverse. The result is that the acquisition contracts customarily contain a detailed series of provisions making representations and warranties about the ownership, financial operations and condition and many other aspects of the business. If the representations and warranties are untrue or are breached, the buyer has a variety of remedies including cancellation of the transaction, rescission of a completed transaction or monetary damages.

The representations and warranties are strongly negotiated and carefully drafted to allocate risk in a manner acceptable to the buyer and seller. While the variations are endless, buyers usually demand and sellers fairly readily provide strong protection about subjects which are and should be certain such as corporate authorization and ownership of shares or assets being sold. Protection limited in scope and time is usually given for less certain items such as the salability of inventories and collectibility of inventories. Limited protection, if any, will usually be given for items which are uncertain in nature and potentially affected by the buyer's activities after the acquisition, such as retention of customers and employees and condition of equipment.

The representations and warranties are usually keyed to three different dates: (1) the date of seller's last financial statements used as a basic for the transaction, (2) the contract date and (3) the closing date. The acquisition contract will require that the representations and warranties be true, accurate and complete on each of those dates. The contract will also provide for survival of all or some of the representations and warranties after the closing of the acquisition for agreed time periods which customarily range from permanent for matters relating to title to relatively brief periods for financial matters and condition of facilities and equipment. The survival provisions will be coordinated with the indemnity provisions in the acquisitions contract.

The buyer customarily also provides representations and warranties. If an acquisition is for cash, they may be quite brief and consist primarily of matters relating to corporate authorization and the availability of financing. If the buyer will pay for a period of time or will issue stock or securities, the representations and warranties will be more numerous and detailed and may correspond in some situations to the protections provided by the seller.

Numerous examples of representations and warranties are contained in the forms of acquisition contracts in this chapter and Chapters 15 and 16.

Covenants. Acquisition contracts customarily contain a number of covenants (promises) by the seller and buyer to take, or refrain from, certain actions. Some are to be accomplished by the closing and others apply after the closing. For example, they may agree to apply for government clearances or for consents of lenders and customers. They may agree to complete a "due diligence" review. The buyer may agree to obtain financing commitments within a specified time period. The seller may agree to obtain title insurance commitments. Each will agree to maintain the secrecy of confidential proprietary information furnished by the other party. The buyer may agree to employee some or all of the existing employees and to continue all or part of their compensation arrangements. The seller may agree not to compete for some time period after the closing. Examples of covenants are shown in the forms of acquisition contracts contained in this chapter and Chapters 15 and 16.

Conditions. In an acquisition contract, conditions are the "out" clauses excusing performance by buyer or seller, or both, if certain events occur or do not occur. For example, both buyer and seller will usually be excused if government agencies decline essential clearances. The seller, and usually also the buyer, will be excused if the buyer does not obtain financing commitments within the time allowed. The buyer will be excused if a material misrepresentation is discovered or a material adverse change in seller's business occurs prior to the closing. Examples of conditions are shown in the forms of acquisition contracts in this chapter and Chapters 15 and 16.

Closing Procedures, Documents and Payments. The acquisition contract specifying a closing place and date will state in detail each step to be taken at the closing. Documents and payments to be delivered will be stated including the medium and means of transmittal of payments. To businessmen, the procedures may seem extraordinarily detailed, but only such detail can prevent a party who wishes to withdraw for selfish reasons from finding excuses for delay or avoidance of obligations. Closings are further discussed in Chapter 17 and examples of closing procedures are shown in the forms of acquisition contracts in this chapter and Chapters 15 and 16.

Indemnities. Some acquisition contracts contain an article which coordinates the contractual protections furnished throughout the contract and describes and limits the procedures and remedies relating to their enforcement. Without this article, the buyer and seller can nevertheless exercise their rights if a misrepresentation or breach of warranty is discovered, a covenant is breached or a condition is not fulfilled. However, especially when a lengthy contract is prepared for the sale of a large or complicated business, it is well worthwhile to include an article stating what will happen if events do not occur as expected. While entrepreneurial businessmen may chide the buyers for introducing an element of negative thinking, the importance of the potential consequences of a default on business, financial and human expectations mandates that businessmen think about the "unthinkable" in some transactions.

Termination and Default. Relatively simply acquisition contracts may include termination and default provisions in several articles such as those containing covenants and conditions. The buyer and seller can rely on these provisions and basic principles of contract law in matters relating to termination and default. When the transaction is complex, involves multiple parties or public companies, it is often worthwhile to prepare a separate article on termination and default. The article can specify how a decision to terminate will be made among multiple parties who may become entitled to exercise or waive a right to terminate or declare a default. It can include a requirement of notice of defaults and a right to cure. It can provide for remedies such as specific and liquidated damages and can also limit remedies in time, scope and amount. It can include a final date, called "drop dead date," at which the contract will terminate if it has not been closed although no default has occurred. An example of a brief separate article on termination and default is contained in the Agreement and Plan of Reorganization in Chapter 16.

General Provisions. An acquisition contract customarily includes a final article containing miscellaneous provisions of a legal nature. Common examples are amendment procedures, notice procedures, assignment restrictions and procedures, governing law, consents to jurisdiction and an acknowledgement that the contract is the entire agreement. The general provisions may also include provisions sometimes found in other articles such as finder's fees, transaction costs, survival of representations and warranties and future cooperation. Examples of articles containing general provisions are found in the form contracts in this chapter and Chapters 15 and 16.

Signatures. The signature page in an acquisition contract usually requires only the corporate signatures of the buyer and seller. However, it can become more complex, especially when stock is being sold by a large number of shareholders. For example, signatures by joint owners or owners by the entireties may be necessary. Signatures by agents, executors, administrators or others acting in representative capacity may be necessary together with powers of attorney, trust agreements, court orders or other evidence of their authority to act.

Exhibits. The exhibits are vital elements of an acquisition contract. They include the documents evidencing the condition of the business as stated in the article on representations and warranties such as asset lists, financial statements, descriptions or copies of major contracts and disclosures of lawsuits, claims and other contingent liabilities. They also include agreed forms of contracts to be signed at the closing such as customer and supply contracts and employment contracts. They may also include special schedules such as a chart allocating the purchase price or a real estate survey showing parcels of land being sold and retained by seller.

Acquisition Contract Checklist

An Acquisition Contract Checklist is included at the end of this chapter. It is intended as a quick reference source for contract preparation. There are, of course, more topics which can be included in acquisition contracts, but the checklist can help professionals to assure that familiar subjects are included unless they are not applicable.

LETTER OF INTENT AND STOCK PURCHASE AGREEMENT TO SELL STOCK FOR CASH AND CONTINGENT PAYMENTS

Forms of a Letter of Intent and a subsequent Stock Purchase Agreement to sell a small electronics corporation to a large computer manufacturer for cash and additional contingent payments based on pre-income tax earnings are provided in the following pages. A Closing Memorandum for the Stock Purchase Agreement is provided in Chapter 17.

The reader should observe that the provisions for the sale of a small business can sometimes be shorter and simpler than those used for a large or complex business. For example, the representations and warranties relating to employee benefit plans and environmental, safety and product liability are much simpler than those used for a larger chemical business in the Assets Purchase Agreement in Chapter 15.

Exhibit 14-1

May 31, 199____

LETTER OF INTENT

VIA FEDERAL EXPRESS

Mr. John L. Smith
Mr. Joseph Johnson
c/o ABC Electronics, Inc.
789 Second Street
Jamestown, New York

Dear Messrs. Smith and Johnson:

We have been discussing a possible acquisition of ABC Electronics Corporation ("ABC"). This letter is intended to summarize the major points discussed in order to establish a basis for further negotiations.

1. Structure and Price. International plans to purchase all the outstanding stock of ABC from you for a cash price of $2,500,000 is cash plus ____% of the average net pre-income tax earnings of ABC for its first two fiscal years ending after the closing. A formula for determining earnings will be included in the Stock Purchase Agreement.

2. Stock Purchase Agreement. We plan to continue negotiations with the objective of preparing and signing a Stock Purchase Agreement on or before July 31, 199__. It is expected that the Stock Purchase Agreement will contain, among other things, the following provisions:

(a) Representation and warranties as to ABC's financial statements and tax returns; salability of inventories and collectibility of receivables; title to your shares and ABC's assets and freedom from litigation, claims and contingent liabilities.

(b) Three year employment contracts for each of you to continue in your present positions at annual salaries of $_____ and $_____, respectively, plus participation in ABC's employee benefit plans provided that you fulfill health and other requirements.

(c) A noncompetition provision in which each of you will agree not to compete with ABC's business for five years after the purchase or one year after any termination of your employment, whichever is longer.

(d) Covenants requiring operation of the business by ABC only in the ordinary course and cooperation with our continuing review of the business until the closing.

(e) Conditions excusing us from closing if any necessary governmental

approvals are not obtained, if any material adverse change in the business occurs, or if any material representations and warranties are no longer accurate on the closing date.

(f) A closing date no later than August 31, 199___.

(g) Survival of representations and warranties for two years and indemnities against their breach.

3. "Due Diligence" Review. *Through July 31, 199___, you will cooperate, and you will cause ABC to cooperate, with our "due diligence" review of its business and financial affairs including access to all books and records and to all officers and mergers. Nevertheless, we will not contact any customers or suppliers without your prior approval and arrangements for the visit or other contact.*

4. "No Shop" Provision. *Through July 31, 199___, you agree not to solicit, negotiate or accept any other offer for sale of ABC and to cause ABC not to solicit, negotiate or accept any offer for a merger or a sale of any material part of its business. During this period, you will maintain free and clear ownership of your ABC shares and will cause ABC to conduct its business only in the ordinary course.*

5. Confidentiality. *We agree to hold in confidence and not to disclose or use for our own benefit any confidential, proprietary information received from you or ABC during our "due diligence" review for a period of three years. Our commitment shall not apply to (A) information already known when received, (B) information in the public domain when received or thereafter in the public domain through sources other than us, (C) information lawfully obtained from a third party not subject to confidentiality obligation to ABC or (D) information developed independently by personnel in our organization who did not have access to your information. We agree to restrict access to your information to persons in our organization who have a need to know and who have signed individual secrecy agreements corresponding to those which we have undertaken. If negotiations are discontinued or the Stock Purchase Agreement does not close for any reason, we will return all documents furnished to us by you and ABC and will keep no copies.*

6. Publicity. *No public announcement of this letter of intent shall be made without your approval and our approval.*

7. Expenses. *If the parties shall not execute and deliver a Stock Purchase Agreement, they shall bear their own expenses and have no further liability or obligations to each other.*

8. Brokers and Finders. *Each party represents and warrants that no broker, finder or other intermediary or consultant introduced them or brought about the proposed sale and agrees to defend and indemnify the other parties against any claim for compensation by any person on the basis of alleged obligations incurred by him or them.*

9. Nonbinding Effect. *This letter of intent is not intended to be a contract or otherwise to create legal obligations of any nature except for those expressly stated in Sections 3 through 8. No contract shall exist until the parties shall execute and deliver a definitive written Stock Purchase Agreement. The parties reserve the*

right to negotiate in their own interests and for their own advantage without any implied obligations based on custom, good faith or reasonable conduct.

If the foregoing conforms to your understanding, please sign and return the enclosed copy of this letter.

Very truly yours,

ACCEPTED: NATIONAL COMPUTERS, INC.

_____ *By* _____
John L. Smith

_____
Joseph Johnson

ABC ELECTRONICS, INC.

By _____

Exhibit 14-2

STOCK PURCHASE AGREEMENT
Index

STOCK PURCHASE AGREEMENT

This Agreement is made on _____, 199__ between JOHN L. SMITH ("Smith") and JOSEPH JOHNSON ("Johnson"), collectively the "Sellers", ABC ELECTRONICS CORPORATION, a Delaware corporation (the "Corporation"), and INTERNATIONAL COMPUTERS, INC., a New York corporation (the "Purchaser"). The Corporation is a party to this Agreement so that it may enter into certain contracts as provided herein, but shall have no rights or obligations under this Agreement except as expressly provided herein.

RECITALS:

A. Sellers each own 10,000 shares of common stock of the Corporation, which shares are all of its issued and outstanding capital stock. Smith is President and Johnson is Vice President of the Corporation and each serves as a director of the Corporation.

B. Sellers wish to sell, and Purchaser wishes to purchase, all of the outstanding stock of the Corporation on the terms and conditions contained in this Agreement including, without limitation, provisions for payment of additional purchase price if the Corporation achieves certain net earnings goals during its first two fiscal years after the closing of this Agreement.

C. The Corporation wishes to continue to employ Smith and Johnson, and they wish to continue to be employed by the Corporation, on the terms and conditions of Employment Contracts attached as Exhibits to this Agreement.

AGREEMENTS:

On the terms and subject to the conditions described herein, the parties agree as follows:

I. THE SALE OF SHARES

1.1 Commitments. Each of the Sellers severally agrees to sell to Purchaser, and Purchaser agrees to purchase from each of them, 10,000 shares of Common Stock of the Corporation for the purchase price provided in Section 1.2.

1.2 Purchase Price. (A) The purchase price for all the shares of Common Stock described in Section 1.1 shall be (A) $2,500,000 payable in cash at the Closing plus (B) _____% of the average net pre-income tax earnings of the Corporation for its first two fiscal years ending after the Closing Date determined in accordance with generally accepted accounting principles consistently applied and the agreed accounting policies provided in Exhibit A (the "Contingent Price"). The Contingent Price shall be payable in cash 120 days after the end of such second fiscal year and shall bear interest at the rate of _____% thereafter if not paid because of dispute or for any other reason. If the calculation of net pre-income tax earnings for *either year shall result in a loss, the amount of such loss shall be deducted in calculating net pre-income tax earnings for the two year period.*

(B) Purchaser shall pay half of the purchase price, including the Contingent Price, to each Seller.

1.3 The Closing. *The closing ("Closing") of this Agreement will be held at the offices of Brown & Williams, 200 Wall Street, New York, NY 10075 on _____, 199__ (the "Closing Date") or at such other time and place as the parties may agree in writing. The obligation of each party to close is subject to its respective conditions stated in Article IV.*

II. REPRESENTATIONS AND WARRANTIES

2.1 The Sellers jointly and severally represent and warrant to the Purchaser as follows:

(a) Corporate Status. *The Corporation is a corporation duly organized and existing in good standing under the laws of the State of Delaware and is qualified to do business with full power, corporate and otherwise, to carry on its business and own its properties. Accurate and complete copies of the Certificate of Incorporation and By-Laws of the Corporation, including all amendments, are attached as* Exhibits B and C. *The Corporation is qualified to do business and in good standing in all jurisdictions where the nature of its activities or ownership of properties requires such qualification and has duly filed all franchise and other tax returns required to be filed by the laws of such states and jurisdictions and has paid all taxes shown to be due and payable in such returns.*

(b) Capitalization. *The present equity capitalization of the Corporation is accurately and completely set forth in* Exhibit D. *All outstanding capital stock of the Corporation is validly issued, fully paid and non-assessable. Except as set forth in* Exhibit D, *the Corporation does not have any authorized, issued or outstanding securities convertible into or exchangeable for capital stock, nor does any person hold any option or right to purchase or otherwise acquire any shares of capital stock or any securities convertible into or exchangeable for such capital stock. The Corporation has not declared, and has no outstanding commitment, to pay any dividend or to make any distribution or transfer of assets to its shareholders or persons affiliated with them. The Corporation has not adopted or committed to any change in its equity capitalization.*

(c) Title to Outstanding Shares. *The Sellers own all 20,000 outstanding shares of Common Stock of the Corporation hereunder free and clear of all pledges, liens, encumbrances, security interest, mortgages, deeds of trust and claims whatsoever and of all restrictions on their respective rights to sell them to Purchaser hereunder. Without limitation, neither the Sellers nor the Corporation are parties to any existing agreement restricting sale or transfer of the shares or granting any person a right to buy them.*

(d) Subsidiaries. *The Corporation has no subsidiaries except those listed in* Exhibit E. *Except as set forth in* Exhibit E, *the Corporation owns all of the authorized and outstanding stock of each of its subsidiaries free and clear of all pledges, liens, encumbrances, security interests, mortgages, deeds of trust, claims or restrictions on the change of control contemplated herein.*

(e) Corporate Authorization. *Execution, delivery and performance of this Agreement has been duly authorized by all requisite corporate action on the part of the Corporation. The Corporation has all necessary power and authority to enter into and perform this Agreement which will not conflict with any law, regulation, restriction or agreement to which it is subject.*

(f) Financial Statements. *(i) The financial statements of the Corporation for its fiscal years ended December 31, 199___ and 199___, audited by Coopers, Andersen, Price & Co., attached as* Exhibit F *reflect fairly the financial condition of the Corporation at such dates and its results of operations, retained earnings and changes in financial position for the fiscal years then ended in accordance with generally accepted accounting principles consistently applied. All material liabilities and obligations, existing and contingent, of the Corporation at December 31, 199___ are fairly reflected or disclosed and described in its financial statements and the notes thereto. Since December 31, 199___, the Corporation has conducted its activities only in the ordinary course and no material change in its financial condition, results of operations or retained earnings occurred during such period. (ii) All inventories reflected in the Corporation's balance sheet at December 31, 199___ are fully usable and salable and all receivables reflected in such balance sheet are collectible except to the extent of the reserves shown therein.*

(g) Taxes. *Sellers have delivered to Purchaser complete and correct copies of the federal, state and local tax returns of the Corporation for each of the five years ended December 31, 199___. Such returns and the information contained therein have been properly and accurately compiled and completed and reflect the tax liabilities of the Corporation for the periods in question. The Corporation has filed all federal, state and local tax returns which are required to be filed and has paid or made adequate provision for the payment of all taxes which have become or may become due in respect of operations during the periods to which such returns relate. The Corporation has delivered to Purchaser complete and correct copies of the reports of any audit of the income tax returns of the Corporation and of any deficiency letter and/or proposed assessment issued at the end of any such audit and all subsequent correspondence and documents relating thereto.*

(h) Litigation, Proceedings or Claims. *Except as described in* Exhibit G, *there is no litigation, governmental proceeding or investigation, or claim pending or threatened against the Corporation or the Sellers or the Corporation's properties or business which might materially and adversely affect its financial condition, business or operations, or against or relating to the transactions contemplated by this Agreement.*

(i) Description of Properties, Contracts and Material Information.

Exhibit H *is an accurate and complete list as of the date of this Agreement of (i) all real property and all major items of equipment presently owned or leased by the Corporation with a brief description of each property and its use, copies of title instruments and leases, and details relating to any liens, encumbrances or claims thereto and any direct or indirect interest therein of any of the Corporation's directors or officers; (ii) all patents, trademarks, trade names, copyrights, including all registration thereof and applications therefor presently owned in whole or in party by the Corporation, and all patent, trademark or copyright licenses to which the Corporation is a party; (iii) all bonds, debentures, notes, stock or other securities other than stock of subsidiaries already listed in Exhibit E, and all accounts receivable other than trade accounts receivable which are not more than 90 days old, held or owned by the Corporation; (iv) all policies of insurance in force covering or owned by the Corporation; (v) all loan agreements or bank credit agreements in effect, setting forth the amount of the original loan, the unpaid balance, the interest rate and payments, the maturity date, any prepayment penalties and the name of the lender; (vi) all material agreements to which the Corporation is a party except that the Corporation may omit agreements made in the ordinary course of business which are terminable by the Corporation by notice of not more than 90 days without penalty or which do not obligate the Corporation in amounts in excess of $25,000 in the aggregate per agreement; (vii) all employment contracts with any officers or employees of the Corporation and the names and current salary rates of all such officers and employees whose current annual salary rate is U.S. $50,000 or more, together with a description of all incentive, compensation, bonus, profit sharing retirement, pension or other similar plans or arrangements for any of such officers or employees and (viii) all agents, consultants and independent contractors retained by the Corporation, with a brief description of the arrangement for compensation, and all persons, if any, holding a power of attorney, to act on its behalf (ix) all agreements and transactions entered into and in force with any officer, director or stockholder of the Corporation or any person related to any of them, except for agreements which are terminable by the Corporation within 90 days without penalty or which do not obligate the Corporation in amounts in excess of $25,000 in the aggregate per agreement. Complete and correct copies of all agreements, instruments or other documents relating to the items referred to above have been delivered or made available to the Purchaser. The Corporation is not in material default on any obligation to be performed by it under any loan, plan or agreement referred to in* Exhibit H, *or in material violation of any law, ordinance, regulation, order or decree applicable to it.*

(j) Legal Compliance. *The Corporation is in compliance with all laws, regulations, permits and orders applicable to its business and assets. Seller has not, and is not, infringing any patent, trademark or copyright or using or disclosing without authorization any trade secret of third parties.*

(k) Employee Relations. *Since January 1, 199___, the Corporation has not experienced any strike, work interruption, organization campaign or other*

concerted action by its employees and has not received any complaint of failure to comply with equal employment opportunity laws.

(l) Employee Benefit Plans. *All employee benefit plans, as defined in the Employee Retirement Income Security Act, covering present and former employees of the Corporation have been fully disclosed to the Purchaser including, without limitation, all commitments to provide employee benefits. Any plans intended to be qualified plans and trusts intended to be exempt organizations under the Internal Revenue Code are qualified and exempt and the Corporation has determination letters evidencing such status. There has been, and is, no reportable event, accumulated funding deficiency, termination liability, withdrawal liability or prohibited transaction in connection with such plans. The Corporation has no obligation to provide post-retirement health, medical, death or other welfare benefits. All group health plans have been maintained in compliance with the Internal Revenue Code. All vacation, severance and similar plans or policies of the Corporation have been fully and accurately disclosed to the Purchaser.*

(m) Environmental, Safety and Product Liability. *Without limitation of other representations and warranties herein, the Corporation and its business and assets are in compliance with, and are not subject to, any liability under federal, state and local environmental laws. The Corporation is not aware of any reason why it will not continue to be able to comply with all its permits or to renew any permit expiring within one year after the date of this Agreement without imposition of standards materially stricter than those now in effect. The Corporation is not subject to any liability with respect to a release or disposal of hazardous waste, hazardous substances or constituents or pollutants. The Corporation is not subject to any liability with respect to defective products regardless of whether such liability results from breach of express or implied warranties or strict liability imposed by reason of misdesign, mismanufacture or failure to warn.*

2.2 Representations and Warranties of Purchaser. *The Purchaser represents and warrants to the Sellers and the Corporation as follows:*

(a) Purchaser is a corporation duly authorized and existing in good standing under the laws of New York with full corporate power and authority to carry out the transactions contemplated by this Agreement.

(b) The execution, delivery and performance by Purchaser of this Agreement and all other agreements and transactions contemplated herein have been authorized on the part of Purchaser by all requisite corporate action and will not violate or conflict with its certificate of incorporation or by-laws or with any law, regulation, judgement, order, restriction or agreement to which Purchaser is a party or to which it is subject.

(c) The shares of Common Stock of the Corporation are being acquired by Purchaser for investment and without any view to, or for resale in connection with, any distribution of such shares within the meaning of the Securities Act of 1933.

(d) No consent, approval, permit, registration, filing or notice to or with any governmental agency or third party is required on the part of Purchaser for the execution, delivery and performance of this Agreement except as expressly provided herein.

(e) This is no litigation or governmental proceeding pending or, to the best of Purchaser's knowledge, threatened against Purchaser that questions the validity or challenges the performance of this Agreement or any action to be taken by Purchaser pursuant to this Agreement.

III. COVENANTS

3.1 Conduct of Business Until Closing. *Pending the Closing, Sellers shall cause the Corporation, and the Corporation agrees, to conduct its business only in the ordinary course. Without limitation of the foregoing, the Corporation shall (A) use its best efforts to preserve intact its business and its assets; (B) maintain its assets in good repair and operating condition except for fire, flood or other Acts of God; (C) continue in full all existing insurance coverage, (D) not enter into any material contract or other transaction without prior written approval of Buyer; (E) use its best efforts to retain employees, customers and suppliers; (F) refrain from any increase in the compensation or benefits of employees or any commitment for an increase; (G) not engage in any inter-company transaction with any of its affiliates except for continuation of transactions in the normal course of business fully disclosed in exhibits to this Agreement; (H) refrain from any sale or transfer or commitment to sell or transfer any of its assets except for sales of products in the ordinary course of business or any action or omission which will subject its assets to any lien, encumbrance, or security interest; (I) refrain, without Purchaser's consent, from any material modification of any of its assets or commitment for any capital expenditure in excess of $_____.*

3.2. Access to the Business and Assets. *Until the Closing, Seller shall consult with Purchaser on the operation of its business and shall afford access to Purchaser and its representatives during normal business hours to all records of its business and Assets and to its employees, accountants, customers and suppliers. However, no investigation by Purchaser shall limit responsibility of Seller for the representations, warranties and agreements herein. Seller shall maintain its assets in good order and repair, but no material alterations or improvements shall be made except with the written approval of Purchaser.*

3.3. Transfers of Certain Properties. *At or prior to the Closing, Sellers shall transfer to the Corporation its assets currently owned by either or both of them but used wholly or partially in its business and listed in Exhibit I-A. At or prior to the Closing, the Corporation shall transfer to Sellers certain assets listed in Exhibit I-B.*

3.4. Property Titles. *Prior to the Closing Date, Sellers shall at its expense furnish to Purchaser a title report and commitment from a title insurer acceptable to Purchaser for the issuance of ALTA title insurance policy insuring that title to all real property owned and to be by the Corporation at the Closing conforms in all respects to the representations and warranties contained in Section 3.1. Such commitment and policy shall contain no exceptions other than the standard printed exceptions contained in all ALTA policies issued for industrial properties by the insurer. The Sellers shall concurrently deliver to Purchaser a current ALTA survey of the real property by a registered land surveyor showing the locations of all buildings, improvements, easements, rights of way and encroachments. Purchaser shall have 10 days after receipt to notify Seller of any objections to title. If Purchaser shall elect to purchase a final policy, Purchaser shall notify Seller at least three business days prior to the Closing Date and shall pay half of the premium therefor.*

3.5. Cooperation After the Closing. *After the Closing, Sellers and Purchaser shall cooperate in transition of ownership of the Corporation from Sellers to Purchaser. Without limitation, if Sellers shall receive any assets of the Corporation after the Closing, they shall promptly deliver such assets to the Corporation. If the Sellers or the Corporation shall need any information for the preparation of tax returns, the other party shall furnish such information in reasonable prior notice.*

3.6. Confidential Information. *All technical and business information furnished by either party to the other party in connection with the transactions contemplated by this Agreement shall be maintained in confidence and shall not be disclosed to third parties or used except for the purposes of this Agreement. The foregoing obligations shall not apply to information which the recipient can show that (a) the information was previously known to it at the time of receipt, (b) was in the public domain at the time of receipt or thereafter entered the public domain without fault of the recipient, (c) corresponds to information which was furnished to the recipient by a third party lawfully entitled to do so, (d) was developed independently by personnel of the recipient who had no access to the information or (e) is required to be disclosed in legal proceedings. If this Agreement shall not be closed, Purchaser shall return to Seller all documents concerning its business or Assets obtained by Purchaser from Seller.*

3.7. Noncompetition. *Sellers each agree not to compete, directly or indirectly, with Purchaser in its business anywhere in the New England states, New York and New Jersey for a period of five years after the Closing Date or a period of one year after termination of employment, whichever is longer. Such competition shall include, without limitation, any employment or consultation with persons engaged or planning to engage in competition with its business and any investment in any such person.*

3.8. Finder's and Other Fees. *Except for a cash fee of $250,000 to be paid by Seller at the Closing to Jackson Brothers, Thomas & Co., Sellers jointly and severally represent to Purchaser that neither of them nor the Corporation, and Purchaser represents to Sellers that Purchaser, has retained any finder, broker or agent or agreed to pay a fee or commission to any such person. Each of them agrees to defend and indemnify the other parties against all loss, liability, cost and expense (including reasonable attorneys fees) in connection with any claim or claims which may be made against the other parties by reason of alleged agreements, understandings or arrangements for such a fee or commission by it.*

IV. CONDITIONS PRECEDENT TO THE OBLIGATIONS OF THE PARTIES

4.1. Conditions to the Obligations of Purchaser. *The obligation of Purchaser to close this Agreement is, at its option, subject to the following conditions:*

(a) Representations and Warranties. *The representations and warranties of Sellers shall continue to be accurate in all respects on the Closing Date, subject to changes occurring in the ordinary course of business and not materially adverse in nature, and they shall have performed all covenants and other obligations under this Agreement required to be performed by them at or before the Closing Date.*

(b) No Material Adverse Change. *There shall have been no material adverse change in its business, assets, financial condition or results of operations of the Corporation.*

(c) Delivery of Certain Documents. *Sellers and the Corporation shall have delivered at the Closing all of the documents described in Article V.*

4.2 Conditions to the Obligations of the Sellers and the Corporation. *The obligations of Sellers to close this Agreement are at the option of each of them, subject to the following conditions:*

(a) Representations and Warranties. *The representations and warranties of Purchaser shall continue to be materially accurate in all respects on the Closing Date and the Purchaser shall have performed all covenants and other agreements herein required to be performed by it on or before the Closing Date.*

(b) Delivery of Certain Documents. *The Purchaser shall have delivered at the Closing the payments and documents described in Article V.*

4.3 Failure of Fulfillment of Conditions; Remedies. *The parties each agree to make all reasonable efforts to fulfill their respective conditions and to cooperate with the other party in fulfillment of its conditions. If any party fails or refuses to perform this Agreement, the other party or parties shall be entitled to specific performance of this Agreement or such other remedies as may be granted in equity or law by a court of competent jurisdiction.*

V. DOCUMENTS TO BE DELIVERED AT THE CLOSING

5.1 Documents Delivered by the Sellers and the Corporation. *At the Closing, the Sellers and the Corporation shall deliver to the Purchaser the following documents:*

(a) *Such evidence of corporate existence, qualification, good standing, incumbency of officers adoption of resolutions and evidence of other corporate procedures and authority as may reasonably be requested by counsel for the Purchaser.*

(b) *Evidence that the property transfers described in Section 3.3 have been made.*

(c) A certificate signed by the Sellers updating and reaffirming the representations and warranties set forth in Section 2.1 and confirming performance of all the covenants set forth in Article III to the extent they are to be performed by them on or before the Closing Date.

(d) A "comfort letter" from Coopers, Anderson, Price & Co., dated the Closing Date, in the form attached as Exhibit J.

(e) A written opinion of Sellers' counsel, dated the Closing Date, in the form attached as Exhibit M.

(f) A release signed by each Seller in the form attached as Exhibit L.

(g) Certificates representing all 20,000 shares of Common stock held by the Shareholders together with stock powers endorsed in blank with the signature guarantees of a bank or member firm of the New York Stock Exchange.

(h) Employment Contracts in the form attached as Exhibit K *signed by the Corporation, Smith and Johnson.*

5.2 Documents to be Delivered by Purchaser. *At the Closing and upon fulfillment of the conditions described at Section 5.1 by the Sellers and the Corporation, the Purchaser shall deliver documents and make payments as follows:*

(a) Such evidence of corporate existence, qualification, good standing, incumbency of officers, adoption of resolutions and evidence of other corporate procedures and authority as may reasonably be requested by counsel for the Seller.

(b) A certificate signed by an officer of the Purchaser updating and reaffirming its representations and warranties set forth in Section 2.2 and confirming performance of all the covenants set forth in Article III to the extent they are to be performed by the Purchaser on or before the Closing date.

(c) A written opinion of Purchaser's counsel, dated the Closing Date, in the form attached as Exhibit M.

(d) A certified or official bank check for $1,250,000 payable to Smith.

(e) A certified or official bank check for $1,250,000 payable to Johnson.

5.3 Simultaneous Delivery. *All documents delivered at the Closing shall be deemed to have been delivered simultaneously.*

VI. GENERAL PROVISIONS

6.1 Survival; Indemnities. *All representations, warranties and agreements of the parties shall survive the Closing, notwithstanding investigations made by the parties. Sellers shall jointly and severally indemnify the Purchaser, and Purchaser shall indemnify Sellers against all loss, liability, damage and expense resulting from untruth, inaccuracy or incompleteness of the information contained in their respective representations and warranties or any failure to perform their respective agreements.*

6.2 Further Actions. *The parties agree to execute and deliver from time to time hereafter any and all such further documents and to take such further actions as shall be reasonably necessary to carry out the transactions contemplated by this Agreement.*

6.3 Nonassignability. *Neither this Agreement nor any rights thereunder may be assigned or otherwise transferred directly or indirectly by any party without the prior written consent of the other parties and any attempt to do so shall be null and void, provided that this Agreement and the rights and obligations herein shall inure to the benefit of, and be binding upon, the executors, administrators, heirs and successors of Smith and Johnson in the event of their death.*

6.4 Entire Agreement. *In entering into and closing this Agreement, no party has relied or shall rely upon any promises, representations and warranties not expressed herein, and this Agreement expresses their entire agreement on the subject matter.*

6.5 Amendment and Waiver. *Neither this Agreement nor any provision or provisions herein may be amended or waived except by a written amendment or new agreement executed by the parties.*

6.6 Governing Law. *The validity, interpretation, performance and enforcement of this Agreement shall be governed by the laws of New York. Each of the parties consents to the jurisdiction of the federal and state courts in New York in all matters relating to this Agreement. Sellers hereby appoint _____ _____ as the agent of each of them to receive process in any legal action or proceeding.*

6.7 Notices. *All notices or other communications hereunder shall be given in writing and shall be deemed to be, if duly given if delivered or mailed, first class postage prepaid, to the following addresses:*

6.8 Expenses. *The Sellers shall pay all costs and expenses incurred by them (including, without limitation, the payment of all fees and expenses of their counsel) and any tax on the sale or transfer of their shares and the Purchaser shall pay all costs and expenses incurred by it (including, without limitation, all fees and expenses of its counsel) in carrying out their respective obligations under this Agreement and the transactions contemplated herein.*

IN WITNESS WHEREOF, the parties have executed and delivered this Agreement as of the   day of   , 199__.

INTERNATIONAL
COMPUTERS, INC.

_____

John Smith

*By*_____

_____

Joseph Johnson

ABC ELECTRONICS
CORPORATION

*By*_____

President

Exhibit 14-3

ACQUISITION CONTRACT CHECKLIST

I.   PARTIES

    A.   *Merger:*

        Constituent corporations transitory subsidiary
        Parent providing shares or funds in triangular merger
        Parent or other shareholders agreeing to vote, refrain from competition, etc.

    B.   *Stock Purchase:*

        Shareholders of corporation to be sold
        Buyer and parent if it will provide shares, funds or other commitments

           NOTE: In a tender offer, the contract consists of the offering statement and letter of transmittal

    C.   *Assets Purchase:*

        Seller and buyer
        Seller's parent or other shareholders agreeing to vote, refrain from competition, etc.
        Buyer's parent agreeing to provide shares, funds or other commitments

II.   RECITALS

        Background and major objectives
        Structure (merger, stock sale or assets sale)
        Plan of reorganization under § 368, IRC, if applicable
        Kind and method of payment

III.   THE TRANSACTION

    A.   *Merger:*

        Mechanical steps to obtain board and shareholder approval and file certificate of merger
        Exchange of securities and shares of acquired corporation for securities, shares and/or cash provided by the acquiring corporation or its parent—usually stated in amounts per share
        Dissenting shareholders (limits and procedures)
        Mechanical steps to accomplish the exchanges
        § 338 (h) (10) election, if applicable

B.   *Stock Sale:*

   *Agreement to sell and buy shares for a price payable in securities,
      shares or money*
   § 338 (h) (10) election, if applicable

C.   *Assets Sale:*

   *Agreement to sell defined assets for a price payable in securities,
      shares or money*
   Definition of assets included and excluded
   Assumption of liabilities and obligations
   Allocation of purchase price among assets

D.   *Common to All Structures:*

   Deferred price payments
   Contingent additional price payments
   Escrow of part of price
   *Methods for determining the price such as market price formulae,
      inventory count and valuation, receivables, etc.*
   *Compliance with § 368 (a) (1) definitions and other requirements
      for a tax-free reorganization, if applicable*
   *Planning for imputed interest, original issue discount (OID) and in-
      stallment sale*
   *Transfer, sales and use, stamp, recording, filing and other taxes in-
      cluding differences in income tax treatment under federal and
      state law*
   *Mechanisms of exchanging shares including endorsement, signature
      guarantees, cash for fractional shares, exchange agent, etc.*

IV.   REPRESENTATIONS AND WARRANTIES

A.   *Seller:*
   1. *Corporate status and good standing of seller and subsidiaries*
   2. *Corporate power and absence of conflict with charter, by-laws,
      agreements, laws, etc.*
   3. *Authorization by board and shareholders, if applicable*
   4. *Capitalization and absence of commitments to make capital
      changes and distributions*
   5. *Title to shares and other securities to be sold or exchanged and
      the fully paid status of shares*
   6. *Title to assets to be sold or exchanged*
   7. *Financial statements, including unaudited interim periods, and
      absence of material adverse changes*
   8. *Tax returns and obligations*
   9. *Contracts, leases, licenses, etc.*

10. *Litigation, claims, investigations, contingent liabilities, etc.*
11. *Compliance with laws, etc.*
12. *Environment and safety*
13. *ERISA and other employee benefit obligations*
14. *Personnel, labor and equal employment*
15. *Insurance*
16. *Intellectual properties*
17. *Government contracts*
18. *Condition of facilities and equipment*
19. *Distributors, agents, consultants, etc.*
20. *Transactions with affiliated persons*
21. *Brokers, finders, etc.*
22. *Full disclosure*
23. *Investment representation as to unregistered shares and securities*

B. *Buyer:*

1. *Corporate status and good standing*
2. *Corporate power and absence of conflict with charter, by-laws, agreements, laws, etc.*
3. *Authorization by board and shareholders, if applicable*
4. *Capitalization and absence of commitments to make capital changes and distributions, if shares or other securities will be issued as payment*
5. *Validity and fully paid status of shares and other securities to be issued as payment*
6. *Financial statements, including unaudited interim reports, and absence of material adverse changes, if shares or other securities will be issued as payment*
7. *Full disclosure in 10-K, 10-Q and 8-K reports, proxy statements and other documents delivered, if shares or other securities will be delivered as payment*
8. *Absence of litigation and need for consents of third parties*

V. COVENANTS

1. *Antitrust and other government clearances and rulings*
2. *Corporate approval steps including board and shareholder meetings, proxy statements and solicitation, etc.*
3. *Tender offer filings and procedures and management recommendations*
4. *Listing of shares and securities*
5. *Registration of shares and securities*
6. *Conduct of the business in ordinary course including restrictions on capital changes and distributions*

7. *Cooperation with "due diligence" review*
8. *Procedures for obtaining title insurance*
9. *Confidentiality*
10. *Noncompetition*
11. *Employment contracts*
12. *Commitments relating to employees and benefits*
13. *Supply and customer contracts*
14. *WARN and Exon-Florio notifications*
15. *Bulk transfer waiver or procedures*
16. *Finders, brokers, etc.*
17. *Restrictive legends on unregistered shares*
18. *Procedures to obtain consents of lessors and parties to material contracts and to transfer permits and registrations*
19. *Indemnification:*
    Representations and warranties
    Covenants
    Liabilities assumed and retained
20. *Agreements to obtain fairness opinions and solvency letters*
21. *Agreements for performance of closing date audits; auditors' reports*
22. *Agreements to remedy environmental violations and conditions likely to result in liability or expense*
23. *Transitional agreements for sharing of facilities, personnel, trademarks, literature, etc.*
24. *Resignations of directors and officers, if applicable*
25. *Amendments of charter, by-laws and contracts essential to the agreements*

VI.   CONDITIONS

A.   *Buyer:*

1. *Continued accuracy of representations and warranties*
2. *No material adverse change*
3. *Performance of seller's covenants including corporate approval*
4. *No adverse government action*
5. *Delivery by seller of specified closing documents*

B.   *Seller:*

1. *Continued accuracy of representations and warranties*
2. *Performance of buyer's covenants*
3. *No adverse government action*
4. *Delivery by buyer of specified closing documents and payments*

VII.   CLOSING DOCUMENTS AND PAYMENTS

A.   *Seller:*

1. *Officers certificate as to corporate documents and approval, incumbency, continued accuracy of representations and warranties, performance of covenants, no material adverse change, etc.*
2. *Evidence of antitrust clearance and other government actions*
3. *Consents to assign contracts, leases, etc.*
4. *Evidence of amendment or termination of shareholders agreement*
5. *"Comfort" letter from auditors*
6. *Solvency letter*
7. *Resignations of directors and officers*
8. *Evidence of filing Certificate of Merger, if a merger*
9. *Evidence of limited exercise of appraisal rights, if a merger*
10. *Stock certificates, endorsed with signature guarantees, if a merger or stock sale*
11. *Bills of sale, deed and assignments, if a sales of assets*
12. *Title insurance binders*
13. *Investment letter, if unregistered securities issued*
14. *Employment contracts*
15. *Supply and purchase contracts*
16. *Tax rulings or opinions*
17. *Non-foreign affidavits under FIRPTA and § 899, IRC if adopted*
18. *Delivery of escrowed shares, securities or money*
19. *Opinion of counsel*
20. *Receipts*

B.   *Buyer:*

1. *Officers' certificate as to corporate documents, and approval, incumbency, continued accuracy of representations and warranties, performance of covenants, no material adverse change, etc.*
2. *Evidence of antitrust clearance, i.e. termination of H-S-R waiting period*
3. *Order accelerating effective date of registration of shares or securities, if applicable*
4. *Evidence of listing shares or securities, if applicable*
5. *Evidence of filing Certificate of Merger, if a merger*
6. *Assumption of liabilities, if an assets purchase*
7. *Evidence of election of buyer officers to officer and directors' positions, if applicable*
8. *Assignment of contracts, leases, etc. if an assets purchase*
9. *Wire transfer or certified check, if price payable in cash*
10. *Stock certificates, promissory notes, etc. if price payable by those instruments*

11.   *BE-13 report and related reports, if applicable*
12.   *Opinion of counsel*
13.   *Receipts*

VIII. TERMINATION

A.   *Events of termination*

    1.   *Mutual agreement*
    2.   *Failure to fulfill conditions*
    3.   *Material breach*
    4.   *Expiration of time limit*

B.   *Methods to terminate*

    1.   *Automatic*
    2.   *Notice*
    3.   *Opportunities to cure*

C.   *Effects of termination*

    1.   *Liability*
    2.   *Costs and expenses*

D.   *Remedies for breach*

    1.   *Money damages*
    2.   *Specific performance and other equitable remedies*
    NOTE: Many acquisition agreements omit termination provisions because their discussion introduces a negative outlook to the negotiations and they tend to be a simple recital of steps which the parties can take without elaboration in the agreement.

IX.   GENERAL PROVISIONS

1.   *Survival of representations, warranties and covenants*
2.   *Integrated agreement*
3.   *Amendment and waiver*
4.   *Nonassignability and binding effect on successors*
5.   *Governing law*
6.   *Notices*
7.   *Publicity*
8.   *Consent to jurisdiction, if appropriate*
9.   *Arbitration, if appropriate*
10.   *Severability, if appropriate*
11.   *Time of the essence, if appropriate*
12.   *Counterparts*
13.   *Expenses*

15

The Acquisition Contract: Asset Purchase Agreements Special Provisions and Agreements

Asset purchase agreements differ in form and substance from the stock purchase agreements described in the previous chapter, but also have many similarities.

The fundamental difference is that an asset purchase agreement must describe in detail all of the business and assets to be purchased and any liabilities and obligations to be assumed. Despite the extra effort required, asset purchases are probably the most common type of business acquisition because freedom from unwanted liabilities makes some troubled businesses salable only by the asset method. The "stepped up" tax basis of assets purchased in a taxable acquisition is also an important factor.

DEFINING THE ASSETS

Where the buyer acquires assets, particularly if the assets do not constitute all of the assets of a seller but only a portion of such assets, the definition of the property being acquired may be complicated.

Division's Assets for Cash.

Article I

Agreement to Sell and Purchase

Subject to the terms and conditions contained in this agreement, seller agrees to sell to buyer, and buyer agrees to purchase from the seller, the assets and property described in Article II hereof, consisting of all of the assets and property of sell-

er's XYZ Division ("division") other than cash, accounts receivable and certain incidental items therein noted. As used herein, the terms "assets and property of division" shall mean property in the possession of division on seller's or division's books and recorded or standing in the name of division.

Article II

Assets and Price

The said assets and property and the purchase price of the said assets and property shall be as follows:

1. *Land listed on Exhibit A, attached hereto*	$ 75,000.00
2. *Buildings and plant known as 1000 West Clinton Street, Chicago, Illinois*	263,000.00
3. *Machinery, equipment tools, jigs, office furniture and fixtures, major items of which are listed on Exhibit B attached hereto*	729,000.00
4. *Nonexpendable dies*	100,000.00
5. *Inventories*	(Book Value)
6. *Prepaid items other than insurance and prepaid royalty*	16,000.00
7. *Patents and patent applications listed on Exhibit D attached hereto and all other miscellaneous assets of division being sold hereunder*	5,000.00
Total	

The preceding clauses illustrate an attempt to define assets of a division of a seller brought by a buyer for cash. As is often done in a cash transaction, the purchase price is allocated to the separate assets by the parties in an attempt to fix the tax consequences of the acquisition. Sometimes in such instances, the purchase price is stated as a lump sum and the parties rely upon their own allocation, outside appraisals and their persuasive powers to convince the Internal Revenue Service of the correctness of the allocation. The inventory value was left blank, to be filled in after the taking of a physical inventory and the pricing of the inventory under a complicated formula.

BUYER'S ASSUMPTION OF LIABILITIES

When the buyer acquires stock of a seller the liabilities of the corporate business continue, since no change in the corporate entity has occurred. On the other hand, when a buyer acquires assets for cash, the buyer generally assumes only liabilities specifically assumed by the buyer in the contract (subject only to bulk sales or similar laws). Defining what liabilities, if any, are assumed by the buyer must be part of the acquisition contract.

Assumption of Liabilities

1. Subject to the provisions of this agreement and plan of reorganization, buyer will assume as of the closing date and pay or discharge the following obligations and liabilities of seller:

(a) Liabilities disclosed on its balance sheet as of April 30, 199__ attached as Exhibit A in the amounts recorded on the books as of closing date, subject to the audit adjustments provided hereinafter;

(b) The law suits numbered 1, 2 and 3 in Exhibit C;

(c) The contracts and agreements listed in Exhibit D; and

(d) Leases and agreements listed in Exhibit F and commitments for the purchase of raw materials and sales of merchandise and under contracts, agreements, and commitments, all as made in the ordinary course and conduct of business since April 30, 199__ the closing date.

Except as set forth in this Section, buyer will assume no other obligations or liabilities (including, without limitation, tort, product liability, environmental or equal employment opportunity) in connection with the purchase of assets. Seller acknowledges that the purchase price is fair and agrees to apply the purchase price promptly to pay or provide fully for all debts and obligations, whether fixed or contingent, taking into account available liability insurance coverage.

INDEMNIFICATION

To the extent that the buyer assumes liabilities and obligations, the seller will usually require that the buyer agree to indemnify and defend the seller against all loss, liability, cost and expense related to the liabilities assumed. This is an important provision because, if the buyer fails to pay and perform as promised, the disappointed creditors are sure to assert claims against the seller and they may sue. The indemnification provision protects the seller against harm from these disputes. The buyer normally agrees to the indemnification provision once it has agreed to the liabilities to be assumed. From the buyer's point of view, if some of the liabilities should be contested, it is better to protect the seller and require his cooperation than to have the seller attempt to defend his own interests in a manner which differs from positions taken by the buyer.

Correspondingly, the buyer will usually require that the seller agree to indemnify and defend the buyer against all loss, liability, cost and expenses related to liabilities not assumed. At first glance, this provision seems simple, but it is often very difficult to negotiate. Sellers readily understand that they should protect the buyer against their problems or failures to pay obvious liabilities such as bank loans, accounts payable and taxes clearly owed prior to the closing date. However, some sellers become very anxious about indemnification of liabilities incurred before the closing date but not identified until thereafter. They begin to fear that the buyer will use the indemnification to recover much of the purchase price by claiming the seller is somehow responsible for operating errors and asset deterioration after the closing. Sellers and their counsel will seek contract language assuring that the buyer cannot shift the post-closing risks of the business back to the seller. A few sellers insist that some or all risks be accepted "AS IS" by the buyer.

The acquisition contract usually also requires that the seller indemnify and defend the buyer against loss, liability, cost and expenses related to the breaches of the representations, warranties and covenants of seller in the acquisition contract. While sellers generally understand that buyers want assurances about the business and assets, they are also concerned about the potential for unfair shifting of risks back to them after the sale. Sellers usually seek to limit the indemnification and survival of the representations and warranties to a period of one or two years after the closing date and to limit the related indemnification to the same period.

Buyers also have anxieties primarily about defects, liabilities and obligations which are identified after the closing date. They fear that the seller will pay, distribute or donate the purchase price to other persons and be unwilling or unable to pay. These anxieties have been greatly compounded by court-developed doctrines of successor liability and the virtual nullification of statutes of limitations during the last two decades with the result that thousands of lawsuits are now brought for alleged injuries and damages traced to "occurrences" which began decades ago.

The indemnification, survival and related provisions in the form of Assets Purchase Agreement presented later in this chapter show techniques which can be used to allocate these risks between a seller and a buyer.

The reader should note the important relationship of insurance coverage to the allocation of risks. To the extent that the risks are covered by liability insurance policies issued by responsible and solvent insurers, the problems of the seller and the buyer are reduced. Unfortunately, many sellers never received or did not retain copies of policies. Insurers and brokers, even the so-called independent brokers, regularly decline to furnish copies of old policies. Thus, it is an important step for the buyer to require the seller to identify and preserve as many older policies as possible. If serious liability problems exist, it may be necessary to retain an insurance archival firm, such as IAG Incorporated, to reconstruct coverage.

Those interested in successor liability generally should review articles titled "Evaluation of Environmental Liability" and "Newly Emerging Liabilities to Employees" in *The Acquisition Yearbook-1991*, Shea, *New York Institute of Finance* (Simon & Schuster), 1991.

REPRESENTATIONS AND WARRANTIES

Examples of representations and warranties contained in an assets acquisition agreement are included in the contract form in this chapter. The reader should observe that they are more detailed than those contained in the contracts in Chapters 14 and 16. This is customary because the seller and buyer must actually decide which assets and liabilities will be transferred and retained. The parties to stock purchase agreements and merger agreements could, and sometimes do, insist on the same degree of detail. However, once they accept the concept that all assets and liabilities will be transferred, they tend to focus on protection relating to major items and to accept (perhaps overlook) lesser items, although some may be significant. Counsel preparing acquisition contracts should keep these tendencies in mind when advising clients.

COVENANTS

The acquisition contract usually contains an article which includes a variety of covenants (promises) to be performed by the seller and buyer before and after the closing. Examples are promises by the seller to conduct the business only in the ordinary course until the closing; promises of buyer and seller to seek and cooperate in obtaining consents of government agencies and other third parties needed for the closing; confidentiality restrictions; noncompetition provisions; contracts for future employment or to purchase or supply products after the closing and commitments to preserve and share documents and other information.

Article IV of the form of Assets Purchase Agreement presented later in this chapter shows examples of covenants.

CONDITIONS PRECEDENT TO THE CLOSING

Both the buyer and seller will require the insertion of specified conditions precedent in the contract. If a condition precedent is not fulfilled, the party affected may refuse to carry out its obligations under the acquisition contract, and not suffer any legal liability as a result of its refusal. The model acquisition contracts in this chapter and in Chapters 14 and 16 contain examples of conditions precedent.

OTHER PROVISIONS

This section contains a number of provisions which illustrate the wide variety of subjects on which buyer and seller should reach agreement, especially in an assets purchase agreement.

(a) Stock for Assets—Section 368(a)(1)(C) Reorganization

As described in Chapter 11, an assets acquisition can meet the requirements for a tax free reorganization under Section 368(a)(1)(C) of the Internal Revenue Code. The following text shows an example of the introduction of such an agreement:

AGREEMENT AND PLAN OF REORGANIZATION ("Agreement") made as of the ____ day of November, 1990, by and between BUYER, a New Jersey corporation, having a place of business at 5000 Madison Avenue, New York, New York 10019 ("Buyer"), and SELLER, a Wisconsin corporation, having a place of business at 8000 Main Street, Milwaukee, Wisconsin 53502 ("Seller").

WITNESSETH:

The Reorganization, pursuant to the provisions of Section 368(a)(1)(C) of the Internal Revenue Code of 1954, as amended, will comprise the acquisition by

Buyer of substantially all of the property, assets, goodwill and business as a going concern of Seller subject to certain liabilities of Seller as hereinafter provided, in exchange solely for a part of Buyer's voting stock and the prompt dissolution of Seller and the distribution of said stock to the shareholders of Seller according to their respective interests, all upon and subject to the terms and conditions of the Agreement hereinafter set forth.

In order to consummate the Plan of Reorganization herein set forth and in consideration of the mutual benefits to be derived therefrom and of the mutual agreements hereinafter contained, the parties thereto do represent, warrant, covenant and agree as follows:

(b) All of Seller's Assets.

Assets to Be Acquired by Buyer

On the closing date hereinafter provided, and upon the terms and conditions herein provided, buyer shall acquire all of seller's assets, business and properties, including without limitation upon the generality of the foregoing, all of seller's right, title and interest in and to its real estate, plants, structures, fixtures, processes, equipment, machinery, tools, dies, jigs, appliances, cash, notes and accounts receivable, executory contracts and purchase orders for the furnishing of goods or the rendition of services to seller; its inventories, materials and supplies, (including raw materials, work in process and manufactured products and prototype models); its patents, inventions, licenses, trademarks and trade names of every sort and kind; its books of account and records which in any way relate to the conduct of its business; the name "XYZ" as a trademark and trade name, together with the goodwill symbolized by said name and by the business, and all other franchises or other privileges used, or of use in, or acquired for use by or in connection with the business, including gas, power, light, water and other tributory and utility properties being and intended to be all of the assets, business and properties of every kind and nature, and wherever situated, of seller.

(c) Seller's Tax Refund Claims Excluded.

Excluded from this sale are: claims for, and the proceeds (including interest) of, refunds of federal income taxes paid in respect of income of seller for any of the three calendar years next preceding the year in which the closing date shall occur, whether or not in being or known at the closing date and including, but not by way of limitation, any claims for refund founded upon or arising by reason of a loss realized by seller in respect of the transactions contemplated by this agreement. Seller hereby indemnifies and agrees to save buyer harmless in respect of federal income tax deficiencies for any of such three calendar years, but only up to the aggregate amount of refunds of such taxes received in respect of such years and hereby reserved to seller. All proceeds (including interest) of claims for refund of federal income taxes paid in respect of income of seller for the fourth year prior to the year in which the closing date shall occur and preceding years, whether or not in being or known at the closing date, shall pass to buyer; and seller undertakes diligently to file and press any such refund claims, under the direction and at the expense of buyer, and to pay to buyer the proceeds realized therefrom.

THE PURCHASE PRICE

Sometimes the purchase price is a fixed number of dollars or a fixed number of shares of stock of the buyer. On other occasions, however, formulae are utilized to define the amount of cash or stock the buyer will pay; sometimes these formulae are based upon future earnings of the seller's business.

(a) A Definition of the Price of Inventory.

The purchase price of the inventories shall be the value of the inventories as at the closing date at the lower of cost or replacement market value in accordance with good accounting practice consistently followed by seller at seller's division ("division"), subject to the modifications set forth below. The inventory valuation shall be based on a physical count conducted at the plant of division immediately following the closing date pursuant to procedures satisfactory to Right, Right, Right & Co., buyer's independent auditors. As soon as practicable after the physical count, buyer shall cause the inventories to be valued in accordance with the principles set forth herein. The expense of taking and pricing inventories shall be borne equally by buyer and seller, except that seller will pay in any event the amount accrued at the closing date by division for auditing purposes. In determining the value of the inventories, Exhibit I, which describes inventory valuation methods of division, shall be deemed in accordance with good accounting practice.

This provision providing a method of valuing inventory permits the attachment of an exhibit to include the detail with which the value of inventory must sometimes be defined.

(b) A Formula Price Based on Market Value of Buyer's Stock:

The stock to be delivered by buyer pursuant to this agreement and plan of reorganization shall be the voting common stock of buyer, approved for listing on official notice of issuance, of the same class of voting common stock which is at present issued and outstanding, and which shares buyer shall have full and lawful authority to deliver, and which, when so delivered, shall have full and equal voting rights and shall be fully paid and nonassessable.

The number of shares of such stock to be delivered shall be determined by the method of computation as provided in (a) below, but subject to the limitations provided in (b) and (c) below, and then subject to adjustment as provided in (d) below.

(a) Initial computation: In making the initial computation the parties shall determine a number of full shares which have a total value as nearly equal to

$6,370,000.00 as is practicable, by dividing into $6,370,000.00 the average of the closing quotations of buyer's voting common stock on the New York Stock Exchange for a period beginning on and including December 20, 199___, and ending on and including January 20, 199___.

(b) High limitation: If the number of shares as computed in (a) above is exceeds 79,494 shares, such number of shares computed shall be deemed to be 79,494 shares.

(c) Low limitation: If the number of shares as computed in (a) above is less than 70,876 shares, such number of shares computed shall be deemed to be 70,876 shares.

(d) Adjustment: The total number of shares of stock to be delivered as computed in accordance with (a) above, and subjected to the limitations in (b) and (c) above, ("Total Shares") shall then be subject to downward adjustment as follows:

For each share of seller's Class A and Class B common stock "dissenting" the Total Shares shall be reduced by that fraction of the Total Shares which has as its numerator the number one, and as its denominator, the number 192,816.

The term "dissenting" as used herein means the action of any shareholder of seller in respect of holdings of seller's shares, or a portion thereof, in demanding payment therefor as provided in Section 180.72 of Chapter 180, Title XVII of the Wisconsin Business Corporation Law.

In no event shall the Total Shares exceed 79,494 shares nor be less than 70,876 shares (except in the case of stock splits or combinations of shares requiring proportionate adjustment of the number of shares to carry out the intent of this agreement and plan of reorganization).

The preceding provision illustrates one method for a buyer and seller to agree on a dollar purchase price and convert it into shares. The averaging of closing prices is an attempt to relate the number of shares delivered at the closing to the agreed upon dollar price on a realistic basis. The upper and lower limits of shares to be delivered result from an attempt on the part of the buyer to protect the earnings per share from the seller's business by limiting the shares delivered by the buyer. The reduction in shares delivered by the buyer as a result of dissenting shareholders of the seller is required where the seller's shareholders have a right to dissent in a merger or assets transaction.

(c) A Formula Price Based on Future Earnings of Seller's Business.

The following clause provides for the payment of additional purchase price by the buyer based upon earnings of the seller's business, after allowing a pre-tax return to buyer of 20 percent of buyer's aggregate investment in the seller's business:

The balance of the purchase price for seller's assets shall be determined in accordance with the following procedures:

(a) For each of the calendar years 199___ through 199___, the pre-tax profit of the business acquired by buyer hereunder shall be determined in accordance with the usual accounting practice of buyer as of the end of such years.

(b) For each of the calendar years 199__ through 199__, the aforesaid pre-tax profit shall be applied as follows:

(i) That portion of the pre-tax profit equal to 20 percent of the total of the initial purchase price determined in accordance with paragraph 1 above when added to the "average additional investment" in the operation of the business acquired by buyer hereunder in the form of working capital or contribution of assets or cash to capital made by buyer from the closing date to the end of the year in question (such total hereinafter referred to as the "aggregate buyer investment"), shall be retained by buyer.

The "average additional investment" shall be determined for any period by averaging the monthly totals of such additional investment as reflected on the monthly balance sheets during such period, and multiplying such monthly average by the number of months in the period in question.

(ii) The remainder of the pre-tax profit for such years, after the setting aside of the amount noted in (i) above the account of buyer, will be divided between buyer and seller in the following proportions:

> *Buyer   60%*
> *Seller   40%*

Seller's proportion will be paid within three months following the year for which it was determined as additional purchase price for the assets noted in paragraph 1(a) above;

(iii) If the pre-tax profit for any of the calendar years 199__ through 199__ is less than 20 percent of the aggregate buyer investment determined in accordance with paragraph (b)(i) above, the pre-tax profit for subsequent years will be retained by buyer to the extent necessary to make up past deficiencies.

(c) In no event will the aggregate of all payments to seller under this agreement exceed a maximum sum of $1,250,000.

A contingent price, where a buyer pays a seller a greater purchase price if the seller's future earnings justify such greater price, may bring a buyer and seller to agree on price where their estimates of the present value of a business are far apart. The buyer may say, "All right if you think your business will earn that much in the future, I'll pay your price, provided your estimate of future earnings is realized." In such provisions for determining the price on the basis of earnings, the definition of future net earnings of the seller's business must be drafted with great care to avoid future disputes between the parties.

(d) Contingent Price Formula—Detailed Definition of Future Earnings.

Exhibit 15–3 contains a contractual provision by which a buyer agrees to pay a contingent price based partially on future earnings during a period of years after the acquisition. The accounting principles and policies to be used in determining

1. Employee Stock Options.

In some instances, a buyer will refuse to assume any liability for previously outstanding stock options of seller's employees. In others, the buyer will agree to substitute options on his stock for the options held on the seller's stock. Such substitution may be made without tax consequence to the employees of seller, provided the substitution complies with the requirements of the Internal Revenue Code. Generally, under these requirements the substituted option may not place the employee in a better financial position than under the old option.

When the buyer assumes no liability for outstanding options:

The liabilities assumed by buyer hereunder shall not include any obligation on the part of buyer with respect to the stock options outstanding on the date of this agreement for employees of seller. To the extent that seller shall settle or satisfy its obligations under such options after the date of this agreement by either buying shares in the open market for such purpose or by making cash payments, such expenditures shall be for its own account and shall be credited on the closing date against the purchase price to be paid by buyer hereunder. The purchase of its shares by seller for this purpose shall not constitute a violation of the covenant by seller contained in Section 3(e) of Article IV.

When the buyer will substitute buyer's options:

Buyer shall substitute for the stock options granted under seller's incentive option plan, to the extent that such options have not become exercisable prior to the closing date, options to purchase shares of buyer's common stock in lieu of shares of capital stock of seller, on a basis which will comply with the Internal Revenue Code and which, subject to such compliance, will on the closing date be as favorable to the holders of such options as their options with respect to seller's capital stock.

2. A Collective Bargaining Agreement.

Buyer will assume all obligations for hourly-paid employees concurred after the closing date under the agreement between division and International Union of Electrical, Radio and Machine Workers, A.F.L.-C.I.O., Local 204, with respect to all employees transferred to buyer as provided in paragraph (a) above. The parties will take all steps necessary and use their best efforts to amend the said agreement in such fashion as to provide two separate agreements, one covering the employees to be transferred to buyer and the other covering employees retained on the seller's payroll located at the Los Angeles plant.

3. Employee Security Clearances.

With respect to the employees of division taken over by buyer as of the closing date, seller will retain all personnel security clearance records and will, to the extent permitted by government regulations, make such records available to buyer as required from time to time.

4. Books, Records, and Classified Documents.

A sale of a division in which classified documents are involved:

Books and Records

(a) With the exception of division's (1) books of account, income tax returns and correspondence and documents relating thereto, (2) document log recording income and outgoing transmission of classified documents, (3) record of reproduction of classified documents, (4) certification of distribution of classified documents, (5) accounting for all secret security information and (6) visitors register, on the closing date seller will deliver to buyer all of division's correspondence, files, drawings, data and other records, papers and documents and manuals or portions thereof relating specifically to, or used by, division. With respect to those classified documents which are to be transferred to buyer hereunder, seller and buyer will take all steps necessary to obtain the consent for the transfer of such documents from the governmental authorities respectively involved or for other disposition of such documents. Pending transfer, responsibility for and custody of such classified documents will rest in seller.

5. Avoiding Double Dividend to Seller's Stockholders.

Should the record date for the payment of the next quarterly dividend on buyer's common stock (buyer's date) occur subsequent to the record date for the payment of the next quarterly dividend on seller's common or preferred stock (seller's record date) then, the closing date shall not, in any event, occur on any date subsequent to the seller's record date and before the buyer's record date. It is the intention of the parties that the shareholders of seller not receive both the next regular buyer's dividend and the next regular seller's dividend.

6. Transfer of Seller's Assets to Buyer's Subsidiary Rather Than to Buyer.

This may be accomplished tax-free under the Internal Revenue Code:

On the Closing Date the Stockholder will transfer to Buyer or the Buyer's Subsidiary, as Buyer may elect, the number of shares of Common Stock of each Corporation set forth on Exhibit A hereto as issued and outstanding, such shares to constitute all of the outstanding capital stock of each Corporation. All certificates representing shares of such stock shall be in form for transfer by delivery and all transfer taxes payable on transfer thereof shall be paid by the Stockholder.

7. Novation of Customer Contracts.

Often, particularly when government contracts are involved, the question of whether the buyer or seller should be responsible for performance becomes of importance. Sometimes, where contracts are not novated, the buyer agrees to perform for the seller's account, but on other occasions the buyer agrees to perform for its own account—as in the provision below:

> *It is agreed by the parties hereto that the contracts listed on Schedule B are contracts which are to be the subject of novation agreements between buyer, seller, and the third parties to the contracts. Seller and buyer agree that they will use their best efforts to effect such novations. The work called for under such contracts from and after such novations, which shall be as of the closing date, shall be performed by buyer for the account of buyer and buyer shall hold seller free from any loss arising from any claim or litigation arising from such work. From and after the closing date, buyer shall assume all losses and retain all profits arising from such contracts.*
>
> *In the event that novation agreements are not entered into through factors beyond the control of either party hereto, then buyer shall, nevertheless, perform such work as is required for the account of buyer and profits or losses therefrom shall be treated the same as if such contracts were novated.*
>
> *With respect to any cost-plus-fixed-fee contract or field service contract listed in Schedule B, if additional funding of any contract appears necessary prior to transfer, buyer and seller will coordinate in a request, as may be mutually considered appropriate and timely, for such additional funding.*

When the buyer agrees to perform non-novated contracts for the account of the seller:

> *Buyer and seller agree to use their best efforts to effect novations of the aforesaid obligations and liabilities assumed by buyer hereunder. If any customer contracts to be assumed by buyer hereunder are not assignable by their terms and the parties are unable to effect novations of them, buyer will nevertheless perform the work thereunder for the account of seller at the price and in accordance with the other terms and conditions provided in such customer contracts. Except as just noted, the work under all sales contracts and commitments assumed by buyer hereunder will be performed by buyer for its account and buyer will indemnify and hold seller harmless from and against any loss or liability arising from any claim or litigation relating to work performed by buyer.*

8. A Covenant Not to Compete.

From a business point of view a buyer may want a seller not to compete in the business which the buyer is acquiring. This is particularly true where a buyer is acquiring a division or product line of the seller, rather than the whole of the seller's business and the employees intend to remain with the seller. From the buyer's point of view, if the buyer is at all vulnerable under the antitrust laws, it should weigh the economic value of the covenant not to compete against the legal implications. Furthermore, the buyer should keep the covenant not to compete within legal bounds or it will not be enforceable. If the seller is a diversified company, it must be careful to define a noncompetition area as narrowly as possible to avoid restriction on normal future growth. A clause to reconcile these viewpoints, where a division was sold, follows:

Covenant Not to Compete

A. Subject to the exceptions herein provided, seller agrees that for a period of two (2) years after the closing date, seller will not, directly or indirectly, engage in the United States in the manufacture, distribution, or contract development of the following division products:

1. An electronic data display system which internally generates alphanumeric characters and geometric symbols and displays them on the face of a cathode ray tube in response to external signals;

2. Simulators for training of crews of manned aircraft in operation of the following airborne equipment; radar, electronic countermeasures, gunnery and bombing systems;

3. Radar transponder beacons designed to assist in the radar tracking of drones, missiles and aircraft; and

4. General purpose automatic test equipment employing the concept of standard modular units of the general type described in that certain brochure captioned "Soldier, Series 500" published by seller (division), or the specific modular units described therein as an end product for use in such equipment.

Provided, however, that seller may develop, manufacture or distribute any of the above products as and only as a part of a system or major sub-system of substantially larger scope.

B. Seller further agrees that for a period of two (2) years from closing date, seller will not directly or indirectly within the United States (1) solicit or accept work which is a direct follow-on to work under contracts performed or being performed by division prior to closing date except as a second source to buyer or (2) represent, in connection with seller proposals for new business, that it retains the specific group of technical talent through which seller performed on division contracts prior to the closing date or through which seller performed on contracts at the Electronic Division, El Paso, California, on the products defined in paragraph A above. This restriction does not extend under any circumstances and in any manner to a description of the qualifications and experience of individuals within seller.

C. Buyer agrees that the foregoing covenants not to compete and restrictions imposed upon seller shall become nonoperable in their entirety in the event of a declared national defense emergency or a state of war and shall become nonoperable with respect to any product or system defined above, the marketing of which buyer ceases to actively pursue or which the United States government strongly urges seller to supply.

D. Nothing contained in the foregoing paragraphs shall be construed as restricting seller from the manufacture, distribution or contract development of any of the foregoing products through a business acquired by seller after the closing date which business is partly but not primarily engaged in the manufacture, distribution or contract development of any of the foregoing products.

E. Seller agrees that it will not during the above-mentioned two (2) year period, directly or indirectly endeavor to recruit any employees of buyer, including but not limited to division employees whom buyer elects to retain.

9. Noninfringement and Invention Assignment.

Particularly when a seller's business involves technical know-how or trade secrets, a buyer may wish to receive assurances that the seller's processes or products do not infringe any other inventions, that seller is not improperly utilizing another's trade secrets, and that the seller's employees have properly assigned all inventions and know-how to seller. The representation set forth below treats these areas in one clause, although, often, the two areas are treated in separate clauses in acquisition contracts:

Except as may be set forth in the Schedule referred to in Section 5.5, Seller has never been charged with infringement or violation of any adversely held patent, trademark, trade name or copyright and there are no unexpired patents, except patents under which Seller is licensed, with claims reading on products of seller or on apparatus or methods employed by Seller in manufacturing or producing the same, or any patented invention or application therefor which would materially and adversely affect any product or operation of Seller, nor is Seller using or in any way making use of any patentable or unpatentable inventions, or any confidential information or trade secrets, of any former employer of any present or past employee of Seller except as a result of the acquisition by either of them of the business of such former employer. All engineering and technical employees of the Seller engaged in research and development work are obliged by the terms of their employment to assign to Seller any improvements in their respective products or in new products in their respective fields of activity, or in methods or machines for making any such products, which they have devised or invented, either solely or jointly with others.

10. SEC Registration of Buyer's Stock.

(i) No SEC Registration—Stock Legend.

When a buyer delivers stock in payment of an acquisition and the stock is not to be registered with the SEC, the contract often provides that the buyer may imprint a legend on its stock certificates, as follows:

All certificates representing shares of Buyer's Common Stock issued to the Stockholders of the merger of Seller into Buyer shall bear the following legend:

The shares represented by this Certificate have not been registered under the Securities Act of 1933, as amended. The shares have been acquired for investment and may not be sold, offered for sale or transferred in the absence of an effective registration statement for the shares under the Securities Act of 1933, as amended, or an opinion of counsel to the Company that registration is not required under said Act.

(ii) Agreement to Register in the Future.

Sometimes a seller's stockholders will only accept unregistered stock, where a buyer will contract to register its stock in the future. The following clause sets forth in some detail the elements that should be contained in an agreement by a buyer to register its stock in the future:

(i) Buyer agrees that if at any time two years after the closing, either Stockholder so requests in writing, it will, within 90 days after receipt of such request, file a registration statement with the Securities and Exchange Commission relating to all or part of the Buyer's Common Stock delivered to the Stockholders on the merger of Seller into Buyer, subject to the limitations hereinafter set forth, and will thereafter use its best efforts to cause such registration statement to become effective, (ii) Buyer agrees that, if at any time after the Closing and on or before the second anniversary thereof, it determines to register for sale, for its account, any of its common stock under the Securities Act of 1933, as amended, on Form S-3, S-1 or any forms replacing such forms it will give written notice thereof to Stockholders, and if so requested, in writing, by a Stockholder within 10 days after the date of the giving of such written notice, Buyer will, subject to the limitations hereinafter set forth, include among the shares which it shall then register, all or part of the Buyer's common stock delivered to the Stockholders on the merger of Seller into Buyer as the Stockholder shall request, and (iii) the rights granted to the Stockholders under sub-sections (i) and (ii) of this section shall be subject to all of the following limitations:

(1) Such rights shall relate only to shares of buyer's Common Stock delivered to the Stockholders upon the merger of Seller into Buyer;

(2) Any notice by Stockholder to Buyer pursuant to sub-sections (i) and (ii) of this

section must specify the number of shares which the Stockholder wishes to have registered and shall include a statement that it is the Stockholder's then present intention of selling the number of shares which he requests to be registered upon the date of the registration statement relating thereto;

(3) Any registration under sub-section (i) and (ii) of this section above shall be at Buyer's expense, except that the Stockholder shall pay any underwriter's discounts and commissions and all stock transfer taxes relating to the shares which he sells;

(4) The Stockholders shall be entitled to demand registration under sub-section (i) above only one time;

(5) The Stockholders shall not be entitled to register any shares of Buyer's Common Stock pursuant to sub-section (i) or (ii) of this section, (a) if counsel to Buyer is of the opinion that the Stockholders may sell the shares of Buyer's Common Stock received by them on the merger of Seller into Buyer, without registration under the Securities Act of 1933, as amended or (b) if the Stockholders are then permitted to sell the shares under any rule adopted by the Securities and Exchange Commission pursuant to the Securities Act of 1933, as amended, permitting sales in a manner and with quantitative limitations similar to those contained in Rule 144 adopted by said Commission as presently in effect.

11. Publicity.

As a practical matter, plans for publicity should be coordinated before a contract is signed, but the first draft of a contract containing a publicity clause may act as a reminder and an understanding of the need for a carefully planned approach to suppliers and customers:

Buyer and seller agree that all notices to third parties and all other publicity concerning the transactions contemplated by this agreement shall be jointly planned and coordinated by both parties, and neither party shall act unilaterally in this regard without the prior approval of the other, such approval not to be unreasonably withheld.

12. Specific Performance.

The following provision is addressed to the legal remedies available upon breach of an acquisition contract and constitutes an attempt to provide for specific performance of an acquisition or rescission of the contract:

The parties mutually acknowledge and agree that in the event of any default by either party under this agreement and plan of reorganization the injury to the aggrieved party will be irreparable and damages will be inadequate, and that in addition to any other remedy provided by law the aggrieved party shall, at its option, be entitled to either specific performance of all covenants provided in this agreement and plan of reorganization or to rescission thereof.

13. Transfer, Sales and Use, Mortgage, Recording, and Property Taxes

Seller agrees to pay all documentary stamp, recording taxes and fees imposed upon the transfer of the business and assets to buyer. Buyer shall pay all sales and use taxes on such transfers. Buyer shall also pay all taxes and fees upon mortgages, security interests and the recording and filing of instruments and notices related to them. Real and personal property taxes for the fiscal years of the taxing authorities in which the closing occurs shall be prorated on the basis of such fiscal years and in accordance with local custom as verified by the title company furnishing title insurance pursuant to this agreement.

FORMS OF ASSETS PURCHASE AGREEMENT
AND ESCROW AGREEMENT

A form of an Assets Purchase Agreement for the sale of a chemical product line together with the plant and other assets used in its manufacture and sale is provided in the following pages. An Escrow Agreement for part of the purchase price is also provided.

The Index to the Assets Purchase Agreement shows the wide variety of subjects which require attention in an assets acquisition. A chemical business was chosen because it provides examples of provisions dealing with assumption of liabilities, indemnification, environmental, safety, ERISA, confidentiality, noncompetition and other provisions which illustrate why and how an assets purchase is accomplished.

Exhibit 15–1

ASSETS PURCHASE AGREEMENT

Index

ASSETS PURCHASE AGREEMENT

This Agreement is made on _____, 199__ between INDUS-TRIAL CHEMICALS, INC., a Delaware corporation ("Seller") and CHEMICAL SPECIALTIES, INC., a Delaware corporation ("Purchaser").

RECITALS:

A. Seller is engaged, among other things, in a business (the "Business") consisting of the manufacture and sale of alkyd resin and polyester resin products. Seller owns assets ("Assets") consisting of a plant at Newark, New Jersey (the "Newark Plant") and other tangible and intangible properties used in the Business.

B. Seller wishes to sell to Purchaser, and Purchaser wishes to purchase from Seller, the Business and Assets on the terms and conditions contained in this Agreement.

AGREEMENTS:

I. SALE AND PURCHASE

1.1 Business and Assets. *Relying upon the representations and warranties and subject to the terms and conditions contained herein, Seller agrees to sell, and Purchaser agrees to purchase, the Business and all the Assets, wherever located, used by Seller primarily in the Business, including certain Assets now shared by the Business and other businesses of Seller and its subsidiaries. Such assets are described, without limitation, in* Exhibit A. *The Assets exclude cash, short-term investments, the main frame computer and business equipment located at Seller's headquarters office building, and warehouses located at Hartford, Connecticut and Richmond, Virginia.*

1.2 Purchase Price; Allocation; Escrow Agreement.

(A) At the Closing, Purchaser shall pay to Seller for the Assets a cash price of $17,000,000 plus an additional cash price equal to:

(i) the estimated book value as of the Closing Date, determined as set forth in Exhibit B, *of raw material, work-in process and finished product inventories (excluding inventories which are obsolete, off-specification or excessive in relation to the last 12 months sales), subject to adjustment after the Closing as described in Section 1.5, and*

(ii) the estimated book value of receivables as of the Closing Date, based on the prior month end figures, excluding receivables past due over 90 days and items owing for unauthorized customer deductions, subject to repurchase as provided in Section 1.5

(B) The purchase price shall be payable by wire transfer to the account of Seller at such bank in the United States as Seller shall designate with appropriate payment instructions prior to the Closing Date.

(C) The purchase price shall be allocated to the Assets for federal, state and local income tax purposes by Seller and Purchaser as provided in Exhibit B.

(D) At the Closing, Seller shall withhold $1,700,000 of the purchase price and shall deposit such amount in escrow with Second National Bank of New York, as Escrow Agent pursuant to the Escrow Agreement attached as Annex I.

1.3 Liabilities and Obligations.

(A) Purchaser shall not assume or otherwise be liable for any liabilities or obligations, fixed or contingent, known or unknown, first incurred by Seller or to which its business or assets first became subject prior to the Closing Date. Nevertheless, Purchaser shall assume the performance from and after the Closing Date of those contracts, leases, licenses permits, registrations and other obligations continuing by their terms after the Closing Date which are fully and accurately disclosed in the exhibits described in Section 3.1.

(B) Provided that Purchaser exercises reasonable care regarding storage and delivery, Seller shall be responsible for product liability with respect to products included in the finished product inventories sold to Purchaser except to the extent that liability arises from any express recommendation by Purchaser of the use of products for unsuitable applications or failure by Purchaser to label or furnish material safety data sheets to customers. Purchaser shall be responsible for any product liability for Products manufactured after the Closing Date.

1.4 Indemnification.

(A) Seller shall defend and indemnify Purchaser and its shareholders, directors and officers against all loss, liability, cost and expense (including reasonable attorneys' fees) related to (a) any misrepresentation made in or pursuant to this Agreement and any breach of a warranty or agreement herein, (b) all liabilities and obligations relating to the Business or Assets not expressly assumed by Purchaser in Section 1.3.

(B) Purchaser shall defend and indemnify Seller against all loss, liability, cost and expense (including reasonable attorneys' fees) related to the performance after the Closing Date of the Contracts, permits and other continuing contractual obligations expressly assumed pursuant to Section 1.3.

1.5 Adjustments to Purchase Price After the Closing.

(A) Inventories

(i) On the Closing Date, Seller shall take a physical inventory of the raw material, work-in-process and finished product inventories and shall deliver a valuation statement to Purchaser within ten business days after the Closing Date.

The valuation statement shall contain a detailed listing and valuation of all such inventories in accordance with Section 1.2 of this Section.

(ii) Purchaser shall provide representatives to participate in the physical inventory. They shall note, during each day of the tally, any objections to the count. Upon any objection to the count, Seller's representatives shall recheck arithmetic or recount to the extent reasonably necessary to reconcile discrepancies in the count. Purchaser's representatives may also object during the count to the condition, obsolescence or other matters affecting quality of the inventories, but failure to so object shall not waive any right to object to the valuation.

(iii) The inventories shall be valued as of the close of business on the Closing Date at book value, which shall be the lower of market value (less 10% to cover the cost of getting the products to market) or cost. The methods to be used in such valuation are described in Exhibit B.

(iv) Promptly after receipt of the valuation statement, Seller or Purchaser shall pay in cash to the other party the difference between the estimated price paid for the inventories at the Closing and the amount (net of disputed inventories) shown in the valuation statement. If there is any dispute as to valuation, it shall be submitted with appropriate documentation to Coopers, Andersen, Price & Co., independent accounts, whose decision shall be final and payment shall be made within five business days after the decision. Fees and disbursements of the independent accountants shall be borne by the party losing the dispute.

(B) Receivables

(i) Within ten business days after the Closing Date, Seller shall deliver to Purchaser a complete list of receivables, excluding receivables past due over 90 days, prepared as of the Closing Date in accordance with Section 1.2. Within five business days after the delivery of such list, Seller or Purchaser shall pay to the other party any difference between the amount of the receivables shown in such list and the estimated amount paid on the Closing Date pursuant to Section 1.5.

(ii) For 90 days after the Closing, Purchaser shall make reasonable efforts consistent with its customary practices to collect the receivables assigned. At the end of such period, Purchaser may reassign any uncollected receivables to Seller together with the related invoices and collection files. Seller shall reimburse Purchaser in cash for the full face amount of such uncollected receivables within five days after such reassignment.

1.6 Maleic Anhydride Purchase Contract. *On the Closing Date, Seller and Purchaser shall execute a Maleic Anhydride Purchase Contract in the form attached to this Agreement as Annex II.*

1.7 Proration of Certain Items. *Seller and Purchaser shall prorate as of the Closing Date all rents, royalties, real and personal property taxes, prepaid items and deposits and shall credit or debit the net amount as appropriate. Proration of property taxes shall be calculated in accordance with local custom as confirmed by the title insurer.*

1.8 Transfer Taxes and Fees. *Seller shall pay, or reimburse Purchaser for, any sales, use, transfer or other taxes and fees imposed on the transfer of the Assets by Seller to Purchaser and upon registration or recording of any instruments effecting such transfer. Purchaser shall pay the cost of the title insurance policy described in Section 6.9.*

II. THE CLOSING

Subject to the conditions stated in Article V, the closing (the "Closing") of this Agreement shall take place at the Newark Plant at 10:00 A.M. on _____ _____, 199__ (the "Closing Date"). The Closing shall be deemed effective at the close of the business on the Closing Date.

III. REPRESENTATIONS AND WARRANTIES

3.1 Representations and Warranties of Seller. *Seller represents, warrants and agrees as follows:*

(a) Corporate Standing. *Seller is a corporation duly organized and existing in good standing under the laws of Delaware; is duly qualified to do business and in good standing in the State of Delaware; has filed all tax returns and paid all franchise, income and real personal property taxes and assessments to such jurisdictions as affect its right to sell or its title to the properties covered by this Agreement except taxes not yet due and payable; and has all requisite power to enter into and perform this Agreement.*

(b) Corporate Authorization. *Seller has taken all requisite action, corporate and otherwise, to authorize the execution and performance of this Agreement including the approval of its board of directors. No approval by Seller's stockholders is required. The execution and performance of this Agreement will not violate any provision of Seller's Certificate of Incorporation or By-Laws, or any agreement to which it is a party or to which Seller or the Business or Assets is subject, or of any law or regulation or any order in any action or proceeding to which it is a party or which affects its business or properties.*

(c) Financial Data and Other Information. *Unaudited financial data of the Business consisting of certain balance sheet items for the years ended December 31, 199__ and 199__ and the six-month period ended June 30, 199__ and statements of operating earnings (before tax) for the years and period then ended are attached as* Exhibit C. *Except as explained in footnotes thereto, such financial data fairly present the results of operations of the Business in accordance with generally accepted accounting principles consistently applied. There has been no material change in the Business or Assets since June 30, 199__.*

(d) Properties. *The Assets listed in Exhibit A are all of the properties of every kind located at the Plant or which have been used primarily in the Business since January 1, 199__ except for properties sold or disposed of in the ordinary course of business. Except as described in* Exhibit A, *Seller owns good and marketable title in fee simple to all the Assets, free and clear of all other claims of ownership, leases, licenses, easements, liens, encumbrances, charges, security interests, conditions and restrictions except for rights-of-way of utilities, public roadways and railroad rights-of-way passing over or through its real property and matters of record which do not affect marketability and the lien of property taxes not yet due and payable. There are no existing violations of zoning ordinances and restrictions and no encroachments either on Seller's real property or by Seller on any adjoining property except as set forth in* Exhibit A. *None of the Assets is subject to any agreement or commitment for sale or disposition, or has been disposed of, except for (i) inventories being sold in the ordinary course of business and (ii) dispositions of properties for depreciation or obsolescence in the ordinary course of business.*

(e) Inventories. *A complete and accurate list of the places where all inventories are located, including estimates of the types and quantities of inventories at each location, is attached as* Exhibit D. *All raw material, work-in-process and finished inventories sold to Purchaser in accordance with Section 1.5 will be free of defects, meet applicable specifications and be salable to customers in the ordinary course of business.*

(f) Receivables. *All receivables (net of reserves) on Seller's books as of the Closing Date will be collectible in full within 90 days after the Closing Date.*

(g) Contracts, Leases, Licenses and other Continuing Contractual Obligations. *An accurate and complete list of all contracts, leases, licenses and other contractual obligations relating to the Business or the Assets is attached as* Exhibit F. *In preparing* Exhibit F, *Seller may omit each purchase order for the purchase of goods or services if the aggregate amount to be sold or purchased over the term of the purchase order is less than $20,000. Seller may also omit any office equipment lease calling for rental payments less than $5,000 over the term of the lease. Seller does not know of any existing failure or refusal by the other party to any of such contracts, leases, licenses or contractual obligations to perform any of them or plan to terminate or modify any of them.*

(h) Environmental and Safety Matters. *(i) Except as disclosed in* Exhibit G, *the Business and Assets are in compliance with, and are not subject to any liability under, each applicable federal, state and local environmental and safety laws, regulations and codes ("Environmental Laws") other than violations which are not in the aggregate material to the Business or the Assets. Without limitation, except as so disclosed, (A) Seller holds all permits and registrations required by the Environmental Laws and is in compliance with them; (B) Seller has prepared and maintained all records and filed all notices and reports required by the Environmental Laws; (C) none of Seller's properties or facilities contains any asbestos-containing material, polychlorinated biphynyl dielectric fluid, underground storage tank or is contaminated*

with any hazardous substance or constituent or any pollutant regardless of whether its presence originated prior to Seller's ownership or operation or was caused by outside sources such as migration from another property or a spill by common carrier, supplier, customer or tenant; (D) Seller has not incurred any liability, existing or contingent, for releases or offsite disposal of hazardous wastes, substances or constituents or pollutants and has not received any notice that it has or may be named as a party potentially responsible for any such release or disposal and (E) Seller is in compliance with all occupational safety and health standards required by the Environmental Laws and has not received notice of any work-related chronic illness or injury among its employees except accidents accurately reported in its OSHA 200 log.

(ii) Except as disclosed in Exhibit B, *to the best of Seller's knowledge, each of Seller's permits and registrations can be transferred or reissued, if necessary, to Purchaser without material modification and Seller knows of no reason why any of them cannot be renewed upon expiration of their current term without imposition of materially stricter conditions if such expiration will occur within one year from the date of this Agreement.*

(iii) Except as disclosed in Exhibit G, *to the best of Seller's knowledge, none of the products, raw materials, components, catalysts, intermediates, by-products or other substances used in its business is the subject of any study, investigation or proceeding conducted or sponsored by any governmental agency under the Environmental Laws.*

(i) Customer and Suppliers List. *An accurate and complete list of each customer who purchased products during 199__ and the first six month period of 199__ and each supplier who furnished raw materials or services in an aggregate amount exceeding $20,000 during such year and period is attached as* Exhibit H *and includes the products purchased, unit volume and dollar volume for each customer. No customer or supplier has advised Seller since January 1, 199__ that it expects to discontinue or materially reduce its purchases or its supply of raw materials or services except as described in* Exhibit H.

(j) Insurance. *An accurate and complete list of all insurance policies held by Seller, including all liability policies held during the 20 year period preceding the Closing Date, with respect to the Business or Assets is attached as* Exhibit I. *Such list shall contain the name and address of the insurer and broker, the policy number and a brief description of the coverage and the extent to which aggregate limits of coverage have been exhausted by claim payments. Seller shall maintain all its insurance in effect through the Closing. If any of the Assets shall be the subject of any loss or damage covered by such insurance and Purchaser shall elect to close, Seller shall assign to Purchaser the right to receive the insurance proceeds.*

(k) Intellectual Property. *An accurate and complete list of all patents and trademarks and applications and proposals therefor derived for or used in the Business is set forth on* Exhibit A. *Seller has not licensed or otherwise authorized anyone to use such patents, trademarks or applications or*

any trade secrets of the Business including, but not limited to, customer lists and business opportunities, except as fully described in Exhibit J. *Seller has not received any claim that any of its products, processes or equipment infringes patents, trademarks or trade secrets of third parties except as described in* Exhibit J. *Seller holds all licenses necessary to use its existing processes and equipment and to manufacture and sell the Products without infringement or violation of any patent, trademark or trade secret rights of any third party.*

(l) Legal Matters. *An accurate and complete list describing all lawsuits, administrative proceedings, investigations and claims pending or threatened with respect to the Business or the Assets is attached as* Exhibit K. *Seller has and is conducting the Business and operating the Assets in compliance with all applicable federal, state and local laws and regulations except as described in* Exhibit K.

(m) Condition of Facilities and Plant Equipment. *Except as disclosed in* Exhibit L, *all facilities and equipment at the Newark Plant are in good condition and repair (fair wear and tear excepted), and have received customary maintenance (including planned overhauls and annual maintenance turnarounds) through the date of this Agreement.*

(n) Personnel and Labor Matters. *An accurate and complete list of all employees who are employed full-time in the Business and their duties, compensation and benefits is attached as* Exhibit M. *Seller has not increased the compensation or benefits of any employee since January 1, 199__ except as described in* Exhibit M. *Seller has no agreement or understanding with any of such employees with respect to their duties, compensation or benefits except as described in* Exhibit M. *Seller is a party to a written agreement with respect to ownership and assignment of inventions and ownership, non-use and nondisclosure of trade secrets with all of such employees and all employees whose employment terminated within the past two years except as described in* Exhibit M. *Seller has not experienced any strike, work stoppage or other concerted work action since January 1, 199__. To the best of its knowledge, Seller is and has been in compliance with all equal employment opportunity laws. Seller does not know of any organization campaign or plan of any labor union to seek representation of any employees of the Business except as described in* Exhibit M.

(o) Approvals, Test Ratings, Etc. *An accurate and complete list of all approvals, ratings or certifications by independent testing organizations and customers of its products which are part of the Business is attached as* Exhibit N. *Seller has received no notice that any of them has or will be withdrawn for any reason.*

(p) Distributors, Agents, Warehouses, Etc. *An accurate and complete list of all distributors, agents and off-site warehouses used in connection with the Business is attached as* Exhibit O.

(q) List of Intra-Company Transactions. *An accurate and complete list of all intra-company sales, services and transfers and of all As-*

sets shared between the Business and other businesses conducted by Seller and its subsidiaries and affiliates is attached as Exhibit P.

(r) Toxic Substances. *A complete and accurate list of all materials used in the Business at the Newark Plant by Seller, which are listed as toxic or hazardous substances in the regulations of the Occupational Safety and Health Administration, 29 CFR § 1910.1000 et seq. or in the regulations of the U.S. Environmental Protection Agency under the Community Right to Know Act, 40 CFR § 11001 et seq. is attached as* Exhibit Q.

(s) Employee Benefit Plans. *All employee benefit plans (as defined in Section 3(3) of ERISA) covering former an current employees of Seller or under which Seller has any obligation or liability are listed and identified as "Benefit Plans" in* Exhibit R. *Seller does not contribute to or have any obligation or liability with respect to any multiemployer plan (as defined in Section 3(37)) of ERISA) to provide retiree medical or other benefits to present or former employees of the Business.*

The Benefit Plans are and have been administered in compliance with their terms and the applicable requirements prescribed by ERISA, the applicable provisions of the Code, and any other applicable Regulation. None of the Benefit Plans which are "employee welfare plans" as defined in Section 3(1) of ERISA are funded through a trust. The transactions contemplated by this Agreement will not result in liability for severance pay to the employees of the Subsidiary.

There are no pending or, to the best of Seller's knowledge, threatened claims by or on behalf of the Benefit Plans, by any employee or beneficiary which allege a breach of fiduciary duty or violation of other applicable state or federal law which could result in any liability under ERISA or any other law.

Each Benefit Plan which is an employee pension benefit plan, as defined in Section 3(2) of ERISA (collectively, the "Pension Plans") which is intended to be "qualified" under Section 401(a) of the Code is so qualified and has received a favorable determination letter from the IRS as to its qualified status. To the best of Seller's knowledge, nothing has occurred since the respective dates of such letters that would adversely affect such qualification.

None of the Pension Plans (or any pension plan maintained by a trade or business under common control with the Seller within the meaning of Section 414(b) or (c) of the Code) which are subject to Title IV of ERISA have completely terminated or been the subject of a "reportable event" as defined in Section 4043 of ERISA. None of the Pension Plans has been partially terminated or incurred a complete discontinuance of contributions. Neither Seller nor any entity which would be considered a single employer with the Seller under Section 414(b), (c), (m) or (o) of the Code has incurred any liability under Sections 412 or 4971 of the Code and no lien has been imposed on the assets of the Subsidiary or its affiliates pursuant to Section 412 of the Code. No Pension Plan has incurred an "accumulated funding deficiency" (whether or not waived) within the meaning of Section 412 of the Code. No amendment has been made to a Pension Plan with respect to which security is required under Section 401(a)(29) of the Code. There have been no prohibited transactions (as such term is defined in Section 4975 of the Code or in Part 4 of the Title I of ERISA) with respect to any Benefit Plan, and no penalty or tax under Section 501(i) of ERISA or Section 4975 of the Code has been imposed upon the Company or the Subsidiary that could subject Purchaser to a tax or penalty on prohibited transactions.

None of the Pension Plans has "unfunded benefit liabilities" within the meaning of Section 4001(a)(18) of ERISA. Using the actuarial assumptions used for funding purposes for the 1989 plan year, the fair market value of the assets of each Pension Plan will exceed the "projected benefit obligations" (within the meaning of Statement of Financial Accounting Standards No. 87) of such Plan as of the date hereof and the Closing. None of the Pension Plans hold any shares of stock or other securities of the Company or any of its affiliates.

The Seller has delivered to Purchaser correct and complete copies, initialed by representatives of the Company and Purchaser for identification purposes, of (a) the Benefit Plans and Pension Plans and all trust agreements and other funding vehicles relating thereto, (b) the most recent IRS determination letter relating to each Pension Plan for which a letter of determination was obtained, (c) to the extent required to be filed, the most recent Annual Report (Form 5500 Series) and accompanying schedules of each Benefit or Pension Plan, as filed with the Internal Revenue Service, (d) if available, any summary plan description relating to the Benefit or Pension Plans, (e) if available, the most recent certified financial statements of each Benefit or Pension Plan and (f) the most recent actuarial valuation report for each Pension Plan.

All group health plans (as defined in Section 162(i) of the Code) covering the employees of the Subsidiary, and any trade or businesses which would be treated as a single employer with the Subsidiary under Section 414(b), (c), (m) or (o) of the Code, have been maintained in compliance with the continuation coverage requirements of Section 4980B of the Code and Part 6 of Title I or ERISA.

3.2 Representations and Warranties of Purchaser. *Purchaser represents and warrants as follows:*

(a) Corporate Standing. *Purchaser is a corporation duly organized and existing in good standing under the laws of the State of New York; is duly qualified and in good standing in the State of New Jersey; has paid all franchise and other taxes to each jurisdiction which affect its right to enter into and perform this Agreement and has all requisite power to enter into and perform this Agreement.*

(b) Corporate Authorization. *Purchaser has taken all requisite action, corporate and otherwise, to authorize the execution and performance of this Agreement and the matters contemplated hereto, including the approval of its board of directors. No approval by Purchaser's stockholders is required. The execution and performance of this Agreement will not violate any provision of Purchaser's Certificate of Incorporation or By-Laws, or any agreement to which it is a party or to which it is subject, or any order in any action or proceedings to which it is a party or which affects its business or properties.*

(c) No consent, approval, permit, registration, filing or notice to or with any governmental agency or third party is required on the part of Purchaser for the execution, delivery and performance of this Agreement except as expressly provided herein.

(d) There is no litigation or governmental proceeding pending or, to the best of Purchaser's knowledge, threatened against Purchaser that questions the validity or challenges the performance of this Agreement or any action to be taken by Purchaser pursuant to this Agreement.

IV. COVENANTS

4.1 Antitrust Clearance.

(A) Each party agrees to prepare and file promptly after the date of this Agreement a notification and report pursuant to the Hart-Scott-Rodino Federal Trade Commission Improvements Act (the "HSR Act") with the Department of Justice (DOJ) and Federal Trade Commission (FTC). If either party shall report information possessed by the other party in order to prepare its notification and report, the party having the information shall furnish it to counsel for the requesting party but may require that counsel refrain from disclosing such information to the requesting party.

(B) Each party shall furnish to the DOJ or FTC such further information as it may reasonably request to evaluate the sale of the Business and Assets and shall exercise reasonable diligence to obtain termination of the waiting period under the HSR Act without any adverse action by the applicable agency. Such obligation to exercise diligence shall not require either party to agree to any modification of this Agreement or to agree to divest or restrict the Business or the Assets or any other business or assets.

4.2 Conduct of Business Until Closing. *Pending the Closing, Seller shall conduct the Business only in the ordinary course. Without limitation of the foregoing, Seller shall, with respect to the Business, (A) use its best efforts to preserve intact the Business and the Assets; (B) maintain the Assets in good repair and operating condition except for fire, flood or other acts of God; (C) continue in full all existing insurance coverage; (D) not enter into any material contract or other transaction without prior written approval of Buyer; (E) use its best efforts to retain employees, customers and suppliers; (F) refrain from any increase in the compensation or benefits of employees or commitment for any increase; (G) not engage in any inter-company transaction with Seller or any of its subsidiaries except for continuation of support ser-*

vices and other transactions which have been in the normal course of business; (H) refrain from any transfer or commitment to transfer any of the Assets except for sales of Products in the ordinary course of business or to subject the Assets to any lien, encumbrance or security interest; (I) refrain, without Purchaser's consent, from any material modification of any of the Assets or commitment for any capital expenditure in excess of $10,000 and (J) refrain, without Purchaser's consent, from entering into any contract for the sale of Products or purchase of raw materials for any aggregate amount in excess of $10,000 or a period longer than 90 days.

4.3 Access to the Business and Assets. *Until the Closing, Seller shall consult with Purchaser on the operation of the Business and shall afford access to Purchaser during normal business hours to all records of the Business and Assets and to its employees, accountants, customers and suppliers. However, no investigation by Purchaser shall limit responsibility of Seller for the representations, warranties and agreements herein. Seller shall maintain the Assets in good order and repair, but no alterations shall be made except with the written approval of Purchaser. No Assets shall be purchased or sold or transferred to other plant locations except for the sale of Products and purchase of raw materials or suppliers in the ordinary course of business.*

4.4 Cooperation in Sharing Records. *Within 30 days after the Closing, Seller shall transfer to Purchaser all business records and historical information pertaining specifically to the Business, except that Seller shall retain copies of (a) documents pertaining to its disposal or shipment of wastes from the Newark Plant and (b) its personnel records pertaining to employees at the Newark Plant. Both Purchaser and Seller shall retain their respective records pertaining to the Business for no less than six years. Each party shall furnish from time to time, as requested by the other party, such records or information (other than confidential trade secrets) pertaining to the Business as required for the requesting party to conduct its operations or fulfill its legal obligations. After the expiration of this six year retention period, neither party shall discard or dispose of any such records or information without thirty days prior written notice to the other party, advising the other of the materials to be discarded or disposed of and offering the other the opportunity to retrieve such materials for retention at its own facilities.*

4.5 Cooperation After the Closing.

(A) If Seller is unable to assign any supply or sale contracts, leases, licenses or permits to be transferred to Purchaser under this Agreement and Purchaser nevertheless elects to close this Agreement, Seller shall continue to perform such contracts, lease, licenses or permits for the account of Purchaser, but Purchaser shall reimburse Seller's actual out-of-pocket costs. After the Closing, Seller shall execute and deliver from time to time such fur-

ther assignments and other documents as Purchaser shall reasonably request to effect or evidence the assignments and transfers of title contemplated by this Agreement.

(B) If Seller shall (i) discover in its possession or control after the Closing any Assets which were not delivered at the Closing or (ii) shall receive payment of any receivable transferred hereunder, Seller shall promptly notify Purchaser and shall deliver the same to Purchaser. Should Seller receive or learn of any business opportunity or other benefit pertaining to the Business or Assets, Seller shall use best faith efforts promptly to notify Purchaser thereof or to refer same to Purchaser.

(C) Seller shall at its expense arrange for the proper disposal prior to the Closing of all waste generated by the Business or stored at the Newark Plant. Seller shall further at its expense arrange for the proper disposal promptly after the Closing of all inventories found during the physical inventory pursuant to Section 1.5 to be obsolete, off-specification or excessive in relation to the last 12 months sales. Such disposal may include the sale of such inventory, but any sale shall not be made without first offering to Purchaser right of first refusal.

4.6 Confidential Information.

(A) Prior to the Closing, all technical and business information furnished by either party to the other party in connection with the transactions contemplated by this Agreement shall be maintained in confidence and shall not be disclosed to third parties or used except where the recipient can show that (a) the information was previously known to it at the time of receipt, (b) was in the public domain at the time of receipt or thereafter entered the public domain without fault of the recipient, (c) corresponds to information which was furnished to the recipient by a third party lawfully entitled to do so or (d) was developed independently by personnel of the recipient who had no access to the information. If this Agreement shall not be closed, Purchaser shall return to Seller all documents concerning the Business or Assets obtained by Purchaser from Seller.

(B) After the Closing, except as allowed under Article 6.3, Seller shall neither disclose nor use any technical or business information included as part of the Assets and shall take appropriate action to require its employees to refrain from any such disclosure or use. Also after the Closing Purchaser shall neither disclose nor use any technical or business information of Seller not related to the Business, but obtained by Purchaser through its due diligence activities prior to the Closing or through its hiring of Seller's employees.

4.7 Bulk Sales Law. *The parties waive compliance with the bulk sales provisions of Section 6 of the Uniform Commerical Code as in effect in New Jersey and Seller hereby agrees to indemnify Purchaser against all loss, liability, cost and expense which may result from such noncompliance.*

4.8 Personnel Arrangements.

(A) Purchaser agrees to make offers of employment to those employees of Seller who are so identified in Exhibit M and Seller consents to such offers of employment. Seller agrees to make reasonable efforts to such employees to accept employment with Purchaser. For a period of two years after the Closing Date, Seller shall not solicit or rehire any of such employees who accept employment with Purchaser without the prior written consent of Purchaser. This Section shall not imply any obligation of Purchaser to retain any employees in employment for any time period or limit its freedom to change their responsibilities or compensation after the Closing.

(B) Purchaser will not assume or continue any of the existing pension or other employee benefit plans of Seller. Seller agrees to provide vested rights as of the Closing Date under its existing defined benefit pension plan to each of the salaried employees participating therein on the date of this Agreement. As soon as reasonably practicable, Seller shall distribute in cash or in fully paid annuities an amount equal to the present value of accrued benefits of each such participant on the Closing Date. Seller shall defend and indemnify Purchaser against all loss, liability, cost or expense related to Seller's employee benefit plans.

4.9 Non-Competition. *Seller and subsidiaries shall not compete with Purchaser in the manufacture or sale of the products which are part of the Business anywhere in the New England and Mid-Atlantic States for a period of four years after the Closing Date. In reaching the foregoing Agreement, Seller acknowledges that other products may be substitutes for products. Therefore, Seller shall not sell products which are known to be substitutes for the products which are part of the Business. Seller shall require any person to whom any significant part of its business or to whom any subsidiary or the business of any subsidiary is sold or transferred to assume the obligations of this Section.*

4.10 Real Property Title Matters. *Within 10 days after the execution of this Agreement, Seller shall at its expense furnish to Purchaser a title report and commitment from a title insurer acceptable to Purchaser for the issuance of an ALTA title insurance policy insuring that title to all real property to be acquired by Purchaser at the Closing conforms in all respects to the representations and warranties contained in Section 3.1(d). Such commitment and policy shall contain no exceptions other than the standard printed exceptions contained in all ALTA policies issued for industrial properties by the insurer. Purchaser shall have 10 days after receipt to notify Seller of any objections to title. If Purchaser so objects, Seller shall have 10 days to clear title to meet such objections and shall use its best efforts to do so, but shall not be obligated to commence a lawsuit against anyone as part of such efforts. If Purchaser has no objection or if Seller clears all title objections, Seller shall arrange at its ex-*

pense for the title insurer to issue a title policy conforming to the commitment at the Closing.

4.11 Environmental Cleanup Responsibility Act.

(A) Seller shall promptly take such steps as shall be required by the New Jersey Environmental Cleanup Responsibility Act (ECRA) to notify the New Jersey Department of Environmental Protection (NJDEP) of the proposed sale and either to (A) file a negative declaration with the NJDEP or (B) seek an administrative consent order of the NJDEP under which Seller shall develop and carry out a cleanup plan for the Newark Plant at its expense including, without limitation, a trust fund, letter of credit or other financial security in an amount and kind acceptable to NJDEP.

(B) If Seller shall file a negative declaration which is not approved within 45 days by NJDEP, Seller shall seek an administrative consent order and carry out and perform a cleanup plan as provided above.

(C) Seller shall hire at its expense such environmental consultants and contractors (reasonably satisfactory to Purchaser) as shall be necessary to perform the cleanup plan with reasonable promptness and efficiency. Purchaser shall afford access after the Closing to Seller and its consultants and contractors to perform the cleanup. Seller shall assure that the cleanup is performed in a manner which does not significantly interfere with Purchaser's operations.

(D) Seller shall be entitled to terminate this Agreement if it cannot within _____ days after the date of this Agreement obtain an administrative consent order authorizing a cleanup plan which can be performed for a cost reasonably estimated to cost no more than $_____.

(E) Purchaser shall be entitled to terminate this Agreement if Seller cannot within _____ days after the date of this Agreement obtain an administrative consent order which can be performed without substantial interruption or interference with operations at the Newark Plant.

4.12 Finder's and Other Fees.
Seller and Purchaser each severally represent that neither of them has retained any finder, broker or agent or agreed to pay any fee or commission to any such person. Each of them agrees to defend and indemnify the other party against all loss, liability, cost and expense (including reasonable attorneys' fees) in connection with any claim or claims which may be made against the other party by reason of alleged agreements, understandings or arrangements for such a fee or commission made by either of them.

4.13 Labels, Business Forms, Packaging, Signs, Literature and Other Materials.
Seller has retained and the Assets do not include any trademarks or tradenames containing the name "Industrial Chemicals." Notwithstanding such retention, Purchaser shall not be required to remove such tradenames or

trademarks from existing labels, containers and printed material or matter used in the Business, provided, however, that, commencing as promptly as possible after the Closing Date, Products shipped by Purchaser shall have affixed thereto a stamp, sticker or other evidence of the fact that the Business has been sold to Purchaser. Purchaser shall further exercise diligent efforts to remove or modify all labels, business forms, packaging, signs, literature and other materials which use such names as soon as reasonably practicable after the Closing Date in the ordinary course of business, but in no event later than six months after the Closing Date.

V. CONDITIONS PRECEDENT TO THE OBLIGATIONS OF SELLER AND PURCHASER

5.1 Conditions of the Obligation of Purchaser. *The obligation of Purchaser to close this Agreement is, at its option, subject to the following conditions:*

(a) Representations and Warranties. *The representations and warranties of Seller shall continue to be accurate in all respects on the Closing Date, except for changes occurring in the ordinary course of business and not materially adverse in nature, and Seller shall have performed all the agreements required herein to be performed by it on or before the Closing Date.*

(b) No Material Adverse Change. *There shall have been no material adverse change in the Business or Assets and have no material loss, destruction or damage to the plants or major items of equipment to be sold by fire, flood, windstorm or other Act of God. The risk of such loss, destruction or damage to property shall remain with Seller until the Closing.*

(c) Delivery of Certain Documents. *Seller shall have delivered at the Closing all of the documents described in Section 6.1.*

(d) No Adverse Governmental Action. *No governmental agency shall have commenced or advised that it plans any lawsuit or administrative proceeding to prevent or restrict the transactions contemplated by this Agreement or to require any later divestiture of all or any part of the Business or Assets.*

(e) Other Documents. *Such other documents as counsel for the Purchaser may reasonably request.*

5.2 Conditions of the Obligation of Seller. *The obligation of Seller to close this Agreement is, at its option, subject to the following conditions:*

(a) Representations and Warranties. *The representations and warranties of Purchaser shall continue to be accurate in all respects on the Closing Date and purchaser shall have performed all agreements herein required to be performed by it on or before the Closing Date.*

(b) Delivery of Certain Documents. *Purchaser shall have delivered at the Closing the payment and documents described in Section 6.2.*

(c) Other Documents. *Such other documents as counsel for the Purchaser may reasonably request.*

5.3 Failure of Fulfillment of Conditions; Remedies. *Seller and Purchaser agree to make reasonable efforts to fulfill their respective conditions and to cooperate with the other party in fulfillment of such conditions. If this Agreement shall be terminated prior to the Closing Date for inability of either party, after reasonable efforts, to fulfill its conditions, the parties shall each bear their own expenses and shall have no liability to the other party for damages or expenses. If either party fails to use reasonable efforts to fulfill its conditions or otherwise fails or refuses to perform this Agreement, the other party shall be entitled to specific performance of this Agreement and to damage and such other remedies as may be granted in equity or by law by a court of competent jurisdiction.*

VI. DOCUMENTS TO BE DELIVERED AT THE CLOSING

6.1 Documents of Seller. *At the closing, Seller shall deliver to Purchaser the following documents:*

(a) Deeds for Real Property. *A special warranty deed to the real property described in Exhibit A, subject only to exceptions permitted by this Agreement, together with a title policy described in Section 4.10.*

(b) General Bill of Sale. *A general bill of sale conveying the Assets (tangible and intangible) of the Business subject only to exceptions permitted by this Agreement.*

(c) Specific Assignments of Contracts, Etc. *To the extent assignable, specific assignments of all contracts, leases and other continuing contractual obligations described in Exhibit F together with all necessary consents which may be required to validly assign the same.*

(d) Specific Assignments of Environmental Permits. *To the extent assignable, specific assignments or other arrangements for transfer of environmental permits listed in Exhibit G together with evidence of the consent of each applicable environmental agency to the transfer of such permits without modifications.*

(e) Specific Assignments of Patents and Trademarks. *Specific assignments of all patents, trademarks and applications therefor in form satisfactory for recording with the patent office or registries of the nations where the same are held.*

(f) Reaffirmation of Representations and Warranties. *A certificate signed by the President or a Vice President of Seller reaffirming as of the Closing Date the representations and warranties set forth in Section 3.1, subject to changes occurring in the ordinary course of business and not materially adverse in nature.*

(g) Corporate Resolutions. *Certified corporate resolutions authorizing the execution and performance of this Agreement by Seller.*

(h) Consents and Approvals. *Evidence of the consent and/or approval of all third parties for the transfer without material modification of all*

contracts, leases, permits and other Assets which require a third party consent or approval for such transfer.

(i) Antitrust. *A letter from the DOJ or FTC or other evidence that the waiting period under the HSR Act has expired or been terminated.*

(j) A copy of an approved negative declaration or administrative consent order issued by the NJDEP and signed by Seller pursuant to Section 6.11.

(k) The Maleic Anhydride Purchase Contract executed by Seller.

(l) The Escrow Agreement executed by Seller.

6.2 Documents to Be Delivered by Purchaser. *Purchaser shall deliver at the Closing:*

(a) Purchase Price. *Wire transfer of the purchase price to the account of Seller, less $1,700,000 deposited with the Escrow Agent.*

(b) Corporate Resolutions. *Certified corporate resolutions authorizing the execution and performance of this Agreement by Purchaser.*

(c) Reaffirmation of Representations and Warranties. *A certificate singed by the President or a Vice President of Purchaser reaffirming as of the Closing Date the representations and warranties set forth in Section 3.2, subject to changes occurring in the ordinary course of business and not materially adverse in nature.*

(d) Assumption Agreements. *Assumption agreements evidencing the assumption by Purchaser of the contracts, leases and other continuing contractual obligations provided in Section 1.3(B).*

(e) The Maleic Anhydride Purchase Contract executed by Purchaser.

(f) The Escrow Agreement executed by Purchaser and a receipt of the Escrow Agent for the $1,700,000 escrow deposit.

VII. GENERAL PROVISIONS

7.1 Successors and Assigns. *This Agreement shall be binding upon and shall inure to the benefit of Seller and Purchaser and their respective successors and assigns, but any attempt by either party to assign this Agreement shall be void without prior written consent of the other party. Nevertheless, Purchaser may assign this Agreement to a wholly owned subsidiary or a purchaser of substantially all of its chemical business, provided that the assignee assumes in writing all of the assignor's obligations hereunder.*

7.2 Strict Compliance. *Failure of any party hereto to insist upon strict observance of or compliance with all of the provisions of this Agreement in any one or more instances shall not be deemed to be a waiver of its right to insist upon such observance or compliance with such provisions in the future or with any other provisions of this Agreement.*

7.3 Entire Agreement. *This Agreement, including the attached Exhibits, constitutes the entire agreement between the parties as to its subject mat-*

ter and there are no other agreements or warranties, express or implied, made by Seller or Purchaser with respect thereto.

7.4 Notices. *All notices pursuant to this Agreement shall be given in writing either by prepaid telex, courier or first class mail addressed as follows:*

If to Seller:

If to Purchaser:

7.5 Amendment: *This Agreement may be amended only by a document in writing stating expressly that it is intended to be an amendment of this Agreement and signed by an officer of both Seller and Purchaser.*

7.6 Survival of Representations and Warranties. *The representations and warranties made herein shall survive and shall not be terminated or otherwise extinguished by the Closing under this Agreement on the Closing Date.*

7.7 Governing Law. *The validity, interpretation, performance and enforcement of this Agreement shall be governed by the laws of the State of New York, without regard to any conflict of laws, principles which may result in application of the law of any other state or jurisdiction, except for such compliance with federal laws and state and local laws in the State of New Jersey as shall be required for its performance.*

7.8 Severability. *If any provision or provisions of this Agreement shall be found to be invalid or unenforceable, the remaining provisions shall be deemed independent and shall continue in full force and effect.*

7.9 Public Communications. *Seller and Purchaser agree not to issue any press releases or other communications in relation to the transactions contemplated by this Agreement without prior consultation of the other party.*

IN WITNESS WHEREOF, the parties have caused this instrument to be signed by their duly authorized officers, as of the day and year first hereinabove written.

INDUSTRIAL CHEMICALS, INC.

By: _____

CHEMICAL SPECIALTIES, INC.

By: _____

Exhibit 15–2

ESCROW AGREEMENT

This Escrow Agreement is made on _____, 199__ between INDUSTRIAL CHEMICALS, INC., a Delaware Corporation ("Seller") and CHEMICAL SPECIALTIES, INC., a New York corporation ("Purchaser") and SECOND NATIONAL BANK OF NEW YORK, a national banking association ("Escrow Agent").

RECITALS:

A. Pursuant to an Assets Purchase Agreement dated _____, 199__ (the "Purchase Agreement"), Seller has agreed to sell its alkyd and polyester resin business (the "Business") and related assets ("Assets") to Purchaser for a price of $16,000,000 plus the value of inventories and receivables of the Business.

B. Section 1.4(A) of the Purchase Agreement provides in substance that Seller shall indemnify Purchaser against all loss, liability, cost and expense related to any breaches by Seller of the representations, warranties and covenants contained in the Purchase Agreement.

C. The parties have agreed to secure the foregoing net current asset and indemnification obligations of Seller by a deposit of $1,700,000 of the price in escrow to be held and applied on the terms and conditions of this Agreement.

AGREEMENTS:

In consideration of the mutual promises herein contained, the parties agree as follows:

1. APPOINTMENT OF ESCROW AGENT.

Seller and Purchaser hereby appoint Escrow Agent, and Escrow Agent hereby accepts such appointment, to serve until the termination of this Agreement as provided in Section 6 or as otherwise provided in Section 9. Purchaser agrees to pay the fees and expenses of Escrow Agent set forth in Exhibit A.

2. DEPOSITS IN THE ESCROW FUND

To secure indemnification provisions of the Purchase Agreement, Seller and Purchaser hereby deposit $1,700,000 in cash in escrow with the Escrow Agent which hereby acknowledges its receipt. Such amount plus interest and minus disbursements, is called the "Escrow Fund."

3. CLAIMS AGAINST THE ESCROW FUND

(A) During the term of this Agreement, the Purchaser may deliver written

notice (a "Claim Notice") to the Escrow Agent and the Seller of claims under the indemnification provisions of the Purchase Agreement specifying the known facts relating to each claim and the amount or estimated amount thereof.

(B) The Seller shall have 10 days from the delivery of any Claim Notice to deliver a notice (a "Dispute Notice") indicating any dispute as to liability or as to the amount of the claim or claims therein together with the facts alleged to support such dispute.

(C) If the Purchaser asserts a claim in the manner specified in this Section and the Seller accepts such claim or fails to dispute such claim by a Dispute Notice given within the time permitted, Escrow Agent shall pay from the Escrow Fund to Purchaser the amount of the claim as specified in the Claim Notice plus interest from the Closing Date to the date of payment.

(D) If the Seller shall properly deliver a Dispute Notice with respect to any claim described in a Claim Notice, Escrow Agent shall reserve an amount from the Escrow Fund equal to the amount or estimated amount of the disputed claim alleged in the Claim Notice and shall hold such amount plus interest attributable thereto until it shall receive written notice, signed by both Seller and Purchaser, furnishing agreed instructions with regard to payment or nonpayment of the claim.

(E) Whenever any amount is paid from the Escrow Fund, interest earned thereon from the effective date to the date of such payment shall be distributed by the Escrow Agent to the person or persons receiving the payment. The Seller and Purchaser agree to cooperate in the calculation of interest hereunder.

4. TERMINATION.

(A) All Claim Notices must be served by Purchaser within one year after the Closing Date, as defined in the Purchase Agreement. If no Claim Notices are delivered within such time period, or if all claims alleged in Claim Notices delivered during such period have been paid or withdrawn, Escrow Agent shall promptly thereafter pay the Escrow Fund to the Seller.

(B) If any Claim Notice has been delivered and remains unresolved at the end of 18 months after the Closing Date, Escrow Agent shall continue to hold such amount of the Escrow Fund as shall relate to the subject matter of each unresolved Claim Notice until it has been resolved. The balance of the Escrow Fund shall be distributed to the Seller. Within 10 days after the resolution of all Claim Notices and payment of all amounts owed to Purchaser, Escrow Agent shall release from escrow and deliver to the Seller any then remaining balance of the Escrow Fund, at which time this Agreement shall terminate.

(C) If any Claim Notice remains unresolved two years after the Closing Date as defined in the Purchase Agreement, at its discretion, Escrow Agent may commence in a court of competent jurisdiction an interpleader action seeking a declaration of the rights of the parties. Escrow Agent may also, at its discretion, deposit the Escrow Fund with such court and shall thereupon be discharged of any and all further duties and liability under this Agreement.

5. NONALIENATION OF INTERESTS IN THE ESCROW FUND.

The rights of Seller in the Escrow Fund shall be non-assignable except by operation of law and any attempt to assign its interest shall be null and void. Such right shall not be evidenced by any formal certificate.

6. INVESTMENT OF ESCROW FUNDS.

(A) Escrow Agent shall invest the cash deposited with it pursuant to this Agreement in such manner as Purchaser from time to time may direct, provided that all of such investments shall be obligations of or guaranteed by the United States of America, or in certificates of deposit in commercial banks with capital exceeding $1,000,000,000 (collectively, "Permitted Investments") or in money market funds which are invested solely in Permitted Investments; provided, further, that the maturities of Permitted Investments shall be such as to permit Escrow Agent to make prompt payment of the Escrow Fund to persons entitled thereto.

(B) Escrow Agent shall not be responsible for, and Purchaser shall replace, any monies lost through any investment made at Purchaser's direction pursuant to Section 6(A) hereof.

7. DUTIES AND LIABILITIES OF ESCROW AGENT; EXPENSES; RESIGNATION.

(A) Escrow Agent shall have no duties or obligations as Escrow Agent hereunder except the ministerial duties and obligations specifically set forth herein which shall be determined solely by the express provisions hereof. In performing any of its duties under this Agreement, Escrow Agent shall not incur any liability to anyone for damages, losses or expenses, except for Escrow Agent's willful default, gross negligence or breach of trust. Accordingly, Escrow Agent shall not incur any such liability for (1) any action that is taken or omitted in good faith upon advice of its counsel given regarding any question relating to the duties and responsibilities of Escrow Agent under this Agreement or (2) any action taken or omitted in reliance upon any instrument, including any notice, written statement or receipt given pursuant to this Agreement, that Escrow Agent shall in good faith believe to be genuine, to have been signed or delivered by a proper person or persons and to conform to the provisions of this Agreement.

(B) Seller and Purchaser jointly and severally will indemnify and hold harmless Escrow Agent against any losses, claims, damages, liabilities and expenses, including reasonable costs of investigation and counsel fees and disbursements that may be imposed on Escrow Agent or incurred by Escrow Agent in connection with its acceptance of appointment of the performance of its duties under this Agreement, including any litigation arising from this Agreement or involving the subject matter hereof, unless any such loss, claim, damage, liability or expense shall be the result of Escrow Agent's gross negligence, willful default or breach of trust.

(C) Escrow Agent shall be entitled to resign by written notice to each of other parties to this Agreement. Such resignation, however, shall not be effective until

the later of the following events: (i) Seller and Purchaser have agreed upon and appointed a successor which has agreed in writing to act as Escrow Agent thereunder, (ii) a successor has been judicially appointed and agreed in writing to act hereunder or (iii) 120 days from the date the written notice of resignation is given to Seller and Purchaser. The foregoing provision shall not limit the rights of Escrow Agent under subsection (B) of this Section.

(D) Escrow Agent shall furnish to the parties monthly reports of income earned and receipts and disbursements. Upon resignation or other termination of its duties hereunder, Escrow Agent shall deliver cancelled checks, Claim Notices, Dispute Notices and other records to the successor Escrow Agent, if any, and otherwise to Purchaser. Seller shall be entitled to a copy of such records.

8. COOPERATION.

Subject to the terms and conditions of this Agreement, each party shall use its best efforts to carry out the transactions contemplated by this Agreement.

9. PARTIES IN INTEREST; ASSIGNMENT.

This Agreement shall inure to the benefit of and be binding on the parties and their respective successors and assigns. Except when expressly permitted by this Agreement or approved by each party, any assignment of this Agreement by any party without the prior written consent of the other parties shall be void. Nothing in this Agreement is intended to confer any rights or remedies on anyone other than a party to this Agreement or the holder of a valid assignment of rights under this Agreement.

10. GOVERNING LAW.

The validity, interpretation, performance and enforcement of this Agreement shall be governed in all respects by the laws of the State of New York without regard to any conflict of interests principles that may apply the law of any other state.

11. AMENDMENTS OR SUPPLEMENTS TO AGREEMENT.

This Agreement may not be amended or supplemented except by a written instrument duly executed by each party.

12. ENTIRE AGREEMENT.

This Agreement, and any documents delivered under this Agreement, sets forth the entire agreement among the parties with respect to its subject matter and supersedes all prior agreements or understandings among the parties regarding those matters.

13. NOTICES.

All notices, requests, demands and other communications under this Agreement shall be in writing and shall be deemed to have been duly given if either deliv-

ered personally or sent by telex or telegram or by certified or registered mail, return receipt requested, with postage prepaid to the parties at their respective addresses set forth below:

If to Seller:

If to Purchaser:

If to Escrow Agent:

14. COUNTERPARTS.

This Agreement may be executed in two or more counterparts, each of which is an original, all of which together shall be deemed to be one and the same instrument.

IN WITNESS WHEREOF, this Escrow Agreement has been executed as of the day and year first above written.

INDUSTRIAL CHEMICALS, INC.
"Seller"

By _____

CHEMICAL SPECIALTIES, INC.
"Purchaser"

By _____

SECOND NATIONAL BANK
"Escrow Agent"

By _____

Exhibit 15–3

CONTINGENT PRICE FORMULA

Detailed Definition of Future Earnings

The following clause illustrates the detail with which future earnings of a seller are often defined to determine an installment price based upon the seller's projected earnings. The more carefully the accounting principles to determine future earnings are set forth, the less likelihood that disputes will arise in the future as to items of income to be included and expenses to be subtracted:

Determination of Shares to be Delivered on the Closing Date.

The number of shares to be delivered by Buyer to Seller on the closing date shall be determined by dividing the average closing price of Buyer's common shares on the New York Stock Exchange for each of the days for which a closing price is quoted during the period (Valuation Period) commencing with the date of execution of this Agreement and Plan of Reorganization and ending on December 13, 199__, into Seven Million Dollars ($7,000,000.00). Any fractional shares produced by such computation shall be rounded to the next full share. For purposes of this Article, the first business day following the expiration of the Valuation Period, i.e. December 14, 199__, shall be deemed the Valuation Date.

Determination of Contingent Shares to be Delivered by Buyer.

In addition to the shares of the common stock of Buyer to be delivered to Seller on the closing date, Buyer shall issue and deliver to Seller, or the designees of Seller at the times hereinafter set forth such number of shares, if any (hereinafter called Contingent Shares), as shall be determined in accordance with, and subject to the limitations set forth in Sections _____ and _____, below.

For purposes of Section _____ below, the following definitions shall apply:

a. PAT: shall mean consolidated after tax earnings of Seller, for any period under consideration computed in accordance with the accounting principles set forth in Appendix II.

b. BASE: shall mean $550,000.

c. PAT INCREMENT: shall mean the increase in PAT over BASE for the fiscal year ending September 30, 199__; for each of the fiscal years ending September 30, 199__, through 199__ inclusive, it shall mean the increase in PAT over BASE or over highest preceding Contingent Year PAT, if any such preceding Contingent Year PAT is higher than BASE, but not exceeding Two Hundred Thousand Dollars ($200,000.00) with respect to any Contingent Year except the fiscal year ending September 30, 199__.

d. PAT DECREMENT: shall mean the decrease in PAT below BASE for the fiscal year ending September 30, 199__, for each of the fiscal years ending September 30, 199__; through 199__ inclusive, it shall mean the decrease in PAT below BASE, or below the highest preceding Contingent Year PAT, if any such preceding Contingent Year PAT is higher than BASE.

e. EXCESS PAT INCREMENT: shall mean that portion of PAT INCREMENT with respect to any Contingent Year, which exceeds Two Hundred Thousand Dollars ($200,000.00) after giving effect to EXCESS PAT INCREMENTS and PAT DECREMENTS, if any, for preceding Contingent Years.

f. Contingent Year: shall mean each of the fiscal years ending September 30, 199__, through September 30, 199__, inclusive.

Contingent shares, if any, to be issued hereunder shall be determined on the basis of the after-tax consolidated earnings of Seller for each Contingent Year, computed in accordance with the accounting principles set forth in Appendix II or any amendment thereof. Such determination shall be made as promptly as possible following the close of each Contingent Year under consideration, and in any event within sixty (60) days of the close of such Contingent Year.

The number of contingent shares to be issued with respect to any Contingent Year shall be determined by dividing the average of the closing prices for each of the days for which a closing price is quoted for the month of October following the close of such Contingent Year into the product of five (5) multiplied by the PAT INCREMENT for such year, after giving effect to carryforwards of EXCESS PAT INCREMENTS and PAT DECREMENTS for prior Contingent Years.

Special Provisions Regarding Contingent Shares.

The obligation of Buyer to issue Contingent Shares and the right of Sellers to receive Contingent Shares shall be subject to the following limitations: (i) Except with respect to the last Contingent Year ending September 30, 199__, the total value of Contingent Shares, (computed with respect to each Contingent Year by multiplying the number of Contingent Shares issued for such Contingent Year by the average price determined pursuant to Section ____ above with respect to such Contingent Year) to be issued and delivered by Buyer with respect to any one Contingent Year shall not exceed one million dollars ($1,000,000.00); (ii) the cumulative total value of all Contingent Shares to be issued and delivered by Buyer, computed as aforesaid, shall not exceed four million dollars ($4,000,000.00); (iii) the cumulative total number of contingent Shares to be issued and delivered with respect to all Contingent Years shall not exceed one hundred ten thousand (110,000) shares.

Buyer shall have the right to set-off against the total value of shares otherwise required to be issued and delivered with respect to any Contingent Year or Contingent Years, the amount of any liability of Seller or Seller's Stockholders pursuant to their indemnity obligations under the provisions of the indemnity agreement of Seller and Seller's Stockholders delivered at the closing.

The total value of the Contingent Shares to be issued with respect to each Contingent Year shall include interest, computed at the date of determination of the amount of Contingent Shares payable, by application of Column(a) of Table I-PRESENT VALUE OF DEFERRED PAYMENT —of Treasury Department Regulation 1.483-1(g)(2). The number of shares designated as being in payment of interest shall be determined by dividing the total interest computed as above by the per share value of the Contingent Shares determined pursuant to Section ____ above. Separate certificates shall be issued for the portion of the Contingent Shares deemed to be in payment of principal and the portion deemed to be in payment of interest. Fractional shares resulting from such computation shall not be issued, but shall be rounded to the next full share subject to the maximum limitation set forth in Section ____.

In the event, prior to distribution of Contingent Shares with respect to any Contingent Year, the number of the one dollar ($1.00) par value common shares of Buyer outstanding, shall be increased or decreased as the result of any stock split or recapitalization, or the shares of the common stock of Buyer shall be changed into or exchanged for a different number or kind of shares or securities of Buyer then an appropriate and proportionate adjustment shall be made in the number or kind of shares, or both, of Buyer thereafter to be delivered with respect to Contingent Years, including an appropriate and proportionate increase or decrease in the maximum number of shares which may be received under this Agreement and Plan of Reorganization but in no event shall Seller or its designees receive other than voting stock of Buyer. No adjustment shall be made hereunder with respect to stock dividends not exceeding three percentum (3%) of Buyer's outstanding stock, per year.

The preceding clauses relating to the determination of contingent shares to be paid by the buyer make reference to accounting principles set forth in Appendix II of the acquisition contract.

APPENDIX II

*Accounting Principles for the Preparation of Financial
Statements for the Determination of Contingent
Share Payments
For the Fiscal Year Ending September 30, 199__:*

1. *Unless otherwise stated hereafter, the accounting principles employed shall be the same as those applied on a consistent basis in preceding years.*
2. *In the preparation of a pro forma combined balance sheet and income statement covering the five corporations and the partnership required under the agreement, these statements should reflect the elimination of all inter-company profits in inventories, and the provision for full U.S. corporate income taxes on the profits of foreign subsidiaries as though earnings were repatriated on a current basis.*

3. *In the determination of net income for Seller Subsidiary of Canada, Limited, provision will be made for the following extraordinary charges.*
   a. *Write down to the lower of cost or market value (at September ___, 199___) those securities held as an investment at that date.*
   b. *Provision for a 15% designated surplus tax which after the acquisition will be levied under Section 105B of the Canadian Income Tax Act upon the distribution of existing earnings and profits of the Canadian Company.*
4. *Any significant inconsistencies in accounting principles and practices, as between the various corporations, will be spelled out by the audit of the Seller's certified public accountants in appropriate notes to the audited pro forma combined statements and covering transmittal letter.*
5. *Extraordinary charges for write-down of securities and provision for 15% designated surplus tax with respect to Seller's Subsidiary of Canada, Limited, provided for in Item 3 above shall be excluded from the determination of "minimum" pro forma combined after-tax earnings for the year ended September ___, 199___, provided for in Section 9.08 of the Reorganization Agreement.*

For Fiscal Years—September 30, 199___, through September 30, 199___:

1. *Depreciation will be computed on a basis consistent with that used for the fiscal year ended September 30, 199___ for all plant, property, and equipment. These depreciation policies are as follows:*
   a. *Book and tax depreciation are the same.*
   b. *Additional first year depreciation of 20% is taken for both book and tax purposes on qualified assets.*
   c. *Depreciation methods are as follows:*
      (1) *Items with a useful life of 3 years or less are depreciated straight-line.*
      (2) *Generally, items over 3 years, declining balance.*
      (3) *One-half year's depreciation is taken in the year acquired and also in the last year of useful life.*
      (4) *Molds, patterns, and tools are usually 3 years straight-line.*
      (5) *Most office furniture and equipment is 10 years double-declining balance.*
      (6) *Paved parking lot—15 years straight-line.*
      (7) *Most buildings and additions—20 years straight-line.*
      (8) *Most plant machinery—10 years double-declining balance.*
      (9) *Items costing under $400 but with lives over 3 years—double-declining balance (this is usually a 5-year life).*
2. *Prior period adjustments and extraordinary items, as defined in APB Opinion 9, APB Opinion 20 and FASB Statement 16 will be excluded from the determination of after-tax consolidated earnings for the then-current year.*

3. *Inventories will be costed on the basis consistently employed by the Seller in prior years, i.e. at standard cost using the first-in, first-out method of costing and providing for a write-down to market value where cost exceeds market at balance sheet dates.*

4. *Comprehensive U.S. income taxes will be provided for and deducted in determining after-tax consolidated earnings based upon the consolidated taxable income shown by the books of account for the Seller, excluding as a tax reduction any amortization of capitalized patent or other costs arising upon dissolution of the partnership. Full U.S. income taxes will also be provided on the profits of foreign subsidiaries.*

5. *Sales of finished goods of their manufacture by Seller to Buyer and Buyer's subsidiaries will be on a "most favored distributor" basis.*

6. *Sales of finished goods of their manufacture by Buyer and Buyer's subdiaries to the Seller will be on a "most favored distributor" basis.*

7. *All cash in excess of normal working capital needs will be remitted to Buyer weekly. In recognition of the need for funds for capital investment, Buyer will provide funds up to $250,000 each year for approved capital projects, or $1,000,000 for the four years, plus any additional amounts generated as a result of the liquidation of assets not in the normal course of business, without a charge for interest. Seller will be charged interest at a rate equal to 1/2 of 1 percent over the prime bank rate for funds provided by Buyer in excess of expenditures for capital projects and will be credited with interest at the same rate for funds remitted to Buyer in excess of such capital expenditures, provided such credit for interest shall not exceed $7,000 per year.*

8. *Specific service requests by Seller to Buyer for technical aid, special research programs, advertising, etc., will be charged to Seller on the basis of cost.*

9. *General services, such as auditing, tax, legal, etc., provided or paid for by Buyer for the Seller in lieu of obtaining such services from other sources will be charged to Seller on a basis consistent with Buyer's current accounting practices. However, charges for such services shall be limited to services provided and shall not exceed costs at which Seller could reasonably expect to obtain similar services from other sources. Arbitrary charges by Buyer for management or administrative services or similar charges which are neither controllable by Seller nor properly chargeable against the operations of Seller will be excluded from the determination of after-tax consolidated earnings.*

10. *Consolidated income for the Seller shall exclude any amortization of capitalized royalty rights or other costs arising upon the dissolution of the partnership.*

11. *Except as indicated above, the accounting principles currently followed by the Seller are to be consistently applied throughout the periods upon which payment of the contingent shares are based.*

The foregoing clauses contain provisions to determine the number of contingent shares payable to a seller under a formula based upon future earnings of the seller, as well as detailed accounting principles to be applied in computing those earnings. The "seller" in the particular situation, included a combination of three corporations (one a foreign corporation) and two partnerships. The detailed provisions in the acquisition contract and in the appendix of accounting principles illustrate some fundamentals which should be considered in drafting clauses to provide for future installment payments of buyer's stock based upon a seller's future earnings.

Two fundamental determinations are involved.

First, the acquisition contract should contain a formula under which the future earnings of a seller are to be converted into shares of stock of the buyer. Such a formula may involve:

1. Definitions of the seller's fiscal years to be utilized in determining future earnings—the buyout period.
2. The amount of future earnings for each fiscal year in the buyout period which will result in payment of additional stock.
3. A determination whether the earnings of the seller during the contingency payment period are to be considered on a cumulative basis.
4. A choice of stock price averaging periods or formulae for converting the seller's future earnings into additional shares of stock, and
5. Dates for delivery of the buyer's stock.

Second, the acquisition contract or a related document should contain a detailed accounting definition of the accounting principles to be applied in computing the earnings of the seller during the buyout period. The accounting definitions should include resolution of matters such as those listed below to make the determination of earnings:

1. Whether the basic accounting principles to be employed should be those used in the past by either the buyer or the seller.
2. Inconsistencies from such accounting principles in determining future earnings of the seller during the buyout period should be set forth in detail.
3. Unique circumstances involving the seller's business, such as treatment of intercompany transactions where subsidiaries are involved or foreign taxes where foreign subsidiaries are involved, should be provided for.
4. The depreciation policies should be provided for in detail, including consideration of the following:
   a. Relationship of book and tax depreciation.
   b. The extent to which determination of depreciation is made on other than a straight-line basis.
   c. Detailed depreciation methods involving such aspects as (i) items with useful life of 3 years or less, (ii) items of useful life in excess of 3 years; (iii) whether one-half year's depreciation is taken in year of acquisition of the asset; (iv) depreciation on molds, patterns and tools; (v) deprecia-

tion on furniture and fixtures; (vi) depreciation on unique assets such as parking facilities; (vii) depreciation on real estate and (viii) depreciation on plant and machinery.

5. Treatment of prior period adjustments and extraordinary items.
6. Treatment of inventories.
7. Computation of taxes where foreign jurisdictions and different entities are involved.
8. Determination of prices where future sales of products and supplies between buyer and seller and their subsidiaries may be involved.
9. Working capital to be made available to seller and treatment of interest charges between buyer and seller with respect to funds respectively made available to each other.
10. Charges for special services such as accounting, legal and other general and administrative services to be made available to seller.

16

The Acquisition Contract: Merger Agreements

As originally prepared, this chapter described and provided forms for traditional two-party merger agreements.

In recent years, two-party mergers have become an infrequent choice as an acquisition structure because of the major risks which may inadvertently be assumed if the buyer succeeds by operation of law to the liabilities and obligations of the seller. One example will be sufficient to illustrate. On May 1, 1967, GAF Corporation, a leading manufacturer of film and specialty chemicals, acquired by merger The Ruberoid Company, a leading manufacturer of building materials. The building materials included asbestos insulation products produced for national defense and protection of buildings against fire. About a decade later, lawsuits for bodily injury began against GAF and other asbestos producers. They grew from hundreds to thousands and then tens of thousands and were supplemented by lawsuits for the cost of removal of the asbestos from buildings.

During the past decade, the triangular merger has replaced the two-party merger to an important extent. The buyer (or an intermediate subsidiary) organizes a transitory subsidiary which receives the proceeds of equity and debt financing. In a forward triangular merger, the seller corporation is then merged into the transitory subsidiary which is the surviving corporation. In a reverse triangular merger, the transitory corporation is merged into the seller corporation. In either situation, the essential effect is that minority shareholders are bound by the vote of the shareholders holding the amount of shares required by the state statute or its certificate of incorporation. In either situation, the surviving corporation is a wholly owned subsidiary of the buyer.

TAX-FREE REORGANIZATION USING
A TRIANGULAR MERGER

The first form in this chapter is an Agreement and Plan of Merger and Reorganization. It provides for the acquisition of ABC Advertising, Inc., a small privately owned advertising corporation, by Titan International, Inc., a large publicly owned diversified advertising corporation. The structure is a reverse triangular merger. The price is paid solely in voting common stock and the transaction is structured as a "tax free" reorganization under Section 368 of the Internal Revenue Code. The Agreement includes provisions for employment contracts and participation in buyer's management committee. The Agreement is conditioned on a favorable vote of two-thirds of the shareholders of the small corporation and that there be no exercise of dissenters' appraisal rights.

The reader should compare the representations and warranties of Titan in Section 2.2 with those given in the acquisition agreements providing for a cash purchase price. Even though Titan is a large, successful company, it has asked the shareholders of ABC to accept Titan's Common Stock in payment. The Common Stock will not be registered by reason of the private offering exemptions. The Agreement evidences that financial and business information about Titan has been furnished to the ABC shareholders. The representations and warranties protect the ABC shareholders if the information contains material misstatements or omissions.

The Agreement requires termination of a pre-existing shareholders agreement, execution of a new shareholders agreement and execution of employment agreements between ABC and its two most senior executives.

The reader should note the reference in Section 5.2.6 to a letter to be delivered by ABC as to certain tax matters. This letter evidences business purposes, continuity of interest, absence of "step" transactions and other facts necessary to confirm tax free reorganization status.

A "CASH OUT" TRANSACTION USING
A TRIANGULAR MERGER

The second form in this chapter is Article I of a Merger Agreement by which Universal Manufacturing, Inc., a large manufacturing corporation, will acquire Modern Tool & Die Corporation, a medium-sized, publicly owned computer manufacturer, for cash. The transaction is a reverse triangular merger. The transaction is sometimes called a "cash out" merger because it enables the buyer to acquire 100% of the outstanding stock of the seller, provided that holders of the amount of shares required by statute or charter vote in favor of the merger. Shareholders who vote against the merger can exercise dissenters' appraisal rights to seek a higher cash price, but cannot continue to retain their shares.

Some provisions of special interest in the Agreement include a condition excusing the buyer if the exercise of dissenters' appraisal rights exceeds an agreed limit; a provision for adjustment of the price based on an audit of net worth on the effective date of the merger; provisions for exchange of stock certificates by the public share-holders; provisions for withholding in escrow of part of the price payable to the largest shareholders; provisions to obtain antitrust clearance; provisions for preparation and clearance of a proxy statement and arrangements for a special shareholders meeting and a "no shop" provision. Readers should observe that Sections 1.10 through 1.13 would usually appear in the article containing covenants.

A form of Exchange Agreement is provided on the pages following the Merger Agreement.

Exhibit 16-1

AGREEMENT AND PLAN OF MERGER AND REORGANIZATION

Table of Contents

ARTICLE I
THE MERGER

ARTICLE II
REPRESENTATIONS AND WARRANTIES

ARTICLE III
COVENANTS OF ABC

ARTICLE IV
COVENANTS OF TITAN AND MERGER CORPORATION

ARTICLE V
CONDITIONS PRECEDENT

ARTICLE VI
TERMINATION, AMENDMENT, WAIVER

ARTICLE VII
DEFINITIONS, MISCELLANEOUS

AGREEMENT AND PLAN OF
MERGER AND REORGANIZATION

This AGREEMENT AND PLAN OF MERGER AND REORGANIZA-TION (the "Agreement"), is dated as of September 1, 199__, among ABC Advertising, Inc. ("ABC"), a New York corporation"), Titan Merger Corporation ("Merger Corporation"), a New York corporation, and Titan, International Inc. ("Titan"), a New York corporation and the holder of all of the issued and outstanding capital stock of Merger Corporation.

WHEREAS, ABC, Titan and Merger Corporation deem it advisable and in the best interest of each of them and of their respective stockholders that Merger Corporation be merged into ABC pursuant to the Business Corporation Law of the State of New York in a transaction intended to qualify as a "reorganization" as that term is used in Section 368 of the Internal Revenue Code of 1954, as amended (the "Code"), and upon the terms and conditions contained in this Agreement;

NOW, THEREFORE, ABC, Merger Corporation and Titan hereby agree as follows:

1.1. Constituent, Surviving Corporations. ABC and Merger Corporation shall be the constituent corporations to the Merger. (Such terms and certain other capitalized terms used herein are defined in Section 7.1.) At the Effective Time, Merger Corporation shall be merged into ABC in accordance with the Business Corporation Law of the State of New York and ABC shall be the surviving corporation of the Merger (sometimes called the "Surviving Corporation"). The name, identity, existence, rights, privileges, powers, franchises, properties and assets, and the liabilities and obligations of ABC, shall continue unaffected and unimpaired by the Merger. At the Effective Time, the identity and separate existence of Merger Corporation shall cease, and all rights, privileges, powers, franchises, properties and assets of Merger Corporation shall be vested in ABC. For accounting purposes, the Merger shall be deemed effective as of 12:01 a.m., October 1, 199__.

1.2. Certificate of Incorporation; By-Laws. At the Effective Time, the Certificate of Incorporation of ABC shall be amended to read in its entirety as set forth in Exhibit A and such Certificate of Incorporation, as so amended, shall be the Certificate of Incorporation of the Surviving Corporation until further amended as provided therein or by law. At the Effective Time, the By-Laws of ABC shall be amended to read in their entirety as set forth in Exhibit B and such By-Laws, as so amended, shall be the By-Laws of the Surviving Corporation, until further amended as provided therein or by law.

1.3. Officers and Directors. Each officer and director of ABC immediately prior to the Effective Time shall continue as an officer or director of the Surviving Corporation until his successor has been elected or appointed and qualified, or as otherwise provided in the Articles of Incorporation or By-Laws of the Surviving Corporation.

1.4. Conversion of Merger Corporation Common Stock. *At the Effective Time, each share of Merger Corporation Common Stock issued and outstanding immediately prior to the Effective Time shall, by virtue of the Merger and without any action on the part of the holder thereof, be converted into and become one fully paid and nonassessable share of Common Stock, $1.00 par value, of the Surviving Corporation.*

1.5. Conversion of ABC Common Stock. *Subject to the conditions and limitations set forth in this Agreement, at the Effective Time, each share of ABC Common Stock issued and outstanding immediately prior to the Effective Time shall, by virtue of the Merger and without any action on the part of the holder thereof, be converted into and become 150 shares of Titan Common Stock. Each such share of Titan Common Stock shall be validly issued, fully paid and nonassessable. All shares of ABC Common Stock held by its stockholders at the Effective Time shall cease to exist, and the certificates for such shares shall thereupon be cancelled and shall be converted into shares of Titan Common Stock.*

1.6. Fractional Shares. *No fractional shares of Titan Common Stock shall be issued pursuant to the Merger. Any fractional shares of Titan Common Stock resulting from the computations herein shall be converted into cash at the closing price per share of Titan Common Stock (the "Cash Conversion Rate") on the last business day prior to the Closing Date.*

1.7. Issuance of Titan Shares; Delivery of Cash. *Subject to the terms and conditions hereof, at the Effective Time, upon surrender to Titan by each stockholder of ABC of certificates for all the shares of ABC Common Stock held by such stockholder, Titan will issue and deliver to each such stockholder of ABC (a) certificates representing the number of shares of Titan Common Stock into which the shares of ABC Common Stock held by such stockholder and outstanding at the Effective Time are to be converted in accordance with Section 1.5 and (b) in lieu of any fractional share, an amount of cash determined by multiplying the Cash Conversion Rate times the fractional share interest to which such stockholder would otherwise be entitled. If any certificate for shares of Titan Common Stock is to be issued in a name other than that in which a certificate for shares of ABC Common Stock so surrendered is then registered, such surrender shall be accompanied by payment of any applicable transfer taxes and documents required for a valid transfer.*

1.8. Changes in Titan Capitalization. *In case Titan shall declare, pay, make or effect any stock dividend or other distribution in respect of the Titan Common Stock payable in shares of capital stock of Titan, any stock split or other subdivision of outstanding shares of Titan Common Stock into a larger number of shares, any combination of outstanding shares of Titan Common Stock into a smaller number of shares or any reclassification of Titan Common Stock into other shares of capital stock or securities, the record or effective time for which shall occur between the date of this Agreement and the Effective Time, appropriate adjustment shall be made in the ration for the conversion of shares of ABC Common Stock into shares of Titan Common Stock.*

ARTICLE II
REPRESENTATIONS AND WARRANTIES

2.1. Representations and Warranties of ABC. *ABC represents and warrants to Titan and Merger Corporation as follows:*

2.1.1. ABC Corporate Status. *ABC is a corporation duly organized, validly existing and in good standing under the laws of the State of New York with full corporate power and authority to carry on its business as now conducted and to own or lease and operate its properties and is qualified and in good standing in all places where such business is now conducted and such properties are now owned, leased or operated. ABC has delivered to Titan and Merger Corporation complete and correct copies of its Articles of Incorporation and By-Laws, as amended through the date of this Agreement.*

2.1.2. ABC Capitalization. *The authorized capital stock of ABC consists of 20,000 shares of Common Stock, $.01 par value, of which 10,000 shares are issued and outstanding. There are no shares of ABC Common Stock held in treasury. All such issued and outstanding shares of ABC Common Stock have been duly authorized and validly issued and are fully paid and nonassessable. There are no preemptive or similar rights on the part of any holders of any class of securities of ABC. No options, warrants, conversion or other rights, agreements or commitments of any kind obligating ABC, contingent or otherwise, to issue or sell any shares of its capital stock of any class or any securities convertible into or exchangeable for any such shares, are outstanding, and no authorization therefor has been given. A complete and correct list of ABC's stockholders and the number of shares held by each of them is attached as Schedule 1.*

2.1.3. ABC Subsidiaries. *ABC has no subsidiaries.*

2.1.4. Authority for Agreement. *ABC has the corporate power and authority to execute and deliver this Agreement and to carry out its obligations hereunder. The execution and delivery of this Agreement and the consummation of the Merger and the other transactions contemplated hereby have been duly authorized by ABC's Board of Directors and subject to the approval of this Agreement by its stockholders, this Agreement constitutes the valid and legally binding obligation of ABC in accordance with its terms. The execution and delivery of this Agreement and the consummation of the Merger and the other transactions contemplated hereby will not conflict with or result in any violation of or default under any provision of the Certificate of Incorporation or By-Laws of ABC or any mortgage, indenture, lease, agreement or other instrument, permit, concession, grant, franchise, license, judgment, order, decree, statute, law, ordinance, rule or regulation applicable to ABC or any of its properties. No consent, approval, order or authorization of, or registration, decla-*

ration or filing with any governmental authority is required in connection with the execution and delivery of this Agreement or the consummation of the Merger and the transactions contemplated hereby by ABC (including the transfer to the Surviving Corporation of all of the rights and assets of ABC), except for the filing with the Department of State of New York of the Certificate of Merger.

2.1.5. Financial Statements. ABC has delivered to Titan and Merger Corporation copies of the ABC Financial Statements. The ABC Financial Statements are complete and correct in all material respects and have been prepared in accordance with generally accepted accounting principles applied on a consistent basis throughout the periods covered thereby and the periods preceding the periods so covered, except as may be indicated in the notes thereto. The balance sheets included in the ABC Financial Statements present fairly its financial position of ABC as at the respective dates therefor and the statements of income and of changes in financial position included in the ABC Financial Statements present fairly its results of operations and changes in financial position for the respective periods. At June 30, 199___, ABC had no known material liabilities, whether absolute, accrued, contingent or otherwise and whether due or to become due, which were not appropriately reflected or reserved against in the balance sheet as at such date and the notes thereto included in the ABC Financial Statements or described in Annex A to this Agreement.

2.1.6. Absence of Changes. Since June 30, 199___ ABC has not:

(a) undergone any change in its condition (financial or other), properties, assets, liabilities, business, operations or prospects other than changes in the ordinary course of business which have not been, either in any case or in the aggregate, materially adverse to ABC;

(b) declared, set aside, made or paid any dividend or other distribution in respect of its capital stock or purchased or redeemed, directly or indirectly, any shares of its capital stock;

(c) issued or sold any shares of its capital stock of any class or any options, warrants, conversion or other rights to purchase any such shares or any securities convertible into or exchangeable for such shares, except that it has issued and sold 500 shares of its Common Stock upon exercise of stock options, which shares are reflected in Schedule 1;

(d) incurred any indebtedness for borrowed money or issued or sold any debt securities:

(e) mortgaged, pledged or subjected to any lien, lease, security interest or other charge or encumbrance any of its properties or assets, tangible or intangible;

(f) acquired or disposed of any assets or properties of material value except in the ordinary course of business;

(g) forgiven or cancelled any debts or claims, or waiver any rights except in the ordinary course of business and as described in Annex A to this Agreement;

(h) entered into any material transaction other than in the ordinary course of business;

(i) granted to any salaried employee having annual direct remuneration in excess of $50,000 or any officer any increase in compensation in any form, or any severance or termination pay, or entered into any employment agreement with any officer or salaried employee which is not terminable by the employer, without cause and without penalty, upon notice of 30 days or less;

(j) adopted or amended in any material respect, any collective bargaining, bonus, profit-sharing, compensation, stock option, pension, retirement, deferred compensation or other plan, agreement, trust, fund or arrangement or other plan, agreement, trust, fund or arrangement for the benefit of employees (whether or not legally binding);

(k) suffered any damage, destruction or loss (whether or not covered by insurance) which materially and adversely affects (in any case or in the aggregate) its condition (financial or other), properties, assets, business, operations or prospects;

(l) suffered any strike or other labor trouble materially adversely affecting the business, operations or prospects of ABC;

(m) suffered any loss of employees, customers or clients that materially and adversely affects its business; or

(n) incurred any liability or obligation (whether absolute, accrued, contingent or otherwise) material to ABC, except in the ordinary course of business.

2.1.7. Taxes. ABC has filed all federal, state, county, municipal and foreign tax returns, reports and declarations which are required to be filed by it and has paid all taxes which have become due pursuant thereto and all other taxes, assessments and other governmental charges imposed by law upon it or any of its properties, assets, income, receipts, payrolls, transactions, capital, net worth or franchises, other than those not delinquent. ABC has not received any notice of deficiency or assessment of additional taxes. United States federal income tax returns for ABC have been examined and closed by the Internal Revenue Service for all years through December 31, 199__. ABC has not granted any waiver of any statute of limitation with respect to, or any extension of a period for the assessment of, any federal, state, county, municipal or foreign income tax. The accruals and reserves for taxes reflected in the consolidated balance sheets of ABC included in the ABC Financial Statements are adequate to cover all taxes due and payable or accruable (including interest and penalties, if any, thereon) in accordance with generally accepted accounting principles as a result of ABC's operations for all periods prior to the dates indicated in such Financial Statements.

2.1.8. Properties. A complete and correct list of all real properties and interests therein owned or leased by ABC is attached as Schedule 2. ABC has good and marketable title to all such real properties listed as owned by it and to all property reflected in the ABC Financial Statements as of June 30, 199__ or acquired after such date (except to the extent disposed of since such date in the ordinary course of business), and valid leasehold interests in all such real properties listed as leased by it and all tangible and intangible properties leased by it, in each case free and clear of all mortgagees, liens, charges, incumbrances, easements, security interests, pledges or title imperfections. ABC has delivered complete and correct copies of all such leases of real property and material personal property to Titan and Merger Corporation; all such leases are valid, subsisting and effective in accordance with their terms and in good standing and there does not exist thereunder any default or event or conditions which, after notice or lapse of time or both, would constitute a default thereunder. All structures and other improvements located on such real properties and all such tangible personal property are in good operating condition and repair, subject to ordinary wear and tear.

2.1.9. Material Contracts. A complete and correct list attached as Schedule 3 includes all agreements, contracts and commitments of the following types, written or oral, to which ABC is a party or by which it or any of its properties is bound as of the date hereof: (a) mortgages, indentures, security agreements and other agreements and instruments relating to the borrowing of money or extension of credit; (b) employment and consulting agreements; (c) collective bargaining agreements; (d) bonus, profit-sharing, compensation, stock option, pension, retirement, deferred compensation or other plans, agreements, trusts, funds or arrangements for the benefit of employees (whether or not legally binding); (e) agreements, orders or commitments for the purchase by ABC of materials, supplies or finished products exceeding $100,000; (f) agreements, orders or commitments for the sale by ABC of its products or services exceeding $200,000; (g) licenses of patent, trademark and other industrial property rights; (h) agreements or commitments for capital expenditures; (i) brokerage or finder's agreements; (j) joint venture agreements and (k) other agreements, contracts and commitments which in any case involve payments or receipts of more than $100,000. ABC has delivered or made available to Titan and Merger Corporation complete and correct copies of all written agreements, contracts and commitments, together with all amendments thereto, and accurate descriptions of all oral agreements listed in Schedule 3. Such agreements, contracts and commitments are in full force and effect and, except as disclosed in Schedule 3, all parties to such agreements, contracts and commitments have, to the best of ABC's knowledge and belief, in all material respects performed all obligations required to be performed by them to date and are not in default in any material respect. No agreement, contract or commitment to which ABC is a party or by which it or any of its properties is bound contains any provision which is unusually burdensome, restrictive or unfavorable to ABC or which materially adversely affects or in the future may (so far as ABC can now foresee) materially adversely affect the condition, properties, assets, liabilities, business, operations or prospects of ABC. ABC does not have outstanding any power of attorney, except routine powers of attorney relating to representation before governmental agencies or given in connection with qualification to conduct business in another jurisdiction.

2.1.10. ERISA. All employee benefit plans established, maintained or contributed to by ABC comply in all material respects with the requirements of ERISA and no such plan which is subject to Part 3 of Subtitle B of Title 1 of ERISA has incurred any "accumulated funding deficiency" within the meaning of Section 302 of ERISA or Section 412 of the Code and ABC has not incurred any liability on account of such an "accumulated funding deficiency" with respect to any employee benefit plan subject to ERISA. No material liability to the Pension Benefit Guaranty Corporation established under ERISA has been incurred with respect to any plan subject to ERISA and ABC has not incurred any liability for any tax imposed by Section 4975 of the Code.

2.1.11. Accounts Receivable. The accounts receivable reflected in the balance sheet included in the ABC Financial Statements as of June 30, 199__ (Except those collected since such date) and such additional accounts receivable as are reflected on ABC's books on the date hereof, are good and collectible except to the extent reserved against thereon or except as described in Annex A to this Agreement. ABC has furnished to Titan and Merger Corporation a complete and correct list of the amount of ABC's accounts receivable as of the date hereof and the ages (to the nearest month) of such receivables.

2.1.12. Patents, Trademarks, Etc. ABC owns no patents, patent applications, trade names, trademarks, trademark applications, copyrights, and copyright applications and there are no patents, trade names, trademarks, copyrights, inventions, processes, designs, formulae, trade secrets, know-how and other industrial property rights necessary for the conduct of its business.

2.1.13. Insurance. A complete and correct list and accurate summary description of, all insurance policies of ABC for the past five years is attached as Schedule 4. ABC has delivered to Titan and Merger Corporation complete and correct copies of all such policies together with all riders and amendments thereto and copies of the insurers' loss and claim reports. Such policies are in full force and effect, and all premiums due thereon have been paid. ABC has complied in all material respects with the provisions of such policies.

2.1.14. Clients. A complete and correct list of all clients of ABC is attached as Schedule 5.

2.1.15. Bank Accounts. ABC has delivered to Titan and Merger Corporation a complete and correct list of each bank in which ABC has an account or safe deposit box together with the names of all persons authorized to draw thereon or have access thereto.

2.1.16. Litigation. There are no judicial or administrative actions, suits, proceedings or investigations pending or, to the best of ABC's knowledge, threatened which might result in any material adverse change in the conditions (financial or other), properties, assets, business, operations or prospects of ABC or in any material liabilities on the part of ABC, or which question the validity of this Agreement or of any action taken or to be taken in connection therewith. There are no citations, fines or penalties heretofore asserted against ABC under any federal, state or local law which remain unpaid.

2.1.17. Compliance with Laws; Governmental Authorizations. *ABC is not in violation or default in any material respect under any statute, law, ordinance, rule, regulation, judgment, order, decree, permit, concession, grant, franchise, license or other governmental authorization or approval applicable to it or any of its properties, nor has it failed to comply in any such material respect with any standards now or hereafter applicable to it under any such existing statute, law, ordinance, rule, regulation, judgment, order, decree, permit, concession, grant, franchise, license or other governmental authorization or approval. All permits, concessions, grants, franchises, licenses and other governmental authorizations and approvals necessary for the conduct of the business of ABC have been duly obtained and are in full force and effect, and there are no proceedings pending or threatened which may result in the revocation, cancellation or suspension, or any materially adverse modification, of any thereof; the consummation of the Merger and the other transactions contemplated hereby will not result in any such revocation, cancellation, suspension or modification; and the Surviving Corporation shall be able, immediately following the Effective Time and without any further action, to exercise all rights thereunder which ABC could have exercised immediately prior to the Effective Time.*

2.1.18. Brokers, Finders, Etc. *All negotiations relating to this Agreement and the transactions contemplated hereby have been carried on without the intervention of any person acting on behalf of ABC in such manner as to give rise to any valid claim against any of ABC, Titan or Merger Corporation for any brokerage or finder's commission, fee or similar compensation.*

2.1.19. Disclosure. *Neither this Agreement nor any attached Schedules, nor any certificate or other document furnished by ABC to Titan or Merger Corporation pursuant hereto contains any untrue statement of a material fact or omits to state a material fact necessary to make the statements contained therein and herein not misleading. There is no fact known to ABC which materially adversely affects, or in the future may (so far as ABC can now reasonably foresee) materially adversely affect its condition (financial or other), properties, assets, liabilities, business, operations or prospects of ABC which has not been set forth herein or in the attached Schedules or Annexes.*

2.2. Representations and Warranties of Titan and Merger Corporation. *Titan and Merger Corporation represent and warrant to ABC as follows:*

2.2.1. Titan Corporate Status. *Titan is a corporation duly organized, validly existing and in good standing under the laws of the State of New York with full corporate power and authority to carry on its business as now conducted. Titan had delivered to ABC complete and correct copies of its Certificate of Incorporation and By-Laws, as amended and in effect on the date hereof.*

2.2.2. Titan Capitalization. *The authorized capital stock of Titan consists of: 10,000,000 shares of Common Stock, $1.00 par value, of which 5,500,000 shares were issued and outstanding as at June 30, 199___. All such issued and outstand-*

ing shares of Titan Common Stock have been duly authorized and validly issued and are fully paid and nonassessable. No options, warrants, conversion or other rights, agreements or commitments of any kind obligating Titan, contingently or otherwise, to issue or sell any shares of its capital stock of any class or any such shares, are outstanding, and no authorization therefor has been given, except for options for the purchase of no more than 250,000 shares authorized to be granted under employee stock option and purchase plans of Titan, of which options to purchase 180,000 of such shares were outstanding as of June 30, 199___.

2.3.3. **Merger Corporation Corporate Status.** *Merger Corporation is a corporation duly organized, validly exiting and in good standing under the laws of the Sate of New York with full corporate power and authority to enter into this Agreement and to carry out the transactions contemplated hereby. Merger Corporation has delivered to ABC complete and correct copies of its Articles of Incorporation and By-Laws, as amended through the date of this Agreement. The authorized capital stock of Merger Corporation consists of 1,000 shares of Common Stock, $1.00 par value, all of which are duly authorized, validly issued and outstanding, fully paid and nonassessable, and owned of record and beneficially by Titan.*

2.2.4. **Authority for Agreement.** *Titan and Merger Corporation have the corporate power and authority to execute and deliver this Agreement and to carry out their respective obligations hereunder. The execution and delivery of this Agreement and the consummation of the Merger and the other transactions contemplated hereby will, prior to the Effective Time, be duly authorized by the respective Boards of Directors of Merger Corporation and Titan; the approval of this Agreement by Titan as the sole stockholder of Merger Corporation will, prior to the Effective Time, be duly authorized by the Board of Directors of Titan; and as of the Effective Time this Agreement will constitute the valid and legally binding obligation of Titan and Merger Corporation. The execution and delivery of this Agreement and the consummation of the Merger and the other transactions contemplated hereby will not conflict with or result in any violation of or default under any provision of the Certificate of Incorporation or By-Laws of Titan or the Articles of Incorporation or By-Laws of Merger Corporation or any mortgage, indenture, lease, agreement or other instrument, permit, concession, grant, franchise, license, judgement, order, decree, statute, law, ordinance, rule or regulation applicable to Titan or Merger Corporation or any of their respective properties. No consent, approval, order or authorization of, or registration, declaration or filing with any governmental authority is required in connection with the execution and delivery of this Agreement or the consummation of the Merger and the other transactions contemplated hereby by Titan and Merger Corporation except for the filing with the Department of State of New York of the Certificate of Merger.*

2.2.5. **Financial Statements.** *Titan has delivered to ABC the Titan Financial Statements. The Titan Financial Statements are complete and correct in all material respects and have been prepared in accordance with generally accepted accounting principles applied on a consistent basis throughout the periods covered* *thereby and the periods preceding the periods so covered, except as may be indicated in the notes thereto. The consolidated balance sheets included in the Titan Financial Statements present fairly the consolidated financial position of Titan and its consolidated subsidiaries as at the respective dates thereof and the statements of consolidated income and of changes in consolidated financial position included in the Titan Financial Statements present fairly the consolidated results of operations and changes in financial position of Titan and its consolidated subsidiaries for the respective periods indicated, subject in the case of the financial statements as of March 31 and June 30, 199__ to normal year-end audit adjustments. At December 31, 199__, Titan and its consolidated subsidiaries had no known material liabilities, whether absolute, accrued, contingent or otherwise and whether due or to become due, which were not appropriately reflected or reserved against in the consolidated balance sheet as at such date and in the notes thereto included in the Titan Financial statements.*

2.2.6. Absence of Changes. *Since December 31, 199__, none of the Titan Companies has undergone any material change in its condition (financial or other), properties, assets, liabilities, business, operations or prospects, other than changes in the ordinary course of business which in the aggregate have not been materially adverse to the Titan Companies on a consolidated basis.*

2.2.7. Litigation. *Except for the matters described in Titan's Annual Report for the year ended December 31, 199__ on Form 10-K, and in Titan's Quarterly Reports on Form 10-Q for the quarters ended March 31 and June 30, 199__, there are no judaical or administrative actions, suits, proceedings or investigations pending or, to Titan's knowledge, threatened which might result in any material adverse change in the condition (financial or other), properties, assets, business, operations or prospects of the Titan Companies on a consolidated basis or in any material liability on the part of the Titan Companies on a consolidated basis, or which question the validity of this Agreement or of any action taken or to be taken in connection herewith.*

2.2.8. Compliance with Laws; Governmental Authorizations. *None of the Titan Companies is in violation or default in any respect material to the Titan Companies on a consolidated basis under any statute, law, ordinance, rule, regulation, judgment, order, decree, permit, concession, grant, franchise, license or other governmental authorization or approval applicable to it or any of its properties. All permits, concessions, grants, franchises, licenses and other governmental authorizations and approvals necessary for the conduct of the business of each of the Titan Companies have been duly obtained and are in full force and effect, and there are no proceedings pending or threatened which may result in the revocation, cancellation or suspension, or any materially adverse modification, of any thereof; the consummation of the Merger and the other transactions contemplated hereby will not result in any such revocation, cancellation, suspension or modification.*

2.2.9. SEC Reports. *Titan has furnished to ABC copies of Titan's (a) Annual Report for the year ended December 31, 199__ on Form 10-K as filed with the*

Securities and Exchange Commission, (b) Quarterly Reports for the quarters ended March 31 and June 30, 199__ on Form 10-Q as filed with the Securities and Exchange Commission, (c) proxy statements for the Annual Meeting of Stockholders held on April 15, 199__, as mailed to Titan's stockholders and filed with the Securities and Exchange Commission and (d) 199__ Annual Report to Stockholders, as mailed to Titan's stockholders and, to the best of Titan's knowledge, the information contained therein did not, on the respective dates of items (a) through (d) of this section, and as it may have been amended or supplemented at the date hereof, does not, contain any untrue statement of a material fact or omit to state any material fact necessary in order to make the statements therein, in light of the circumstances under which they were made, not misleading.

2.2.10. Disclosure. *Neither this Agreement nor any certificate prepared by Titan or Merger Corporation pursuant hereto, and furnished to ABC pursuant hereto, contains any untrue statement of a material fact or omits to state a material fact necessary to make the statements contained herein or therein not misleading.*

2.2.11. Titan Stock. *The shares of Titan Common Stock to be issued pursuant to the Merger will, prior to the Effective Time, have been duly authorized, and all of such shares, when so issued, will be validly issued and outstanding, fully paid and nonassessable, and no stockholder of Titan will have any preemptive right in respect thereof.*

2.2.12. Brokers, Finders, Etc. *All negotiations relating to this Agreement and the transactions contemplated hereby have been carried on without the intervention of any person acting on behalf of Titan or Merger Corporation in such manner as to give rise to any valid claim against ABC, Titan, or Merger Corporation for any brokerage or finder's commission, fee or similar compensation.*

ARTICLE III
COVENANTS OF ABC

3.1. Conduct of Business. *From the date hereof to the Effective Time, except as otherwise consented to by Titan and Merger Corporation in writing, ABC shall:*

(a) carry on its business in, and only in, the usual, regular and ordinary course in substantially the same manner as heretofore and, to the extent consistent with such business, use all reasonable efforts to preserve intact its present business organization, keep available the services of its present officers and employees, and preserve its relationship with clients, customers, suppliers and others having business dealings with it to the end that its goodwill and going business shall be unimpaired at the Effective Time;

(b) maintain all its material structures, equipment and other tangible

personal property in good repair, order and condition, except for depletion, depreciation, ordinary wear and tear and damage by unavoidable casualty;

(c) keep in full force and effect insurance comparable in amount and scope of coverage to insurance now carried by it other than life insurance policies discontinued pursuant to the written request of Titan;

(d) perform in all material respects all of its obligations under agreements, contracts and instruments relating to or affecting its properties, assets and business;

(e) maintain its books of account and records in the usual, regular and ordinary manner;

(f) comply in all material respects with all statutes, laws, ordinances, rules and regulations applicable to it and to the conduct of its business;

(g) except as disclosed to Titan and Merger Corporation, not amend its Articles of Incorporation or By-Laws;

(h) not enter into or assume any agreement, contract or commitment of the character referred to in clauses (a) through (k) of Section 2.1.9, except in the ordinary course of business;

(i) not merge or consolidate with, or agree to merge or consolidate with, or purchase substantially all of the assets of, or otherwise acquire any business or any corporation, partnership, association or other business organization or division thereof;

(j) not take, or permit to be taken, any action which is represented and warranted in clauses (a) through (n) of Section 2.1.6 not to have been taken since June 30, 199__; and

(k) promptly advise Titan in writing of any materially adverse change in the financial condition, operations, business or prospects of ABC.

3.2. Access and Information. *ABC shall give Titan and Merger Corporation and their representatives full access to its properties, books, records, contracts and commitments and will furnish all such information and documents relating to its properties and business as Titan or Merger Corporation may reasonably request. In the event this Agreement is terminated and the Merger abandoned, Titan and Merger Corporation will keep confidential any information (unless readily ascertainable from public information or sources or otherwise required by law to be disclosed) obtained from ABC in connection with the Merger and will return to ABC all documents, work papers and other written material obtained by Titan or Merger Corporation from ABC.*

3.3. Subsequent Financial Statements. *With respect to each fiscal quarter ending more than 45 days prior to the Effective Time, ABC will deliver to Titan and Merger Corporation, no later than 45 days after the end of such fiscal quarter, an unaudited consolidated balance sheet of ABC as of the last day of such fiscal quarter and the statements of income, changes in stockholders' equity and changes in financial position of ABC for the fiscal period then ended, certified as to completeness and accuracy by the chief financial officer of ABC.*

ARTICLE IV
COVENANTS OF TITAN AND MERGER CORPORATION

4.1. Certificate of Merger. *Upon the fulfillment of all of the conditions precedent to the obligations of ABC contained herein, Merger Corporation will cause to be executed and filed, pursuant to Section 904 of the Business Corporation Act of the State of New York, a Certificate of Merger (the "Certificate of Merger") in the office of the Secretary of State of New York with respect to the Merger.*

4.2. Subsequent Financial Statements. *With respect to each fiscal quarter ending more than 45 days prior to the effective Time, Titan will deliver to ABC, not later than 45 days after the end of such fiscal quarter, an unaudited consolidated balance sheet of Titan and its consolidated subsidiaries as at the last day of such fiscal quarter and the consolidated statements of income, changes in stockholders' equity and changes in financial position of Titan and its consolidated subsidiaries for the fiscal period then ended prepared in conformity with the requirements of Form 10-Q under the Securities Exchange Act of 1934, as amended.*

ARTICLE V
CONDITIONS PRECEDENT

5.1. Conditions to Obligations of Each Party. *The obligations of ABC and Merger Corporation to effect the Merger and of Titan to deliver the shares of Titan Common Stock issuable pursuant to the Merger shall be subject to the fulfillment at or prior to the Effective Time of the following conditions:*

5.1.1. Stockholder Approval. *This Agreement and the Merger shall have been approved by the unanimous affirmative vote of at least two-thirds of all the holders of the outstanding shares of ABC Common Stock without any exercise of dissenter's appraisal rights.*

5.1.2. No Injunction, Etc. *No action or proceeding shall have been instituted by any public authority or private person prior to the Effective Time before any court or administrative body to restrain, enjoin or otherwise prevent the consummation of the Merger or the transactions contemplated hereby or to recover any damages or obtain other relief as a result of the Merger.*

5.1.3. Governmental Compliance. *All permits, approvals and consents of any governmental body or agency, which Titan or ABC may reasonably deem necessary or appropriate, shall have been obtained.*

5.2. Conditions to the Obligations of Titan and Merger Corporation. *The obligation of Titan and Merger Corporation to effect the Merger shall be subject to the fulfillment, at or prior to the Effective Time (or waiver by them), of the following additional conditions:*

5.2.1. ABC Representation, Performance. *The representations and warran-*

ties of ABC contained in section 2.1 shall be true at and as of the date hereof and shall be repeated and shall be true at and as of the Effective Time with the same effect as though made at and as of the Effective Time. ABC shall have duly performed and complied with all agreements and conditions required by this Agreement to be performed or complied with by it prior to or at the Effective Time. ABC shall have delivered to Titan and Merger Corporation, a certificate, dated the date of the Effective Time, and signed by its Chairman or its President and by its chief financial officer to the effect set forth above in this Section 5.2.1.

5.2.2. Shareholders' Agreement. *The Shareholders' Agreement, dated as of September 15, 1987, among ABC and its shareholders shall have been terminated.*

5.2.3. Stockholders' Restrictive Agreement. *Each ABC stockholder shall have executed and delivered to Titan and Merger Corporation an agreement substantially in the form of the attached Exhibit C.*

5.2.4. Employment Agreements. *ABC and each of James Brown and Thomas Gray shall have executed an Employment Agreement, substantially in the form attached as Exhibit D (the "Employment Agreements").*

5.2.5. Consents. *Any required consent to the Merger under any agreement or contract, the withholding of which would have a material adverse effect on the properties or business of ABC, shall have been obtained.*

5.2.6. Letter as to Certain Tax Matters. *ABC shall have delivered to Titan and Merger Corporation a letter in the form attached as Exhibit E as to certain matters relating to the qualification of the Merger within the meaning of Section 368 of the Code.*

5.2.7. Opinion of Counsel. *Titan and Merger Corporation shall have received a favorable opinion, addressed to them and dated the date of the Effective Time, of Casey, Stern & White, counsel for ABC, satisfactory in substance and form to Titan, Merger Corporation and their counsel, to the effect that: (a) ABC is a corporation duly organized, validly existing and in good standing under the laws of the State of New York and has all requisite corporate power and authority to own and lease its properties and to carry on its business and to enter into this Agreement, consummate the Merger, and carry out the transactions contemplated hereby; (b) the authorized and outstanding capital stock of ABC is as stated in such opinion (which statement shall be consistent with ABC's representations, warranties and agreements herein), and all outstanding shares of such capital stock are duly authorized, validly issued, fully paid and nonassessable, except for the liability for debts, wages and salaries due and owing to any of its laborers, servants or employees, other than contractors for services performed by them for ABC as is imposed on stockholders of closely held corporations by Section 630 of the Business Corporation Law of New York and, to the best of its knowledge, there is no basis for the imposition of such liability on the stockholders of ABC; (c) this Agreement has been duly authorized by all necessary corporate action on the part of ABC, its directors and its stockholders, has been duly executed and delivered by the duly author-*

ized officers of ABC and constitutes the valid and legally binding obligation of ABC enforceable in accordance with its terms; (d) except as set forth in Section 2.1.4, no order, authorization, consent or approval of, or registration, declaration or filing with any governmental authority is required in connection with the consummation by ABC of the transactions contemplated by this Agreement, or to enable the Surviving Corporation to exercise all rights under all permits, concessions, grants, franchises, licenses and other governmental authorizations and approvals which ABC would have exercised immediately prior to the Effective Time; (e) the execution, delivery and performance of this Agreement by ABC and the consummation by ABC of the transactions contemplated hereby will not constitute a breach or violation of or default under the articles of Incorporation or By-Laws of ABC or under any indenture, mortgage, lease or other agreement or instruction, known to such counsel, to which ABC is party or by which it or its properties are bound, or under any judgment, decree or order applicable to ABC or its properties; (f) to the best of such counsel's knowledge, there are no judicial or administrative proceedings or investigations pending or threatened which question the validity of this Agreement or any action taken or to be taken pursuant hereto; (g) to the best of such counsel's knowledge, there are no judicial or administrative actions, suits, proceedings or investigations pending or, to ABC's knowledge, threatened, which might result in any material adverse change in the conditions (financial or other), properties, assets, business, operations, or prospects of ABC or in any material liability on the part of ABC, or which question the validity of this Agreement or of any action taken or to be taken in connection herewith, nor are there any citations, fines or penalties heretofore asserted against ABC under any federal, state or local law which remain unpaid; (h) upon the filing of the Certificate of Merger, the Merger shall have been duly consummated in accordance with the Business Corporation Law of the State of New York with the effect provided therein, and the shares of ABC Common Stock shall have been cancelled and converted and the shares of Merger Corporation Common Stock shall have been converted as provided in Sections 1.4 and 1.5, hereof; (i) the Stockholders' Restrictive Agreement has been duly executed and delivered by each ABC Stockholder and constitutes the valid and legally binding obligation of each ABC Stockholder enforceable in accordance with its terms and (j) such other matters as Titan, Merger Corporation or their counsel may reasonably request.

5.2.8. Corporation Proceedings. *All corporate and other proceedings in connection with the Merger and the other transactions contemplated by this Agreement, and all documents and instruments incident thereto, shall be satisfactory in substance and form to Titan and Merger Corporation and their counsel, and Titan and Merger Corporation and their counsel shall have received all such documents and instruments, or copies thereof, certified if requested, as may be reasonably requested.*

5.3. Conditions to Obligation of ABC to Effect Merger. *The obligation of ABC to effect the Merger shall be subject to the fulfillment, at or prior to the Effective Time (or waiver by ABC), of the following additional conditions:*

5.3.1. Titan, Merger Corporation Representations, Performance, Etc. *The representations and warranties of Titan and Merger Corporation contained in Section 2.2. shall be true at and as of the date hereof and shall be repeated and shall be true at and as of the Effective Time with the same effect as though made at and as of such time (except for changes, not material in the aggregate, in the number of outstanding shares of Titan Common Stock and the number of outstanding employee stock options). Titan and Merger Corporation shall have duly performed and complied with all agreements and conditions required by this Agreement to be performed or complied with by them prior to or at the Effective Time. Titan shall have delivered to ABC a certificate dated the date of the Effective Time and signed by its Chairman, President or any Vice President and by its chief financial officer to such effect.*

5.3.2. Opinion of Counsel. *ABC shall have received a favorable opinion, addressed to ABC and dated the date of the Effective Time, of Brenner, Schwartz & Kelly, counsel for Titan and Merger Corporation, satisfactory in substance and form to ABC and its counsel, to the effect that: (a) Titan is a corporation duly organized, validly existing and in good standing under the laws of the State of New York and has all requisite corporate power and authority to carry on its business as described in the documents referred to in Section 2.2.1 and to enter into this Agreement and carry out the transactions contemplated hereby; (b) Merger Corporation is a corporation duly organized, validly existing and in good standing under the laws of the State of New York and has all requisite corporate power and authority to enter into this Agreement, consummate the Merger and carry out the other transactions contemplated hereby; (c) this Agreement has been duly authorized by all necessary corporate action on the part of Titan and Merger Corporation, has been duly executed and delivered by the respective duly authorized officers of Titan and Merger Corporation and constitutes the valid and legally binding obligation of Titan and Merger Corporation, respectively, enforceable in accordance with its terms; (d) the share of Titan Common Stock issued at the Effective Time pursuant to the Merger are duly authorized, validly issued, fully paid and nonassessable, and no stockholder of Titan has or will have a preemptive right of subscription or purchase in respect thereof; (e) except as provided in Section 2.2.4, no order, authorization, consent or approval of, or registration, declaration or filing with any governmental authority is required in connection with the consummation by Titan and Merger Corporation of the transactions contemplated by this Agreement; (f) the execution, delivery and performance of this Agreement by Titan and Merger Corporation and the consummation by them of the transactions contemplated hereby will not constitute a breach or violation of or default under the Certificate of Incorporation or By-Laws of Titan or Merger Corporation or under any indenture, mortgage, lease or other agreement or instrument, known to such counsel, to which either is a party or by which either or its properties are bound, or under any judgment, decree or order of any governmental authority having jurisdiction over Titan or Merger Corporation or their respective properties known to such counsel; (g) to the best of such counsel's knowledge, there are no judicial or administrative pro-*

ceedings or investigations pending or threatened which question the validity of this Agreement or any action taken or to be taken pursuant hereto; (h) upon the filing of the Certificate of Merger, the Merger shall have been duly consummated in accordance with the Business Corporation Law of the State of New York with the effect provided therein, and the shares of ABC Common Stock shall have been cancelled and converted and the shares of Merger Corporation Common Stock shall have been converted as provided in Sections 1.4 and 1.5 hereof; (i) the Merger will qualify as a reorganization within the meaning of Section 368 of the Code; no gain or loss will be recognized to the ABC stockholders upon the exchange of their shares of ABC Common Stock for shares of Titan Common Stock (except for fractional share interests); the basis of the shares of Titan Common Stock received by the ABC stockholders will be the same as the basis of the ABC Common Stock exchanged therefor; the holding period of the shares of Titan Common Stock received by ABC stockholders will include the holding period of the shares of ABC Common Stock exchanged therefor, provided that such shares of ABC Common Stock were held as capital assets on the date of the merger and (j) such other matters as ABC or its counsel may reasonably request.

5.3.3. Corporate Proceedings. *All corporate and other proceedings in connection with the Merger and the other transactions contemplated by this Agreement, and all documents and instruments incident thereto, shall be satisfactory in substance and form to ABC and its counsel, and ABC and its counsel shall have received all such documents and instruments, or copies thereof, certified if requested, as may be reasonably requested.*

ARTICLE VI
TERMINATION, AMENDMENT, WAIVER

6.1. Automatic Termination. *This Agreement shall automatically terminate and the Merger shall automatically be abandoned without any further action on the part of any party hereto on December 31, 199__ if the Merger shall not have theretofore become effective.*

6.2. Termination. *This Agreement may be terminated and the Merger abandoned at any time (whether before or after the approval thereof by the stockholders of ABC or Merger Corporation or both) prior to the Effective Time:*

(a) by mutual consent of the Boards of Directors of ABC, Titan and Merger corporation evidenced by appropriate resolutions;

(b) by Titan or Merger Corporation by notice to ABC (i) if any of the conditions set forth in Section 5.1 or 5.2 shall not have been fulfilled by November 10, 199__ or (ii) if any material default under or material breach of any agreement or condition of this Agreement, or any material misrepresentation or material breach of any warranty contained herein, on the part of ABC shall have occurred and shall not have been cured; or

(c) by ABC by notice to Titan and Merger Corporation (i) if any of the conditions set forth in Section 5.1 or 5.3 shall not have been fulfilled by November 10, 199__, (ii) if any material default under or material breach of any agreement or condition of this Agreement, or any material misrepresentation or material breach of any warranty contained herein, on the part of Titan or Merger Corporation shall have occurred and shall not have been cured.

6.3. Effect of Termination. *In the event of the termination of this Agreement and abandonment of the Merger pursuant to the provisions of Section 6.1 or 6.2 hereof, this Agreement shall become void and have no effect, without any liability on the part of any party thereto or its directors, officers or stockholders in respect of this Agreement, except the liabilities of each of the parties hereto to pay the expenses incurred by it or on its behalf.*

6.4. Amendment. *This Agreement may be amended by action of the Boards of Directors of the parties hereto (or a duly authorized committee thereof) at any time before or after approval hereof by the stockholders of ABC, but after any such approval no amendment shall be made which substantially changes the terms hereof without the further approval of such stockholders. This Agreement may not be amended except by an instrument in writing duly executed and delivered on behalf of each of the parties hereto.*

6.5. Extension; Waiver. *At any time prior to the Effective Time, the Boards of Directors of Titan or Merger Corporation, on the one hand, or ABC, on the other (or a duly authorized committee of any of them), may (a) extend the time for the performance of any of the obligations or other acts of the other, (b) waive any inaccuracies in the representations and warranties of the other parties contained herein or in any document or instrument delivered pursuant hereto and (c) waive compliance by the other with any of the agreements or conditions contained herein. Any agreement on the part of a party hereto to any such extension or waiver shall be valid if set forth in an instrument in writing duly executed and delivered on behalf of such party.*

ARTICLE VII
DEFINITIONS, MISCELLANEOUS

7.1. Definition of Certain Terms. *As used herein, the following terms shall have the following meanings:*

> Agreement: *this Agreement and Plan of Merger and Reorganization.*
> Cash Conversion Rate: *as defined in Section 1.6.*
> Code: *the Internal Revenue Code of 1986, as amended.*
> ABC: *as defined in the first paragraph of this Agreement.*
> ABC Common Stock: *shares of Common Stock, par value $.01, of ABC.*
> ABC Financial Statements: *the consolidated financial statements of ABC for the years ended, December 31, 19____ to December 31, 19____, in-*

clusive, including the notes thereto, certified by Thatcher, Romano & Lury, which financial statements include in each case a balance sheet, a statement of income, a statement of changes in stockholders' equity and a statement of changes in financial position.

Effective Time: *the time at which the Certificate of Merger is filed with the Department of State of New York in accordance with Section 904 of the Business Corporation Law of New York.*

ERISA: *the Employment Retirement Income Security Act of 1974, as amended.*

Merger: *the merger of Merger Corporation into ABC in accordance with the terms and conditions of this Agreement.*

Merger Corporation: *as defined in the first paragraph of this Agreement.*

Titan: *as defined in the first paragraph of this Agreement.*

TItan Common Stock: *shares of Common Stock, par value $1.00 of Titan.*

Titan Companies: *Titan and Titan Subsidiaries.*

Titan Financial Statements: *(a) the consolidated financial statements of Titan and its consolidated subsidiaries, and for the years ended December 31, 199__ to December 31, 199__, inclusive, certified by Coopers, Andersen, Price & Co. and (b) the unaudited consolidated financial statements of Titan and its consolidated subsidiaries as at, and for the three-month period ended March 31, 199__, and the three-month and six-month period ended, June 30, 199__, which financial statements include in each case a consolidated balance sheet, a consolidated statement of income, a consolidated statement of changes in stockholders' equity and a consolidated statement of changes in financial position.*

Titan Subsidiary: *any corporation, association, or other business entity a majority (by number of votes) of the shares of capital stock (or other voting interests) of which is owned or controlled by Titan or another Titan Subsidiary.*

Stockholders' Restrictive Agreement: *as defined in Section 5.2.4.*

Surviving Corporation: *as defined in Section 1.1.*

7.2. Survival of Representations and Warranties. *The representations and Merger Corporation contained in Article II and the agreements of ABC and of Titan and Merger Corporation contained in Articles III and IV shall survive for a period of 18 months after the Effective Time, provided that the representations and warranties contained in Section 2.1.7 shall survive until 60 days after the final determination of the tax liabilities of ABC for the fiscal years ended April 30, 199__ through 199__. Each stockholder of ABC, by virtue of being entitled to receive any Titan common Stock as a result of the Merger, hereby agrees to indemnify Titan and Merger Corporation for any losses, liabilities, costs or expenses incurred by Titan or Merger Corporation arising or resulting from (i) any of the representations or warranties of ABC not being true and correct as of the date hereof and as of the Effective Time or (ii) ABC failing to perform any agreement contained in this Agreement and required to be performed by ABC at or before the Effective Time, provided that the extent of any ABC stockholder's liability hereunder shall be limited to an amount equal to the number of shares of Titan Common Stock received by such stockholder as a result of the Merger multiplied by the Cash Conversion Rate. With respect to liability under Section 2.1.7 hereof for United States federal income tax through 199__, any ABC stockholder, to the extent potentially liable and at his own expense, may participate in contesting such liability, unless Titan determines in good faith that such participation will materially affect other interests of Titan.*

7.3. Expenses. *ABC and Titan Merger Corporation shall assume and bear all expenses, costs and fees incurred or assumed by such party in the preparation and execution of this Agreement and compliance herewith, whether or not the Merger herein provided for shall be consummated, and Titan and ABC shall indemnify and hold each other harmless from and against any and all liabilities or claims in respect of any such expenses, costs or fees.*

7.4. Notices. *All notices, consents, requests, instructions, approvals and other communications provided for herein and all legal process in regard hereto shall be validly given, made or served, if in writing and delivered personally or sent by registered or certified mail, postage prepaid, (i) if to Titan or Merger Corporation, to _____ and; (ii) if to ABC, to _____, or, in each case, at such other address as may be specified in writing to the other parties.*

7.5. Miscellaneous. *The headings contained in this Agreement are for reference purposes only and shall not affect in any way the meaning or interpretation of this Agreement. This Agreement constitutes the entire agreement and supersedes all prior agreements and understandings, both written and oral, among the parties with respect to the subject matter hereof. This Agreement may be executed in several counterparts, each of which shall be deemed an original, and all of which shall constitute one and the same instrument. This Agreement shall be governed in all respects, including validity, interpretation and effect, by the laws of the State of New York.*

IN WITNESS WHEREOF, the parties have duly executed this Agreement as of the date first above written.

ABC ADVERTISING. INC.

Attest:

By _____
       Title:

_____
       Secretary

TITAN MERGER CORPORATION

Attest:

By _____
       Title:

_____
       Secretary

TITAN INTERNATIONAL INC.

Attest:

By _____
       Title:

_____
       Secretary

Exhibit 16–2

MERGER AGREEMENT

Index

MERGER AGREEMENT

This Merger Agreement is made on June 28, 199__ by and between MOD-ERN TOOL & DIE CORPORATION, a New York corporation ("Modern"), certain shareholders of Modern whose names and signatures appear at the end of this Agreement (the "Principal Shareholders"), UNIVERSAL MERGER CORPORA-TION, a New York corporation ("Merger Corporation") and UNIVERSAL MAN-UFACTURING, INC., a Delaware corporation ("Universal"), the holder of all of the issued and outstanding capital stock of Merger Corporation.

WHEREAS, the parties deem it advisable and in the best interests of each of Modern and Merger Corporation and their respective stockholders that Merger Corporation be merged into Modern pursuant to the Business Corporation Law ("BCL") of the State of New York upon the terms and conditions contained in this Agreement which shall constitute the plan of merger pursuant to Section 902 of the BCL;

NOW, THEREFORE, the parties agree as follows:

ARTICLE I
THE MERGER

1.1. Constituent and Surviving Corporations. *Modern and Merger Corporation shall be the constituent corporations to the Merger. At the Effective Time, Merger Corporation shall be merged into Modern in accordance with the BCL, and Modern shall be the surviving corporation (herein sometimes called the "Surviving Corporation") of the merger. The name, identity, existence, rights, privileges, powers, franchises, properties and assets and the liabilities and obligations of Modern shall continue unaffected and unimpaired by the Merger. Upon the filing of a Certificate of Merger with the Department of State of New York (the "Effective Time"), the identity and separate existence of Merger Corporation shall cease and all rights, privileges, powers, franchises, properties and assets and the liabilities and obligations of Merger Corporation shall be vested in Modern. For accounting purposes, the merger shall be deemed effective as of 12:01 a.m., September 30, 199__, hereinafter called the Effective Time.*

1.2. Certificate of Incorporation; By-Laws. *At the Effective Time, the Certificate of Incorporation of Modern shall be amended to read in its entirety as set forth in the Certificate of Merger attached as Exhibit A and, as so amended, shall be the Certificate of Incorporation of the Surviving Corporation until further amended as provided therein or by law. At the Effective Time, the By-Laws of Modern shall be amended to read in their entirety as set forth in the attached Exhibit B and, as so amended, shall be the By-Laws of the Surviving Corporation until further amended as provided therein or by law.*

1.3. Officers and Directors.*Each of the Principal Shareholders and each other director of Modern immediately prior to the Effective Time shall submit his or her resignation as an officer and/or director of Modern as of the Effective Time. The directors of the Surviving Corporation shall be the persons serving as directors of Merger Corporation immediately prior to the Effective Time. The officers of the Surviving Corporation shall be elected by the Board of Directors at a meeting held promptly after the Effective Time.*

1.4. Conversion of Merger Corporation Common Stock. *At the Effective Time, each share of Merger Corporation Common Stock issued and outstanding immediately prior to the Effective Time shall, by virtue of the Merger and without any action on the part of the holder thereof, be converted into and become one fully paid and nonassessable share of Common Stock, $1.00 par value, of the Surviving Corporation.*

1.5. Conversion of Modern Common Stock. *Subject to the conditions and limitations set forth in this Agreement, at the Effective Time each share of Modern Common Stock issued and outstanding at the Effective Time by virtue of the Merger and without any action on the part of the holder thereof, shall cease to exist and be converted into and become $17.50 cash, payable without interest (the "Merger Price"). Nevertheless, subject to Section _____, holders of shares ("Dissenting Shares") who have taken all necessary steps under Section 623 of the BCL to dissent and demand payment and are otherwise entitled to payment thereunder shall receive such amount as they become entitled to receive thereunder. All certificates representing shares of Modern Common Stock held by its stockholders at the Effective Time shall thereafter be surrendered for cancellation in exchange for the Merger Price or, in the case of holders of Dissenting Shares, into such amount as they are entitled to receive under Section 623 of the BCL.*

If a holder of Dissenting Shares shall withdraw his or her demand for appraisal with the consent of Modern, if required by the BCL, or shall become ineligible for such appraisal (through failure to perfect or otherwise), then, as of the Effective Time of the occurrence of such withdrawal or ineligibility, which ever last occurs, such shareholder shall receive the Merger Price. Modern will not voluntarily make any payment or commitment with respect to any demands for appraisal and shall not, except with the prior written consent of Universal, settle or offer to settle any such demands. Each holder of Dissenting Shares shall have only such rights and remedies as are granted to such a holder under Section 623 of the BCL.

1.6. Stock Options and Related Matters. *At the Effective Time, holders of outstanding options to purchase Modern Common Stock heretofore granted under an employee stock option plan, program or arrangement will receive in settlement (whether such options are immediately exercisable or not) a cash payment from Modern in an amount equal to the excess, if any, of the Merger Price over the exercise price per share for each of the options. At the Effective Time, all such outstanding options shall be converted into, and thereafter represent only the right to receive, the cash settlement amount provided in this Section. At the Effective Time, each employee stock option, stock bonus or stock award plan of the Company which provides for the issuance of Modern Common Stock shall be terminated and no further stock awards, stock options or stock appreciation rights shall be granted thereunder.*

1.7. Payment of the Merger Price; Exchange Agent. *(a) From and after the Effective Time, a bank or trust company to be designated by Universal (the "Exchange Agent") shall act as exchange agent pursuant to the Exchange Agency Agreement attached as Exhibit C in effecting the exchange of cash for certificates which, prior to the Effective Time, represented Modern Common Stock.*

(b) If all of the conditions to their obligations described in Article IV have been met or waived in writing, Universal shall provide funds to Merger Corporation and Merger Corporation shall, immediately prior to the Effective Time, deposit in trust with the Exchange Agent funds in an aggregate amount equal to the product obtained by multiplying the number of shares of Modern Common Stock outstanding at the close of the business of Modern on the date immediately before the date of the Effective Time (other than shares held in the treasury of Modern and its subsidiaries) by the Merger Price. However, such amount shall be reduced by the amounts payable to the Escrow Agent pursuant to Section 1.8 of this Agreement. The net amount so deposited is called the "Payment Fund." The Exchange Agent shall be instructed in the Exchange Agency Agreement that payments to be made to the Principal Shareholders (but not to any other stockholders of Modern) from the Payment Fund shall be subject to reduction pursuant to Section 1.8. The Payment Fund shall be invested by the Exchange Agent as directed by the Surviving Corporation and any net earnings shall be paid to the Surviving Corporation as and when requested by the Surviving Corporation.

(c) If all the conditions to their obligations described in Article IV have been met or waived in writing, Universal shall provide funds to Merger Corporation and Merger Corporation shall pay to Modern an amount in cash sufficient to make the payments to holders of options to purchase Modern Common Stock as provided in Section 1.6.

(d) The Exchange Agent, pursuant to irrevocable instructions, shall make the payments described in Section 1.5 out of the Payment Fund. The Payment Fund shall not be used for any purpose other than as provided herein. Promptly following determination of the maximum number of shares which the holders thereof have claimed are Dissenting Shares, the Exchange Agent shall promptly repay to the Surviving Corporation from the Payment Fund an amount equal to the product obtained by multiplying the number of such Dissenting Shares by the Merger Price.

(e) Promptly after the Effective Time, the Exchange Agent shall mail to each record holder of certificates which immediately prior to the Effective Time represented shares of Modern Common Stock a form of letter of transmittal and instructions for use in surrendering such certificates and receiving payment therefor.

(f) Upon the surrender of each certificate in proper form pursuant to applicable instructions and with appropriate endorsements, signature guarantees and evidence of authority of those endorsing in a representative capacity, the holder shall be paid within 10 days of the surrender of his certificate, without interest thereon,

the amount of cash to which he is then entitled hereunder and such certificate shall forthwith be cancelled. Until so surrendered and exchanged, each such certificate shall represent solely the right to receive the cash into which the shares have been converted. Each holder must surrender his certificates in order to be paid the cash to which he is otherwise entitled. If any cash to be paid in the Merger is to be paid to a person other than the holder in whose name a certificate is registered, it shall be a condition of such exchange that the certificate surrendered shall be properly endorsed or otherwise in proper form for transfer and that the person requesting such exchange shall pay to the Exchange Agent any transfer or other taxes and fees required by reason of the payment of such cash to a person other than the registered holder of the certificate surrendered, or shall establish to the satisfaction of the Exchange Agent that such tax has been paid or is not applicable. Notwithstanding the foregoing, neither the Exchange Agent nor any party hereto shall be liable to a holder of Shares for any cash delivered pursuant hereto to a public official pursuant to applicable abandoned property laws.

(g) Promptly following the date which is six months after the Effective Time, the Exchange Agent shall return to the Surviving Corporation all cash, certificates and other instruments in its possession relating to the transactions described in this Agreement and the Exchange Agent's duties shall terminate. Thereafter, holders of certificates representing Modern Common Stock may surrender such certificates to the Surviving Corporation and (subject to applicable abandoned property, escheat and similar laws) receive such amount, without interest, as they may be entitled to receive hereunder, but shall have no greater rights against the Surviving Corporation than may be accorded to general creditors of the Surviving Corporation under New York law.

(h) After the Effective Time, there shall be no transfers on the stock transfer books of the Surviving Corporation of any shares of Modern Common Stock. If, after the Effective Time, certificates previously representing shares of Modern Common Stock are presented to the Surviving Corporation or the Exchange Agent, they shall be cancelled and exchanged as provided herein.

1.8. Escrow Fund. An aggregate amount in cash equal to $2,500,000 (the "Escrow Fund") shall be deducted from the amount payable to the Principal Shareholders pursuant to Section 1.5. The amounts so deducted shall be paid as of the Effective Time to Second National Bank, as Escrow Agent (the "Escrow Agent") under the Indemnity and Escrow Agreement attached as Exhibit D (the "Escrow Agreement"). The Escrow Fund shall be for the purposes stated in the Escrow Agreement, and shall be administered and repaid to Universal and/or distributed to the Principal Shareholders as provided therein.

1.9. Determination of Net Worth. (a) Modern shall retain Coopers, Andersen, Price & Co. to audit Modern's balance sheet as of December 31, 199___. If the Merger is not consummated, half of the fees and expenses incurred by Modern for such audit will be reimbursed by Universal. Such fees and expenses shall not be taken into account in determining Modern's net worth as herein provided.

(b) Modern's net worth shall be calculated in the manner prescribed in Section _____ hereof and shall be not less than $5,000,000 as of June 30, 199__ .

(c) If Modern's net worth shall be less than $5,000,000 as of June 30, 199__, and Universal shall elect to close this Agreement, the amount payable to the Principal Shareholders in connection with the Merger shall be subject to deduction of an amount equal to the deficiency in Modern's net worth below $1,800,000, but in no event by more than $2,500,000. Such deduction shall be accomplished by repaying the amount of such deficiency to Universal from the Escrow Fund to the extent funds are available.

1.10. Hart-Scott-Rodino Act Compliance. *Modern, Universal and Merger Corporation shall prepare and file as soon as practicable after the date of this Agreement their respective notifications and reports with the U.S. Department of Justice (DOJ) and the Federal Trade Commission (FTC) pursuant to Section 7A of the Hart-Scott-Rodino Federal Trade Commission Improvements Act. Each of them shall thereafter promptly respond to requests of the DOJ or FTC for additional information and shall seek early termination of the waiting period.*

1.11. Proxy Statement; Other Filings. *Modern shall prepare a proxy statement and solicit proxies with respect to the Merger in compliance with the Exchange Act and the rules and regulations of the Commission. Modern shall file the proxy statement and proxy with the Commission and shall use its reasonable efforts to obtain prompt clearance by the Commission. The proxy statement (including the favorable recommendation of Modern's board of directors) and proxy shall be promptly mailed by Modern to its shareholders after SEC clearance has been obtained. Modern shall also promptly prepare and file any other filings required under federal or state securities laws relating to the Merger and the transactions contemplated herein. Modern and Universal each shall use its best efforts to obtain and furnish the information required to be included in the Proxy Statement and any other filings. Such information shall be accurate and complete in all material respects and shall not omit to state any material fact required to make such information not false or misleading. The Proxy Statement and any other filing shall comply as to form in all material respects with all applicable requirements of law.*

1.12. Meeting of Shareholders. *Modern shall take all action necessary to call, give notice, convene and hold a meeting of its shareholders as promptly as practicable to consider and vote upon the adoption of this Merger Agreement.*

1.13. No Shopping. *Modern shall not, directly or indirectly, through any officer, director, agent or otherwise, (i) solicit, initiate or encourage the submission of inquiries, proposals or offers relating to any acquisition or purchase of assets of or any equity interest in, Modern or any of its subsidiaries or any tender offer, exchange offer, merger, consolidation, business combination, sale of substantial assets or of a substantial amount of assets, sale of securities, liquidation, dissolution or similar transactions involving Modern, or (ii) enter into or participate in any discussions or negotiations regarding any of the foregoing, or furnish to any other person any information with respect to the business, properties or assets of Mod-*

ern or any of the foregoing, or (iii) otherwise cooperate in any way with, or assist to participate in, facilitate or encourage, any effort or attempt by any other Person to do or seek any of the foregoing.

1.14. Certificate of Merger. *Upon the fulfillment of all of the conditions precedent to the respective obligations of the parties, Merger Corporation and Modern will cause to be executed and filed, pursuant to Section 904 of the BCL, a Certificate of Merger in the office of the Secretary of State of New York with respect to the Merger.*

1.15. Further Agreements. *(a) Each party shall use its best efforts to take all such action as may be necessary or appropriate in order to effectuate the merger under the BCL as promptly as possible including, without limitation, the filing under the BCL of a Certificate of Merger consistent with the terms of this Agreement. If at any time after the Effective Time, any further action is necessary or desirable to carry out the purposes of this Agreement and to vest the Surviving Corporation with full right, title and possession to all assets, property, rights, privileges, powers and franchises of either of the Constituent Corporations, the officers of such corporations are fully authorized in the name of their corporation or otherwise to take, and shall take, all such lawful and necessary action.*

(b) Each Principal Shareholder hereby agrees to retain all of his shares of Modern Common Stock held on the date of this Agreement and to vote them in favor of the Merger at the shareholders meeting called for that purpose and any and all adjournments thereof.

(For remainder of Agreement, see Index and other Forms of Agreements in this chapter and other chapters.)

Exhibit 16-3

UNIVERSAL MANUFACTURING, INC.
456 Third Street
New York, N.Y. 10085

_____, *199__*

Second National Bank of New York,
*   as Exchange Agent*
300 Wall Street
New York, New York 10075

    Re: Exchange Agency Agreement

Dear Sirs:

    Universal Merger Corporation, A New York corporation ("Merger Corporation"), Universal Manufacturing, Inc., a Delaware corporation and the holder of all of the issued and outstanding capital stock of Merger Corporation ("Universal"), Modern Tool & Die Corporation, a New York corporation ("Modern") and certain shareholders of Modern whose names appear at the end of the Merger Agreement have entered into a Merger Agreement, dated _____, 199__ (the "Merger Agreement"), a copy of which is attached hereto as Exhibit A.

    Pursuant to the Merger Agreement, among other things, (i) Merger Corporation will be merged into Modern (the "Merger") and Modern will be the surviving corporation (sometimes called "Surviving Corporation"). At the Effective Time, each share of Modern Common Stock issued and outstanding immediately prior to the merger will cease to exist and be converted into a right to receive a cash payment of $17.50 per share payable without interest except for Dissenting Shares as provided in Section 1.5 Agreement (the "Merger Price").

    Modern, Universal and Merger Corporation hereby appoint you and you hereby agree to act as Exchange Agent ("Exchange Agent") in connection with the Merger, to effectuate the exchange for cash for certificates which, prior to the Effective Time, represented Modern Common Stock ("Certificates") and such other duties as are expressly provided herein.

1. The Payment Fund.

    If all conditions described in Article IV of the Merger Agreement have been met or waived in writing, Universal will provide funds to Merger Corporation and Merger Corporation will, immediately prior to the Effective Time, deposit in trust with Exchange Agent funds an aggregate amount equal to the product obtained by multiplying (i) the number of shares of Modern Common Stock outstanding at the close of business of Modern on the date immediately before the date of the Effective Time (other than shares held in the treasury of Modern), by (ii) the Merger Price. However, the amount deposited will be reduced by the amounts payable pursuant to Section 1.9 of the Merger Agreement. Such net amount deposited by Merger Corporation with Exchange Agent shall be called the "Payment Fund."

The Payment Fund shall not be used for any purpose other than as provided herein.

Promptly following determination of the maximum number of shares which the holders thereof have claimed are Dissenting Shares, Exchange Agent shall pay to Surviving Corporation from the Payment Fund an amount equal to the product obtained by multiplying the number of shares claimed as Dissenting Shares by the Merger Price.

2. Payment of Payment Fund.

Exchange Agent shall invest all amounts deposited with it pursuant to the Agreement as may be directed from time to time by Surviving Corporation, provided that all of such investments shall be obligations of or guaranteed by the United States of America, certificates of deposit in commercial banks with capital exceeding $1,000,000,000 (collectively, "Permitted Investments") or in money market funds which are invested solely in Permitted Investments. The maturities of permitted Investments shall be such as to permit Exchange Agent to make payment of (i) the Payment Fund to persons entitled thereto and Merger Corporation (ii) any net earnings of the Payment Fund to Surviving Corporation as and when requested by Surviving Corporation

3. Transmittal Letters and Instructions to Surrender Certificates.

Promptly after the Effective Time, Modern shall cause National Stock Transfer Company (the "Transfer Agent") to deliver to Exchange Agent the names and addresses of the record holders of Modern Common Stock as of the close of business on the day immediately preceding the date of the Effective Time of the Merger, and Exchange Agent shall mail to each record holder of Certificates (i) a form of letter of transmittal ("Letter of Transmittal") and instructions ("Instructions") in the forms attached hereto as Exhibits B and C, respectively, for use in surrendering Certificates and receiving payment therefor; (ii) a notice advising such holder of the effectiveness of the Merger and (iii) a self-addressed return envelope.

Exchange Agent shall examine the Letters of Transmittal and Certificates delivered to Exchange Agent to ascertain whether (i) the Letters of Transmittal are filled out and executed in accordance with the Instructions and (ii) the Certificates appear to be properly surrendered and endorsed for transfer. In each case where some irregularity exists, Exchange Agent shall endeavor to take such action as may be necessary to cause such irregularity to be corrected.

Upon receipt by Exchange Agent of any request for payment of the Merger Price in respect of Certificates which have been lost, stolen or destroyed, Exchange Agent shall notify Surviving Corporation thereof and shall not pay any portion of the Merger Price in respect of such lost, stolen or destroyed Certificate unless and until the person making such request shall have provided to Exchange Agent suitable evidence of such loss, destruction or theft, in proper form pursuant to the Letters of Transmittal and the Instructions, including without limitation, an affidavit of loss and an indemnity bond in form satisfactory to Exchange Agent.

4. Surrender and Cancellation of Certificates; Payment for Shares.

(a) Within ten days of a delivery of a properly completed Letter of Transmittal and the surrender of a Certificate properly endorsed for transfer and otherwise in compliance with the Instructions, Exchange Agent, subject to the provisions of paragraph 4(b), shall pay the Merger Price for shares represented by such Certificates to the holder thereof or its properly designated transferee, without interest thereon, and such Certificate shall forthwith be cancelled by Exchange Agent. No payment shall be made by Exchange Agent as to any Modern Common Stock until a Certificate or Certificates representing such shares are received by Exchange Agent, or the proper lost certificate procedure, as provided in paragraph 3, has been completed. If any payments are to be made to a person other than the holder in whose name a Certificate is registered, it shall be a condition of such exchange that the Certificate surrendered shall be properly endorsed or otherwise in proper form for transfer and that the person requesting such exchange shall pay to Exchange Agent any transfer or other taxes and fees required by reason of the payment of such cash to a person other than the registered holder of the Certificate surrendered, or shall establish to the satisfaction of Exchange Agent that such tax has been paid or is not applicable. Notwithstanding the foregoing, neither Exchange Agent nor any party hereto shall be liable to a holder of shares for any cash delivered pursuant hereto to a public official pursuant to applicable abandoned property laws.

(b) The aggregate Merger Price payable to Exchange Agent from the Payment Fund to each of the persons named as Principal Shareholders in the Merger Agreement shall be reduced by \$_____. The aggregate amount of such reduction shall be deposited in escrow pursuant to Section 1.8 of the Merger Agreement.

(c) Promptly following the date which is six calendar months after the Effective Time, Exchange Agent shall return to Surviving Corporation all cash, Certificates and other instruments in its possession relating to the transactions described in this Agreement and Exchange Agent's duties shall terminate. Thereafter, holders of Certificates shall be entitled to look only to the Surviving Corporation for payment for shares represented by Certificates.

5. Duties and Responsibilities of Exchange Agent.

As Exchange Agent hereunder you:
(i) shall have no duties or obligations other than those specifically set forth herein;
(ii) will be regarded as making no representations and having no responsibili-

ties as to the validity, sufficiency, value or genuineness of any Certificates or the shares represented thereby deposited with you hereunder except for willful wrongdoing or gross negligence in the performance of the duties expressly assumed by you hereunder;

(iii) shall not be obligated to take any legal action hereunder which might in your judgment involve any expense or liability, unless you shall have been furnished with such indemnity as shall be reasonably satisfactory to you;

(iv) may rely on and shall be protected in acting in reliance upon any opinion, notice, letter, telegram or other document delivered to you and believed by you to be genuine and to have been signed by the proper party or parties;

(v) may rely on and shall be protected in acting upon written or oral instructions with respect to any matter relating to your actions as Exchange Agent under this Agreement;

(vi) may consult counsel satisfactory to you (including counsel for Universal) and the opinion of such counsel shall be full and complete authorization and protection in respect to any action taken, suffered or omitted by you hereunder and in good faith and in accordance with the opinion of such counsel; and

(vii) shall not be called upon at any time to advise any person surrendering shares hereunder as to the wisdom of surrendering shares or as to the market value of decline or appreciation in market value of any share.

6. Indemnification.

Universal and Surviving Corporation hereby agree to indemnify and hold harmless Exchange Agent against any loss, liability or expense incurred without negligence or bad faith on the part of Exchange Agent arising out of or in connection with the performance of its duties hereunder, including the costs and expenses of defending any claim of liability which may arise against it hereunder.

7. Removal or Resignation of Exchange Agent.

Universal may remove Exchange Agent at any time upon written notice to be delivered to Exchange Agent. Exchange Agent may resign by written notice to the parties hereto; provided that such resignation shall not be effective until Universal has appointed a successor Exchange Agent which has agreed in writing to act hereunder.

8. Parties in Interest; Assignment.

This Agreement shall inure to the benefit of, and the obligations created hereby shall be binding upon, the successors and permitted assigns of the parties hereto. Any assignment of this Agreement by any party without the prior written consent of the other parties shall be void. Nothing in this Agreement is intended to confer any rights or remedies on anyone other than a party to this Agreement or the holder of a valid assignment of rights under this Agreement.

9. Compensation to Exchange Agent.

For its services rendered hereunder, Exchange Agent shall be entitled to the compensation set forth in Annex I *hereto.*

10. Notices.

All notices, checks, Letters of Transmittal and other communications delivered in connection with this Agreement shall be validly given or made, if in writing and delivered personally or sent by registered or first class mail, postage prepaid, if to record holders of Modern Common Stock, to their respective addresses set forth pursuant to paragraph 3 or, if to the parties hereto, to their respective addresses set forth below:

If to Universal, to:

456 Third Street
New York, NY 10085
Attention: Vice President and
General Counsel

If to Modern, to:

789 Fourth Street
White Plains, NY 10599
Attention: Financial Vice President

If to Escrow Agent, to:

300 Wall Street
New York, NY 10075
Attention: Corporate Service Dept.

11. Amendment.

This Amendment may not be amended except by an instrument in writing duly executed and delivered on behalf of each of the parties hereto.

12. Definition of Certain Terms.

As used herein, the following terms shall have the following meanings:

Modern Common Stock: *shares of common stock, par value $1.00, of Modern.*

Dissenting Shares: *shares of Modern Common Stock of holders who have taken all necessary steps under Section 623 of the Business Corporation Law of the State of New York to dissent and demand payment of the fair value of their shares.*

Effective Time: *the time at which the Certificate of Merger is filed with the Department of State of New York in accordance with Section 904 of the Business Corporation Law of the State of New York.*

13. Miscellaneous.

The headings contained herein are for reference purposes only and shall not affect in any way the meaning or interpretation of this Agreement. This Agreement constitutes the entire agreement and supersedes all prior agreements and understandings, both written and oral, among the parties with respect to the subject matter hereof. This Agreement may be executed in counterparts and each shall be deemed an original, and all of which shall constitute one and the same instrument. This Agreement shall be construed and enforced in accordance with the laws of the State of New York.

Please acknowledge receipt of this Agreement and confirm your acceptance of the arrangements herein provided by signing and returning to us the enclosed copy of this Agreement.

Very truly yours,

UNIVERSAL MANUFACTURING, INC.

By: _____

UNIVERSAL MERGER CORPORATION

By: _____

MODERN TOOL & DIE CORPORATION

By: _____

ACCEPTED AND AGREED:

DATE: _____

SECOND NATIONAL BANK OF NEW YORK,
  as Exchange Agent

By: _____

17

Closing an Acquisition

OVERVIEW

Those attending an acquisition closing for the first time are usually amazed at the large numbers of documents being signed and delivered in multiple copies. Veterans will humorously inquire whether the lawyers hope to charge by the pound for the paperwork. However, they know that each document has a function in completing the acquisition.

The closing of an acquisition is an event governed by the acquisition contract. Its objective is to permit sellers, buyers, lenders and others to complete their transactions in a coordinated manner subject only to risks they have agreed to undertake.

Although rarely stated in words, buyers cannot pay the price and assume the risk of later delivery of documents transferring the business. Sellers cannot transfer the business and risk a later failure or refusal by the buyer to pay and deliver commitments. Lenders cannot advance funds and hope that the borrower will later provide a valid promissory note and mortgage on the acquired assets. None of them can risk delivering their money or assets, only to learn later that a government agency has disapproved the acquisition or that taxes will be imposed differently than expected.

The "simultaneous" closing provides a method to eliminate or reduce these risks. A closing date and place are chosen and inserted in the acquisition contract. The lawyers and their clients then prepare documents to be delivered and payments to be made simultaneously or in an agreed sequence on the closing date. When the date arrives, all documents are placed on the table in a conference room at the office where the closing is held. They are carefully reviewed and signed. When everyone is satisfied with the documents, they are exchanged and funds or securities are transferred in payment.

No one must risk future performance by others except as agreed in the acquisition contract and related contracts. When the last steps are completed, the businessmen and professionals usually relax, shake hands and enjoy a lunch or dinner to celebrate the acquisition and start new working relations on a cordial note.

TIMING

Selection of a closing date depends on an estimate of time required to accomplish the steps which are conditions to the obligations of seller and buyer to complete the acquisition.

An acquisition contract can sometimes be signed and closed on the same day. In situations where confidentiality is important or negotiations have been difficult, the buyer and seller may agree that an immediate closing is best. This is possible if the contract conditions are fairly simple and steps can be taken to fulfill them at or prior to the closing. For example, when a buyer will pay cash from its treasury for a privately owned business and no approvals or rulings are needed from government agencies, it is common to instruct the lawyers to prepare the closing documents together with the acquisition contract so that the acquisition can be closed immediately.

Many acquisitions, however, are subject to the fulfillment of conditions which are time-consuming and perhaps also difficult to accomplish. Examples are government approvals or clearances, tax rulings, registration and listing of securities, favorable votes by public shareholders, consents by customers and suppliers to the assignment of important contracts, negotiations with labor unions and sometimes the completion of a "due diligence" investigation. Although most acquisition contracts do not contain a condition excusing the buyer if it cannot obtain financing, the buyer may want some time to arrange a loan on favorable terms. In these situations, both buyer and seller will recognize that the acquisition cannot be closed quickly, but will want the protection of a signed contract before undertaking difficult, costly and time-consuming efforts. The acquisition contract will usually provide for a closing within a short period after the last of the conditions is fulfilled, but will also state that the contract will terminate if the conditions are not fulfilled by a final date, sometimes called a "drop dead" date.

BASIC PROCEDURES

Closing procedures follow different patterns depending on the acquisition structure: merger, stock purchase or assets purchase. They differ again if multiple party transactions are involved including triangular mergers. They become still more complex and must be very carefully planned when combined with the closing of loans used to pay the acquisition price.

Merger. The closing of a merger must be timed so that closing documents evidencing fulfillment of all conditions can be reviewed and approved in time to authorize filing certificates of merger with state government authorities followed by transfers of funds as provided in the merger agreement. Without careful advance preparation, it can be difficult to complete a merger in a single day. To do so, it has become customary to hold a preclosing on the day prior to the merger during which all available documents are reviewed and often also signed but not delivered. This shortens the steps to be taken on the morning of the closing and permits early instructions to service companies waiting in state capitols to file the previously signed certificates of merger. The price can then be paid and documents exchanged. Because the surviving corporation succeeds by operation of law to all assets, rights, liabilities and obligations, there is no need for deeds, bills of sale, assignments and assumption agreements. There is also no need for shareholders of the merged corporation to transfer their shares which are automatically cancelled, but the merger agreement will usually require the shareholders to surrender their certificates in return for their share of the purchase price.

Stock acquisition (private company). The closing of a stock acquisition of a privately owned corporation is relatively simple. The necessary steps can usually be taken entirely in the closing room. Ownership is transferred by delivering stock certificates endorsed or accompanied by assignment forms signed by the stockholders. It is best to review in advance the stock records and the outstanding certificates in order to resolve problems of lost certificates, certificates held as pledges by lenders and certificates registered in the names of deceased family members, minors, trusts and estates. With preparation and a preclosing, there should be ample time to permit clearance of wire transfers on the closing date.

Stock acquisition (public company). The closing of a stock acquisition of a publicly owned corporation is handled using the services of a depository or exchange agent, usually a bank experienced in corporate trust services. In a cash tender offer, letters of transmittal with detailed instructions are mailed to the shareholders. Those shareholders who wish to tender shares sign the letter of transmittal and send it with their stock certificates to the depository. If the tender offer is hostile, there is no closing of the usual kind. The bidder notifies the depository of acceptance of the tenders once all conditions are met and the bid has been kept open long enough to meet legal requirements. If more shares are tendered than the bidder offered to buy, the depository prorates the shares accepted. The depository then mails checks for the shares purchased and certificates for shares not purchased to the shareholders who tendered. If the tender offer is friendly, a closing may take place on the date the bidder accepts the shares tendered.

Exchange offer. An exchange offer to shareholders of a publicly owned corporation is handled by procedures similar to those used for a tender offer. However, prospectuses must be mailed to the public shareholders as well as letters of transmittal. The exchange agent will handle certificates submitted in response to an exchange offer in a manner similar to the depository in a tender offer.

Assets acquisition. The closing of an assets acquisition is detailed and time-consuming. However, they are very common because they enable a buyer to choose, with some exceptions, the assets to be purchased and the liabilities to be assumed. To close an assets acquisition, it is necessary to transfer the assets and any assumed liabilities and obligations individually or in groups:

- Deeds are used to transfer owned real property. They are presigned and recorded on the closing date.

- A general bill of sale is used to transfer inventories, accounts receivable, equipment and miscellaneous assets.
- Specific bills of sale or other documents are used to transfer motor vehicles, permits, patents and other special assets.
- A general form of assignment, assumption and indemnity agreement can be used for most contracts, accounts payable, purchase orders and other continuing obligations.
- Specific assignment, assumption and indemnity agreements may be necessary for leases, some types of contracts, and permits which impose continuing obligations. For example, novation agreements are needed to assign government contracts. Consents of the other party are needed to assign most leases and formal contracts with customers and suppliers.
- Commitments for title insurance are reviewed and the insurer's requirements are met by satisfaction and release of mortgages, payment of any overdue taxes and clearance of any other title defects so that the final policy will contain only standard exceptions and other items acceptable to the buyer such as sewer and power line easements and railroad rights of way.
- Transfer taxes and recording fees and any applicable sales taxes are paid and annual real and personal property taxes are prorated together with other items such as rents, deposits, fuel and water.

Indemnity provisions are an important part of agreements assuming liabilities and obligations. If an event after the closing results in a claim, the seller will frequently be included and will want reimbursement of its costs and expenses, especially if the claim results in litigation.

CLOSING DOCUMENTS

Some closing documents are commonly used at closings regardless of whether the transaction is a merger, stock purchase or assets purchase. While these documents also differ depending on the nature of the transaction, a list of documents frequently used is as follows:

Certificates of incorporation
Good-standing certificates
By-laws
Enabling resolutions adopted by directors and shareholders
Incumbency certificates
Evidence that the Hart-Scott-Rodino waiting period, if applicable, has expired
Order of the Securities Exchange Commission declaring the registration statement effective, if the buyer will issue securities for distribution to public shareholders of seller
Approval or clearance by other government agencies
Tax rulings from the Internal Revenue Service or state tax agencies.

Letter evidencing listing of securities for trading on a stock exchange or the NASDAQ system

"Comfort" letters from accountants on financial statements delivered by seller or buyer

Legal opinions

Solvency letters (leveraged buyouts)

Fairness opinions (management buyouts, sales to "white knights" and other transactions where management decisions may be questioned by shareholders) Promissory note and mortgage if seller financing is used

Instructions for delivery of securities or wire transfer of funds

Receipts for securities or cash funds

Escrow agreements for funds withheld from the purchase price to secure price adjustments, representations and warranties and indemnities.

ACTIVITIES CONCURRENT WITH CLOSINGS

Before and during a closing, other important activities may be taking place and must be coordinated with the closing:

- An audit of the seller's financial condition
- Registration of securities with the SEC
- Compliance with state securities laws
- Compliance with requirements in state corporation laws, certificate of incorporation or by-laws that the acquisition be approved by votes of specified percentages of shareholders
- Stock exchange listing and rules
- Tax rulings from the Internal Revenue Service
- Antitrust clearance
- Escrow agreements

Audits. In many acquisitions, the price depends partially on the amount and value of the seller's assets on the closing date, particularly inventories and receivables. In all assets acquisitions and in stock and merger acquisitions where the acquired corporation is a subsidiary, there is a real possibility that interdivision or intercompany transactions or operating losses will deplete assets or increase liabilities before the closing date. The depletion can occur without knowledge of seller's management. Thus, it is common to arrange a full audit or at least a balance sheet audit as of the closing date. The price paid on the closing date is based on an estimate subject to adjustment when the audit results are reviewed and accepted.

Securities Registration—Federal Laws. If the purchase price will be paid in stock or other securities and no exemption from the Securities Act of 1933 is available, the buyer's counsel should commence preparing a registration statement as soon as possible and file it with the SEC even before the acquisition contract is signed. A special Form S-4 may be available or Form S-1 can be used. Counsel should recognize that previous ability of the buyer to meet SEC registration requirements does not mean that they can be met if the acquisition material and the seller has been privately owned and does not have financial statements that are adequate to meet SEC requirements. Counsel should review Regulations S-K and S-X to determine the requirements for the registration statement including financial statements audited by independent accountants who can render an unqualified opinion. If a problem is identified, it can sometimes be resolved by a conference with the accounting staff or the SEC who have long taken pride in achieving substance over form. If the problem is substantial, however, the acquisition may need to be restructured and renegotiated.

State "blue sky" laws. Chapter 6 summarizes briefly the effect of so-called state blue sky laws on acquisitions where securities form a part of the purchase price, and the effect of such laws should have been provided for in the acquisition contract. In some instances, notwithstanding that registration of securities is not required with the Securities and Exchange Commission under the Securities Act of 1933, a state will require registration with or notice to a state securities commission. Since state blue sky laws may void a buyer's delivery of its stock and give a seller the right to monetary recovery after receipt of a buyer's stock issued without compliance with such laws, before closing the transaction, the buyer should assure itself of compliance. Consider California law, since the California Corporation Code is probably as restrictive as the laws of any other state. To indicate the completeness of the information that a buyer must reveal in its application for the qualification of its securities under the California Corporation Code, a standard form of facing page of an application follows on page 497.

State corporation laws, the corporate character and bylaws. In addition, the parties must comply with the corporation laws of the states involved. Chapter 6 outlines the requirement of various state laws that the shareholders of a seller approve a sale of assets by a required favorable voting percentage. Therefore, in an assets transaction, for the seller legally to convey assets to the buyer necessary shareholder approval must usually be obtained. The required approval may generally be obtained at an annual or special shareholders meeting called for the specific purpose of considering the sale of the assets to the seller. Not only the laws of the state of incorporation, but also the corporate charter or the bylaws of the seller, will fix the period of time which must elapse from sending notice of a meeting to the seller's shareholders and holding the meeting. Such period of time must, of course, be taken into account in establishing the timetable for the closing, and should have been taken into account in drafting the acquisition agreement.

Stock exchange rules and listing. As noted in Chapter 6, under the Rules of the New York Stock Exchange a buyer must obtain the approval of its stockholders before the Exchange will list stock where directors or officers have an interest in the seller, or where an increase of 18.5 percent in the outstanding stock of the buyer will result from the acquisition, or where the size of the buyer will increase by 18.5 percent. Where the circumstances of an acquisition involve any of these three situations, the buyer must obtain approval of its shareholders although state law or its charter does not require such approval.

Effective Date_____

Orders Issued_____

```
┌─────────────────────────────────┐
│     DEPARTMENT OF CORPORATIONS  │
│              FILE NO.           │
└─────────────────────────────────┘
```
(Insert file number of previous filings of Applicant
before the Department, if any)

FEE:_____
(To be completed by Applicant)

Date of Application:_____

DEPARTMENT OF CORPORATIONS
STATE OF CALIFORNIA
FACING PAGE

APPLICATION FOR QUALIFICATION OF SECURITIES, UNDER THE CORPORATE SECURITIES LAW OF 1968,
BY *(Check Only One)*

☐ COORDINATION, SECTION 25111   ☐ NEGOTIATING PERMIT, SECTION 25102(c)
☐ NOTIFICATION, SECTION 25112   ☐ POST-EFFECTIVE ⎫ AMENDMENT NUMBER _____ TO
☐ PERMIT,   SECTION 25113   ☐ PRE-EFFECTIVE ⎭ APPLICATION FILED UNDER SECTION _____
☐ PERMIT,   SECTION 25121   DATED _____

This application is for an ☐ open or ☐ limited offering qualification as defined in Section 260.001 of the rules (check as applicable)

1. Name of applicant	

2. (a) Is applicant a corporation, partnership, trust or other entity?_____
   (b) State of incorporation or jurisdiction under which organized?_____
   (c) If a corporation, is applicant in good standing in the State of its incorporation? (Indicate "yes" or "no")_____
   (d) Is applicant a registered investment company? (Indicate "yes" or "no")_____

3. Address of principal executive office of applicant

Number and Street	City	State	Zip Code

4. Name and address of person to whom correspondence regarding this application should be addressed.

5.

(a) Description of Securities (See instructions on reverse side)	(b) Total number of shares or units of each class of securities being qualified in California (e.g., "20,000")	(c) Proposed maximum offering price per unit (e.g., "$10")	(d) Proposed maximum aggregate offering price for securities being qualified in California (e.g., "$200,000") Note: Fee calculated on total of this column	(e) Does a public market exist for this class of securities? (Indicate "yes" or "no." If "yes," insert CUSIP number.)

6. Consideration to be paid for securities if other than cash and the aggregate value ascribed thereto by the Board of Directors of the issuer, e.g., "Real Property, $100,000," "Assets of a going business, $50,000."

7. There is no adverse order, judgment or decree entered in connection with the offering by any State regulatory authority, any court or the Securities and Exchange Commission, except as follows: *(If none, so state)*

260.110 (5-74)

Disregarding the need to hold special meetings as a result of stock exchange rules, when a buyer is listed on an exchange and intends to utilize newly issued shares of stock to make an acquisition, it must generally list the stock on the particular exchange. Such listing involves the preparation of a listing application, normally not difficult, but nevertheless another item involving passage of time which must be prepared before the closing. For example, where the buyer will list stock on the New York Stock Exchange, the acquisition contract should provide for a period of approximately three weeks to prepare the application and obtain the approval of the application by the Committee on Stock Listings of the Exchange—although, when necessary, approval has been obtained in a shorter period of time.

The following form is an application for listing on the New York Stock Exchange:

LISTING APPLICATION TO
NEW YORK STOCK EXCHANGE   *June 17, 199 ___*

BUYER

12,592 ADDITIONAL SHARES OF COMMON STOCK
IN EXCHANGE FOR THE ASSETS OF SELLER

Number of Shares of Common Stock   Number of Holders of Common Stock
issued and outstanding as of ___ at May 31, 199____ : 29,295
May 31, 199____ : 5,553,610 _____
(including 47,956 shares in the   _____
treasury)

DESCRIPTION OF TRANSACTION

The Buyer will acquire substantially all the property, assets, goodwill, and business, subject to stated liabilities of the seller, in exchange for _____ shares of its Common Stock. No officer or director of the Buyer or any of its subsidiaries has any interest, direct or indirect, in the Seller.

The Seller manufactures and sells bicycles, wagons, and hobby toy items. This acquisition will afford the Buyer entry into that segment of the toy industry as an addition to its present products for the recreation and leisure-time field.

Reference is made to Exhibit A hereto for a description of the history and business and for the financial statements of the Seller.

The acquisition of the Seller will be treated as a "pooling of interests" for accounting purposes. Peck & Peck, independent public accountants of the Buyer, have reviewed the proposed accounting treatment and approve it as being in accordance with generally accepted accounting practice.

It is the present intention of the Buyer that the Seller will operate as a subsidiary in the recreational segment of its business.

RECENT DEVELOPMENTS

The buyer has released publicly notice of all important developments relating to its business.

AUTHORITY FOR ISSUE

On May 3, 199_____ , the Board of Directors authorized management to negotiate and acquire the Seller and on June 7, 199_____ , the Board of Directors approved the Agreement and Plan of Reorganization dated June 6th, 199_____ , and authorized the issuance and listing of the _____ shares of the Buyer's Common Stock. No further corporate authorization is required for the issuance of the Buyer's Common Stock.

OPINION OF COUNSEL

There has been filed in support of the Application, the Opinion dated June 10, 199_____ , of Jones, Jones & Jones, New York, New York, stating that all proceedings necessary to authorize the issue of the shares of Common Stock covered by this Application in connection with said acquisition of the Seller, have been duly taken and the issue and delivery of certificates representing such shares of Common Stock of the Buyer have been duly authorized; that said shares when issued in the manner now contemplated will be validly issued and outstanding, fully-paid, and non-assessable with no personal liability attaching to the holders thereof under the laws of the State of Delaware, the State of incorporation of the Buyer, or under the laws of the State of New York, the State in which the Buyer has an executive office; and registration of said shares under the Securities Act of 1933 is not required since the issuance and delivery of such shares to the Seller for distribution to its shareholders (who have represented that they are acquiring the Buyer's Common Stock strictly for investment with no intention of selling or distributing any thereof in any manner which would render the issuance of such shares subject to the registration requirements of said Act) will not involve a "public offering" within the meaning of Section 4(2) of said Act.

BUYER

*By   John Johnson
President*

The listing application includes a balance sheet, a statement of income and retained earnings, a description of the history and business of the seller, an accountant's report and an officer's certificate as to the accuracy of the financials, which have here been omitted. Also, the Exchange may require other supporting documents such as an opinion of counsel as to the need to register the buyer's shares, an accountant's opinion as to "pooling of interests" accounting treatment, an undertaking to advise the Exchange when the shares have been delivered for the purpose described in the listing application and other documents which may be pertinent to the particular listing of the stock. The form of listing application, upon approval, is subject to receiving "official notice of issuance," since stock may not be listed unless it has actually been issued. Where the buyer's transfer agent does not attend the closing, the transfer agent will officially notify the Exchange of the issuance of the stock after it gives the certificates to the custodian (normally an officer of the buyer) for delivery at the closing. Upon receipt of notice from the transfer agent, the stock is listed by the Exchange. Then, after the stock has been delivered at the closing in exchange for the seller's assets or stock, the custodian should send a notice to the stock exchange that the transaction has been completed. A form of such notice is found later in this chapter. On the other hand, when the transfer agent attends the closing, the agent normally will not give official notice of issuance until the transaction has been closed.

Tax rulings. One condition precedent frequently present in the contract is the prior receipt by one or both parties of a tax ruling from the Commissioner of Internal Revenue that the acquisition will be a tax-free acquisition. The application for such a ruling should be made to the Commissioner of Internal Revenue, Rulings and Corporate Reorganization Division, Washington, D.C. No standard form of ruling application exists. However, as a suggested basic approach to the ruling application, the applicant should reveal all facts and circumstances of the proposed transaction in the application. The ruling should, of course, also set forth the applicant's contentions and the sections of the Internal Revenue Code under which it believes the acquisition should be treated as tax-free. If a favorable ruling is obtained, a copy of the ruling will be required to be attached to the income tax return of the applicant filed for the fiscal year in which the acquisition takes place.

Normally, a revenue agent examining the tax return will accept the tax effect of the transaction as expressed in the copy of the ruling attached to the return. However, if there is a deviation in the form of the transaction as it actually took place from the form of transaction as proposed in the ruling application and repeated in the ruling itself, the examining agent may, if circumstances warrant, take the position that the acquisition is taxable, in spite of the ruling.

Antitrust clearance. The United States Department of Justice is willing to consider proposed acquisitions to determine whether they would violate the antitrust laws. Experts in the field, however, often advise the parties not to avail themselves of this opportunity to obtain an informal ruling from the Justice Department. In those instances where the parties fear that under Section 7 of the Clayton Act discussed in Chapter 6, the acquisition is such a borderline case that the consent of the Justice Department will probably not be forthcoming, it is often advised that the parties make their own determination and act accordingly.

However, in those instances where the contract provides for prior clearance of the acquisition with the Justice Department, the parties may approach the Justice Department on an informal basis. Either the buyer or seller may make an appointment with the Justice Department and then describe the details of the proposed acquisition. In coming to its conclusion, the Justice Department will naturally request material such as the form of the proposed acquisition agreement, financial and distribution data of the industry involved, the relationship between the buyer and seller and other miscellaneous items such as major supplier and customer contracts and distributorship agreements. Should the parties be fortunate and obtain Justice Department clearance, they still, however, have no binding assurance that the Federal Trade Commission may not institute a proceeding to upset the acquisition on its own initiative. Thus, they should consider a similar approach to the FTC to obtain a clearance if the FTC appears likely to exercise jurisdiction with respect to the acquisition.

Preparation for closing requires detailed study, listing and preparation of all documents required for the closing, plus agreement by the lawyers for the buyer and seller, prior to the closing, that the documents are in proper form. The lawyers for both the buyer and seller should prepare drafts of the necessary documents and exchange the drafts well in advance of the closing to assure that both counsel are satisfied and that no unexpected difficulties with forms of documents will arise at the closing.

Conducting the closing. As well as preparing for the closing, the lawyers carry the burden of conducting the closing. The attorneys for both parties should prepare for the closing as carefully as possible. Clients will become impatient if, at the closing, necessary documents have not been prepared in advance and the closing is delayed to amend or prepare such documents. Where stock is exchanged for stock, the closing often may be quite simple. On the other hand, when assets are being acquired, closing the transaction may require many title documents to be exchanged, and unless careful preparations have been made, the closing may become emotional and tedious. In those instances where numerous documents must be exchanged, the lawyers may arrange a preclosing exchange of executed documents, to be held in escrow, making the actual closing as painless as possible.

Concurrent loan closing. When the buyer pays the purchase price from its internal funds or from previously arranged lines of credit, payments are handled as part of the steps included in the simultaneous closing. For many years, payments were made by certified or official bank checks. However, wire transfers have been used in recent years, even for relatively small acquisitions. The closing should be conducted, if possible, so that wire transfer instructions can be given during banking hours and transfers can be completed and confirmed on the closing date.

When the buyer plans special loans to finance the purchase price, the acquisition closing must usually be coordinated with a concurrent loan closing. Especially when the loans will be secured by mortgages and security interests in the assets of the acquired business, the steps can be quite intricate and will not occur simultaneously. On the contrary, actions must be arranged in a sequential order so that the loan funds can be advanced; properties cleared of existing mortgages, security interests and liens; new mortgages, security interests and liens can be recorded and title insurance commitments can be issued in acceptable form. Extensive prior planning and arrangements must be made including arrangements to record pre-signed documents and pay filing fees and transfer taxes. Failure to do so could prevent the closing on the planned schedule and considerable extra effort and cost.

Closing memoranda and checklists. Prior to a closing, the lawyers prepare and exchange checklists identifying the documents to be furnished at the closing.

They also exchange proposed forms of the documents. They usually engage in some negotiation to obtain all documents necessary to protect their clients' interests and to obtain full and proper wording of the documents with the same objective. Experienced lawyers know that it is prudent to require all necessary documents and actions at or before the closing. Acquisition team members scatter soon after the closing to pursue other activities which become their new priorities. Obtaining documents and other actions after the incentive of the closing deadline has passed can be a frustrating experience.

As part of the closing, the lawyers usually also prepare a closing memorandum outlining the key events before, during and after the closing. The document provides a useful overview and record of the transaction. At times, the actions to be performed after the closing are phrased as commitments and the parties sign the closing memorandum.

A form of Closing Memorandum is attached as Exhibit 17–1.

Exhibit 17–1

CLOSING MEMORANDUM

Stock Purchase Agreement dated _____, 199__

This Closing Memorandum describes the actions taken at the closing of the Stock Purchase Agreement dated _____, 199__ between John L. Smith and Joseph Johnson, ABC Electronics Corporation and International Computers, Inc. All capitalized terms herein shall have the meanings assigned to them in the Stock Purchase Agreement unless otherwise stated.

The closing as held on _____, 199__ at the offices of Brown & Williams, 200 Wall Street, New York, New York 10075 at 9:30 A.M.

I.   *PERSONS PRESENT AT THE CLOSING*

   A list of the persons present at the Closing is attached as Exhibit A.

II.   *EVENTS PRIOR TO THE CLOSING*

   The following events occurred prior to the Closing:

   1. A letter of intent was executed on _____, 199__.

   2. A press release was issued on _____, 199__.

   3. A business "due diligence" review of the Corporation was performed by representatives of the Purchaser between _____, 199__ and _____, 199__.

   4. The Board of Directors of the Corporation approved the Stock Purchase Agreement on _____, 199__.

   5. The Board of Directors of the Purchaser approved the Stock Purchase Agreement on _____, 199__.

   6. The Stock Purchase Agreement was signed by the Sellers, the Corporation and the Purchaser on _____, 199__.

   7. On _____, 199__, the Sellers transferred to the Corporation the assets listed in Exhibit 1–A and the Corproation transferred to the Sellers the assets listed in Exhibit 1–B pursuant to Section 3.3 of the Stock Purchase Agreement.

   8. On _____, 199__, Sellers delivered to the Purchaser a preliminary title report and commitment of Reliable Title Guarantee Co. and a current survey by G. Washington & Associates, registered land surveyors, pursuant to Section 3.4 of the Stock Purchase Agreement.

   9. On _____, 199__, the Sellers and the Corporation executed an agreement terminating a Shareholders Agreement dated January 1, 199__ between them and releasing all rights thereunder. Jason Burton, a former shareholder, also signed the termination and release agreement.

   10. On _____, 199__ Northeastern Computers, Inc.

executed a consent to the continuation of its five year contract dated March 17, 199__ notwithstanding the change of ownership of the Corporation.

III. EVENTS OCCURRING AT THE CLOSING

Except as otherwise indicated, all actions at the Closing were deemed to take place simultaneously and all documents were dated as of the Closing Date.

A. Documents Delivered by Sellers. *The following documents were delivered by the Sellers and the Corporation to the Purchaser:*

(a) Certificate of Incorporation of the Corporation and all amendments, certified by the Secretary of State of Delaware, and a long firm good standing certificate of the Secretary of State of Delaware.

(b) Good standing certificate of the Secretary of State of New York.

(c) Secretary's Certificate as to the Certificate of Incorporation, By-Laws and certain corporate resolutions of the Corporation.

(d) Evidence of the property transfers required by Section 5.1(b).

(e) Certificate signed by the Sellers pursuant to Section 5.1(c).

(f) "Comfort letter" of Coopers, Price, Anderson & Co. pursuant to Section 5.1(d).

(g) Opinion of Davis, Sullivan & Weiss pursuant to Section 5.1(e).

(h) Releases signed by each Seller pursuant to Section 5.1(f).

(i) Certificates representing 20,000 shares of Common Stock of the Corporation endorsed by the Sellers.

(j) Employment Contracts signed by the Corporation and each of the Sellers.

(k) Evidence of payment of a finder's fee of $250,000 of Jackson Brothers, Thomas & Co.

(l) Receipts for $1,250,000 signed by each of the Sellers.

B. Documents and Payments Delivered by Purchaser. *The following documents and payments were delivered by the Purchaser to the Sellers:*

(a) Certificate of Incorporation of the Purchaser and all amendments, certified by the Secretary of State of New York, and a long form good standing certificate of the Secretary of State of New York.

(b) Secretary's Certificate as to the Certificate of Incorporation, By-Laws and certain corporate resolutions of the Purchaser.

(c) Officers' Certificate pursuant to Section 5.2(b).

(d) Opinion of Brown & Williams pursuant to Section 5.2(c).

(e) Wire transfer of $1,250,000 to the account of Smith pursuant to Section 5.2(d).

(f) Wire transfer of $1,250,000 to the account of Johnson pursuant to Section 5.2(e).

C. Other Actions Taken at the Closing. *The Sellers, the Corporation and Purchaser also took the following actions at the Closing:*

(a) With Purchaser's approval, the Corporation and Sellers exe-

cuted an Interim Lease Agreement providing for continued use by the Corporation of the Main Street Warehouse owned by Sellers.

(b) Purchaser ordered a final title insurance policy to be issued by Reliable Title Insurance Co. and Sellers and Purchaser each paid half the premium invoice of the title insurer. In order to clear title, Sellers delivered payment to the title insurer to discharge an outstanding assessment for road paving and a release of a mechanic's lien for roofing repairs.

IV. EVENTS AFTER THE CLOSING

By agreement between Sellers, the Corporation and Purchaser, the following actions will be taken after the Closing:

1. A press release, letter to employees, letter to customers and letter to suppliers will be sent by the Corporation containing text attached to this Memorandum.

2. Purchaser will deliver to Sellers a copy of the final insurance policy issued by Reliable Title Insurance Co.

SELLERS:

ABC ELECTRONICS CORPORATION

_____

John L. Smith

By _____

INTERNATIONAL COMPUTERS, INC.

_____

Joseph Johnson

By _____

Exhibit A

Persons Present at the Closing

Sellers:

>   *John L. Smith*
>   *Joseph Johnson*

Sellers' Accountants:

>   *Thomas L. Stern representing Coopers, Price, Anderson & Co.*

Sellers' Counsel:

>   *Jonathan Weiss representing Davis, Sullivan & Weiss*

Purchaser:

>   *James A. Callaghan, Senior Vice President*
>   *Douglas J. Waters, Financial Vice President*
>   *Jane C. Ripley, Corporate Secretary*

Purchaser's Counsel:

>   *Marsha O. Delaney and Mark Cooper representing Brown & Williams*

Title Insurer:

>   *Claire T. Wendt representing Reliable Title Insurance Co.*

Financial Consultant:

>   *Anthony Vilanova and Mary Wong representing Jackson Brothers,
>   Thomas & Co.*

18

After the Acquisition

POST-CLOSING PRIORITIES

The period shortly after the closing is a time when critical steps must be taken to integrate the acquired business with the buyer organization. Within a few months, skillful buyers will take initiatives to achieve the synergies which were the acquisition objectives. On the other hand, some buyers will plant seeds which can lead to disintegration of the acquired business.

During the same period, a variety of legal, accounting, tax, insurance, employee benefits and other steps must be taken, or should be taken because they may be difficult or impossible at later times.

Both of these priorities are discussed in this chapter.

INTEGRATING THE ACQUIRED BUSINESS

In the authors' experience, few subjects consume more time during acquisition negotiations than discussions of the future of the combined businesses. All too often, however, the plans do not work as expected for several reasons:

- Acquisition negotiations are usually conducted confidentially between top management representatives who tend to focus primarily on management and financial issues rather than integration of operations.
- Negotiations are necessarily at arm's length and lack the cooperation needed for strategic operations planning.
- Concessions made during acquisitions sometimes impair future operating efficiency.
- After management-driven or financially motivated acquisitions, integration of operations is sometimes delegated to operating officers and managers who had little or no participation in the evaluation and planning. While most will use their best efforts, some will see the situation as a threat to their position

505

or as an opportunity to seize power. Some will be apathetic, especially if they feel that management should not have omitted them from the planning.

How can businesses be skillfully integrated? The authors recommend the following:

First, planners should recognize that every acquisition involves integration, even when the buyer promises extensive autonomy to management of the acquired business. For example, financial reporting, budgets, cash management, taxes, insurance, general personnel policies, employee benefits and other activities are commonly integrated even when the acquired business is successful and will have operational freedom.

Second, the chief executive and senior managers of the seller should decide whether they can work within the buyer's management structure which will inevitably impose some degree of review and approval of their decisions. For some entrepreneurial CEOs, especially if they are also founders, an honest answer may be "No." If so, they should consider their alternatives ranging from retirement with consulting contracts to discontinuance of negotiations.

Third, buyer methods should not be imposed on seller operations until the working professionals in both organizations have exchanged visits to each of their workplaces and understood the advantages and disadvantages of the existing methods used by each of them.

Fourth, buyer management should begin steps toward integration by early involvement of its operational personnel, preferably during the "due diligence" review. As sales managers, engineers and others interact, opportunities and problems will be identified and can be planned and negotiated.

Fifth, buyer management should not force integration of businesses that initially seem to be similar, but experience shows are not.

The third recommendation is important in order to avoid classic mistakes made in many acquisitions. For one example, buyer management often expects to achieve economies by purchasing bulk raw materials at costs lower than a smaller seller could achieve. However, if their suppliers cannot make timely deliveries of products usable in seller's manufacturing processes and meeting specifications for seller's products, the economies will not be achieved and sales and customers may be lost.

For another example, buyer management may seek to increase sales of the seller's products by introducing national account customers who buy in large volume at discount prices. However, the acquired business may lack processes and equipment suitable for a high volume, low margin commodity business. If so, it may lose money on the higher sales volume, displease the national account customers, and lose regional and local customers who were pushed aside.

For still another example, integration of financial services often includes credit functions. Many customers won and kept by a seller's business for years have been jeopardized by peremptory long distance calls from buyer credit managers unaware of longstanding credit arrangements with the seller. It may be necessary for a buyer to tighten credit standards for some or all of seller's customers, but the change should be handled as a joint credit and marketing project coordinated among buyer and seller management and their sales and credit personnel.

The fourth recommendation is very important. Actual achievement of the synergies sought by top management depends on operating personnel. If some or all of them cannot be achieved, it is best to know while the acquisition is being negotiated. If that is impossible, it is still best to identify opportunities and problems as soon as possible. For example, some years ago, top management of a major corporation bought a small startup manufacturer major with unused capacity for manufacture of a product used in large quantities by the corporation. For technical reasons unknown to top management, the type of product produced by the small manufacturer could not be used at the large corporation's plants. Fortunately, during exchange visits of personnel, an engineer with the large corporation suggested a process change which greatly speeded production and reduced costs. Within months, the small manufacturing plant achieved full sales at excellent profit margins to outside customers.

The fifth recommendation requires that corporate management monitor the integration planning and progress and be prepared to pursue alternatives or turn back if necessary. For example, a manufacturer of industrial commodity products may encounter difficulties in attempting to integrate its sales and marketing staffs with those of an acquired high technology product manufacturer or a prestigious brand name retail product manufacturer. Corporate managers may believe that the sales and marketing departments of the acquired business are greatly overstaffed and overpaid because they have not dealt with customers who need heavy technical support or who will buy only if the product is supported by extensive advertising and "point of purchase" programs. They may also believe that their own sales and marketing personnel are qualified to handle the products of the acquired business. Acting prematurely based on such beliefs can be disastrous. Careful review may, of course, show that technical or marketing support can be reduced and that sales and marketing personnel can be trained to handle the products of the acquired business. However, corporate management should not create pressures for premature integration that risk loss of customers.

SHUTDOWNS, CUTBACKS AND LAYOFFS

A primary objective of some business combinations has been to achieve cost reductions by elimination of duplicative facilities and work forces. These objectives, of course, may reduce competition and are subject to review under the antitrust laws as described in Chapter 5. However, acquisitions with these objectives have been allowed in declining industries such as railroads, steel and cement. History has shown that the combined businesses were seldom successful unless programs other than cost reductions were introduced. Some of the reasons are discussed later.

Cost reductions are not a primary objective for most acquisitions. However, opportunities exist after most acquisitions. Some are virtually automatic. For example, after a publicly owned corporation is acquired, the need for its public and shareholder relations departments disappear together with part of the work done by its accounting, legal and other departments. It is also relatively easy to eliminate obvious waste such as "no show" jobs, nepotism, personal expenses charged to the business and the like. Cutting these items often improves morale among responsible employees. Other cost reductions are more difficult to evaluate and implement because each operation and employee is contributing some value but the result is unprofitable.

In the authors' opinion, every important cost reduction program must be part of a credible turnaround and future growth program or it is likely to fail. For example, if workers know that a business has products or processes that are technologically obsolete, they will want to know that cost savings will be applied to a realistic modernization program. If not, they will recognize that the cost reductions only delay the inevitable and will resist extra work and other sacrifices. Motivated employees will seek new employment and other employees will become more apathetic.

A cost reduction program should also be intelligently and fairly administered. Elimination of productive departments and people in the seller organization in favor of weaker departments and people in the buyer organization will be seen as "politics" and morale will plunge. Cuts of promising projects and respected people in research, marketing and other long term activities will be recognized as jeopardizing the future. Hastily implemented programs will be seen as a "quick fix" unlikely to achieve permanent results.

One of the authors participated in a remarkably successful turnaround of a major corporation which had encountered severe difficulties for over a decade. Some of the most important methods were as follows:

- Visible sharing by senior management in hard work, risk and austerity budgets.
- Implementation of personnel reductions over a short time period, accompanied by significant bonus and incentive programs for remaining employees asked and given freedom to assume more responsibilities.
- Careful listening and planning to match cost reductions burdens on productivity
- Use of funds created by savings, even when still scarce, to buy long-needed equipment to improve product quality and manufacturing efficiency.
- Continuous emphasis that contributions to the business would be obtained, recognized and rewarded wherever found. Real awards for accomplishments by operating and administrative workers were given by top management.
- Reduction of bureaucracy by accountability systems including eventual replacement of managers who could not develop and successfully implement improvements or who stifled employee innovation and growth.

The authors recommend an article titled "Cost Cutting: How to Do It Right," *Fortune,* April 9, 1990 as an unusually observant discussion of the reasons why some cost reduction programs fail and others succeed. The article recommends six short rules which are more realistic than those found in many lengthy discussions.

Another article containing a number of perceptive observations and recommendations is "Taking the Humane Approach to Postacquisition Layoffs," *Mergers & Acquisitions,* Panos, March/April, 1989.

A BUSINESS INTEGRATION CHECKLIST

Reassure seller's employees, customers, suppliers, creditors and other key people of continuity or give fair notice of interruptions of ongoing relationships

Exchange of management knowhow

Exchange of technical knowhow

Exchange of marketing and sales knowhow

Exchange of production knowhow

Exchange of support services knowhow

Coordinate marketing and sales functions to allow "one stop shopping" for customers

Combine warehouses

Combine outbound freight and distribution

Combine agents and distributors

Coordinate purchasing functions to obtain volume discounts

Coordinate inbound freight

Refinance loans, if assumed

Coordinate service functions including accounting, advertising, credit, engineering, environmental, insurance, legal, pension, public relations, quality control, research, treasury, transportation

Redesign products using acquired knowhow

Redesign manufacturing processes using acquired knowhow

Plan the marketing and sale of new products or products produced by new processes

POST-CLOSING CHECKLIST

File Form 8-K with the SEC

File affidavit with the IRS under FIRPTA

File Forms BE-13 with the DOC

File applicable tax elections and reports such as an election under Section 338(h)(10) of the Internal Revenue Code, the information required by Regulation Section 1.368-3 for a tax free reorganization and the report required by Section 382 of the Code for an ownership shift

Obtain issuance of formal title insurance policies

Record assets at "stepped up" values for tax and accounting purposes

Obtain issuance of formal endorsements or policies evidencing coverage of seller's operations and properties if seller's policies will not continue in effect

Issue new stock options if seller employees were made eligible for buyer's stock option plan

Issue benefit booklets and certificates evidencing coverage under buyer's life, medical and other insurance and benefit booklets

Arrange for seller's employees to read and sign corporate code of conduct

Coordinate plans providing retirement benefits including pension, 401(k), medical and life

Monitor investment and disbursement of securities or funds with an exchange agent

Monitor investment and disbursement of funds with an escrow agent and claims filed against the funds

Obtain and preserve recorded originals of real estate deeds and mortgages and furnish evidence of payment of fees and taxes to persons responsible for corporate tax returns

Monitor sales of shares covered by any shelf registration statement including compliance with Rule 10b–6

Alert any new corporate officers and directors of the need to file Forms 3 and 4 with the SEC and furnish forms and instructions

Verify that any 5% beneficial stockholder has filed a Schedule 13–D

Obtain Forms W–4 for new employees

File Forms 1099 for funds disbursed

Change corporate name and signatories on seller bank accounts to the extent necessary

Cancel and obtain premium refunds on insurance policies discontinued

Complete environmental permit transfers and reissues and complete compliance with environmental cleanup laws, if required

MAINTAINING OLDER LIABILITY INSURANCE COVERAGE

To the extent not completed prior to an acquisition, one of the most important post-closing projects may be identifying and obtaining evidence of seller's historical insurance coverage.

In recent years, the courts have found a growing array of reasons for imposing liability on buyers for claims of bodily injury and property damage allegedly caused by defective products or hazardous emissions and wastes generated or disposed of by acquired businesses. Because many courts interpret statutory time limits on the right to sue as running from the date when the claimant allegedly discovered the injury or damage, the claims may be covered by insurance policies written decades ago. Indeed, the coverage furnished by those policies is probably more favorable to the insured than coverage written in recent years.

Older liability policies are valuable assets for the following reasons:

• Injury or damage commencing with exposure to defective products or releases of hazardous emissions or wastes during the policy period may be covered even though they do not manifest themselves until years later.

• Some contain no aggregate limits on liability.

• Some provide separate bodily injury and property damage limits.

• Some contain an obligation to defend separate from the liability limits and the obligation may be unlimited in amount.

• Many contain no pollution exclusion and others contain a pollution exclusion applicable only to some kinds of pollution.

• Few contain the large, self-insured retention and deductible provisions found in most recent policies.

It is a shocking experience to be sued for injuries claimed to have been caused by products sold 30 years ago or industrial waste delivered to a state licensed contractor 20 years ago. It is even more shocking to be sued when the claims relate to an acquired business. Nevertheless, many buyers complete acquisitions without obtaining evidence of the seller's historical liability coverage. They happily switch coverage to new brokers and carriers with the result that they drop to the bottom of the priority list with the seller's broker and insurers who happily discard policies, files and other coverage records. When claims are received, their current insurers deny coverage and the old insurers deny they ever insured the seller.

Unless the nature of an acquired business makes liability remote, the authors recommend that buyers make a determined effort to obtain old liability policies and related records before or as soon as possible after an acquisition. For those who do not take these steps and are confronted by a later lawsuit, there is at least one firm, IAG Incorporated, which specializes in insurance portfolio reconstruction including the coverage slips issued by syndicates at Lloyds and London companies. See "Insurance Archaeology in Mergers and Acquisitions," Mulrennan, *The Acquisition Yearbook—1991*, New York Institute of Finance (Simon & Schuster), 1991.

INTEGRATING PENSION PLANS

The task of integrating defined benefits pension plans is important and closely regulated by provisions of ERISA designed to protect workers and the major accumulations of funds in these plans.

Effects of Acquisition Structure

The choices of the seller and the buyer for continuation or termination of pension plans are affected by the form of the transaction, i.e. merger, stock purchase or assets purchase.

In a merger, the buyer succeeds by operation of law to all rights and obligations of the seller. Thus, pension plans automatically continue, but the buyer can merge, freeze or terminate such plans after the merger.

In a stock purchase, the corporation continues its own rights and obligations. The buyer does not directly succeed to rights and obligations for the plan, but can elect new management that will continue, merge, freeze or terminate the plan.

In an assets purchase, the seller's employees (or the employees of the division being sold) are terminated and some or all may be hired by the buyer. The buyer can adopt the seller's plan, but is not required to do so. If a buyer does not adopt the plan, the seller can freeze or terminate it.

Alternatives Regarding Seller's Plans

Continuation of Seller's Plans. Continuation of a seller's plan can be accomplished by resolutions of the buyer's board of directors adopting the plan and authorizing an assignment and assumption of the related group annuity contract or trust agreement. A determination letter is customarily obtained from the IRS. PBGC regulations provide that a transaction involving a change in the contributing sponsor is a reportable event if the plan has unfunded vested benefits of $1 million or more.

Split-Off and Continuation of Part of Seller's Plans. When a seller has a pension plan covering multiple businesses, whether operated as subsidiaries or unincorporated divisions, a buyer of one of the businesses can assume the seller's plan by arranging a split-off (spinoff) transaction. The buyer can adopt a plan corresponding to seller's plan and a trust to fund its benefits. The seller can then split the assets of the trust under its plan into assets allocable to its retained employees and assets allocable to employees of the business being sold. These assets can be transferred to the trust established by the buyer.

Defined contribution plans can easily be split on the basis of the individual accounts of the participants. Actuarial calculations are required to split the assets of a defined benefit plan.

I.R.C. Secs. 414(1) and 411(d)(6) require that each participant be entitled immediately after the transfer to a benefit that would, if the plan were then terminated, be equal to or greater than the benefit he or she would have been entitled to receive immediately before the transfer if the plan were terminated. See Reg. Sec. 1.414(1)–1(n); ERISA Sec. 4044 and Revenue Rulings 86–47 and 86–48.

Merger of Seller's Plans into Buyer's Plans. After an acquisition, a buyer may wish to include the employees of the acquired business in its own pension plans. This can be accomplished by merging the seller's pension plan into the buyer's pension plan. The steps involve amending the seller's plan, prospectively or retroactively, to become identical to the buyer's plan and making similar amendments to the annuity contracts or trust agreements used to fund the plans.

A merger of defined contribution plans can be accomplished easily. The balance in the individual account of each participant in the merged plan must be the same as it was in the predecessor plan immediately before the merger. IRS. Reg. Sec. 1.414(1)-1(d).

A merger of defined benefit plans involves complex actuarial calculations because each participant must be entitled to a benefit immediately after the companies' merger that is at least equal to the benefit the participant had been terminated immediately before the merger. The sufficiency of the plan assets to meet this requirements can be evidenced by preparing a schedule of benefits or retaining sufficient data for five years to permit preparation of such a schedule. A buyer will not usually wish to merge pension plans that are considerably different in benefits or funding sufficiency, except perhaps prospectively. See IRS Reg. Sec. 1.414(1)-1.

Freezes. As an alternative to continuation or termination, an employer can "freeze" a defined benefit pension plan by amending its benefit provisions to eliminate benefits accruing on and after the amendment date. Benefits accrued before the amendment date cannot be reduced by such an amendment. See I.R.C. Sec. 411(d)(6). A 15-day notice must be given to all plan participants and beneficiaries and to the unions representing them pursuant to ERISA Sec. 204(h).

Freezing a plan can provide important financial relief to an employer, but does not eliminate all continuing costs. Administration and reporting requirements must continue to be met. Premiums must continue to be paid to the PBGC under ERISA Sec. 4007(a). Contributions will continue to be made to fund benefits committed before the amendment date including any amounts owed for deficiencies.

If there is a complete discontinuance of contributions, the rights of all participating employees to accrued benefits, to the extent then funded, must become vested. See I.R.C. Sec. 411(d)(3) and IRS Regulation Sec. 1.411(d)-2.

On the other hand, an employer that freezes and continues a plan can benefit from favorable actuarial experience, such as employee turnover and investment appreciation. In addition, individuals designated by the employer can continue to act as plan administrator, investment manager and trustee. These advantages should be compared to ongoing costs including PBGC premiums as increased by OBRA.

The Tax Reform Act of 1986 requires that any plan, including a frozen defined benefit plan, cover at least 50 employees or, if less, 40 percent of all the employees of the employer. See I.R.C. Sec. 401(a)(26). A frozen plan that initially meets this requirement may lose its qualification over a period of years unless it is terminated or merged into another plan.

Curtailment of Benefits. It is also possible to curtail benefits under a plan by amending its provisions to reduce benefits accruing after the date of the amendment, but consideration should be given to whether a partial termination may result. See IRS Reg. Sec. 1.411(d)-2.

Termination. Under Sec. 4041 or ERISA, as amended by SEPPAA, an employer can voluntarily terminate a defined-benefit pension plan only by meeting the criteria for a standard termination or a distress termination. Both methods of termination require that notice be sent to the PBGC, all participants and beneficiaries, and any union or other person representing them. A voluntary termination may not proceed if it would violate an existing collective bargaining agreement. ERISA Sec. 4041. See proposed PBGC Regulations to be added as 29 C.F.R. Parts 2616 and 2617, announced at 52 Fed. Reg. 3318 (Sept. 2, 1987.)

ERISA Sec. 4069(a) imposes termination liability on any person and its controlled group (determined as of the termination date) if such entities entered into any transaction within the preceding five years of the termination, a principal purpose of which was to evade their liability under ERISA.

This provision creates potential seller liability whether a merger, stock sale or assets sale is made. There may be risk of use of ERISA Sec. 4069(a) to impose seller liability after leveraged buy-out transactions if the buyer terminates a plan within five years. The courts will presumably examine original capital adequacy and cash flow projections in determining whether there was a purpose to evade.

From the point of view of the buyer, a stock purchase does not provide its usual insulation from direct liability for obligations of an acquired subsidiary because ERISA Sec. 4062 imposes termination liability on all members of a controlled group. Further, an acquired subsidiary may have contingent liability if it was a member of a controlled group sponsoring a pension plan before the sale. Thus, the buyer must carefully review not only the pension obligations of the subsidiary but also those of its affiliates, and must obtain indemnification or other protection against them.

From the point of view of the buyer, any liability in an assets purchase should arise only if a plan is assumed in the acquisition contract. The language of ERISA Sec. 4069(a) does not appear to apply to a buyer if the buyer does not assume a plan. Nevertheless, claims based on such theories as successor liability and the practical merger doctrine are possible, so the buyer should inquire how the seller plans to meet any termination liability if a plan is not assumed. It should also obtain indemnification or other protection against such liability.

CLAIMS AFTER THE CLOSING

Among the difficult tasks after a closing are the investigation, evaluation and assertion of claims against the seller or buyer and sometimes against their directors, officers and shareholders. The claims generally are in the following categories:

- Amounts owed under purchase price adjustment provisions, usually based on an audit as of the closing date.
- Breach of representations and warranties in the acquisition contract as supplemented or limited by indemnification provisions.
- Disputes about nondelivery of assets and failures to continue to purchase or supply products or services.
- Breach of employment or consulting contracts.
- Breach of confidentiality and noncompetition provisions in the acquisition contract.

Many items must be checked in a closing date audit including timely and accurate recording of sales and costs, especially for items in transit. The most important items, however, are usually inventories and receivables. Ideally, procedures for both items will be stated on the acquisition contract. If not, orderly procedures should be established for the inventory count and valuation. First, establish who will take the inventory and who will review. Second, establish how much time will be allowed for objections. For count, the time should be short. More time is need for quality, including obsolescence, because discussions with manufacturing and sales personnel may be needed to decide whether some items should be written down or written off. If inventories or receivables are written off, it is customary to give the seller a reasonable opportunity to sell or collect them if a method can be found which will not conflict with the ongoing business.

Claims for breaches of representations and warranties tend to be more sensitive than price adjustments resulting from closing date audits. The authors recommend that financial and legal personnel be instructed to assemble quietly the data for and against claims and to submit a full report to top management before any claims are made. Staff professionals do not usually know the full history of the acquisition negotiations. Senior management should assure that proposed claims are within the spirit of the negotiations as well as the language of the acquisition contract. Otherwise, claims perceived as unfair or petty may jeopardize ongoing relationships.

At the other extreme, some breaches of representations and warranties are so fundamental that they may decide to seek rescission of the acquisition itself and monetary damages. For example, if the seller concealed the imminent loss of a major customer or fraudulently overstated sales or understated costs, a court judgment for money damages may be inadequate to make the buyer whole. If so, a court can order that the acquisition be unwound. However, the courts are usually reluctant to order and supervise such a drastic remedy. They will usually measure the financial loss and provide a monetary remedy.

One of the authors has participated in transactions involving the repurchase of a business by a seller. In each situation, disputes existed as to whether the seller had misrepresented the business or the buyer had inadequately managed the business after the closing. However, it was agreed that the business had a better chance of survival in the hands of the seller. Much credit is due to businessmen who can overcome disappointment and disputes to achieve a transaction which preserves a business otherwise likely to be lost.

When an acquisition is negotiated and closed quickly, the buyer may find it did not fully identify the assets and liabilities included or obtained from commitments for relationships between buyer's business and retained seller's businesses. For example, a division of a corporate business often shares facilities and services, buys components and sells products to other corporate divisions and subsidiaries. Privately owned businesses often deploy assets among a variety of corporations, partnerships and trusts owned by family members and friends. After the closing, the buyer may find it is dealing with a variety of people who were not part of the acquisition negotiations and who have no intention of sacrificing their own interests. For example, an eager buyer may rely on a verbal assurance from a corporate seller that its ABC Division will be happy to continue to supply components, only to receive a 15% price increase shortly after the closing. A verbal assurance that the XYZ subsidiary will continue to buy may last a few months. XYZ may then introduce a second supplier in order to assure that price and quality are competitive. Protests to the seller generally bring polite expressions of sympathy, and perhaps minor adjustments, but important changes will rarely be made unless the acquisition contract requires them. In these situations, the buyer should realistically evaluate its legal rights, if any, and enforce them. If its rights are deficient, the best course is to negotiate courteously for the best obtainable terms and rapidly seek alternate suppliers and customers. Misdirected anger and accusations are likely to be ineffective and even counterproductive.

Employment contract disputes are relatively rare if the contracts are limited to working executives and managers who will continue to perform their duties in much the same manner after the closing. They tend to see the contract as welcome security against unforeseen change. Unfortunately, disputes with former chief executives and other top management members are common, especially if one or more were founders. The executives complain that they do not have freedom to do their jobs effectively and are burdened by "red tape" and second-guessing. The buyer complains that they are refusing to work as team players and perform the normal duties of business managers. These disputes must be resolved under the terms of the employment contracts and also the confidentiality and noncompetition provisions in the acquisition contract. If differences become irreconcilable, it is usually best to negotiate a settlement which preserves the most important values for the buyer and the executives.

In the authors' experience, it is a mistake for either side to be excessively rigid about resolving differences in "chemistry" between a buyer organization and senior executives. When disputes are forced to the wall, the result may be firings or resignations, perhaps followed by attempts to compete and lawsuits claiming misuse of proprietary information and breach of noncompetition provisions. These lawsuits are unpredictable and both sides have a lot to lose. At one extreme, some executives have lost their employment and investments made in new businesses. At the other extreme, some buyers have been held liable for wrongful discharge. Still others found they could not prevent the former executive from establishing a new business outside the protection of confidentiality and noncompetition provisions.

One example will illustrate this last point. Some years ago, the chief executive and founder of a company sold to a large public corporation resigned after policy disputes with the buyer's management. A respected scientist, he made no effort to compete, but organized a company whose unrelated products involved technology more scientifically challenging than those of his former company. Even without invitations, research managers gradually left the buyer organization to seek employment with the new company whose work had greater scientific appeal. The buyer eventually closed the company it had bought.

CONCLUSION

The authors hope that this chapter, together with the discussion in Chapter 1, will help the reader to see that acquisitions are part of business life. Corporate development activities that precede an acquisition and integration activities afterwards are at least as important, and often more important, than the acquisition itself. M&A professionals commonly refer to companies as having successful or unsuccessful acquisition programs, but the real test is whether the overall corporate business is successful and the acquisition contributes to the success. Indeed, if business integration is successful, memory of the separate business will gradually fade except on occasions when it is appropriate to remember founders and others who contributed to the early development of the corporate business.

Index of Forms and Checklists

Subject Index

Weighting techniques, financial statement valuation, 88-89
Williams Act, tender offers, 228-29

Y

Young founders, and divestiture, 18-19

Z

Zero coupon notes, 29-30